MCSE Database Design on SQL Server 7

Chris Leonard
Brad Schulz
Greg "Buck" Woody
Jose Amado-Blanco
Pam Barker

MCSE Database Design on SQL Server 7 Exam Prep

Limits Of Liability And Disclaimer Of Warranty

The author and publisher of this book have used their best efforts in preparing the book and the programs contained in it. These efforts include the development, research, and testing of the theories and programs to determine their effectiveness. The author and publisher make no warranty of any kind, expressed or implied, with regard to these programs or the documentation contained in this book.

The author and publisher shall not be liable in the event of incidental or consequential damages in connection with, or arising out of, the furnishing, performance, or use of the programs, associated instructions, and/or claims of productivity gains.

Trademarks

Trademarked names appear throughout this book. Rather than list the names and entities that own the trademarks or insert a trademark symbol with each mention of the trademarked name, the publisher states that it is using the names for editorial purposes only and to the benefit of the trademark owner, with no intention of infringing upon that trademark.

The Coriolis Group, LLC
14455 N. Hayden Road, Suite 220
Scottsdale, Arizona 85260

480/483-0192
FAX 480/483-0193
http://www.coriolis.com

Library of Congress Cataloging-in-Publication Data
MCSE database design on SQL Server 7 exam prep/Christopher A. Leonard ... [et al.]
p. cm.
Includes index.
ISBN 1-57610-519-9
1. Electronic data processing personnel--Certification. 2. Microsoft software--Examinations--Study guides. 3. Database design--Examinations--Study guides. 4. SQL server. I. Title: Database design on SQL Server 7. II. Leonard, Christopher A.
QA76.3 .M328 1999
005.75'85--dc21 99-042704
CIP

Printed in the United States of America
10 9 8 7 6 5 4 3 2 1

President, CEO
Keith Weiskamp

Publisher
Steve Sayre

Acquisitions Editor
Jeff Kellum

Marketing Specialist
Cynthia Caldwell

Project Editor
Greg Balas

Technical Reviewer
David Anstey

Production Coordinator
Laura Wellander

Cover Design
Jesse Dunn

Layout Design
April Nielsen

CD-ROM Developer
Robert Clarfield

14455 North Hayden Road, Suite 220 • Scottsdale, Arizona 85260

Coriolis: The Training And Certification Destination™

Thank you for purchasing one of our innovative certification study guides, just one of the many members of the Coriolis family of certification products.

Certification Insider Press™ has long believed that achieving your IT certification is more of a road trip than anything else. This is why most of our readers consider us their *Training And Certification Destination.* By providing a one-stop shop for the most innovative and unique training materials, our readers know we are the first place to look when it comes to achieving their certification. As one reader put it, "I plan on using your books for all of the exams I take."

To help you reach your goals, we've listened to others like you, and we've designed our entire product line around you and the way you like to study, learn, and master challenging subjects. Our approach is *The Smartest Way To Get Certified*™.

In addition to our highly popular *Exam Cram* and *Exam Prep* guides, we have a number of new products. We recently launched Exam Cram Live!, two-day seminars based on *Exam Cram* material. We've also developed a new series of books and study aides—*Practice Tests Exam Crams* and *Exam Cram Flash Cards*—designed to make your studying fun as well as productive.

Our commitment to being the Training And Certification Destination does not stop there. We just introduced *Exam Cram Insider*, a biweekly newsletter containing the latest in certification news, study tips, and announcements from Certification Insider Press. (To subscribe, send an email to **eci@coriolis.com** and type "subscribe insider" in the body of the email.) We also recently announced the launch of the Certified Crammer Society and the Coriolis Help Center—two new additions to the Certification Insider Press family.

We'd like to hear from you. Help us continue to provide the very best certification study materials possible. Write us or email us at **cipq@coriolis.com** and let us know how our books have helped you study, or tell us about new features that you'd like us to add. If you send us a story about how we've helped you, and we use it in one of our books, we'll send you an official Coriolis shirt for your efforts.

Good luck with your certification exam and your career. Thank you for allowing us to help you achieve your goals.

Keith Weiskamp

Keith Weiskamp
President and CEO

Look For These Other Books From The Coriolis Group:

MCSE Database Design on SQL Server 7 Exam Cram
Jeffrey Garbus, David Pacuzzi, and Alvin Chang

MCSE Administering SQL Server 7 Exam Prep
Brian Talbert

MCSE SQL 7 System Administration Prep and Cram Pack
Certification Insider Press

MCSE SQL 7 Database Design and Administration Practice Tests Exam Cram
Geoffrey Alexander and Joseph Alexander

To my dear wife, Margie, whose steadfast love and support have upheld me throughout the course of this project. I hope I never come to take for granted your faith in me and in God's ability to lead us through times like this. You are a praiseworthy woman, and I know that I am blessed to be sharing this Great Adventure with you. I love you!

—Chris Leonard

❧

To my beloved wife, Donna, and my children, Austin, Alix, and Aaron, who I love dearly and are my pride and joys. You have been exceedingly understanding and patient with me for these four months during this project for which, I wholly dedicate this book to you. I can't wait to see what God's plan is for all of our lives!

—Brad Schulz

❧

To Jo Anna, who taught me the infinite joy of learning.

—Greg "Buck" Woody

❧

This book is dedicated to all database administrators, designers, and developers from whom I continue to learn everyday.

—Jose Amado-Blanco

❧

To my husband, John, and sons, Ron and John Jr., who continue to support me and encourage me. Thank you for your love and encouragement and unwavering support. The three of you are the lights of my life and I am exceedingly blessed to have you.

—Pam Barker

❧

About The Authors

Chris Leonard has worked with database technologies for over 10 years, both as a developer and as a DBA. He is currently a DBA for a Fortune 250 company in the Tampa Bay area that relies heavily on the Microsoft SQL Servers he builds and administers, using them to store hundreds of megabytes of critical information. He has worked extensively with other database servers as well, including IBM DB2, Oracle, and Sybase. Chris's background also includes broad teaching experience.

Brad Schulz is a principal consultant with Tech Data Corp. in Tampa, Florida. He has worked with SQL Server 7 for almost one-and-a-half years and participated in the beta product evaluations. He has also worked with large-scale database systems and computer technology in general for 15 years. Brad was a founder of two companies in the exciting telecommunications business and has traveled an interesting path from his Electrical Engineering background at the University of Louisville.

Greg "Buck" Woody is a database administrator (DBA) for a consulting firm in Tampa, Florida. He has worked with computer technology for 17 years, in roles as varied as a technical trainer, network administrator, manager, and DBA. He has worked with Microsoft products since DOS 2.0, and with SQL Server since version 4.2. Buck holds certifications from Microsoft (MCSE), Novell, and Sun Microsystems. He graduated with honors from Tampa College with a Business degree.

Jose Amado-Blanco is an independent database administrator consultant in Sybase and SQL Server who works in the Tampa area of Florida. He obtained his college and Master in Science degrees from the Moscow Economic-Statistic Institute. Jose has been working with computer technology for 11 years, in diverse environments such as mainframes, PCs, and client server. He has worked with Sybase since version 4.2 and with SQL Server since version 6.5. He is a Microsoft Certified Professional in SQL Server.

Pam Barker has used all of the major database management systems at one time or another in designing and constructing applications during her 17-year career as a DBA. As some of these DBMSs were in version 1.0 releases at the time, Pam is pleased to have been able to observe first-hand the evolution and development of database systems. In addition, she has authored and delivered database design and programming courses for several national training companies. Pam currently manages a DBA team for a high-tech Fortune 500 company based in the Tampa, Florida area where she lives with her husband and two sons.

ACKNOWLEDGMENTS

To my beloved children Gabe, Abby, and Nicholas: Thanks for all your hugs and prayers! Daddy loves you very much. To Tennessee Cabin Press: We did it! To Doug and Amy: Special thanks for helping far beyond expectations. Finally, to my Lord: You are my life. I hereby declare my work on this project to be solely *Soli* [SDG].

—*Chris Leonard*

Deep gratitude goes again to my family, and to my co-authors for inviting me to join them on this project. Many thanks to Buck for keeping us on schedule, to Mike Good for his contributions, to Rob and Ian at Microsoft, and to Jeff Kellum and Greg Balas at Coriolis. Finally, high praises go to my Lord. Selah!

—*Brad Schulz*

I would like to acknowledge the sacrifices and encouragement my family has given me through this process and the dedication and hard work that my co-authors have shown. I would also like to acknowledge all the professionals of the Tampa SQL User's Group who help me learn more about SQL Server each day.

—*Greg "Buck" Woody*

I want to thank my wife, son, and daughter for their patience and support. I also want to thank Karen Brown for her special editorial work, Marty Hensler for the lengthy SQL discussions we have had, and Mark Yelton for his initial editions. Finally, thanks to my dad for teaching me that hard work pays off.

—*Jose Amado-Blanco*

Over the years I have worked with many exceptional DBA's and information technology professionals. The knowledge and insight that I have gleaned from them has helped me enormously both in my career and in the preparation of this book.

—*Pam Barker*

Contents At A Glance

TABLE OF CONTENTS

CHAPTER 8
TRANSACT-SQL SCRIPTING AND COMMAND BATCHES 265

CHAPTER 9
SUMMARIZING AND TRANSFORMING DATA 309

INTRODUCTION

Welcome to *MCSE Database Design on SQL Server 7 Exam Prep.* This new book from Certification Insider Press offers you interactive activities and numerous hands-on projects that reinforce key concepts and help you prepare for the exam. This book also features troubleshooting tips for solutions to common problems that you will encounter. We feel that this book is much more than a study-guide for an exam. It represents many years of combined SQL Server experience that will aid you in real-world activities in your professional career.

The companion interactive CD-ROM features a unique test simulation environment with two complete practice exams that allow you to test your skills and knowledge, making this the perfect study guide for the Microsoft certification exams. The exam questions have been specially written based on the content of the book to reinforce what you have learned. These materials have been specifically designed to help individuals prepare for Microsoft Certification Exam 70-029, *Designing and Implementing Databases on Microsoft SQL Server 7.* Answers to end-of-chapter review questions and projects are also found on the CD-ROM.

The big technology question for the technology professional is "Are you certified?" Certification is rapidly becoming the key to professional career enhancement for network engineers, technicians, software developers, Web designers, and even professional office workers.

If you're ready to dig right in, skip to the "About The Book" section later in this introduction.

WHY BECOME A MICROSOFT CERTIFIED PROFESSIONAL?

Becoming a Microsoft Certified Professional (MCP) can open many doors for you. Obtaining the appropriate Microsoft Certified Professional credentials can provide a formal record of your skills to potential employers. Certification can be equally effective in helping you secure a raise or promotion.

The Microsoft Certified System Engineer (MCSE) program is made up of a series of core and elective exams in several different tracks. Combinations of individual exams can lead to certification in a specific track. Most tracks require you to pass a combination of core and elective exams. (Exam 70-029, *Designing and Implementing Databases on Microsoft SQL Server 7*, is an elective exam.) Your MCSE credentials tell a potential employer that you are an expert. You'll find that this exam is very versatile, and is valid for many certification tracks. This exam is a core requirement for the new Microsoft Certified Database Administrator (MCDBA) certification. You also earn elective credit toward (MCSE+I) certification, and elective credit toward (MCSD) certification. Passing this exam is very useful in all Microsoft certifications.

Want To Know More About Microsoft Certification?

There are many additional benefits to achieving Microsoft certified status. These benefits apply to you as well as to your potential employer. As a Microsoft Certified Professional, you will be recognized as an expert on Microsoft products, have access to ongoing technical information from Microsoft, and receive special invitations to Microsoft conferences and events. You can obtain a comprehensive, interactive tool that provides full details about the Microsoft Certified Professional Program online at **www.microsoft.com/train_cert/cert**. For more information on texts from Certification Insider Press that will help prepare you for certification exams, visit our site at **www.certificationinsider.com**.

A Microsoft Certified Professional receives the following benefits:

- Microsoft Certified Professional wall certificate. Also, within a few weeks after you have passed any exam, Microsoft sends you a Microsoft Certified Professional Transcript that shows which exams you have passed.
- License to use the Microsoft Certified Professional logo. You are licensed to use the logo in your advertisements, promotions, proposals, and other materials, including business cards, letterheads, advertising circulars, brochures, yellow page advertisements, mailings, banners, resumes, and invitations.
- Microsoft Certified Professional logo sheet. Before using the camera-ready logo, you must agree to the terms of the licensing agreement.
- Access to technical and product information directly from Microsoft through a secured area of the MCP Web site. Dedicated forums on CompuServe (GO MECFORUM) and The Microsoft Network enable Microsoft Certified Professionals to communicate directly with Microsoft and one another.
- One-year subscription to *Microsoft Certified Professional Magazine,* a career and professional development magazine created especially for Microsoft Certified Professionals.

- Invitations to Microsoft conferences, technical training sessions, and special events.

A Microsoft Certified Systems Engineer receives all the benefits mentioned above and the following additional benefits:

- Microsoft Certified Systems Engineer logos and other materials to help you identify yourself as a Microsoft Certified Systems Engineer to colleagues or clients.
- One-year subscription to the Microsoft TechNet Technical Information Network.
- One-year subscription to the Microsoft Beta Evaluation program. This benefit provides you with up to 12 free monthly beta software CDs for many of Microsoft's newest software products. This enables you to become familiar with new versions of Microsoft products before they are generally available. This benefit also includes access to a private CompuServe forum where you can exchange information with other program members and find information from Microsoft on current beta issues and product information.

Certify Me!

So you are ready to become a Microsoft Certified Professional. The examinations are administered through Sylvan Prometric (formerly Drake Prometric) and Virtual University Enterprises, or VUE (a division of National Computer Systems, Inc.) and are offered at more than 1,000 authorized testing centers around the world. Microsoft evaluates certification status based on current exam records. Your current exam record is the set of exams you have passed. To maintain Microsoft Certified Professional status, you must remain current on all the requirements for your certification.

Registering for an exam is easy. To register to take an exam with Sylvan Prometric, call (800) 755-EXAM (3926). Dial (612) 896-7000 or (612) 820-5707 if you cannot place a call to an 800 number from your location. To register with VUE, contact them at (888) 837-8616 or online at their Web site at **www.vue.com/ms**. You must schedule the exam at least one day before the day you want to take the exam. Taking the exam automatically enrolls you in the Microsoft Certified Professional program; you do not need to submit an application to Microsoft Corporation.

When you call to register, have the following information ready:

- Your name, organization (if any), mailing address, and phone number.
- A unique ID number (for example, your Social Security number).
- The number of the exam you wish to take (70-029 for the SQL Server 7 Design exam).

- A method of payment (for example, credit card number). If you pay by check, payment is due before the examination can be scheduled. The fee to take each exam is currently $100.

Additional Resources

One of the best sources of information about Microsoft certification tests comes from Microsoft itself. Because its products and technologies—and the tests that go with them—change frequently, the best place to go for exam-related information is online.

If you haven't already visited the Microsoft Certified Professional or Training and Certification pages, do so right now. As of this writing, the Microsoft Training and Certification page resides at **www.microsoft.com/train_cert** and the Microsoft Certified Professional page is at **www.microsoft.com/mcp**. Note that it may not be there by the time you read this, or it may have been replaced by something new, because the Microsoft site changes regularly. If this happens please read the next section, "Coping With Change On The Web."

The menu options in the home page's left-hand column point to important sources of information in the Training and Certification pages. Here's what to check out:

- **Train_Cert Summaries/By Product** Use this to jump to product-based summaries of all classroom education, training materials, study guides, and other information for specific products. In the Back Office section, under the heading "SQL Server 7," you'll find an entire page of information about SQL Server 7 training and certification, including links to the specific 70-029 test. This tells you a lot about your training and preparation options, and mentions all the tests that relate to SQL Server 7.
- **Search/Find an Exam** Pulls up a search tool that lets you list all Microsoft exams and locate all exams pertinent to any Microsoft certification (MCP, MCSD, MCSE, MCT, and so on), or those exams that cover a particular product. This tool is quite useful not only to examine the options, but also to obtain specific test preparation information, because each exam has its own associated preparation guide.
- **Downloads** Here, you'll find a list of the files and practice tests that Microsoft makes available to the public. These include several items worth downloading, especially the Certification Update, the Personal Exam Prep (PEP) tests, various assessment exams, and a general Exam Study Guide. Try to peruse these materials before taking your first test.

Of course, these are just the high points of what's available in the Microsoft Training and Certification pages. As you browse through them—and we strongly recommend that you do—you'll probably find other information we didn't mention here that is every bit as interesting and compelling.

Coping With Change On The Web

Sooner or later, all the specifics we've shared with you about the Microsoft Training and Certification pages, and all the other Web-based resources we mention throughout the rest of this book, will go stale or be replaced by newer information. In some cases, the URLs you find here may lead you to their replacements; in other cases, the URLs will go nowhere, leaving you with the dreaded 404 error message, *File not found*.

When that happens, please don't give up. There's always a way to find what you want on the Web, if you're willing to invest some time and energy. To begin with, most large or complex Web sites—and Microsoft's qualifies on both counts—offer a search engine. As long as you can get to the site itself, you can use this tool to help you find what you need.

The more particular or focused you can make a search request, the more likely it is that the results will include information you can use. You can search for Training and Certification will produce a lot of data about the subject in general. If you're specifically looking for, for example, the Preparation Guide for Exam 70-029, *Designing and Implementing Databases on Microsoft SQL Server 7*, you'll be more likely to get there quickly if you use a search string such as: *Exam 70-029* AND *Preparation Guide*. Likewise, if you want to find the Training and Certification downloads, try a search string such as: *Training and Certification* AND *download page*.

Finally, don't be afraid to use general search tools like **www.search.com**, **www.altavista.com**, or **www.excite.com** to find related information. Although Microsoft offers the best information about its certification exams online, there are plenty of third-party sources of information, training, and assistance in this area that do not have to follow a party line like Microsoft does. The bottom line is: If you can't find something where the book says it lives, start looking around.

About The Book

Career opportunities abound for well-prepared database designers and administrators. This book is designed as your doorway into database design and administration through Microsoft SQL Server 7. If you are new to SQL Server or database programming, this book is your beginning to an exciting future.

Others who have prior experience with SQL Server or perhaps an earlier version will find that this book adds depth and breadth to that experience. In addition, this text provides the knowledge you need to prepare for Microsoft's certification exam 70-029, *Designing and Implementing Databases on Microsoft SQL Server* 7. As of this printing, the exam is nonadaptive, and focuses on exhibits and application style questions. The practice exams in this book and on the CD are styled to prepare you for these questions.

Because SQL Server is closely tied to Windows NT Server, it is marvelously scalable and fits into both large and small organizations. It provides the cornerstone on which to build a multitier design for an application, an Internet Web site, or an Intranet. A new feature allows SQL Server to be installed on Windows 95, Windows 98 and Windows NT Workstation as well. The success of Windows SQL Server 7 is reflected in the huge number of software vendors and developers who develop in this environment or who have switched from other environments to Windows SQL Server.

When you complete this book, you will be at the threshold of a SQL design or administration career that can be very fulfilling and challenging. This is a rapidly advancing field that offers ample opportunity for personal growth and for making a contribution to your business or organization. The book is intended to provide you with knowledge that you can apply right away and a sound basis for understanding the changes that you will encounter in the future. It also is intended to give you the hands-on skills you need to be a valued professional in your organization.

The book is filled with hands-on projects that cover every aspect of programming and designing databases using SQL Server 7. The projects are designed to make what you learn come alive through a story of a new DBA that you can follow and allows you to actually perform the tasks discussed. Also, every chapter includes a range of practice questions to help prepare you for the Microsoft certification exam. All of these features are offered to reinforce your learning, so you'll feel confident in the knowledge you have gained from each chapter.

Chapter 1, "An Overview Of Microsoft SQL Server 7" provides a brief history of Relational Database Management Systems, particularly the Microsoft SQL Server product, as well as explaining its components, hardware, and software requirements.

In Chapter 2, "SQL Database Architecture" you are given a detailed look at the architecture and SQL design for databases.

Chapter 3, "Developing A Logical Database Design" explains the process for designing the model used to create the database project, which is very important for a successful application implementation.

We continue our look at this important process in Chapter 4, "Deriving The Physical Design." The mapping of the logical design to the physical layout is described in great detail in this chapter.

After reviewing the important building blocks of a database design, Chapter 5, "Tables" steps you through the proper planning process for designing your tables.

Chapter 6, "Indexes" steps you through configuring the Indexes you'll need to ensure that your design is optimized for speed.

Chapter 7, "Retrieving And Modifying Data" teaches you the basics about interacting with your SQL Server data, and explains important strategies for accessing and changing data quickly.

Chapter 8, "Transact-SQL Scripting And Command Batches" discusses ways to use multiple SQL Server commands together to accomplish jobs that no single command could achieve.

In Chapter 9, "Summarzing And Transforming Data" you will learn how to develop and fine-tune queries for summarizing and accumulating data.

Chapter 10, "Views" discusses in greater detail SQL Server's ability to create logical tables that restrict access to sensitive data and can simplify a programmer's interaction with the database.

Creating batches of database entries, as well as how to manage locks is discussed in Chapter 11, "Transactions And Locking". You will learn about the types of SQL Server locks, as well as the different methods for handling transactions here.

In Chapter 12, "Stored Procedures" we begin to look at some of the issues involving database programming. Chapter 12 provides a detailed discussion of stored procedures and their use.

Chapter 13, "Triggers" continues the discussion of database integrity, focusing on triggers, as well as the advantages and disadvantages associated with them.

In Chapter 14, "Creating The Physical Database" we will complete the process begun in Chapters 3 and 4. We will discuss the proper way to build you database using Microsoft's tools for SQL Server 7.

Often data resides outside a SQL Server. Chapter 15, "Remote Data Sources" discusses the process of accessing data from other database platforms such as Oracle. You'll also learn to attach spreadsheets and other office automation products and access them within SQL Server.

Chapter 16, "Data Transfers" discusses the process for importing data into your database. A powerful new tool, Microsoft's Data Transformation Services, is explained in this chapter.

Another new feature is the Full-Text capabilities in SQL Server 7. Chapter 17, "Implementing Full-Text Search" discusses the methods of implementing this exciting innovation.

Chapter 18, "Maintaining A Database" discusses the tricks of the trade for maintaining your database so that it runs with peak efficiency and shows you how to perform preventative maintenance to help avoid system downtime.

Chapter 19, "Diagnosing Problems And Improving Query Performance" completes our study of SQL Server 7 by examining the techniques used to examine the performance of your queries.

We also have included some helpful appendixes and a glossary.

Features

To aid you in fully understanding SQL Server 7 concepts, there are many features in this book designed to improve its value:

- **Chapter objectives** Each chapter in this book begins with a detailed list of the concepts to be mastered within that chapter. This list provides you with a quick reference to the contents of that chapter, as well as a useful study aid.
- **Illustrations and tables** Numerous illustrations of screenshots and components aid you in the visualization of common setup steps, theories, and concepts. In addition, many tables provide details and comparisons of both practical and theoretical information.
- **Hands-on projects** Although it is important to understand the theory behind server and networking technology, nothing can improve upon real-world experience. To this end, along with theoretical explanations, each chapter provides numerous hands-on projects aimed at providing you with real-world implementation experience.
- **Chapter summaries** Each chapter's text is followed by a summary of the concepts it has introduced. These summaries provide a helpful way to recap and revisit the ideas covered in each chapter.
- **Review questions** End-of-chapter assessment begins with a set of review questions that reinforce the ideas introduced in each chapter. These questions not only ensure that you have mastered the concepts, but are also written to help prepare you for the Microsoft certification examination.

Text And Graphic Conventions

Wherever appropriate, additional information and exercises have been added to this book to help you better understand what is being discussed in the chapter. Icons throughout the text alert you to additional materials. The icons used in this book are as follows:

The Note icon is used to present additional helpful material related to the subject being described.

Each hands-on activity in this book is preceded by the Hands-On Project icon and a description of the exercise that follows.

Tips are included from the author's experience that provide extra information about how to attack a problem, how to set up Proxy Server for a particular need, or what to do in certain real-world situations.

WHERE SHOULD YOU START?

This book is intended to be read in sequence, from beginning to end. Each chapter builds upon those that precede it, to provide a solid understanding of SQL Server 7. After completing the chapters, you may find it useful to go back through the book and use the review questions and projects to prepare for the Microsoft certification test for Designing and Implementing Databases on Microsoft SQL Server 7 *SQL* (Exam 70-029). Readers are also encouraged to investigate the many pointers to online and printed sources of additional information that are cited throughout this book. You'll find that much of the information in this book will serve as a good reference throughout your experience with SQL Server 7.

SYSTEM REQUIREMENTS

To complete the projects and assignments in the book, you will need access to SQL Server 7. These projects are not mandatory; however, the projects will give you experience using this resource as a prospective server administrator.

The recommended software and hardware configurations are described in the following sections.

SQL Server 7

SQL Server 7 system requirements include the following:

- Windows 95, 98, Windows NT Workstation 4 or Windows NT Server 4
- Pentium class computer with 32MB of RAM minimum
- VGA monitor
- Mouse or pointing device
- Hard disk with at least 125MB free
- CD-ROM drive

System Requirements For Exam Prep Software

System requirements for the software include the following:

- 8MB RAM (16MB recommended)
- VGA/256 Color display or better
- 6X CD-ROM Drive
- Windows NT 4 or Windows 95

About The CD-ROM

To become certified, you must pass rigorous certification exams that provide a valid and reliable measure of technical proficiency and expertise. The CD-ROM that comes with this book can be used in conjunction with the book to help you assess your progress in the event you choose to pursue Microsoft Professional Certification. The CD-ROM contains specially designed test simulation software that features practice exams. These content-based questions were expertly prepared to test your readiness for the official Microsoft certification examination on SQL Server 7 (Exam 70-029).

Practice Exam Features

The practice exams include the following features:

- Two complete tests.
- 80 questions on each test.
- 120-minute timed test to ensure exam readiness.
- Questions that can be marked and answered later.
- Graphical representation of your test grade.
- Grades are categorized by chapter.

Solutions To End-Of-Chapter Questions And Projects

For further help in making sure you are prepared for the SQL Server 7 certification exam, we have included solutions for the end-of-chapter review questions and hands-on projects on the CD-ROM.

Berg Software

This software includes an evaluation version of *ProcedurePro*, which allows users to generate commonly required stored procedures easily for tables on Microsoft SQL Server versions 6.5 and 7.

Hands-On Projects Sample Databases And Source Code

Certain projects and examples from the book are included for reference.

CHAPTER ONE

AN OVERVIEW OF MICROSOFT SQL SERVER 7

After Reading This Chapter And Completing The Exercises, You Will Be Able To:

- Define the new features in Microsoft SQL Server 7
- Identify the improvements from version 6.5
- Learn the tools included with Microsoft SQL Server 7 and their purposes

Microsoft SQL Server version 7 is a great leap forward in technology from the previous versions of Microsoft's flagship relational database product. It provides greater speed, flexibility, more automation, and better data migration tools than all of its predecessors. A relational database provides greater flexibility in designing and changing a database than does a non-relational one, and Microsoft's newest product provides not only this flexibility but also a lot of power that scales from small computers with personal operating systems up to clustered enterprise servers. You will face many questions about these features and enhancements in the SQL Server 7 Design and Implementation exam.

This chapter will introduce you to the improvements in Microsoft SQL Server 7. This information about some of these new features is but the tip of the iceberg. Much of this information is necessary background material for using the product and for questions found on the exam. Some of the concepts may be old hat to a seasoned Database Administrator (DBA), but a quick review of the chapter will introduce the concepts and terms that we will use throughout the book.

Microsoft SQL Server Version 7

Microsoft SQL Server was born in the late '80s in collaboration among Microsoft, Ashton-Tate (of Dbase fame), and Sybase Corporation to create a relational database to run on IBM's OS/2 operating system. Relational data-bases view data as *tables* or *sets*, and database syntax or operators allow the user to join the tables or produce horizontal or vertical subsets from these tables.

Mainframe databases usually consist of files of data, usually unrelated.

Data is the facts, figures, and details stored in a database; *information* is meaning derived from data. A *datum* is one unit of data.

Programmers designed the data files and then related them using programs, but it became quite complex to manage the changes. Data using this format is often stored redundantly, meaning that the information in one file may have to be stored again in another file to relate it (see Figure 1.1).

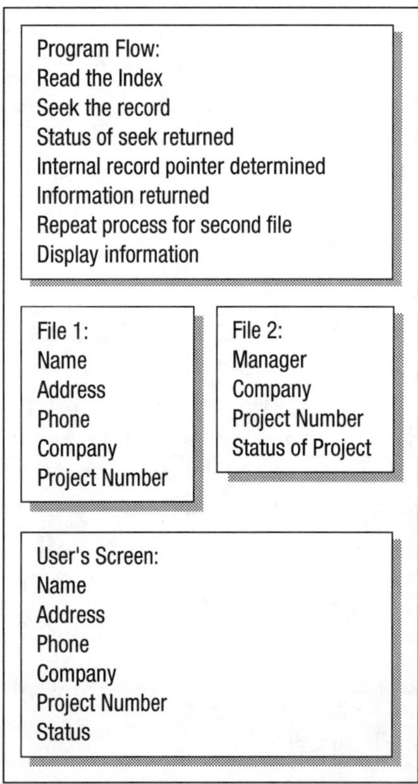

Figure 1.1 File database structure and relations.

Relational databases use a data storage engine, and usually use commands called *Structured Query Language*, or *SQL*, originally created by an IBM researcher in the 1970s. The SQL language allows rapid changes to be made to the data or its structure very quickly, without having to move the data out first. Data can be related using one or more fields in the related tables in what is known as a *join* (see Figure 1.2).

Ashton-Tate left the partnership when Microsoft decided to create its own operating system, known as *Windows NT*. Microsoft SQL Server was released as version 4.2 in 1988 based on source code licensed from Sybase. Microsoft took full control of the database code and released version 6 in 1996. Version 6.5 was released with many new enhancements, but still had a lot of similarity to Sybase's relational database product.

With SQL Server 7, Microsoft has completely rewritten the base code to be faster, more scalable, and more powerful than any of its previous versions. Microsoft SQL Server 7 began development in May 1996. Three beta versions were released in June 1997, December 1997, and June 1998. The product was released to the market on November 25, 1998. That may seem like a short time to create a product of such magnitude (and it is), but the product had a total of 623 builds, or testing versions. (The official build number of the released product

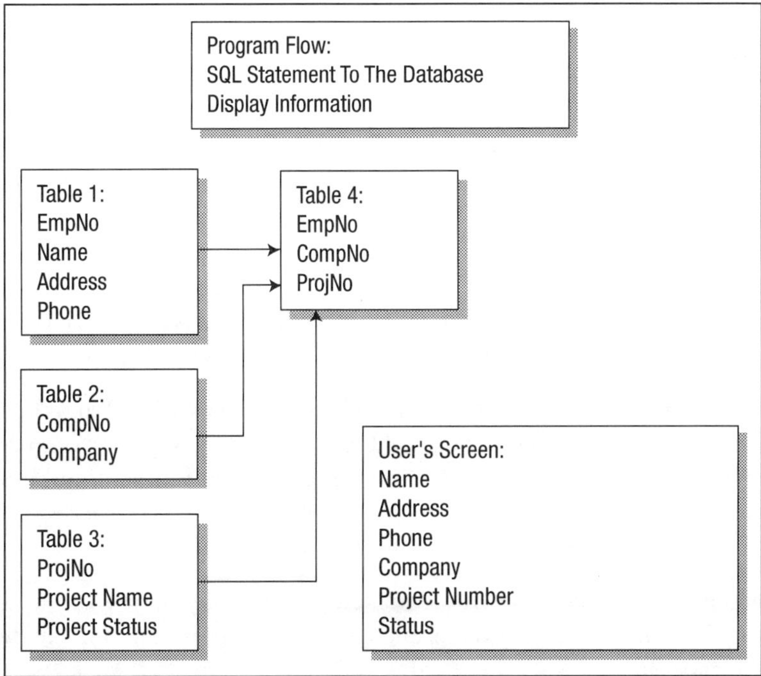

Figure 1.2 SQL relational tables.

is 623.07.) More than 100,000 sites were involved in beta testing, not least of all Microsoft, which uses SQL Server for all of the systems developed internally by its own Information Technology group. During the testing of version 7, more than 1,200 databases received from 31 countries were migrated to version 7. During this time, approximately 3.5 million hours of testing occurred, and more than 16 million functional tests were performed. SQL Server 7 was definitely not a new product when it hit the market.

Features In Microsoft SQL Server 7

Microsoft has introduced many new features with version 7. Among them are speed, tuning, platforms, upgrades, and data transformations. Let's examine each of these.

Speed

Until version 7, the SQL Server core database engine components had not changed much from the source code licensed from Sybase. SQL Server 7 has been completely redesigned to take full advantage of today's more powerful processors and larger storage options. Microsoft SQL Server 7 has been optimized to be faster than previous Microsoft databases by being able to split one *query* (a database access request) across many processors, and to decide when it is best to do so. This allows the maximum use of all CPUs in a computer during requests.

New indexing options also allow for faster access to data when sorts or specific queries are used. The size of *pages* (more on this later) that SQL Server 7 uses has been increased from 2K in version 6.5 to 8K. Think of two people carrying firewood to a campsite. If they move at the same speed, but the second person carries four times as much firewood, then the second person is able to get more wood to the campsite at one time. In a similar fashion, SQL Server 7 can bring back more data at one time and has to make fewer trips to the database engine to do so.

Another speed enhancement is the *Tabular Data Stream (TDS)* that the query processor engine uses. The TDS is the protocol used by SQL Server to communicate with the server. TDS is a logical data stream protocol, and rides on a lower-level communication protocol. This allows much faster access to the database architecture than in previous versions.

The Query Optimizer has been automated to constantly update old statistics (using sampling) on the database, enabling up-to-the-minute information for the query plan.

A *query plan* is a read-only data structure that is stored in memory; it can be used by any number of users. No user information is stored in the query plan, and never more than one or two copies of the query plan are in memory. This process makes the return of data faster. Query plans are also now shared across connections, which gives the processor more time to return data. The server does this by assigning to the query plan an identification number that can be referenced later. The query processor also uses index intersection and union strategies to filter data even before it gets rows from the database.

Tuning

One of the largest improvements to SQL Server is the *automatic tuning* that takes place in SQL Server 7. Prior to this version (and still in most other relational database products from competing companies), one of the most time-consuming and difficult tasks a DBA had was to tune the dozens of interrelated settings that controlled buffers, memory, and the like to keep the database running in optimal fashion. Microsoft spent a great deal of time on the programming of SQL Server 7 so that the server can *watch* the way that users are accessing the data and can make these parameter changes automatically. You still have the option to set the parameters manually, but in most cases this would actually slow down the data-base. Plenty of integration with the NT operating system allows this dynamic tuning to take place.

Platforms

Most relational database products run only on fairly large-scale computers and usually on only a Network Operating System (NOS). This always presented a problem for developers who wished to have demonstration versions of their software or for users to run their applications on a disconnected network (like laptops). By enabling SQL Server to run the same code base on Windows 95, Windows 98, and Windows NT Workstation and Server, Microsoft enables the distribution of applications using SQL Server. Providing the capability to run on these smaller footprint operating systems also allows the added benefit of setting up replication for road warriors or laptop users who collect information in the field and then transfer information to the network server.

Upgrades

Because many companies (including Microsoft) adopted the earlier versions of Microsoft's relational database, they became concerned about the time and effort involved in moving data and programs to a new version. Realizing that they cannot make sales if this concern were not addressed, Microsoft expended a great deal of effort in making this transition as painless as possible. Microsoft also kept a keen eye on the competition, making many enhancements to this upgrade process so that a company can migrate from those platforms, too. Even so, version 6.5 backups are not compatible with version 7's restore feature.

Note: Every product sold at Microsoft is recorded on a SQL Server database.

Data Transformations

Another difficult database task is moving data out of a particular relational database pro-duct into other database products or foreign file formats. To answer this demand, Microsoft has created the *Data Transformation Service (DTS)*, a product unto itself in power and flexibility. This tool allows data to be moved to and from Microsoft SQL Server 7 using graphical wizards or programs. DTS can even transform data en route; it can also be used to transfer and transform data between any two OLE DB-compliant database products and is useful for data warehousing.

Improvements From Microsoft SQL Server 6.5

Microsoft has made significant improvements in several areas of SQL Server 7 over version 6.5. Not all of these are important to memorize, but knowing the differences can help you with upgrading from SQL Server 6.5 and will also assist you with questions on Microsoft's exam. Let's examine some of the major areas.

New Support For Windows 95 And Windows 98 Servers

The Windows 95, Windows 98, and Windows NT Workstation (or Windows 2000 Professional) operating systems can now host the SQL Server Engine, as well as Windows NT Workstation. Previously, Windows NT Work-station could act as a full SQL server, although this broke the licensing agreement with Microsoft for SQL Server. Many developers felt this was the only way to create and test applications locally. Microsoft had provided a version of SQL Server designed to run on Windows NT Workstation, but slight differences from the full server version made the testing impractical. A major change is that Windows NT Workstation does not allow the installation of the standard edition of Microsoft SQL Server. With the Windows 95 and Windows 98 operating systems now supported, users can run their demonstration or embedded database code on these operating systems. Laptop computers are supported with merge replication and conflict resolution. SQL Server 7 for Windows 95 and Windows 98 operating systems is fully featured, with the exception of operating system limitations. Symmetric multiprocessors, named *pipes*, full-text search, asynchronous I/O, and integrated security features are not supported on Windows 95 or Windows 98 due to operating system limitations. See Table 1.1 for a list of the major changes from version 6.5 to 7.

Table 1.1 List of the major changes from version 6.5 to 7 of SQL Server.

Item	SQL Server 7	SQL Server 6.5
File Size	32TB	32GB
Objects	2,147,483,647	2,000,000,000
Database total size	1,048,516TB	1TB
Columns (in one table)	1,024	250
Row length (bytes)	8,060	1,962
Character column (bytes)	8,000	255
SELECT tables limit	32	16
Memory use per user	24K	44K
Memory use per open database	2,880 bytes	1,144 bytes per server plus 160 bytes per database
Memory use per open object	276 bytes	240 bytes
Memory size per lock	96 bytes	60 bytes

Dynamic Database Size Management

In version 6.5 and below, databases were assigned to SQL Server logical *devices*, which were then assigned to files. It was very important to document those devices and configurations in case a rebuild was required. Databases for SQL Server 7 are created based on operating system files. You can create databases in version 7 with one **CREATE DATABASE** statement. You can also use a graphical method (which we'll examine in Chapter 12) to create a new database or to alter an existing database.

A SQL Server 7 database consists of two or more files. One file (or more) holds the data, and the other file is used for the transaction log.

In a SQL Server 7 file, the first data file is called the *primary file*, and has an extension of .mdf. Any other files used to store data for a database are called *secondary* and have an extension of .ndf. The transaction log file (there can be only one) has an extension of .ldf.

You can use more files for one database, but only one database can be contained in a file. A SQL Server 7 setting allows a database file to expand automatically so that you don't have to watch the space you're using as the data grows or run any new commands against the database. When you create a database, you can specify a growth increment. As the file gets full, it will grow by the size you indicated in the growth increment. You should also specify a file size; if you don't, the file can continue to grow until it has used all available space on the disk. Another enhancement is that when a database is *dropped* (deleted), the files for that database are also deleted. In previous versions of SQL Server, the files remained intact after you deleted the database and an operating system command was necessary to remove the deleted database.

You can *detach* a database, which removes the database from the server but keeps the files intact on the operating system. The useful part of this feature is that the data-base can then be *attached* to the same or even another server. This feature makes the database very portable. The database is left in exactly the same state it was in when it was detached, and can even be copied and distributed to multiple locations or servers. A good use for this feature would be in a testing environ-ment. You could detach the database, back up those files, and then re-attach it to the same server. By restoring the database files from the backup, the database could be attached to a new server so that a *clean* testing database is available.

Wizards

Wizards are graphical software programs that guide you through complex database tasks. Microsoft SQL Server 7 has enhanced old wizards and added new ones—more than 25—that step through some rather complicated tasks quite simply. You should be familiar with the operations you can and cannot do with a wizard. Here are some of the current wizards:

- Database
  - Create Database
  - Create Diagram
  - Create Index
  - Create Login
  - Create Stored Procedures
  - Create View
- Management
  - Backup
  - Create Job
  - Create Trace
  - Database Maintenance Plan
  - Index Tuning
- Setup
  - Version Upgrade

- Data Transformation Services (DTS)
    - Import
    - Export
- Replication
    - Configure Publishing And Distribution
    - Create Publication
    - Pull Subscription
    - Push Subscription
- Others
    - Full-text Indexing
    - ODBC Driver
    - Web Assistant

Locking Enhancements

Locks on a database occur when two or more users try to query, update, or delete the same datum at the same time. If one user reads from the database that the company has five units available to sell and attempts to sell all five, and meanwhile another user reads that the company has five units and attempts to sell all five, a problem can quickly develop. To correct this problem, data is *locked*, or prevented from access, while one user takes ownership of it. While this user updates the data, all other users are unable to access it.

Lock settings are always a trade-off between performance and security. As the number of transactions increase, locking can become quite an issue. Microsoft SQL Server 6.5 used page locking, preventing users from modifying an entire 2K page of data until the first process had finished with the data. To solve this problem, lock settings are now dynamic, and a cost is determined to choose the type and number of locks on the database. *Full row-level locking* is the default. This means that only the row requested is locked. However, SQL Server 7 will dynamically scale to page or table locking based on a cost algorithm.

SQL Server 7 supports full row-level locking not only for data rows but for index entries as well. A lock manager automatically adjusts the locks it uses for large databases. Setting the number and type of locks was previously somewhere between an art and black magic, which is the stuff better left to something like a lock manager.

Transact-SQL Enhancements

Transact-SQL (or T-SQL) is Microsoft's extension, or broadening, of the set of commands available in the ANSI version of the Structured Query Language. Some of these commands will appear on the test. You should be familiar with not only the syntax of these commands but also how they are used. New or enhanced T-SQL commands include:

- **ALTER PROCEDURE** *Procedures* are code stored in the database that performs various activities on data. Previously a procedure had to be dropped and created again to make a change. **ALTER PROCEDURE** allows the procedure to be changes without having to drop it first.
- **ALTER TRIGGER** *Triggers* are actions tied to a table that contain code that *fires* when an event happens in that table. A classic use for triggers is to have them modify another table when changing data, thereby enforcing referential integrity (RI), something very important to a database. This new statement allows changes to be made *on the fly*, even by code, that would change a trigger from perhaps a **DELETE** to an **UPDATE**.
- **ALTER VIEW** *Views* are queries against one or more tables that create a new (logical) collection of that data. Views allow you to show only portions of a table or group of tables that looks just like a table to other users or programs. This new enhancement changes a previously created view without affecting any other stored procedures or triggers.
- **ALTER TABLE** *Tables* are the collection of data by rows and columns, and are the heart of relational database storage. This enhancement modifies a table definition by altering, adding, or deleting columns and constraints (for referential integrity) or by disabling or enabling constraints and triggers.
- **BULK INSERT** This command copies data into a database table or view using a user-defined format. It can be executed within transactions (more on transactions later). When you *undo* (roll back) this statement using multiple batches, all batches are rolled back.
- **COMMIT WORK** *Transactions* are groups of things you'd like the server to keep together—for instance, adding both the client's name and address to several tables at once. If a client's record isn't saved, no reason exists to save the address, either. By placing **BEGIN TRANSACTION** before the commands, you enter and **COMMIT WORK** after the commands, the entire group is kept together. Another command, **COMMIT TRANSACTION**, has been around for at least two versions, but the new command makes SQL Server 7 ANSI-92 compliant. ANSI-92 is a standard for SQL database products.
- **DENY** This command denies permission from a user and prevents the user from inheriting the permission through subsequent group or role

memberships. We'll see how these things are interrelated in the Security section. The things the user or group can be denied can include:

- **CREATE DATABASE**
- **CREATE DEFAULT**
- **CREATE PROCEDURE**
- **CREATE RULE**
- **CREATE TABLE**
- **CREATE VIEW**
- **BACKUP DATABASE**
- **BACKUP LOG**

This is another command that makes SQL Server 7 ANSI-92 compliant.

- **RESTORE** The previous command for restoring a database was called **LOAD**. It's still there for backward compatibility, but **RESTORE** does much more. The Database Administration exam goes into much more detail than the study for this exam requires, but this book will touch on this command and the commands that go with it that are enhanced, such as:
  - **RESTORE FILELISTONLY**
  - **RESTORE HEADERONLY**
  - **RESTORE LABELONLY**
  - **RESTORE VERIFYONLY**
- **ROLLBACK WORK** When a transaction (the group of data we wanted to keep together) is sent to the database (committed), you can undo that group of work with this command. Another command exists like this one (**ROLLBACK TRANSACTION**), but **ROLLBACK WORK** (you guessed it) makes SQL Server 7 ANSI-92 compliant. This command also has one other important difference: When you *nest* (place one inside another) transactions, **ROLLBACK WORK** always rolls back to the *first* **BEGIN TRANSACTION** statement and it decrements the **@@TRANCOUNT** system function to 0.

New Programming Interfaces

Users don't access Microsoft SQL Server databases directly. Applications are written to access the data in SQL Server. These programs can include the utilities that come with SQL Server, such as the Enterprise Manager or Query Analyzer (more on that follows) or other applications. Programmers wishing to access SQL Server can use the Component Object Model (COM) or the Microsoft ActiveX Data Objects (ADO) interface.

COM

The Component Object Model (COM) is the framework that Microsoft and other vendors developed for designing applications. COM is the most important programming initiative in the Microsoft coding environment. Microsoft reports that COM is in use on well over 150 million systems worldwide. COM is a well-defined and freely available specification and reference for writing code. Major system vendors such as Hewlett Packard, Digital Equipment Corporation, Siemens-Nixdorf, and Silicon Graphics have announced plans to ship COM on Unix and other operating systems within a year of this writing.

COM is basically a software architecture that allows applications to be built from binary software components. COM is the underlying architecture that forms software services, such as Object Linking and Embedding (OLE). OLE services are used in creating things like compound documents, custom controls, inter-application scripting, data transfer, and other software interactions.

COM is also a binary standard for component interoperability and is programming language-independent. It is used on all Microsoft platforms and even the Apple Macintosh operating system, as well as some varieties of Unix. COM uses a single programming model for components to communicate within the same process.

OLE DB

OLE DB is an Application Programming Interface (API) that allows COM applications to place and retrieve data from various data sources. An OLE DB data source can include data stored in many different formats, not just Microsoft SQL Server 7 databases.

When an application is written using OLE DB, an OLE DB provider accesses the data source. Microsoft SQL Server 7 has a native OLE DB Provider for SQL Server that can be used by OLE DB applications to access the data in SQL Server. In SQL Server 6 and 6.5, OLE DB applications had to use Open Database Connectivity calls (ODBC) to access the data.

OLE DB is the API that Microsoft recommended for tools, utilities, or even system-level development for access to SQL Server features that are not available using the ADO interface.

ADO

The ADO interface is essentially built on top of OLE DB. ADO is a new data access interface used to transfer data to and from with any OLE DB-compliant data source. ADO sits at the application level for use with OLE DB. The ADO interface is installed as part of the SQL Server installation.

Replication Enhancements

Microsoft SQL Server made big inroads into the Relational Database Management System (RDBMS) market when it introduced replication in version 6. SQL Server 7 continues to enhance this function and the replication feature continues to build on the *publish and subscribe* metaphor.

Some of the new APIs support two-way (*bidirectional*) replication with other Relational Database Management Servers, such as Oracle, DB2, Sybase, and Informix. These APIs also allow replication with nonrelational database file formats. Previously, only after-market products were available to perform these functions, and they were neither inexpensive nor simple to learn.

A new type of replication has been added called *merge replication*. This type of replication is used for disconnected applications like laptops and offices with remote network links. The value of this feature will be much appreciated by the companies who base their programming efforts on SQL Server and wish to demonstrate the product on their sales forces' laptop computers.

Microsoft provides enhanced transactional replication with a redesigned distribution database for scalability, *pull* and *anonymous* subscribers, and stored procedure replication. The administration of replication has been simplified with the addition of a new interface. More wizards have also been added. SQL Server 7 includes integrated monitoring and replication agents for the replication features as well.

SQL Server Agent

The SQL Server Executive from the previous versions of Microsoft SQL has been changed to the *SQL Server Agent* in version 7. The *SQL Server Agent* performs the functions previously served by the SQL Server Executive, such as the following:

- Job scheduling and execution
- Alert creation and notification

The SQL Server Agent is a service that can be independently controlled from the Services applet in the Control Panel. One of the new enhancements for this service is the ability to create and control jobs that run on many servers. To set up the Agent, first configure the *Operators*, then you can assign alerts to those Operators. See Figure 1.3 to view a SQL Server Agent panel.

Once you've created the operators and set alerts for them, you can create *jobs*. Jobs contain steps, schedules, and notifications. Steps are enhanced in SQL Server 7 and can include the following items (from the drop-down list):

- Active scripting
- CmdExec

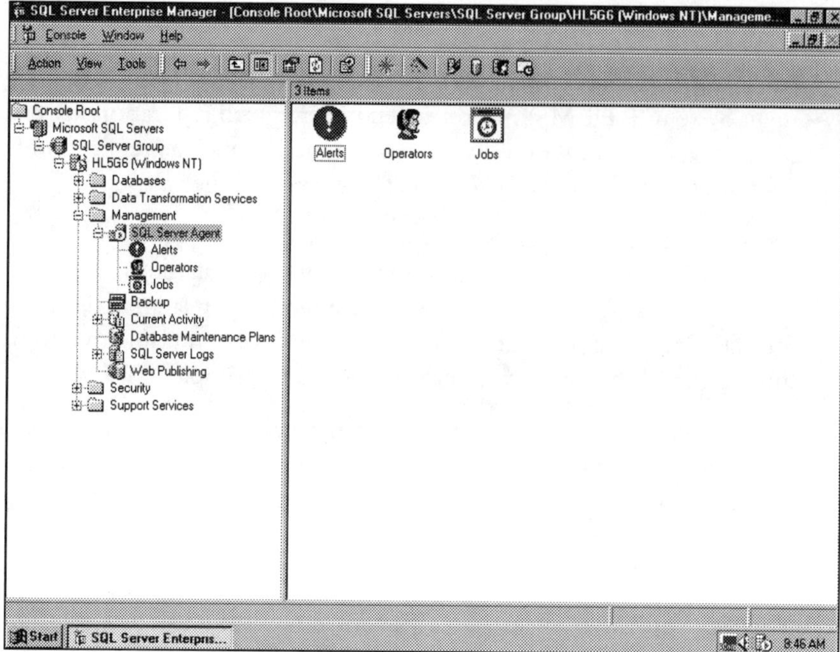

Figure 1.3 SQL Server Agent panel.

- Distribution
- Logreader
- Merge
- Snapshot
- TSQL

These steps can be set to continue based on a status of successful completion, unsuccessful completion, or whenever the job completes to move on to the next step. The scheduler allows the job to be run one time, on a recurring basis, when the SQL Server Agent is started, or even when the CPU is at an idle threshold.

SQL Server Agent information is stored in the *msdb* database.

Full-Text Search

A new feature in Microsoft SQL Server 7 is called the *full-text search.* You can create support for text searching on character-based data in SQL Server tables. The process involves creating indexes of specified words in selected columns of selected tables. You use the T-SQL language to use these indexes to support searches. You can manage full-text indexes from SQL Server Enterprise Manager or through stored procedures. Be warned: Full-text searching requires increased overhead in CPU cycles, as well as administration time

Improved Support For Data Warehousing

Microsoft SQL Server 7 also includes the *Online Analytical Processing Server,* called the *Microsoft SQL Server OLAP Services*. Database users in a typical operational database use something called *Online Transaction Processing (OLTP)*. The difference between OLAP and OLTP is in the way the data is stored. OLAP data is stored in a nonnormalized form, whereas OLTP data is stored in a normalized form. An OLAP server provides summarized data in a specially grouped form that provides information to a Decision Support Service (DSS) for analysis.

The Microsoft SQL Server OLAP Services provides multidimensional data analysis normally found in add-on tools for other database products.

The Microsoft OLAP Server supports Multidimensional Online Analytical Processing (MOLAP), Relational Online Analytical Processing (ROLAP), and Hybrid Online Analytical Processing (HOLAP) implementations of Data Warehousing.

The Microsoft SQL Server OLAP Service provides *Distributed Merge Replication.* This feature keeps changes from those remote databases in synchronization with the master database. This can be done over the Internet or even over Remote Access Service (RAS). You can also integrate the Microsoft SQL Server OLAP Service with Microsoft Office, most notably the pivot tables found in Microsoft Excel.

Tools

Microsoft has added many new tools to work with SQL Server 7. We will look at the biggest changes that have been made in the graphical tools suite, and we'll also examine a few of the more important command-line tools that have been updated. All the graphical tools are encased within Microsoft's newest management framework called the Microsoft Management Console (MMC) (see Figure 1.4).

SQL Server Enterprise Manager is now a *snap-in* component to the MMC, which allows it to share the same interface with other BackOffice tools. The MMC can simplify enterprise management tasks by combining the various management tools required to operate a network server into the same framework. The MMC is automatically installed along with SQL Server Enterprise Manager.

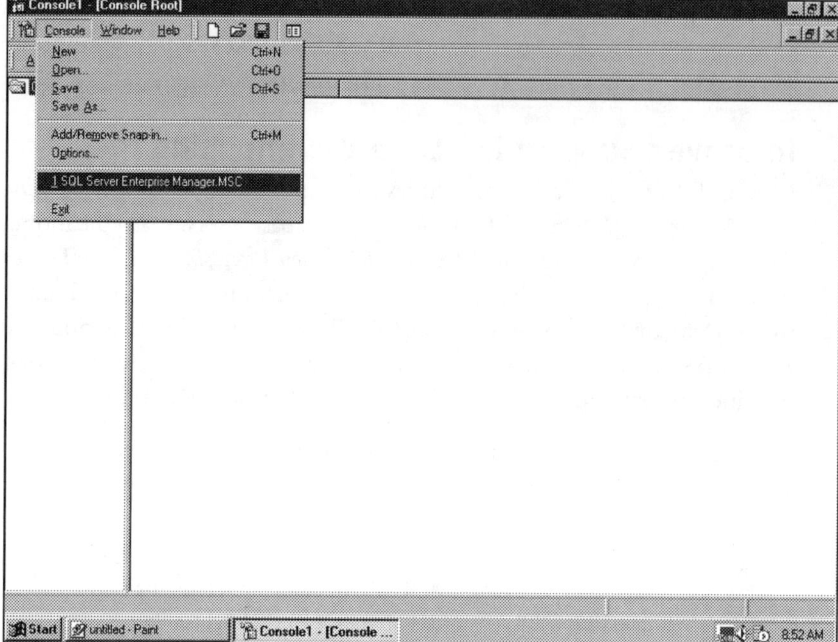

Figure 1.4 The Microsoft Management Console.

Enterprise Manager

The *SQL Server Enterprise Manager* is the graphical utility used to configure and manage all of your SQL Server and SQL Server objects, whether local to you or not. SQL Server Enterprise Manager includes a scheduler so that you can set events or management tasks to run at whatever time you choose. This scheduler is independent of the Scheduler Control Panel applet that runs on the Windows NT operating system (see Figure 1.5).

The Enterprise Manager also includes a graphical workspace for setting up the various administrators' information for alert capability. Using the Enterprise Manager, you can configure beeper numbers, email addresses, and network addresses of the people you would like to notify when an error or even a user-defined event occurs. One of the useful parts of this feature is the ability to add times and dates when a particular operator should be notified. This is a great feature if you'd rather not be awakened at 2 A.M. in the morning to be notified that the backup was successful. In addition the Enterprise Manager has a built-in replication management interface that permits you to quickly determine the state of the replication scheme you've created.

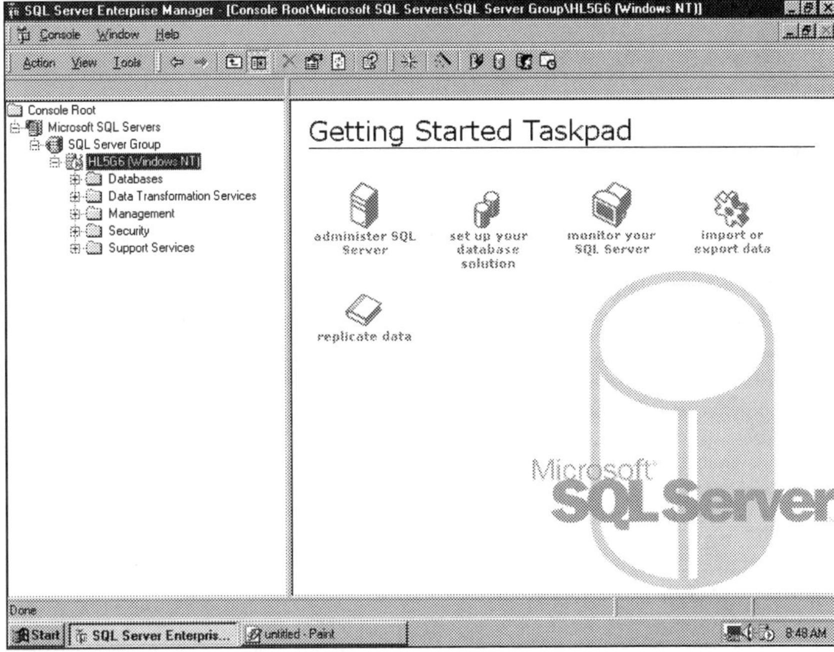

Figure 1.5 SQL Enterprise Manager.

You can also use SQL Server Enterprise Manager to graphically perform the following:

- Manage logins, permissions, and users
- Manage backup services and databases
- Create scripts
- Back up the database and transaction logs
- Create full-text indexes, database diagrams, and database maintenance plans
- Manage tables, views, stored procedures, triggers, indexes, rules, defaults, and user-defined data types
- Import and export data
- Transform data
- Perform Web administrator tasks

Query Analyzer

The Microsoft SQL Server Query Analyzer in version 7 replaces the ISQL_w and MSQuery tools from version 6.5 (see Figure 1.6).

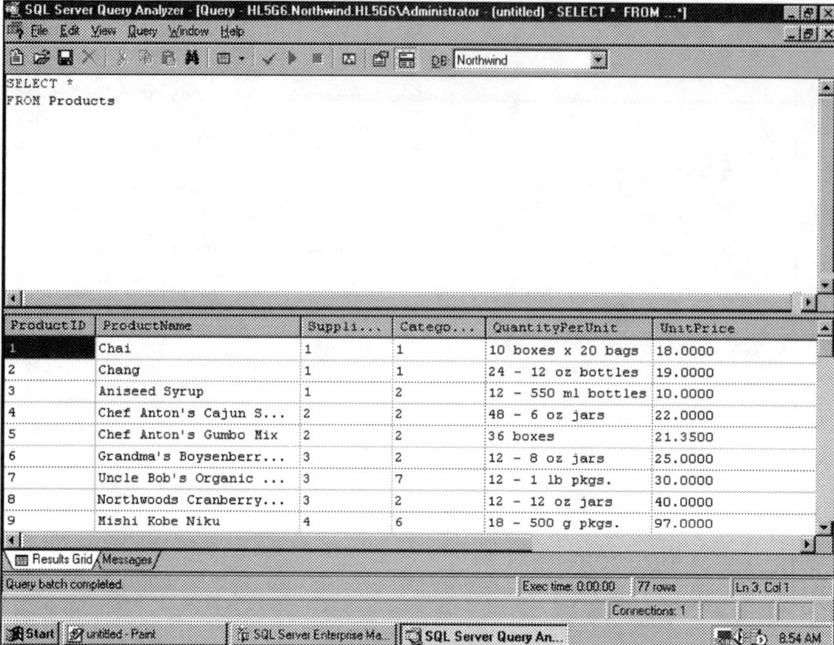

Figure 1.6 SQL Query Analyzer with grid display.

The *Query Analyzer* is a graphical tool that permits you to write queries and execute those queries against the SQL Server 7 database. With this tool you can also execute multiple queries simultaneously. One of the enhanced features is the ability to view the results as a grid. The query panel is also color-coded to easily denote keywords and variables.

The *Execution Plan* option graphically displays the data retrieval methods chosen by the Microsoft SQL Server query optimizer. This plan display uses icons to show the specific statements and queries in SQL Server. You can also analyze the query plan and receive assistance for improving the query's performance. The SQL Server Query Analyzer also displays suggestions for more indexes or statistics on nonindexed columns that would speed the retrieval of data. The Query Analyzer does this by showing the statistics that are missing and allows you to make changes to the structure of the database or query that will correct the errors.

SQL Profiler

The Microsoft SQL Server Profiler in version 7 replaces the Trace utility found in SQL Server 6.5. This tool can capture a continuous record of all server activity as it happens (see Figure 1.7).

SQL Server Profiler monitors any events produced by SQL Server and can filter events based on user-specified criteria. SQL Server Profiler can output to the

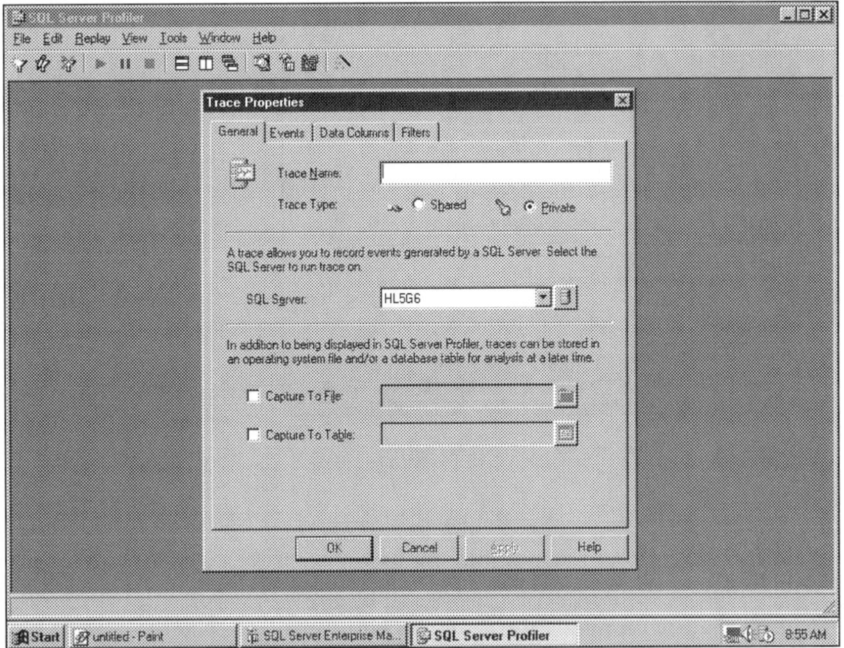

Figure 1.7 SQL Server Profiler.

screen, to a file, or even a table within SQL Server 7. The SQL Server Profiler allows you to replay traces, allowing you to run a sequence of events over and over again for testing or debugging. With SQL Server Profiler you can monitor T-SQL statements, batches, object usage, locking, security events, errors, and other SQL Server objects. You can also monitor queries, stored procedures, locks, and transactions, as well as log changes and replay captured data on another server by running the activity captured on the first server.

Index Tuning Wizard

A difficult part of optimizing a database is picking the best possible index arrangements. Almost no other setting can gain or lose as much performance as having proper indexes on the database. On the other hand, completely understanding not only SQL Server internals and processes but also the interrelation of all tables and access methods of a database is a daunting task, to say the least. On large databases, tuning can quickly become an overly complex task. A new enhancement to SQL Server in version 7 is the addition of an Index Tuning Wizard that can examine the database and make indexing recommendations for that structure (see Figure 1.8).

To diagnose a database accurately, the wizard needs a sample of work done on that database by users, called a *workload*. If you don't have a representative of this workload or it isn't feasible to perform one, SQL Server 7 can generate one for

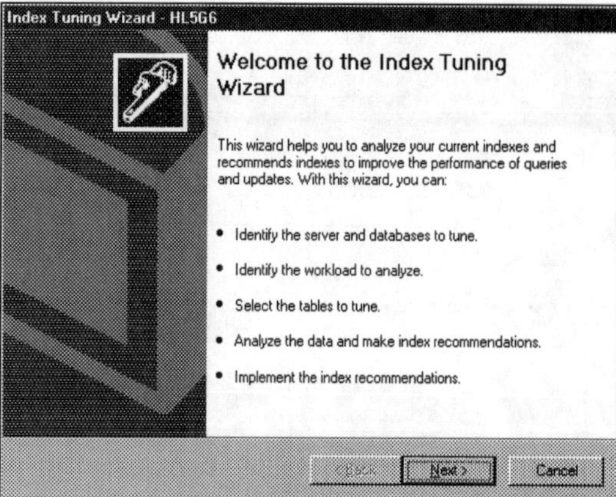

Figure 1.8 The Index Tuning Wizard.

you. Once you've created your workload and it's been examined, the Index Tuning Wizard can recommend the best indexes for a database. It can also analyze what effects the proposed changes might have. If you're not happy with a particular recommendation, you can customize it. Once the wizard has made the recommendations, you can implement the changes immediately, schedule the changes to be made later, or even save the recommendations to a SQL script.

Data Transformation Services (DTS)

The DTS Wizard can assemble data from many sources and *pump* (the Microsoft term) that data into a SQL Server database or even other databases or files. This data can be transformed while transferring the data using ActiveX or SQL scripts. Data can also be modified allowing multiple tables from a sending database to be merged into one table on a receiving database. Because DTS uses any OLE DB source, you could use this tool to transfer data between DB2 and Oracle, on a periodic scheduled basis (see Figure 1.9).

DTS can graphically replace the **BCP** command with a graphical import utility. With DTS you also have the ability to define a series of related *jobs* to perform during the transformation. These jobs can be programs, SQL statements, batch files, or any other valid command. You also set the steps or sequence in which these jobs should be performed. As an example, you could transfer a table, copy a file, send a notification, and then transfer the next table.

DTS operations can be scheduled, allowing you to automate the transfer of data. You can also set the DTS commands (grouped as a *package*) to be called from a stored procedure. This feature would allow you to set a condition on a table to perform the transfer if it reaches a certain limit or contains a certain value.

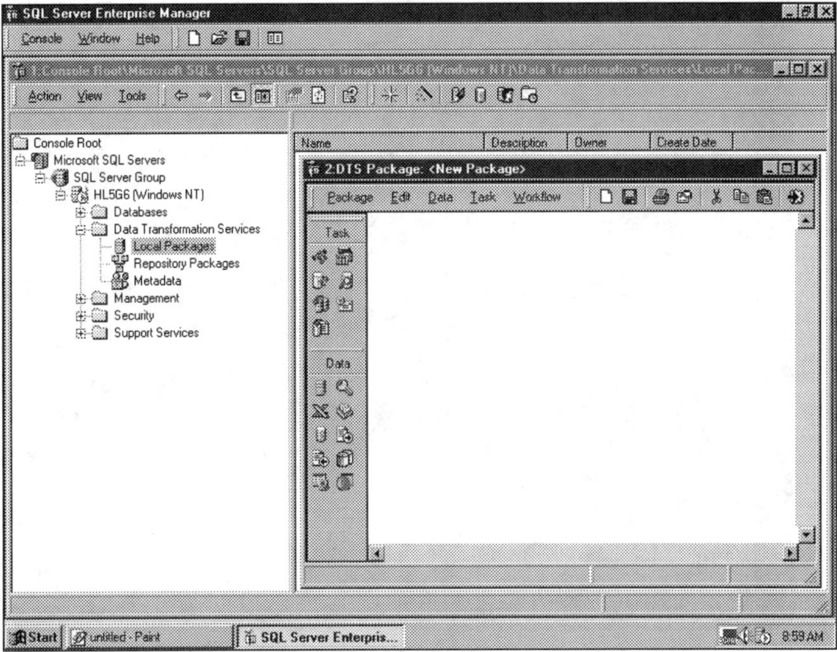

Figure 1.9 Data Transformation Services.

osql

The *osql utility* is a command-line utility to execute T-SQL statements and scripts (see Figure 1.10). The osql utility is an ODBC client like isql, which is based on DB-Library. The difference is that the osql utility uses the ODBC database Application Programming Interface (API). Both osql and isql are provided with the Microsoft SQL Server version 7 installation. The *isql* utility, however, does not support some SQL Server version 7 features. For example, isql cannot access columns defined with the ntext data type and truncates any char, varchar, nchar, or nvarchar columns that are longer than 255 bytes. Other than that, both osql and isql allow the same commands to be run.

SQL Scheduler

This tool, which is configured within the Enterprise Manager, allows you to set up dates, times, and recurrence patterns for activities to happen within SQL Server 7. This tool controls activities such as backups and maintenance that you need to occur automatically or when you are not available (see Figure 1.11).

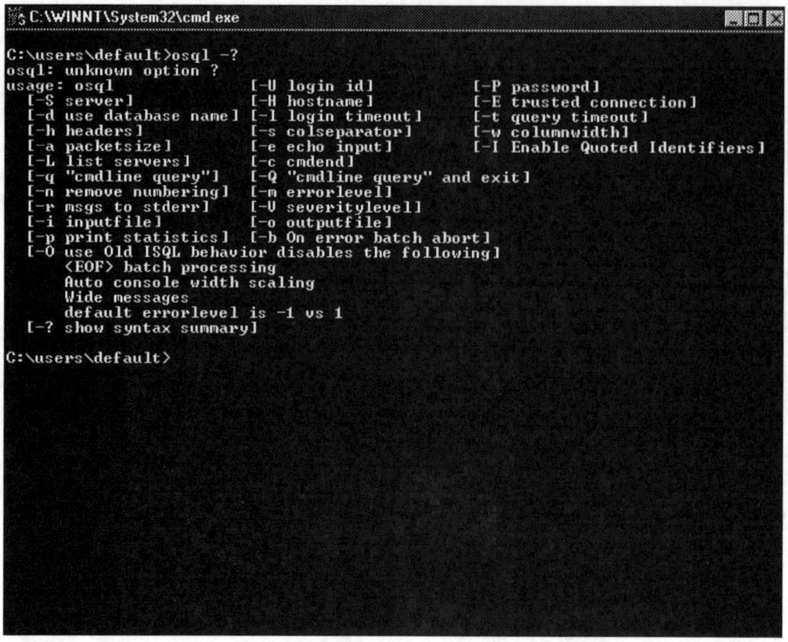
C:\WINNT\System32\cmd.exe
C:\users\default>osql -?
osql: unknown option ?
usage: osql [-U login id] [-P password]
[-S server] [-H hostname] [-E trusted connection]
[-d use database name] [-l login timeout] [-t query timeout]
[-h headers] [-s colseparator] [-w columnwidth]
[-a packetsize] [-e echo input] [-I Enable Quoted Identifiers]
[-L list servers] [-c cmdend]
[-q "cmdline query"] [-Q "cmdline query" and exit]
[-n remove numbering] [-m errorlevel]
[-r msgs to stderr] [-V severitylevel]
[-i inputfile] [-o outputfile]
[-p print statistics] [-b On error batch abort]
[-O use Old ISQL behavior disables the following]
<EOF> batch processing
Auto console width scaling
Wide messages
default errorlevel is -1 vs 1
[-? show syntax summary]
C:\users\default>

Figure 1.10 osql command line.

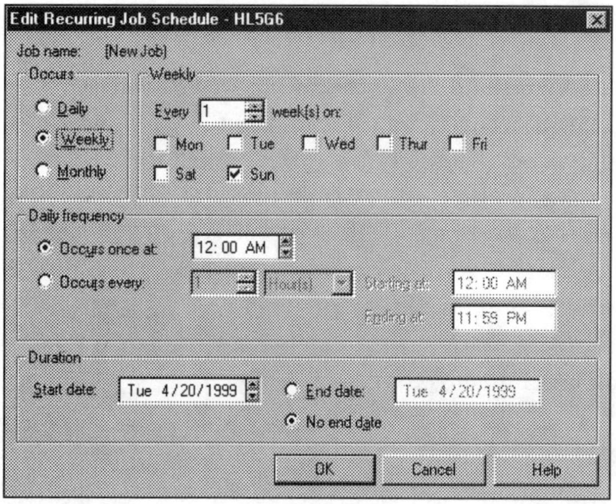
Edit Recurring Job Schedule - HL5G6
Job name: [New Job]
Occurs
Daily
Weekly
Monthly
Weekly
Every 1 week(s) on:
Mon Tue Wed Thur Fri
Sat Sun
Daily frequency
Occurs once at: 12:00 AM
Occurs every: 1 Hour(s) Starting at: 12:00 AM
Ending at: 11:59 PM
Duration
Start date: Tue 4/20/1999
End date: Tue 4/20/1999
No end date
OK
Cancel
Help

Figure 1.11 SQL scheduler.

The Database Diagram Tool

One of the best ways to create complex database designs is to visualize graphically the relationships between tables. In the past a database was designed by creating large diagrams called *Entity Relationship Diagrams* (*ERD*). This process was very expensive and took quite a bit of training on the graphical tool required to create these diagrams. Microsoft includes a new tool in SQL Server 7 that allows you

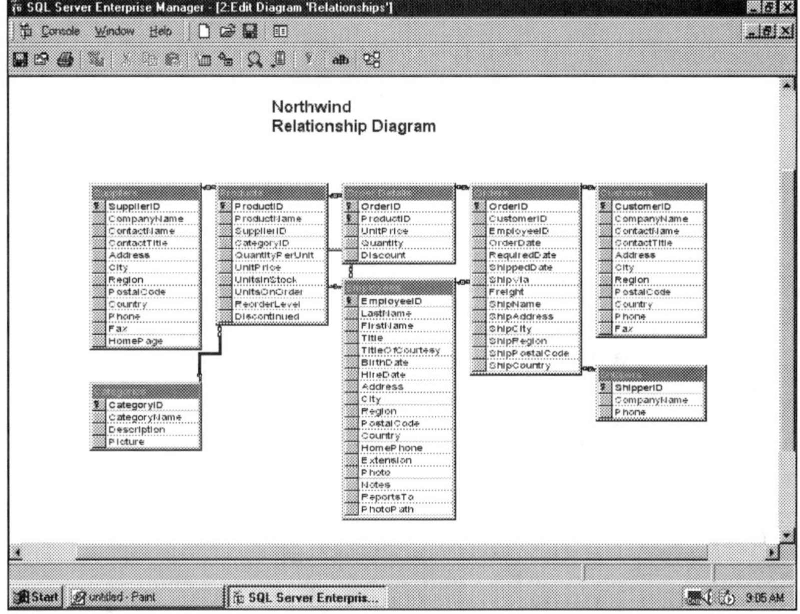

Figure 1.12 Database Diagram tool.

to create the diagram of your database graphically; then with one click, the tool will create the database for you (see Figure 1.12).

You can also save database diagrams and transport them to another server for creation or print them. If you choose the latter option, make sure you have lots of paper.

ERDs can also be reverse-engineered from an existing database. This can be very useful for programming meetings or management reports.

The Database Diagram tool can also alter tables and other structures within the database without destroying the current data in the database.

Database diagrams are saved in the *dtproperties* table of the database.

Chapter Summary

This chapter introduced you to Microsoft's newest database, SQL Server version 7. Many questions you will face on the exam will concern the enhancements to the previous version of SQL Server, 6.5:

- SQL Server 7 is a relational database. A relational database uses an engine to control the data formats for the data, allowing you to change the file without destroying the data.
- Microsoft SQL Server 7 has been enhanced to provide greater speed by increased page and extent sizes, multiprocessor optimization, and a new query optimization.
- SQL Server 7 has also been enhanced by providing automatic tuning of many parameters, which had to be set by hand in previous versions.
- Microsoft Windows 9x, Windows NT Workstation (Windows 2000 Professional), and Windows NT Server (Windows 2000 Server) are supported by SQL Server. Some options are not available on the Windows 9x platforms, such as symmetric multiprocessor support, named pipes, full-text search, asynchronous I/O, and integrated security. You can install a limited connection version of SQL Server 7 on Windows NT Workstation (Windows 2000 Professional), but not the full connection version.
- Microsoft has included a full upgrade path from versions 6 and 6.5, but you cannot upgrade from version 4.2. The path for upgrading version 4.2 is to upgrade it to version 6.5 and then upgrade the databases to version 7. SQL Server 7 also contains the Data Transformation Services, which can migrate data from other database servers.
- SQL Server 7 has many more different file and memory sizes than previous versions. See Table 1.1 for details.
- SQL Server 7 databases and transaction logs can be set to grow automatically with or without limits. You can set the increment for growth.
- Many new wizards for SQL Server 7 have been created.
- Locking for SQL Server 7 is controlled automatically, and now includes row-level locking. This enhances availability of data to the users. SQL Server 7 automatically selects between page and row-level locks based on cost.
- Many new Transact SQL (T-SQL) commands have been added, and several previous commands have been enhanced or have had their syntax altered.
- New or enhanced programming interfaces have been added to SQL Server 7, including Component Object Model (COM) techniques such as Object Linking and Embedding DB (OLE DB) and ActiveX Data Objects (ADO).
- Microsoft has enhanced the replication of SQL Server by adding new types of replication, such as Merge Replication, which provides for disconnected database replication.
- The SQL Server Agent has replaced the SQL Server Executive from version 6.5. The SQL Server Agent performs job scheduling and execution and alert

creation and notification. Information on the configuration of the SQL Server Agent is stored in the msdb database.

- SQL Server 7 includes a new feature called Full-Text Search. This feature performs searches using common English questions rather than T-SQL commands. This process is accomplished using special indexes on the database.
- SQL Server 7 supports Online Analytical Processing (OLAP) including relational, multidimensional, and hybrid Online Analytical Processing.
- New tools included with SQL Server 7 also include the Microsoft Management Console (MMC) to graphically manage the server. The Enterprise Manager is a snap-in to the MMC that performs most all tasks on the database, such as security and schema manipulation.
- The Query Analyzer in version 7 replaces the **ISQL_w** from version 6.5. It's new features are color coding, a grid results pane, and a graphical query plan display.
- The SQL Profiler is a new tool that replaces the Trace utility in version 6.5. This tool can capture and filter events on the database and play those events against another database.
- The Index Tuning Wizard performs an analysis on a database based on a workload, which is a capture of standard activity on a database. If this test is impossible or impractical to perform, SQL Server can generate activity on the database for you.
- The new osql command-line utility works in the same way the isql utility did in version 6.5, but osql works on an ODBC level. Both of these commands allow you to run T-SQL commands from the command line.
- The Database Diagram tool creates Entity Relationship Diagrams (ERDs) and can use those graphical plans of a database to create a new database or modify an existing one. Database diagrams are saved in the dtproperties table of the database.

Review Questions

1. The definition of *data* is:
   a. Information about a person, place, or thing
   b. A discrete piece of information
   c. Facts, figures, and details stored in a database
   d. The lowest level of information stored in a database

2. Microsoft SQL Server 7 is a new and fairly untested database product.
   a. True
   b. False

3. What is the page size in Microsoft SQL Server 7?
   a. 2K
   b. 4K
   c. 64K
   d. 8K

4. What is a query plan?
   a. A statistical engine used by SQL Server version 7
   b. A read-only data structure that is stored in memory
   c. A graphical plan set by each user
   d. The plan created by developers to assist the database in finding data

5. Database backups from SQL Server 6.5 are compatible with SQL Server 7.
   a. True
   b. False

6. SQL Server 7 uses what size for a row length?
   a. 1,962 bytes
   b. 1,024 bytes
   c. 250 bytes
   d. 8,060 bytes

7. How much memory is consumed per open database in SQL Server version 7?
   a. 1,144 bytes per server plus 160 bytes per database
   b. 8,060 bytes
   c. 2,880 bytes
   d. 1,024 bytes

8. What is the extension used for the first data file in SQL Server 7?
   a. .mdf
   b. .ndf
   c. .ldf
   d. .msf

9. What is the Component Object Model?
   a. A database design model
   b. The object model used for writing Structured Query Language code
   c. The framework that Microsoft and other vendors developed for designing applications
   d. A model for designing triggers in Microsoft SQL Server 7 databases

10. The SQL Server Agent replaces which tool from SQL Server 6.5?
    a. SQL Server Scheduler
    b. SQL Server Enterprise Manager
    c. SQL Server Executive
    d. isql

Hands-On Projects

This exercise assumes a test Windows NT 4 server with Service Pack 4 installed. Read the instructions carefully and do not perform this install on your production machine unless you understand the options presented. If you are unsure about an option, cancel the installation and read the *Books Online* about the option to be installed.

Susan Rogers was (to say the least) a little concerned. Her boss had just come in and told her that she was going to be working on a new project. Her company had decided to write its own software for its distribution system and wanted her to do the database design for it.

Susan had started with Fitness Unlimited (a supplier for sports superstores) two years ago, and had been working in the Information Systems department since that time. She had been working with databases for a while, but more as a maintenance Database Administrator than as a designer of one. "Oh," her boss had said, "we'll probably want to get you certified in this stuff as well. I spoke with upper management, and when you're certified there's a promotion for you. Let me know when you're ready to take those tests." He disappeared out of her cubicle.

She felt her pulse move up a notch. Susan knew she could do the job with enough time to figure out what was needed, but to take the certification exams as well? She felt she had a lot to learn, and was a little intimidated by all the information she'd have to become familiar with by the end of the project.

The first thing Susan did was to install SQL Server 7 on her server. That wasn't too difficult, because she had installed Microsoft SQL Server 6.5 in the past. When she had installed version 6.5, she was asked questions by the install program, and the senior DBAs gave her the values to enter. This time she was on her own.

She began by installing the prerequisites for the SQL Server installation:

Project 1.1

To install SQL Server 7 prerequisites, perform the following:

1. Insert the SQL 7 CD.
2. Click on Install Prerequisites at the graphical main screen that displays. If your system has been set to not auto-play CDs, then open the drive letter that corresponds to your CD-ROM drive with the Explorer and run the autoplay.exe file you see there.
3. Click on NT 4 at the SQL Server 7 Prerequisites screen.
4. Click on Minimal Install at the next SQL Server 7 Prerequisites screen.
5. Click on Next at the Internet Explorer 4.01 SP1 Active Setup screen.
6. Click on I Accept The Agreement at the License Agreement screen, then Next.
7. Click on United States at the Active Channel Selection screen.
8. Leave the folder selections as defaults at the Destination Folder screen.
9. If any files on your system are newer, click on No To All when presented with the overwrite message.
10. Click on OK when prompted for the reboot.

When that was done, Susan began the installation of the SQL Server program. She answered the questions during the installation for the most part by taking the defaults.

To Install SQL Server 7, perform the following:

1. Insert the SQL 7 CD.
2. Click on Install SQL Server 7 Components at the graphical main screen that displays. If your system has been set to not auto-play CDs, then open the drive letter which corresponds to your CD-ROM drive with the Explorer and run the autoplay.exe file you see there.
3. Click on SQL Server—Standard Edition at the SQL install graphical screen.
4. Click on Local Install at the Select Install Method screen.
5. Click on Next at the Welcome screen.

6. Click on Yes at the Software License Agreement screen.
7. Enter the name and company at the User Information screen, then click on Next.
8. Enter the license code at the Setup screen, then click on Next.
9. Click on OK at the next Setup screen.
10. Click on Typical—Set the proper directories—click on Next at the Setup Type screen.
11. Select the radio button that begins Use The Same… Then set the account and password for the service (this account must be a domain admin with access to a mail account) and then click on Next at the Services Accounts screen.
12. Click on Per Seat, then on Continue at the Choose Licensing Mode screen.
13. Click on I Agree and then on OK at the Per Seat Licensing screen.
14. Click on Next at the Start Copying Files screen.
15. Select Finish at the final graphical screen and allow the machine to reboot.

Next, Susan installed the Administration portion on her own workstation, and installed *SQL 7 Books Online* to be local to her machine, so she wouldn't have to keep the CD in her drive. She was pretty pleased with herself at this point, because the database appeared to be up and running.

Then, Susan opened the *SQL 7 Books Online* and began reading at the section marked, "Getting Started." That's when she saw the section marked "Installing And Running SQL Server" and groaned, "I've just started, and already I began without reading the documentation first." It was her first lesson, and she promised herself it wasn't a mistake she'd make again.

Project 1.2

To locate and search a topic using *Books Online:*

1. Click on the Start menu.
2. Move the pointer to Programs, then locate Microsoft SQL Server 7, then *Books Online.*
3. Click on the Search tab or press Alt+S.
4. Type "backup" in the dialog box.
5. Click on List Topics, or press Alt+L, or press Enter.
6. Locate the topic entitled Managing Backups and double-click on it.
7. Click on the Favorites tab.
8. Click on the Add button.

To open the graphical manager for each tool described in this chapter:

1. Click on the Start menu.
2. Move the pointer to Programs, then locate Microsoft SQL Server 7, then Enterprise Manager.
3. Double-click on the program group marked SQL Server Group in the tree pane.
4. If you don't see your server listed, right-click on the SQL Server Group and select New SQL Server Registration. Complete the wizard, and your server will display in the selection.
5. If the server has a circle with a red square next to its name, right-click on the server name and select Start from the menu. In a few moments, the red square should turn to a green triangle. This means your server is now running.
6. Double-click on the name of your server (or click on the plus sign once) and the tree pane will expand.
7. Click on each icon once in the tree pane, and notice the changes in the information pane on the right as you do.
8. Expand each plus sign you see by one click, then continue clicking the icons to see their display.

Susan read the information from *Books Onine* and noted the new enhancements to SQL Server 7, especially noting that the memory requirements for user connections and how locks had changed. She felt this would be valuable information in the future to properly size the memory in her server.

The next thing Susan did was to browse the Internet to find out what was going to be required of her to pass the Microsoft Certified Database Administrator exam. She located the following information at **www.microsoft.com/train_cert**:

Microsoft certification for database administrators (MCDBA) consists of four core exams and one elective exam. The four core exams are as follows:

- System Administration for SQL Server 7
- Implementing a Database in SQL Server 7
- Implementing and Supporting Windows NT 4
- Implementing and Supporting Windows NT 4 in the Enterprise

The elective course can be Microsoft Visual Basic, Microsoft Visual C++, Data Warehousing, IIS, or TCP/IP.

Susan also searched Microsoft's TechNet and the Web for information relating to COM, OLE DB, ADO and other programming specifications regarding SQL Server. "If I'm going to have to support the programmers and write procedures," she said, "I'll need to understand the latest buzzwords."

Chapter Two

SQL Database Architecture

After Reading This Chapter And Completing The Exercises, You Will Be Able To:

- Understand and describe the theory behind the relational model
- Understand the external, conceptual, and internal views of the relational database architecture
- Describe the structures within a relational database
- Understand the basics of relational algebra
- Describe the use of SQL in managing and manipulating the database environment
- Describe at a high level logical database components found in a database
- Understand the role of pages, extents, database files, and filegroups in supporting the physical structure of the database

Before we can properly discuss the various objects within a database and how to manage them, we need to have a background into what these objects are and how they are used. In this chapter we'll begin that discussion, and then in Chapters 3 and 4 we'll more fully develop those concepts.

The Relational Data Model

Microsoft SQL Server is based on the formal theory known as the *relational data model*. When we describe a database system as relational, we are simply referring to a database management system that is constructed according to the basic principles of this underlying theoretical model.

The relational model is a method for representing and manipulating data. It also provides techniques for defining data structure, data integrity, and data manipulation methods. Before delving into a more rigorous explanation of the relational model, it might be helpful to first describe very generally two important characteristics of relational databases. The users perceive data as tables—and only as tables—with each table comprising a two-dimensional view of a body of data. This table has rows, with each row containing a consistent set of data that can be vertically represented as columns. Also, the operators or syntax available to the user will generate new logical tables from existing tables. For example, language is available to retrieve a subset of rows or columns from a table, with the result in turn having the appearance of a new table.

Let's consider the following example where we have the single table *Suppliers* and we are looking for contact information for all companies located in the UK. The retrieval is performed using Structured Query Language (SQL) that will be further described in this chapter and in detail in subsequent chapters in this book:

```
select CompanyName, ContactName, Phone from Suppliers
where Country = 'UK'

CompanyName                ContactName        Phone
------------------------   ----------------   --------------
Exotic Liquids             Charlotte Cooper   (171) 555-2222
Specialty Biscuits, Ltd.   Peter Wilson       (161) 555-4448

(2 row(s) affected)
```

The original *Suppliers* table had 12 columns and 29 rows, and in this example we have specified a subset of data that is presented as a two-dimensional table.

The Architecture Of A Relational Database System

In order to translate the relatively abstract notion of tables and operators into a computer-based system that can be programmed and managed, we will first consider the three levels that make up the architecture of a relational database system:

- **The internal level** This level involves the disk or storage units and is concerned with the way in which data is physically stored. Aspects such as disk location and allocation of space are often considered at this level. In addition to such elements, specific data types and table definitions or layouts are maintained here.
- **The external level** This level is the closest to users. External levels present data and allow users to have an interface in which they can specify the data to be viewed or updated. At the external level, data can be manipulated using a wide variety of tools and specific subsets of data can be customized for each user.
- **The conceptual level** This level provides a form of interaction between the previous two levels and, most important, allows one level to be changed or customized without having to affect the other.

Figure 2.1 depicts the relationship of these levels or views to each other and will allow us to explore this concept in more detail.

At the external level, users might purchase report writers or query tools to specify the data subsets that they wish to browse or manipulate. They might also use predefined programs developed in languages such as Microsoft Visual Basic or C++

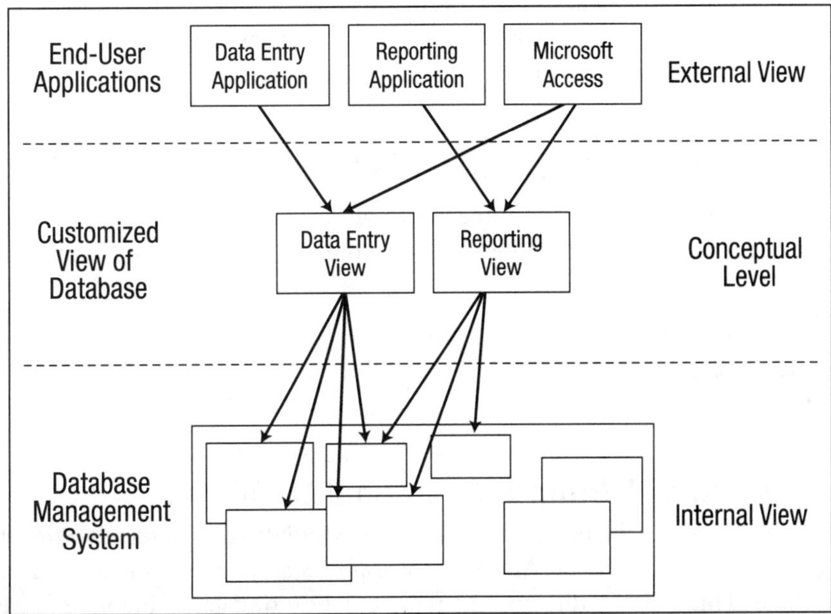

Figure 2.1 The architecture of a relational database system.

because these programs provide a customized presentation layer. The data view presented to each user is often controlled and customized by the interface program being used. The external level is usually created by a programmer according to design specifications and may be customized by the end user using provided tools.

The conceptual view is a view of the database content with an overall *schema* or arrangement of data. This view includes such components as security, integrity, and rules. Many conceptual views are possible, based on subsets of data that is tailored to fit the needs of specific users, such as data entry clerks who update data or analysts who only run reports. The database administrator who has responsibility for database analysis and design, as well as creation, usually con-trols this level.

At the lowest level, the internal view defines how a database record is organized, such as the data types, the lengths, and the order of the data presented. In addition, the organization of the database records into groups or tables onto physical components, such as databases, pages, extents, and so forth, is a part of this level. The data-base administrator and the system administrator share responsibility for definition of this level.

It is important to note that each of these levels can be altered independently of each other. This is one of the most important strengths of the relational database architecture. As a database grows, additional disk space can be added and a group of records can be relocated without affecting the conceptual or external view. When business needs change, new tables can be added or existing elements can be modified without affecting existing user queries.

Further Definition Of The Relational Model

The relational model has three important generic elements that we will now review in some detail before we look at their implementation in Microsoft SQL Server 7:

- Database structures
- Data integrity
- Data manipulation

Structures Within A Relational Database

The following formal terminology is often used when describing the elements of a relational database: An *entity* corresponds to what has so far been called a table. This is a two-dimensional representation of data. In Figure 2.2, we see the *Products* relation that contains information about the items sold by the Northwind company.

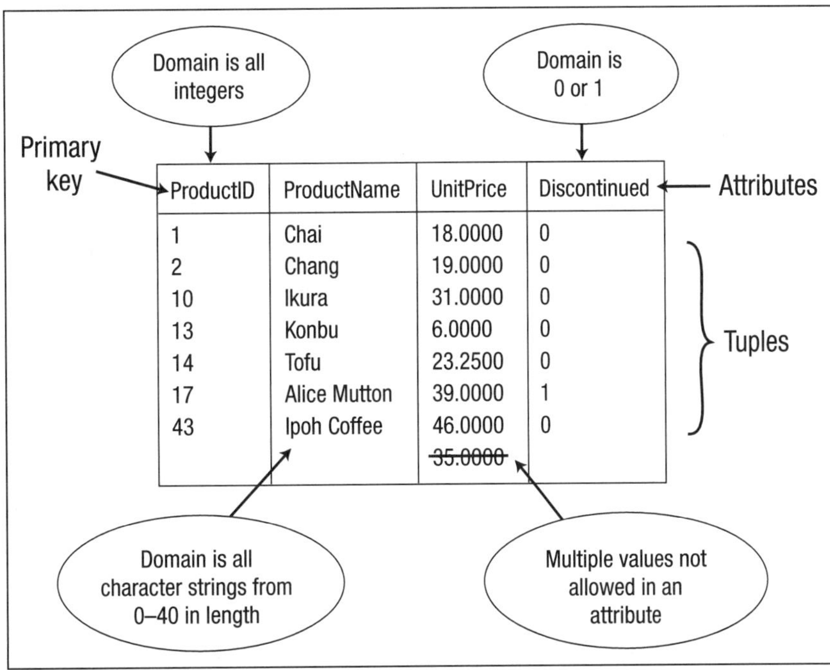

Figure 2.2 The *Products* relation.

A *tuple* compares to a record or row. Each table can contain many tuples. In the *Products* table example, there are seven records or tuples describing our inventory with each record describing one product. An *attribute* is a column or data element in a row. Each row has one or more attributes. In our sample table, four attributes were selected for display. The *primary key* is a unique identifier for a table. It is made up of one column or a combination of columns. Values in the primary key cannot be duplicated within a table. The column *ProductID* is unique within our sample table, and no value can appear more than once.

A *domain* is a pool of values representing the universe of possible data values for a specific column or attribute. In the case of the *ProductID* column, the domain might be made up of all integers. Constraints are shown on the the *Discontinued* column which has additional restrictions defined through a *constraint* (constraints will be discus-sed later in this chapter). It has only two possible data values: 0 or 1.

While a relation can be defined as a two-dimensional representation of data, some special characteristics are also important to consider. These properties further set apart a relational database system from a traditional file-based database system.

These additional properties of relations are as follows: No duplicate tuples (or records) exist within a table. Just as in mathematical sets, duplicate elements are not allowed, in a relation each tuple must be distinct and unique from every other tuple. In other words, no record may look exactly like another record, with every value in every column in one record matching a second record.

Tuples are arranged without any particular order from top to bottom. Whereas physical data can be stored in a certain order within a file for retrieval, logical data can be presented in any order. The sequencing of the data has no effect on the syntax of the queries that might be specified. Attributes are arranged without any order from left to right. Conceptually, we can consider each tuple to be defined by a set of attributes, with each attribute being referenced by name and never by position.

All attribute values are *atomic*, or single-valued. Most simply, at any intersection of row and column one and only one value will exist, never a set of values. When we look at the record for Ipoh Coffee in the *Products* table in Figure 2.2, we notice that two values for *UnitPrice* are specified. We will need to come up with another way of specifying a discounted price, as any attribute instance can have only one value; we will look for a solution to this dilemma in Chapter 3.

Domains

In the complex world of a relational database, the smallest unit of data is the individual data value at the intersection of each column and record. These values are atomic, that is, they cannot be further decomposed into smaller elements.

A *domain* is the set of all possible values for a particular data element. For example, in our *Products* table the attribute *ProductName* has as its domain all character strings from 0 to 40 characters in length. In this chapter we will introduce constraints and other methods that will allow us to further specify the set of valid values that will comprise a domain. We do this by applying specific business rules. For example, a negative *UnitPrice* might not be appropriate in our *Products* table.

Relational Databases

Now that we have defined the elements of a relational database system, we can in turn define a relational database: a *database* is a collection of relations or tables where the data will vary over time. Each table represents a collection of data about a specific business object or process, such as *Products*, *Customers*, and *Orders*. Furthermore, the collection of data represents the enterprise or some portion of the enterprise with data values being inserted, updated, and deleted to reflect the changing business environment.

Data in a relational database is both *integrated* and *shared*. For example, at the Northwind Company our data entry users can coexist with our reporting users as they share the usage of some tables at the same time as they use integrated data, such as specific customer information that is not shared.

A few points here are important to consider: The data is integrated because the data is contained in a collection of otherwise distinct and separate data files or tables with most or all redundant information removed. The product name appears only in the *Products* table, but can be referred to when querying the *Orders* table. Also, the data is shared because each element of data can be read or updated by many users and for different purposes. For example, the shipping clerk will require a much different picture than a supervisor in the purchasing department.

Data Integrity

Each database has very specific integrity rules that are defined by the business processes supported. For example, the quantity ordered must always be a positive number, the part description must always be entered in uppercase and not contain special characters, and the vendor number must match a vendor number that is in the *Vendor* table and has an active flag. However, two general integrity rules apply to every relational database: the *entity integrity* rule and the *referential integrity* rule. Because these two rules refer to primary and foreign keys, these concepts will be defined first.

Primary Keys

As was previously noted, each relation or table must have a unique identifier or *key*. Therefore, each relation has at least one *candidate* key, where each candidate key is simply a possible unique key. Most relations have only one candidate key that by default becomes the primary key. Where more than one candidate key exists, we will choose one and the remaining candidate keys will usually become *alternate* keys.

For example, the *Products* table shown in Figure 2.3 has two candidate keys: *ProductID* and *ProductName*. Both are unique in our example and either one could be a primary key. However, we will choose *ProductId* to be the primary key and *ProductName* will become an alternate key. The reasons why we would choose this structure will be discussed in detail in Chapters 3 and 4.

Primary keys are an important concept because they provide the only way of exactly addressing a specific record or tuple in a table. Without a primary key, a query might return multiple records. No consistent method would further specify criteria that would reduce the record set to just one. Imagine two men in the same family named John. If you couldn't add the qualifier Senior or Junior to the name, who would answer when you called out, "John"?

Foreign Keys

As we process orders for the Northwind Company, it becomes clear that we cannot process an order for a product unless that product is described in our product table. If we allowed nonexistent part numbers to be entered, we would not have integrity or validity in our database.

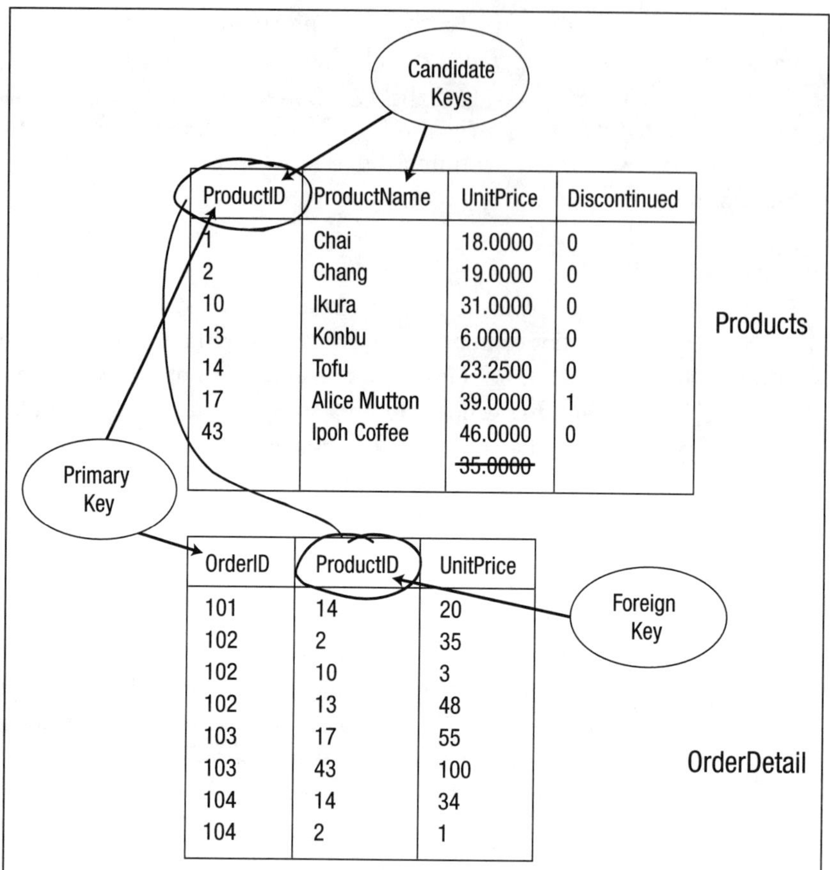

ProductID	ProductName	UnitPrice	Discontinued
1	Chai	18.0000	0
2	Chang	19.0000	0
10	Ikura	31.0000	0
13	Konbu	6.0000	0
14	Tofu	23.2500	0
17	Alice Mutton	39.0000	1
43	Ipoh Coffee	46.0000	0
		~~35.0000~~	

OrderID	ProductID	UnitPrice
101	14	20
102	2	35
102	10	3
102	13	48
103	17	55
103	43	100
104	14	34
104	2	1

Figure 2.3 *ProductID* and *ProductName* Candidate Keys in the *Products* table.

This is an example of a *foreign key* relationship, where a foreign key is an attribute (or combination of attributes) whose value is required to match that of the primary key of some other relation. The foreign key (or secondary key) and its corresponding *primary key* are defined to share the same underlying domain.

Our product and order example is shown in the tables used in Figure 2.3. Here, the primary key *ProductID* in the *Products* table is used as a foreign key *ProductID* in the *OrderDetails* table. In both tables the *ProductID* column must have the same domain. They must have the same data types and constraining business rules.

Foreign keys to primary key matches are *references* between one table and another. They can be thought of as the glue that holds a relational database together. By specifying foreign to primary key relationships, the database designer is building into the database structure the business rules that need to be enforced.

Integrity Rules

Now that the concept of primary and foreign keys has been covered, we can define the integrity rules that govern relational databases:

- **Entity integrity** No attribute that either comprises the whole primary key or a portion of the primary key can accept **NULL** values. A **NULL** *value* is not a zero or nothing, it means that the data has not yet been defined. If **NULL** values were allowed, this would imply that it is possible to have records that could not be identified. This would clearly contradict our earlier position that each record must be uniquely addressable.
- **Referential integrity** If a record in one table references a record in another table, then that second record must already exist. This relationship is defined via a foreign key relationship, as shown in Figure 2.3. In this example we cannot insert a record in the *OrderDetails* table and specify a *ProductID* that is not in the *Products* table.

Conversely, it is possible for a foreign key to have a **NULL** value. For example, our business rule might state that it is permissible to have a price adjustment recorded in the *OrderDetails* table with a blank *ProductID* attribute. We will some detailed examples of these types of conditions in Chapters 3 and 4.

Data Manipulation

The last part of the relational model allows us to manipulate the data previously defined via structures and integrity rules. Data manipulation is performed using operators that are based on relational algebra. This allows for such set functions as union, intersection, difference, and Cartesian product, in addition to the special relational operators: *select*, *project*, *join*, and *divide*. The operators are depicted in Figure 2.4 and are further described as follows:

- **Select** Extracts specified records from a specific relation—restricts data according to specified criteria. (Do not confuse with the SQL **SELECT** statement, which is much more powerful than the algebraic Select function).
- **Project** Extracts specified attributes from a specific relation—You can specify a subset of attributes in any order.
- **Product** Produces a Cartesian product of all possible combinations of pairs of tuples.
- **Union** Produces a superset of all tuples appearing in either or both of two specified relations.
- **Intersect** Produces a subset of all tuples appearing in both tables.
- **Difference** Produces a relation containing all records appearing in the first table but not in the second.

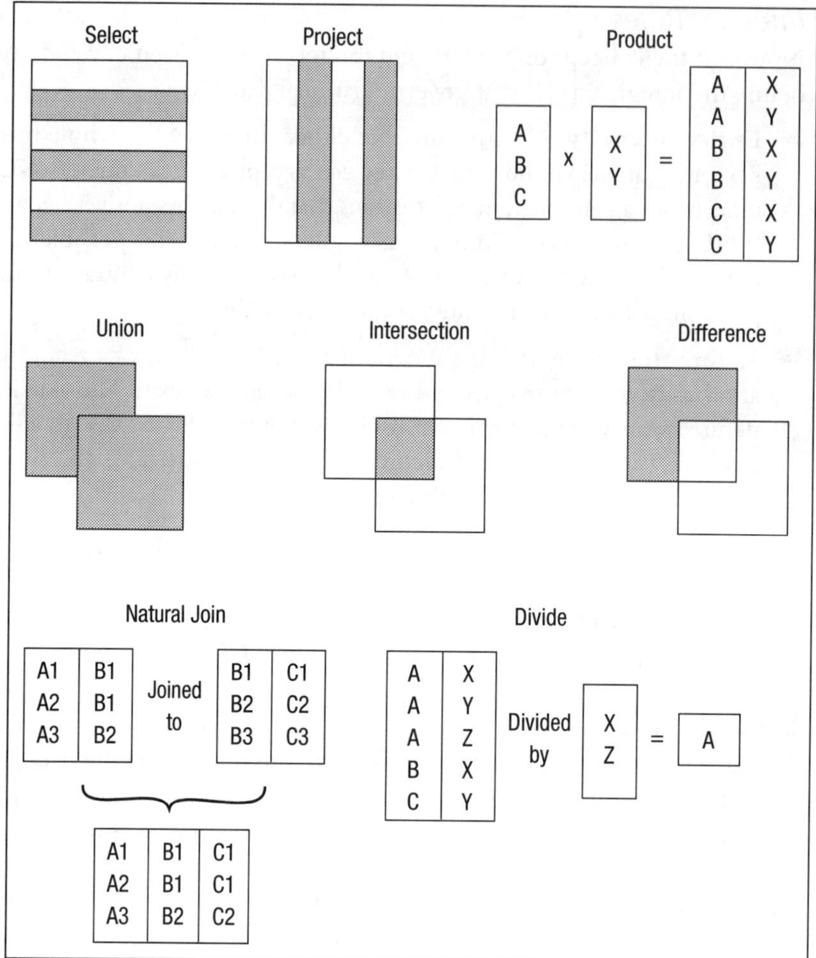

Figure 2.4 Relational algebra.

- **Join** Builds a resulting relation from two specified relations, where the resulting relation contains all possible concatenated pairs of tuples from the two original relations. In the example, record B3, C3 in the second table does not have a natural join to any records in the first table and will not exist in the resulting table.
- **Divide** Builds a resulting relation of all matches between a two-attribute and a one-attribute relation (or primary key). In the example, the C and Y attributes in the first table do not have matches in the second table.

When considering these algebraic operations, note this important property: The output of each operation is always another table. As a result, multiple operations can be nested with a table produced by one operation becoming input into a subsequent operation.

A theoretical alternative to using relational algebra as a model is using relational calculus. Relational calculus defines queries that specify the items a predicate must satisfy. The relational calculus model allows for additional expressions for predicates such as *exist, in,* and *between*. This model also provides for greater richness and flexibility in the language.

Structured Query Language

As the theory of relational algebra and relational calculus was transformed into a useful query language, several intermediate languages, such as *Information System Base Language* (*ISBL*) and *SQUARE,* were developed by IBM before the theory finally evolved into the language we now know as Structured Query Language or SQL.

The SQL language is a hybrid based on relational algebra and relational calculus with the addition of further features that enable arithmetic comparisons and operations, assignment of values, and the application of aggregate functions to a group.

If we look back at some of the simplest concepts of relational algebra, the select and the intersection, we can see a direct correlation in SQL select syntax. Just as we described three components of the relational model, we will see that the SQL syntax falls into three categories: *Data Definition Language* (*DDL*), where tables and other supporting structures can be defined; *Data Control Language* (*DCL*), which allows rules for data integrity and data security to be specified; and *Data Manipulation Language* (*DML*), which specifies methods by which data can be retrieved for viewing or updating.

Microsoft SQL Server uses Transact-SQL. T-SQL is a greatly enhanced version of the American National Standards Institute (ANSI) standard for SQL. The version of SQL supported in Microsoft SQL 7 is ANSI SQL-92, which is the standard specification for SQL published in 1992; however, Microsoft has increased the power of SQL by adding many extensions that improve the functionality and utility of this language.

SQL Server Database Architecture

Earlier in this chapter we discussed the three levels that make up the architecture of a relational database system (the internal, external, and conceptual levels). At that time, our discussion was relatively abstract, but now we will use Figure 2.5 to show at a high level how Microsoft has implemented this architecture in SQL Server. These levels are: as follows:

- **Internal level** Data is stored in a consolidated and centralized location on a database server. Data redundancy is eliminated, as multiple users do not need to maintain personal copies of the data. Only the data results from a user's

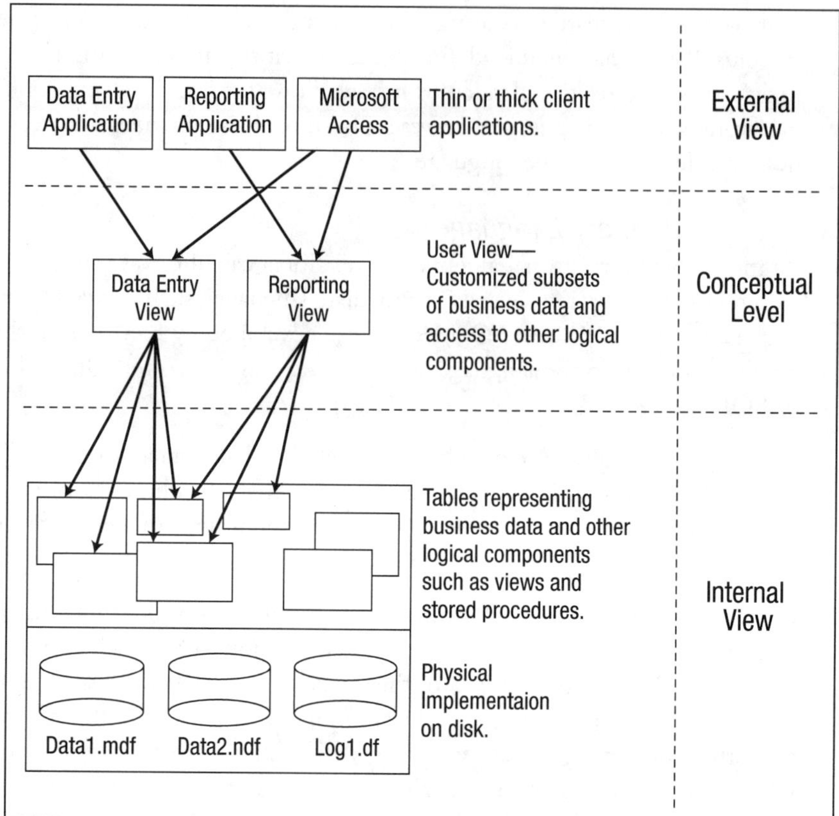

Figure 2.5 Internal, External, and Conceptual views of a relational database system.

query are returned to the client, cutting down on unnecessary network traffic.

- **External level** The data is presented to the user with the correct and appro-priate security, integrity, and business rules as defined within the database. This allows for consistent presentation of data and equal enforcement of all rules. The client can be a *thick* client where the application also contains business logic, as well as the code required to both query and display data to the end-user. The application containing business rules can be placed on a shared server with a *thin* client that simply formats an input query and displays results.
- **Conceptual level** SQL Server provides redirection or *mapping*, which allows a user to specify a table without having to know which disk device it is on or which data files are in use. Furthermore, a system administrator can relo-cate tables to new disk drives in order to improve read/write performance and be assured that all programs and queries will continue to

function. At this level, access to tables, views, and other logical database components can be defined.

All file-based systems have an internal level where data is written to or read from disk, as well as an external level that presents a user interface and application-specific business rules. An important aspect of relational database systems is the middle level, where a mapping from logical components, such as tables, views, data integrity rules, and other objects, to physical structures, such as files, pages, and extents, can be defined.

Logical Database Components

When a user or programmer views a database, a number of database objects can be listed or accessed:

- Constraints
- Defaults
- Indexes
- Keys
- Stored procedures
- Tables
- Triggers
- User-defined data types
- Views

By utilizing these objects, the user or programmer will be able to manipulate or view predefined data using standard and consistent methods. The following sections will introduce these logical database components, and later chapters will go into much greater detail.

Tables

Each database is comprised of a number of *tables*. Each table describes some object important to the business process or function represented in the database. In the *Northwind* database, tables describing customers, products, orders, and employees enable a distribution business to function.

User-Defined Data Types

In order to create a table, each column or attribute must be defined by both name and data type. A number of standard data types are provided with SQL Server. These include integers of various lengths, character and variable character, as well as datetime, identifier, and image data types. However, it is also possible to create database-specific, user-defined data types that can enable more consistent mapping of data across many tables.

For example, an indicator data type might always need to be one character in length and not allow **NULLs**. Using a user-defined data type in the database, you would define the indicator once and then use it many times in subsequent table definitions.

Views

Each time a table is created in a database, database space is set aside for the table. If the new table were created as a result of executing a **SELECT** statement against an existing table, the data would be redundantly stored. The data will become outdated as soon as the original table changes unless additional update steps are coded into either the client application or the database.

An alternative is the use of *views* that define a *virtual* table that can be queried or updated like a real table. Rather than storing the resulting table on disk, the query statements used to define the view are stored in the database. The server executes the query when the view is referenced in a SQL statement. This keeps the virtual table up to date.

In a view, data subsets can be specified, multiple tables can be joined, or data results can be calculated or aggregated. Views provide another way of specifying a consistent data access method that can be used by a large number of end users.

Stored Procedure

A *stored procedure* is a group of Transact-SQL statements stored together as a single named object in a database. By using stored procedures, consistent application logic can be defined and then utilized by any number of end-user applications, batch scripts, and even *ad hoc* queries.

For example, suppose that you have analyzed an automatic inventory restocking process. This process requires computation of back-order quantities and units preallocated to customers, as well as analysis of previous vendor's fulfillment times on other orders. Writing this logic into a stored procedure (and requiring the item number as input) will enable this code to be run at any time in a consistent fashion. In addition, conditional logic in the stored procedure can be used to evaluate the results of the SQL statement to determine if subsequent statements should be executed. This process results in improved performance, as the intermediate data results are stored as memory variables rather than being returned to the client application.

Using stored procedures is an important component in shielding both users and programmers from having to deal with the details of table structures and business logic. Once a specific business process has been coded into a stored procedure, tested, and made available, all processes can use that stored procedure. When business rules change, programs will not need to be modified as long as the input and outputs for the stored procedure are not altered.

Constraints

Constraints are the first line of defense when defining the data values allowed in a column or domain and should always be used in preference to triggers, rules, and defaults. While a data type such as integer will by default narrow down the allowed data values to only whole numbers, thus excluding characters and decimals, this is frequently not sufficient for defining a domain of valid values. There are five types of constraints available:

- **NOT NULL** This specifies that a column value must be entered, that is, it may not contain a **NULL** value.
- **CHECK** This specifies a range or list of valid values. For example, a supplier number must be between 1 and 10,000.
- **UNIQUE** This ensures that the data in a group of columns will be unique for all rows in the table. For a group of columns specified in the uniqueness constraint, no two rows in a table are allowed to have the same non-**NULL** values for the group of columns.
- **PRIMARY KEY** These are made up of the column or group of columns that uniquely identify a single record in a table.
- **FOREIGN KEY** These identify a data relationship between two tables in a database. A **FOREIGN KEY** in one table points to a key in another table. When a **FOREIGN KEY** constraint is defined, it will not be possible to insert a row with a **FOREIGN KEY** value that does not exist in the referenced table. It is also important to remember that it will not be possible to delete that record from the referenced table if there are any **FOREIGN KEY** values referencing that row.

Rules

Rules are similar to check constraints and are provided for backward compatibility with earlier versions of Microsoft SQL Server.

Defaults

When defined, a *default* is the value assigned to a column when it is not otherwise specified when inserting a record into a table. A default must evaluate to a constant, but can also be a mathematical expression or a built-in function. For example, a time-stamp field might be identified to have a default that is evaluated by the **getdate()** function whenever a record is inserted into the table.

Triggers

Triggers are similar to stored procedures because they are groups of Transact-SQL code executed as a unit and stored in the database with an associated name. They are very powerful and will be executed for any **INSERT**, **UPDATE**, or **DELETE** statement that is executed against the base table. Triggers can be used to define additional integrity checking or specific business rules within the database. Similar to stored procedures, they help to provide consistency by moving processing out of front-end programs and scripts and into the database.

Indexes

An *index* is a physical structure associated with a table that is created by the database administrator to improve the speed of data retrieval. When a table is first created, data is stored in an unorganized structure known as a *heap,* and any data access will require a scan of the entire table looking for rows that match the specified qualifications.

The two types of indexes are:

- **Clustered indexes** The data in the table is physically resorted according to the columns specified in the index.
- **Nonclustered indexes** The index structure is physically separated from the table and pointers from the index refer back to specific data pages.

Either type of index can be further specified to be either *unique* or *nonunique*. If an index is unique, then only one row may contain that specific grouping of data values.

Physical Database Components

As a table grows in size, more and more space on disk will be consumed. Though it is not necessary to worry about the low-level calls that write to disk, it is a good idea to understand how data is written to disk and organized. This knowledge will ultimately improve the speed and reliability of databases you might design.

Significant changes were made in SQL Server 7 so that it could support continuous scalability, performance, and functionality improvements. Where the previous physical architecture of devices, segments, and 2K pages was an outcome of the smaller systems for which SQL Server 6.5 was originally developed, the SQL Server 7 architecture is ready to take advantage of improvements in the Microsoft Windows NT operating system and computing hardware.

Pages And Extents

The smallest unit in SQL Server 7 is a *page*, which is 8K or 128 pages per megabyte. Each page has 96 bytes set aside to describe the type of page, the amount of free space remaining, and the object ID of the object owning the page. Multiple records (even from multiple tables) are stored on the page with offsets providing fast access to each record, as shown in Figure 2.6.

This improvement in size to an 8K page from the 2K page that was available in SQL Server 6.5 has enabled the maximum number of columns per row to

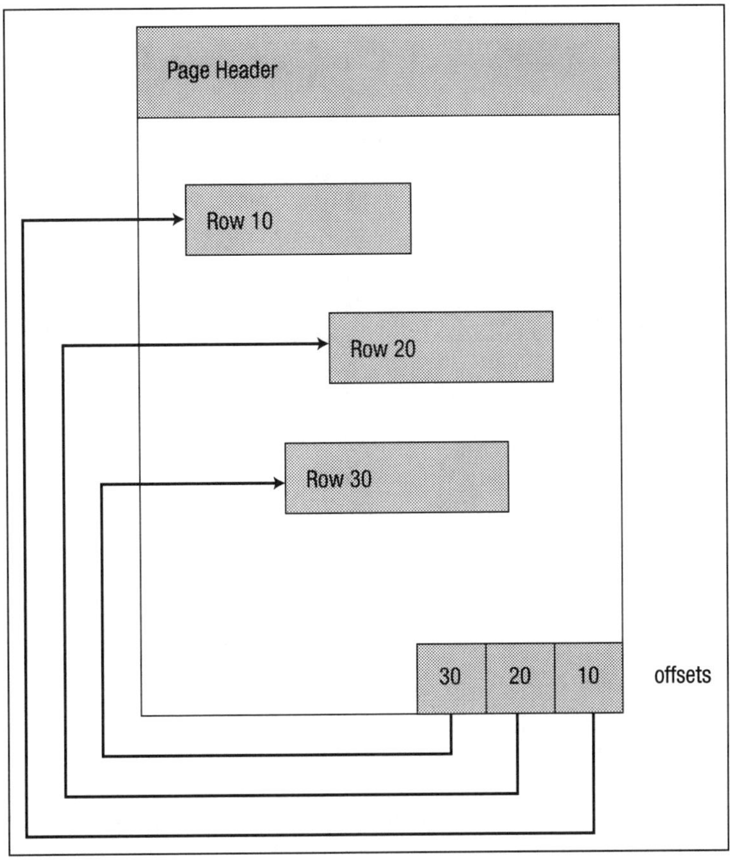

Figure 2.6 SQL Server data page.

increase to 1,024K. This provides for significant performance improvements as rows are only compacted when necessary and an offset or slot array allows for a binary search of specific data on a page.

Data rows are placed in sequence in the next available space starting immediately after the header. A row-offset table at the end of the page contains an entry for every record on the page and records how far from the first byte of the page the beginning of the record is. Six types of pages are in a typical SQL Server database, as shown in Table 2.1.

Extents are the building blocks from which tables and indexes are constructed. An extent is eight contiguous pages, or 64K, or 16 extents per MB. In order to maximize efficiency when allocating space, tables or indexes will be assigned to mixed extents where up to eight tables or indexes share the extent when first created. When the table or page requires eight pages or more, additional space will be allocated on uniform extents where all the pages are owned by a single table or index.

Table 2.1 Types of data pages.

Page Type	Description
Data	Data rows containing all data except for **TEXT**, **NTEXT**, and **IMAGE** data
Index	Index entries
Text/Image	**TEXT**, **NTEXT**, and **IMAGE** data
Global Allocation Map	Information about allocated extents
Page Free Space	Information about available free space
Index Allocation Map	Information about extents used by a table or index

Database Files And Filegroups

In reengineering SQL Server 7's use of files to support databases, Microsoft has considered the future of relational database and planned for improved scalability and performance. Unlike the SQL Server 6.5's use of segments and device files, SQL Server 7 provides a much simpler space management scheme.

The following are some important notes regarding file management in SQL Server 7:

- A database consists of one or more database files.
- Database files can grow or shrink automatically as data is added or deleted.
- Data and logs no longer reside in a single file.
- Database files can logically grouped into filegroups for ease and consistency of handling.
- Database objects can be placed into any filegroup; functionally similar to segments, but much easier to maintain.
- A file can only be used by one database.

The three types of database files are:

- **Primary data files** Every database has one primary file that points to all of the other files required by the database. The recommended extension for primary data files is .mdf.
- **Secondary data files** All data files after the primary data file are secondary data files. A database does not have to have a secondary data file; others may have many secondary data files. The recommended file extension is .ndf.
- **Log files** Every database has at least one log file to hold the transaction log—information that is needed to roll back an individual transaction or recover a database. The recommended file extension is .ldf.

Each database file has two names: The logical and the physical name. The name must follow all SQL rules for names and must be unique to the database.

Also, the physical file name is the actual name of the underlying disk file. The name must be assigned consistently with NT or Windows 95/98 rules for file names. Figure 2.7 depicts an example of the relationship between logical and physical file names.

In order to improve the administration of multiple files, a database administrator can group database files into filegroups, which allow for more discrete placement of data and indexes on specific disk devices. This improves disk reads and writes, as well as overall performance. As with most things, economies of scale prevail when using filegroups, as the benefits are negligible (or even nonexistent) with smaller and less complex databases. However, for high-end, high-volume systems, the degree of control that can be gained by precise placement of data is signifi-cant. In addition, by managing multiple filegroups, different backup schemes may be used and different types of disk devices and RAID methodologies can be employed.

There are three types of filegroups:

- **The primary filegroup** Contains the primary data file (.mdf) and any other files (.ndf and .ldf) not put into another filegroup.
- **User-defined filegroups** You can specify these at the time you create a data-base; these can contain secondary (.ndf) and log (.ldf) files. You can add on any number of user-defined filegroups.
- **A default filegroup** You can specify ones that contain the pages for all tables and indexes not placed in other specific filegroups. Only one filegroup in a database at a time can be the default, and it can be either the primary or a user-defined filegroup.

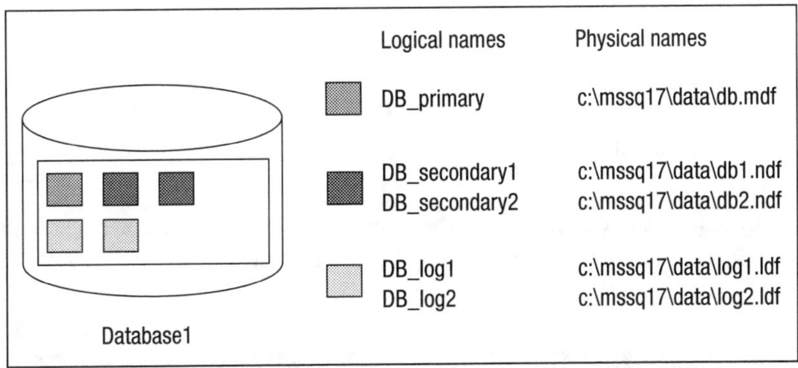

Figure 2.7 Relationship of logical to physical file names.

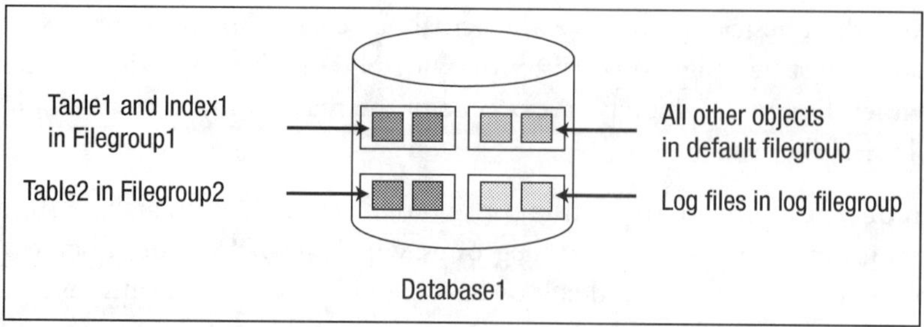

Figure 2.8 Databases, files, and filegroups.

In Figure 2.8, a possible database configuration suitable for a high-end system is shown. Notice that *Table1*, *Index1*, and *Table2* are placed specifically on separate disk devices to separate high-volume disk read/write operations from the rest of the database.

Space Allocation

As the database grows, SQL Server will allocate more pages to those objects that require them and reuse space freed up by deleted data. This functionality provides less expensive extent allocation and a big performance gain due to the fact that free space information is densely packed so each read to retrieve allocation information is very efficient. Allocation information is not chained, which simplifies the maintenance of this information and improves overall database reliability as broken chains are no longer an issue.

Two types of allocation maps are used to store information about the allocation of extents:

- **Global Allocation Map (GAM)** These pages record which extents have been allocated. Each GAM has capacity for 64,000 extents or nearly 4GB of data.
- **Shared Global Allocation Map (SGAM)** These pages record which extents are currently used as mixed extents and have at least one unused and available page. Each SGAM cover 64,000 extents or nearly 4GB of data.

As shown in Table 2.2, each of these structures contains a bit for each mapped extent to indicate the current status of the extent.

Table 2.2 Bit patterns in GAM and SGAM.

Current Use of Extent	GAM Bit Setting	SGAM Bit Setting
Free, not in use	1	0
Uniform extent, or full mixed extent	0	0
Mixed extent with free pages	0	1

By using these bits and interrogating GAM and SGAM for the next available uniform or mixed extent and flipping the values, SQL Server is freed from having to manage chains of allocation information. This results in a much faster and more reliable allocation of space. As page chains are largely done away with, the need to perform consistency checks and other repair operations on tables has become obsolete.

Chapter Summary

The relational model provides tools defining data structures, data integrity rules, and data manipulation methods. The relational model has two important characteristics: Data is perceived using a two-dimensional table. Also, when manipulating tables, the results will be presented in the form of new tables.

Three components of the relational architecture to consider when reviewing the implementation of the relational model are as follows:

- **The internal level** The organization of data on disk.
- **The external level** How data is presented to end users.
- **The conceptual level** Indirection between the other two levels that allows one to be changed without affecting the other.

In addition, we covered the following items:

- **Relation** Also called a *table*, this represents a two-dimensional view of data.
- **Tuple** Corresponds to a record or view. Any table will have one to many tuples.
- **Attribute** A column or data element in a table row.
- **Primary key** A unique identifier for a table that can be made up of one or many columns.
- **Domain** The pool of valid values available for use in a specific column.
- **Data** In a relational database, data is both *integrated* and *shared*.
- **Foreign key relationships** Allow for a relationship between two tables to be defined via matching data values.

The entity integrity rule does not allow for **NULL** values to be inserted into a primary key. According to the referential integrity rule, if a record in one table references a value in a second table, then that second record must exist. This allows for business rules to be defined in the database itself

Eight operators are available in relational algebra: select, project, product, union, intersect, difference, join, and divide. SQL is a hybrid based on relational algebra and relational calculus and has been enhanced with features that allow for arithmetic comparisons and operations, assignment of values, and the application of aggregate functions to a group. Transact-SQL is based on the ANSI standard SQL-92, but has been substantially enhanced with many extensions specific to Microsoft SQL Server 7.

Logical database components introduced in this chapter include constraints, defaults, indexes, keys, stored procedures, triggers, user-defined data types, and views. The smallest unit in SQL Server 7 is a page that is 8K in size.

An extent is comprised of eight contiguous pages and may be either mixed where multiple table or indexes share the extent or uniform where a single table or index owns all the pages.

The three types of database files are:

- **Primary data files** Each database has only one.
- **Secondary data files** A database can have none or many.
- **Log files** Each database must have one, but could have multiple.

Each database file will have both a logical and physical name providing an additional level of indirection. Database files are organized into filegroups, with each database having at least a primary filegroup that is also the default. But a database could also have user-defined filegroups that can contain secondary data and log files.

SQL Server will allocate space dynamically, as more is required and will shrink the database as data is deleted. Extents are managed using a Global Allocation Map and a Shared Global Allocation Map.

Review Questions

1. A relation is a three-dimensional representation of data with the dimensions being rows or records, columns or attributes, and time.
   a. True
   b. False
2. Each attribute value is atomic or single-valued; a given attribute cannot have more than one value.
   a. True
   b. False

3. The following is an example of which integrity rule? The *Products* table in the *Northwind* database may not have a **NULL** entered in the *ProductID* column that is defined at the primary key.
   a. Domain integrity
   b. Entity integrity
   c. Primary integrity
   d. Referential integrity

4. The following is an example of which relational algebra operator? Given a 10-column table, select five specific columns into the result set.
   a. Difference operator
   b. Divide operator
   c. Project operator
   d. Select operator

5. When the following objects are created in a SQL Server database, which will result in the query that created the object being stored in the system catalog with an identifying name? (Choose all correct answers.)
   a. Constraint
   b. Stored procedure
   c. Table
   d. Trigger
   e. View

6. Which of the following are examples of constraints? (Choose all correct answers.)
   a. Clustered
   b. Not **NULL**
   c. Primary key
   d. Rule
   e. Unique

7. Which of the following are types of database files? (Choose all correct answers.)
   a. Global allocation files
   b. Index allocation files
   c. Log files
   d. Primary files

8. Which of the following are types of data pages? (Choose all correct answers.)
   a. Global Allocation Map
   b. Log map
   c. Index allocation map
   d. Page free space

9. Which of the following are reasons for a database administrator to use filegroups when creating a database? (Choose all correct answers.)
   a. Change to a nondefault extent size
   b. Improve disk performance by placing data and indexes on specific disk devices
   c. Use different backup schemes for different filegroups
   d. Use nonunique indexes instead of unique indexes

10. Which of the following accurately describe characteristics of data in relational databases?
    a. Data is integrated and shared.
    b. Data is integrated, but not shared.
    c. Data is shared, but not integrated.
    d. Data is not integrated and not shared.

11. The smallest unit in SQL Server's physical structure is:
    a. Database file
    b. Extent
    c. Filegroup
    d. Page

12. Which of the following are names that can be given to a database file? (Choose all correct answers.)
    a. Group file name
    b. Logical file name
    c. Physical file name
    d. Primary file name

13. Which statements are true regarding file management in SQL Server 7? (Choose all correct answers.)
    a. Every database must have one and only one primary file.
    b. Every database must have at least one secondary file.
    c. Every database must have only one log file.
    d. Every database must have at least one log file.

14. Which statements are true regarding database file names? (Choose all correct answers.)
    a. Each file will have a logical file name that must be unique to the server.
    b. Each file will have a logical file name that must be unique to the database.
    c. Each file will have a physical file name that must follow Windows NT/95/98 naming rules.
    d. Each file will have a secondary file name that is used by the backup utility.

15. Which of the following can be assigned as a default value for a column? (Choose all correct answers.)
    a. Constant
    b. Foreign key value in another table
    c. Mathematical expression
    d. Transact-SQL built-in function

HANDS-ON PROJECTS

Susan began her new role by researching the objects that make up the database. She had been working with databases as a maintenance DBA and had been exposed to them before, but she hadn't given them a great deal of thought. She knew that to fill her new job adequately, she'd have to be familiar with each object and how it would be used properly. She opened the Enterprise Manager and began slowly examining each object.

Project 2.1

In this chapter you were introduced to nine logical database components: constraints, defaults, indexes, keys, stored procedures, tables, triggers, user-defined data types, and views. Though later chapters will explore these in detail, you will review the *Northwind* database now and look at a few examples:

1. Start SQL Server Enterprise Manager and continue expanding the plus signs next to MS SQL Server, SQL Server Group, and then the name of your SQL Server installation. Then expand Databases and finally *Northwind*. You will then see a listing that contains tables, views, stored procedures, rules, defaults, and user-defined data types as well as some other items that will not be covered just now. Notice that you do not see constraints, indexes, keys, and triggers listed separately.
2. Click on the Tables icon first, which will cause a list of all tables in the *Northwind* database to be displayed in the right-hand pane.
3. In the right-hand pane, select the table *Orders* by double-clicking on the table icon to the left of the name.

4. This will display a smaller window that will show details regarding the attributes or columns that comprise this table. In addition, you will notice a key icon placed next to the column *OrderID* that denotes that this column is a primary key. In addition, this column may not contain **NULLS**, as the **NULLS** column is not checked. Scroll down a bit in the window and you will notice that the column *Freight* has a default value of 0 specified. All columns other than *OrderID* can accept nulls.
5. You can obtain an alternative and more detailed view of this table by using the system stored procedure **sp_help**. After canceling from the table detail window, start a SQL session by selecting Tools | SQL Server Query Analyzer. In the small window labeled DB at the top of the form, click on the pull-down arrow and select *Northwind*.
6. In the input window, type **sp_help *Orders***, and execute the statement by clicking on the green arrow at the top of the screen. A second pane will open and display the results of this statement.
7. Move your cursor to the bottom pane, and use the scroll bars to move through the output. You will notice information regarding column names, data types, and nullability characteristics similarly to what you previously saw. (You will need to scroll to the right to see the full display.)
8. However, as you scroll down, you will see additional details. For example, the table is located in the **PRIMARY** filegroup. This table has nine indexes, with one of them being a clustered unique index on *OrderID*. This column is also the primary key for this table. (Remember that you will also need to scroll to the right to see additional details.) All indexes are also located in the **PRIMARY** filegroup.
9. Continue to scroll down, and you will notice information regarding constraints and defaults on this table. You'll see one default, as noted previously, and three foreign keys with one primary unique key. As you scroll right you will see which table each foreign key references.
10. And, lastly, a foreign key in another table *Order Detail* is referencing the *Orders* table via the column *OrderIDI,* as noted in the section labeled Table Is Referenced By.
11. Switch back to the Enterprise Manager window and click on the icon next to Views. The right-hand pane lists all views in the database. Scroll down and click on Quarterly Orders, and the Properties window displays the SQL syntax that was used to create this view. You will notice that the tables *Customers* and *Orders* were specified in the join. This is the join that will be executed when a SQL select statement is executed against this view. Cancel the Properties window.
12. In the left-hand pane, click on the icon next to Stored Procedures. The right-hand pane display will be refreshed and will now display a list of all stored

procedures in the *Northwind* database. Click on **CustOrderOrders** and the Properties window will show you the SQL syntax used to create this object. This SQL syntax following the "as" clause will be executed whenever this stored procedure is called with an input parameter of a customer number. Cancel the Properties window.

13. Click on the icon next to Rules in the left-hand pane; the right-hand pane will display nothing, as no rules have been created in this database. This reflects that constraints have effectively replaced rules.
14. Now click on the icon next to Defaults in the left-hand pane. The right-hand pane is still blank. However, we had noted previously that there was a default on the column *Freight* in the table *Orders*. You may notice that you don't see that default listed here. In Chapter 5, you will learn the two methods used to create defaults: a fault definition created using the **DEFAULT** keyword when a table is created or altered, or a default object that is then bound to the already created table. In the *Northwind* database, all defaults were created using the first method.
15. The last object type we will examine here is the User Defined Data Type. You can click on the icon in the left-hand pane, but no objects display in the right-hand side. These will be covered in detail in Chapter 5.

Project 2.2

You will now explore how the *Northwind* database uses logical and physical files and filegroups. This project will only be an introduction, as Chapter 14 will show you these tools in much more detail:

1. In your Enterprise Manager window, double-click on the *Northwind* database. Information in the left pane about tables will be replaced with high-level information about the database. You will see the database creation date, its total size (the default is .62MB), and other information. Select database properties from the right-hand pane, and a new window displaying additional details about the database will display. You will notice that the physical NT or Windows 95/98 file that contains this database is named C:\MSSQL7\DATA\Northwind.mdf and that 3MB have been allocated in this file. In addition, SQL Server will automatically grow this file as more data is added to the database. Scroll to the right and you will notice that this file is located in the **PRIMARY** filegroup. This file also has the logical name *Northwind,* which is how the file location is specified in SQL statements.
2. Notice that the only file displayed is the primary data file that has the extension .mdf. Click the tab at the top of the window labeled Transaction Log and you will see a 1MB transaction log file located in the same directory as the data file, but named Northwind.ldf. This file has the logical name Northwind_log.

CHAPTER THREE

3

DEVELOPING A LOGICAL DATABASE DESIGN

After Reading This Chapter And Completing The Exercises, You Will Be Able To:

- Understand the database development life cycle
- Understand the top-down and bottom-up approaches to developing database requirements
- Develop and refine an entity-relationship model that accurately documents business processes and functions
- Remove redundant data elements from the entity-relationship model through normalization
- Complete the database design by documenting insert/update rules and defining domains

A number of steps are involved in transforming what might be a loose set of business and functional requirements into a fully implemented database design. This chapter will focus on the data analysis and design portion of the database life cycle, with special emphasis on logical data modeling. Chapter 4 will complete the logical design and transform it into a physical database.

THE DATABASE LIFE CYCLE

Databases that support required business functions with good performance, accurate data, and proper flexibility need up-front planning before the DBA creates the first table. The following is a brief overview of the steps in the life cycle of a database. See Figure 3.1 for an illustration of these steps:

1. Database requirements are determined by interviewing both the producers and users of data. A formal specification (usually in a narrative form) is produced that lists items such as the data elements required, their sources, data relationships, and rules for integrity, security, and performance.
2. A logical design is developed using data modeling techniques. As part of this process, redundant data will be removed and the natural relationships between sets of data will be defined.

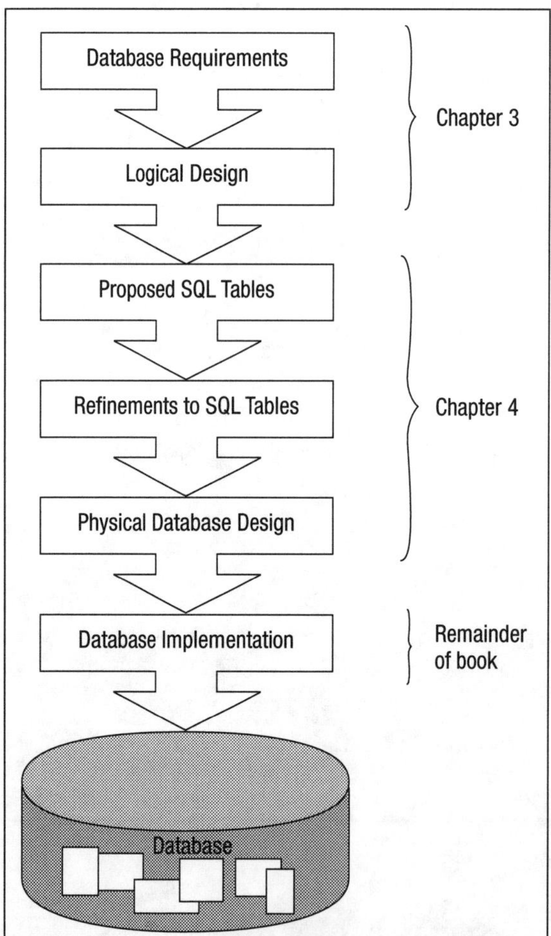

Figure 3.1 Database life cycle.

3. A proposed set of SQL tables is laid out on paper or with software tools using the logical design as the initial specification.
4. The business rules defined in the logical design are translated into the physical database design. The DBA will create database components, such as constraints, triggers, indexes, and keys, to ensure that all previously defined rules for integrity, security, and processing have been met.
5. The set of tables produced is refined. Factors such as data update rates and read frequencies, data volume, growth patterns, and archiving requirements are considered. At this point, it is not unusual to add some of the redundant data at the expense of disk storage in order to improve overall query speed.
6. The design is now ready for implementation, and the DBA will begin to create the database and populate it with tables, triggers, stored procedures, and other objects.

In this chapter, the focus will be on Step 2, though some coverage of Step 1 will be provided. Chapter 4 will present methods for successfully completing the next three steps.

Gathering Database Requirements

Because many books are available on systems analysis and design, including a number that focus on the requirements gathering phase, we won't discuss this topic here in great detail. However, it is worthwhile noting that two approaches are commonly seen in database design that will affect the process used for gathering requirements: *bottom-up* and *top-down*.

In the bottom-up approach, information on all data elements of interest is gathered and categorized into groups, cross-referenced using dictionary tools, and described using spreadsheets and other special-purpose tools. This approach is rather simplistic and often ignores the big picture of the business processes being described or fails to consider alternative design approaches. Limitations to the design produced by this approach are often only obvious after much time and effort has gone into further refinements and even implementation.

By using the top-down approach, you can avoid many of these pitfalls. The design staff will normally use experts who understand the business process being analyzed. With this knowledge, the designer can focus on important data elements, identify the major processes and issues, and begin to present alternative solutions. This approach will also allow long-range planning to be more readily incorporated into the design.

For example, in the bottom-up approach, the designer of a new human resources system might start listing all of the data elements needed to describe an employee. All of these data elements will be put through a somewhat mechanical design process. A reasonably good design, perhaps using an employee number to identify the employee, may very well be produced.

However, by taking the top-down approach, the designer will examine the process of hiring and determine that an employee who is assigned an employee number is first a candidate who has submitted a résumé and is going through the interview process. An employee number at this point doesn't make sense, but some sort of candidate identification will be required.

A somewhat different design can be derived using the top-down approach, as opposed to the bottom-up approach. The top-down design often appears to better reflect real-world experiences.

Logical Database Design

In Chapter 2, the three levels of the database architecture were introduced:

- **The external level** This defines the view of data that end users will see when they are using customized applications, reporting tools, and other client applications.
- **The internal level** This is where the databases, tables, and other objects are created in files spaces on disks controlled by the relational database manage-ment system.
- **The conceptual level** This provides a level of indirection and allows the external views to be mapped to the internal level.

The details regarding integrated and customized data views at the conceptual level can be expressed via a *logical database design*—a specification that defines the data attributes and the relationships among the attributes that support a business process or function.

It is important to follow a consistent and thorough methodology through the logical database design process; many formal methodologies exist. The following is a checklist of the basic steps that should be used:

1. Analyze and identify major entities, or data objects.
2. Identify the relationships between entities, including all characteristics of the relationship.
3. Identify primary and alternate keys for all entities.
4. Review relationships and establish foreign keys.
5. Referring back to original database requirements, add in remaining nonkey attributes.
6. Normalize the entities removing redundant data and repeating groups.
7. Complete the database design by documenting insert/update rules, data domains, and other business rules.

These steps will be described and illustrated throughout this chapter with a number of examples to demonstrate some of the variations that you might see in actual practice.

Two key processes are employed during the logical design phase of a project to identify and define the data attributes and to refine the relationships. Both of these methods will be described in some detail in this chapter:

- **Entity-relationship modeling** The process of describing and relating entities, relationships, and attributes.
- **Normalization** The processing of verifying that attributes associated with entities are assigned consistently and in such a way that redundancy is eliminated.

Entity-Relationship Modeling

The process of entity-relationship modeling was first described by P. P. Chen in 1976 and was later extended by other researchers and analysts to support the design of relational database systems. The *entity-relationship model* (*ER model*) or *entity-relationship diagram* (*ERD*) is a graphical representation of the data structure. This diagram becomes the basis for effective communication among the programming team and with the end user. Whereas a paper narrative or a spreadsheet of data attributes becomes difficult to understand or unwieldy, the ER model is often much easier to grasp, even for the end user.

The original Chen notation used in constructing a graphical ER model consisted of rectangles and diamonds connected by lines. Over time, other designers have developed a variety of annotation methods to describe details of the ER model. Boxes and arrows will be used in this book to represent entities and relationships.

In addition, many specialized software products exist that can greatly simplify the preparation of ER models and will eliminate the otherwise arduous work that would be required to construct models by hand. These products also provide additional tools, such as data dictionaries and interfaces to process modeling that provide enhanced capability for documenting the database design. SQL Server 7 includes a graphical tool in Enterprise Manager that allows the DBA to create database diagrams that both document the physical database and create or modify database objects.

Basic Objects

Several basic objects make up the ER model. These include the following:

- **Entities** Data objects that describe a person, place, thing, or event, such as employee, company, publisher, author, patient, hospital, and admission.
- **Relationships** Associations between entities that are usually described by a verb phrase, such as employs, publishes, teaches.

- **Attributes** The elements that provide description and detail about entities and relationships and might include such elements as employee name, department name, author name, publishing date, diagnosis, and assigned bed.

Entity

The basic building block of an ER model is an *entity* or a *data object* that describes a person, place, thing, or event. As we begin to define the entities that are required to support the ordering process for Northwind, a distributor of gourmet food products, we might start to think about entities such as *product* that describes things, a *customer* that describes people, and an *order* that describes events.

An *entity instance* is a specific occurrence of an entity; for example, a product, such as Ipoh coffee, or a specific customer, such as B's Beverages. Considering entity instances will help to validate the design as it progresses. The entities *customer* and *order* are represented as rectangles as shown in Figure 3.2.

Relationships

Relationships define associations between entities and allow for one entity to act on another. For example, a customer *places* an order and an order *is placed by* a customer. At its simplest, a relationship is graphically represented as a line with an arrow as shown in Figure 3.2. The arrow will go *from* one entity *to* another where the *from* entity is the parent and the *to* entity is the child.

The relationship can generally be stated as some action of the parent on the child. For example, teacher teaches class, customer places order, project team has member. Though the reverse relationship descriptions are not always labeled on an ER model, it is expected that the reverse relationship is also true—class is taught by teacher, order is placed by customer, member is assigned to project team.

A *relationship instance* represents a specific occurrence of a relationship, such as a specific customer order. Degree, connectivity, existence, and role further describe relationships; these elements will be defined in the section "Characteristics Of Relationships."

Attributes

Once an entity or relationship has been defined, additional details about those objects will be required (and can be provided) via *attributes*. For the Northwind customer, we will want to know such things as customer number, name, credit limit, date of last order, contact name, and so forth. The relationship between customer and order can be further described by such attributes as *order date* and *order ID*.

Consider two types of attributes:

- **Identifiers** These uniquely describe a specific entity or relationship instance and may be composed one or more attributes, such as *customer number, order ID*.

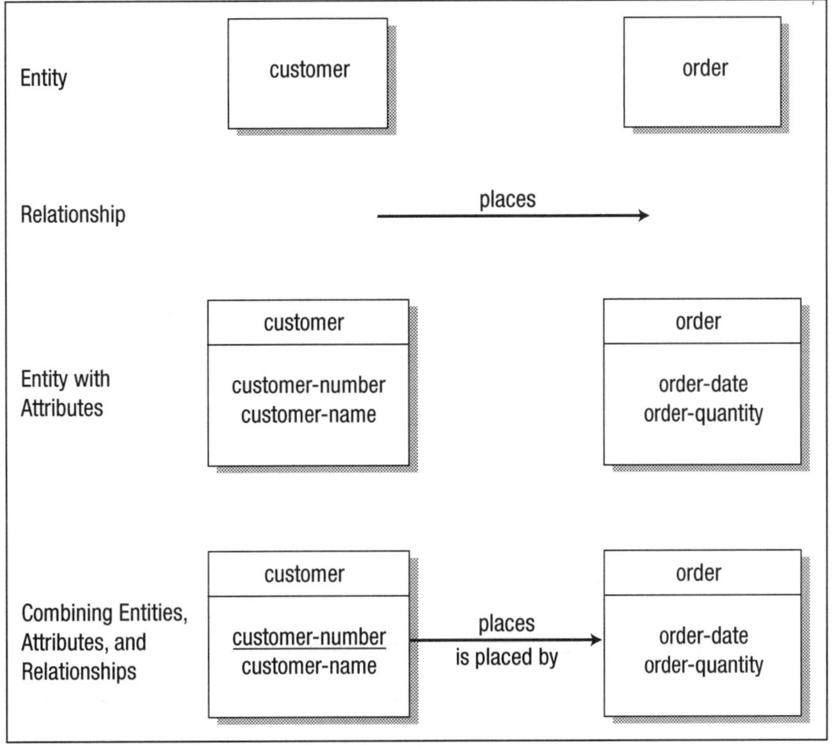

Figure 3.2 Basic objects in an ER model.

- **Descriptors** These provide additional information about the entity or relationship, such as *customer name, credit limit, order date.*

As shown in Figure 3.2, attributes can be listed within the entity box with the addition of an underline for those attributes that are identifiers.

Characteristics Of Relationships

Now that we have reviewed the basic building blocks of the ER model, we will delve further into additional characteristics of relationships and discuss these elements:

- Degree
- Connectivity
- Cardinality
- Existence

These elements are very important, as they will ultimately be used to define the referential integrity rules that we will enforce via database objects, such as constraints, triggers, keys, and others.

Degree Of A Relationship

The number of entities associated with a relationship is defined by its degree. Relationships of degree 1, 2, or 3 are also known as *unary*, *binary*, and *ternary* relationships, respectively. Typically, relationships will be binary with a degree of 2. In fact, it is often very rare to see relationships of degree 1 or 3 even represented in a data model. However, an example of each type is shown in Figure 3.3.

A *binary relationship* is an association between two entities. For example, relationships can be defined between hospitals and patients, author and publishers, authors and books, customers and orders. Likewise, a *unary relationship* describes an association between two instances of the same entity. For example, in a human resources system, another employee manages an employee. This relationship is also described as being *recursive*.

Very occasionally, if it is impossible to break down the relationship between three entities into two binary relationships, a *ternary* relationship results. For example, a doctoral candidate writes a thesis at a college or university. It is impossible to describe the relationship between author and thesis without including the relationship to the degree-granting institution.

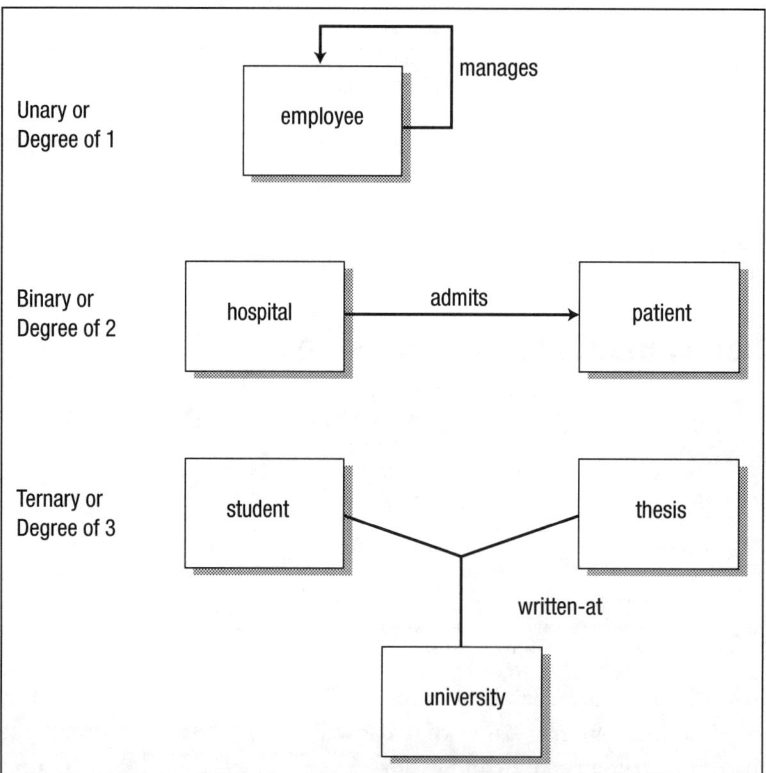

Figure 3.3 Degree of a relationship.

Connectivity And Cardinality Of A Relationship

We had previously mentioned that each entity is composed of one or more entity instances, such as Island Trading, Maison Dewey, and others representing a customer. By specifying the *connectivity of a relationship,* we can describe how many entity instances are required on either side of the relationship. Connectivity values are either one or many. For example, if we are designing a class scheduling system, a teacher teaches many classes, but one teacher teaches a class. In this case we have connectivity of one on the teacher side of the relationship and connectivity of many on the class side as depicted in Figure 3.4.

In addition, we can use the *cardinality* of the relationship to further define exactly *how many* the many relationship is. For example, if the teacher can teach many classes but no more than five, a one-to-five relationship exists between teacher and class where five is the largest class load.

Existence Of An Entity In A Relationship

When the existence of one entity instance depends on the existence of another instance in another entity, this is called *existence dependency* or simply *existence*. Furthermore, existence is either *optional* or *mandatory*. Let's consider some examples in Figure 3.5. A customer may or may not have ordered a

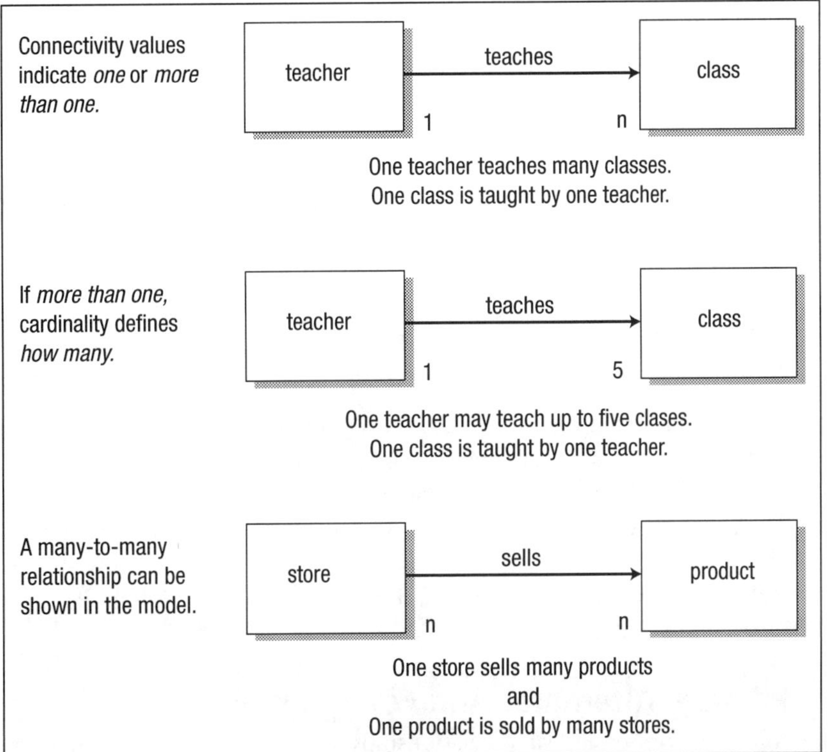

Figure 3.4 Connectivity and cardinality of a relationship.

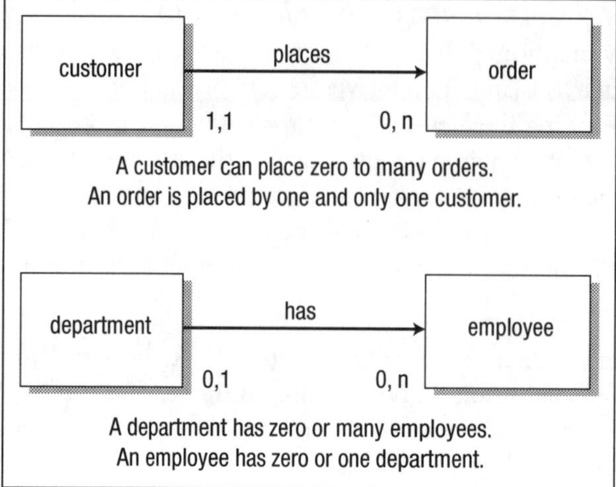

Figure 3.5 Existence of a relationship.

product from Northwind. Therefore, the existence of a relationship from customer to order is optional. On the other hand, an order cannot exist without a customer and the relationship of order to customer is mandatory.

In the case of a human resources system, an employee can be hired but not yet assigned to a department; the relationship from employee to department is optional. Likewise, a department may be newly formed and without employees. In this case, the relationship from department to employee is also optional.

Many-To-Many Relationships

As you work through your database design and ER model, you may come across the special case of many-to-many relationships where the minimum cardinality on both sides of the relationship is greater than one. For example, information technology staff is assigned to projects in Figure 3.6. And, as is typical with short-staffed IT departments, *employee is assigned to many projects* and *project is staffed by many employees* as shown in the first model.

A new entity assignment will allow two one-to-many relationships to be defined. The new relationships are *employee is assigned to project assignment* and *project has assigned to it project assignment*. Though the wording may seem awkward, by adding this new entity, it is much easier to describe the process flow. In addition, the project-assignment entity can now be described with attributes, such as date assigned, hours worked, percent complete. The intermediate entity is frequently called an *associative entity*.

Primary, Alternate, And Foreign Keys

After the entities and their relationships have been charted, the next step is to identify primary, alternate, and foreign keys for all entities.

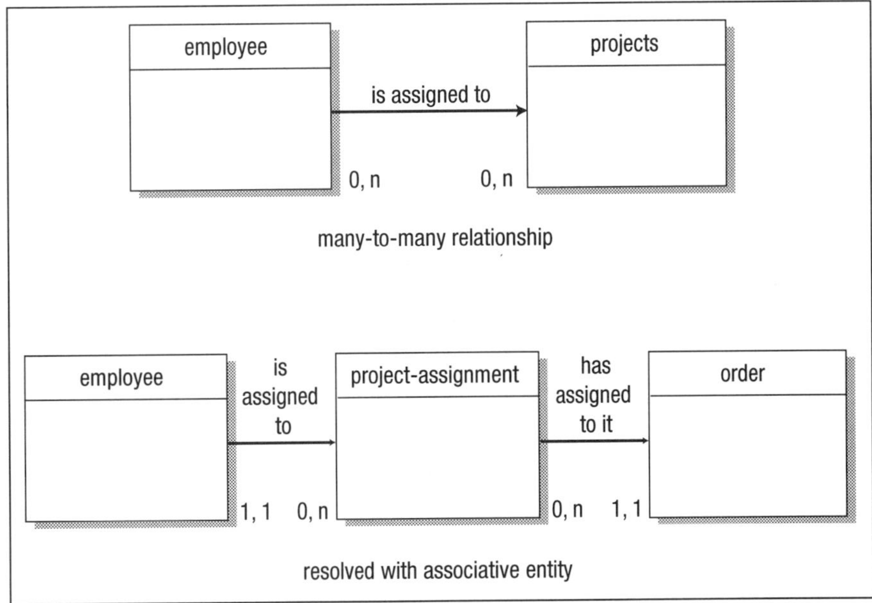

Figure 3.6 Many-to-many relationships.

Primary And Alternate Keys

Taking one entity at a time, first identify each *candidate key* which is an attribute that uniquely identifies each entity instance. A candidate key may be composed of only one or several attributes, in which case it is called a *composite key*. Furthermore, the candidate key cannot be unknown or nullable. One candidate key will be chosen as the primary key, and the remaining candidate keys will be *alternate keys*.

For example, a hospital system has the entity *patient* with the following possibilities for candidate keys:

- **Patient name** In a large hospital system, it is impossible to ensure uniqueness.
- **Patient name plus date of birth** Looks more promising than the first choice, but still not guaranteed to be unique with common names.
- **Social Security number** Not all patients have a Social Security number; for example, foreign visitors, students and workers on visas.
- **Patient number** A system-generated unique number appears to be the best available choice.

Let's consider another example—the *patient-visit* entity in the same hospital system:

- **Patient number and visit date-time** This composite key is unique.
- **Patient number and visit number** This composite key containing a system-generated number in place of the visit date-time is also unique.

You will notice that the alternative candidate keys overlap. Both keys contain patient number and one other attribute. In addition, either key works equally well as a primary key. You simply choose one candidate key as the primary, the other becomes the alternate key.

On an ER model, the primary key will be underlined, and alternate keys will be labeled *ak1, ak2,* and so forth, as shown in Figure 3.7. You will note we have an *employee* entity that contains candidate keys *employee number* and *social security number.* If our analysis verifies that each of these numbers is unique, then we can simply select one as the primary key and denote the other as an alternate. In our second example, the *order detail* entity has candidate keys *order number, order line number,* and *order number,* and we have selected *part number* after we verified that each part number in an order will only appear once.

When we transform our logical model into the physical design, we may elect to switch our primary key for one of the alternate keys due to storage and performance considerations. Having the alternate keys identified now will allow us to easily evaluate them later and select the best key to implement.

Foreign Keys

Foreign keys allow us to specify the attributes or data that joins two entities. We have already identified the relationship with the arrow shown, but the foreign key will provide further details regarding the underlying business rules. The foreign key attribute or attributes will be placed in the child entity. This foreign key will join the entity instance back to a corresponding entity instance in the parent entity. As the key originates in the parent entity, it is considered *foreign* to the child.

For example, the *teacher* entity shown in Figure 3.8 has a primary key of *teacher number.* The *class* entity has a primary key of *class number.* We will add the teacher number to the *class* entity to reflect the relationship between the two entities. Note that we have identified in parentheses the source entity of the *teacher number* attribute. This will help us later when we begin to transform our logical model into a physical design and begin to create data objects.

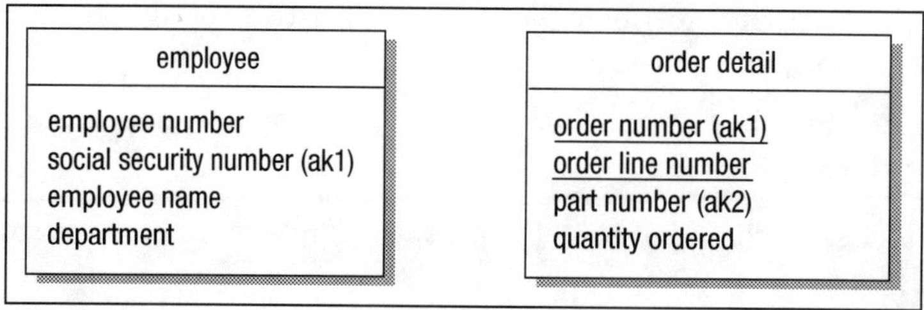

Figure 3.7 Primary and alternate keys.

We have discussed the two entities *patient* and *patient-visit* where *patient number* is the primary key *in patient* and *patient-visit* has a composite primary key *of patient number* and *visit number*. Notice that the foreign key *patient number* that joins these two entities also participates in the primary key.

Nonkey Attributes

In order to complete the ER model, nonkey attributes that had been identified in the preparation of original database requirement will be added to the appropriate entities. *Nonkey attributes* are facts about the entity that describe or quantify the entity. Examples of nonkey attributes are items like quantity, name, color, size, address, date, and so forth.

After identifying a nonkey attribute, place it with an entity where the attribute is dependent on the whole primary key. For example, *order quantity* will describe *order* and *order line* in the *order detail* entity, but *customer ID* will describe *order* in the *order entity*. Placing *customer ID* in the *order detail* entity will create data inaccuracies later. These attributes are simply placed inside the appropriate entity box. Their placement has no particular order.

As you are placing attributes, you may occasionally come across some that seem to describe a relationship, rather than either of the entities. Often these relationships are events that require location or date information that is specific to the event. For example, in Figure 3.9, the original two entities, *doctor* and *patient*, have been expanded into three attributes. They have been added to describe the treatment received. Before adding the *treatment* entity, attributes such as *treatment*

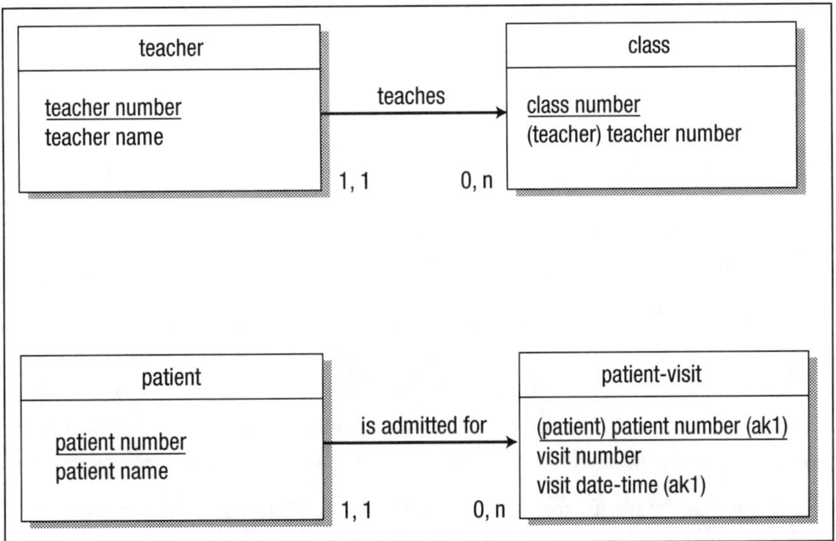

Figure 3.8 Foreign keys.

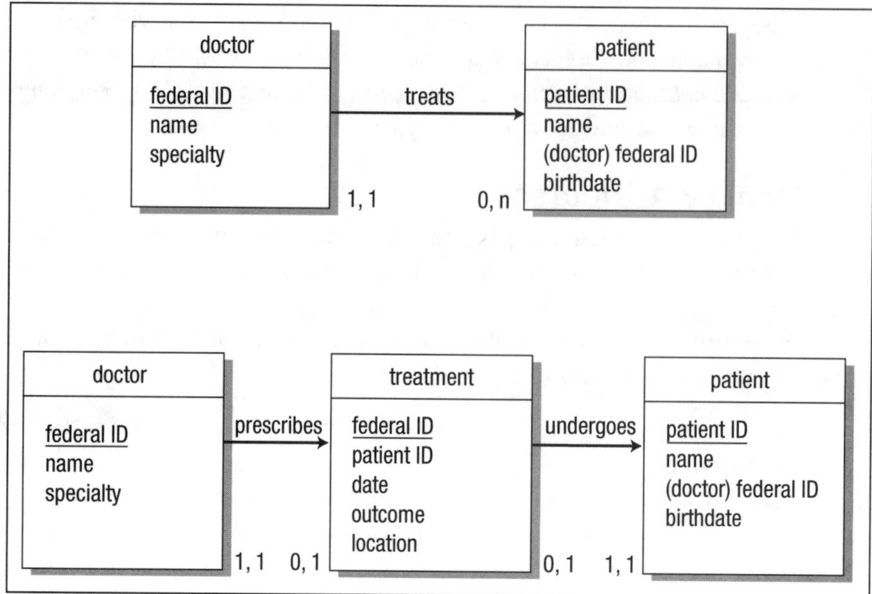

Figure 3.9 Attributes that describe a relationship.

date, outcome, location of treatment (outpatient or inpatient), didn't properly belong with either the *doctor* or the *patient* entity.

AN ER MODEL OF NORTHWIND (PART 1)

Now that we have learned the basics of ER modeling techniques, let's take a look at our distribution company, Northwind. This company buys gourmet and imported food products from suppliers and sells them to customers, such as stores and other resellers. You have been asked to develop an ER model for the portion of the business that purchases product from suppliers.

The first step is to develop a narrative description of the process that you intend to model. Included in the following narrative is some detail regarding data sources and data relationships:

Northwind buys products from suppliers with whom they already have a business relationship. Information about a supplier will be captured when contact is first made. At a minimum, the supplier ID and the supplier name must be entered. Some suppliers are located in multiple locations with specific contact information for each location.

The products being stocked are gourmet food items. Some of the products have been discontinued, while others are still in an active state. Products will also be divided into categories so that a catalog can be produced. At a minimum, the product ID and the product name must be entered when a new product is set up.

The next step is to take this information and begin to identify the possible entities. It appears that *supplier* is an obvious entity with several business rules already defined. *Product* is another possible entity, or perhaps two product entities are necessary: one for *active product* and another for *discontinued product*. Two product entities might make sense in those circumstances where the business process is very different for those two groupings. That does not seem to be the case here, as no description is in the narrative of return or clearance activities for the discontinued product. Therefore, one entity to describe all products will be sufficient with an active flag, as well as a category as descriptive attributes. In Figure 3.10, the entities for *supplier* and *product* have been defined.

Our next step is to identify the relationship; that is, *supplier supplies product*. Because two entities are participating, this relationship is binary or of degree 2. We must consider the connectivity of the relationship next. As we review our database requirements, it appears that one supplier can sell many products. But what about the reverse: Can one product be sold by more than one supplier? If that were the case, we would have a many-to-many relationship expressed in our model. As it appears that our requirements are not complete, some phone calls are made, and the issue is settled—each product is only purchased from one supplier.

Next we will give some thought to cardinality. Is there any reason to believe that a supplier can sell only one product or a maximum number of products to Northwind? In fact, no limits exist and the relationship will be defined as *one* on the supplier side and *many* on the product side.

The last item to consider in reviewing the relationship between *supplier* and *product* is existence. Is it necessary for one or more products to exist for an instance of supplier? Again, a phone call is made, and the answer is no. The *supplier* record can exist without entries in the *product* entity. On the other hand, a *product* cannot exist without a *supplier* record; that fact was included in the original requirements. The relationship is mandatory on the *product* side and optional on the *supplier* side. The relationship can now be fully expressed as *supplier supplies zero-to-many product* and *product is supplied by one and only one supplier* and is properly annotated in the ER model shown in Figure 3.11.

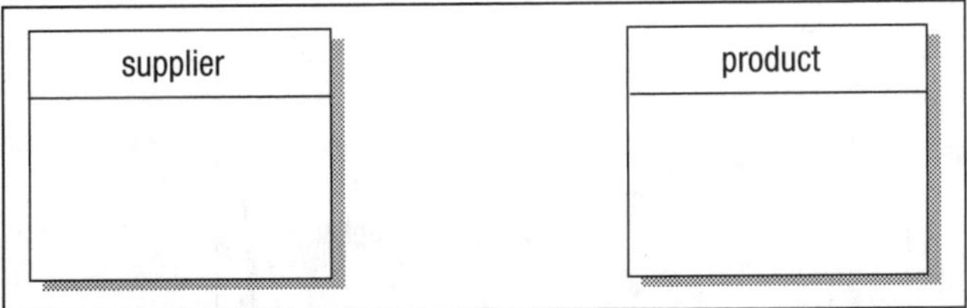

Figure 3.10 Supplier and product entities.

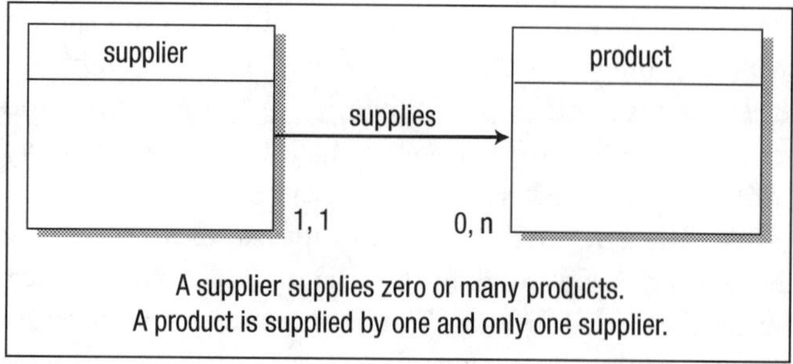

Figure 3.11 Relationship between supplier and product.

By saying the relationship in a full sentence and in each direction, you can validate that the business rule expressed in the model is in fact correct.

With the two entities and the relationship defined and all attributes listed, we will now define the primary keys. The primary key will uniquely identify each entity instance or record, and a foreign key will define the data relationship between the two entities via joining attributes. First, we'll determine a primary key for the *supplier* entity. We have a single candidate key, *supplier ID*. Remember that *supplier name* was a possible candidate key because it is a required field, but it is not unique. It is possible that we might have two records for the same supplier located in different locations.

In the *product entity* we have two candidate keys: *product ID* and *product name*. Though both work equally well as primary keys, we will choose *product ID*. We have noted a functional relationship between supplier and product, and we will define the relationship via a foreign key (*supplier ID*)—the primary key in the supplier entity. The primary keys will be annotated on the model with underlines and the foreign key source will be identified with parentheses as seen in Figure 3.12.

We have now completed our ER model to the point of specifying two entities and a relationship, along with primary and foreign keys and all attributes known so far. We will continue to refine our logical database design for supplier and product through the remainder of this chapter.

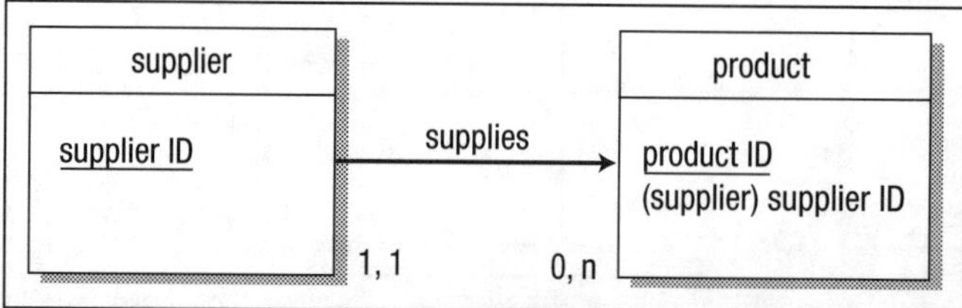

Figure 3.12 ER model for supplier and product.

Data Normalization

Once the ER model has been completed, we can further refine it by removing repeating groups and redundant data elements. This process is called *normalization* and will result in a database design that provides several advantages:

- Less disk space will be required because no data elements—except for foreign keys—will be stored in multiple locations.
- Data inconsistencies that can be introduced when updates and deletes occur will be largely eliminated. For example, if one instance of a duplicated data element is updated or the instance in which it is located is deleted, what should happen to the remaining data elements?
- The database design that results from the normalization process will be better able to support later changes in scope or business process without major modification.

It is important to note that the normalization process is focused solely on the data and the meaning of the data and will not take into account the computing environment, the transaction rates, or data volumes. Though normalization will often have a positive impact on these elements, tuning for these elements will be considered after the logical design process is complete.

After performing the normalization steps, the database will be in a normal form. These forms are numbered sequentially to represent the level of normalization. Whereas the normal forms will be presented in sequence as if this were a step-by-step process, the end result of attaining a third normal form or higher is the goal. Most database designers will refine their design and remove flaws using intuition and experience and bring their design directly to the desired third normal form.

First Normal Form

An entity is in *first normal form* if no repeating groups exist. Any repeating groups or multivalued variables should be moved to a child entity. In a class registration system developed for a community school, the analyst might have initially designed a nonnormalized student entity as shown in Figure 3.13. In this example student information, such as student number, name, and other information, including up to two classes is listed. At first glance, this may appear to be a very reasonable design, because students can only take up to two evening classes. Problems will exist with the design, however, if changes are required in the physical database due to the school choosing to offer classes on Fridays or Saturdays.

Notice in Figure 3.13 that the repeating groups in the sample data go across the page; this is a telltale sign that repeating groups or multivalued variables are

student number	student name	class1 code	class1 name	class1 days	class1 teacher	teacher1 office	class2 code	class2 name	class2 days	class2 teacher	teacher2 office
1	Ron	C101	Cars	MT	Smith	B23	S101	Stocks	WR	Brown	B35
2	John	M101	Music	WR	Jones	A35					
3	Emily	A101	Art	MT	Jones	A35	M101	Music	WR	Jones	A35

Nonnormalized Data

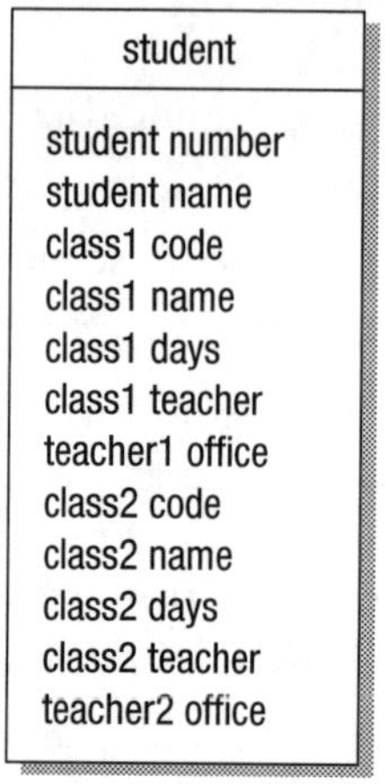

student
student number student name class1 code class1 name class1 days class1 teacher teacher1 office class2 code class2 name class2 days class2 teacher teacher2 office

Nonnormalized Entity

Figure 3.13 Nonnormalized data.

present. In Figure 3.14, the design has been transformed into first normal form with the addition of a child entity that contains the class information. Now, the data that previously went across the page is listed down the page with the same number of records, as each student has class instances. The database design has been simplified as a result and is now ready for further normalization.

Second Normal Form

In the *second normal form*, all attributes that do not describe the whole primary key or alternate key are removed. If you refer to Figure 3.14, you will notice the nonkey attributes *class name*, *class days*, and others in the *schedule* entity, which only describes a portion of the key, the *class code*. To achieve second normal form, these attributes, along with a copy of their primary key, are moved to a new entity and related back to the schedule entity via a foreign key relationship. The results are shown in Figure 3.15.

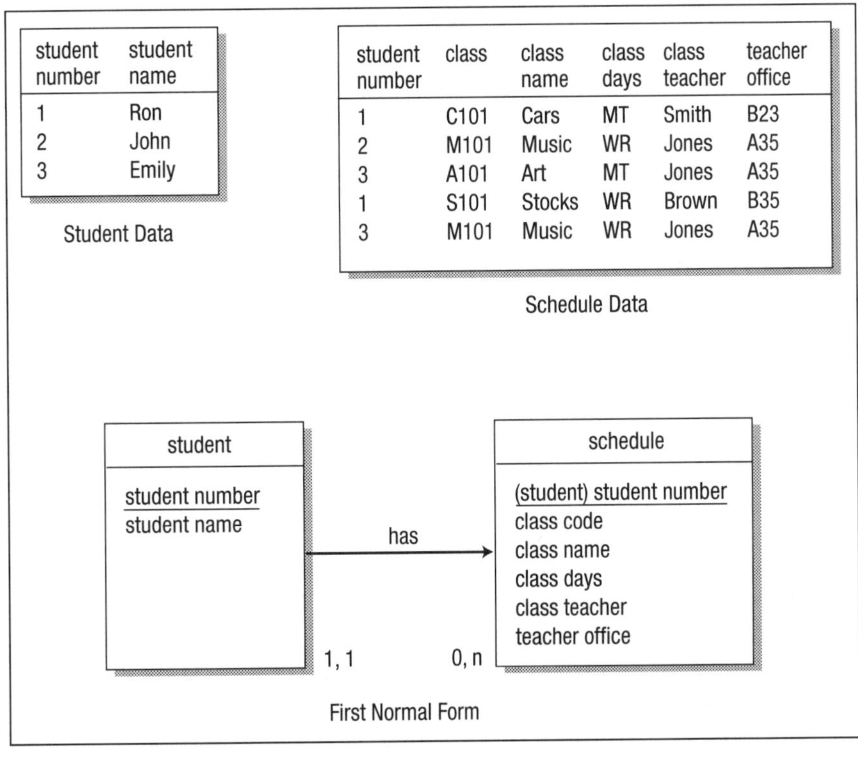

Figure 3.14 First normal form.

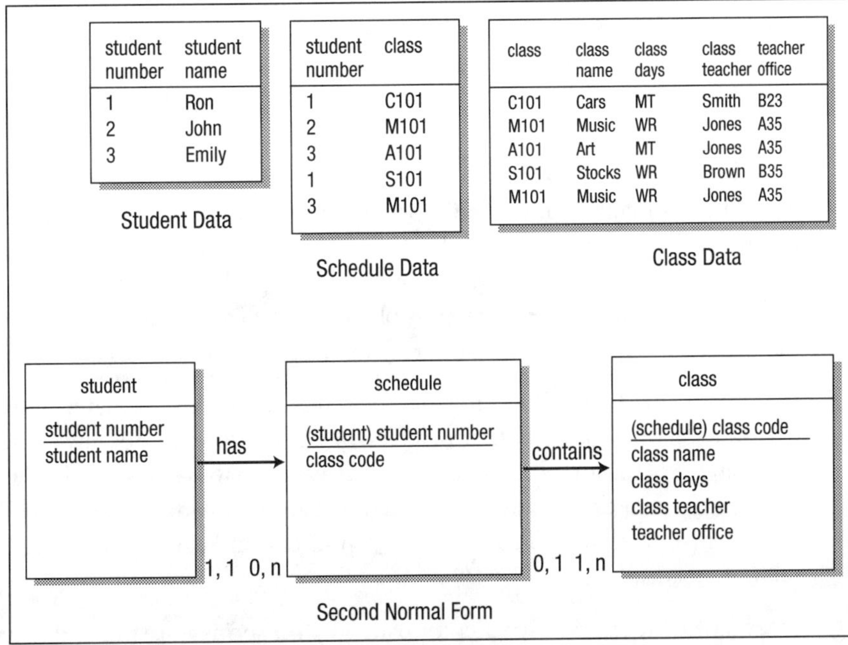

Figure 3.15 Second normal form.

The result is an additional reduction in redundancy, as well as an elimination of a possible data update anomaly. If you refer back to the schedule data in Figure 3.14, you will notice that some classes have multiple instances. This will require a change in class schedule or assigned teacher to be updated in not just one but multiple records. Often examining the data will point out data redundancies or opportunities for normalization that are not as obvious in the ER model.

Third Normal Form

All nonkey attributes that depend on other nonkey attributes (except for alternate keys) are removed to achieve *third normal form*. In other words, each nonkey attribute must depend only on the entire primary key or alternate key (second normal form) and nothing but the primary key or alternate key. Refer to the class data depicted in Figure 3.15. Notice that the value for *teacher office* is the same even though the teacher is assigned to different classes. The value of *teacher office* is dependent on the teacher name and not the class being taught.

As noted in the previous discussion of the second normal form, we have introduced a possible accuracy issue, because multiple records would now need to be updated if a teacher's office assignment changed. In addition, we have an even more difficult problem with this design, because we could lose teacher information altogether. Imagine that we have a teacher who is temporarily not assigned to any classes. No entity instances will be in the *class* entity that reference that teacher, and all information about that teacher will be lost.

The solution is to move the attribute *teacher office* into a new entity and define a relationship via a foreign key back to the *class* entity as presented in Figure 3.16. Now an instance for a new teacher who is not yet assigned to any classes can be created. The data loss situation for a teacher on sabbatical has been removed.

Boyce-Codd Normal Form

Typically, normalization to third normal form is sufficient. However, some additional normalization is available for specific special cases. The *Boyce-Codd normal form* addresses the scenario where multiple, composite, overlapping candidate keys exist. By examining every possible choice of candidate key and ensuring that each key is in third normal form, additional redundancies are removed.

An entity is in Boyce-Codd normal form if each attribute is determined only by a full candidate key—either primary or alternate—and not any subsets of a candidate key. In our example in Figure 3.17, we have represented data for race car teams where each team has one or more drivers: A driver can only drive on one team, each team can have multiple sponsors, and each sponsor can support multiple teams.

By creating an entity with a composite key on sponsor, team, and driver, the relation is in third normal form. However, we will have a data anomaly if

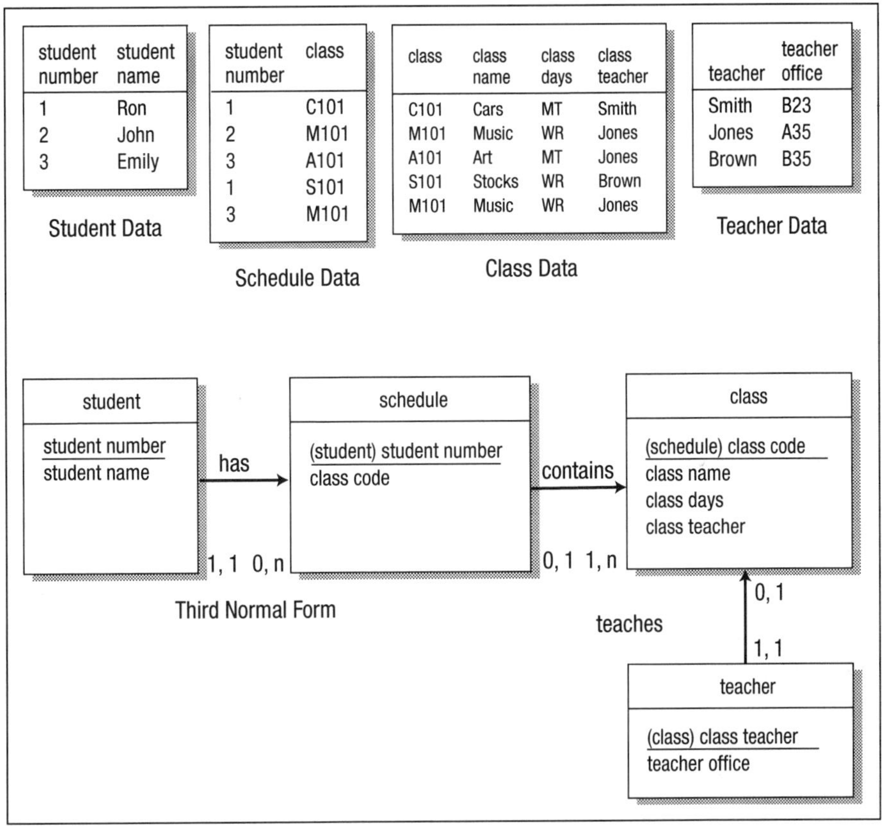

Figure 3.16 Third normal form.

Dino Oil stops sponsoring the Blue team, because we will not have any record of Jonathan driving for that team and we will lose all of the associated detail.

By decomposing this single entity into two as shown in Figure 3.18, we will be able to avoid possible data loss. Furthermore, we have introduced additional flexibility in creating new instances of *team sponsor* and *driver assignment* with only a small amount of additional overhead.

Completing The Normalization Process

Two other normal forms are available for the advanced database administrator to use:

- **Fourth normal form** This further refines potential repeating groups into separate entities by removing any multivalued components of the primary key to new entities.
- **Fifth normal form** This addresses pair-wise cyclical dependencies within composite primary keys.

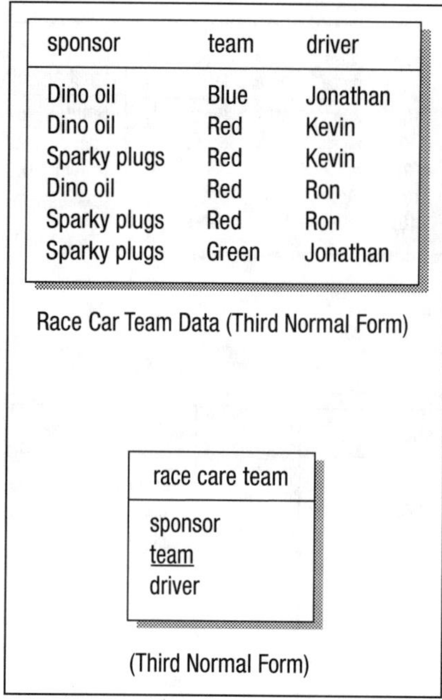

Figure 3.17 Race car team in third normal form.

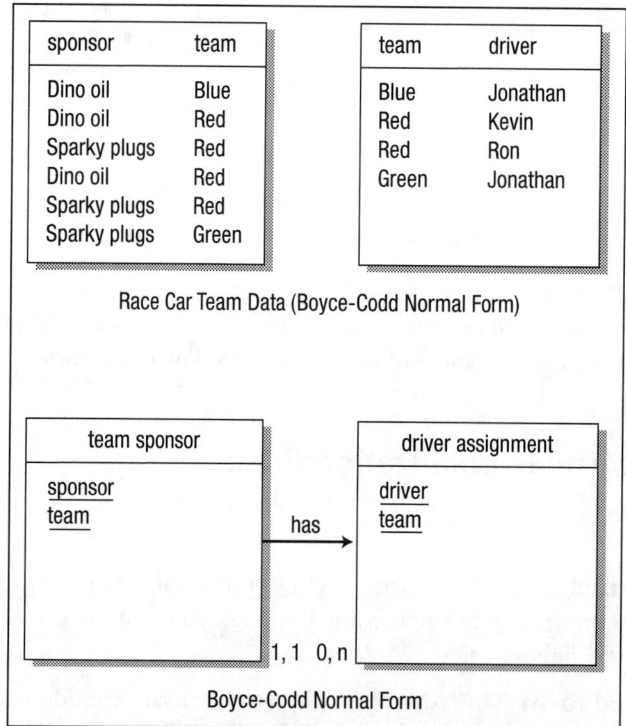

Figure 3.18 Race car team in Boyce-Codd normal form.

Though designing a logical model that is completely normalized is the ultimate goal of any data modeler, these additional forms are not frequently used and will not be discussed in this book.

One word of caution is required here. Do not make the mistake of overnormalizing a database. This is done by splitting a fully normalized entity into two smaller entities. If you notice that you have entities on your model with one-to-one relationships instead of one-to-many relationships, then you have gone too far. This construct does not violate any normalization principles, but you will have added unnecessary complexity to your model.

Another consideration when reviewing your ER model is the effect of time on data relationships. For example, your model might have *customer* and *order* entities where *customer places order*. In the *customer* entity you might have the *address* to which the *order* was shipped. If you have a business requirement to be able to support sales tax audits that will need a report of where each order was shipped, having the *customer address* only in the *customer* entity will not satisfy this need. The *customer address* can be changed at any time to reflect new information received, and this has the affect of rewriting your order history. The solution is to place the *customer address* in the *order* entity as well, where it forever serves as a record of the actual shipping address for that order. This appears at first glance to be a clear violation of our rules of normalization, because we are introducing duplicate customer address data. However, different business meanings are assigned to the two customer addresses—current address versus shipped address.

It might appear that creating an ER model and normalizing data is an art, not a science. Although we have described some rules and recommendations that may seem somewhat mechanical, the nuances of your particular business process and your interpretation of your user requirements are key. The most important rule is that the model should represent how *your* business operates and functions, with an eye toward database performance.

An ER Model Of Northwind (Part 2)

Now that you learned the basic principles of data normalization, we will return to the Northwind ER model that we had partially completed earlier and normalize it. Remembering that one of the main goals of normalization is to eliminate redundancy; it is often helpful to simply begin by looking for repeating groups and other data that doesn't seem to describe the primary key. Though we described the normal forms in a stepwise fashion, we are not in practice going to progress through first normal form, second normal form, and so on. Instead, we will identify the nonnormalized data and eliminate it as we discover it. Our goal is to perfect a third normal form ER model.

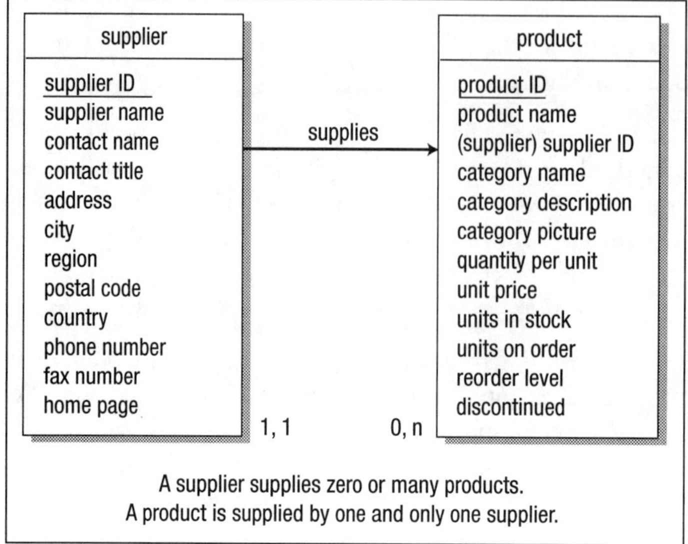

Figure 3.19 ER model for supplier and product.

The ER model as depicted in Figure 3.19 shows two entities that have the relationship, primary keys, and foreign key defined. As we review the model, we notice no repeating groups.

We review the supplier entity and note that most attributes seem to describe *supplier id*. We do pause over *contact title* as it seems to describe *contact name* rather than *supplier ID*—a violation of the third normal form. This data will be moved to a separate contact entity.

As *contact name* might be duplicated, we'll add a *contact ID* as our primary unique key as shown in Figure 3.20. The attribute *supplier ID* will be copied to the *contact* entity as a foreign key and part of the primary key. Reviewing our require-ments, it appears that *contact information* is optional and this will be noted in the relationship. We have now established the relationship *supplier is represented by zero or one contacts* and *contact represents one and only one supplier.*

Similarly, we observe that the *category information* in the *product* entity describes *category name* rather than *product ID*. This data will also be moved to its own entity. A primary key of *category name* and a foreign key in the *product* entity will replace the original attributes. Note that the *category* entity is the parent in the relationship and *product* is the child. The relationship can be presented as *category describes zero to many products* and *product is described by zero to one categories*. This relationship is optional on both sides, that is, a *product* does not need a *category* and a *category* may not be assigned to a *product*. We have now completed the ER model for Northwind's stocking process. However, we will continue to develop the logical design required to support this business function.

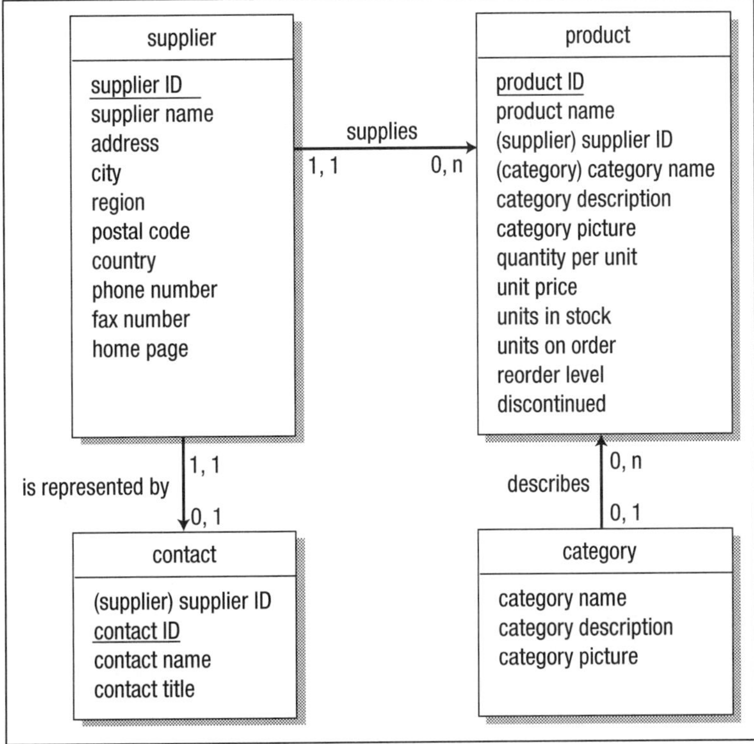

Figure 3.20 Normalized ER model for supplier and product.

Business Rules

We have discussed enough about the process of logical database design to build an ER model that will reflect the data structures required to support a business operation. The model alone does not completely address data integrity. Identifying primary and foreign keys to ensure entity and relational integrity is only a start. By defining additional business rules, you ensure that your logical design accurately reflects the actual practices used.

We will discuss three types of business rules:

- Insert/update rules that address integrity of relations
- Domains that address integrity of attributes
- Special processing requirements not previously defined

If you are using a specialized software tool to create your ER model, you may have the capability within that tool to document these business rules and link them to the appropriate entities and relationships. If your software is limited, you might need to use spreadsheets and other external documents.

Insert/Update Rules

An insert/update rule defines the conditions under which a primary or foreign key may be inserted, updated, or deleted. These rules are also sometimes called *existence constraints* because the existence or nonexistence of another entity will control the completion of the operation on the first entity. For example, a *customer* cannot place an order for a nonexistent *product*. Therefore, an *order* instance cannot be entered if a *product* instance does not exist. In addition, a *product* instance cannot be deleted if orders for that *product* exist.

Insert Rules

Insert rules document how the parent instance controls the inserting of new instances into the child.

The six insert constraints areas follows:

- **Dependent** Insert a child record only when a matching parent instance already exists.
- **Automatic** Always permit insertion of child record; if parent instance does not exist, create it.
- **Nullify** Always permit insertion of child record; if parent instance does not exist, set foreign key in child to **NULL**.
- **Default** Always permit insertion of child record; if parent instance does not exist, set foreign key in child to predefined default.
- **Customized** Permit insertion of child instance only if special circumstances are met.
- **No effect** Always permit insertion of child instance; do not check parent instance.

By analyzing the business model, each relationship in the model will be defined by an insert constraint. For example, in Figure 3.21 we have a representation of the relationship we had previously identified between supplier and product in our Northwind ER model.

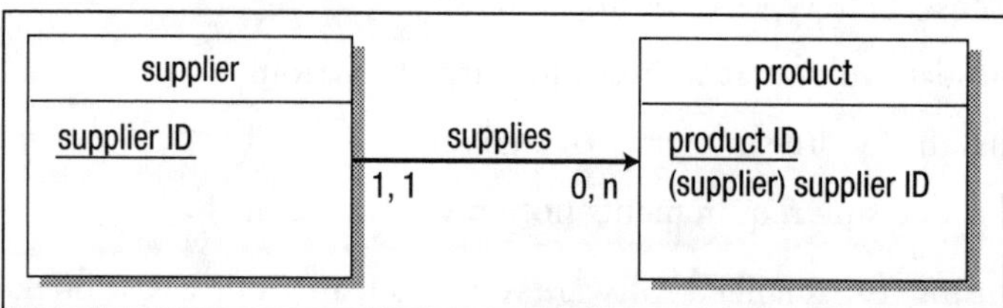

Figure 3.21 ER model for supplier and product.

Six possible constraints will control the insertion of new records or the update of the *supplier ID* attribute in the product entity:

- **Dependent** The product must be supplied from an existing supplier.
- **Automatic** The product may be supplied from an existing or new supplier. If the supplier is new, a corresponding instance is added to supplier.
- **Nullify** The product must either be supplied be from an existing supplier or the supplier ID will be set to **NULL**, indicating that no supplier exists.
- **Default** The product must either be supplied from an existing supplier or a default supplier.
- **Customized** The product must be supplied from the supplier who has the best credit terms available. Any number of customized rules are available.
- **No effect** The product may be supplied from any supplier whether the supplier is on the approved list or not.

Delete Rules

Just as are six types of insert rules exist, six types of delete rules control when a parent instance will be deleted:

- **Restrict** Delete a parent instance only when no matching child instances exist.
- **Cascade** Always permit deletion of parent instance and then cascade the deletion to all matching child instances.
- **Nullify** Always permit deletion of parent instance. If any matching child entity instances exist, then set their foreign keys to **NULL**.
- **Default** Always permit deletion of parent instance. If any matching child entity instances exist, then set their foreign keys to a predefined default.
- **Customized** Permit deletion of parent instance only if special circumstances are met.
- **No effect** Always permit deletion of parent instances; do not check child record.

Just as we did previously with insert rules, we will want to evaluate and identify a delete constraint for each relationship in our data model.

When we examine the relationship between supplier and product in our Northwind model in Figure 3.21, six constraints control the deletion of a supplier instance and how changes are rippled out to the product instance. We can select from the following:

- **Restrict** Supplier cannot be terminated if he is presently supplying parts.
- **Cascade** If the supplier is terminated, then remove any supplied parts from the product list.

- **Nullify** If the supplier is terminated, then update the product list to reflect an unassigned vendor.
- **Default** If the supplier is terminated, then reassign all items in the product list to the default supplier.
- **Customized** If the supplier supplies more than ten items in the product list, then cancel the deletion and send an email to the department head.
- **No effect** The supplier is terminated without any checks being performed; some items in the product list may be left behind.

Selecting Insert And Delete Constraints

Only by analyzing and then understanding your business requirements will you be able to pick the rules that are right for your logical database design. It is generally a good idea to avoid the nullify insert and delete rules and choose the default insert and delete rules instead. Though foreign keys can be nullable, it is generally better to assign a default value, even if it is a blank string or zero. This will simplify processing in the physical database environment. And, of course, the no effect insert and delete may simplify coding the front-end application as the insert and delete operation are always permitted to complete. However, you are opening yourself up for major data integrity issues if this is implemented without proper consideration for the consequences.

Data Domains

A *domain* is simply a set of valid values for an attribute. Or, to be more precise, a domain represents a pool from which one or more attributes may draw their values. For example, the set of state codes represent a set of 50 values from which values can be drawn for such attributes as supplier state, customer state, employee state, and the like. Table 3.1 lists the characteristics that are typically used to describe a domain.

The most rigorous method for defining domains is to define each domain explicitly and then associate it with one or more attributes. However, most data modeling tools are not designed to support separate named domains, and this method is not used very often. The most frequently used method for defining data domains is simply to assign domain characteristics, such as data type, length, allowable values, and so forth, to each attribute. Next, evaluate the entire set of attributes in the ER model to determine if any two or more attributes share the same domain.

Some characteristics of domains do not change no matter which entity the attribute is located in. For example, data type and length are inflexible. On the other hand, characteristics such as nullability and uniqueness will be affected when an attribute is participating in a primary or foreign key. For example,

Table 3.1

Domain Characteristics	Examples
Data type	integer, character, date
Length	10 digits, 35 characters
Format	yy/mm/dd (to describe a date), xxx-xxx-xxxxx (to describe a phone number)
Allowable values	0 < x < 100, x in ('A','B','C'), x in set of valid state codes
Meaning	age of employee, age of machinery, date paid, date hired
Uniqueness	unique, nonunique
NULL support	not nullable, nullable
Default value	0, 'false', current date

department numbers will always be numeric, but they may be unique and not **NULL** in the *department* table where they are the primary keys. They might also be nonunique and nullable in the *employee* table where it is used to describe an employee instance.

Attributes assigned to different entities may also have different sets of allowable values, depending on their business context. For example, the domain of *area code* may be all telephone area codes in the United States when the attribute is associated with the entity representing U.S. suppliers. But when the same attribute is associated with the entity representing employees, the list of allowable values might be restricted to just the few area codes in the area surrounding the employer's location.

Other Business Rules

At this point in your logical model, you should have the majority of your business rules embodied. Some rules remain that could be so specific that they are still not represented in any of these constructs. In these cases it becomes necessary to specify *triggering operations* that will specify the rules under which insert, update, and delete operations on attributes can be carried out. For example, it might be necessary in the human resources model to specify the following business rule that will require a triggering option:

The sum of the employees 401K contributions to all available accounts cannot be greater than 15 percent of base salary.

These operations should be clearly documented in the design documentation so that implementation during a later phase can be completed.

Chapter Summary

We have discussed the following items in this chapter:

- Databases that will support required business functionality must first begin with a solid database design based on business rules and requirements.
- In gathering database requirements, two methods can be used: *top-down*, where emphasis is placed on process, or *bottom-up*, where the emphasis is on individual data elements; the top-down approach generally provides better results.
- The logical database design will express details regarding the conceptual level that maps the external user views of data to the internal database representations on disk and in tables.
- Entity-relationship modeling is the cornerstone of logical database design, because many of the details of the design can be expressed graphically with boxes and arrows.
- The basic objects in an ER model are entities, relationships, and attributes.
- An entity is a data object that describes a person, place, thing, or event.
- A relationship defines an association between entities and allows for one entity to act on another. The relationship generally represents some action of the parent entity on a child entity.
- Attributes provide additional detail about the business objects and functions represented by entities and relationships.
- Two types of attributes exist: identifiers that uniquely identify a specific entity or relationship instance, and descriptors that provide additional information about the entity or relationship.
- Relationships are further described by the following characteristics: degree, connectivity, cardinality, and existence.
- The degree of a relationship defines how many entities are participating in the relationship: one, two, or three.
- The connectivity of a relationship describes how many entity instances are required on each side of the relationship; values are either one or many.
- Cardinality further defines exactly how many entity instances are involved; that is a specific number.
- The existence of one entity on another entity is either optional or mandatory.
- Many-to-many relationships are special cases that can be resolved into two one-to-many relationships by creating an associative entity.
- Candidate keys are all keys that uniquely identify each entity instance.

- A composite key is composed of more than one attribute.
- A primary key is selected from all available candidate keys.
- Candidate keys not selected to be the primary key become alternate keys.
- Foreign keys specify the attributes that join two entities. As the key originates in the parent as a primary key, it is considered foreign in the child.
- Nonkey attributes should be placed with those entities where the attribute dependent on the whole primary key.
- Normalization is the process of removing repeating groups and other redundant data elements from the ER model.
- Advantages of normalization include a reduction in disk space in the implemented model, elimination of data inconsistencies that can occur during updates on nonnormalized data, and a database design that is better able to support future modifications.
- An entity is in first normal form if no repeating groups exist.
- In the second normal form, all attributes that do not describe the whole primary key are removed to other entities.
- In third normal form, all nonkey attributes that depend on other nonkey attributes (except for alternate keys) are removed.
- The Boyce-Codd normal form addresses the scenario where multiple, composite, overlapping candidate keys exist. Each key must be in third normal form.
- Do not over normalize by splitting an entity into two entities joined via a one-to-one relationship as this adds unneeded complexity to the model.
- Though the entity-relationship model does a very thorough job of documenting data objects and relationships, not all of the business rules that ensure entity and relational integrity can be defined in the model.
- Insert rules will describe how the parent instance controls the inserting of new instances into the child entity.
- The six insert constraints are: dependent, automatic, nullify, default, customized, and no effect.
- Delete rules will describe how a parent instance will be deleted when a corresponding child record is deleted.
- The six delete constraints are: restrict, cascade, nullify, default, customized, and no effect.
- A domain represents a pool of valid values from which one or more attributes can be selected.
- Characteristics typically used to describe domains include data type, length, format, allowable values, meaning, uniqueness, **NULL** support, and default value.

3

- Business rules not previously defined by primary and foreign keys, insert/update rules, and relationships can be specified by triggering operations which represent specific actions to be carried out after an insert, update, or delete.

Review Questions

1. As you are creating an entity-relationship model, which of the following steps will be included during the process? (Choose all correct answers.)
   a. Analyze the business process and create a requirements documents.
   b. Analyze and identify major entities or data objects.
   c. Normalize the entities removing data redundancy.
   d. Create a proposed set of SQL tables and indexes.

2. Which of the following are basic objects defined in the entity-relationship model? (Choose all correct answers.)
   a. Entities
   b. Indexes
   c. Relationships
   d. Domains

3. Which of the following correctly describe the characteristics of an entity?
   a. Entities represent people, places, things, or events.
   b. In an ER model, entities are represented as diamonds.
   c. An entity instance represents the entire population that comprises that entity.
   d. Entities will be described by degree.

4. Which of the following correctly describe the characteristics of a relationship? (Choose all correct answers.)
   a. When a relationship line is drawn, the arrow is pointing toward the child entity.
   b. Connectivity describes how many entities are joined with the relationship: 1, 2, or 3.
   c. Existence describes whether the relationship is optional or mandatory.
   d. Cardinality describes how many entity instances will participate in the relationship.

5. Given the business requirements that passengers book air flights, which correctly describes the entities and relationships that might be derived from this limited description? (Choose all correct answers.)
   a. Two entities exist: *passenger* and *flight*.
   b. The relationship will be drawn so that the arrow is going from *passenger* to *flight*.
   c. The degree of the relationship is two.
   d. The relationship is mandatory on both sides.
   e. This is a many-to-many relationship.

6. Given the business requirement that real estate broker lists property, which correctly describes the relationship that might be derived from this limited description? (Choose all correct answers.)
   a. The relationship will be drawn so that the arrow is going from *property* to *broker*.
   b. The connectivity on the *broker* side of the relationship is one.
   c. The connectivity on the *property* side of the relationship is one.
   d. The existence of the relationship is optional on the *broker* side.
   e. The existence of the relationship is optional on the *property* side.

7. Given the business requirement that assemblies are manufactured from subassemblies, which statement correctly describes the relationship (hint: this is a recursive relationship) that might be derived from this limited description? (Choose all correct answers.)
   a. The arrow on the relationship line will represent subassemblies.
   b. The connectivity on the assembly side of the relationship is one.
   c. The connectivity on the subassembly side of the relationship is one.
   d. The existence of the relationship is optional on the assembly side.
   e. The existence of the relationship is optional on the subassembly side.

8. Which of the following statements correctly identifies characteristics of a candidate key? (Choose all correct answers.)
   a. A candidate key may contain one or more attributes.
   b. Only one of the attributes may be nullable.
   c. Candidate keys not chosen to be a primary key will become foreign keys.
   d. A candidate key uniquely identifies an entity instance.

9. Consider the entity *airline flight* and the attributes *flight number, date, time, origination airport, destination airport, type of jet*, and *passenger capacity*. From the following, select the candidate keys. (Choose all correct answers.)
   a. *flight number*
   b. *flight number, date, time*
   c. *origination airport, destination airport, type of jet*
   d. *origination airport, destination airport, date, time*
   e. *origination airport, destination airport, date, time, type of jet*

10. Consider the entity *property* (U.S. real estate listed by broker) and the following attributes: *street address, city, state, zip, dimensions, county, plat book description, nearest cross street, zoning*. From the following, select the candidate keys. (Choose all correct answers.)
    a. *street address, city, state*
    b. *street address, city, state, zip*
    c. *street address, city, state, zip, county*
    d. *county, plat book description*
    e. *county, zoning, nearest cross street*

11. Which of the following statements correctly describe foreign keys? (Choose all correct answers.)
    a. Foreign keys specify which attribute or attributes join two entities.
    b. The data that comprised the foreign key originates in the child entity and is added to the parent entity to reflect the relationship between the two entities.
    c. It is possible to have a relationship between two entities and not have a foreign key identified.
    d. It is possible for a single entity to contain multiple foreign keys if the entity participates in multiple relationships.

12. Which of the following statements correctly describe the normalization process? (Choose all correct answers.)
    a. A benefit of normalization is that less disk space will be required when the logical model is converted to a physical database.
    b. The database is usually normalized to the second normal form; only in rare cases will a third normal form be derived.
    c. A frequent characteristic of a nonnormalized database design is the presence of repeating groups of data.
    d. A nonnormalized database design will frequently have inconsistencies during database update and insert operations.

13. Which of the following are correct statements regarding the normal forms? (Choose all correct answers.)
    a. In first normal form, all repeating groups are identified and moved to a child entity.
    b. In second normal form, attributes that do not describe the primary key are identified and moved to a child entity.
    c. In second normal form, attributes that do not describe the primary key are identified and moved to a new parent entity and linked back to the original entity via a foreign key.
    d. In third normal form, each nonkey attribute must depend on the primary key and only the primary key.

The following information is provided for questions 14 through 16. You have been asked to model an airline ticketing system and are currently working on the logical database design. You have an ER model with three entities: *passenger*, *flight*, *ticket*. Passengers, flights, and tickets are identified by unique numbers.

You have been given the following business requirements: A passenger purchases a ticket for a scheduled flight; a passenger can cancel a flight and retain the ticket for a future flight; a passenger can request that all flights be canceled and money returned; a flight cannot be canceled if tickets have been purchased.

14. Which of the following statements correctly describe the relationships between the entities? (Choose all correct answers.)
    a. *Passenger* and *flight* are child entities, and *ticket* is the parent entity to *passenger* and *flight*.
    b. The existence of the relationship between *ticket* and *passenger* is optional on the *ticket* side and mandatory on the *passenger* side.
    c. The existence of the relationship between *ticket* and *flight* is optional on the *ticket* side and mandatory on the *flight* side.
    d. The connectivity of the relationship between *ticket* and *passenger* is one on the *ticket* side and many on the *passenger* side.
    e. The connectivity of the relationship between *ticket* and *flight* is many on the *ticket* side and one on the *flight* side.

15. Which of the following statements correctly describe the foreign keys? (Choose all correct answers.)
    a. The *passenger* entity will contain the foreign key flight number.
    b. The *ticket* entity will contain the foreign key flight number.
    c. The *flight* entity will contain the foreign key ticket number.
    d. The *ticket* entity will contain the foreign key passenger number.
    e. The *passenger* entity will contain the foreign key ticket number.

16. Given the stated business requirements, which of the following insert rules will apply?
    a. Dependent rule on relationship between passenger and ticket
    b. Dependent rule on relationship between ticket and flight
    c. Default rule on relationship between passenger and ticket
    d. Default rule on relationship between ticket and flight

17. Given the stated business requirements, which of the following update rules will apply? (Choose all correct answers.)
    a. Restrict rule on relationship between passenger and ticket
    b. Restrict rule on relationship between ticket and flight
    c. Cascade rule on relationship between passenger and ticket
    d. Cascade rule on relationship between ticket and flight
    e. Nullify rule on relationship between passenger and ticket
    f. Nullify rule on relationship between ticket and flight

HANDS-ON PROJECTS

Susan had taken a look at the architecture that she would be using to design her database. She took a deep breath and logged on to her workstation. She knew that the design portion of her job was probably the farthest-reaching of the tasks she'd be asked to do. If the design were poor, she knew the rest of the project would be tough to do correctly. She started her design by assessing the business rules she'd been given by the development group.

Project 3.1

You have been asked to analyze the customer ordering process for the Northwind Company and create a logical database design. The following business requirements document was put together by the business analyst assigned to your project team.

The Northwind Company sells gourmet and imported foods to customers who are food shops, markets, and restaurants. The individual placing the order is typically the owner, but sometimes a purchasing agent is the representative. Each company that purchases from Northwind has a single designated contact. Each company has been given a unique five-character alphanumeric customer code.

After a customer has been set up in the order entry system, the contact buyer can place an order for products available from Northwind. When an order is placed, the customer can specify their choice of shipping method from available shippers with whom Northwind does business. If the customer does not specify a shipper, Northwind will ship the product via United Package. In addition, the customer can specify an alternative shipping location. This is especially helpful for stores or restaurants with multiple locations. If an alternative location is not specified, the order will be shipped to the address the customer already has on file.

The customer can also order in advance of their needs and specify a future date on which they would like to receive the product. The customer can order multiples of any available item and discounts can be applied against any item purchased. Products may be back-ordered if Northwind does not have the desired product in stock. Customers can order more than one item at a time.

The following data elements describing customers have been identified and should be included in the database design: *CustomerID*, *CompanyName*, *ContactName*, *ContactTitle*, *Address*, *City*, *Region*, *PostalCode*, *Country*, *Phone*, and *Fax*.

Order information includes the following: *OrderID*, *OrderDate*, *RequiredDate*, *ShippedDate*, *ShipVia*, *ShipperCompanyName*, *ShipperPhone*, *Freight*, *ShipName*, *ShipAddress*, *ShipCity*, *ShipRegion*, *ShipPostalCode*, *ShipCountry*, *ProductID*, *Product Name*, *UnitPrice*, *UnitsInStock*, *Quantity*, and *Discount*.

Create an ER model for Northwind using the previously defined business requirements. Use the following checklist when creating your model:

1. On a piece of paper, create the entities *Customers*, *Orders*, and *Order Details*.
2. Define the relationships by reviewing the following for each: Which entity is the parent? Which is the child? Give the relationship an appropriate name. What is the connectivity (one or many) on the parent side? On the child side? Is the existence optional or mandatory on the parent side? On the child side?

   Draw in the relationship with an arrow on the child side and label it with a name. Add connectivity and existence information to both the parent and child ends of the relationship.

   Verify the relationship by stating it in a phrase that links the parent to the child and in a second phrase that links the child to the parent.
3. Review the data attributes that describe *Customers*, *Orders*, and *Order Details* and determine which are the candidate keys for each entity. Remember that the candidate key must be unique and nonnullable.

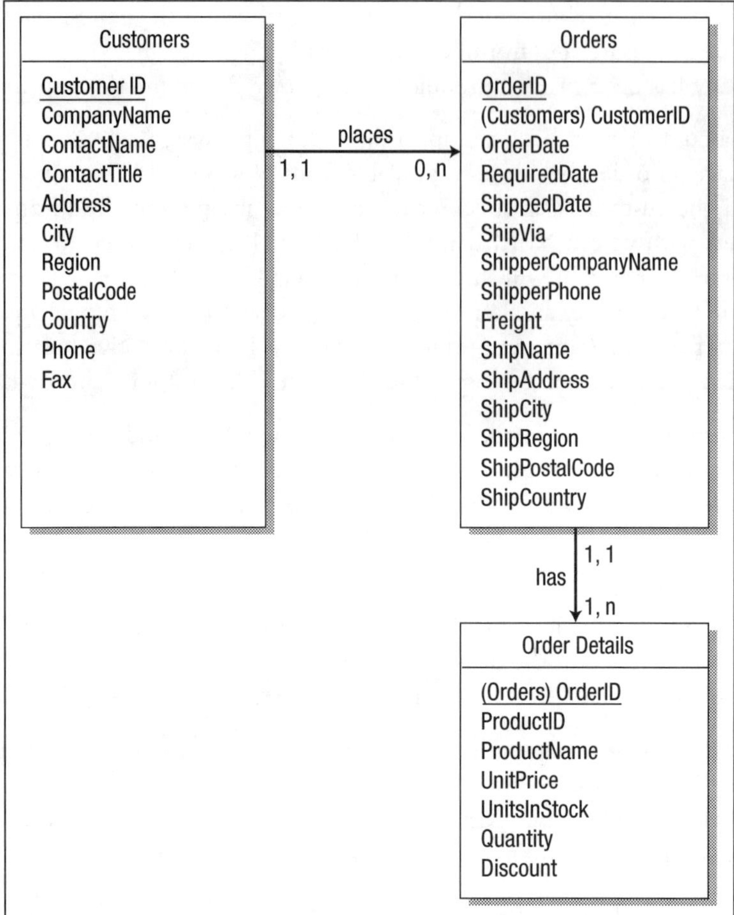

Figure 3.22 ER Model for Northwind customers and orders.

4. For each entity, review the candidate keys and select the appropriate primary key. Candidate keys not selected become alternate keys. Annotate the model by underlining the primary keys and adding the AK to alternate keys.
5. As relationships exist between *Customer*, *Orders*, and *Order Details*, verify that a foreign key has been added to each child table and add the name of the parent table in parentheses to identify the data source.
6. Add the remaining attributes that are nonkeys and place them within the appropriate entity boxes.
7. Compare your work against Figure 3.22.

Susan had spent a couple of days creating her initial model. She put it aside over the weekend and then on Monday came in to work on normalizing the design. She took out her notes on normalizing the database and began going over her checklist and the database model.

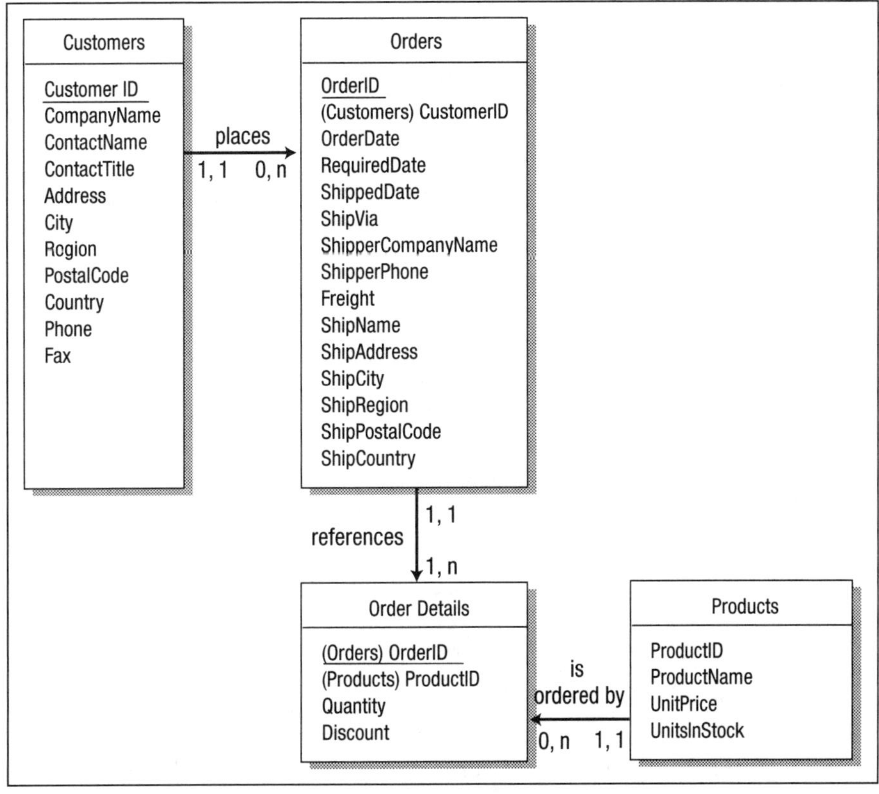

Figure 3.23 ER model for Northwind customers and orders—second normal form.

Project 3.2

Review the ER model created in the previous section and normalize it to third normal form. Use the following checklist as you perform this work:

1. Review the nonkey attributes in each of the entities looking for repeating groups. If none are there, the model is in first normal form.
2. Review the model looking for nonkey attributes that describe only a portion of the primary key. Remove those attributes into a new entity and define the relationship. When complete, the model will be in second normal form, as shown in Figure 3.23.
3. Review the model looking for nonkey attributes that describe other nonkey attributes rather than the primary or alternate key. Remove those attributes into a new entity and define the relationship. When complete, the model will be in third normal form, as shown in Figure 3.24.

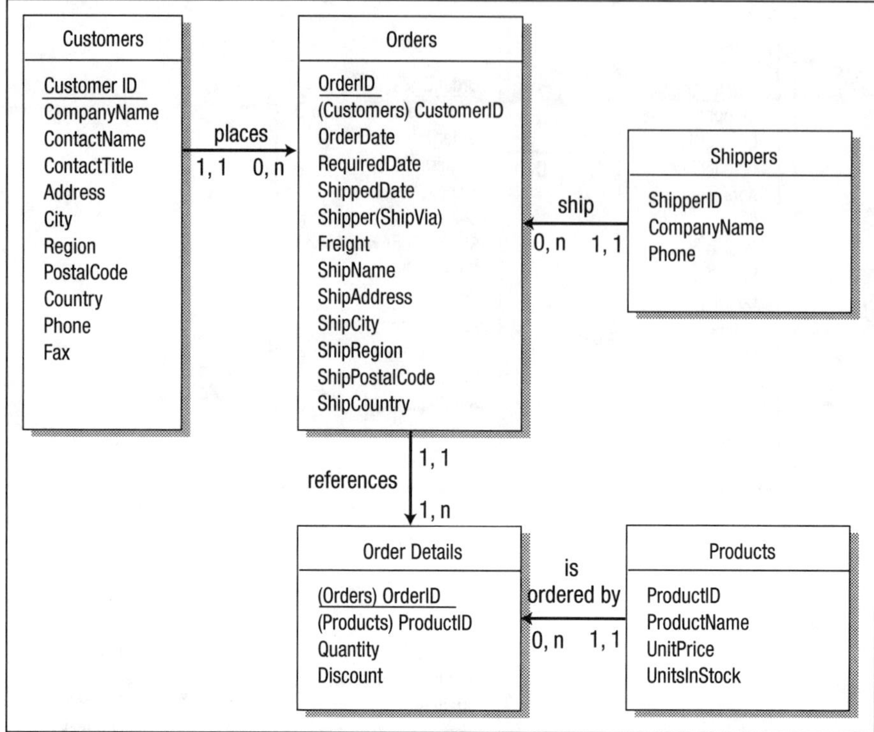

Figure 3.24 ER model for Northwind customers and orders—third normal form.

Table 3.2 Insert/update rules for Northwind customers and orders.

Rules	Parent	Child
Insert-Dependent	Customers	Orders
Insert-Dependent	Shippers	Orders
Insert-Dependent	Products	Order Details
Insert-Default	Shippers	Orders
Delete-Restrict	Customer	Orders
Delete-Restrict	Shippers	Orders
Delete-Restrict	Products	Order Details

Complete the logical database design for Northwind by defining the business rules that will ensure entity and referential integrity.

1. Review the model and the business requirements, considering both insert rules that define when and how a parent will allow a child instance to be added and delete rules that define the affect on the child record when a parent record is deleted.
2. Table 3.2 shows the results of analysis of the *Northwind* model.

3. The next step is to define data domains. Whereas data domains should be defined for each and every attribute, for this project the following attributes have been selected as representative examples: *CustomerID*, *CompanyName*, *ContactName*, *Address*, *OrderDate*, *RequiredDate*, *ShippedDate*, *Quantity*, and *ShipAddress*.
4. For each attribute, define the following characteristics: meaning, data type, length, allowable values, uniqueness, null support, and default value. Use the business requirements specified at the beginning of this project, as well as your own experience as a data analyst and DBA to complete this.

Table 3.3 shows a possible set of results for this domain analysis.

Table 3.3 Possible set of results for domain analysis.

Attribute	Data Type	Length	Allowable	Unique Values	NULL	Default	Meaning Value
CustomerID	Integer	4	Y	N		Sequential number to each unique customer	
Company Name	Character	40	N	N		Business name	
Contact Name	Character	40	N	N		Individual who places order	
Address	Character	40		N	N	Shipping address	
OrderDate	Date	—	N	N		Today	Date when order is placed; can be replaced with other date value
Required Date	Date	—	>=Today	N	Y	Today	Date when customer desires order to be shipped
ShippedDate	Date	—	>=Today	N	Y	Date on which product was actually shipped	
Quantity	Integer	2	>0	N	N	Quantity ordered	
ShipAddress	Character	30		N	N	Address	Address to which order should be shipped

CHAPTER FOUR

DERIVING THE PHYSICAL DESIGN

After Reading This Chapter And Completing The Exercises, You Will Be Able To:

- Complete the database life cycle by understanding the process of translating a logical database design into a physical database
- Correlate the objects in a logical model to the objects in a physical model
- Utilize the diagram editor in SQL Server Enterprise Manager to document the physical design and generate the Transact-SQL required to create tables, primary keys, indexes, and foreign keys
- Understand some of the design considerations involved in implementing an Online Transaction Processing versus a Decision Support System database
- Understand the factors that should be considered when designing and choosing indexes

In Chapter 3, we described several methods for creating a logical database design that graphically documented business and functional requirements. In Chapter 4 we will translate this logical design into the physical database design.

Physical Design In The Database Life Cycle

In Chapter 3 you learned about the database life cycle. This life cycle is a process of defining business requirements, developing a logical database design, and then implementing the logical design into a physical database design. This database design can support the original business requirements, as well as future requirements. Figure 4.1 illustrates the steps included in the full database life cycle.

The focus in Chapter 3 was on the first two steps: the specification of business requirements and the logical database design. These steps involved tools such as used entity-relationship models, normalization techniques, and the definition of business rules.

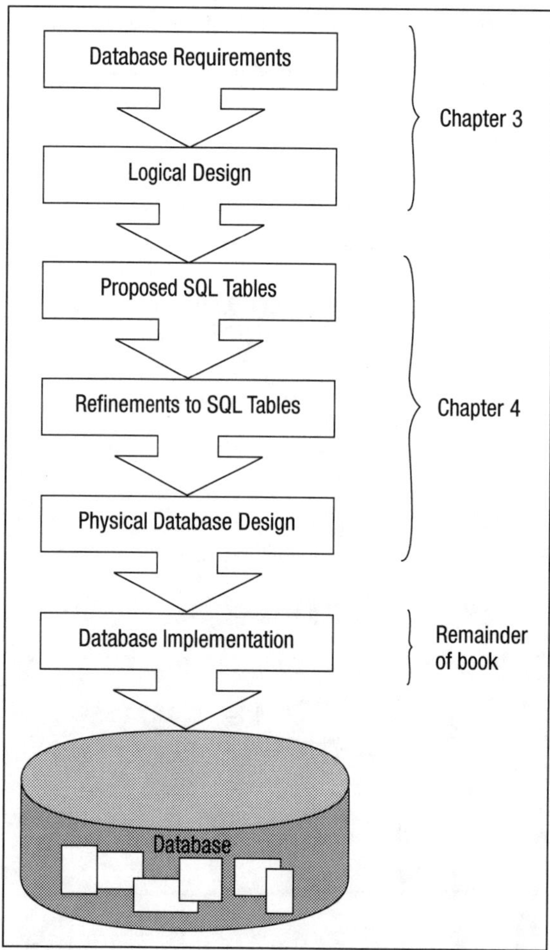

Figure 4.1 Database life cycle.

In Chapter 4, we will complete the database life cycle using the following steps:

1. Lay out on paper the preliminary set of SQL tables using the previously created logical design. You might also use software tools.
2. Transform the business rules defined in the logical design into the physical database design. The DBA will then create database components, such as constraints, triggers, indexes, and keys. This will ensure that all previously defined rules for integrity, security, and processing have been met.
3. Refine the set of tables produced. Factors such as data update rates and read frequencies, data volume, growth patterns, and archiving requirements are considered. At this point, it is not unusual to add redundant data at the expense of disk storage in order to improve overall query speed.

After completing these steps, the physical database design is ready for implementation. The DBA will create the database and populate it with tables, triggers, stored procedures, and other objects.

As you convert the logical database design into a physical design, you will start to notice a correlation between the following logical and physical design objects:

- Entities are converted to tables.
- Relationships are converted to primary and foreign keys and indexes.
- Relationship attributes control the uniqueness of indexes and nullability of attributes.
- Domains will be defined by constraints.
- Business rules will be enforced by foreign keys and triggers.

Although we have discussed this translation process as a series of steps, the experienced DBA will often begin making design decisions based on expected query types, query volumes, update methods, and expected growth. This will be done even as the physical database design is being created. In this chapter we will consider all of these factors that affect performance as we translate our logical model into a physical design.

For some database designers, performance of the completed physical design may not be considered during the design process. An expectation may be present that the data volumes will not be large or that the machine supporting the database will have adequate memory and CPU power available. Unfortunately, as the database grows and users' expectations evolve, it will be extremely difficult to improve retroactively the performance of the database by making design changes. Considerable rework and the subsequent chain of testing and data conversion might be required.

You should begin by considering performance, as well as data integrity and business functionality requirements during the physical design process. This will help you produce a database design that will be able to support the application and user population through many cycles of enhancements and modifications.

Database Design Considerations

Before delving into the details of translating a logical database design into a physical design, it will be helpful to consider the overall goals of the database being designed. For example, is this database oriented toward *online transaction processing (OLTP)*, meaning that the volume of inserts, updates, and deletes will be heavy? Often very few records are queried with each SQL statement, but records are frequently changed.

Concurrency, which is the ability to support multiple updates simultaneously, is an important consideration. In an order entry system, it is important that two order-takers do not allocate the same item out of inventory. We expect that the database will ensure that first one, and then the other order-taker will view and then update inventory figures.

In addition, *atomicity* is crucial for data accuracy. Atomicity is the ability to isolate transactions so that a unit of work comprised of one or more SQL statements is either entirely committed or rolled back. In an order entry system, our business requirements state that we must reduce the customer's credit limit at the time the order is placed. We want to ensure that we decrement the credit limit in the customer record in the same transaction where we place orders. We do this by inserting records into the order header and order detail tables. If any one of these statements fail, we want all the data to be rolled back. If all the statements are successful, they will be committed. Only then will the results be visible to the other order entry clerks.

Decisions made now about indexes and keys will play a role as they will promote faster data access and ensure additional data integrity. We will examine these considerations in detail in Chapter 11.

A database designed for OLTP will be highly normalized with the data spread among smaller and narrower table structures. The indexes in these databases will be designed specifically for the queries being performed. Data that is not referenced frequently or is no longer current is often removed into separate tables or databases. This historical data can then be referenced and will not slow down users who are executing update queries.

Physical table indexes must be carefully scrutinized. If an index is not used to support a query, it should be removed. Each update to a base table will also require updates to the associated indexes. Indexes should be kept as narrow as possible. A common technique is to use an alternate index to supplement an existing index. At first glance, this may seem harmful because an additional index has been added, but it is much more efficient to query information by one field than by three.

Databases designed for decision support are optimized for data that changes infrequently or via batch update methods. A typical scenario is to build a *decision support system* (*DSS*) database where data is stored in one or more OLTP databases. This data is copied to the DSS database on a scheduled basis, often during off-hours or periods of light activity.

Although you can't ignore the indexes required to support batch updating, the primary purpose of the database will be to support *ad hoc* queries, standard queries, and reports. It is common to see many indexes on each table with important columns participating in multiple indexes.

The tables required to support reporting functions are often heavily denormalized so that queries or reports can be run against a smaller number of larger tables. Data is often pre-summarized so that commonly run queries do not repeatedly perform the same calculations.

A typical DSS database to support sales analysis will be updated with nightly batch jobs. These jobs might copy customer and order information from the OLTP databases supporting order processing. Although the OLTP database may have only active orders in the order table, the DSS database will have all orders, regardless of status. The DSS database might also contain supporting information from tables, such as product, sales territory, and others, so that excessive table joins are avoided.

Indexes in the OLTP database on an order table will be few in number to reflect the limited number of ways in which order information can be accessed. The DSS database will have many indexes on the order table to reflect the wide variety of possible queries that might be executed against it.

Database Diagrams

When a physical database design is first laid out, you can use tools such as paper and pencil and graphical software such as database modeling tools. Specialized software often has the capability of creating the Transact-SQL statements necessary to create or modify database structures. Advanced tools can also *reverse-engineer* data-base structures by importing definitions about database objects directly from SQL Server into the tool and then producing default graphical representations that can be further refined.

It is also possible to use a tool provided by Microsoft as part of SQL Server Enterprise Manager to create database diagrams. These database diagrams can be used for two different functions:

- To depict in a graphical format the relationships between tables, also depicting tables and their keys.
- To create or alter the physical structure of a database by creating, dropping, or modifying tables.

Figure 4.2 shows SQL Server Enterprise with the *Northwind* database diagrams selected in the left-hand pane. Currently only a single diagram named *Relationships* has been defined and is listed in the right-hand pane.

After double-clicking on the diagram named *Relationships*, a graphical representation of all of the tables in the *Northwind* database is displayed, as shown in Figure 4.3. Notice the lines between the tables that indicate relationships; many of these lines are further annotated with a key symbol to indicate a foreign key relationship. Primary keys in each table are noted with a key symbol as well.

As we translate our logical model to a physical database design, the Enterprise Manager diagram tool will be our preferred method for initially defining our table structures and then refining them. All of these tasks can be carried out by utilizing specific Transaction-SQL statements that you can create and then execute utilizing Query Analyzer.

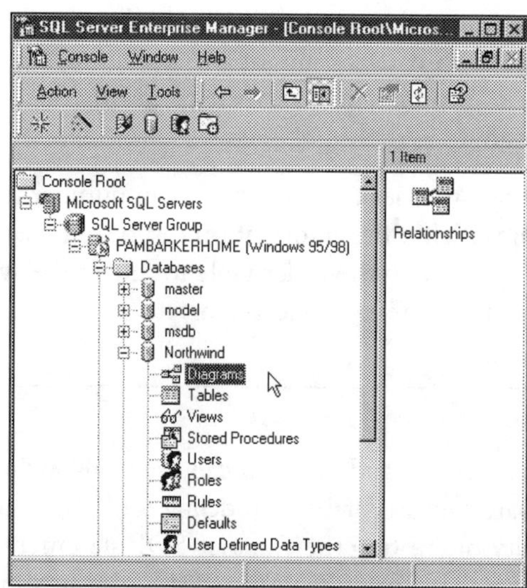

Figure 4.2 Enterprise Manager database diagrams.

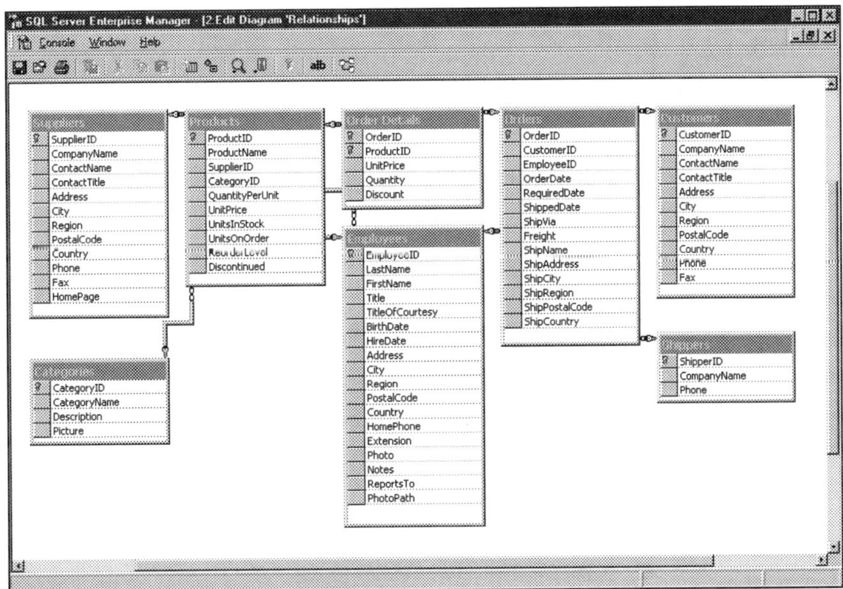

Figure 4.3 Database diagram *Relationships* for the *Northwind* database.

Database diagrams provide an easy way to perform a number of useful tasks. Here are a few examples:

- Create Transact-SQL code to create, alter, or drop database objects without having to know or write the Transact-SQL code to do so.
- Create Transact-SQL code that can be saved and then executed immediately or later.
- The DBA can visually review the proposed table structures in the diagram and others can print them for review.
- Create special-purpose diagrams that focus on specific departments or business functions as subsets of a larger diagram.

Although we will cover many of the useful elements of the diagraming tool in this chapter, don't forget to look at SQL Server *Books Online* for details that may not be described here.

Preliminary Physical Design

The first step in translating a logical database design into a physical design is to create a preliminary proposal for a set of tables that will be appropriate to the logical design. Keep in mind the following ideas as you carry out this process:

- The translation process usually maintains a one-for-one correspondence between each entity in the ER model and a table. Usually, a one-for-one correspondence exists between attributes and columns.
- The database design should be consistent; that is, every integrity and business rule defined in the logical model should be accounted for in the physical design.

Following are the basic steps to include when creating this preliminary physical design:

1. For each entity in the ER model, identify a corresponding table.
2. For each attribute, identify a corresponding column. Consider column name, data type and length, nullability, and default values.
3. For each table and column, consider data integrity by defining primary keys, indexes including alternates, foreign key relationships, domain definitions, and column constraints.

Table Definitions

As you lay out your preliminary physical design, you should plan to create a table for each entity defined in your ER model. Do not combine entities with similar data or keys and do not separate entities. Considerations such as denormalization will be considered after the preliminary design is completed. After the design is complete, it will become easier to see how changes in table structures will improve or degrade queries and updates.

Naming conventions that can be followed for the life of the project should be initiated at this point. If databases and tables have been created for other projects, use those established naming conventions whenever possible. Typically, a glossary of acceptable abbreviations is created and is used consistently for all projects. It may be necessary to consider the use of upper, lower, or mixed case, depending on the specifics of your SQL Server installation (some installed character sets are case specific).

It is generally best to select table names that are intuitive to the development staff, as well as any potential end-users that might have direct access to the data-base. Though table names in SQL Server 7 can be up to 128 characters in length, choose names that are meaningful but practical for those who will need to reference them.

Table names can have underscores or dashes to separate name components, for example, *Order_Header* or *Customer-History*. Spaces can also be used, as in the name *Order Details*, although this is not normally done because square braces need to be used as delimiters when specifying this name in a Transact-SQL statement, for example, *[Order Details]*.

If supporting end-user queries is important and your database object names are not friendly or consistent, a very effective option is to create *views* that have the appropriate names, including column names. See Chapter 10 for details on this topic.

Column Definitions

Refer to your ER model with the documented attributes. Translate each attribute into a column. Use consistent and appropriate names as previously defined in your name glossary. For example, use *nbr* or *no* for number or *cust* for customer if you prefer an abbreviation. Underscores are often used to separate portions of the name. For example, customer name and customer number become: *cust_name* and *cust_nbr*.

Typically, names are composed of a general class such as *address* or *qty* and are then modified with prefixes or suffixes that provide an additional description. Examples include *cust_address, order_qty, shipped_qty, returned_qty*.

When translating attributes into columns, avoid the temptation to combine data elements into a single column. For example, a project number might be composed of a department code and a sequence number, and it may seem appropriate to simply create column called *project_nbr* of the appropriate length. By specifying two separate columns of the appropriate data types, it will be relatively easy to validate that a department code is valid by using a foreign key. SQL Server can also verify that the sequence number is entered as only numeric data. This same validation becomes difficult when these columns are combined.

You can place the columns in any order. Typically, the order of columns in a table will be identical to those in the ER model: Primary key columns lead the order, and subsequent columns generally are grouped according to business function or relative importance.

Column Attributes

For each column, you must consider attributes, such as data type, length, nullability, and default values. Some columns might be suited to being classified as *identity* columns; SQL Server will determine the next appropriate data value when each new row is inserted. This section will introduce the physical properties of columns and Chapter 5 will cover this subject in greater detail.

In making decisions about the physical implementation of these column attributes, the DBA will refer to the logical database design performed earlier. The domain analysis is especially important. The DBA will also look at other tables and columns created in the database in order to ensure consistency and will make appropriate adjustments.

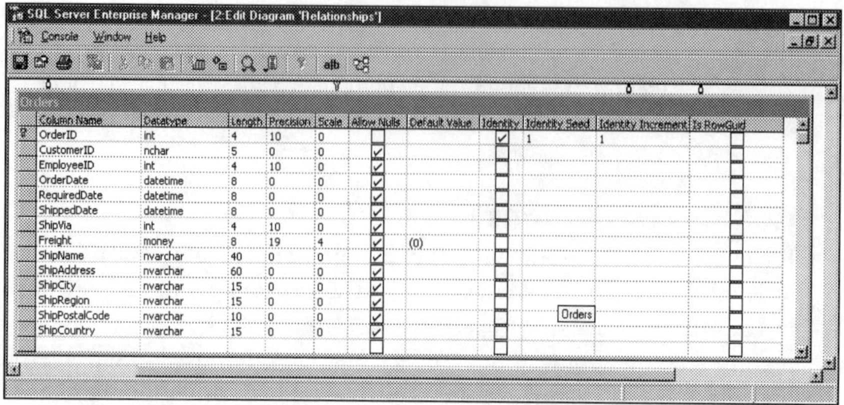

Figure 4.4 Column properties for the *Orders* table.

Figure 4.4 shows the column properties that are defined in SQL Server for the *Orders* table in the *Northwind* database. This window has been displayed by right-clicking on the *Orders* table and then selecting Column Properties from the pop-up menu. To revert to the original display, right-click on the table and then select Column Names from the pop-up menu.

A wide range of character, numeric, and date data types, and special data types, such as binary and money, are available. An important component of the initial validation of data entered into a table is the appropriateness of the data instance for the defined data type. For example, although the column *dept_number* can certainly be defined as a character data type, defining the column as a integer will ensure that a data entry clerk does not key in a "O" instead of a "0" if the values for this column should always be numeric.

You will also need to determine the length for each column. The domain analysis performed earlier will help to determine the appropriate choice. For example, the range of expected values will enable the DBA to decide between a one-, two-, or four-byte integer. For floating point numbers, specify the additional property of precision. For decimal numbers, the properties of precision and scale will be completed.

Define columns holding character data as fixed length or variable length. Generally, it is better to define columns as fixed length, unless it is known that data values will vary widely in length. This is the normal procedure, because there is extra overhead in storing the length definition with each value.

Each column will also need to be defined as either nullable or not nullable. Generally, you should define them as not nullable; only define them as nullable where appropriate to the business function being supported. Defining a column as nullable should be the exception rather than the rule.

Remember that a **NULL** is a special case, meaning that the data is *unknown* or *unavailable* or *to be filled in later*. A **NULL** does not have the same meaning as a blank or a zero value. Advantages of **NULL** include their special handling in aggregate functions as shown in Chapter 9. Disadvantages include the special coding that may be required in Transact-SQL statements as described in Chapter 7.

You can specify default values within the column properties window as well. This is shown in Figure 4.4 for the *Freight* column that has a default value of 0. When a new record is inserted into the *Orders* table and a specific value is not provided by the user for *Freight*, a zero value will be provided by SQL Server.

For columns where a unique value is desired and no business meaning is attached to a specific value, the *identity* property can be selected for any column that is of the integer type. In Figure 4.4, the column *OrderID* has been defined as a four-byte integer identity column. With each new row inserted into this table, SQL Server will reference values stored in its system tables to determine the next available value. This guarantees uniqueness and simplifies application and database coding. A starting value, as well as an incrementing value can be specified. Chapter 5 will provide additional details and examples of how this might be implemented.

Keep in mind that *identity* columns are never appropriate for such data elements as Social Security numbers or document numbers that must trace back to pre-printed forms. The last column, *rowguid*, will be evaluated and checked only if replication processing is a consideration for this table.

PHYSICAL DESIGN FOR NORTHWIND (PART 1)

In Chapter 3, we created a logical design for Northwind, a distributor of gourmet and imported food products. Our initial business requirements focused on the portion of the business that purchases products from suppliers. The ER model produced as a result of this analysis is shown in Figure 4.5.

We have four tables in this logical model. We will expect to have four tables in our preliminary physical design with each data attribute that is identified in the ER model mapped to the physical design. You will create your physical design using the SQL Server Enterprise Manager's diagramming component. First, create an empty *Northwind* database by right-clicking on databases and selecting New Database from the resulting pop-up menu. Then type the database name into the Database Properties pop-up window. For now the default database size, location, and so forth will be sufficient.

After expanding the plus sign next to the new database name, right-click on the Diagrams item and select New Database Diagrams. This opens up a blank window where you can create a new database diagram. From the toolbar at the top of the diagramming window, select the New Tables icon and provide a table

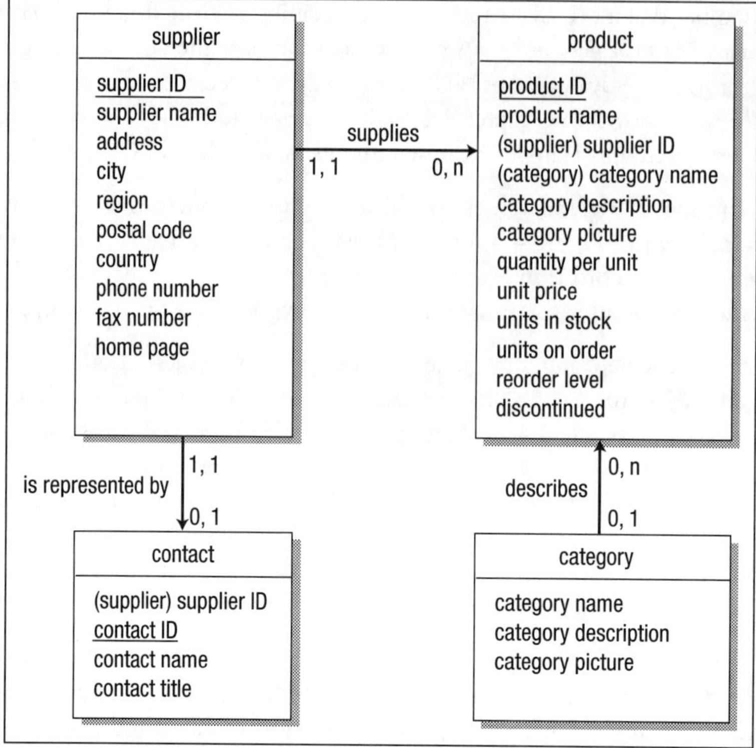

Figure 4.5 ER model for Northwind.

name. A table with no column definitions will then display in the diagram. Right-click on the table and select Column Properties from the pop-up properties window. Fill in the column name, data type, length, and attributes as specified in your domain analysis. Repeat this process for each of the four tables. When you are finished, your preliminary table design will look like the one shown in Figure 4.6.

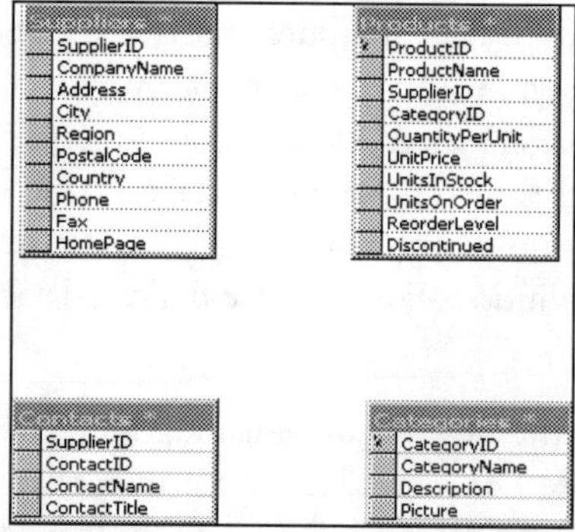

Figure 4.6 Tables defined for *Northwind.*

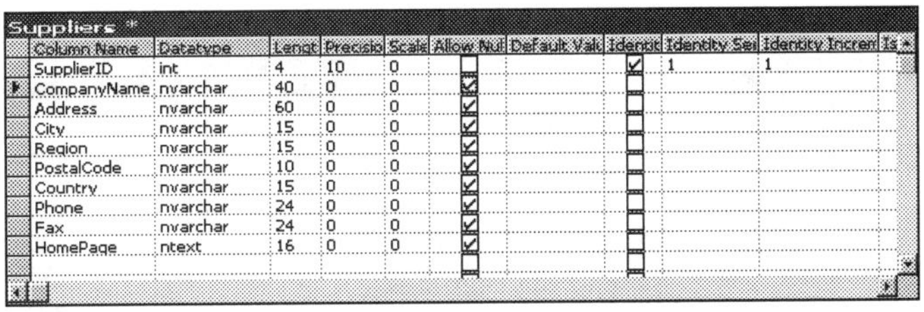

Suppliers *

Column Name	Datatype	Lengt	Precisio	Scale	Allow Nul	Default Valu	Identit	Identity Sec	Identity Incren	Is
SupplierID	int	4	10	0			✓	1	1	
CompanyName	nvarchar	40	0	0	✓					
Address	nvarchar	60	0	0	✓					
City	nvarchar	15	0	0	✓					
Region	nvarchar	15	0	0	✓					
PostalCode	nvarchar	10	0	0	✓					
Country	nvarchar	15	0	0	✓					
Phone	nvarchar	24	0	0	✓					
Fax	nvarchar	24	0	0	✓					
HomePage	ntext	16	0	0	✓					

Figure 4.7 *Suppliers* table.

Details of the column definitions for the *Suppliers* table is shown in Figure 4.7. Notice that the *SupplierID* column has been defined as an identity column, because no business function is associated with specific values and we have chosen to let the database determine the next available value. All columns are defined to be not nullable and none have defaults. It will be necessary during data entry to specify a value for each column.

Logical Data Integrity

We have now completed the basics of our physical database design and have already addressed some elements of integrity. We examined and then specified such column attributes as nullability and default values, which are elements that contribute to domain integrity.

In Chapter 3 we learned about several other types of integrity that are important. This integrity ensures a complete and accurate implementation of our business rules into our logical database design. A brief description of each follows:

- **Entity integrity** Ensures that any given row in a table will be uniquely identified.
- **Domain integrity** Verifies that data entered in a column will be accurate and valid, for example, will be of the correct data type, and will come from the list of valid values.
- **Referential integrity** Enforces the predefined relationships between tables as data is entered and deleted and ensures that key values are consistent across all tables containing those key values. For example, when data is entered, references to nonexistent data are not allowed; when data is deleted, all references to that key are also deleted.
- **User-defined integrity** Enforces all other business rules, for example, a customer cannot place an order for a product when the amount they owe for current orders is overdue.

Table 4.1 lists the possible implementation methods for each of these types of integrity.

Table 4.1 Integrity implementation methods.

Type Of Integrity	Implementation Method
Entity	**PRIMARY KEY** constraint
	UNIQUE constraint
	IDENTITY property
Domain	**DEFAULT** definition
	FOREIGN KEY constraint
	CHECK constraint
	NOT NULL attribute
Referential	**FOREIGN KEY** constraint
	CHECK constraint
User-Defined	Stored procedures
	Triggers

In the following sections, we will review the various methods that can be used to implement these integrities in the physical database design.

Primary Keys And Unique Constraints

Each table in the physical design should have a *primary key* that is an attribute or set of attributes that uniquely identifies an instance within that table. The primary key must exist for each and every instance within that table; therefore, no column in the key can be nullable. The primary key will enforce entity integrity. Examples of primary keys include *EmployeeID* for an *Employee* table or the combination of *CustomerNbr*, *ContactName* for a *CustomerContact* table.

When a primary key constraint is defined for a table, SQL Server will automatically create a unique index containing the same key columns. This index also allows for fast retrieval of data when the primary key columns are specified in the **WHERE** clause of a SQL **SELECT**, **UPDATE**, or **DELETE** statement.

Although a table can only have one primary key, it can have multiple unique constraints. For example, the table *Employee* has the primary key *EmployeeID*, along with the associated unique constraint on *EmployeeID*. The alternate key, *SocialSecurityNbr*, can be defined to be an index with a unique constraint.

Indexes defined by the primary key or as a unique constraint may be clustered or nonclustered. A *clustered* index is one in which the data is physically reorganized, so a table may have only one clustered index. We will discuss indexes in great detail in Chapter 6. Unless specified, the primary key index will be clustered and the unique constraint index will be nonclustered. Analysis of potential queries may indicate that better performance can be obtained by making one of the unique constraint indexes the clustered index.

However, one consideration to keep in mind when defining indexes (especially the clustered index), is the importance of keeping the index short and as compact as possible. A short index allows more data values to fit on an index page, thus reducing disk I/O.

4

When the primary key and index is broad or composed of multiple columns, an excellent alternative is a special case of a manufactured key, called a *surrogate key*. You can define the surrogate key as the primary key, you can use it to define foreign key relationships to other tables where only a single column will be copied to the foreign key tables, and you can use it to join other tables. You can still define the original, multicolumn key with a unique constraint and it can be available for specifying subsets of data to be retrieved. Generally, the surrogate key will be defined as either an *identity* column or an integer data type with values controlled by the front-end application.

Primary keys are specified in the Enterprise Manager diagramming tool by highlighting the desired column or columns in a table, right-clicking them, and then selecting Set Primary Key from the properties window. A key icon will appear next to the column name. This is shown in Figure 4.8.

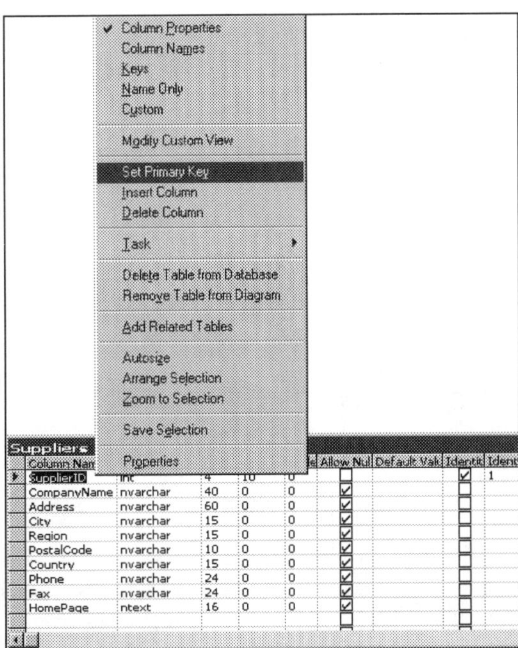

Figure 4.8 Setting the primary key.

Foreign Keys

A powerful function of relational database design and implementation is the ability to define foreign relationships that allow tables to be joined. By defining a foreign key relationship, you can also define and maintain referential and domain integrity.

The method of enforcing referential integrity through foreign key constraints is often called *declarative referential integrity (DRI)*, because the referential integrity rules are *declared* at the time a table is created. For example, in the *Northwind* database the line drawn between the two tables (shown in the diagram in Figure 4.9), a foreign key relationship between the *Products* and *Order Details* tables. Note the key shown on the end of the line closest to the *Products* table. The column *ProductID* is a primary key in that table and is a foreign key in the *Order Details* table.

Although the names of the columns participating in a foreign key relationship may be different, it is generally a good practice to match the names in both tables. The data types of the related columns must be identical, except for nullability and variable-length attributes. For example, the primary key *CustomerIDI,* which is not nullable, can be referenced by the foreign key *CustomerNumber*, which is nullable. Further, a column defined as *char(30)* can reference a column defined as *varchar(30)*.

Although a foreign key constraint is generally linked to a primary key in another table, you can define the foreign key to reference the columns of any unique constraint or alternate index. This may be useful in the case of an *employee* table, where the primary key is *employee_nbr*, but an alternate unique index has been specified on *social_security_nbr*. The *social_security_nbr* column can be used in a foreign key relationship between the *employee* table and the *401k* table.

In Chapter 3, we described the special case of a *unary* or *recursive relationship*, where a relationship existed between two instances of the same entity. A common

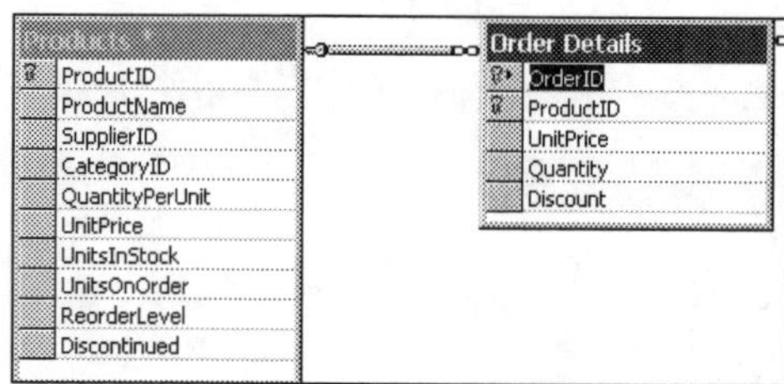

Figure 4.9 A foreign key relationship.

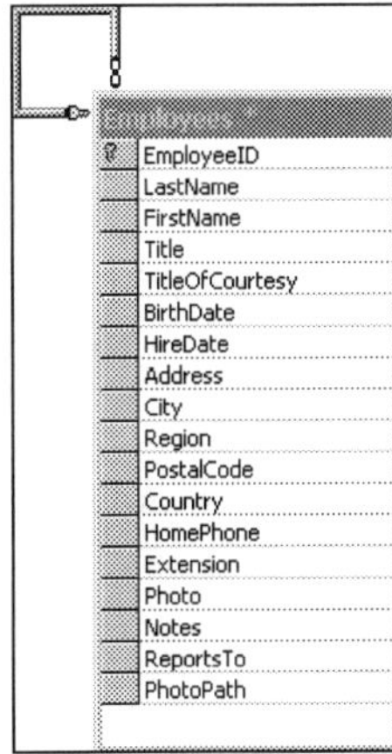

Figure 4.10 Foreign keys in a recursive relationship.

example is a human resources system where another employee manages an employee. You can also express this type of recursive relationship as a foreign key relationship as shown in Figure 4.10.

In this example, another employee supervises an employee and a relationship is defined between the primary key *EmployeeID* and the foreign key *ReportsTo*. It is very important to note that unlike primary keys, when foreign keys are defined, an index on the foreign key is not built automatically. You will often want to add an index, generally nonunique, on the foreign key to speed up join queries.

For good join performance, it is important that multicolumn indexes that are built to support foreign keys are defined in the same order as the corresponding primary index. A potential negative impact exists in terms of modifying performance when foreign keys are defined. Every foreign key relationship defined will add additional steps to the processing that SQL Server must carry out for inserts, updates, and deletes. This could ultimately consume significant resources as the required I/O to validate data against large table increases.

For example, a foreign key relationship exists between the *Products* and *Order Detail* tables on the *ProductID* column. For every insert into the table *Order Detail* or update of *ProductID*, a corresponding check of the *Products* table is necessary in order to verify that a valid product number has been specified. If an invalid product number has been specified, the insert or update terminates with an exception.

Foreign keys are defined in the database diagram editor of Enterprise Manager by highlighting the column or columns participating as the primary key and then dragging the cursor over to the table that contains the foreign key.

Check Constraint

A self-contained method of enforcing domain integrity is performed through the use of *check constraints*. This ensures that data values entered will be in an expected range. Check constraints allow a record to be updated or inserted if the constraint does not evaluate to **FALSE**. Keep in mind that this means that if the constraint evaluates to **TRUE** or **UNKNOWN**, the update will be allowed. You can specify check constraints on the table or column.

Examples of check constraints that you might specify on the column include the following:

```
EmployeeID >= 0 and EmployeeID <= 9999
```

```
RequiredDate >= OrderDate
```

```
OrderDate <= getdate()
```

Note that it is possible to use an **AND**'ed expression in the constraint. In addition, a constraint on one column can reference a value in a second column. In the third example, the check constraint is referencing a system function.

A few extra steps are added to the query execution plan when you define a check constraint, but this is typically a much less expensive operation than the foreign key constraint. A check constraint requires some additional logical processing, as opposed to the additional I/O required to probe a second table with a foreign key constraint.

You can define a check constraint on a table so that any update operation against any column as well as all insert and deletes will be validated against the constraint. For example, to verify that an employee does not update his or her own employee record, you can define the following constraint:

```
suser_id(null) <> EmployeeID
```

A possible performance penalty in terms of CPU exists for this type of constraint, as it will be evaluated in every possible insert or update condition. However, no additional overhead in terms of disk I/O will be added.

User-Defined Integrity

In Chapter 3, we introduced the concept of insert/update rules that define the conditions under which a primary or foreign key may be inserted, updated, or deleted. The foreign key constraints previously described prevent updates that reference data that is not in the primary key table. They also prevent deletions from the primary key table when referencing records that are in the foreign key table. These actions may not be enough protection in all cases. For example, under some conditions a delete or update operation should be allowed to continue. As these types of scenarios cannot be coded with the constraints previously desc-ribed, the DBA can use database triggers to define the specific actions required.

Five types of actions exist for either updates or deletes that you can code using triggers:

4

- **No effect or restrict** The delete of a parent is prevented when one or more child records exist. The update of the joining column in a parent is prevented when one or more child records exist.
- **Cascade** All matching rows in the child will be deleted. When a joining column in a parent is updated, cascade the change to all of the child records.
- **Default** The delete of the parent row is permitted and all foreign key values in the child table are set to a default value. The update of the joining column in the parent row is permitted and all foreign key values in the child table are set to a default value.
- **Nullify** The delete of the parent row is permitted and all foreign key values in the child table are set to **NULL**. The update of the joining column in the parent row is permitted and all foreign key values in the child table are set to **NULL**.
- **Customized** Permit deletion of update of parent record only in special cases as defined by the trigger code.

When using custom trigger code to handle referential integrity between parent and child tables, it is better to not define foreign key constraints. You might define them simply for documentation purposes with the *no check* option so that the constraint will not be enforced. As a constraint is checked prior to a trigger, it is possible to have a situation where a constraint will cause an insert or update to fail and the trigger that handles data cleanup will not be executed. In these cases you should remove the constraint or modify it to include the *no check* option. Also, ensure that the trigger is coded to properly handle all desired referential integrity.

Physical Design For Northwind (Part 2)

So far, four tables have been created using the SQL Server Enterprise Manager diagram tool to support the product ordering function of *Northwind*; these tables are shown in Figure 4.11.

The next step is to define primary keys for each table:

- *SupplierID* for the *Suppliers* table
- *ProductID* for the *Products* table

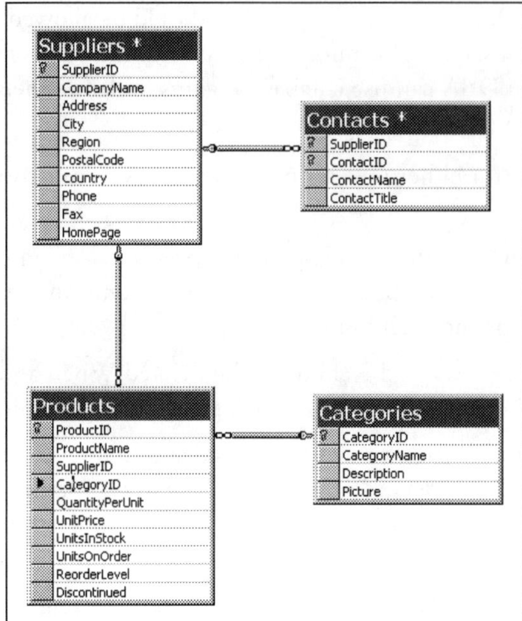

Figure 4.11 Tables defined for *Northwind*.

- *SupplierID*, *ContactID* for the *Contacts* table
- *CategoryID* for the *Categories* table

Highlight the column or columns that should be primary keys and right-click to open the properties window and select Set Primary Key. A key icon next to the column name will mark the primary key. Remember that a unique, clustered index will also be created on the same column or columns as the primary key.

Define foreign key constraints between the following parent and child tables:

- *CategoryID* in the *Categories* table to *Products*
- *SupplierID* in the *Suppliers* table to *Contacts*
- *SupplierID* in the *Suppliers* table to *Products*

Foreign keys are defined in the diagram editor by highlighting the column or columns participating in the primary key and then dragging the cursor over to the child table that contains the foreign key.

No indexes will be created on the foreign keys just defined. Therefore, an important step to remember is to create those nonunique, nonclustered indexes with the same column in the same order as the keys just created. Chapter 6 will describe the syntax for this index creation.

By completing these primary and foreign key definitions, you define the relationships between suppliers and the products they supply. You can use categories to describe products. And each supplier has one or more contacts. In addition, it will not be possible to perform the following actions because of the foreign key constraints that have been defined:

- Delete a category record if a product is assigned to it.
- Update a category ID if a product is assigned to it.
- Delete a supplier record if a product is supplied by that supplier or if a contact is known for that supplier
- Update a supplier ID if a product is supplied by that supplier or if a contact is know for that supplier.

According to the provided business requirements, the following check constraints should be defined at the column level:

- *QuantityPerUnit* in the *Products* table should be greater than 0.
- *Discontinued* in the *Products* table should be either Y or N.
- *Region* in the *Suppliers* table should be in the following list of valid values: N, S, E, or W.

Performance Expectations

Before a physical database design is ready for implementation, the DBA will attempt to tune the design by selecting from various implementation options based on processing and performance requirements.

Many possible types of systems exist, ranging from OLTP to DSS. Some systems contain multiple gigabytes of data and some support hundreds of users. Therefore a discussion of design for performance becomes somewhat generalized. In preparing for a performance analysis, the following are some expected characteristics that you should investigate:

- **Type of processing** Update versus insert versus delete
- **Type of selection criteria** Especially on frequently used queries or long-running queries that will require special analysis
- **Data volumes** Both total numbers of rows searched, as well as total tables size that reflects numbers of pages searched
- **Data returned** Number of records returned
- **Visibility of system** To end-users
- **Relationship** To day-to-day operations and support of external customers
- **Type of processing** Online versus batch
- **Type of queries** Standard and predefined versus *ad hoc*

- **Business processing** Number of business documents or processes supported on a daily, weekly, or monthly basis; for example, number of orders placed, or number of customer calls answered
- **Growth of business** Expected increase in number of business documents or processes supported
- **Expected execution times** Of key queried or batch processes
- **Throughput-peak transaction rate** Versus average over the day
- **Growth of systems load** Expected growth in transaction rates

If all of this information is not available, the process of gathering as much of this information as possible will enable the DBA to better understand how to complete the database design.

Indexes For Performance

When reviewing the physical database design and table indexes, you should consider the following:

- Smaller tables (less than 100 rows) used for data validations and lookup will not need an index, because the process of scanning the base rows versus performing the index lookup may be faster.
- By default, SQL Server will create a clustered index on the columns designated for the primary key. Generally, queries executed against the primary key return a single record. If queries returning groups of similar data, for example:

  ```
  customer name like 'Acme%'
  territory = 'A'
  ```

  are frequently executed, it might be useful to cluster that index instead.
- Indexes will speed up the selection of data, but will always slow down inserts, updates, deletes, bulk copies, and other processing.
- Adding additional indexes will also increase overall database size, which will increase the amount of time it takes to perform a database backup or restore, perform index maintenance using **UPDATE STATISTICS**, and so forth.
- Tables that are modified on a moderate to frequent basis with more than four indexes should be evaluated carefully to ensure that all indexes are needed.
- Keep in mind the concept of *index coverage*, which will enable the query optimizer to find all of the data it needs to perform a query in an index alone. Sometimes, the addition of a single column is all that is required to avoid the extra overhead of accessing the base table.

- Define the sequence of columns in multicolumn indexes so that as many queries as possible can use the index. Remember that an index containing *col1, col2, col3* will be used by queries with selection criteria *col1* or *col1, col2,* or *col1, col2, col3*. Selection criteria only specifying *col2* or *col3* or *col2, col3* in combination will not use this index.
- Try not add an index on a column that is frequently updated, because every update will need to be propagated out to the index and could impose a severe performance penalty.
- When enough disk space on different devices is available, plan on creating nonclustered indexes in different filegroups than the base table in order to take advantage of increased I/O throughput.
- Where tables are rapidly growing and being updated frequently, consider a very small index fillfactor (more on this in Chapter 6) in order to minimize the negative effects of an index.
- Conversely, where tables are static and not changing, consider a very high index fillfactor in order to maximize the number of records read with each disk I/O.
- Plan to monitor indexes for fragmentation and to run the **UPDATE STATISTICS** command when data distributions change in order to ensure that the correct indexes continue to be used by the query optimizer.
- Perhaps the most important note is to test and benchmark important queries against multiple indexing schemes in a database that has a set of data that closely approximates production volumes and data distributions. Remember that all queries will run quickly against a table with 1,000 records. Remember to benchmark, benchmark, benchmark.

DENORMALIZATION

In Chapter 3, we were careful to construct a logical data model that achieved third normal form by removing all repeating groups and ensuring that each table only contained attributes that defined the primary key.

We evaluate the preliminary physical design that is derived from the logical model by directly translating each logical entity to a physical table. During this process we may note areas where it makes to sense to combine data tables, include duplicate data elements, or store derived data elements.

When considering duplicating data to improve data lookup performance in frequently accessed queries, consider the volatility of the data being duplicated. If this duplicate data changes frequently, the cost of the update may outweigh the benefit to query speed. On the other hand, judicious use of *duplicate data* can be very beneficial. For example, consider an order entry system where data about vendor (including location) is stored in the vendor table. The product table has a foreign key for vendor, along with information about products that can be sold to customers.

If the location of the vendor is important to order processing, product lookups frequently reference the *vendor* table in addition to the *product* table. By duplicating location data into the product table, a table join can be avoided. The only expense is the duplicate update that is performed whenever the vendor location changes.

In a database designed to be in third normal form, *derived data* (data that is computed or aggregates from other data elements) is calculated from the base data each time it is needed. For example, imagine an order entry system with an order header table that has one or more order detail records for each header. In this system each record contains a quantity ordered for each product. It is possible to calculate the value of each order line by multiplying the stored unit price by the stored quantity ordered. We would then sum each line to produce a total value for the order. This is very repetitive, especially in a busy OLTP system.

It might be more advantageous to store this derived data in the order header and order detail tables. The extended price at the line level can be stored in the order detail. The sum of the extended prices for each detail record can be stored in the order header table.

Table Definitions

Making changes to table structures is not as easy as adding an index or adding duplicate data. This process potentially affects a number of queries and triggers that might need to be redesigned, or recoded and then retested. At times it will make sense to combine tables or to *partition* tables horizontally or vertically.

When reviewing the database design, it may be advantageous to join tables that are always referenced together or where the relationship is very close to being one-to-one. For example, in a project management database where employees are tracked against their assignments, the original logical and physical design might have specified separate tables for employee and projects, because it is expected that employees might be assigned to either zero, one, or many projects.

Further analysis of data and queries has now shown that the majority of employees are assigned to only one project. In this case, it makes sense to fold the project information into the employee table and expand the primary key on the table to include project identification to ensure uniqueness for the small number of employees with multiple projects.

Table partitioning, either horizontally or vertically, offers advantages in both DSS and OLTP databases. *Horizontal table partitioning* is used as a logical way to divide data between two or more tables of identical structures on the basis of a data value. Let's examine a typical example of the use of horizontal table partitioning in order to separate active from inactive data.

In a call center application, customer service representatives take customer calls, route, and then close the calls. Though a call history is periodically queried regarding previous issues, the majority of the work is focused on taking a new call, routing, and closing the call. In this situation, it would be advantageous to move calls to a *call history* table, thus removing them from the *active call* table. This keeps the active call tables smaller, and also allows the call center staff to quickly check for open calls in their assigned queues, update the calls with additional details, and route them on to the next support person.

A potential disadvantage of such a design is that extra work is involved in inserting the call information into the call history table and deleting the call from the active call table with each call closure. This design strategy will probably work best in situations where each call is accessed often and is updated while still open. The benefit is diminished in systems where calls are simply opened and then closed.

Horizontal table partitioning is also useful when separating data for reporting purposes in a DSS database. For example, detailed sales data for each region of a large company might be separated into individual region tables for specific analysis. This will provide a smaller table improving query performance. In addition, a smaller table will be easier to manage when database utilities need to be run. Aggregated or summary data reflecting all regions would still be maintained in the appropriate rollup tables.

Vertical table partitioning is a function of separating individual groups of columns into separate tables and duplicating the primary keys into tables with one-to-one relationships. This partitioning is useful when data in the same table is updated or managed by different departments.

In a database where employee information is maintained by the human resources and payroll departments, pockets of employee information exist that are specific to one department, but not the other. For example, the human resources department enters and updates such fields as start date, promoted date, department code, job code, and so forth. The payroll department updates data on a more frequent basis and focuses on such fields as salary-to-date, deduction codes, and other fields affecting each pay period.

All of these fields describe a single employee instance and can be held in a single employee table with an employee number as key. It may be helpful to provide a table specific to the payroll department so that frequent updates do not impact the human resources department. The human resources department updates its set of employee data less frequently, but runs frequent reports analyzing head-count, reporting on overdue performance evaluations, and so forth.

Security

It is important to determine how application and database security will be implemented while reviewing and completing the physical database design. The exclusive use of stored procedures to access the data will simplify security. Using stored procedures is the preferred method, as no other object access needs to be granted. Instead, privileges to execute stored procedures can be granted to specific user names, Windows NT groups, and SQL Server roles.

Please see *SQL Server 7 Books Online* for an explanation of the implementation of database and application security via Windows NT groups and SQL Server roles.

Although an OLTP database is generally designed for specific queries and updates, databases designed for DSS require table access. In this case, an analysis of access rights should be completed as part of the database requirements.

In reviewing the required database rights, the DBA needs to determine which user group should be able to access which data. In some cases, specific columns or records may be off-limits to particular database users. The use of physical table partitioning (as described earlier) or the use of views (discussed further in Chapter 10) that logically partition the data are helpful in achieving the desired data protection. After creating the appropriate physical tables or views, specific access privileges can be granted to the appropriate groups and roles.

Physical Design For Northwind (Part 3)

The physical database design for the Northwind company is almost completed, as shown in Figure 4.12. We defined primary and foreign keys, as well as check constraints. Before wrapping up the database design, we will review the table definitions to ensure that they are optimized for the expected database usage.

As this is an OLTP database supporting data entry clerks processing orders, avoiding unnecessary table joins is important. As specified in the logical data model, we have created a *Contacts* table that has a foreign key relationship to the *Suppliers* table. This structure supports a one-to-many relationship between *Suppliers* and *Contacts*. Additional analysis reveals that the companies that Northwind does business with are small and have one contact individual.

If we elect to fold the contact information into the *Suppliers* table, we can accommodate multiple contacts by expanding the primary key in the *Suppliers*

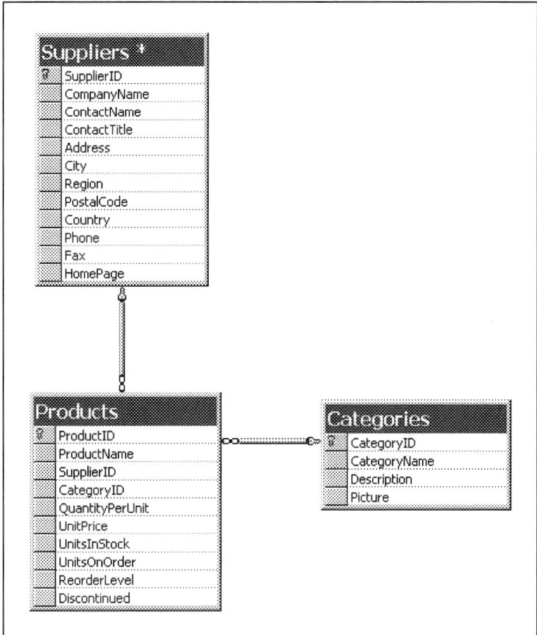

Figure 4.12 Complete physical database design for Northwind.

table to include either *ContactID* or *ContactName*. If a business case can be justified with the original analyst, the *Suppliers* table can be modified to include *ContactName* and *ContactTitle* as attributes. This change will only allow a single contact for each supplying company.

After reviewing the database requirements and deciding that a single contact is sufficient, the complete database design is shown in Figure 4.12.

Keep in mind that this design decision may be the easiest to implement at this stage, but will be difficult to reverse, should business changes reveal that multiple contacts are required.

Impact Of Database Design

Choices made as the physical database design is derived will impact the resulting database and the application it supports in a number of areas:

- **Database performance** Too many (or not enough) indexes will slow down query and update performance. Too many indexes or indexes that are too broad will increase disk I/O.
- **Data integrity** Use of **PRIMARY KEY**, **UNIQUE**, **CHECK**, and **FOREIGN KEY** constraints, along with triggers, will ensure that data is entered accurately and as required by the business functionality being supported.

- **Database Maintenance** Reducing the table size by creating surrogate keys instead of propagating wide keys, as well as partitioning the tables horizontally or vertically where appropriate, can reduce table size and make it easier to execute **DBCC** and **UPDATE STATISTICS** utilities.
- **Extensibility** Normalized table design will lay a foundation that can be readily modified as business functionality changes.
- **Scalability** Properly locating tables and indexes into separate file groups will enable placement on separate and larger physical drives as the database grows in both size and transaction rate.
- **Availability** Database backups, **DBCC** commands, and **UPDATE STATISTIC** commands may slow down or block user access. By dividing data into smaller chunks, the DBA will have more flexibility in executing these commands and will be able to improve system availability.
- **Security** Separating sensitive data from more generally available, public data through views and table partitioning will enable easier implementation of the desired database security.

Chapter Summary

We have discussed the following items in this chapter:

- The process of translating a logical database design into a physical database design begins by defining a preliminary set of SQL tables where a one-for-one correspondence exists between each entity and attribute and table and column.
- Using the business rules defined in the logical model as keys, relationships, domains, and business rules, the physical model is enhanced to include primary and foreign keys, unique constraints, check constraints, and triggers.
- Query and update performance are important factors that cannot be overlooked in the physical design process, because it might be very difficult to retrofit changes to improve performance after implementation into production.
- Databases oriented toward online transaction processing (OLTP) support a high volume of queries and updates.
- Concurrency is the ability to support multiple update simultaneously and is often an important design consideration for OLTP databases.
- OLTP databases also require highly atomic transactions. Atomic transactions can be isolated to a unit of work that can be rolled back or committed entirely.
- OLTP databases are usually highly normalized and will have few indexes on each table.

- Decision support (DSS) databases are optimized for queries that frequently read and return large data volumes.
- DSS databases are often denormalized and contain duplicate or derived data in order to minimize table joins. Usually these tables have many indexes to support a wide variety of queries.
- You can use the diagram editor in Enterprise Manager to graphically depict the physical database design. It can also generate the Transact-SQL statements needed to create tables, primary and foreign keys, indexes, and constraints.
- The domain analysis prepared during the logical database design helps determine the correct data types and lengths, nullability, defaults, and check constraints for each column.
- Consistency in choosing table and column names during the physical design process will make the jobs of the DBAs and developers easier.
- Each table should have a primary key that is composed of one or more columns that uniquely identify each record in the table. When a primary key is created, a clustered, unique index on the same column(s) is built automatically.
- A surrogate key can be used to replace a primary key that is composed of many columns. This eliminates the duplication of this broad key throughout the database.
- You can use foreign keys to define relationships between tables and to enforce referential integrity. Each relationship in the logical model is translated into a foreign key.
- An index on the child table is not built automatically when a foreign key is defined; generally, an index should be built to improve join performance.
- Check constraints are self-constrained validations at the column or table level that further enforce domain integrity.
- User-defined integrity will be implemented via triggers or stored procedures, which can also enforce the following referential integrity rules between parent and child tables: no affect or restrict, cascade, default, nullify, and customized.
- Performance expectations for the database being developed should be documented ahead of time with the database design, then benchmarked to determine if the performance requirements have been met.
- Physical databases will frequently be denormalized. They will not implemented as fully third normal designs. By adding duplicate or derived data, disk I/O can be reduced and database performance improved.

- Tables can be partitioned horizontally on the basis of a predefined data value in order to reduce the size of tables being actively updated or to separate data into departmental tables or views.
- Tables can also be partitioned vertically in order to support different business functions that might have very different requirements for updates and security.

Review Questions

1. Which of the following are characteristics of a database designed to support OLTP? (Choose all correct answers.)
   a. Each table will be heavily indexed.
   b. The ability to support concurrency is an important design objective.
   c. Tables will be highly normalized with data spread among smaller, narrower tables.
   d. Tables will be highly denormalized with duplicate and derived data added to speed up query processing.

2. Which of the following tasks can be performed using the diagram editor in the SQL Server Enterprise Manager? (Choose all correct answers.)
   a. Document the logical database design.
   b. Document the physical database design.
   c. Generate SQL code to create tables, primary keys, foreign keys, and indexes.
   d. Generate SQL code to create triggers to maintain user-defined referential integrity.

3. Which of the following steps are included when creating a preliminary physical design? (Choose all correct answers.)
   a. For each entity, define an equivalent table.
   b. For each relationship, create a primary key constraint.
   c. Review the domain analysis to determine data types, lengths, nullability, and so on.
   d. For each attribute, define an equivalent column.

4. Which of the following statements regarding the implementation of data integrity are true? (Choose all correct answers.)
   a. A primary key ensures referential integrity.
   b. A unique constraint ensures entity integrity.

c. A default or check constraint ensures domain integrity.

d. A foreign key ensures domain integrity.

5. Which of the following statements correctly describe foreign key constraints?

   a. The names and data types of the columns participating in a foreign key relationship must be identical.

   b. A foreign key in a child table is linked to a primary key in a parent table.

   c. When a foreign key relationship is defined between two tables, you cannot enter data values into the table holding the primary key that are not present in the table holding the foreign key.

   d. Because no impact on performance happens when implementing foreign keys, they should be used freely to define referential integrity.

6. Which of the following statements regarding primary keys and unique constraints is true?

   a. After creating a primary key, the DBA must remember to also create a unique, clustered index containing the same columns.

   b. Whereas a table can have only one unique index, it can have multiple unique constraints defined.

   c. Indexes should be as narrow as possible, because this allows more data values to fit on an index page and reduces disk I/O.

   d. Only one of the columns in a primary key may be nullable.

7. Which of the following statements regarding check constraints are true? (Choose all correct answers.)

   a. As little additional disk I/O occurs when implementing check constraints, their impact on update performance is minimal.

   b. Check constraints can reference data in other tables.

   c. Check constraints can reference system functions, such as **getdate()**.

   d. Check constraints can reference data in another column in the same row.

8. Which of the following statements regarding user-defined integrities are true? (Choose all correct answers.)

   a. Coding triggers or stored procedures to handle integrities is necessary when the default behaviors defined by foreign key constraints are not correct.

   b. If a foreign key constraint and a trigger are defined, the trigger will fire first, and only if it succeeds will the foreign key constraint be evaluated.

c. When a *nullify* integrity is coded, the delete of the parent row is permitted and any matching foreign key values in the child are set to **NULL**.

d. When a *cascade* integrity is coded, the deletion of the parent row is permitted and all matching rows in the child row are deleted as well. When a joining column in the parent is updated, update the foreign key in the child as well.

9. Which of the following statements regarding measuring performance is true?

   a. It is not necessary to measure quantitatively performance because your users will tell you if the system is fast enough.

   b. Having a way to benchmark different indexes and key structures in the development environment improves the quality of the delivered physical database design.

   c. It is only necessary to measure query performance or update performance, because either one ensures that your physical database design is correct.

   d. It is possible to accurately measure performance by creating a database containing a subset of the data volume expected in production as long as all of the indexes are in place.

10. Which of the following statements regarding the affect of index selection on performance are true? (Choose all correct answers.)

    a. Adding an index on a column whose value changes frequently improves performance.

    b. An index containing the columns *a1*, *b2*, *c3* improves the performance of queries using the selection criteria of either *a1*, *b2*, or *c3*.

    c. Adding an extra column to an index so that all data needed for a query can be found in just the index will improve performance.

    d. Adding more indexes to a table may speed up query performance, but almost certainly slows down modify performance.

11. Which of the following statements regarding denormalization are true? (Choose all correct answers.)

    a. The process of denormalization will add duplicate data elements to the physical model in order to improve data integrity.

    b. Data added during the process of denormalization can be either duplicate data or data calculated from other fields.

    c. Foreign keys can be defined to maintain the duplicate data created during normalization.

    d. Some overhead during updates will be added when duplicate or derived data is added to the database design.

12. Which of these statements regarding modification to table definitions in the physical database design are true? (Choose all correct answers.)
    a. As the database design is reviewed, some tables might be combined and other tables might be split apart in order to improve database performance.
    b. Horizontal table partitioning is used to separate active data from inactive data or to split data from multiple departments into individual department tables.
    c. Partitioning data into smaller tables may improve system availability, because smaller tables will not need as much time for backups, restores, index rebuilds, or **UPDATE STATISTICS**.
    d. As it is easy to modify the database design to either partition or join tables, a review of the table design can be deferred until of the development of stored procedures and triggers has been completed.

13. Which of the following statements regarding security are true? (Choose all correct answers.)
    a. Databases designed for decision support use stored procedures exclusively to access data.
    b. Using stored procedures exclusively to query and update data simplifies security, because no direct access to tables or views will need to be granted.
    c. Table partitioning—either horizontal or vertical—will help in managing security, because sensitive data can be separated into separate tables or views.
    d. An analysis of access rights either to stored procedures or to base tables should be performed during the physical design using the specifications defined in the original database requirements document.

14. Which of the following statements regarding physical database design is correct?
    a. Although physical database design has a large impact on query and update performance, it has a negligible impact on data integrity.
    b. A fully normalized database design is better suited than a heavily denormalized database design to supporting future business functionality that might need to be added to the database.
    c. It is best to place all tables and indexes in the same filegroup so that space management can be simplified.
    d. Indexes that contain columns not required for the supported queries are faster than narrower indexes.

15. Which of the following statements regarding the impact of physical database design on performance are true? (Choose all correct answers.)
    a. A physical database design that exactly matches the logical database design is always the fastest.
    b. If two DBAs are asked to produce a physical database design using the same logical model, a possibility exists that the two physical designs will be very different, but both will perform very well.
    c. If update performance on a table is not up to par, adding more indexes to the fields being updated will improve performance.
    d. By using such features as primary keys, unique constraints, and foreign keys, you can manage and control data integrity.

Hands-On Projects

Susan had performed the logical design of her database using the SQL Server Enterprise Manager's graphical Database Design tool. She printed the diagram for the design review team and pored over the details with the developers. After a few modifications to the diagram, she headed back to her cubicle and made the changes to the diagram. She had access to other design tools, but she wanted to immerse herself in Microsoft's products so she would be ready for the MCDBA exam. She was surprised to find that the tool was quite usable for this task.

Project 4.1

In this project you will transform the logical database design created in Project 3.1 and 3.2 into a physical database design that can support the customer ordering process for the Northwind Company.

Refer back to the Hands-On Projects section in Chapter 3 for business requirements and the completed ER model in Figure 3.24. Use the database diagram tool in SQL Server Enterprise Manager and the following checklist to create a preliminary physical design that contains all tables, columns, primary keys, and foreign key constraints. The preliminary physical design will be a one-for-one translation of each entity in the ER model into a table.

1. Open SQL Server Enterprise Manager and create an empty *Northwinds* database. In the left-hand pane, right-click on databases and select New Database from the resulting pop-up window. Type the database name "*Northwinds4*" into the Database Properties pop-up window. The default database size, location, and so forth will be sufficient.
2. After expanding the plus sign next to the new database name, right-click on the Diagrams item and select New Diagrams. This opens up a blank window where you can create a new database diagram.

3. From the toolbar at the top of the diagramming window, select the New Tables icon and provide a table name in the pop-up window. A table with no column definitions will display in the diagram. Right-click on the table and select Column Properties from the pop-up properties menu. Fill in the column name, data type, length, and attributes for each column.
4. Repeat this process for each table in your physical model.
5. Create primary keys by highlighting the column or columns in the table that should be primary keys and right-click to open the properties pop-up window. On this window, select Set Primary Key. The primary key will be marked by a key icon next to the column name.
6. Repeat this process for each table in your physical model.
7. Define the foreign key constraints by highlighting the column or columns participating in the primary key and then dragging the cursor over to the child table that contains the foreign key.

After Susan created her design and had her meetings with the design team, she read the business requirements once again. She then decided on the final constraints she would need on the database and turned once again to the Diagram Tool to do the job.

Project 4.2

Complete the physical database design by adding the check constraints and default values that were defined during the domain analysis in Project 3.2 and that are shown in Figure 3.25.

Because it will be necessary to recompute frequently the total dollar amount of the order, as well as the dollar amount for each order line when orders are shipped, billed, and then processed for payment, add the appropriate columns in the database diagram for these fields.

In further analyzing business requirements, several alternate indexes appear to be necessary. Therefore, we will add indexes on the *ShipVia* column in the *Orders* table so that all orders being sent via the same shipper can be processed together. In addition, an index on *ContactName* in the *Customers* table will be helpful for lookup when a contact calls in to place order.

Use the following as a checklist when making these modifications to your database diagram:

1. To add check constraints and default values, right-click on the desired column name and from the pop-up window select Column Properties. Add constraints and defaults to the appropriate columns. To hide these column details, right-click again and select Column Names from the pop-up menu.

2. To insert new columns into a table, highlight the column above which the new column should be placed, right-click, and from the pop-up window select Insert Column.
3. To create an index on one or more columns, select the desired table by placing the cursor on any column, right-click to display a pop-up properties window, and select Properties, which is the very last item. Select the Indexes/Keys tab in the Properties window. Select New to create a new index, which will be given a default name. In the columns window, use the pull-down menu to choose the columns to be indexed. Select Close when done.
4. To generate and view the Transact-SQL code that will be executed to create these database objects, right-click anywhere in the background of the diagram and select Save Change Script from the pop-up window. You will be able to view the SQL code and, optionally, save it to a text file.
5. Save the diagram by choosing the Save icon from the tool bar. A Save window will confirm that you are ready to also save these changes to the database.

CHAPTER FIVE

TABLES

After Reading This Chapter And Completing The Exercises, You Will Be Able To:

- Define column data types
- Define identity columns
- Define row global unique identifier columns
- Create column defaults
- Create column rules
- Create column-level and table-level constraints
- Create tables
- Alter tables
- Drop tables
- Name the most important system tables

Tables are the database objects where the data is stored. They are composed of columns (*fields*) that run vertically and the rows (*records*) containing the data that run horizontally. Tables store not only the user's data, but also data that SQL Server uses to function.

TABLE TYPES

SQL Server 7 has two types of tables, *temporary* and *permanent*. *Temporary* tables are just that: temporary. They are created and destroyed during a session. Temporary tables can be *local* or *global*, depending on their lifetime and visibility. Let's take a look at each kind.

A *local* temporary table is visible only in the current session. A local temporary table is indicated by the # sign preceding the table name, such as **#<table_name>**.

A *global* temporary table is visible to all sessions. This type of table is available to be used by all users who are connected to the server. A global table is indicated by the ## sign preceding its name, such as **##<table_name>**.

A local temporary table is dropped when the user that created it disconnects from SQL Server 7. A global temporary table is dropped once all users who were using it disconnect from the SQL Server. Temporary tables are always created on the *tempdb* database.

Permanent tables are, of course, permanently recorded in the database unless you (or someone else) drops them. Permanent tables can be created by the system or by a user.

When creating tables, you need to consider the following rules:

- The combination of table owner and table name has to be unique within a database.
- A table name can be 128 characters long (116 if it is a temporary table).
- A table can have up to 1,024 columns.
- Each column name within a table must be unique.
- The first character of a table name (and a column name) has to be a letter (as defined in the Unicode Standard 2). You can also use the symbols _ and @. If the table name has embedded spaces, you must delimit it with brackets, for example, [*table name*]. A table or column name cannot be a Transact-SQL (T-SQL) reserved word.

The Unicode Standard 2 defines a letter as any Latin character from a-z and A-Z and any other letter character from other languages.

Column Data Types

A *data type* defines the type of data stored in a column. It helps enforce data integrity because the data stored in the column has to conform to the column's data type; for example, you cannot store character data in a column that has a *money* data type assigned to it. Using strict data types for table columns also helps optimize performance and storage space for the type of data being stored.

SQL Server 7 has several system data types, and it's important that you become familiar with them for the exam and for the real world:

5

- **Binary data** Consists of hexadecimal numbers.
  - **binary[(n)]:** Fixed-length of n bytes (n is a value between 1 and 8,000 bytes).
  - **varbinary[(n)]:** Variable-length of n bytes (n is a value between 1 and 8,000 bytes).
  - **image:** Variable-length (maximum length is 2^{31}-1 (2,147,483,647) bytes).
- **Character data** Consists of alphanumeric characters and symbols.
  - **char(n):** Fixed-length of n characters (n is a value between 1 and 8,000 characters).
  - **varchar(n):** Variable-length of n characters (n is a value between 1 and 8,000 characters).
  - **text:** Variable-length of characters (maximum length is 2^{31}-1 (2,147,483,647) characters).
- **Unicode data** Consists of all characters defined on all character sets, that is, any character defined by the Unicode Standard. This type takes double the space of a non-Unicode data type.
  - **nchar(n):** Fixed-length of n unicode characters (n is a value between 1 and 4,000 characters).
  - **nvarchar(n):** Variable-length of n unicode characters (n is a value between 1 and 4,000 characters).
  - **ntext:** Variable-length of unicode characters (maximum length is 2^{30}-1 (1,073,741,823) characters).
- **Integer data** Consists of positive and negative whole numbers.
  - **integer** or **int:** Whole numbers between -2^{31} (-2,147,483,648) and 2^{31} (2,147,483,648).

    - **smallint:** Whole numbers between -2^{15} (-32,768) and $2^{15}-1$ (32,767).
    - **tinyint:** Whole numbers between 0 and 255.
- **Decimal data** Consists of data with a fixed precision and scale.
    - **decimal [(p, s)]** or **dec [(p, s)]:** Exact number between $-10^{38}-1$ and $10^{38}-1$.
    - **numeric [(p, s)]:** Exact number between $-10^{38}-1$ and $10^{38}-1$.
    - ***p* (precision):** The maximum number of digits to the right and left of the decimal point.
    - ***s* (scale):** The maximum number of digits after the decimal point.
- **Approximate data** Consists of data without a fixed precision.
    - **float [(p)]**: Floating precision number between -1.79E+308 and 1.79E+308 (p indicates the precision and is a value between 1 and 53).
    - **real:** Floating precision number between -3.40E+308 and 3.40E+38.
- **Monetary data** Consists of money type data. Can be positive or negative.
    - **money:** Monetary values between -2^{63} (-922,337,203,685,477.5808) and $2^{63}-1$ (922,337,203,685,477.5807).
    - **smallmoney:** Monetary data between -214,743.3648 and 214,743.3647.
- **Date and time data** Consists of a date and a time value.
    - **datetime:** Dates between 1/1/1753 and 12/31/9999.
    - **smalldatetime:** Dates between 1/1/1900 and 6/6/2079.
- **Special data**
    - **timestamp:** A number in binary format representing the sequence of activity on a row. (The timestamp number has nothing to do with a date and time of an insert or update of a row.)
    - **bit:** A value of 1 or 0.You can string eight bits together and still take up only one byte of space.
    - **uniqueidentifier:** A 16-byte binary value that operates as a *Globally Unique Identification Number* (*GUID*). Each GUID is always unique.

SQL Server 7 also allows you to create *user-defined* data types based on the system data types. The system stored procedure **sp_addtype** is used to create user-defined data types. The syntax for **sp_addtype** is:

```
sp_addtype [@typename=]<name>, [@phystype=]<system_data_type>
                    [, NULL|NOT NULL]
where <name> is the name of the user defined data type,
and <system_data_type> is one of the above
mentioned system data types.
```

```
NULL|NOT NULL specifies whether the
user-defined data type will allow null values.
```

In the *Northwind* database, a user-defined data type can be created for phone numbers. The user-defined data type can be created with the following syntax:

```
sp_addtype 'phone_dtype', 'nvarchar(24)', 'null'
```

As a result, when defining the *Customers, Shippers,* and *Suppliers* tables, the user-defined data type will be assigned to the *phone number* columns. This ensures that when you create tables and use the data type **phone_dtype**, the phone number data type will be defined consistently across the database.

To drop an already defined user-defined data type, use the system stored procedure **sp_droptype** as follows:

```
sp_droptype phone_dtype
```

A user-defined data type cannot be dropped if tables or other database objects reference it, if the user-defined data type is used within a table definition, or if a rule or default is bound to it.

NULL/NOT NULL Columns

Another decision that has to be made when defining a table is whether the columns will allow null values. To specify this, use the keyword **NULL** or **NOT NULL** when defining the column.

All of the previously mentioned data types (except for the **bit** type) allow **NULLS**. A **NULL** *value* is not the same as an *empty string* or a zero value. A **NULL** value means that the value is unknown or undefined *at this time*. Keep in mind, however, that a column defined as allowing **NULLS** cannot be part of a primary key.

Listing 5.1 shows a **CREATE** statement that defines a column that allows **NULL** values and defines two columns that do not allow **NULL** values.

Listing 5.1 Defining a column that allows **NULL** and **NOT NULL** values.

```
CREATE TABLE Shippers (
     ShipperID integer NOT NULL,
     CompanyName nvarchar(40) NOT NULL,
     Phone nvarchar(24) NULL)
GO
```

Identity Columns

An *identity column* is a column that auto-increments its value every time a record is inserted into the table.

Only one identity column can exist per table and only columns of integer and decimal data types defined as **NOT NULL** can be identity columns.

When you define an identity column, you can specify the *seed* and *increment*. The seed is the starting value of the column; the increment is how much the value will be incremented each time a record is inserted into the table. If they are not specified, the default of (1. 1) will be assigned.

It is guaranteed that the value in an identity column is unique within the table. That is why an identity column is often used as the **PRIMARY KEY** of the table. The system variable **@@IDENTITY** contains the last identity value generated by a statement that inserts data into a table.

Listing 5.2 shows how you would define an identity column on a table and demonstrates the values of the system variable **@@IDENTITY**.

Listing 5.2 Defining an identity column on a table and demonstrating the values of the system variable **@@IDENTITY**.

```
CREATE TABLE Shippers (
     ShipperID integer identity(2, 3) NOT NULL,
     CompanyName nvarchar(40) NOT NULL,
     Phone nvarchar(24) NULL )
GO
INSERT INTO Shippers (CompanyName, Phone)
VALUES ('Sports Inc.', '1234567')
GO
SELECT 'First identity value inserted:', @@IDENTITY
GO
INSERT INTO Shippers (CompanyName, Phone)
VALUES ('Groceries Inc.', '2345678')
GO
SELECT 'Second identity value inserted:', @@IDENTITY
GO
SELECT * FROM Shippers
GO
```

```
The results of the previous statements are as follows:
--------------- ------
First identity value inserted: 2
```

```
-------------- -----
Second identity value inserted: 5

ShipperID  CompanyName        Phone
---------  -------------      -------
2          Sports Inc.        1234567
5          Groceries Inc.     2345678
```

Inserting Explicit Values Into An Identity Column

Sometimes you might need to insert explicit values into an identity column because gaps have occurred. In order to accomplish this you need to first issue the **SET IDENTITY INSERT <table_name> ON | OFF** command.

Note that the first inserted **ShipperID** value is 2 and the second is 5 since we defined the seed value as 2 and the increment as 3, such as (2, 3).

Checking And Correcting Identity Column Values

To check the current identity value of a column, use the **DBCC CHECKIDENT** command. If necessary, this command also corrects the value. This command has been greatly improved in SQL Server 7; now it allows you to reseed an identity column. The syntax is: **DBCC CHECKIDENT(<table_name> [, { NORESEED | RESEED [, <reseed_value> }].**

Row Global Unique Identifier Column

A *row global unique identifier* column is an identifier column that contains values unique across *all* databases on the network. This column must be of data type **uniqueidentifier** and must have the **ROWGUIDCOL** column property set when defining it.

Row global unique identifier columns are used when data from different databases will be merged into one database. You can see a model of this type of column in Listing 5.3.

Tables participating in Merge Replication must have a row global unique identifier column.

When defining a row global unique identifier, you need to consider the following rules:

- Use only one **ROWGUIDCOL** column per table.
- To insert a unique value, use the **NEWID** function.
- To ensure the uniqueness of the values, define a **UNIQUE** constraint on the column.

Listing 5.3 Defining a row global unique identifier column.

```
CREATE TABLE [example guid] (
     kgid uniqueidentifier ROWGUIDCOL not null,
     firstname char(15) not null,
     lastname varchar(80) not null )
GO
INSERT INTO [example guid] VALUES (NEWID(), 'Bill', 'Green')
GO
PRINT 'Rows in the [example guid] table:'
PRINT ''
SELECT * FROM [example guid]
GO
```

The results of the above statements are as follows:

```
Rows in the [example guid] table:

kgid                                 firstname  lastname
------------------------------------ ---------- --------
7EBCA30A-ED18-11D2-A978-00600837930F Bill       Green
```

DEFAULTS

A *default* is a value that is inserted into a column during an insert operation when no explicit value is given in the insert statement. Defaults cannot be enforced on an identity column or on a timestamp data type.

SQL Server 7 supports two ways for defining a default for a column. The first is to create a default object and bind it to a column (this feature is supported for backward compatibility with previous versions of Microsoft SQL Server).

Default Object

A *default object* is created using the **CREATE DEFAULT** statement, like this:

```
CREATE DEFAULT <default_name> AS <constant_value>
```

Once a default object is created, you have to bind it to a column or to a user-defined data type using the stored procedure **sp_bindefault**:

```
sp_bindefault [@defname=] 'default_name',
                        [@objname=] 'object_name'
                        [, [@futureonly=] 'futureonly'|NULL ]
```

Note the terms used in the preceding statement:

➤ **default_name** Default created with the **CREATE DEFAULT** command.

- **object_name** Table and column or user-defined data type to which the default will be bound.
- **futureonly** Used only when binding to a user-defined data type. If used, the default will only be bound to new columns with the specified user-defined data type.
- If **NULL** is specified, all columns with the specified user-defined data type will inherit the default.

In order to drop a default object, you must first *unbind* it from the columns or user-defined data types that it is bound to.

To unbind a default, use the stored procedure **sp_unbindefault**, like this:

```
sp_unbindefault [@objname=] 'object_name'
            [, [@futureonly=] 'futureonly'|NULL ]
```

To drop a default use the **DROP DEFAULT** command, which looks like this:

```
DROP DEFAULT <default_name1> [, <default_name2>…]
```

Listing 5.4 shows how to create a default object and bind it to the *Country* column of the *Customers* table.

Listing 5.4 Creating a default object.

```
CREATE DEFAULT def_country AS 'USA'
GO
sp_bindefault def_country, 'Customers.Country'
GO
```

After binding the default to the column, if no value is supplied for the *Country* column during an insert of a row, the default value of **USA** will be assigned to the *Country* column.

Default Definition

The second way to create a default for a column is to create a default definition. A *default definition* (in some parts of the SQL Server 7 documentation they are referred to as *default constraints*) is created when creating or altering a table using the property:

```
DEFAULT <constant_expression>
```

where the **<constant_expression>** is a literal value, a system function, or a **NULL** value.

Listing 5.5 shows how a default definition can be created when defining a table. In this case, if a value for the *Country* column is not specified when a row is inserted into the table, the default value of **USA** will be used.

Listing 5.5 Creating a default definition when defining a table.

```
CREATE TABLE Customers (
     CustomerID nchar(5) not null,
     CompanyName nvarchar(40) not null,
     Address nvarchar(60) not null,
     City nvarchar(15) not null,
     State nvarchar(10) not null,
     Country nvarchar(15) not null DEFAULT ('USA')
)
GO
INSERT INTO Customers (CustomerID, CompanyName, Address, City, State)
VALUES ( '1111', 'Green Inc.', '19008 Dale Mabry', 'Tampa', 'FL' )
GO
SELECT CompanyName, City, State, Country FROM Customers
GO
```

The results of the preceding statements are as follows:

```
CompanyName       City        State       Country
-----------       -----       -----       -------
Green Inc.        Tampa       FL          USA
```

As you can see, the default value of **USA** was assigned to the *Country* column, because no value was supplied in the insert statement. This is shown in Listing 5.6.

Listing 5.6 Using a system function with a default definition.

```
CREATE TABLE DEFAULT_example (
     employeeid integer identity (1, 1) not null,
     address   varchar(100) not null,
     city char(15) not null,
     state char(2) not null,
     country char(10) not null,
     last_updated datetime not null DEFAULT GETDATE()
)
GO
```

RULES

A *rule* is an object that specifies which values are acceptable in a column when performing an insert or update process. Since rules are supported for backward compatibility (they have been replaced by constraints in SQL Server version 7), we will give a brief explanation of them.

A *rule object* is created with the **CREATE RULE** command. After creating a rule object, you need to bind it to a column or a user-defined data type with the help of the **sp_bindrule** stored procedure with this syntax:

5

```
sp_bindrule [@rulename=] 'rule_name'],
                    [@objname=] 'object_name'
                    [, [@futureonly=] 'futureonly'|NULL ]
```

Note the following terms in the preceding statement:

- The **'rule_name'** is the rule created with the **CREATE RULE** command, and **'object_name'** is the table and column or user-defined data type to which the rule will be bound.
- The **'futureonly'** clause is only used when binding to a user-defined data type. If used, the rule will only be bound to new columns with the specified user-defined data type.
- If **NULL** is specified, all columns with the specified user-defined data type will inherit the rule.

When a rule is bound to a table column, the current data of the column is not validated against the rule. In order to drop a rule object, you must first unbind it from the columns or user-defined data types that it is bound to. To unbind a rule, use the stored procedure **sp_unbindrule**:

```
        [@objname=] 'object_name'
[, [@futureonly=] 'futureonly'|NULL ].
```

To drop a rule use the command:

```
DROP RULE <rule_name1> [, <rule_name2>…].
```

You can bind only one rule to a column or to a user-defined data type.

Whenever possible, use **CHECK** constraints instead of rules, because **CHECK** constraints improve performance.

Listing 5.7 creates a rule object and binds it to the *Country* column of the *Customers'* table. The rule restricts the values allowed in the *Country* column to **USA** and **CANADA**.

Listing 5.7 Creating a rule object.

```
CREATE RULE rule_country AS @country IN ( 'USA', 'CANADA' )
GO
sp_bindrule rule_country, 'Customers.Country'
GO
```

Column-Level And Table-Level Constraints

You can enforce database integrity two ways within SQL Server 7. You can either use rules and triggers, or you can define *constraints*, which are rules on what the data in a table can be. Constraints are defined when a table is created using the **CREATE TABLE** statement or you can add them afterward using the **ALTER TABLE** statement. When defining constraints you can supply a *constraint name* or you can allow SQL Server 7 to generate one automatically.

Two types of constraints exist: *column-level* and *table-level.*

- **Column-level constraint** A column-level constraint is declared when the column is being defined and applies only to that column of the table.
- **Table-level constraint** A table-level constraint is declared independently from the column definition and may apply to more than one column. A **DEFAULT** constraint cannot be defined as table-level constraint.

You can define all column-level constraints as table-level constraints.

To view all constraints that are associated with a table, you can use the system stored procedure **sp_helpconstraint <table_name>**.

Constraints can be divided into different classes:

- **CHECK** constraints
- **PRIMARY KEY** constraints
- **FOREIGN KEY** constraints
- **UNIQUE** constraints

CHECK Constraints

A **CHECK** constraint is used to enforce domain integrity during an insert or update. A **CHECK** constraint evaluates to True or False and only those values that evaluate to True are accepted. You can specify a set or range of values that a column can accept. You can define more than one **CHECK** constraint on a column. The syntax for a **CHECK** constraint is as follows:

```
[CONSTRAINT <constraint_name>]
     CHECK
      [NOT FOR REPLICATION]
      (expression).
```


The **NOT FOR REPLICATION** keyword is used to prevent enforcement of the constraint during a replication process. Remember that **(expression)** must always evaluate to True or False.

In Listing 5.8, the **CHECK** constraint restricts the values being inserted or updated into the *BirthDate* column to be less than the current date.

Listing 5.8 Defining a **CHECK** constraint at the column level.

```
CREATE TABLE Employees_a (
          EmployeeID integer IDENTITY (1, 1) NOT NULL ,
          LastName nvarchar(20) NOT NULL ,
          FirstName nvarchar(10) NOT NULL ,
          Title nvarchar(30) NULL ,
          BirthDate datetime NULL CHECK (BirthDate < getdate()),
          HireDate datetime NULL ,
          Phone nvarchar(24) NULL ,
          Extension nvarchar(4) NULL
     )
     GO
```

In Listing 5.9, the **CHECK** constraint restricts the values being inserted or updated into the *BirthDate* column to be less than the current date, additionally, the value has to be less than the value in the *HireDate* column.

Listing 5.9 Defining a **CHECK** constraint at the column level.

```
CREATE TABLE Employees_b (
          EmployeeID integer IDENTITY (1, 1) NOT NULL ,
          LastName nvarchar(20) NOT NULL ,
          FirstName nvarchar(10) NOT NULL ,
          Title nvarchar(30) NULL ,
          BirthDate datetime NULL,
          HireDate datetime NULL ,
```

```
        Phone nvarchar(24) NULL ,
        Extension nvarchar (4) NULL,
        CHECK (BirthDate < getdate() and  BirthDate < HireDate)
)
GO
```

PRIMARY KEY Constraint

A **PRIMARY KEY** constraint is used to enforce the *entity* integrity of a table. A **PRIMARY KEY** is defined on the column (or a minimal set of columns) that uniquely identify a row in a table. When a **PRIMARY KEY** constraint is created, SQL Server 7 automatically creates a unique index on the columns that define the constraint. The syntax for a column-level **PRIMARY KEY** constraint is as follows:

```
[CONSTRAINT <constraint_name>]
      PRIMARY KEY  [CLUSTERD|NONCLUSTERED]
      [WITH FILLFACTOR = <fillfactor>]
      [ON <filegroup>|DEFAULT].
```

The syntax for a table-level **PRIMARY KEY** constraint is as follows:

```
[CONSTRAINT <constraint_name>]
      PRIMARY KEY [CLUSTERD|NONCLUSTERED]
(column1 [, column2 [,…column16]])
      [WITH FILLFACTOR = <fillfactor>]
      [ON <filegroup>|DEFAULT].
```

Each table can have only one **PRIMARY KEY** constraint defined.

The columns that define the **PRIMARY KEY** cannot allow **NULL** values. By default, a **PRIMARY KEY** is created as **CLUSTERED**.

The **WITH FILLFACTOR** option is used to specify what percentage of the index pages will be filled when creating the unique index (this option will be discussed in Chapter 6).

The **ON <filegroup> | DEFAULT** option is used to specify on which filegroup the unique index will be created. If the **ON** option is not specified, the index will be created in the same filegroup as the table (filegroups will be discussed in Chapter 14).

In Listing 5.10, a **PRIMARY KEY** constraint is created on the *ShipperID* column. The **Primary Key index** will be saved on the **PRIMARY** filegroup.

Listing 5.10 A column-level **PRIMARY KEY** constraint.

```
Column-level constraint:
     CREATE TABLE Shippers (
          ShipperID integer identity NOT NULL CONSTRAINT PK_Shippers
               PRIMARY KEY CLUSTERED (ShipperID) ON 'PRIMARY',
          CompanyName nvarchar(40) NOT NULL ,
          Phone nvarchar(24) NULL
     )
     GO
```

5

In Listing 5.11, a **PRIMARY KEY** constraint is created on the *OrderID* and *ProductID* columns. The **Primary Key** index will be saved on the default filegroup.

Listing 5.11 A table-level **PRIMARY KEY** constraint.

```
Table-level constraint:
     CREATE TABLE [Order Details] (
          OrderID integer NOT NULL ,
          ProductID integer NOT NULL ,
          UnitPrice money NOT NULL ,
          Quantity smallint NOT NULL ,
          Discount real NOT NULL ,
          CONSTRAINT PK_Order_Details
               PRIMARY KEY  CLUSTERED (OrderID, ProductID)
     )
     GO
```

UNIQUE Constraint

A **UNIQUE** constraint is used to make sure that a column does not allow duplicate values. When a **UNIQUE** constraint is created, SQL Server 7 automatically creates a unique index on the columns that define the constraint. The syntax for a **UNIQUE** column-level constraint is as follows:

```
[CONSTRAINT <constraint_name>]
     UNIQUE [CLUSTERD|NONCLUSTERED]
      [WITH FILLFACTOR = <fillfactor>]
      [ON <filegroup>|DEFAULT]
```

The syntax for a **UNIQUE** table-level constraint is as follows:

```
[CONSTRAINT <constraint_name>]
     UNIQUE [CLUSTERD|NONCLUSTERED]
      (column1 [, column2 [,… column16]])
      [WITH FILLFACTOR = <fillfactor>]
      [ON <filegroup>|DEFAULT].
```

The **WITH FILLFACTOR** option is used to specify what percentage of the index pages will be filled when creating the unique index (this option will be discussed in Chapter 6).

The **ON <filegroup> | DEFAULT** option is used to specify on which filegroup the unique index will be created. If the **ON** option is not specified, the index will be created in the same filegroup as the table (filegroups will be discussed in Chapter 14).

Several differences exist between a **UNIQUE** constraint and a **PRIMARY KEY** constraint:

- You can define up to 250 **UNIQUE** constraints on a table (249 nonclustered and 1 clustered).

You can define only one **PRIMARY KEY** constraint on a table.

- You can define a **UNIQUE** constraint on a column that allows **NULL** values. You cannot define a **PRIMARY KEY** constraint on a column that allows **NULL** values.
- A **UNIQUE** constraint by default is nonclustered. A **PRIMARY KEY** constraint by default is clustered.

In Listing 5.12, a **UNIQUE KEY** constraint is created on the *Isbn* column. The *Unique Key* index will be saved on the default filegroup.

Listing 5.12 A definition of a column-level and a table-level **UNIQUE** constraint.

```
– Defined as a column-level constraint:
    CREATE TABLE UNIQUE_ example_1 (
         bookid integer identity (1, 1) not null
              PRIMARY KEY NONCLUSTERED,
         title varchar(100) not null,
         authorid integer not null,
         isbn char(15) not null
              CONSTRAINT col_unique UNIQUE NONCLUSTERED
    )
    GO

– Defined as a table-level constraint:
    CREATE TABLE UNIQUE_ example_2 (
         bookid integer identity (1, 1) not null
              PRIMARY KEY NONCLUSTERED,
         title varchar(100) not null,
```

```
        authorid integer not null,
        isbn char(15) not null,
        CONSTRAINT tab_unique UNIQUE NONCLUSTERED (isbn)
    )
    GO
```

FOREIGN KEY Constraint

A **FOREIGN KEY** constraint enforces *referential integrity* for the values of a column or group of columns. It is used to identify relationships between tables by ensuring that the values placed in one table reference another table. This is commonly used to make sure that a product sale is recorded only if a customer exists, for instance. A **FOREIGN KEY** constraint references a column or columns defined as a **PRIMARY KEY** constraint or as a **UNIQUE** constraint in the referenced table.

SQL Server 7 supports 253 **FOREIGN KEY** constraints per table.

The syntax for a column-level **FOREIGN KEY** constraint is as follows:

```
[CONSTRAINT <constraint_name>] [FOREIGN KEY]
     REFERENCES ref_table (ref_columns) [NOT FOR REPLICATION]
```

The syntax for a table-level **FOREIGN KEY** constraint is as follows:

```
[CONSTRAINT <constraint_name>] FOREIGN KEY (column1[,…column n])
     REFERENCES ref_table (ref_columns) [NOT FOR REPLICATION]
```

Where the **ref_table** is the table being referenced (which must have a **PRIMARY KEY** or **UNIQUE** constraint) and the **ref_columns** clause describes the columns that are being referenced. The **NOT FOR REPLICATION** keyword is used to not enforce the constraint during a replication process.

A **FOREIGN KEY** constraint makes having orphaned records impossible, because of the following:

- Rows cannot be inserted into a child table if there is no corresponding value in the parent table.
- Rows from a parent table cannot be deleted if a **FOREIGN KEY** is referencing them.
- A **PRIMARY KEY** or **UNIQUE KEY** value cannot be changed if a **FOREIGN KEY** is referencing it.

SQL Server 7 does not support cross-database referential integrity using **FOREIGN KEY** constraints. Cross-database referential integrity can be applied using triggers.

The **FOREIGN KEY** constraints defined in Listing 5.13 do not allow a row to be inserted into the *[Order Details]* table, unless there is a corresponding **OrderID** in the *Orders* table, and a corresponding *ProductID* in the *Products* table.

Listing 5.13 Defining a column-level and a table-level **FOREIGN KEY** constraint in one statement.

```
CREATE TABLE [Order Details] (
     OrderID integer NOT NULL CONSTRAINT FK_Order_Details_Orders
          FOREIGN KEY REFERENCES Orders (OrderID),
     ProductID integer NOT NULL,
     UnitPrice money NOT NULL,
     Quantity smallint NOT NULL,
     Discount real NOT NULL,
     CONSTRAINT FK_Order_Details_Products
          FOREIGN KEY (ProductID) REFERENCES Products (ProductID)
)
GO
```

CREATING TABLES

Tables can be created using the **CREATE TABLE** statement. Remember that when creating a table you must determine the following items:

- The columns' data type
- Will the columns accept null values?
- Will there be an identity column?
- Will there be a row global unique identifier column?
- Will there be any column-level or table-level constraints?
- Will there be any computed column?

The syntax for the **CREATE TABLE** statement is as follows:

```
CREATE TABLE [<database>.[<owner>].]<.table_name>
( <col>  { <data_type>
                   [NOT NULL|NULL]
                   [ [IDENTITY [(<seed>,<increment>)]]|
                     [ROWGUIDCOL]|
                     [DEFAULT <constant_expression>] ]|
```

```
                    [[CONSTRAINT <constraint_name>]
                       PRIMARY KEY [CLUSTERED|NONCLUSTERED]
                              [WITH FILLFACTOR = <fillfactor>]
                              [ON <filegroup>|DEFAULT]|
                       UNIQUE [CLUSTERED|NONCLUSTERED]
                              [WITH FILLFACTOR = <fillfactor>]
                              [ON <filegroup>|DEFAULT]|
                       [FOREIGN KEY] REFERENCES <ref_table> (ref_columns)
             [NOT FOR REPLICATION]|
                       CHECK [NOT FOR REPLICATION] (logical expression) ]
               |AS <computed_column_expression>
            }
   [, <col2> .....[,<coln>]]

   [, [CONSTRAINT <constraint_name>]
        PRIMARY KEY [CLUSTERED|NONCLUSTERED]  (col1[,col2...] )
                [WITH FILLFACTOR = <fillfactor>] [ON <filegroup>|
                DEFAULT]|
        UNIQUE [CLUSTERED|NONCLUSTERED] (col1[,col2...] )
                [WITH FILLFACTOR = <fillfactor>] [ON <filegroup>|
                DEFAULT]|
        FOREIGN KEY (col1[, col2...] ) REFERENCES <ref_table>
(ref_columns)
           [NOT FOR REPLICATION]|
        CHECK [NOT FOR REPLICATION] (logical expression),
[<definition_of_next_table_constraint>] ]
)
[ON <filegroup>|DEFAULT]
[TEXTIMAGE_ON <filegroup>|DEFAULT]
```

The only option of the above syntax that we've not already covered is the creation of a computed column. The data in a computed column is not physically stored in the table. In a computed column only the column definition is stored.

A computed column cannot be part of a **PRIMARY KEY** constraint, a **UNIQUE** constraint, a **FOREIGN KEY** constraint, a **DEFAULT** constraint, or an index.

Computed columns cannot be modified; SQL Server 7 calculates the value automatically when data is inserted or updated.

The computed expression **(<computed_column_expression>)** can be a non-computed column name, a constant, a function, a variable, or any combination of any of these.

The table option **ON <filegroup> | DEFAULT** is used to specify on which database **filegroup** the table will be stored.

The table option **ON <filegroup>|DEFAULT** is also used for **PRIMARY KEY** and **UNIQUE** constraints.

The option **TEXTIMAGE_ON <filegroup> | DEFAULT]** is used to specify on which database filegroup the columns of data type **text**, **ntext**, and **image** will be stored.

Listing 5.14 illustrates the process to define a computed column on a table.

Listing 5.14 Defining a computed column on a table.

```
CREATE TABLE [Order Details] (
     OrderID integer NOT NULL ,
     ProductID integer NOT NULL ,
     UnitPrice money NOT NULL ,
     Qty smallint NOT NULL ,
     Discount real NOT NULL,
     TotalCost AS (UnitPrice * Qty) - (UnitPrice * Qty * Discount)
)
GO
```

ALTERING TABLES

A new feature in Microsoft SQL Server 7 is that once a table has been created, you can modify its definition. The **ALTER TABLE** command allows you to add or remove columns, change column definitions, add or drop the **Row Global Unique Identifier** property, add or remove constraints, enable or disable **FOREIGN KEY** and **CHECK** constraints, and enable or disable triggers.

Adding A Column

When adding a column to a table, the same questions apply as when you are creating a table:

- What is the columns' data type?
- Will the column accept **NULL** values?
- Will the column be an identity column?
- Will the column be a row global unique identifier column?
- Will the column have a column-level constraint associated with it?

To add a column that does not allow **NULL** values you must specify a default value for the column.

The syntax of the **ALTER TABLE** statement for adding a column to a table is as follows:

```
ALTER TABLE <table_name>
      ADD <col1> { <data_type>
                                 [NULL|NOT NULL]
                                 [ [DEFAULT <constant_expression>]|
                                   [IDENTITY [(<seed>, <increment>)
                                        [NOT FOR REPLICATION]]|
                                   [ROWGUIDCOL] ]
                                 [ [CONSTRAINT <constraint_name>]
                                   [PRIMARY KEY [CLUSTERED|
                                   NONCLUSTERED]]
                                        [WITH FILLFACTOR = <fillfactor>]
                                        [ON <filegroup>|DEFAULT]]|
                                   [UNIQUE [CLUSTERED|NONCLUSTERED]]
                                        [WITH FILLFACTOR = <fillfactor>]
                                        [ON <filegroup>|DEFAULT]]|
                                   [FOREIGN KEY]
                                        REFERENCES <ref_table>
(<ref_columns>)|
                                   CHECK [NOT FOR REPLICATION]
(<logical_expression>)
                             |AS <computed_column_expression>
                         }
               [, <col2> ....]
```

Listing 5.15 shows how to add a column that does not allow **NULLS** to a table. This statement will add a new column to the table and will save the current date and time in the newly added *LastUpdated* column.

Listing 5.15 Adding a column that does not allow **NULLS** to an existing table.

```
ALTER TABLE Orders ADD LastUpdated datetime NOT NULL DEFAULT getdate()
```

Dropping A Column

Another of the features that SQL Server 7 has added with the **ALTER TABLE** statement is the ability to drop a column from a table dynamically. In prior versions of SQL Server, you had to export the data from the table, drop and re-create the table and then import the data back to the table.

The syntax for dropping a column is as follows:

```
ALTER TABLE <table_name> DROP COLUMN <col1>[, <col2>…]
```

Columns that are being replicated, that are part of an index or a constraint, or have a default assigned to it, cannot be dropped. Listing 5.16 shows how the column added in Listing 5.15 can be dropped. (The example assumes that the **DEFAULT** constraint that was added has already been dropped.)

Listing 5.16 Dropping a column.

```
ALTER TABLE Orders DROP COLUMN LastUpdated
```

Modifying A Column Definition

In prior versions of Microsoft SQL Server, it was impossible to change a data type definition of a column without having to drop and re-create the table. This has changed in SQL Server 7. Now the data type and the **NULL|NOT NULL** attribute of a column can be changed dynamically.

Just remember that you can change the data type as long as the data that is saved in the table permits those changes. For example, if a column is of data type **char(10)** and you want to change the column definition to an integer type, the statement will not return an error as long as the data in the column are all numbers between -2^{31} (-2,147,483,648) and 2^{31} (2,147,483,648). The syntax for modifying a column is as follows:

```
ALTER TABLE <table_name>
     ALTER COLUMN <col1> [<new_data_type> [NULL|NOT NULL]]
```

If one on the following conditions is true, the column cannot be modified:

- The column is a row unique identifier column (**ROWGUIDCOL**).
- The column is a computed column.
- The column is used in the expression of a computed column.
- The column is being replicated.
- The column is part of a **PRIMARY KEY** or **FOREIGN KEY** constraint.
- The column is of **text**, **image**, **ntext**, or **timestamp** data type.
- The column was used in a **CREATE STATISTICS** statement.
- The column is part of an index (with the exception of when the size of a *varchar* or *varbinary* column is being increased).
- The column is part of a **CHECK** or **UNIQUE** constraint and you are not modifying the length of a **varchar** or **varbinary** column.
- The column has a default associated to it and you are changing the columns' data type.

Listing 5.17 shows how a data type of a column and its **NULL | NOT NULL** property can be changed.

Listing 5.17 Changing a data type of a column.

```
ALTER TABLE Shippers ALTER COLUMN CompanyName nvarchar(100) NULL
```

Adding/Dropping The Row Global Unique Identifier Property (ROWGUIDCOL)

The **ALTER TABLE** statement allows you to add or drop the row global unique identifier property to a column.

Remember that **ROWGUIDCOL** property can only be added to a column if the column is of **uniqueidentifier** data type.

The syntax for adding and/or dropping the **ROWGUIDCOL** property is as follows:

```
ALTER TABLE <table_name>
      ALTER COLUMN <col1> ADD|DROP ROWGUIDCOL
```

Listing 5.18 shows how a row unique identifier property can be dropped from a table.

Listing 5.18 Dropping a row unique identifier property from a table.

```
ALTER TABLE [example guid] ALTER COLUMN kgid DROP ROWGUIDCOL
```

Adding A Constraint

A **PRIMARY KEY**, **UNIQUE**, **FOREIGN KEY**, **DEFAULT**, or **CHECK** constraint can be added to a table at any time using the **ALTER TABLE** statement. The syntax for adding a constraint is as follows:

```
ALTER TABLE <table_name> [WITH CHECK|WITH NOCHECK]
     ADD [CONSTRAINT <constraint_name>]
           PRIMARY KEY [CLUSTERED|NONCLUSTERED] (<col1>[, <col2>...])
                  [WITH FILLFACTOR = <fillfactor>] [ON <filegroup>|
                  DEFAULT]|
           UNIQUE [CLUSTERED|NONCLUSTERED] (<col1>[, <col2>...])
                  [WITH FILLFACTOR = <fillfactor>] [ON <filegroup>|
                  DEFAULT]|
           FOREIGN KEY [(<col1>[, <col2>...])]
                REFERENCES <ref_table> [(<ref_col1>[, <rec_col2>...])]
                [NOT FOR REPLICATION]|
           DEFAULT <constant_expression> FOR <col_name>|
           CHECK [NOT FOR REPLICATION] (<logical_expression>)
```

The **ALTER TABLE** statement offers two additional options that are not available in the **CREATE TABLE** statement:

- The **WITH CHECK | WITH NOCHECK** option is used with the **FOREIGN KEY** and **CHECK** constraint. If you do not want the existing data in the table to be verified when adding a constraint, specify the **WITH NOCHECK** option. The data that is added or updated after adding the constraint will always be validated. The default option is to validate the data, such as **WITH CHECK**.
- The **FOR <col_name>** option is used when adding a **DEFAULT** constraint to specify the column to which this constraint is associated.

Listing 5.19 shows how to add a **FOREIGN KEY** constraint to a table. Note that the keywords **WITH NOCHECK** are used, meaning that the data in the table will not be validated against the constraint that is added.

Listing 5.19 Adding a **FOREIGN KEY** constraint to an existing table.

```
ALTER TABLE dbo.Orders WITH NOCHECK ADD CONSTRAINT FK_Orders
     FOREIGN KEY (CustomerID) REFERENCES dbo.Customers (CustomerID)
```

Dropping A Constraint

The **ALTER TABLE** statement can also be used to drop a constraint. The syntax for dropping a constraint is as follows:

```
ALTER TABLE <table_name> DROP [CONSTRAINT] <constraint_name>
```

Listing 5.20 shows how to drop a constraint.

Listing 5.20 Dropping a constraint.

```
ALTER TABLE dbo.Orders DROP CONSTRAINT FK_Orders
```

Enabling And Disabling A FOREIGN KEY And CHECK Constraint

If you need to disable the validation of a **FOREIGN KEY** or **CHECK** constraint while inserting or updating data to a table, you can use the **ALTER TABLE** command. In prior versions of Microsoft SQL Server, it was necessary to drop the constraint, insert or update the data, and then re-create the constraint. With SQL Server 7 all you have to do is disable the validation of the constraint before loading or updating data, and then enable the constraint. The syntax for enabling and disabling a **FOREIGN KEY** and **CHECK** constraint is the following:

```
ALTER TABLE <table_name> CHECK|NOCHECK CONSTRAINT
    ALL|<constraint_name1>[, <constraint_name2>, ....]
```

To enable or disable all constraints use the option **ALL**, otherwise specify the name of the constraint. Listing 5.21 shows how all **FOREIGN KEY** and **CHECK** constraints on a table can be disabled.

Listing 5.21 Disabling all **FOREIGN KEY** and **CHECK** constraints on a table.

```
ALTER TABLE Orders NOCHECK CONSTRAINT ALL
```

Enabling And Disabling A Trigger

The last use of the **ALTER TABLE** statement is to enable or disable the firing of a trigger when an **INSERT**, **UPDATE**, or **DELETE** statement is executed against a table. The syntax for this case is as follows:


```
ALTER TABLE <table_name> ENABLE|DISABLE TRIGGER
                ALL|<trigger_name1>[, <trigger_name2>...]
```

To enable or disable all triggers of a table use the option **ALL**, otherwise specify the name of the trigger. Listing 5.22 shows how to disable the firing of all triggers of a table.

Listing 5.22 Disabling the firing of all triggers of a table.

```
ALTER TABLE Employees DISABLE TRIGGER ALL
```

Dropping Tables

When a table is dropped, all data, indexes, triggers, and constraints associated with it are removed from the database. A table that is being referenced by **FOREIGN KEY** constraints cannot be dropped. To drop a table you use the **DROP TABLE** statement. The syntax is as follows:

```
DROP TABLE <table_name>
```

Listing 5.23 shows how to drop a table.

Listing 5.23 Dropping a table.

```
DROP TABLE Orders
```

System Tables

SQL Server 7 stores its information in system tables. Each database has a group of 18 system tables that store database-level system information known as the *database catalog*. A list of the database catalog is provided in Table 5.1.

The *master* database also contains additional system tables that store server-level information known as the *system catalog*. A list of the system catalog is provided in Table 5.2.

Table 5.1 Database catalog tables (in all databases).

Table Name	Brief Description
sysallocations	Has one row for each allocation unit.
syscolumns	Has a row for every column of a table and view and a row for every parameter of a stored procedure.
syscomments	Has the original SQL statements for each database view, rule, trigger, stored procedure, **CHECK** constraint and **DEFAULT** constraint.
sysconstraints	Has the mapping of each constraint with the object that owns it.
sysdepends	Has the dependency information for each database object.
sysfilegroups	Has one row for each filegroup in a database.
sysfiles	Has one row for each file in a database.
sysforeignkeys	Has information of **FOREIGN KEY** constraints.
sysfulltextcatalogs	Has the set of full-text catalogs.
sysindexes	Has a row for each table and index.
sysindexkeys	Has information of the columns of an index
sysmembers	Has a row for each member of a database role.
sysobjects	Has a row for each database object.
syspermissions	Has information about granted and denied permissions.
sysprotects	Has information of permissions applied to security accounts.
sysreferences	Has the mapping of each **FOREIGN KEY** constraint to the referenced columns.
systypes	Has the system and user-defined data types.
sysusers	Has a row for each database user or role.

System tables should not be modified directly with an **INSERT**, **UPDATE** or **DELETE** statement. If any application needs the *metadata* (which is data about data) from the system tables, it should use the system functions, system stored procedures, or system information schema views.

Chapter Summary

In this chapter you learned the following:

- SQL Server 7 has several system data types. You can also create user-defined data types using the **sp_addtype** system stored procedure. To drop a user-defined data type use the **sp_droptype** system stored procedure.

Table 5.2 System catalog tables (only in the master database).

Table Name	Brief Description
sysaltfile	Has a row for each file in a database.
syscacheobjects	Has information of the cache usage.
syscharsets	Has a row for each character set and sort order used.
sysconfigures	Has configuration option settings.
syscurconfigs	Has current configuration option settings.
sysdatabases	Has a row for each database.
sysdevices	Has a row for each backup file and database file.
syslanguages	Has a row for each defined language.
syslockinfo	Has information of lock requests.
syslogins	Has one row for each login account.
sysmessages	Has a row for each possible system error or warning.
sysoledbusers	Has a row for each user mapped to a linked server.
sysperfinfo	Has a row for reach SQL Server 7 performance monitor counter.
sysprocesses	Has a row for each process running in SQL Server 7.
sysremotelogins	Has a row for each remote user allowed to call remote stored procedures.
sysservers	Has a row for each linked server.

5

- SQL Server 7 has two types of tables: *temporary* tables and *permanent* tables.
- When creating a table you have to make important decisions about what columns the table will have, the data type of the columns, the **NULL | NOT NULL** condition of the columns, and whether or not there will be an identity column or row unique identifier column defined.
- You also have to decide what constraints the table will have in order to ensure data integrity, and on which filegroup the table will be stored.
- You create a table with the **CREATE TABLE** statement.
- Constraints can be defined at a column level or at a table level.
- You can alter a table with the **ALTER TABLE** statement. This statement allows you to add and remove columns, change column definitions, add and drop the row unique identifier property (**ROWGUIDCOL**) of a column, add and drop constraints, and enable and disable constraints and triggers.

Review Questions

1. A temporary table is created in the:
   a. *Master* database
   b. Current database
   c. *tempdb* database
   d. *msdb* database

2. Which of the following statements creates a temporary table? (Choose all correct answers.)
   a. **CREATE TABLE #authors (AuthorID int, Name nvarchar(30))**
   b. **CREATE TABLE authors (AuthorID int, Name nvarchar(30))**
   c. **CREATE TABLE [Order Details] (OrderID int, ProductID integer)**
   d. **CREATE TABLE ##[Order Details] (OrderID int, ProductID integer)**

3. The Unicode data types take half the space the non-Unicode data.
   a. True
   b. False

4. The data type unique identifier is used with:
   a. Row global unique identifier column
   b. Identity column
   c. Monetary column
   d. Non-**NULL** columns

5. The user-defined data type **zipcode_dtype** can be dropped with:
   a. **drop datatype zipcode_dtype**
   b. **sp_droptype zipcode_dtype**
   c. **sp_drop_datatype zipcode_dtype**
   d. **sp_delete_datatype zipcode_dtype**

6. A null value is the same as an empty string.
   a. True
   b. False

7. According to the following example, what will the next value of the *OrderID* column be?

```
CREATE TABLE Order (OrderID integer IDENTITY(1,3), CustomerID int,
                              OrderDate datetime)
GO
INSERT INTO Order (CustomerID, OrderDate) VALUES ( 123, getdate() )
INSERT INTO Order (CustomerID, OrderDate) VALUES ( 234, getdate() )
GO
```

   a. 7
   b. 6
   c. 3
   d. 9

8. A unique value in a row global unique identifier is guaranteed:
   a. Because SQL Server 7 auto-generates a value each time a row is inserted into the table.
   b. Using triggers and stored procedures
   c. Using the **NEWID()** system function
   d. None of the above.

9. Which of the following commands correctly define a row global unique identifier column?
   a. **CREATE TABLE table2 (id uniqueidentifier rowguidcol not null, ...)**
   b. **CREATE TABLE table2 (id integer rowguidcol not null, .)**
   c. **CREATE TABLE table2 (id uniqueidentifier not null, ...)**
   d. **CREATE TABLE table2 (id float rowguidcol not null, ...)**

10. A default definition can be created:
    a. When creating a table
    b. When altering a table
    c. a and b.
    d. None of the above.

11. A check constraint is used to enforce:
    a. Domain integrity
    b. Referential integrity
    c. Entity integrity
    d. Database integrity

12. If a table was created with the following command:

```
        CREATE TABLE Customer (
                CustomerID int identity not null,
                CustomerName nvarchar(100),
                Address nvarchar(50),
City nvarchar(5),
State nvarchar(2),
                CONSTRAINT chk_Customer CHECK (State in
('FL', 'CA', 'NY'))
                        NOT FOR REPLICATION
)
GO
```

Which of the following is true? (Choose all correct answers.)

   a. Only customers from Florida, California, or New York can be inserted.
   b. Customers from all states can be inserted.
   c. Customers from Florida, California, and New York cannot be replicated to another table.
   d. During a replication process the constraint is not validated.

13. Which of the following is not true about a **PRIMARY KEY** constraint? (Choose all correct answers.)

   a. There can be more than one **PRIMARY KEY** constraint per table.
   b. A column that allow **NULL** values can be part of a **PRIMARY KEY** constraint.
   c. When a **PRIMARY KEY** constraint is defined SQL Server 7 automatically generates a unique index.
   d. A **PRIMARY KEY** constraint has to be clustered.

14. According to the following **CREATE** statement, where will the unique index be saved?:

```
CREATE TABLE Orders (
        OrderID int IDENTITY (1, 1) NOT NULL PRIMARY KEY CLUSTERED,
        OrderDate datetime NULL ,
        RequiredDate datetime NULL ,
        ShippedDate datetime NULL
)
GO
```

a. On the *tempdb* filegroup
b. On the same *filegroup* as the table
c. On the *filegroup* that is reserved only for indexes
d. On the log *filegroup*

15. The keyword **REFERENCES** is used when defining a:
    a. **CHECK** constraint
    b. **PRIMARY KEY** constraint
    c. **UNIQUE** constraint
    d. **FOREIGN KEY** constraint

5

16. If the following **ALTER TABLE** command is issued, what will it cause?

```
ALTER TABLE Sales DISABLE TRIGGER ALL
```

    a. Delete triggers will not fire when rows are deleted.
    b. Insert triggers will not fire when rows are inserted.
    c. Update triggers will not fire when rows are updated.
    d. All of the above.

17. If the following check constraint is defined on a column, which of the following values will it accept? (Choose all correct answers.)

```
CHECK ( id LIKE '[0-9] [0-9] [0-9] [0-9] [0-9] [0-9] [0-9]' )
```

    a. '5487921'
    b. '456-884'
    c. '9095846'
    d. '84A8795'

HANDS-ON PROJECTS

These activities assume that you are already connected to the *Northwind* database using the Query Analyzer.

Susan experienced a little trouble with the table layouts during her design of the database. There were places that would allow for data corruption and in some instances the design didn't work at all. She leaned back in her chair and said, "I'll have to call a meeting about this." She opened her email and began, "To: Design Team…"

Project 5.1

In this activity you will create two tables. One of the tables will have an identity column. You will also define some constraints while creating the tables.

1. Create the *Benefits* table. It has an *id* column and a *description* column. You need to ensure that the *id* column is unique.

To ensure the uniqueness of the *id* column you define it as an *identity* column and you create a **PRIMARY KEY** constraint on it.

In the Query Analyzer tool, type the following command and execute it:

```
CREATE TABLE Benefits (
     BenefitID integer identity not null PRIMARY KEY CLUSTERED,
     BenefitDescription nvarchar(300) not null )
GO
```

2. Create the *Employee Benefits* table. This table contains all the benefits per employee. It also has the date the benefit started and the date it ended if applicable.

To ensure the uniqueness of the rows in the table you define a **PRIMARY KEY** constraint on the *EmployeeID* and *BenefitID* columns.

In order to enforce referential integrity, you also need to define a **FOREIGN KEY** constraint that references the *EmployeeID* column of the *Employees* table, and a **FOREIGN KEY** constraint that references the *BenefitID* column of the *Benefits* table.

In the Query Analyzer tool, type the following command and execute it.

```
CREATE TABLE [Employee Benefits] (
     EmployeeID int not null
          FOREIGN KEY REFERENCES Employees (EmployeeID),
     BenefitID  int not null REFERENCES Benefits (BenefitID),
     StartDate datetime not null DEFAULT getdate(),
     EndDate datetime null,
     PRIMARY KEY (EmployeeID, BenefitID)
)
GO
```

After studying the design of her tables, Susan found that the data types in the tables were not optimized for storage or in some cases, speed. She used an **ALTER TABLE** statement to make the changes. She changed a date field that had originally been defined as **char**.

Two of the tables had no primary key fields, so she added a column with the **identity** type. She then noticed one table in the database that could be used in a data warehousing application later, so she planned ahead and assigned its primary key as a row global unique identifier.

5

Project 5.2

In this activity you add a column and a **CHECK** constraint to a table.

1. You need to add a column to the *Employees* table of the *Northwind* database that will contain the email address for each employee. The data type of the column will be the user-defined data type that was created in the steps above.

In the Query Analyzer window type the following command and execute it:

```
ALTER TABLE Employees ADD EmailAddress email_dtype
GO
```

2. You need to add a **CHECK** constraint to the *Employee Benefits* table to make sure that the *EndDate* can never be smaller than the *StartDate*.

In the Query Analyzer window type the following command and execute it:

```
ALTER TABLE [Employee Benefits]
     ADD CONSTRAINT Chk_StartDate CHECK (EndDate >= StartDate)
GO
```

She also noticed that as records were added into the *customer_order* table, the *shipping_method* column wasn't always filled out. She set a default on the column to the value "**ground**". Susan felt that this would be a safe value, since it was the slowest and least expensive option that a customer would pick, the **bottom** value. She also defined a rule on the *shipping_method* column that restricted the entries to known countries.

CHAPTER SIX

INDEXES

After Reading This Chapter And Completing The Exercises, You Will Be Able To:

- Describe and create single-column and composite (multicolumn) indexes
- Describe index intersection and covered indexes
- Describe and create clustered indexes
- Describe and create nonclustered indexes
- Describe and create unique and nonunique indexes
- Determine the appropriate fill factor for an index
- Rebuild indexes
- Tune indexes
- Update the distribution statistic of an index

Indexes are one of the banes and boons of the administrator's job. Indexes can make or break the performance of a database, and knowing how to wield them properly is very important. It is very important to manage your indexes on a continuing basis. It only makes sense that Microsoft gives this subject a great deal of weight. After all, one of the key measures of a database's speed is how quickly it can retrieve data. Indexes are one of the main factors in how this happens.

Index Basics

A database is of little help if you cannot access the data quickly. An *index* is a database object that makes it possible to find data in a table quickly by means of minimizing the input and output operations when executing queries. An index points the server to the proper location of the data quickly.

Indexes are an important part of any SQL Server database; they have several advantages. The primary one is to increase the speed of data access. Indexes are also used to enforce **PRIMARY KEY** and **UNIQUE** constraints (see Chapter 5).

SQL Server 7 uses a *balanced tree* structure (called a *B-Tree* structure) to save information in an index. A B-Tree index structure has several levels of index pages; the number of levels depends on the size of the table and the number of columns used to define the index. The uppermost page of the B-Tree index structure is called the *root page*. A pointer to the root page is found in the *sysindexes* table. The bottommost pages of the index structure are called *leaf pages*. The pages in-between the root and leaf pages are known as *nonleaf pages*.

Indexes increase the speed of search operations; however, you'll need to be careful when creating an index, because defining too many indexes can affect the performance of **INSERT**, **UPDATE**, and **DELETE** operations. Not only does the data in the table get modified, but the data in the index pages is also maintained dynamically by SQL Server. This can cause the **INSERT**, **UPDATE**, or **DELETE** operation to take longer than expected by adding extra steps.

Each index has a *distribution statistics* page related to it. These statistics help the optimizer estimate the number of rows that will match a typical index key. They also tell the optimizer the approximate shape of the index distribution. Keeping the distribution statistics up to date is very important so the query optimizer can make intelligent decisions about querying a table. These statistics can be updated automatically by SQL Server 7, or you can do it manually using the **UPDATE STATISTICS** command.

When creating an index keep in mind that:

- If a table is very small (usually fits on one page allocation unit), you don't need to create an index, because it will not be used.
- Only the owner of the table is allowed to create an index in that table.
- The maximum number of columns that can participate in an index is 16.
- The maximum number of indexes allowed on a table is 250 (one clustered index and 249 nonclustered indexes).
- The maximum length of all the columns defined on an index is 900 bytes long.

- Columns that contain only a few unique values (two to four) are not good candidates for an index. Most probably, a table scan will be performed even if an index is defined. An index can be any of the following:
  - Single-column or multicolumn (composite)
  - Clustered or nonclustered
  - Unique or nonunique

6

Single-Column Index And Composite (Multicolumn) Index

An index created on one column is known as a *single-column index*. Indexes created on more than one column are known as *multicolumn indexes* or *composite indexes*. Though SQL Server 7 allows multicolumn indexes, it is a good practice to keep indexes as compact as possible (both in number of columns defining the index and in size of the columns). Indexes of fewer columns and on narrower columns take less disk space and require less maintenance overhead because more entries can be saved on one index page.

When creating a composite index, specify the more selective column first. The distribution statistics of an index only keeps samples (steps) for the first column of a composite index (see "Statistics" later in this chapter).

Index Intersection And Covered Indexes

In SQL Server version 7, Microsoft introduced the possibility of using more than one index per table to solve a query. This is called *index intersection*. SQL Server 7 selects small subsets of data returned from using each index, and then intersects all returned subsets. The final result will be those rows that meet the criteria of all used indexes.

SQL Server 7 also supports *covering* indexes. A *covered index* is created when all columns of a query are part of the index. In this situation, it is not necessary to retrieve data from the data pages; all the information needed is on the index pages. This technique dramatically reduces I/O operations.

For example, if your query statement is as follows:

```
SELECT col1, col2, col3
FROM table1
WHERE col1 = 10 AND col2 < 100
```

If your index is defined on *col1*, *col2*, and *col3*, then all information will be retrieved directly from the index pages. SQL Server 7 also combines the usage of index intersection and covered indexes. If one index does not cover the query but two or more indexes will, SQL Server will consider joining the indexes.

Clustered Index

A *clustered* index determines in which physical order the data is saved in the table. This is the reason why a table can have only one clustered index. A clustered index can be unique or nonunique, and it can be defined on one column or on multiple columns. To define a clustered index, specify the **CLUSTERED** clause when creating the index.

As we mentioned earlier, the structure of every index consists of a root page, nonleaf pages and leaf pages. In the case of a clustered index, the leaf pages are the actual data pages sorted by the column(s) used when the index was created. Figure 6.1 illustrates the B-Tree structure of a clustered index.

It is very important to correctly select the column(s) that will be part of the clustered index. Clustered indexes perform very well on:

- Column(s) often searched by ranges of values (such as queries that use the **BETWEEN**, >, <, >=, and <= operators on the **WHERE** clause). Because the data is physically stored in a sorted order of the index, SQL Server 7 uses the clustered index to find the first value and then scans the data pages until the last value is found.

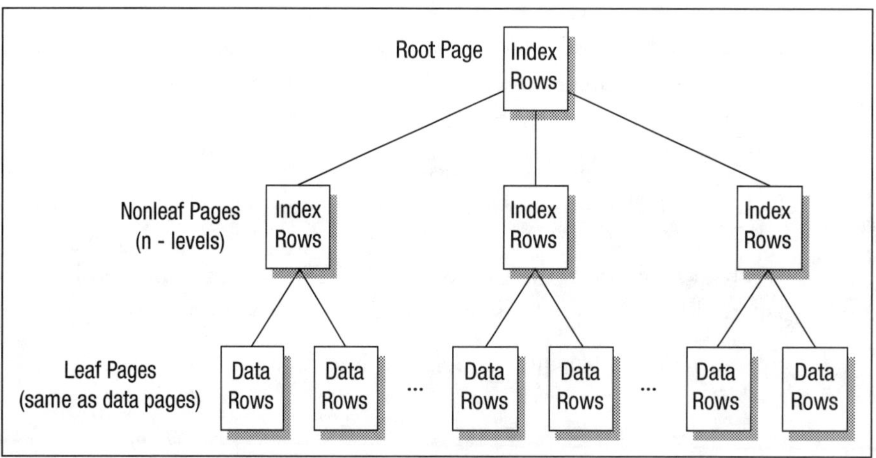

Figure 6.1 B-Tree structure of a clustered index.

- Column(s) by which the query result set is sorted (such as, column(s) participating in the **ORDER BY** clause of a query). In this case, SQL Server 7 does not need to create a worktable to perform the sort.
- Column(s) that participate in a **GROUP BY** clause of a query.
- Column(s) that uniquely define the rows in a table, if no other index will be defined on the table, or if it is an OLTP system requiring immediate access.
- Column(s) that do not get updated often.
- Column(s) that have a small numbers of different values (for example a column with ZIP codes). If the column has very few different values, for example male or female, you should not define an index at all.
- Queries that return a large number of rows.
- Column(s) that form a foreign key because they are generally nonunique.
- Column(s) of **integer** data type.

Be aware that:

- A clustered index should not be defined on a column that increments its value sequentially (like an *identity* column). This will cause a *hot spot* on disk, because all inserts will be done on the last data page.
- If a column that is part of a clustered index is updated, the whole row will have to be moved in order to maintain the rows in physical order, thus causing extra disk I/O.
- When creating a clustered index, consider available space. Creating a clustered index requires 120 percent of the size of the table to be available in the database.

Tables without a clustered index, known as *heap tables,* store data in no particular order.

Nonclustered Index

A nonclustered index can be unique or nonunique and can be defined on one column or on multiple columns. To define a nonclustered index, specify the **NONCLUSTERED** clause when creating the index. (The **NONCLUSTERED** clause is the default. Not specifying it has the same effect as specifying it). The structure of a nonclustered index is very similar to a clustered index. Figure 6.2 illustrates the B-Tree structure of a nonclustered index.

A nonclustered index differentiates itself from a clustered index in that:

- The data in the table is not stored in the order of the nonclustered index.

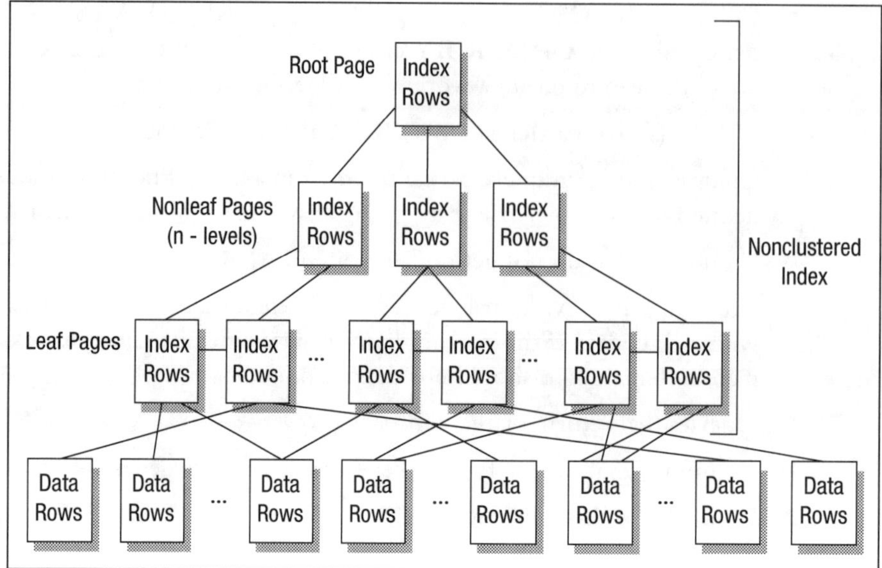

Figure 6.2 B-Tree structure of a nonclustered index.

- The leaf pages of a nonclustered index do not hold the data of the table. The leaf pages of the nonclustered index contain index rows that point to the data pages of the table. These pointers are known as *row locators*.

If a table does not have a clustered index and one is created, all the nonclustered indexes are re-created automatically to use clustered keys as the row locators.

If a clustered index of a table is dropped, all the nonclustered indexes are automatically re-created to use the row identifiers as row locators. A nonclustered index can be created on a table that has a clustered index or on a heap table. A table can have 249 nonclustered indexes.

Nonclustered indexes perform very well on:

- Columns that are very selective, that is columns that contain large sets of different values (for example, columns that contain unique values).
- Columns often used on **WHERE** clauses. This is preferable if the columns limit the amount of returned rows to a small set.
- Covered queries. A covered query occurs when all the columns that participate in the **WHERE** clause are part of an index or indexes. If your table is not frequently updated, consider defining a nonclustered index for each column frequently used in your queries. This allows SQL Server to use the covering index technique explained previously.
- Queries returning a small set of rows.

Row Indicators

A row locator can be the clustered key (if the table has a clustered index) or a row identifier (if the table is a heap table). The row identifier consists of the file number, the page number, and the row location of the data row in the data page.

UNIQUE INDEX

A *unique index* is an index that does not allow duplicate values on the columns participating on the index. To define a unique index, specify the **UNIQUE** clause when creating the index. Remember that when a **PRIMARY KEY** or **UNIQUE** constraint is defined, SQL Server 7 automatically creates a unique index on the columns that enforce the constraint. Both clustered and nonclustered indexes can be defined as unique indexes.

6

SQL Server 7 checks for the existence of duplicate values when:

- Creating a unique index. If duplicate values exist, an error is returned and the index is not created.

A unique index can be created on a column that allows **NULL** values. However if the column has a **NULL** value in more than one row, a unique index is not allowed. The same applies for creating a unique index on multiple columns.

- A unique index has been created and an **UPDATE** statement is performed. If one or more rows of the **UPDATE** statement will cause duplicate values to exist, the whole transaction is rolled back and an error message is returned.
- A unique index exists on a table and an **INSERT** statement is performed. The clause that was used to define the unique index determines the behavior of SQL Server 7 when one or more duplicate rows are encountered.

If the unique index was created *without* the **IGNORE_DUP_KEY** clause, the whole transaction is rolled back and an error message is returned.

If the unique index was created *with* the **IGNORE_DUP_KEY** clause, the rows without duplicate values will be inserted. The rows that have duplicate values will not be inserted and a warning message is displayed.

For example, imagine that you have two tables (*TableA* and *TableB*) with the exact same structure and that *TableA* has a unique index defined. *TableB* has ten rows, seven of which already exist in *TableA*. If the unique key was created without the **IGNORE_DUP_KEY** clause, and the following statement is executed:

```
INSERT INTO TableA SELECT * FROM TableB
```

This returns an error stating that duplicate keys cannot be inserted and no rows will be inserted. On the other hand, if the unique key was created with the **IGNORE_DUP_KEY** clause, the statement would insert the three rows that do not exist in *TableA* and return a warning stating that duplicate keys were ignored.

Fill Factors

The *fill factor* option controls how full (by percentage) the index leaf pages will be when an index is created. Remember; in the case of a clustered index, the index leaf pages are the same as the data pages; in the case of a nonclustered index, the index leaf pages point to the data pages. When a row is inserted into a full index page, SQL Server 7 performs a *page split*. A page split consists of moving approximately half of the rows of the full page to a new page (generally in another place of the hard drive) in order to make room for the inserted row. Page splits are a very costly operation because of the extra I/O involved. Also, any future read operations to the table suffer because of the data not being in sequential pages.

The fill factor percentage is an advanced server-wide configuration option that can be changed using the **sp_configure** system stored procedure. The new percentage specified will only take effect on new indexes created after stopping and restarting SQL Server 7:

```
sp_configure 'fill factor (%)', <percent>
```

The fill factor server-wide setting can be overwritten for each index when it is created using the **FILLFACTOR** clause of the **CREATE INDEX** command, or when the index is rebuilt using the fill factor parameter of the **DBCC DBREINDEX**.

The *fill factor percentage* is saved in the *sysindexes* table and is applied only when an index is created or when it is rebuilt. The fill factor percentage is not maintained when rows are added, updated, or deleted.

Valid values for the fill factor are as follows:

- **0 (Default value)** A fill factor of 0 means that the index leaf pages will be 100 percent full and that space for at least one row will be left in the nonleaf index pages.
- **1–99** A fill factor between 1 and 99 means that the index leaf pages will be *X* percent full (1–99 percent). It leaves space free in the nonleaf pages for at least one more entry.

- **100** A fill factor of 100 means that the index leaf pages will be 100 percent full and that no space will be left in the nonleaf index pages.

Listing 6.1 shows how the fill factor server-wide configuration can be changed to have the leaf index pages 75 percent full after an index has been created. Notice that for the new setting to take effect, the **reconfigure with override** statement has to be issued and that SQL Server will have to be stopped and restarted.

Listing 6.1 Changing the fill factor server-wide configuration.

```
sp_configure 'fill factor (%)', 75
GO
reconfigure with override
GO
```


Usually the default fill factor value (0 percent) performs well; however, in some cases you might find it beneficial to change the default value. A fill factor of 100 percent should only be used on read-only tables where insert operations will not be performed. A fill factor of 100 percent will reduce the physical size of the index, because all pages (leaf and nonleaf) will be completely full. Remember, if a row is inserted, a page split will occur.

A fill factor between 1 and 99 percent should be used when you know that the table will have inserts and updates. A smaller fill factor will leave more free space on the leaf pages, causing less page splitting to occur. A very low fill factor should be used only on those tables where a lot of rows will be inserted. Keep in mind that smaller fill factors cause less page splitting and also cause an index to take more physical space.

The **SQL Server: Access Methods—Page Splits** counter from Performance Monitor can help you fine-tune the fill factor. If this counter is greater than 0, check how fragmented the table is (how much page splitting has occurred) by using the **DBCC SHOWCONTIG** command. A large amount of page splitting in a short period of time might be an indication that you need to decrease the fill factor for the indexes on the table. The syntax for the **DBCC SHOWCONTIG** is as follows:

```
DBCC SHOWCONTIG ( <table_id>[, <index_id>] )
```

The following is an example of the output of a **DBCC SHOWCONTIG** command run against the *Order Details* table of the *Northwind* database:

```
DBCC SHOWCONTIG scanning 'Order Details' table...
Table: 'Order Details' (661577395); index ID: 1,
database ID: 6
```

```
TABLE level scan performed.
- Pages Scanned.............................: 9
- Extents Scanned...........................: 6
- Extent Switches...........................: 5
- Avg. Pages per Extent.....................: 1.5
- Scan Density [Best Count:Actual Count]..: 33.33% [2:6]
- Logical Scan Fragmentation ..............: 0.00%
- Extent Scan Fragmentation ...............: 33.33%
- Avg. Bytes Free per Page.................: 671.2
- Avg. Page Density (full).................: 91.71%
DBCC execution completed. If DBCC printed error messages,
contact your system administrator.
```

The most important indicator of the **DBCC SHOWCONTIG** command is *scan density*. A low value for the scan density indicator means that the index leaf pages have a lot of free space. This might be an indicator that page splitting has occurred. In this case, it might be appropriate to rebuild your index.

When tuning fill factors, keep in mind that database reads usually outnumber database writes. Smaller fill factors tend to slow database reads because more pages have to be read (more I/O operations are performed).

PAD_INDEX

As we mentioned earlier, a fill factor primarily affects the index leaf pages. To apply the fill factor percentage to the nonleaf pages, you have to specify the **PAD_INDEX** clause when you create the index. Because **PAD_INDEX** uses the fill factor percentage, it can only be used in conjunction with the **FILLFACTOR** clause.

No matter how small the fill factor specified, the number of rows in a nonleaf index page is never less than two.

Creating An Index

You can create an index using the **CREATE INDEX** command or using the Create Index Wizard. You can't create an index while the database or transaction log is being backed up. Remember that only the table owner (the person who created the table) is allowed to create an index on a table and that when a **PRIMARY KEY** or **UNIQUE** constraint is defined, SQL Server 7 automatically creates a unique index.

CREATE INDEX Command

The syntax for the **CREATE INDEX** command is as follows:

```
CREATE [UNIQUE] [CLUSTERED|NONCLUSTERED] INDEX <index_name>
    ON <table> (<col1>[, <col2>[,...]])
    [WITH  [PAD_INDEX]
                  [[,] FILLFACTOR = <fill_factor_%]]
                  [[,] IGNORE_DUP_KEY]
                  [[,] DROP_EXISTING]
                  [[,] STATISTICS_NORECOMPUTE]
     ]
     [ON <filegroup>]
```


When creating an index the default is nonunique. To create a unique index you must specify the **UNIQUE** clause.

By default, a nonclustered index is created (same as specifying the **NON-CLUSTERED** clause). To create a clustered index you must specify the **CLUSTERED** clause.

An index name must be unique within a table, but not within a database. The first character of an index name has to be a letter as defined in the Unicode Standard 2 or one of the following symbols: _, @, #. If the index name has embedded spaces, you must delimit it with brackets, such as **[index name]**. An index name cannot be a Transact-SQL reserved word.

<col1>[, <col2>[,....]] are the column(s) to which the index applies. To create a composite index, specify the name of the columns in the order of the sort priority of the index. The limit of columns participating in a multicolumn index is 16, and the sum of their lengths cannot be greater then 900 bytes. Computed columns and columns of data type ntext, text, image, or bit cannot be part of an index.

As described earlier, the **PAD_INDEX** and **FILLFFACTOR** options are used to specify what percent of the nonleaf and leaf index pages will be filled when the index is created.

The **IGNORE_DUP_KEY** clause is used only when creating a unique index and controls what will happen if a duplicate key value is inserted (refer to the **UNIQUE** index paragraph).

The **DROP_EXISTING** clause is used to rebuild the specified index. If a **CREATE INDEX** command is executed with an index name that already exists and the **DROP_EXISTING** clause is not specified, an error will be returned. To enhance performance when rebuilding a clustered index on a table that also has nonclustered indexes, use the **DROP_EXISTING** clause instead of the **DROP INDEX** command followed by the **CREATE INDEX** command.

Let's suppose that you need to rebuild the clustered index on a table that also has nonclustered indexes. This is what happens if you drop the clustered index with the **DROP INDEX** command and then create it with the **CREATE INDEX** command:

- When the clustered index is dropped, all nonclustered indexes will be rebuilt automatically to change the row locators to use row identifiers instead of clustered keys.
- When the clustered index is created, all nonclustered indexes will be rebuilt automatically to change the row locators to use clustered keys instead of row indicators.

As you can see, the nonclustered indexes are rebuilt twice. You can avoid this if the **CREATE INDEX** command with the **DROP_EXISTING** clause.

In order to determine which index or indexes are appropriate to use during query processing, SQL Server 7 keeps statistics about the distribution of the key values of each index; this is known as the *distribution statistics*.

To disable the automatic recompilation of the statistics for an index, use the **STATISTICS_NORECOMPUTE** clause when creating the index (see "Statistics" later in the chapter). Use this clause with extreme caution. Outdated distribution statistics could result in SQL Server 7 not picking the optimal execution plan.

The **ON <filegroup>** clause is used to specify on which filegroup the index will be created. If the **ON** option is not specified, the index will be created in the same filegroup as the table (filegroups will be discussed in Chapter 12).

Listing 6.2 shows how to create a clustered index on the *Territories* table of the *Northwind* database. In this example, we are overriding the sever-wide fill factor. After the index has been created, the leaf and nonleaf index pages will be 50 percent full (**FILLFACTOR** and **PAD_INDEX** clauses). Notice how the message received (*Index (ID=2) is being rebuilt*). This means that the nonclustered index that already existed on the table was rebuilt to use the clustered keys as row locators.

Listing 6.2 Creating a clustered index.

```
CREATE CLUSTERED INDEX TerrDesc_CIDX
ON Territories ( TerritoryDescription )
WITH FILLFACTOR = 50, PAD_INDEX
GO
Index (ID = 2) is being rebuilt.
```

Listing 6.3 shows how to create a nonclustered index. Notice how the **NON-CLUSTERED** clause is not specified because it is the default. The index created will not have its distribution statistics automatically updated by SQL Server 7 because it was created with the **STATISTICS_NORECOMPUTE** clause.

Listing 6.3 Creating a nonclustered index.

```
CREATE INDEX ShipName_IDX
ON Orders ( ShipName ) WITH STATISTICS_NORECOMPUTE
GO
The command(s) completed successfully.
```


Listing 6.4 shows how to create a unique clustered index. Notice how the nonclustered index was automatically rebuilt to use the clustered keys as the row indicators **(Index (ID=2) is being rebuilt)**.

Listing 6.4 Creating a unique clustered index.

```
CREATE UNIQUE CLUSTERED INDEX Region_CIDX
ON Region ( RegionDescription )
GO
Index (ID = 2) is being rebuilt.
```

Listing 6.5 shows how to re-create a clustered index using the **CREATE INDEX** command with the **DROP_EXISTING** clause.

Listing 6.5 Re-creating a clustered index.

```
CREATE CLUSTERED INDEX TerrDesc_CIDX
ON Territories ( TerritoryDescription )
WITH DROP_EXISTING
GO
The command(s) completed successfully.
```

Create Index Wizard

You can also create an index using the Create Index Wizard. The Create Index Wizard consists of six screens that take you through the process step by step. You advance from screen to screen by clicking on the Next button. To go back to the prior screen, click on the Back button. The screens are as follows:

- The first screen is the Welcome To The Create Index Wizard screen. This screen explains what can be done with the wizard.
- The second screen is the Select Database And Table screen. In this screen, you select on which table the index will be created and you specify in which database it is saved. The wizard does not allow you to select any table belonging to a system database (*master*, *model*, *msdb*, *tempdb*).

- The third screen is the Current Index Information screen. This screen shows infor-mation of the existing indexes of the table. The information shown is: name, clustered or nonclustered, and columns participating in the index (see Figure 6.3).
- The fourth screen is the Select Columns screen. In this screen you select the column or columns that will participate in the index (see Figure 6.4).
- The fifth screen is the Specify Index Options screen. In this screen you specify if the index is clustered (if a clustered index doesn't already exist on the table), if it is a unique index, and you select the fill factor (see Figure 6.5).

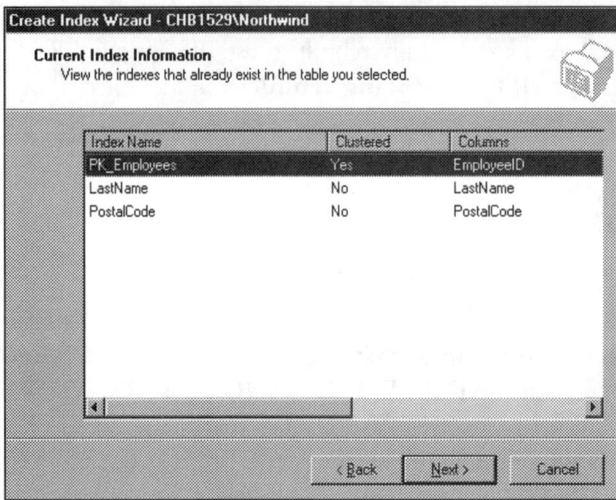

Figure 6.3 Current Index Information screen from the Create Index Wizard.

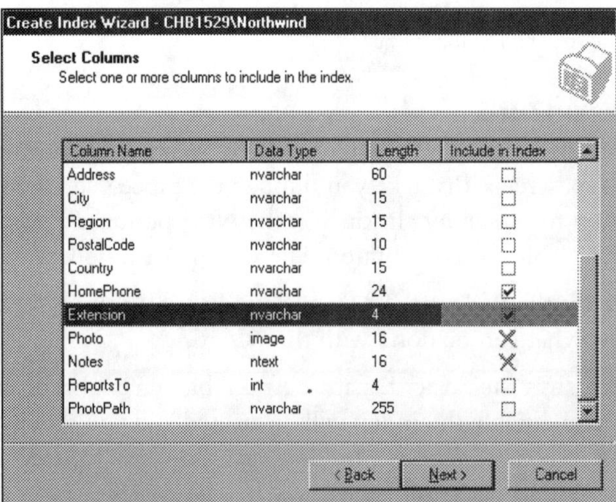

Figure 6.4 Select Column screen from the Create Index Wizard.

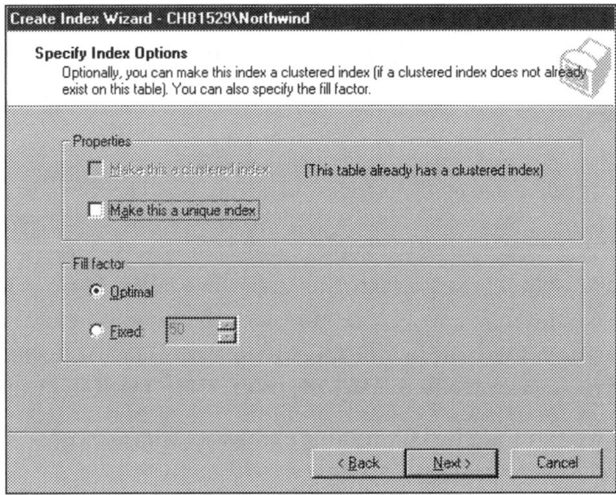

Figure 6.5 Specify Index Options screen from the Create Index Wizard.

➤ The sixth and final screen is the Completing The Create Index Wizard screen. In this screen you can name the index (if you do not like the name generated by the wizard), and you organize the columns by the sort priority of the index (see Figure 6.6). Click on the Finish button to create the index.

DBCC DBREINDEX

The **DBCC DBREINDEX** command is very useful when rebuilding an index or all indexes of a user table without knowing the table's structure. The indexes created by SQL Server to enforce **PRIMARY KEY** and **UNIQUE** constraints

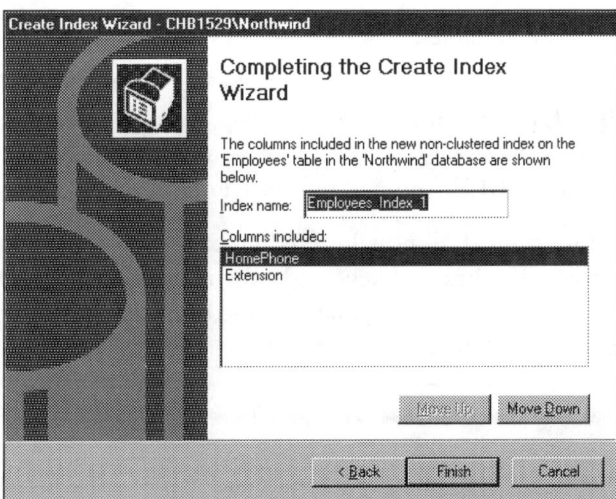

Figure 6.6 Completing The Create Index Wizard screen from the Create Index Wizard.

can also be rebuilt, eliminating the need to drop and re-create the constraints (see Chapter 5). The **DBCC DBREINDEX** command is much more efficient than dropping and re-creating all indexes using **DROP INDEX** and **CREATE INDEX**:

```
DBCC DBREINDEX ( <table_name> [, <index_name> [,<fillfactor>]]) [WITH
NO_INFOMSGS]
```

To rebuild an index with a new fill factor, specify the **<fillfactor>** parameter. If a 0 fill factor is used, the index will be rebuilt with the same fill factor as it was created. A 0 fill factor is the same as not specifying any fill factor. To suppress all the informational messages, specify the **WITH NO_INFOMSGS** clause.

Listing 6.6 demonstrates how to rebuild the *OrdersOrder_Details* index of the *Order Details* table.

Listing 6.6 Rebuilding an index.

```
DBCC DBREINDEX ( [Order Details],
'OrdersOrder_Details' )
GO
Index (ID = 3) is being rebuilt.
DBCC execution completed. If DBCC printed error messages, contact your
system administrator.
```

Dropping An Index

When an index is dropped, all the space occupied by the index is recovered for future use by other database objects. The **DROP INDEX** cannot be used to:

- Drop indexes on system tables.
- Drop an index automatically created by SQL Server 7 when a **PRIMARY KEY** or **UNIQUE** constraint is created. To drop an index created to enforce a **PRIMARY KEY** or **UNIQUE** constraint, you have to drop the constraint using the **ALTER TABLE** command (see Chapter 5).

If a clustered index is dropped, all nonclustered indexes will be automatically rebuilt and will replace the clustered keys with row identifiers. To drop an index you have to specify the index name and table name on which the index was created. The syntax of the **DROP INDEX** command is:

```
DROP INDEX <table_name>.<index_name>[, ....]
```

Listing 6.7 shows how to drop an index. Notice that because the index being dropped is a clustered index, the nonclustered index that exists on the table is rebuilt.

Listing 6.7 Dropping an index.

```
DROP INDEX Territories.TerrDesc_CIDX
GO
The clustered index has been dropped.
Index (ID = 2) is being rebuilt.
```

VIEWING AN INDEX

Once an index has been created on a table, you can view what type of index it is, which columns are part of the index, and the order of columns in the index.

6

You can view the information of the indexes created on a table with the help of the system stored procedure **sp_helpindex**. The syntax of the **sp_helpindex** stored procedure is:

```
sp_helpindex [@objname = ] '<table_name>'
```

The **sp_helpindex** stored procedure returns:

- All the indexes defined on a table
- The type of each index (clustered, nonclustered, unique)
- Whether the index was created because a **PRIMARY KEY** constraint was defined
- Whether the index was created with the **STATISTICS_NORECOMPUTE** clause
- The filegroup where the index is saved
- The column(s) that the index contains

Listing 6.8 shows the output of the **sp_helpindex** stored procedure run in the *Northwind* database against the *Orders* table.

Listing 6.8 Running **sp_helpindex**.

```
sp_helpindex Orders
GO
index_name       index_description                      index_keys
--------------   -----------------------------------    -------------
PK_Orders        clustered, unique, primary key located  OrderID
                 on PRIMARY
CustomerID       nonclustered located on PRIMARY         CustomerID
CustomersOrders  nonclustered located on PRIMARY         CustomerID
EmployeeID       nonclustered located on PRIMARY         EmployeeID
EmployeesOrders  nonclustered located on PRIMARY         EmployeeID
```

```
OrderDate        nonclustered located on PRIMARY        OrderDate
ShippedDate      nonclustered located on PRIMARY        ShippedDate
ShippersOrders   nonclustered located on PRIMARY        ShipVia
ShipPostalCode   nonclustered, stats no recompute       ShipPostalCode
                 located on PRIMARY
```

From the output you can see that the **PK_Orders** index is clustered and unique, and the *ShipPostalCode* index was created with the **STATISTICS_NORECOMPUTE** clause.

You can also view the indexes that a table has with the **sp_help** system stored procedure. This procedure shows the same information that **sp_helpindex** does, plus all the columns that a table contains. The syntax for the **sp_help stored** procedure is:

```
sp_help [[@objname = ] <table_name>]
```

SQL Server 7 introduces a new Transact-SQL function that allows you to find out the property value of an index. The Transact-SQL function is called **INDEXPROPERTY**, and the syntax is as follows:

```
INDEXPROPERTY( <table_ID>, <index_name>, <property> )
```

Note that you must specify the identification number of the table **(<table_ID>)** that contains the index. To find an object identification number, use the **object_id(<object_name>)** function.

<index_name> is the name of the index for which you want the property information, and **<property>** is the database property to return. For a list of all properties, see Table 6.1.

Listing 6.9 shows the output of the **INDEXPROPERTY** function. In this case we are interested in knowing the number of leaf levels that the *CustomerID* index of the *Orders* table of the *Northwind* database has.

Listing 6.9 The **INDEXPROPERTY** function.

```
SELECT INDEXPROPERTY( object_id('Orders'),
'CustomerID', 'IndexDepth')
GO
-----
2
```

Table 6.1 List of properties and their return value.

Property	Property Description	Return Values
IndexDepth	The number of levels in an index.	>1
IsAutoStatistics	Was the index created by the **auto create statistics** option of **sp_dboption**?	1 = True; 0 = False; **NULL** = Invalid input
IsClustered	Is the index clustered?	1 = True; 0 = False; **NULL** = Invalid input
IsStatistics	Was the index created by the **CREATE STATISTICS** statement or by the **auto create statistics** option of **sp_dboption**?	1 = True; 0 = False; **NULL** = Invalid input
IsUnique	Is the index unique?	1 = True; 0 = False; **NULL** = Invalid input
IndexFillFactor	Fill factor with which the index was created. Fill factor percent.	0 to 10
IsPadIndex	Fill factor applied to the nonleaf index pages.	1 = True; 0 = False; **NULL** = Invalid input
IsFulltextKey	Is the index the full-text key for a table?	1 = True; 0 = False; **NULL** = Invalid input
IsHypothetical	Is the index a hypothetical index and cannot be used directly as a data access path?	1 = True; 0 = False; **NULL** = Invalid input

6

STATISTICS

SQL Server 7 keeps statistics about the distribution of values in an index and about the selectivity of those key values. These statistics are called *distribution statistics*; they do not have to fit on one page. The statistics are stored as a long string of bits across multiple pages.

The *selectivity* property of an index describes how many rows can be identified by a certain key value. If the selectivity of an index is very low, SQL Server 7 might never use the index in a query. The query optimizer might determine that it is more effective to use another index or scan the table. Examples of highly selective indexes are unique indexes. The selectivity of an index is based on the number of rows that will be returned (number of rows that meet the value). Normally if the index returns more than 25 percent of the rows, then it is considered *low selective* and will not be used. For example, if in a 1,000-row table there is a column with three values: A (333 rows), B (333 rows), and C (334 rows), and you create an index on it, the optimizer will never use the index.

Some texts give the percentage of rows returned as 20 percent, some 30 percent and others 25 percent. We will use 25 percent for this study. To our knowledge, this is not a test subject, but a concept that gives guidelines.

Distribution statistics for an index are automatically created when the index is created or rebuilt. SQL Server 7 can also maintain statistics for columns that are not part of an index. Statistics for nonindexed columns can be created with help of the **CREATE STATISTICS** command. They can also be created automatically by the query optimizer on columns participating in **WHERE** clauses if the **auto create statistics** database option is set to True (True is the default value).

Distribution statistics on columns that are not part of an index count against the 249 nonclustered indexes per table limit. Statistics cannot be created on computed columns and on columns of data type image, text, and ntext.

Distribution statistics are of no use if they are not kept current. Imagine that you create an index on a column where the table has 2,000 rows. When the index is created, not more than two rows have the same value in the columns. In this example the index is highly selective. If you perform an update to that table and make all values in the column the same, the selectivity of the index is extremely low. Because the distribution statistics have not been updated, the optimizer still thinks that the index should be used to access data. This can cause very slow performance. It is important to keep the distribution statistics current in order to ensure that the optimizer makes the correct decisions on the most efficient way to access data from a table. In order to avoid that kind of situation, distribution statistics must be updated when the data in the table changes. Distribution statistics can be updated with the help of the **UPDATE STATISTICS** command. SQL Server 7 will automatically update the statistics if the **auto update statistics** database option is set to True. Unless otherwise instructed, SQL Server 7 uses a sampling method to update the distribution statistics.

To disable automatic statistics maintenance by SQL Server you can:

- Create the index with the **STATISTICS_NORECOMPUTE** clause (see the previous section, "Creating An Index").
- Use the **NORECOMPUTE** clause of the **UPDATE STATISTICS** and **CREATE STATISTICS** command (explained later in the chapter).

➤ Set the **auto create statistics** and **auto update statistics** database option to false through the GUI or with the help of the **sp_dboption** system stored procedure.

➤ Use the **sp_autostats** system stored procedure.

Unused statistics created automatically by SQL Server 7 are automatically deleted.

Updating Statistics

The **UPDATE STATISTICS** command is used to update the distribution statistics of an index and to update statistics created with the **CREATE STATISTICS** command. **UPDATE STATISTICS** should be run when many rows are added to the table, when many rows are deleted from the table, or when many key values are updated. The syntax for **UPDATE STATISTICS** is as follows:

```
UPDATE STATISTICS <table_name>
     [<index_name>|(<statistics_name>[,....])]
     [WITH [FULLSCAN|SAMPLE <percent_or_number> {PERCENT|ROWS}]
                [[,] [ALL|COLUMNS|INDEX]]
                [[,] NORECOMPUTE]
     ]
```

To update the statistics of an index, specify the index name **(<index_name>)**. To update statistics created with the **CREATE STATISTICS** command, specify the statistics group name **(<statistics_name>)**. If no index name or statistics group name is specified, use the **UPDATE STATISTICS** command to update all distribution statistics related to the table.

Distribution statistics can be updated based on a full analysis of the data in the table (specifying the **FULLSCAN** clause) or based on a sample of the data in the table. Data sampling can be done on:

➤ *A percentage of the rows in the table*—Specify the **SAMPLE <percent> PERCENT** clause.

➤ *A number of rows in the table*—Specify the **SAMPLE <number> ROWS** clause.

If the percentage or number of rows specified will not be enough to create useful statistics, SQL Server 7 will sample enough rows to make the statistics useful.

To update column statistics only, specify the **COLUMNS** clause. If you are updating the statistics for an index you cannot specify this clause. To update only index statistics, specify the **INDEX** clause, and to update all existing statistics, specify the **ALL** clause.

The **NORECOMPUTE** clause disables the automatic update of the distribution statistics. Use this clause carefully, because it may cause the optimizer to make nonoptimal decisions when accessing data.

To update statistics on all user tables, use the **sp_updatestats** system stored procedure.

You can enable or disable automatic update of statistics on an index using the **sp_autostats** system stored procedure.

Listing 6.10 shows how to update the distribution statistics of the *CustomerID* index of the *Orders* table.

Listing 6.10 Updating statistics.

```
UPDATE STATISTICS Orders CustomerID
GO
```

Creating Statistics

Distribution statistics created with the **CREATE STATISTICS** command or those automatically created by SQL Server 7 help the query optimizer make better decisions when querying tables that have no useful indexes. With the help of these statistics, the optimizer will have a better idea of the number of rows in each table participating in the query. The optimizer can then make a decision on whether to use a hash or merge join, or which table to use as the outer table of a nested loop.

To create distribution statistics on a column or set of columns, use the **CREATE STATISTICS** command. The syntax for **CREATE STATISTICS** is:

```
CREATE STATISTICS <statistics_name> ON <table_name> (<col1>[,...])
[WITH [FULLSCAN|SAMPLE <percent> PERCENT]
          [[,] NORECOMPUTE]
]
```

If the **FULLSCAN** clause is specified, all rows in the table will be read to create the statistics. If the **SAMPLE <percent> PERCENT** clause is specified, SQL Server 7 will randomly read a percent of the data to create the statistics, and **<percent>** can be fractional.

If neither the **FULLSCAN** nor the **SAMPLE** clauses are specified, SQL Server will determine what percent of the data will be sampled in order to obtain useful statistics. The **NORECOMPUTE** clause disables the automatic update of the created statistics. Use this clause carefully, because it may cause the optimizer to make nonoptimal decisions when accessing data.

You can also create statistics on all columns in all user tables using the **sp_createstats** system stored procedure.

6

Dropping Statistics

If you need to delete statistics, use the **DROP STATISTICS** command.

```
DROP STATISTICS <table_name>.<statistic_name>[,....]
```

DBCC SHOW_STATISTICS

The **DBCC SHOW_STATISTICS** command is used to obtain information about the current distribution statistics of an index. The output of a **DBCC SHOW_STATISTICS** command gives the following information:

- **Updated** The last time the statistics where updated.
- **Rows** The number of rows in the table.
- **Rows sample** The number of rows sampled when the distribution statistics were created or updated.
- **Steps** The number of distribution steps, which is the number of histogram values in the current distribution statistics.
- **Density** The selectivity of an index (*density*).
- **Average key length** The average length of an index row.
- **All density** The selectivity of the specified column prefix in the index.
- **Columns** The column(s) for which all the density is specified.

Use the **DBCC SHOW_STATISTICS** command to determine if an index is of any use to the optimizer. A low density returned by **DBCC SHOW_STATISTICS** means that the index has high selectivity. An index with high selectivity means that it is useful to the optimizer. The syntax for the **DBCC SHOW_STATISTICS** command is as follows:

```
DBCC SHOW_STATISTICS (<table_name>, <index_name>)
```

Listing 6.11 shows how to find the distribution statistics information for index *LastName* of the *Employees* table in the *Northwind* database.

Listing 6.11 Displaying the distribution statistics.

```
DBCC SHOW_STATISTICS ( 'Employees', 'LastName')
GO
Statistics for INDEX 'LastName'.
Updated              Rows Rows Sampled Steps Density  Average key length
-------------------- ---- ------------ ----- -------  ------------------
May 6 1999 10:10PM 9    9            9     0.1111111 18.222223

(1 row(s) affected)

All density     Columns
----------      --------------------
0.11111111      LastName
0.11111111      LastName, EmployeeID

(2 row(s) affected)

Steps
---------
Buchanan
Callahan
Davolio
Dodsworth
Fuller
King
Leverling
Peacock
Suyama

(9 row(s) affected)
DBCC execution completed. If DBCC printed error messages, contact your
system administrator.
```

If you want to find out the last time the distribution statistics of an index was updated, you can use the system function **STATS_DATE (<table_id>, <index_id>)**.

Index Tuning

Index tuning is one of the most important tasks to allow SQL Server to perform efficiently. No simple rules exist when designing the appropriate set of indexes on a table. One set of indexes may be appropriate in a given moment, but when the data in the tables changes they might become inappropriate. Fortunately, Microsoft has introduced the Index Tuning Wizard, which helps determine which indexes should be created on a database.

Keep in mind the following recommendations:

- Create nonclustered indexes on all columns frequently used in queries to maximize the use of covered indexes.
- Optimize index maintenance by writing queries that update as many rows as possible in a single statement instead of writing multiple queries.
- Consider creating your indexes on a filegroup located on a different physical disk than the data filegroup.
- Keep indexes as narrow (less columns) as possible. The number of index pages that must be maintained increases in direct proportion to the width of the index.
- Keep the statistics for index current.
- Indexes of columns with few unique values (for example, an index on a column that can only have two values) are of no use for the optimizer.

Index Tuning Wizard

The Index Tuning Wizard recommends the best set of indexes that the database should have for a specific workload in order to maximize database performance. A *workload* is a set of SQL commands (**INSERT**, **UPDATE**, **DELETE**, or stored procedure calls) saved as a SQL script or as a SQL Server Profiler output file or table.

The Index Tuning Wizard will only consider the first 32,767 queries for tuning. It does not consider all other queries when the tuning analysis is being performed.

The set of SQL commands should be representative of normal database activity. For example, it makes no sense to create a workload of all commands when a database is going to be populated for the first time, because it does not represent the day-to-day database activity.

The Index Tuning Wizard walks through the process of fine-tuning a set of indexes for a specified workload. The wizard consists of several screens. You move from screen to screen clicking on the Next button; you can always go back to the prior screen by clicking on the Back button.

Let's see how the Index Tuning Wizard works with an example. In this example, we have a very small workload created against the *Orders* table of the *Northwind* database. The indexes defined on the *Orders* table are:

```
index_name                    index_keys
---------------               --------------
PK_Orders                     OrderID
CustomerID                    CustomerID
CustomersOrders               CustomerID
EmployeeID                    EmployeeID
EmployeesOrders               EmployeeID
OrderDate                     OrderDate
ShippedDate                   ShippedDate
ShippersOrders                ShipVia
ShipPostalCode                ShipPostalCode
```

Listing 6.12 shows the commands in the workload.

Listing 6.12 Commands in the workload.

```
SELECT * FROM Orders WHERE ShipName
LIKE 'Que Delícia'
GO
SELECT * FROM Orders WHERE ShipName
LIKE 'Alfreds Futterkiste'
GO
UPDATE Orders SET ShippedDate = getdate()
WHERE ShipName = 'Bólido Comidas preparadas'
GO
UPDATE Orders SET ShippedDate = getdate()
WHERE ShipName = 'Centro comercial Moctezuma'
GO
SELECT * FROM Orders WHERE ShipName
LIKE 'Consolidated Hold%'
GO
SELECT * FROM Orders WHERE ShipName
LIKE 'France%'
GO
UPDATE Orders SET ShippedDate = getdate()
WHERE ShipName = 'GROSELLA-Restaurante'
GO
UPDATE Orders SET ShippedDate = getdate()
WHERE ShipName = 'Lazy K Kountry Store'
GO
SELECT * FROM Orders where ShipName
LIKE 'North/%'
GO
```

Let's analyze all the screens from the Index Tuning Wizard:

- The first screen is the Welcome To The Index Tuning Wizard screen. This is an introductory screen that explains what you can expect from this wizard.
- The second screen is the Select Server And Database screen (see Figure 6.7). As the title suggests, you select which server and database you want to tune. This screen also has two other options:
  - **Keep All Existing Indexes** If you select this option, the wizard recommends only new indexes; it does not give any recommendation as to whether any of the existing indexes are not useful. For better tuning, do not select this option.
  - **Perform Thorough Analysis** For better tuning, select this option. However, the wizard takes longer to perform the analysis.

The execution time of the wizard also increases if the workload file or table increases in the number of SQL comments they contain.

- The third screen is the Identify Workload screen (see Figure 6.8). If you already have a workload file or table, select the I Have A Saved Workload File option, otherwise select I Will Create The Workload File On My Own. If you select this option, the wizard opens the SQL Profiler screen and finishes. No recom-mendations are made because no workload was analyzed.

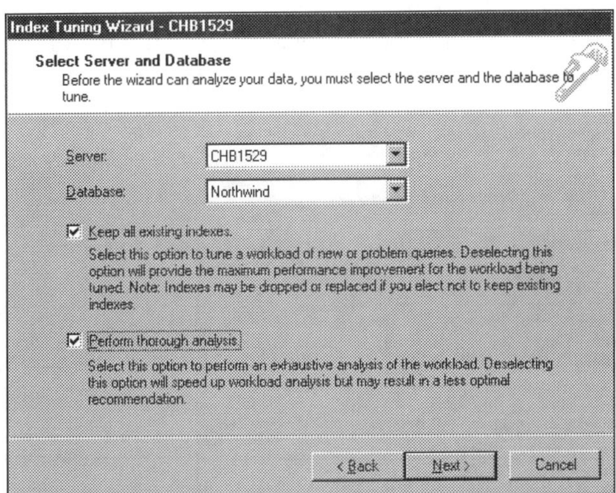

Figure 6.7 Select Server And Database screen from the Index Tuning Wizard.

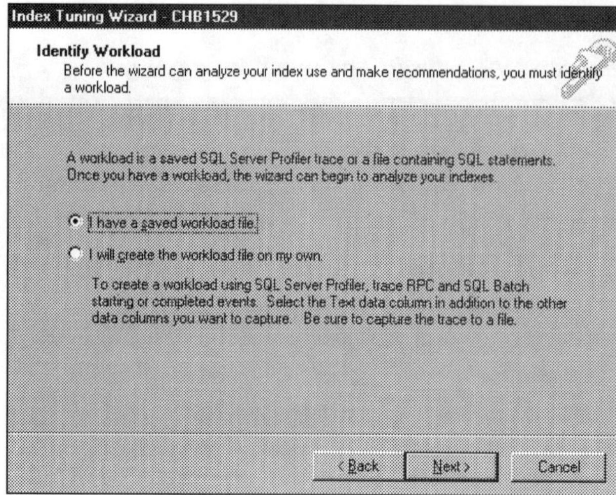

Figure 6.8 Identify Workload screen from the Index Tuning Wizard.

- The fourth screen is the Specify Workload screen (see Figure 6.9). Here, you specify if your workload is saved in a file (SQL Script or SQL Profiler output) or in a table (SQL Profiler output). When you select either of these options, a screen appears for you to select the file or table. If you want to limit the maximum number or queries to tune, the maximum space for the indexes that the wizard recommends, or maximum columns allowed per index recommended by the wizard, click on the Advanced Options button.
- The fifth screen is the Select Tables To Tune screen (see Figure 6.10). By default, the wizard analyzes the entire database. The wizard performs faster if it has fewer tables to analyze. This is the last screen before the analysis begins.

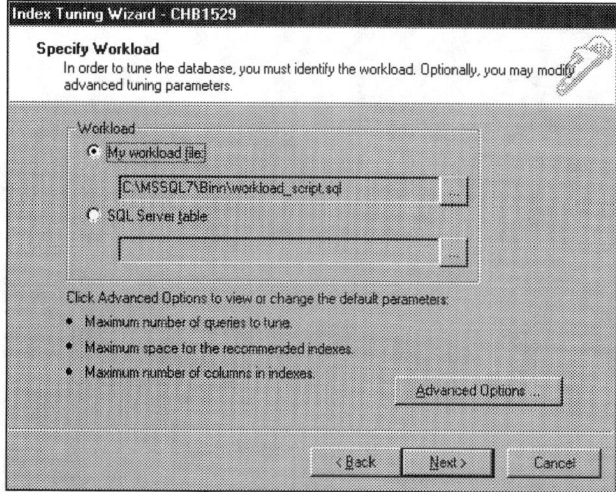

Figure 6.9 Specify Workload screen from the Index Tuning Wizard.

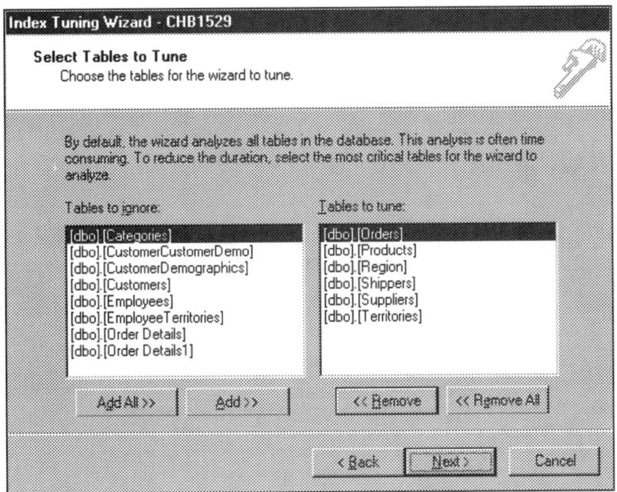

Figure 6.10 Select Tables To Tune screen from the Index Tuning Wizard.

- The sixth screen is the Index Recommendations screen (see Figure 6.11). This screen shows all recommended indexes for the table, whether the indexes exist or not, whether the indexes should be clustered or nonclustered, and what performance improvement should be expected if the changes are implemented. It also creates six reports about the analysis that it performed. To view those reports, click on the Analysis button.
- The seventh screen is the Schedule Index Update Job screen (see Figure 6.12). In this screen, you can instruct the wizard to not implement the

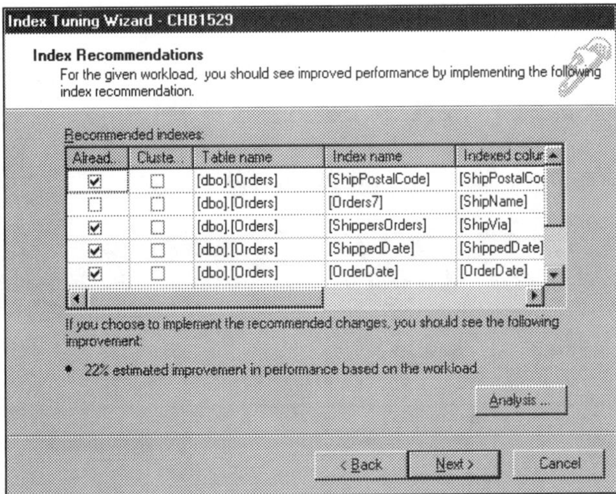

Figure 6.11 Index Recommendations screen from the Index Tuning Wizard.

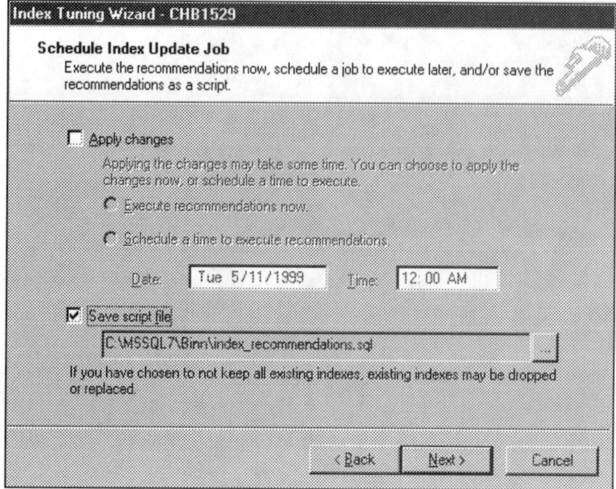

Figure 6.12 Schedule Index Update Job screen from the Index Tuning Wizard.

recommendations, to immediately implement the recommendations, or to schedule the implementation of the recommendations. You can also decide if you want to save the recommendations as a script file.

- The final screen is the Completing The Index Tuning Wizard screen.

For our example, the recommendations made by the wizard are:

- Drop two indexes, one on the *CustomerID* column and the other on the *EmployeeID* column. Notice that two indexes exist on the *CustomerID* column (indexes: *CustomerID* and *CustomersOrders*) and on the *EmployeeID* column (indexes: *EmployeeID* and *EmployeesOrders*).
- Create a new nonclustered index on the *shipname* column.

Listing 6.13 shows the script that was created.

Listing 6.13 Nonclustered index on the *shipname* column.

```
USE [Northwind]
BEGIN TRANSACTION
DROP INDEX [dbo].[orders].[CustomerID]
if (@@error <> 0) rollback transaction
DROP INDEX [dbo].[orders].[EmployeesOrders]
if (@@error <> 0) rollback transaction
CREATE NONCLUSTERED INDEX [orders7]
ON [dbo].[orders]
([shipname])
if (@@error <> 0) rollback transaction
COMMIT TRANSACTION
```

The Index Tuning Wizard will not recommend indexes on the following:

- System tables
- **PRIMARY KEY** and **UNIQUE** constraints
- Tables that do not belong to the selected database, that is, tables being referenced by cross-database queries

Additionally, the Index Tuning Wizard will not make any recommendations if not enough data is in the tables to be analyzed or the recommended indexes will not give a significant performance improvement.

Index Analysis Through The Query Analyzer

Using the Perform Index Analysis option from the Query menu of the Query Analyzer (see Figure 6.13), you can perform simple index analysis. The analysis can only be done on a single query or single batch (do not specify the **GO** statement). Index analysis only recommends creating nonclustered indexes.

6

IMPACT ON TOTAL DATABASE SIZE

Indexes have a great impact on the database size. The index pages created when an index is defined require extra space. Also, keep in mind that the distribution statistics of an index are saved in what is known as *distribution pages*; these pages also require extra space.

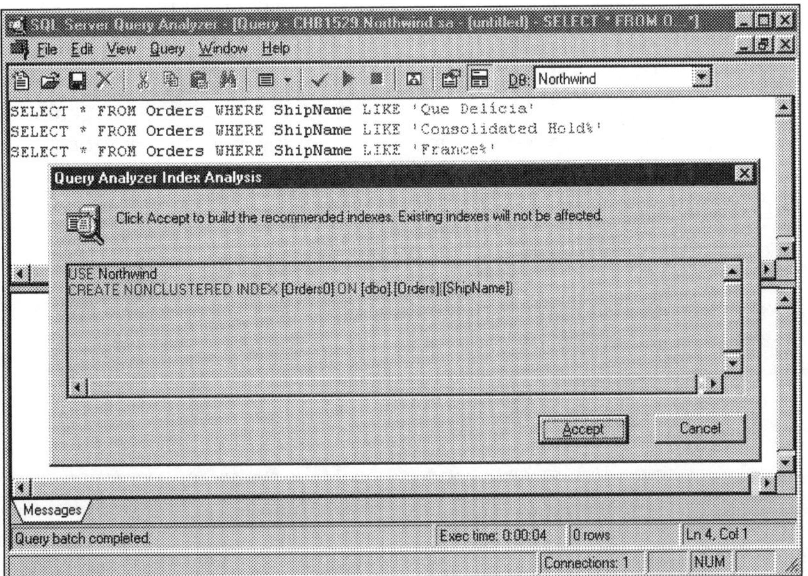

Figure 6.13 Performing index analysis through the Query Analyzer.

The *fill factor* specified when creating an index determines how full the leaf pages of an index will be. The remaining space on the leaf pages is left free for future inserts. Therefore, a smaller fill factor will result in a larger database. For example, if a clustered index is created with a **FILLFACTOR** of 30, the table will take three times more space than if you had specified a **FILLFACTOR** of 100. The reason is that the data pages will only be 30 percent full when the clustered index is created instead of a 100 percent full. The fill factor also determines how full the leaf index pages of a nonclustered index are.

Another index option that affects the total database size is the **PAD_INDEX** option of the **CREATE INDEX** command. This option applies the specified fill factor to the nonleaf index pages.

Use the system stored procedure **sp_spaceused** to determine how much disk space is used by the data and indexes of a table or to find out how much disk space is being used by the entire database.

IMPACT ON QUERY PERFORMANCE

Indexes can have a huge impact on query performance. If no indexes are defined on a table, or if the indexes are not efficient for a query, SQL Server 7 performs *table scans* in order to retrieve data from a table. Full scans of a table generally take longer than when an index is used. SQL Server 7 Query Optimizer determines which is the most efficient way to retrieve the data from a table. Nevertheless, you can override the Query Optimizer by specifying an optimizer hint on the **FROM** clause of a **SELECT** statement. For example, you might instruct the Query Optimizer to use a specific index instead of performing a table scan. The use of optimizer hints is recommended only in extreme situations. Usually the Query Optimizer does the best job. The following is a partial syntax of the **SELECT** statement:

```
SELECT <col1>, ..., <coln>
FROM <table> [WITH] INDEX( <index_id>|<index_name>)
Or (for backward compatibility):
SELECT <col1>, ..., <coln>
FROM <table> [WITH] (INDEX = <index_id>|<index_name>)
```

In the test we have performed only the syntax for backward compatibility works.

An **<index_id>** of 0 instructs the optimizer to perform a table scan. An **<index_id>** of 1 instructs the optimizer to use the clustered index.

Listing 6.14 shows how to force the query optimizer to use the *CustomerID* index of the *Orders* table of the *Northwind* database.

Listing 6.14 Forcing a particular index to be used.

```
SELECT * FROM Orders WITH (INDEX = CustomerID)
WHERE CustomerID = 'VINET'
```

Impact On DML Performance

Too many indexes may cause performance to decrease when adding or deleting many rows in a table or when updating the values of an index column(s). The reason for this is the extra overhead incurred in updating the indexes. At the same time, indexes may improve performance during a **DELETE** or **UPDATE** statement. For example, imagine a 1,000,000-row employee table that does not have an index on the *LastName* column. If the following **DELETE** statement were executed, a costly table scan would be performed. On the other hand, if an index had existed, the query optimizer would have used it to quickly find the rows that needed to be deleted. In this case, the overhead of scanning the table is far more expensive than the overhead of updating the indexes.

```
DELETE FROM Employee WHERE LastName = 'XYZ'
```

If a table is being populated for the first time with a large amount of data, it is recommended that the indexes be created after the data load. The load will be completed much more quickly because the indexes will not have to be maintained as the data is inserted. This is true for any of the load methods, for example, **INSERT** statements, the **BCP** utility, **BULK INSERT** statements, or the Data Transformation Services.

Even though SQL Server 7 automatically updates statistics if the **auto update statistics** database option is set, it is a good practice to update manually the statistics of the indexes of a table after inserting or deleting many rows from a table and after updating many key values. This ensures that the Query Optimizer makes smart decisions in future queries.

As with **SELECT** statements, you can specify index hints in the **FROM** clause of a **INSERT**, **UPDATE**, and **DELETE** statement. Use the index hints with extreme caution.

Chapter Summary

The following concepts have been discussed in this chapter:

- You can create an index on one column (single-column index) or on multiple columns (composite index). Keep an index as compact as possible.

- Only one clustered index can exist per table because the clustered index determines the physical order in which the data is saved. A clustered index can be a single or multicolumn index.
- The leaf pages of a clustered index are the data pages.
- Clustered indexes should be used on columns searched by range values, on columns participating in the **ORDER BY** and **GROUP BY** clauses, on columns that are not updated often, and for queries that return a large number of rows.
- You can have 249 nonclustered indexes; each one can be a single or multi-column index.
- The leaf pages of a nonclustered index point to the data pages.
- The row locators (pointers to the data pages) of a nonclustered index will contain the clustered keys if a clustered index exists on the table. Otherwise, they will contain row identifiers (file number, page number, and row location of the data in the data page).
- You should use a nonclustered index on highly selective columns and on columns often used in **WHERE** clauses that return small amount of rows.
- SQL Server 7 supports index intersection (when more than one index is used to solve a query) and covered indexes (when all the columns of a query can be found on an index so it is not necessary to retrieve data from the data pages).
- Unique indexes do not permit duplicate key values. Clustered and nonclustered indexes can be unique indexes. Single column and multicolumn (composite) indexes can be unique.
- The fill factor determines how full the leaf pages of an index will be after an index is created or rebuilt. A low fill factor may decrease page splitting, but may impact read performance.
- Use the Performance Monitor **SQL Server: Access Methods–Page Splits** counter and the **DBCC SHOWCONTIG** command to monitor page splits.
- The fill factor percentage is a server-wide configuration option that you can override with the **FILLFACTOR** clause of the **CREATE INDEX** statement.
- Specify the **PAD_INDEX** clause of the **CREATE INDEX** statement to apply the fill factor percentage to the nonleaf pages of an index.
- You can create an index with the **CREATE INDEX** statement or with the Create Index Wizard.
- Specify the **IGNORE_DUP_KEY** clause of the **CREATE INDEX** statement to ignore duplicate keys when you perform a batch insert.

- Use the **DROP_EXISTING** clause of the **CREATE INDEX** to re-create a clustered index instead of dropping and re-creating it. The **DROP_EXISTING** clause improves performance.
- You can drop an index with the **DROP INDEX** command. If a clustered index is dropped, all the nonclustered indexes will be automatically re-created.
- Indexes automatically created when a **PRIMARY KEY** or **UNIQUE** constraint is created cannot be dropped with the **DROP INDEX** command.
- You can view all indexes defined on a table with the **sp_helpindex** system stored procedure.
- To view index properties, use the **INDEXPROPERTY()** function.
- The distribution statistics of an index define the selectivity of the index and the distribution of values in the index.
- Use the **UPDATE STATISTICS** command to update the distribution statistics of an index after many rows have been inserted, deleted, or updated in a table.
- SQL Server 7 automatically updates distribution statistics if the **auto update statistics** database option is set to True and if the index was not created with the **STATISTICS_NORECOMPUTE** clause.
- Use the **DBCC SHOW_STATISTICS** command to view the distribution statistics information of an index.
- The Index Tuning Wizard is a wonderful tool to optimize indexes based on a workload of commands.

Review Questions

1. Which of the following are true? (Choose all correct answers.)
    a. A unique index is created when a **PRIMARY KEY** constraint is defined.
    b. A unique index is not created when a **PRIMARY KEY** constraint is defined unless you use the **CREATE INDEX** command.
    c. A unique index is created when a **UNIQUE** constraint is defined.
    d. A unique index is not created when a **UNIQUE** constraint is defined unless you use the **CREATE INDEX** command.

2. Which of the following are true about indexes? (Choose all correct answers.)
    a. They improve query responses.
    b. They are maintained dynamically by SQL Server.
    c. They reduce the size of the database.
    d. All of the above.

3. How many clustered indexes can exist per table?
   a. 1
   b. 249
   c. 250
   d. No limit

4. How many nonclustered indexes can exist per table?
   a. 1
   b. 249
   c. 250
   d. No limit

5. A table with one million rows is used very often in queries. The table is always queried by two columns (*col1* and *col2*) at the same time. Column *col1* is less selective then column *col2*. Which of the following indexing schema is the most appropriate?
   a. A composite index with *col1* as the first column and *col2* as the second column.
   b. A composite index with *col2* as the first column and *col1* as the second column.
   c. An index on column *col1*.
   d. An index on column *col2*.

6. A table with 180,000 rows is queried very often. The table can be queried by different columns. If the table is not updated very often, which is the best indexing schema?
   a. Create a large number of composite indexes.
   b. Create a large number of single-column indexes.
   c. Create a small number of single-column indexes.
   d. Create a small number of composite indexes.

7. Which of the following commands creates a composite index in columns *LastName* and *FirstName* of the *Employees* table?
   a.
   ```
   CREATE INDEX idx1
   ON Employees (LastName, FirstName)
   ```
   b.
   ```
   CREATE INDEX Employees.idx1
   (LastName, FirstName)
   ```
   c.
   ```
   CREATE INDEX idx1
   ON Employees LastName + FirstName
   ```
   d.
   ```
   CREATE INDEX idx1
   ON Employees (FirstName, LastName)
   ```

8. A table with 50,000 rows is never updated. The data is always retrieved by two columns (*col1* and *col2*) at the same time. Column *col1* is more selective than column *col2*. Only one index should be defined on the table. Which is the best indexing schema?

   a. A multicolumn clustered index on (*col1*, *col2*).

   b. A multicolumn clustered index on (*col2*, *col1*).

   c. A multicolumn nonclustered index on (*col1*, *col2*).

   d. A multicolumn nonclustered index on (*col2*, *col1*).

9. Which of the following is true about clustered and nonclustered indexes? (Choose all correct answers.)

   a. A clustered index defines the order the data is physically stored.

   b. Nonclustered indexes perform well when a column is queried with a **BETWEEN** clause.

   c. A clustered index performs well when a large amount of sorted rows are returned.

   d. A clustered and nonclustered index can be unique.

10. Which of the following is true about unique indexes? (Choose all correct answers.)

    a. A unique index can be created on a column with duplicate values only if the **FUTURE_ONLY** clause is used.

    b. A unique index can be created on a column that allows **NULL** values.

    c. A clustered index cannot be unique.

    d. A nonclustered index can be unique.

11. The Employees table has a composite index defined on (*LastName*, *FirstName*). Which of the following queries will make a proper use of the index? (Choose all correct answers.)

    a.
    ```
    SELECT * FROM Employees
    WHERE FirstName = 'Joe' AND LastName = 'Smith'
    ```

    b.
    ```
    SELECT * FROM Employees
    WHERE LastName = 'Smith' AND FirstName = 'Joe'
    ```

    c.
    ```
    SELECT * FROM Employees
    WHERE LastName = 'Smith'
    ```

    d.
    ```
    SELECT * FROM Employees
    WHERE FirstName = 'Joe'
    ```

    e.
    ```
    SELECT * FROM Employees
    WHERE LastName LIKE 'Smi%'
    ```

    f.
    ```
    SELECT * FROM Employees
    WHERE LastName LIKE '%ith'
    ```

12. You have been monitoring the page splits on a table and have noticed that data page splits are happening very often. Which of the following solutions will help most?
    a. Re-create the clustered index with a lower fill factor.
    b. Re-create the clustered index with a higher fill factor.
    c. Re-create the clustered index with the same fill factor.
    d. None of the above.

13. In which of the following situations does a clustered index perform well? (Choose all correct answers.)
    a. Columns searched by range values
    b. Columns that are often updated
    c. Columns participating in the **ORDER BY** clause
    d. Columns that uniquely identify a column

14. In which of the following situations does a nonclustered index perform well?
    a. Queries that return a small number of rows
    b. Columns that are very selective
    c. Columns that are frequently updated
    d. All of the above.

15. *TableA* and *TableB* have the exact same structure. An index was created on *TableA* with the following command:

```
CREATE UNIQUE INDEX idx1
ON TableA (LastName, FirstName)
```

If *TableB* has ten rows, seven of which already exist on *TableA*, what will be the result of the following statement:

```
INSERT INTO TableA
SELECT * FROM TableB
GO
```

    a. No rows will be inserted and an error message will be returned.
    b. Three rows will be inserted and a warning message will be returned.
    c. All ten rows will be inserted.
    d. None of the above.

16. What will be the result of the next command?

```
CREATE INDEX idx1
ON Employees (LastName) WITH PAD_INDEX,
FILLFACTOR = 50
```

a. The nonleaf index pages will be half full.
b. The leaf index pages will be half full.
c. The nonleaf and leaf index pages will be half full.
d. None of the above.

17. You need to re-create a clustered index of a table that also has nonclustered indexes. The recommended way to do this is:

a. Drop the clustered index with the **DROP INDEX** command and create the clustered index again.
b. Drop all indexes (clustered and nonclustered) and create them again.
c. Re-create the clustered index, specifying the **DROP_EXISTING** clause in the **CREATE INDEX** statement.
d. All of the above.

HANDS-ON PROJECTS

These activities assume that you are already connected to the *Northwind* database using the Query Analyzer.

Susan had learned a great deal since she originally started the project. She began by familiarizing herself with SQL Server, and had been involved in the early stages of the design of the database. The physical design had been complete, and now Susan's attention turned to tuning the database. She knew that if the indexes weren't well thought out, she'd be in big trouble when the system went under load.

Susan studied her database and found several tables that didn't have indexes that needed them. She opened *Books Online* and checked the syntax for creating an index.

Project 6.1

In this activity, you create an index according to the following specifications.

The index needs to be on the *ShipName* column of the *Orders* table. All the index pages need to be 80 percent full. Name the index *IDX ShipName*.

In the Query Analyzer, type the following command and execute it:

```
CREATE INDEX [IDX ShipName]
ON Orders (ShipName)
WITH FILLFACTOR = 50, PAD_INDEX
GO
```

Once Susan began her examination of the index, she noticed that a few of the clustered indexes had an ineffective fill factor. She didn't want to drop those indexes and re-create them, so she decided to use the **DBCC REINDEX** command to change the fill factor.

Project 6.2

In this activity, you need to rebuild all indexes from the *Orders* table and apply a new fill factor.

Instead of dropping and re-creating each index separately, we are going to use the **DBCC DBREINDEX** command. You need to apply a new fill factor of 65. In the Query Analyzer, type the following command and execute it:

```
DBCC DBREINDEX ( Orders, '', 65 )
GO
Index (ID = 1) is being rebuilt.
Index (ID = 2) is being rebuilt.
Index (ID = 3) is being rebuilt.
Index (ID = 4) is being rebuilt.
Index (ID = 5) is being rebuilt.
Index (ID = 6) is being rebuilt.
Index (ID = 7) is being rebuilt.
Index (ID = 8) is being rebuilt.
Index (ID = 9) is being rebuilt.
Index (ID = 10) is being rebuilt.
Index (ID = 11) is being rebuilt.
DBCC execution completed. If DBCC printed error messages, contact your
system administrator.
```

Susan noticed that some queries ran slowly even after she created the new indexes. She did some detective work and found that the **auto update statistics** setting had been turned off. She ran the **UPDATE STATISTICS** command and ran the queries again, with far better results.

Chapter 7

Retrieving And Modifying Data

After Reading This Chapter And Completing The Exercises, You Will Be Able To:

- Use **SELECT** statements to retrieve data from tables
- **INSERT** rows of new data into tables
- Remove data using **DELETE** and **TRUNCATE TABLE**
- Modify existing data using **UPDATE**
- Understand the key features of available programming interfaces and the differences between them

Now that you have learned how to design a database and implement tables and indexes, it is time to master the main Transact-SQL commands used to retrieve and modify data stored in these tables. In this chapter, you will learn the essentials of the **SELECT**, **INSERT**, **DELETE**, and **UPDATE** statements.

RETRIEVING DATA WITH SELECT

The **SELECT** statement may be the most fundamental of all Transact-SQL statements. It is usually the first statement a new database programmer learns, and it is the most frequently used statement as well. However, the **SELECT** statement is also very flexible, and can be used to create very sophisticated queries. Although a complete syntax chart for such a flexible statement would be very elaborate, the main clauses of the **SELECT** statement can be summarized as follows:

```
SELECT    select_list
[INTO     new_table]
FROM      data_source
[WHERE    search_condition]
[GROUP BY group_by_expression]
[HAVING   search_condition]
[ORDER BY order_expression]
```

The **GROUP BY** and **HAVING** clauses are covered in Chapter 9. Over the course of this section, we will discuss each of the remaining clauses of the **SELECT** statement. We will begin our discussion of this important command with some very simple **SELECT** statements, and we will begin to build up a sophisticated query arsenal as we systematically discuss the more advanced **SELECT** features.

Simple SELECT Statements

In its simplest form, **SELECT** is used to request a specific group of columns from a single table, as in the following example:

```
SELECT LastName, FirstName, Country, HomePhone
FROM   Employees

Results:
LastName      FirstName  Country   HomePhone
---------     ---------  -------  ----------
Davolio       Nancy      USA       (206) 555-9857
Fuller        Andrew     USA       (206) 555-9482
Leverling     Janet      USA       (206) 555-3412
Peacock       Margaret   USA       (206) 555-8122
Buchanan      Steven     UK        (71) 555-4848
Suyama        Michael    UK        (71) 555-7773
King          Robert     UK        (71) 555-5598
Callahan      Laura      USA       (206) 555-1189
Dodsworth     Anne       UK        (71) 555-4444
```

Specifying The Select List

As you can see in this example, the simplest **SELECT** statements follow the pattern **SELECT** *select_list* **FROM** *data_source*. In a simple query such as this, the *select_list* is a list of columns, and the *data_source* is the name of the table containing those columns.

The *select_list* can contain expressions other than column names. For example, Transact-SQL functions can be used instead of column names. Transact-SQL functions are covered in detail in Chapter 9.

When an asterisk or star character (*) is used in the *select_list,* SQL Server replaces this symbol with list of all of the table's columns. This means that the following two queries are equivalent:

```
/* Explicitly selecting all columns from Employees: */
SELECT EmployeeID, LastName, FirstName, Title, TitleOfCourtesy,
       BirthDate, HireDate, Address, City, Region, PostalCode,
       Country, HomePhone, Extension, Photo, Notes, ReportsTo,
       PhotoPath
FROM   Employees

/* Implicitly selecting all columns from Employees: */
SELECT *
FROM   Employees
```

Although the star notation is obviously more compact, it is often better to explicitly specify the entire column list. For example, suppose your database contains the following table:

```
CREATE TABLE CompactDisc (
    Artist Varchar(50),
    Title  Varchar(50)
)
```

If you write a program to list the information from this table, you could use the star notation, writing **SELECT * FROM CompactDisc**, or you could explicitly name each column, writing **SELECT Artist, Title FROM CompactDisc**. Either query will return the same results. Notice what happens if the database administrator makes a change to the table, adding another column called *NumberOfTracks* and your query explicitly names the columns desired. The output of your query will not change, and so your program will still function correctly. However, if you used the star notation, your query will begin to return all three columns the next time it is compiled. If your program is not prepared for this change, it may crash or return incorrect results.

In relational database terminology, the process of restricting which columns are included in a query's result set is called *projection*.

Column Aliases

SQL Server allows you to rename columns in a result set using column aliases. You can do this in two ways. The first syntax is to use **column_alias = column_expression** in place of a column name. The second method is to specify **column_expression [AS] column_alias** in place of a column name. For example, the following queries both retrieve the *CompanyName* column from the *Shippers* table, but cause the column to be renamed in the result set by using the column alias *Shipper Name*:

```
/* first method: */
SELECT 'Shipper Name' = CompanyName
FROM    Shippers

/* second method: */
SELECT CompanyName AS 'Shipper Name'
FROM   Shippers

Results of either query:
Shipper Name
-------------
Speedy Express
United Package
Federal Shipping
```

Selecting Literal Values

Literal values can be used as expressions on the select list. The following query returns the string *MCDBA* nine times, because the *Employees* table has nine rows:

```
SELECT 'MCDBA' AS Certification
FROM    Employees

Results:
Certification
-------------
MCDBA
MCDBA
MCDBA
MCDBA
MCDBA
MCDBA
MCDBA
MCDBA
MCDBA
```

When selecting literal values, the **FROM** clause is optional if no columns are named in the select list. In such a case, one row is built from the expressions listed. You may still use column aliases to name the *columns*. The following query returns the string *MCDBA* only once:

```
SELECT 'MCDBA' AS Certification
```

```
Results:
Certification
-------------
MCDBA
```

The WHERE Clause

Just as the select list is used to restrict the columns returned by a query, the **WHERE** clause is used to restrict the rows returned. The **WHERE** clause contains *Boolean* (true or false) search conditions that are evaluated for each row in the table. If the search condition is true for a particular row, then that row is included in the query's result set. If the search condition is false for a particular row, then that row is excluded. For example, the following query refines our previous *Employees* query so that only USA employees are included in the result set:

```
SELECT LastName, FirstName, Country, HomePhone
FROM   Employees
WHERE  Country = 'USA'
```

```
Results:
LastName        FirstName  Country   HomePhone
--------        ---------  -------   ---------
Davolio         Nancy      USA       (206) 555-9857
Fuller          Andrew     USA       (206) 555-9482
Leverling       Janet      USA       (206) 555-3412
Peacock         Margaret   USA       (206) 555-8122
Callahan        Laura      USA       (206) 555-1189
```

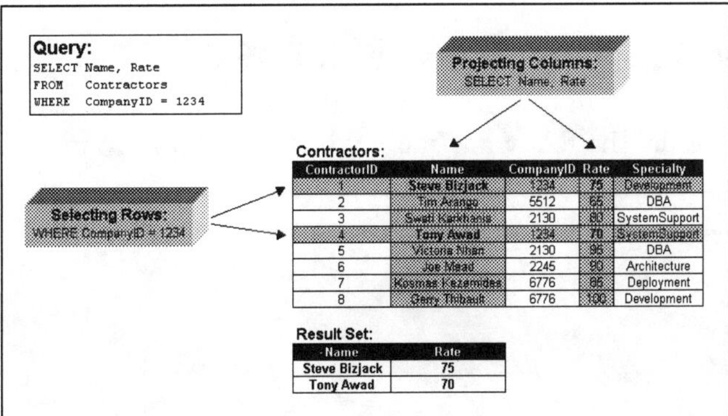

Figure 7.1 Determining a simple query's result set.

Figure 7.1 illustrates how projection (based on a **SELECT** statement's select list) and selection (based on the statement's **WHERE** clause) interact to determine which columns from which rows are included in the result set.

The **WHERE** clause can specify several Boolean search conditions, and these conditions can be combined using logical operators such as **AND**, **OR**, and **NOT**. The following example uses a more complex set of search conditions in the **WHERE** clause to find products that may need to be ordered:

```
SELECT  ProductName, UnitsInStock,
        UnitsOnOrder, ReorderLevel
FROM    Products
WHERE ((UnitsInStock = 0) OR
       (UnitsInStock + UnitsOnOrder < ReorderLevel))
AND    (Discontinued = 0)
```

```
Results:
ProductName             UnitsInStock UnitsOnOrder ReorderLevel
-----------             ------------ ------------ ------------
Nord-Ost Matjeshering   10           0            15
Gorgonzola Telino       0            70           20
Outback Lager           15           10           30
```

When the exact value of a character string is not known, you can still search for it in a **WHERE** clause by using the **LIKE** keyword. **LIKE** works just like = for strings, except that it allows for wildcard characters in the search pattern. The underscore (_) is used to match any single character, and the percent sign (%) is used to match more than one character. For example, the clause **WHERE ColumnA LIKE 'Smit_'** will match the values 'Smith' and 'Smite' or any other five-character value beginning with 'Smit'. Likewise, the clause **WHERE ColumnB LIKE 'A%'** will match any string value beginning with the character 'A'.

Eliminating Duplicate Rows With **DISTINCT**

Sometimes it is desirable to eliminate duplicate rows from a query's result set. For example, consider the following query, which lists all the countries present in the *Employees* table:

```
SELECT Country
FROM   Employees
```

```
Results:
Country
--------
USA
USA
USA
USA
UK
UK
UK
USA
UK
```

This query result is certainly accurate, as it displays the value of the *Country* column for every row in the *Employees* table. However, it is not a very efficient way to determine what countries are represented in the table. The reason is the duplication of countries that compels the reader to scan the output, comparing the rows to each other manually. Eliminating the duplicates would produce a better list of the countries in this table. The keyword **DISTINCT** lets you accomplish this. You may specify either **DISTINCT** or **ALL** before every item on a select list. If you do not specify either, **ALL** is the default. The following query eliminates the duplicate countries by specifying that only **DISTINCT** countries should be returned:

```
SELECT DISTINCT Country
FROM   Employees

Results:
Country
--------
UK
USA
```

Sorting Query Output With ORDER BY

You will frequently want to control the order of the rows in a query's result set. This ability is extremely important for many reporting scenarios. Suppose you were responsible for producing a report of all employees' telephone extensions in a company of 10,000 people. Such a report requires output that is sorted by name; if the report is not sorted as expected, it will be virtually useless.

The **ORDER BY** clause is used to invoke SQL Server's sorting mechanism. The syntax simply requires you to specify each expression that will be used to sort the result set. You may also specify a sort direction for each sort expression of **ASC** for ascending order or **DESC** for descending order. If you do not specify a sort direction for a sort expression, **ASC** is used. The following example retrieves the names of all the employees and guarantees that the result set is sorted in *LastName, FirstName* order. Note that both column names and column aliases can be used as sort expressions:

```
SELECT LastName [Last Name], FirstName [First Name]
FROM   Employees
ORDER  BY [Last Name], FirstName

Results:
Last Name            First Name
----------           ----------
Buchanan             Steven
Callahan             Laura
Davolio              Nancy
Dodsworth            Anne
Fuller               Andrew
King                 Robert
Leverling            Janet
Peacock              Margaret
Suyama               Michael
```

You can also specify column numbers as sort expressions. This means that the previous query could have been written in the following way without changing its behavior:

```
SELECT LastName [Last Name], FirstName [First Name]
FROM   Employees
ORDER  BY 1, 2
```

ORDER BY, when it is present, is usually the last clause specified in a query. The only clauses that can appear after it are all much less common: **COMPUTE [BY]**, **FOR BROWSE**, and the **OPTION** clause used to specify **query_hints**.

Creating Tables With SELECT...INTO

In Chapter 5, you learned how to use the **CREATE TABLE** statement to make new tables in the database. The **SELECT** statement gives you another way to make new tables. When the **SELECT** statement is used with the optional **INTO** clause, no result set is returned to the user. Rather, a new table is created to hold the result set. In the following example, a new temporary table called *#Suppliers* is created as a copy of the current *Suppliers* table:

```
SELECT *
INTO   #Suppliers
FROM   Suppliers

Results:
(29 row(s) affected)
```

Notice that you do not see the contents of the new table unless you subsequently issue another **SELECT** query against it. In order to use **SELECT...INTO**, the database where the new table will be created must have the **select into/bulkcopy** option set (database options are covered in Chapter 14). Beginning with version 7 of SQL Server, this option is always set and cannot be changed. Because temporary tables are always created in *tempdb*, this means that it is always possible to create temporary tables in SQL Server 7 by using the **SELECT...INTO** syntax.

If you administer previous versions of SQL Server, you may want to verify that the **select into/bulkcopy** option is set for *tempdb*. Although this option could be turned off for *tempdb* in previous versions of SQL Server, this is usually not advisable. So much Transact-SQL code has been written assuming that this option is set for *tempdb* that any number of things can go wrong if it is not. In fact, some parts of the SQL Server 6.5 Enterprise Manager, such as the Current Activity monitor, will not work correctly if this option is set.

Although the *#Suppliers* contains a copy of the *Suppliers* data, the definition of the two tables differ in several ways. This is because SQL Server creates the new table with features intended to represent the result set it is derived from. This means that *#Suppliers* has the same column names, data types, and data as the *Suppliers* table. However, it does not inherit any other features from *Suppliers*, such as indexes or constraints, because result sets do not need any of these features. The best way to think of the new table is to regard it as a stored result set.

If you want to use **SELECT...INTO** to create a permanent table, you must first ensure that the **select into/bulkcopy** option is enabled for that database, as previously mentioned. By default, this option is enabled in the sample *Northwind* database. You can check this option, and set it if necessary, using the **sp_dboption** stored procedure, as shown in the following example:

```
/* Check the status of select into/bulkcopy: */
EXEC sp_dboption Northwind, 'select into/bulkcopy'

/* Set the select into/bulkcopy option ON: */
```

```
EXEC sp_dboption Northwind, 'select into/bulkcopy', true

/* Verify that the option has been enabled: */
exec sp_dboption Northwind, 'select into/bulkcopy'

Results:
OptionName                          CurrentSetting
----------                          --------------
select into/bulkcopy                off

OptionName                          CurrentSetting
----------                          --------------
select into/bulkcopy                ON
```

Exercise care when enabling this database option, because it allows certain nonlogged operations, such as **SELECT...INTO**, to be performed in the database. These nonlogged operations can interfere with database and log backup procedures. You shouldn't change this option without consulting the database administrator.

Once the **select into/bulkcopy** option is enabled, you can use **SELECT...INTO** to create permanent tables, as the following example shows:

```
/* Create a permanent table using SELECT...INTO: */
SELECT *
INTO   [Backup Copy Of Shippers]
FROM   Shippers

/* Display the contents of this new permanent table: */
SELECT *
FROM   [Backup Copy Of Shippers]

Results:

(3 row(s) affected)

ShipperID  CompanyName       Phone
---------  -----------       -----
1          Speedy Express    (503) 555-9831
2          United Package    (503) 555-3199
3          Federal Shipping  (503) 555-9931
```

In practice, the most common use of **SELECT...INTO** is to create tables in *tempdb* or to create tables in a development environment. In a production environment, the **select into/bulkcopy** option is likely to be turned off for databases other than *tempdb* in order to enable SQL Server's most reliable backup and recovery strategies.

Using SELECT To Perform Joins

The **SELECT** queries we have looked at so far retrieve data from only one table at a time. However, the **FROM** clause of the **SELECT** statement allows you to name more than one source for the query data. One of the strengths of a relational database is the ability to meaningfully *join* data from different tables on an *ad hoc* basis.

Inner Joins

To understand how joins work, consider the tables *Region* and *Territories* in the *Northwind* database. *Region* has two columns (*RegionID* and *RegionDescription*), whereas the *Territories* table has three columns (*TerritoryID, TerritoryDescription*, and *RegionID*). A one-to-many relationship exists between *Region* and *Territories*: each region may be associated with many territories, but each territory may be associated with, at most, one region.

Suppose you wanted to retrieve the territory description for territory 02116, along with the name of the region associated with that territory. To do this, you might name the columns you want in the select list, specify both tables in the **FROM** clause, and put the correct restriction in the **WHERE** clause so that only data for territory 02116 will be selected. However, when you run your query, you get back more than one answer, as the following query indicates:

```
SELECT TerritoryDescription, RegionDescription
FROM   Territories, Region
WHERE  TerritoryID = '02116'

Results:
TerritoryDescription  RegionDescription
--------------------  -----------------
Boston                Eastern
Boston                Western
Boston                Northern
Boston                Southern
```

Upon inspecting the two tables separately, you find only one row in *Territories* for *TerritoryID* 02116, and that row has a *RegionID* of 1, which corresponds to the eastern region. Therefore, the first row in your result set is valid, but the other rows are not. How did these erroneous rows get into your result set?

The answer is that the query you wrote does not properly join the tables. In order to join the tables meaningfully, you must specify that you are only interested in combinations of data where *Territories.RegionID* is equal to *Region.RegionID*. The incorrect rows in your result set do not meet this test, as can be seen in the following modified query:

```
SELECT TerritoryDescription AS [Territory],
       RegionDescription    AS [Region],
       Territories.RegionID AS [T.RegionID],
       Region.RegionID      AS [R.RegionID]
FROM   Territories, Region
WHERE  TerritoryID = '02116'

Results:
Territory  Region    T.RegionID  R.RegionID
---------  -------   ----------  ----------
Boston     Eastern   1           1
Boston     Western   1           2
Boston     Northern  1           3
Boston     Southern  1           4
```

In relational database terminology, this type of (usually erroneous) query has a special name: it is called a *Cartesian product* or a *cross join*. Both of these terms refer to the fact that no restriction is placed on the way rows from the two tables can be combined. This usually happens when you forget to include the necessary join condition. Suppose, for example, that you write the query **SELECT * FROM Table1, Table2**. If *Table1* has two tuples (or rows) with values (1, 2, 3) and (4, 5, 6) and *Table2* has three tuples (A, B), (C, D), and (E, F), then the result set for this query will contain six tuples representing all possible combinations of rows from these two tables: (1, 2, 3, A, B), (1, 2, 3, C, D), (1, 2, 3, E, F), (4, 5, 6, A, B), (4, 5, 6, C, D), and (4, 5, 6, E, F). In general, the number of rows in a Cartesian product is the number of rows in the first table multiplied by the number of rows in the second table. For large tables, this can create a huge number of unwanted rows, putting a great deal of unwanted strain on your SQL Server.

To resolve this problem, you could add a condition to your **WHERE** clause specifying that you require the *RegionID* values from the two tables to be equal. This query would work properly, as shown in the following example:

```
SELECT TerritoryDescription, RegionDescription
FROM   Territories, Region
WHERE  TerritoryID = '02116'
```

```
AND    Territories.RegionID = Region.RegionID
```

```
Results:
TerritoryDescription  RegionDescription
--------------------  -----------------
Boston                Eastern
```

Because *RegionID* is a column name in both tables, we had to *qualify* this name whenever we used it in this query. SQL Server only requires you to qualify object names as much as is necessary to avoid ambiguity, although it is never an error to qualify an object name more than is necessary. In this case, the fully qualified name of the *RegionID* column in the *Region* table is *Northwind.dbo.Region.RegionID*. More information on fully qualified object names is in Chapter 9, in the discussion of the **PARSENAME** function.

7

This type of join is called an *equijoin* because the *join condition* is an equality test. It is also called an *inner join* because rows from the two tables are combined in a row of the result set only if the requirements of the join condition are met. This method of joining tables, where the join condition is coded as one or more additional conditions inside the **WHERE** clause, has been used by SQL programmers for quite some time. However, a newer method has come into favor over the last several years. This new method uses the keywords **INNER JOIN** inside the **FROM** clause to achieve the same result. Using this approach, the previous query may be rewritten as follows:

```
SELECT TerritoryDescription, RegionDescription
FROM   Territories INNER JOIN Region
ON     Territories.RegionID = Region.RegionID
WHERE  TerritoryID = '02116'
```

This **INNER JOIN** syntax specifies the two tables being joined, as well as the join condition, which appears in the **ON** clause. This example presents the simplest scenario, where only two tables are being joined, and the join condition tests only one column from each table. However, joins can be nested and complex join conditions can be used to test more than one column from each table. The following example, which lists for each *Order Detail* the *Customer*, *Product*, and *Quantity*, shows a set of **INNER JOIN** clauses that connect four tables:

```
SELECT Customers.CompanyName AS Customer,
       Products.ProductName  AS Product,
       Quantity
```

```
FROM (((
Customers INNER JOIN Orders
      ON Customers.CustomerID = Orders.CustomerID)
INNER  JOIN [Order Details]
      ON Orders.OrderID = [Order Details].OrderID)
INNER  JOIN Products
      ON [Order Details].ProductID = Products.ProductID)
```

The default type of join on SQL Server is an **INNER JOIN**. Because of this, the keyword **INNER** is optional.

The important thing is to see how the **INNER JOINS** are built up systematically. If you read this query carefully, you will see that this join is similar to the previous ones we have looked at, although it connects more tables. It follows the same rules as our previous joins. Each **INNER JOIN** clause still has two data sources, just like before, and each **INNER JOIN** has an accompanying **ON** clause. The difference is that now some of the data sources are not tables, but are the results of other joins.

Starting with the innermost parentheses within the **FROM** clause, the first **INNER JOIN** matches data from the *Orders* table and the *Customers* table based on the value of *CustomerID*. Then this intermediate data source is in turn joined to the *Order Details* table based on the value of the *OrderID* column. Finally, we include information from the *Products* table by using the *ProductID* column. In this way we have logically built up a single data source from which to choose columns. This data source has available all of the columns of the four tables that are joined together, but only in combinations that meet the requirements of the join conditions. Whereas most joins you write may not be this complex, you can see that building such sophisticated joins is just a matter of being methodical as you join in one table after another.

Note that the **INNER JOIN** clause moves the join condition out of the **WHERE** clause and into the **FROM** clause, which syntactically emphasizes that the result of the join can be thought of as a virtual table. More significantly, it is much harder to produce accidentally a Cartesian product with this syntax. Without the **INNER JOIN** syntax, we created a Cartesian product by simply writing the seemingly harmless query **SELECT * FROM Table1, Table2**. However, because the **INNER JOIN** clause *requires* the **ON** keyword, coding **SELECT * FROM Table1 INNER JOIN Table2** will just cause a syntax error. If a Cartesian product is actually desired, it can be coded by stating an **ON** condition that is always true, such as **SELECT * FROM Table1 INNER JOIN Table2 ON 1=1**. However, a better way would be to use the special **CROSS JOIN** clause, such as **SELECT * FROM Table1 CROSS JOIN Table2**.

Other Types Of Joins

A *recursive relationship* is one where a table is related to itself. The *Employees* table in the *Northwind* database has a recursive relationship representing employee supervision. Because an employee is supervised by another employee, this relationship has been modeled by including a column called *ReportsTo* in the *Employees* table. This column holds the *EmployeeID* of the employee's supervisor. This is a normal foreign key relationship except that the parent data and the child data come from two different rows in the same table.

To retrieve data from both sides of a recursive relationship, a table is joined to itself. Such joins are called *self-joins* or *auto-joins*. Before writing a self-join, however, you must be able to use *table aliases*. A table alias is another name given to a logical copy of a table (or view) in a query. It is given in the **FROM** clause, immediately following the table name. For the duration of that query, the table alias is used instead of the actual name of the table. Table aliases are frequently used with joins to shorten qualified column names. For example, the following pseudo-query joins two tables based on the value of two common columns. Notice how the repetition of the table names clutters up the query:


```
SELECT TableA.ColumnX, TableA.ColumnY, TableB.ColumnZ
FROM   TableA INNER JOIN TableB
ON     TableA.ColumnX = TableB.ColumnX
AND    TableA.ColumnY = TableB.ColumnY
```

The following query is equivalent to the previous one. By using table aliases, we are able to make this query both easier to read and easier to type:

```
SELECT A.ColumnX, A.ColumnY, B.ColumnZ
FROM   TableA A INNER JOIN TableB B
ON     A.ColumnX = B.ColumnX
AND    A.ColumnY = B.ColumnY
```

Now we are ready to write our self-join. Because a self-join connects a table to itself, table aliases must be used so that SQL Server can tell the two logical instances of the table apart. For example, to query the employee—supervisor relationship we have been talking about, we will need one reference to the *Employees* table for the supervised employees and another for the supervisors. Armed with all this knowledge, you might try to run the following query to list the name of each employee along with the name of his or her supervisor:

```
SELECT EMP.FirstName  + ' ' +  EMP.LastName AS Employee,
       BOSS.FirstName + ' ' + BOSS.LastName AS Supervisor
FROM   Employees EMP INNER JOIN Employees BOSS
ON     EMP.ReportsTo = BOSS.EmployeeID
```

```
Results:
Employee            Supervisor
--------            ----------
Anne Dodsworth      Steven Buchanan
Janet Leverling     Andrew Fuller
Laura Callahan      Andrew Fuller
Margaret Peacock    Andrew Fuller
Michael Suyama      Steven Buchanan
Nancy Davolio       Andrew Fuller
Robert King         Steven Buchanan
Steven Buchanan     Andrew Fuller
```

This query uses + (plus), which is SQL Server's string concatenation operator. You can find a table of SQL Server operators in Chapter 9.

The self-join works by naming the *Employees* table in the **FROM** clause with a table alias of *EMP* and then joining this virtual *EMP* table to the *Employees* table (again), this time with an alias of *BOSS*. Now that this join has been established with its table aliases, notice how the entire rest of the query functions as though the *Employees* table were not named at all. The query is written as though *EMP* and *BOSS* were real tables being joined to each other.

You may have noticed a problem with the output from our last query. The *Employees* table has nine rows, but our output has only eight rows. Andrew Fuller, who shows up in the *Supervisor* column five times, is never listed as an employee. Obviously, Andrew must be an employee, because the supervisor data is also drawn from the *Employees* table. Why is he left off the list of employees?

The answer to this question has to do with the fact that Andrew Fuller has no supervisor. In other words, if you look at his row in the *Employees* table, you will see that the *ReportsTo* column is **NULL**. This implies that the join condition **EMP.ReportsTo = BOSS.EmployeeID** can never be true for Andrew, because the value of *EMP.ReportsTo* is **NULL** for his *EMP* row, and **NULL** can never be equal to anything. In addition, if the join condition cannot be true for Andrew's *EMP* row, his *EMP* row will never be included in the query's result set.

The easiest way to include a row for Andrew in our query output is to change our join from an **INNER JOIN** to an **OUTER JOIN**. Recall that an **INNER JOIN** is a join where rows from the two tables are combined in a row of the result set only if the requirements of the join condition are met. An **OUTER JOIN** can be used to include rows in the result set even if the join conditions are not met. **OUTER JOIN** queries exist solely to solve problems like the one we are having with Andrew.

SQL Server supports three types of **OUTER JOIN** clauses: **LEFT OUTER JOIN**, **RIGHT OUTER JOIN**, and **FULL OUTER JOIN**. In each case, the word "OUTER" is optional. Each of these outer joins will include rows from one or both of the tables, even if the join condition is not met for that row. **LEFT OUTER JOIN** will return the same results as an **INNER JOIN**, but will add to those results information from any row in the first (left) table that cannot be matched to the second (right) table by the join condition. **RIGHT OUTER JOIN** returns the same results as an **INNER JOIN**, but adds to it information from any row in the second (right) table that cannot be matched to the first (left) table by the join condition. **FULL OUTER JOIN** returns the same results as an **INNER JOIN**, but adds to it information from any row in either table that cannot be matched to the other table by the join condition.

7

The following query has only one difference from the previous query: the join type has been changed from **INNER** to **LEFT**. Because the *EMP* table alias is the first (left) table, any *EMP* row that cannot be matched by the join condition will still be included in the result set. In other words, Andrew Fuller will be listed as an employee even though he has no supervisor:

```
SELECT EMP.FirstName  + ' ' +  EMP.LastName AS Employee,
       BOSS.FirstName + ' ' + BOSS.LastName AS Supervisor
FROM   Employees EMP LEFT JOIN Employees BOSS
ON     EMP.ReportsTo = BOSS.EmployeeID
```

```
Results:
Employee            Supervisor
--------            ----------
Andrew Fuller       NULL
Anne Dodsworth      Steven Buchanan
Janet Leverling     Andrew Fuller
Laura Callahan      Andrew Fuller
Margaret Peacock    Andrew Fuller
Michael Suyama      Steven Buchanan
Nancy Davolio       Andrew Fuller
Robert King         Steven Buchanan
Steven Buchanan     Andrew Fuller
```

Notice how SQL Server supplies a **NULL** value for the name of Andrew's supervisor. The reason for this is not the **NULL** value in Andrew's *ReportsTo* column. Rather, SQL Server always responds with **NULL** values when it is asked for information it does not have. In this case, SQL Server is being asked to build a string based on the supervisor's name. Because Andrew has no supervisor, this is information SQL Server does not have, and so it puts a **NULL** value in the appropriate place in the result set. You will see **NULL** values in **OUTER JOIN** result sets whenever the non-null information in that row of the result set could not be matched using the **JOIN** condition.

SQL Server also support another **OUTER JOIN** syntax in which **WHERE** clause operators are used to indicate a join type. For example, a left join between two tables joined by a single column could be written as **SELECT * FROM TableA, TableB WHERE TableA.Col1 *= TableB.Col1**. For right joins, =* is used. You may see this syntax in some databases, especially if you work with any legacy code. However, the **INNER JOIN** and **OUTER JOIN** syntax we have been using for most of this section is preferred for several reasons. First of all, it is less ambiguous than the legacy syntax, and is much less prone to produce accidental Cartesian products. Second, it is not possible to specify a **FULL OUTER JOIN** using the legacy syntax. Finally, the **INNER JOIN** and **OUTER JOIN** syntax is compliant with the ANSI SQL-92 standards, which is an industry-wide SQL syntax that Microsoft and other database vendors have committed to support. You will see the syntax used in this chapter on the exam.

UNION Queries

The **UNION** operator makes it possible to combine two queries so that all rows from each query are returned as a single result set. **UNION** queries are well suited for combining similar information that is contained in more than one data source. For example, the following query lists Northwind's customers, shippers, and suppliers using three query expressions combined by two **UNION** statements:

```
SELECT 'Customer' AS Type, CompanyName AS Company, Phone
FROM    Customers
UNION
SELECT 'Shipper',  CompanyName, Phone
FROM    Shippers
UNION
SELECT 'Supplier', CompanyName, Phone
FROM    Suppliers
ORDER   BY Type, Company
```

```
Results:
Type     Company                            Phone
-----    -------------------                ------
Customer Alfreds Futterkiste                030-0074321
Customer Ana Trujillo Emparedados y helados (5) 555-4729
Customer Wilman Kala                        90-224 8858
Customer Wolski  Zajazd                     (26) 642-7012
Shipper  Federal Shipping                   (503) 555-9931
Shipper  Speedy Express                     (503) 555-9831
Shipper  United Package                     (503) 555-3199
Supplier Aux joyeux ecclésiastiques         (1) 03.83.00.68
```

```
Supplier Bigfoot Breweries                    (503) 555-9931
Supplier Tokyo Traders                        (03) 3555-5011
Supplier Zaanse Snoepfabriek                  (12345) 1212
```

Notice the single **ORDER BY** clause that appears at the end of the query. Technically, the **UNION** operator does not combine entire queries. Rather, it combines what Microsoft calls *query specifications* in order to form a single query. Because a single query can only be sorted one way, a **UNION** query can only have one **ORDER BY** clause. This is why **ORDER BY**, when used in a **UNION** query, only appears once, after the very last query specification.

Also note that in order to rename the columns in the result set, we only had to supply column aliases for the first query specification. In a **UNION** query, the column names are taken from the first query specification.

It is possible for two query specifications to produce duplicate rows. By default, if two such query specifications are combined with the **UNION** operator, these duplicate rows will be removed. To include duplicate rows in a **UNION** query's output, use **UNION ALL** instead of **UNION**. For example, **SELECT ColA FROM TableA UNION ALL SELECT ColB FROM TableB**. Notice that whereas **ALL** is the default for a query specification's **SELECT** list, it is not the default behavior for the **UNION** operator.

Here's a process saving tip: you may want to use **UNION ALL** even when you know that the result set will have no duplicate rows. The reason is that you will save the SQL Server from going through the effort of attempting to detect duplicates. For a large result set, the difference in speed and resource consumption can be substantial.

In order to use **UNION**, the two query specifications involved must be *union-compatible*. This means that each query specification must have the same number of columns and that corresponding columns from each query specification must be of compatible data types. For example, suppose the first query specification has two columns with data types **INT**, and **VARCHAR (20)**. Then the second query specification must also have two columns, where the first column's data type is compatible with **INT** and the second column's data type is compatible with **VARCHAR (20)**. For more information on how SQL Server determines union compatibility, see the topics "Guidelines For Using **UNION** And Data Type Precedence" in the *SQL Server Books Online*.

Whereas **JOIN** statements and **UNION** operators combine data in meaningful ways, they are complementary techniques that are fundamentally different from each other. The following are interesting ways to compare the **UNION** operator with **JOIN** statements:

- **JOIN** statements combine data sources, such as tables or views.
- **UNION** operators combine result sets.
- **JOIN** can be thought of as operating *horizontally* to combine specific rows from two different data sources into a virtual data source that has all of the columns of each original data source.
- **UNION** can be thought of as operating *vertically* to combine all rows from two different result sets into a virtual result set that has all of the rows of each original result set.

Subqueries

A *subquery* or *nested query* is, as its name implies, a query embedded inside another query. It is sometimes called an *inner query* because it is contained inside another query. Likewise, the containing query is sometimes called an *outer query*. The use of subqueries allows a Transact-SQL programmer to achieve some effects that might otherwise require intricately coded stored procedures. In this section, we will examine several ways to use subqueries in **SELECT** statements.

Subqueries Used In Comparisons

Up until now many of our **WHERE** clauses have contained *hard-coded literal values*. An example of a hard-coded literal value is the "5" in the search condition **EmployeeID = 5**. Hard-coded literal values may be acceptable for *ad hoc* (one-time) queries, but they are very inflexible by nature. This makes them poorly suited for database applications because users may be selecting or typing query parameters dynamically at their computer.

In some cases, subqueries may be a better way to build comparisons. Suppose, for example, that we want to find everyone who works in the same country as Nancy Davolio. Without subqueries, we would have to run two queries: the first to find out what Nancy's country is, and the second to find the other employees in that country. With subqueries, we are able to retrieve this information using a single query, as seen in the following code:

```
SELECT FirstName, LastName
FROM   Employees
WHERE  Country =
      (SELECT Country
       FROM   Employees
       WHERE  FirstName = 'Nancy'
       AND    LastName = 'Davolio')
ORDER  BY FirstName, LastName
```

```
Results:
FirstName  LastName
---------  --------
Andrew     Fuller
Janet      Leverling
Laura      Callahan
Margaret   Peacock
Nancy      Davolio
```

This query works because the embedded subquery returns exactly one value, *USA*. After SQL Server retrieves this value, it then inserts it into the outer query in the place of the subquery. This transformation yields the following intermediate query that SQL Server executes in the usual way:


```
/* Intermediate Query Created By SQL Server: */
SELECT FirstName, LastName
FROM   Employees
WHERE  Country = 'USA'
ORDER  BY FirstName, LastName
```

Subqueries Used In The Select List

A subquery can also be used as an expression in the select list. The following query displays the name of the highest-ranking employee in the *Big Boss* column by exploiting the fact that this person has no supervisor. SQL Server calculates this value by first running the subquery to retrieve the value Andrew Fuller. It then uses this literal value as the first expression of the outer query's select list.

```
SELECT (SELECT FirstName + ' ' + LastName
        FROM   Employees
        WHERE  ReportsTo IS NULL
       )   AS  [Big Boss],
       FirstName + ' ' + LastName AS Employee
FROM   Employees
ORDER  BY Employee

Big Boss       Employee
--------       ---------
Andrew Fuller  Andrew Fuller
Andrew Fuller  Anne Dodsworth
Andrew Fuller  Janet Leverling
Andrew Fuller  Laura Callahan
Andrew Fuller  Margaret Peacock
Andrew Fuller  Michael Suyama
Andrew Fuller  Nancy Davolio
Andrew Fuller  Robert King
Andrew Fuller  Steven Buchanan
```

Because the subqueries discussed so far return only a single value, they are sometimes referred to as *scalar subqueries*.

Subqueries That Return Groups Of Values

Not all subqueries return a single value. Consider the following query:

```
SELECT DISTINCT OrderID AS [Beverage Orders]
FROM   [Order Details]
WHERE  ProductID IN
     ( SELECT ProductID
       FROM   Products INNER JOIN Categories
       ON     Products.CategoryID = Categories.CategoryID
       WHERE  Categories.CategoryName = 'Beverages'
     )
ORDER  BY OrderID

Results:
Beverage Orders
---------------
10253
10254
10255
...
11075
11077
```

This query uses an embedded subquery to look up the *ProductID* for every product in the *Beverages* category. Because more than one such product may exist (in fact, 12 exist), we cannot use a simple comparison operator, such as equals (=). This is because it makes no sense to ask whether a particular *ProductID* value is equal to a group of 12 *ProductID* values.

Transact-SQL provides a group of logical operators for situations like this. In our example, we have used the logical operator **IN**. This operator has the syntax **single_value IN set_of_values** and returns true if the **single_value** is included in the **set_of_values**. For our query, this means that the result set will include any row from *[Order Details]* where the *ProductID* is associated with the beverage category. The entire list of set operators is discussed in Chapter 9.

Testing Existence With Subqueries

Another logical operator that is frequently used with subqueries is **EXISTS**. The following query uses **EXISTS** to display the same information displayed by the previous query—the list of *Orders* that include the sale of at least one beverage:

```
SELECT DISTINCT OrderID AS [Beverage Orders]
FROM   [Order Details]
WHERE  EXISTS
    (  SELECT *
       FROM   Products INNER JOIN Categories
       ON     Products.CategoryID = Categories.CategoryID
       WHERE  Categories.CategoryName = 'Beverages'
       AND    [Order Details].ProductID = Products.ProductID
    )
ORDER  BY OrderID

Results:
Beverage Orders
---------------
10253
10254
10255
...
11075
11077
```


The **EXISTS** operator will return "true" if the subquery following it returns a nonempty result set. Because **EXISTS** tests for the existence of rows, but does not return any values from that row, you don't need to specify specific columns in the subquery's select list. Because of this, the select list of an **EXISTS** subquery is usually represented by an asterisk (*).

Correlated Subqueries

Whenever a subquery requires information from its outer query, the subquery is called a *correlated subquery*. In this particular query, the inner query checks for products that are associated with the *Beverages* category *and* whose *ProductID* matches the *ProductID* column in the *Order Details* table. It is this dependence on the value of *[Order Details].ProductID* that makes this inner query a correlated subquery. SQL Server is often able to determine a query execution strategy requiring a noncorrelated subquery to be executed only once for its entire outer query. A correlated subquery, however, must be executed once for each row evaluated by the outer query, because it depends on the outer query to supply information it needs.

Table aliases are often used with correlated subqueries, in which case the table alias may be called a *correlation name*. Here is an example of a correlated subquery that uses correlation names. This query displays a cross-reference showing which customers have used which shippers:

```
SELECT CUST.CompanyName AS Customer,
       SHIP.CompanyName AS Shipper
FROM   Customers CUST, Shippers SHIP
WHERE  EXISTS
     ( SELECT *
       FROM   Orders ORD
       WHERE  ORD.CustomerID = CUST.CustomerID
       AND    ORD.ShipVia    = SHIP.ShipperID
     )
ORDER  BY Customer, Shipper
```

Results:

```
Customer                            Shipper
-------------------                 --------
Alfreds Futterkiste                 Federal Shipping
Alfreds Futterkiste                 Speedy Express
Alfreds Futterkiste                 United Package
Ana Trujillo Emparedados y helados  Federal Shipping
Ana Trujillo Emparedados y helados  Speedy Express
Antonio Moreno Taquería             Federal Shipping
Wilman Kala                         Federal Shipping
Wilman Kala                         Speedy Express
Wolski  Zajazd                      Federal Shipping
Wolski  Zajazd                      Speedy Express
Wolski  Zajazd                      United Package
```

This is not the only way to write this query. For example, this query could be rewritten as a three-way **INNER JOIN**. It is common for Transact-SQL to offer more than one way to meet a specific query's requirements. As a database administrator or a database programmer, it is important that you understand the performance impact of the way a query is written. Sometimes it results in little or no difference in the efficiency or performance of the query, and sometimes the difference is dramatic. To learn how to write the most efficient queries possible, you will need to master the material in Chapter 19.

One of the topics covered in Chapter 19 will be "Using Optimizer Hints." The **SELECT** statement supports three kinds of hints: table hints, join hints, and query hints. The **INSERT**, **DELETE**, and **UPDATE** statements, which will be introduced later in this chapter, can also accept optimizer hints. In addition to the coverage of hints in Chapter 19, you can read about some basic table hints in Chapter 6.

Derived Tables

Another use of nested queries is to specify a derived table as the data source for a query instead of naming a table or a view. Such a *derived table* must always be given a table alias. For example, the following query is a legal way to display employees' names:

```
SELECT *
FROM
   (SELECT FirstName,
           LastName
    FROM   Employees) AS Emp
```

USING **INSERT** TO ADD DATA

Now that you have learned many ways to use the **SELECT** statement, you probably want to go practice on your own database tables. However, before you can retrieve data *from* tables, you have to put data *into* tables. The most basic way to do this is to use Transact-SQL's **INSERT** statement. In this section, we will look at several different ways to use **INSERT** to add new rows to an existing table.

Using **INSERT** To Add Individual Rows

The first form of **INSERT** statement we will examine is used to add a single row of default values to a table. The basic syntax of this kind of **INSERT** statement is:

```
INSERT [INTO] {table_name|view_name}
DEFAULT VALUES
```

This statement will **INSERT** one row to the table or updateable view named. Each column of the new row will hold the default value for that column. The only table or view in the *Northwind* database that can be used with this type of **INSERT** is the *Orders* table. The following code adds a new row to the *Orders* table:

```
INSERT  INTO Orders
DEFAULT VALUES
```

If you were to run this **INSERT** statement and examine the row it added, you would find that the newly created record is just a template or a generic order. The row contains a new *OrderID* and a *Freight* amount of 0, but all the other columns contain **NULL** values. SQL Server automatically generates the new *OrderID* because *OrderID* is an *identity* column. The *Freight* column is assigned a value of 0 because that is the default value for *Freight*. The other columns are given **NULL** values because, although they do not have system-generated or user-specified default values, they are configured to allow **NULLS**.

The usefulness of such an **INSERT** statement, which may not be obvious at first, is that a row like this can serve as an order *template*. In many applications, a row must be created *before* the user supplies all of the necessary data to populate that row. In such a case, an **INSERT...DEFAULT VALUES** statement makes good sense, because it allows a row to be created that can be populated later with **UPDATE** statements (**UPDATE** is covered later in this chapter).

You may have wondered why *Orders* is the only table in the *Northwind* database that can be used with **INSERT...DEFAULT VALUES**. The reason is that in order to use this form of **INSERT**, each row of the table must have a default value associated with it or it must allow **NULL** values. A default value can be system-generated, as is the case with **TIMESTAMP** or **IDENTITY** columns, or it can be a user-specified **DEFAULT** constraint declared as part of the table's definition. Trying to use **INSERT...DEFAULT VALUES** for a table where these conditions are not met will cause SQL Server to return an error. In the *Northwind* database, the *Orders* table is the only one where all the columns meet these conditions.

Most **INSERT** statements do not use the **DEFAULT VALUES** clause. It is more common to gather the information for a new row first, and then to **INSERT** the entire row, specifying the values for many or all of the columns. The syntax for this type of insert is:

```
INSERT [INTO] {table_name|view_name}
[(column_list)]
VALUES
(expression_list)
```

The *column_list* and the *expression_list* in this statement have a one-to-one relationship: Every column on the column list has a corresponding expression on the expression list. The relationship between these two lists is ordered so that the first expression is used as the value for the first column, the second expression is used for the second column, and so on. The data type of each expression must be compatible with the column it is going to populate. The following example could be used to add a new row to the *Shippers* table:

```
INSERT INTO Shippers (CompanyName, Phone)
VALUES ('Tennessee Cabin Freight', '(555) 555-5555')
```

You may have noticed that the column *ShipperID* was not listed in the column list. This is because the *ShipperID* column is an *identity* column, and so SQL Server will automatically generate its value. This **INSERT** creates a new row that has a system-generated *ShipperID*, a *CompanyName* of 'Tennessee Cabin Freight', and a value of '(555) 555-5555' for the *Phone* column.

It is an error to try to specify a value for an *IDENTITY* column unless the **IDENTITY_INSERT** option is set for the table receiving the **INSERT**. It is always an error to try to specify a value for a *timestamp* column.

The expressions used in the expression list must be *scalar expressions.* A scalar expression is one that must return a single value. Subqueries are not allowed on the expression list.

As this example showed, it is not necessary to include every column from the table on the column list. If a column is omitted from this list, SQL Server generates its value following the same rules it uses for columns created by **INSERT...DEFAULT VALUES**. If a default value is defined for that column, SQL Server will use it. If no default is defined for that column, SQL Server attempts to use a **NULL** value instead. If a column that is not listed in the column list has no default value and does not accept **NULL** values, SQL Server returns an error.

7

The columns in the column list can be named in any order. That is, the following two statements are equivalent:

```
INSERT TableA (Col1, Col2) VALUES (1, 2)
INSERT TableA (Col2, Col1) VALUES (2, 1)
```

Both of the statements above add a single row to *TableA* with **Col1 = 1** and **Col2 = 2**, even though the order of the column list is reversed. Remember that the relationship between the column list and the expression list is based on the order of the lists, not the order of the columns in the table.

If the optional column list is omitted entirely (and you are not using the **DEFAULT VALUES** clause), SQL Server expects you to supply values for each column in the table *in the order that they are defined in the database catalog*. Because no guarantee exists that the number or order of columns in a table will never change, it is not considered good programming practice to omit the column list, unless the query is a one-time, *ad hoc* insert. Even in this case you may want to include the column list just to be safe.

The keywords **DEFAULT** and **NULL** can be used on the column list in place of column values. If **DEFAULT** is specified on the expression list, SQL Server will use the default value for the corresponding column. If none is defined, an error is returned. Likewise, if **NULL** is specified, SQL Server will use a **NULL** value for the corresponding column, and will return an error if that column cannot accept **NULL** values.

Using **INSERT...SELECT** To Insert Multiple Rows

An embedded **SELECT** statement may be used with **INSERT** in place of **VALUES** clause. This creates the following syntax:

```
INSERT [INTO] {table_name|view_name}
[(column_list)]
query_definition
```

When the **INSERT...SELECT** syntax is used, each column in the result set of the **query_definition** must be compatible with its corresponding column in the **column_list**. In other words, the query definition and the column list must be union-compatible. Columns may be omitted from the column list, or the column list may be omitted entirely, according to the same rules that apply to a single-row **INSERT** statement.

The following code creates a new table that is able to hold some of the information stored in the *Employees* table. This new table is populated with an appropriate **INSERT...SELECT** statement, and then displayed using **SELECT**:

```
CREATE TABLE UK_Employees
(UK_EmployeeID INT IDENTITY(1,1),
 FirstName     NVARCHAR(10),
 LastName      NVARCHAR(20),
 City          NVARCHAR(15),
 HomePhone     NVARCHAR(24))

INSERT INTO UK_Employees (FirstName, LastName, City, HomePhone)
SELECT FirstName, LastName, City, HomePhone
FROM   Employees
WHERE  Country = 'UK'

SELECT *
FROM   UK_Employees

Results:
UK_EmployeeID FirstName LastName  City     HomePhone
------------- --------- --------  -----    ---------
1             Steven    Buchanan  London   (71) 555-4848
2             Michael   Suyama    London   (71) 555-7773
3             Robert    King      London   (71) 555-5598
4             Anne      Dodsworth London   (71) 555-4444
```

Using **INSERT...EXECUTE** To Insert Multiple Rows

A final variation on the **INSERT** statement is to use an **EXECUTE** statement to supply the rows to be inserted into the table. **EXECUTE** can invoke a stored procedure or dynamically run a character string that contains a Transact-SQL batch. Stored procedures will the subject of Chapter 12 of this book, whereas Transact-SQL batches are covered in Chapter 8. For now, it is enough to know that these are methods of logically combining multiple Transact-SQL statements. Here is the syntax for this type of **INSERT**:

```
INSERT [INTO] {table_name|view_name}
[(column_list)]
EXEC[UTE] {stored_procedure|(sql_string)}
```

To be used in an **INSERT...EXECUTE** statement, the results of the **EXECUTE** statement must be union-compatible with the columns in the column list. The syntax **EXEC[UTE]** indicates that **EXEC** is a valid abbreviation for **EXECUTE**. The following example creates a two-column table and uses **INSERT...EXECUTE** to populate it using a dynamic SQL batch:


```
CREATE TABLE SimpleInsert
(RowID INT, Sentence NVARCHAR(100))

INSERT SimpleInsert
EXEC ("SELECT 5, 'This sentence is for RowID 5.'")

SELECT *
FROM   SimpleInsert

DROP TABLE SimpleInsert

Results:
RowID       Sentence
-----       ---------
5           This sentence is for RowID 5.
```

The statements **SELECT**, **INSERT**, **DELETE**, and **UPDATE** are collectively called *Data Manipulation Language (DML)* statements. DML is defined to be the subset of SQL that allows data to be retrieved or manipulated. Some people define DML to include only data modification commands but not data retrieval commands, thus excluding **SELECT** from the list of DML commands. However, *SQL Server Books Online* repeatedly makes a point of including **SELECT** as a DML statement.

Other subsets of the SQL language that you may come across in your database reading include *Data Definition Language (DDL)* and *Data Control Language (DCL)*. DDL allows you to define and manipulate the structure of database objects and include the statements to create, alter, and drop different types of database objects, such as **CREATE PROCEDURE**, **ALTER TABLE**, and **DROP USER**. DCL commands, such as **GRANT**, **REVOKE**, and **DENY**, let you control access to database objects.

Removing Rows With DELETE

The **DELETE** statement is used to remove existing rows from tables. In its simplest form, **DELETE** takes the following syntax:

```
DELETE [FROM] {table_name|view_name}
[WHERE search_condition]
```

The **WHERE** clause is identical to the **WHERE** clause of a **SELECT** statement. This means that it can contain comparison tests and subqueries. If the optional **WHERE** clause is omitted, every row will be deleted from the named table.

The code samples for the **DELETE** statement can permanently remove data from your database. They are meant to be studied but not executed. If you do execute these samples, do not ignore the **BEGIN TRANSACTION** and **ROLLBACK TRANSACTION** statements. If you omit these two commands, you may permanently remove data from your copy of the *Northwind* database. If this should happen to you, consult the *SQL Server Books Online* for instructions on how to rebuild your *Northwind* database.

Transaction control, which is a way of ensuring that a entire group of SQL statements either succeeds or fails in a consistent manner, is covered in Chapter 11.

The three **DELETE** statements in Listing 7.1 are combined in a single transaction so that the **DELETE** statements can easily be rolled back (canceled). If you execute the **DELETE** statements from this section exactly as they are given, you will not lose any data. Your output may indicate that a certain number of rows have been deleted, but once the transaction is rolled back the data will still be there.

The first **DELETE** shows that without a **WHERE** clause a **DELETE** statement will remove every row in its table. As the output indicates, all 49 rows in the *EmployeeTerritories* table would be removed by this statement if its transaction were not canceled. The next **DELETE** demonstrates the use of a simple comparison in the **WHERE** clause. If this transaction were committed, this statement would remove 159 rows from the *Order Details* table. The third and final **DELETE** statement in this sample code removes any orders for which no matching *Order Details* records can be found. This **DELETE** will not remove any rows unless it is run after the second **DELETE**.

Listing 7.1 Deleting rows within a transaction so the changes can be canceled.

```
/* Protect your data with a transaction: */
BEGIN TRANSACTION

/* Delete all rows from a table: */
PRINT  'Deleting all rows from EmployeeTerritories...'
DELETE FROM EmployeeTerritories

/* Delete selected rows from a table: */
PRINT  'Deleting Order Details with Quantity > 50...'
DELETE FROM [Order Details]
WHERE Quantity > 50

/* Use a subquery with DELETE: */
PRINT  'Deleting Orders with no matching Order Details...'
DELETE FROM Orders
WHERE NOT EXISTS
    (  SELECT *
       FROM [Order Details]
       WHERE Orders.OrderID = [Order Details].OrderID
    )

/* Cancel your changes: */
ROLLBACK TRANSACTION

Results:
Deleting all rows from EmployeeTerritories...
(49 row(s) affected)

Deleting Order Details with Quantity > 50...
(159 row(s) affected)

Deleting Orders with no matching Order Details...
(10 row(s) affected)
```


Using DELETE...FROM

Although the **WHERE** clause makes **DELETE** a very powerful command, there are times where it is difficult, or even impossible, to specify a search condition that properly identifies the rows you want to remove. In such a case, you should consider the use of the **DELETE...FROM** syntax. This statement is a Microsoft extension to the SQL-92 standard that is only found in Transact-SQL. It allows you to specify multiple data sources that can then be referenced by the **WHERE** clause to identify rows that **DELETE** should remove. The syntax for this statement is:

```
DELETE [FROM] {table_name|view_name}
FROM   data_source
[WHERE search_condition]
```

Notice that the **FROM** on the first line is optional but the **FROM** on the second line is not. This second **FROM** simply allows you to specify additional data sources that can be referenced by the **WHERE** clause. As an example, suppose you have just learned that all of the *Order Details* records associated with Laura Callahan have been incorrectly entered into the database and must be removed immediately. The following query would delete the proper rows:

Don't forget to include the **BEGIN TRANSACTION** and **ROLLBACK TRANSACTION** statements if you run this query on your SQL Server.

```
/* Protect your data with a transaction: */
BEGIN  TRANSACTION

DELETE [Order Details]

FROM   Employees EMP INNER JOIN Orders ORD
ON     EMP.EmployeeID = ORD.EmployeeID
WHERE  EMP.FirstName = 'Laura'
AND    EMP.LastName = 'Callahan'
AND    ORD.OrderID = [Order Details].OrderID

/* Cancel the transaction: */
ROLLBACK TRANSACTION

Results:
(260 row(s) affected)
```

Removing All Rows With TRUNCATE TABLE

The **TRUNCATE TABLE** statement is similar to the **DELETE** statement in that both can be used to remove rows from a table. Beyond that fact, however, the two statements are not very similar. We will briefly highlight these differences while discussing the type of situations for which **TRUNCATE TABLE** is most useful. The syntax of **TRUNCATE TABLE** is quite simple:

```
TRUNCATE TABLE table_name
```

Notice that **TRUNCATE TABLE** does not support **WHERE** clauses or subqueries. This reflects the first (and most important) difference between **TRUNCATE TABLE** and **DELETE**. Simply put, **TRUNCATE TABLE** cannot selectively remove rows the way **DELETE** does. Instead, ***TRUNCATE***

TABLE *always removes every row* from the table. Make sure you understand this: The use of **TRUNCATE TABLE** removes every row from the table named in the query.

If you have not seen the **TRUNCATE TABLE** statement before, you may be wondering how useful this statement could possibly be. After all, instead of **TRUNCATE TABLE table_name**, you could simply write **DELETE table_name** and achieve the same results with less typing.

Although this is true, for several reasons, **TRUNCATE TABLE** is a statement experienced database administrators frequently rely on. The most important reason is that **TRUNCATE TABLE** uses fewer system and transaction log entries than an equivalent **DELETE** statement. **DELETE FROM table_name** will make a transaction log entry *for every row deleted.* **TRUNCATE TABLE** cuts back on this effort significantly by not logging any of the removed rows. Instead, **TRUNCATE TABLE** simply deallocates the data pages holding the rows. This saves a lot of time and effort, because each data page may hold dozens, hundreds, or even thousands of individual data rows. In recent testing, a **TRUNCATE TABLE** statement removed the rows from a table in 10 milliseconds, whereas the equivalent **DELETE** took almost 15 *seconds* to remove the same rows.

When the **TRUNCATE TABLE** statement deallocates pages, *it makes the table behave as though the pages had never been allocated*. One of the implications of this is that if the table contains an *identity* column, that column will be reset to its original **SEED** value.

It is not risky for SQL Server to truncate a table without creating log entries for the deleted rows. Because the **TRUNCATE TABLE** statement itself is logged, it can be rolled forward, if necessary, for recovery purposes. In addition, because the page deallocations are logged also, **TRUNCATE TABLE** can be rolled back during database recovery, or in response to a **ROLLBACK TRANSACTION** statement. For more information about transaction logging and control, please see Chapter 11.

Still, the use of **TRUNCATE TABLE** changes SQL Server's behavior in some subtle ways that you need to understand. In Chapter 13, you will learn about *triggers*. One type of trigger is a *delete trigger*, which is a group of Transact-SQL statements that are automatically executed by SQL Server whenever a row in a table is deleted. SQL Server uses the transaction log when it executes a delete trigger. Because individual row deletions are not logged with **TRUNCATE TABLE**, this statement will not cause delete triggers to be executed. For similar reasons, SQL Server does not allow **TRUNCATE TABLE** to be run against any table that is referenced by a *foreign key*.

Another difference between **DELETE** and **TRUNCATE TABLE** is that permission to execute **DELETE** statements against an object can be granted to any user or role in the database. However, the only users that can issue **TRUNCATE TABLE** are the table's owner and the database owner.

To review, you should consider the following conditions when deciding whether to use **TRUNCATE TABLE** or **DELETE**:

- If you want to remove all rows in a table, **TRUNCATE TABLE** may be appropriate. If rows are to be selectively removed, you must use **DELETE**.
- If the number of rows to be removed is large, consider using **TRUNCATE TABLE** to save time and resources.
- If your table has triggers, and these triggers must be executed even when the table is being emptied of all rows, you must use **DELETE** and not **TRUNCATE TABLE**.
- If your table is referenced by any foreign keys, you must use **DELETE** and not **TRUNCATE TABLE**.
- If your table has an *identity* column, remember that it will be set back to its original **SEED** value after **TRUNCATE TABLE** is run.
- You can grant another user the permission to **DELETE** rows from a table you own, but you cannot grant them the permission to run **TRUNCATE TABLE** against it.

Because **TRUNCATE TABLE** deallocates pages, which are physical database objects and not logical table data, **TRUNCATE TABLE** is considered a Data Definition Language (DDL) statement and not a Data Manipulation Language (DML) statement.

Using UPDATE To Modify Data

When you want to modify data that already exists in a database, you have at least two choices. The first choice would be to record the current values for each column of the row to be updated, delete the row, and finally insert a new row with the proper mix of original and updated column values. A much easier (and more common) approach is to use an **UPDATE** statement to change the data in an existing row. The syntax for a basic **UPDATE** statement is:

```
UPDATE {table_name|view_name}
SET    update_list
FROM   table_source
WHERE  search_condition
```

UPDATE has only one clause we have not already examined in another statement: the **SET** clause. This clause ordinarily introduces a list called an *update_list*. The items on the update list are separated by commas, and each item has the form *column_name = new_value*, such as the phrase *ContactTitle = 'Purchasing Manager'* in the following example, which updates two columns in the *Suppliers* table:

```
UPDATE Suppliers
SET    ContactName = 'T. D. Raines',
       ContactTitle = 'International Sales Manager'
WHERE  SupplierID = 8
```

The **new_value** expression can be a hard-coded literal value, a formula based on Transact-SQL functions, a Transact-SQL variable, the name of another column, or even a subquery that returns a single value. The columns listed in the update list can be listed in any order. If a column in the update list is not updateable, such as an *identity* or *timestamp* column, SQL Server returns an error.

7

Note that the **WHERE** clause given specifies a value for the table's primary key. This means that only one row will match the **WHERE** clause, and that only that row will be updated. Specifying values for the table's entire primary key is not required, but it is a common practice when updating only one row is the desired result. Because a **WHERE** clause acts as a filter, any row that is not excluded by the **WHERE** clause will be updated. This means that all rows in the table will be updated if the **WHERE** clause is omitted.

Using **UPDATE** With Nested Subqueries

Like the **DELETE** statement, **UPDATE** can make use of embedded subqueries. Suppose that Robert King has left Northwind and that his orders are supposed to be credited to his manager for the time being. The following example uses subqueries to perform this **UPDATE**:

```
UPDATE Orders
SET    EmployeeID =
     ( SELECT ReportsTo
       FROM   Employees
       WHERE  EmployeeID = Orders.EmployeeID
     )
WHERE  EmployeeID =
     ( SELECT EmployeeID
       FROM   Employees
       WHERE  FirstName = 'Robert'
       AND    LastName = 'King'
     )
```

Notice that two subqueries are used. The first one finds the row in the *Employees* table that matches the *EmployeeID* in the *Orders* table and retrieves the supervisor's *EmployeeID*, which is held in the *ReportsTo* column. The second subquery restricts the rows to be updated by requiring that the *EmployeeID* in the *Orders* table matches the name Robert King in the *Employees* table.

Using UPDATE...FROM

The **UPDATE** statement shares another feature with the **DELETE** statement. This is the ability to use a **FROM** clause to specify other table sources that can then be referenced by the **UPDATE** statement's **WHERE** clause. This allows **UPDATE** to be very flexible in specifying which rows should receive the update. The following causes the same data modifications as the previous example. This example, however, uses **UPDATE...FROM** instead of using embedded subqueries:

```
UPDATE Orders
SET    EmployeeID = EMP.EmployeeID
FROM   Employees EMP
WHERE  Orders.EmployeeID = EMP.EmployeeID
AND    EMP.FirstName = 'Robert'
AND    EMP.LastName = 'King'
```

As was true with the **DELETE** command, this additional **FROM** clause is a Microsoft Transact-SQL extension to the ANSI SQL standard, and you should not expect to find it on other SQL platforms.

QUERY TOOLS AND INTERFACES

Microsoft ships several tools with SQL Server that let you run queries, view result sets, and analyze queries efficiency. In this section we will briefly discuss these tools and present a summary of the various *Application Programming Interfaces (APIs)* that are available for use with SQL Server.

Query Tools

The query tools provided with SQL Server include the SQL Server Query Analyzer, *osql*, and *isql*. Each tool has particular strengths that make it valuable for filling certain roles during an application's life cycle. We begin this discussion with a review of the SQL Server Query Analyzer.

SQL Server Query Analyzer

The SQL Server Query Analyzer (isqlw.exe) is the new graphical query tool included with SQL Server. It can be started as a standalone application or launched from within the SQL Enterprise Manager by clicking on Query Analyzer in the Tools menu (see Figure 7.2).

You should already be familiar with the Query Analyzer from using it in the previous chapters' examples and case studies. What you may not have discovered is that the Query Analyzer can do a lot more than just execute queries and return the result sets to you. Here is a list of features available in the SQL Server Query Analyzer:

- **Display results in a grid** If you turn on the Results In Grid option on the Query menu, SQL Server will display subsequent query results in a grid. This spreadsheet-like grid is easy to read and has resizable columns.
- **Save and retrieve queries and result sets** The Query Analyzer's file menu has a standard Save command that lets you save queries and result sets. There is also an Open item, allowing you to retrieve these files for later use.
- **Use multiple servers simultaneously** By using the File|Connect menu command, you can establish connections to different SQL Servers at the same time. A separate query window is established for each connection to each server. A shortcut to creating a new connection to the current server is to type Ctrl+N or to click on the New Query icon located at the left end of the toolbar.

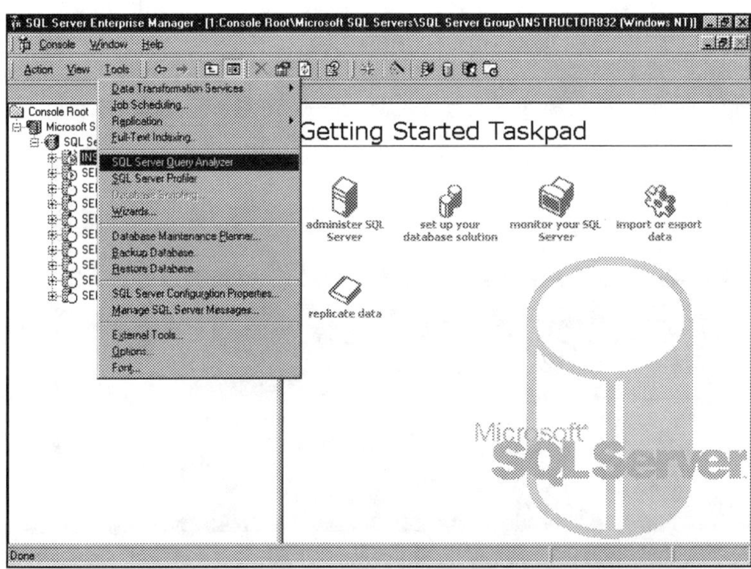

Figure 7.2 Launching the Query Analyzer from SQL Enterprise Manager.

- **Parse queries without executing them** Use the Query|Parse menu command to parse a query to check its syntax without executing it. This is useful for checking each new section of code you add when building a long query. If you parse a 25-statement procedure after every statement you add to it, it is easier to locate syntax errors.
- **Show estimated and actual execution plans** If you turn on the Query|Show Execution Plan option, SQL Server will display a graphical representation of the strategy it uses to run subsequent queries in the current query window. By clicking on Query|Display Estimated Execution Plan, you can see the strategy without executing the query. SQL Server can also display its query plans using text instead of the graphical display. You will learn how to interpret these execution plans in Chapter 18.
- **Perform index analysis** If you select the Perform Index Analysis option from the Query menu, SQL Server will analyze your query and present recommended indexing changes that will speed up the query. As seen in Figure 7.3, you can choose to implement the suggested changes or to cancel them.
- **Setting other query options** The Query|Current Connection Options menu choice lets you set many other configuration options for your current connection. For example, you can turn on or off the display of the number of rows affected by your queries. The display of I/O statistics can be enabled or disabled inside this same dialog box. Query timeout values can be set, and you can specify a custom batch delimiter to use instead of **GO**. You can also specify output formats for result sets and the maximum amount of characters displayed for any column.

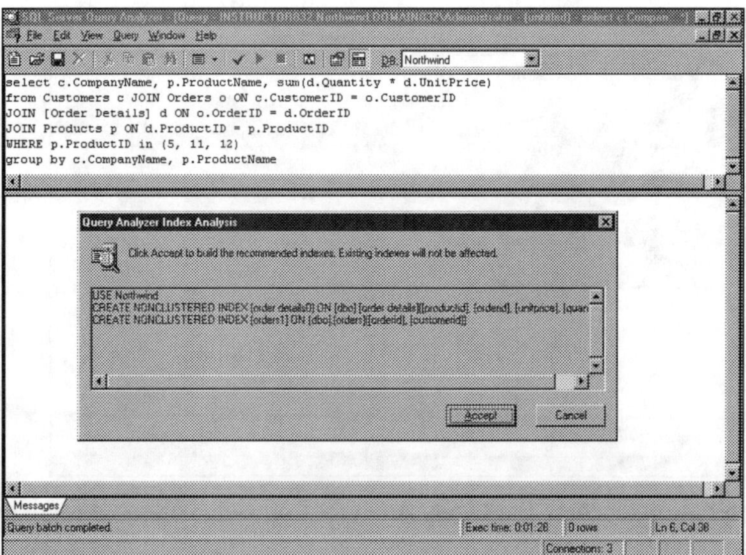

Figure 7.3 Performing index analysis with the Query Analyzer.

Command-Line Query Processors

SQL Server comes with two command-line query processors: *isql* and *osql*. Both are used to execute Transact-SQL statements or entire scripts. The *isql* program is a utility that shipped with previous versions of SQL Server. It is based on the DB-Lib Database Library (DB-Lib) interface, which does not support all the new features of SQL Server 7. The *osql* program is a new query utility in SQL Server version 7. It implements all of the same command-line options that are supported by *isql*, but, because it is built on top of the *Open Database Connectivity* (*ODBC*) interface, it supports all new SQL 7 features. Here is an example showing how to execute a query from the command line using *osql*:

```
osql -S MyServer -E -Q "select * from Northwind..Employees"
```


In this command, the **-S** option tells *osql* that the server name is *MyServer*. The **-E** option establishes a trusted (NT-authenticated) connection, and the **-Q** option passes in a query that *osql* will execute. The same command could be run with *isql* by specifying the same options:

```
isql -S MyServer -E -Q "select * from Northwind..Employees"
```

Both *osql* and *isql* also support nontrusted connections using a **-U** option to specify the SQL Server login name and optionally using **-P** to specify the password. If **-U** is specified by **-P** is not, the program will prompt the user to type in the password. When the password is typed, it is not displayed on the screen. Each program supports many other processing and formatting options, which you can review by executing either command with the **-?** option.

You should use *osql* whenever you are able to choose. Because *osql* is based on the newer ODBC interface, it is likely to be supported by Microsoft for a longer time. Also, remember that *isql* does not support all of the new SQL Server features available in version 7. For example, *isql* cannot read Unicode input files or retrieve **NTEXT** values, whereas *osql* can do both of these things. If no query or input file is specified with these utilities, they start in an interactive mode that allows you to enter the queries you want to run. You must enter a batch delimiter (which is **GO** by default) to run a batch of commands, and you must type "EXIT" to terminate the program. Operating system commands can be run from either *osql* or *isql* by specifying **"!!"** at the beginning of the line, as in this example:

```
osql -S MyServer -E -Q "!!dir"
```

Choosing A Query Tool

For situations when you want an easy-to-use graphical query utility, the SQL Server Query Analyzer is the correct tool to use. It lets you maintain several open connections at once, as well as allowing you to perform standard Windows commands, such as Copy and Paste. This tool also allows you to easily save files, perform analysis of execution plans and index usage. All of these tasks are more difficult to achieve using the command-line query tools. These features make the SQL Server Query Analyzer the tool of choice for developing, debugging, and optimizing Transact-SQL queries and procedures.

You can use the command-line query tools from within operating system scripts. This makes them very well suited to use in nightly batch jobs, so they serve an important function in a typical database application. As already noted, you should use *osql* instead of *isql* when you can. However, in spite of its limitations, in certain situations *isql* is the correct tool to use. For example, if you have a non-Windows client that supports DB-Library connections but does not support ODBC, you must use *isql* instead of *osql*.

Programming Interfaces

Microsoft has created several programming interfaces for use with SQL Server. Microsoft classifies them in terms of maturity, overhead, programmer control, and SQL 7 feature set. Table 7.1 briefly summarizes several of the general-purpose SQL Server programming interfaces. An interface with the value (Native) in the

Table 7.1 General-Purpose SQL Server programming interfaces.

API Name	Maturity	Runs On	Control	SQL 7 Features	Languages
DB-Library	Legacy	(Native)	High	Limited	VC++
DB-Library for VB	Legacy	DB-Lib for C	Low	Limited	VB
ESQL	Legacy	DB-Lib for C	Low	Limited	VC++ and COBOL
DAO	Legacy	ODBC	Low	Limited	VB and VC++
RDO	Established	ODBC	Moderate	Most	VB and VJ++
ODBC	Established	(Native)	High	All (except OLAP)	VC++
OLE DB	Emerging	(Native)	High	All (including OLAP)	VC++
ADO	Emerging	OLE DB	Moderate	Most (including OLAP)	VC++, VJ++, and VB

Note: In these tables, VC++ refers to Microsoft Visual C++, VB refers to Microsoft Visual Basic, and VJ++ refers to Microsoft Visual J++.

Table 7.2 Specialized SQL Server programming interfaces.

API Name	Typical Usage
SQL-DMO	Developing SQL management tools in Visual C++
SQL-Namespace	Incorporating SQL Enterprise Manager components into other applications
Replication Components	Managing replication processes and implementing replication from non-SQL Server data sources
DTS	Managing and executing Data Transformation Services packages
Open Data Services	Creating extended stored procedures

Runs On column is an interface that directly accesses SQL Servers *Tabular Data Stream* (*TDS*) protocol. Table 7.2 lists other more specialized programming interfaces that are available for use with SQL Server. You can find more information on any of these interfaces in *SQL Server Books Online*.

7

Chapter Summary

This chapter showed you how to use the **SELECT** command to retrieve data from a SQL Server table. You can retrieve data from multiple tables simultaneously using **UNION** and **JOIN** queries. You can change data by the **INSERT**, **DELETE**, and **UPDATE** commands. Finally, several programming interfaces are available to use with SQL Server:

- Use the **SELECT** statement's **WHERE** clause to retrieve a subset of the table's rows. Use the *column list*, also called a *select list*, to specify which columns should be in the result set.
- Use **JOIN** clauses to retrieve data from more than one table. Use **UNION** to combine the output of more than one query.
- Use **INNER JOIN** to return combinations of rows from the joined tables that meet the specified *join condition*. If you need to include rows that do not fulfill the join condition, use an *outer join* instead. The types of outer joins are **LEFT**, **RIGHT**, and **FULL**.
- Use *subqueries*, or *nested queries*, to embed one query within another. Some of the uses of subqueries include looking up values in a **WHERE** clause, specifying derived columns in the select list, or using values from the main query to check for the existence of corresponding rows in another table.
- Use **INSERT** to put rows into a table. You can specify the values for a single new row, or you can generate many new rows at one time with a **SELECT** statement or an **EXECUTE** statement.
- Use **DELETE** to remove rows from a table. **DELETE** has a **WHERE** clause and an optional **FROM** clause that restrict which rows it will delete.

- Use **TRUNCATE TABLE** to remove all of the rows in a table more quickly than **DELETE** can, because it logs only page deallocations and not individual row deletions. **TRUNCATE TABLE** always removes every row in the table. You cannot truncate a table that is referenced by a foreign key constraint.
- Use the **UPDATE** statement to change values in existing rows. **UPDATE** has a **WHERE** clause and an optional **FROM** clause that restrict which rows it will modify.
- Use the SQL Server Query Analyzer to develop and run queries with an easy-to-use, graphical interface. Use it also to perform other tasks such as examining query execution plans and performing index analysis. Use *osql* to run Transact-SQL commands in operating system scripts for batch processing. Use *isql* instead of *osql* when a client cannot connect using ODBC.
- APIs exist for use with SQL Server. You should be familiar with the names and uses of the more common APIs.

Review Questions

Unless otherwise specified, these questions use the *Northwind* database schema.

1. Which of the following queries will retrieve the company name for supplier number 12?

   a.
   ```
   SELECT Suppliers.CompanyName
   WHERE SupplierID = 12
   ```
   b.
   ```
   SELECT FROM Suppliers
   CompanyName WHERE CompanyID = 12
   ```
   c.
   ```
   SELECT CompanyID AS CompanyName
   FROM Suppliers
   WHERE CompanyID = 12
   ```
   d.
   ```
   SELECT CompanyName
   FROM Suppliers
   WHERE CompanyID = 12
   ```

2. You want to retrieve information about orders and the salesperson that placed each order. To do this, you know that you must combine data from the *Orders* table with the appropriate data from the *Employees* table. You know that the *EmployeeID* column of the *Orders* table is never **NULL**. Which of the following **FROM** clauses will combine data from the two tables correctly?

a. `FROM Orders, Employees`
b. `FROM Orders O`
   `WHERE O.EmployeeID = Employees.EmployeeID`
c. `FROM Orders O JOIN Employees E`
   `ON O.EmployeeID = E.EmployeeID`
d. `FROM Orders INNER JOIN Employees`

3. You want to retrieve all values from the column *ProductName* in the *Products* table. In the result set, you want the column to be called *Product*. Which of the following queries will produce the desired result? (Choose all correct answers.)

a. `SELECT Product = ProductName`
   `FROM Products`
b. `SELECT ProductName AS Product`
   `FROM Products`
c. `SELECT ProductName = Product`
   `FROM Products`
d. `SELECT ProductName Product`
   `FROM Products`

4. You need to retrieve rows from the *Orders* table for any order that was issued by either Employee 1 or Employee 3 or for which the *CustomerID* is **'VINET'**. Which of the following **WHERE** clauses may be used? (Choose all correct answers.)

a. `WHERE CustomerID = 'VINET'`
   `AND EmployeeID = (1 OR 3)`
b. `WHERE CustomerID = 'VINET'`
   `AND EmployeeID IN (1, 3)`
c. `WHERE CustomerID = 'VINET'`
   `OR EmployeeID IN (1, 3)`
d. `WHERE CustomerID = 'VINET'`
   `OR ((EmployeeID = 1) OR (EmployeeID = 3))`

5. Which **WHERE** clause could be used to find employees with last names containing a lower-case "s"?

a. `SELECT EmployeeID`
   `FROM Employees`
   `WHERE LastName LIKE 's'`
b. `SELECT EmployeeID`
   `FROM Employees`
   `WHERE LastName LIKE '%s%'`

7

c.
```
SELECT EmployeeID
FROM Employees
WHERE LastName = '%s%'
```
d.
```
SELECT EmployeeID
FROM Employees
WHERE LastName LIKE '%s'
OR LastName LIKE 's%'
```

6. You want to retrieve information from the *Employees* table sorted by the hire date, with the earliest dates first. Any employees hired the same day should be sorted by *EmployeeID* within that date, with the smallest *EmployeeID* values first. Which of the following **ORDER BY** clauses is correct?
   a. `ORDER BY HireDate, EmployeeID DESC`
   b. `ORDER BY HireDate ASC, EmployeeID`
   c. `ORDER BY HireDate DESC, EmployeeID`
   d. `ORDER BY HireDate DESC, EmployeeID ASC`

7. Which of the following queries will create a temporary table holding a copy of the data in the *Employees* table for those employees who are not located in the United States?

a.
```
SELECT *
FROM Employees
INTO #Employees
WHERE Country <> 'USA'
```
b.
```
SELECT #Employees
FROM Employees
WHERE Country <> 'USA'
```
c.
```
CREATE TABLE #Employees
AS SELECT *
FROM Employees
WHERE Country <> 'USA'
```
d.
```
SELECT *
INTO #Employees
FROM Employees
WHERE Country <> 'USA'
```

8. You have two queries that run against two different tables. When run separately, each query works correctly. However, when you attempt to combine the queries using the **UNION** operator, you receive an error message. What is a possible cause of this problem?
   a. The second result set has too many columns.
   b. The first column of the first result set is **CHAR (10)**, but the first column of the second result set is **CHAR (8)**.
   c. The third column has different names in each result set.
   d. You cannot use **UNION** to combine separate result sets in this manner.

9. You are embedding a subquery inside another query. The subquery returns three columns. What are valid ways in which this subquery can be used? (Choose all correct answers.)
   a. As a derived column in the select list.
   b. As a derived table in the **FROM** clause.
   c. As a value used in the **WHERE** clause to compare against a column value, as in **WHERE ColumnA = (subquery)**.
   d. To check for the existence of rows in the subquery matching conditions that depend on the outer query, as in **WHERE EXISTS** (subquery).

10. Which syntax can be used to put the company name of every supplier into a temporary table called *#Suppliers*? Assume that the data type of *CompanyName* is **NVARCHAR (40)** and that your Transact-SQL statement(s) must create the temporary table. (Choose all correct answers).
    a.
    ```
    INSERT INTO #Suppliers (CompanyName)
    SELECT CompanyName
    FROM Suppliers
    ```
    b.
    ```
    SELECT CompanyName
    FROM Suppliers
    INTO #Suppliers
    ```
    c.
    ```
    SELECT CompanyName
    INTO #Suppliers
    FROM Suppliers
    ```
    d.
    ```
    CREATE TABLE #Suppliers
    (CompanyName NVARCHAR(40))
    INSERT INTO #Suppliers (CompanyName)
    SELECT CompanyName
    FROM Suppliers
    ```

11. You have archived a copy of all order detail information for order numbers less than 11,000. Which **DELETE** statement will remove the corresponding rows from the *Order Details* table, because they are no longer needed?

    a.
    ```
    DELETE
    FROM [Order Details] < 11000
    ```
    b.
    ```
    DELETE
    WHERE OrderID < 11000
    FROM [Order Details]
    ```
    c.
    ```
    DELETE *
    FROM [Order Details]
    WHERE OrderID < 11000
    ```
    d.
    ```
    DELETE
    FROM [Order Details]
    WHERE OrderID < 11000
    ```

12. **TRUNCATE TABLE** is appropriate to use when you have archived all of the *Orders* records from last year and now you want to quickly delete those records.

    a. True

    b. False

13. The telephone extension for the employee named Anne Dodsworth has changed from 452 to 317. Assuming only one employee has this name, which **UPDATE** statement(s) will make the correct change to the database? (Choose all correct answers.)

    a.
    ```
    UPDATE Employees
    SET Extension = 317
    WHERE EmployeeID =
    (SELECT EmployeeID
    FROM Employees
    WHERE FirstName = 'Anne'
    AND LastName = 'Dodsworth')
    ```
    b.
    ```
    UPDATE Employees
    SET Extension = 317
    WHERE FirstName = 'Anne'
    AND LastName = 'Dodsworth'
    ```

c.
```
UDPATE Employees
CHANGE 452 TO 317
WHERE FirstName = 'Anne'
AND LastName = 'Dodsworth'
```

d.
```
UPDATE Employees
WHERE FirstName = 'Anne'
AND LastName = 'Dodsworth'
SET Extension = 317
```

14. The SQL Server Query Analyzer can be used to execute queries, view query execution plans, and perform index analysis for a query.
    a. True
    b. False

15. Both *isql* and *osql* are based on the intuitive Windows graphical user interface (GUI), and are therefore frequently used for issuing interactive queries against SQL Server.
    a. True
    b. False

16. What are the general-purpose programming interfaces that access the SQL Server TDS stream directly? (Choose all correct answers.)
    a. DB-Library
    b. ODBC
    c. OLE DB
    d. ADO

17. What are two general-purpose programming interfaces for SQL Server that provide an interface around a native interface, making that interface more easily accessible from Microsoft Visual Basic? (Choose all correct answers.)
    a. ESQL
    b. RDO
    c. OLE DB
    d. ADO

HANDS-ON PROJECTS

Project 7.1

In this project you will use the graphical query tool in SQL Server Enterprise Manager.

The *Query Designer* in the *SQL Server Enterprise Manager* allows you to design queries graphically. This tool, though not easy to find, is very easy to use for designing queries, even complex queries such as multitable joins. To use the Query Designer, follow these steps:

1. In SQL Server Enterprise Manager, expand the appropriate icons needed to expose your SQL Server's icon. This group of icons may be different on each machine. For a default installation, you must expand Microsoft SQL Servers and then SQL Server group in order to show the icon for your SQL Server. (In the SQL Enterprise Manager, you expand an icon by clicking on the plus (+) sign next to it.)
2. Expand the Databases folder.
3. Expand the *Northwind* database.
4. Click on the Tables icon. The list of tables in the *Northwind* database will appear in the pane on the right side of the screen.
5. Right-click on the *Customers* table. From the menu, select Open Table|Return All Rows. You can see this menu structure in Figure 7.4.

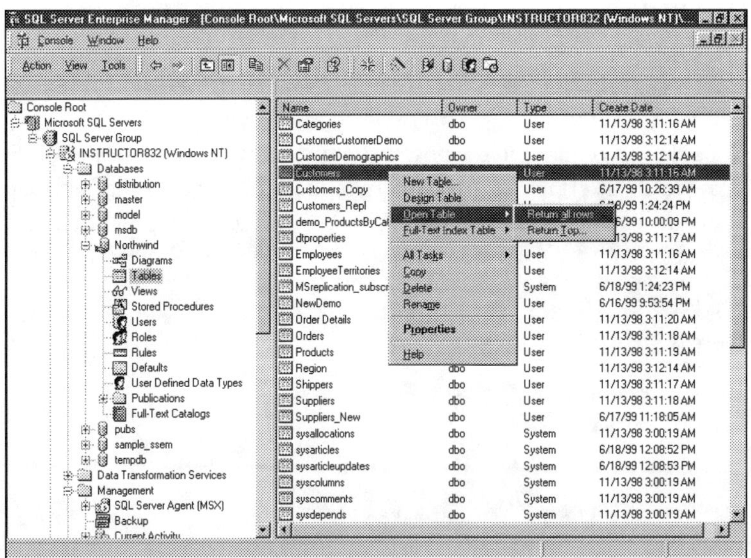

Figure 7.4 Opening the Query Design tool.

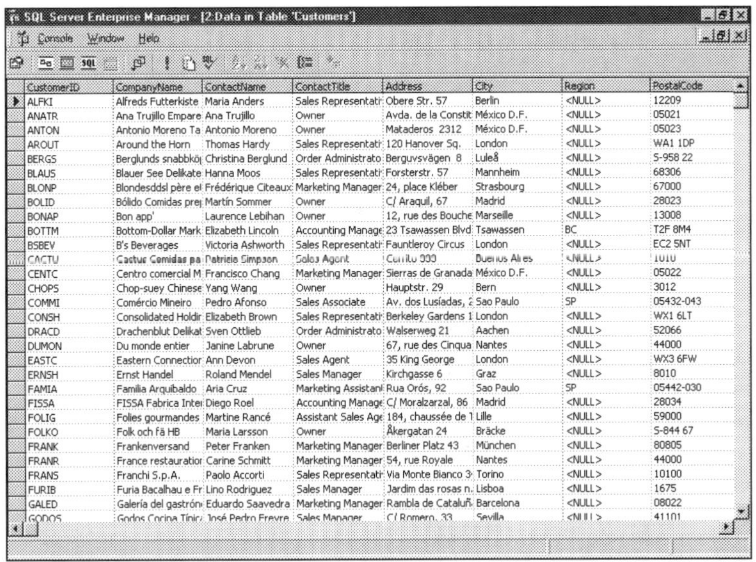

CustomerID	CompanyName	ContactName	ContactTitle	Address	City	Region	PostalCode
ALFKI	Alfreds Futterkiste	Maria Anders	Sales Representati	Obere Str. 57	Berlin	<NULL>	12209
ANATR	Ana Trujillo Empare	Ana Trujillo	Owner	Avda. de la Constit	México D.F.	<NULL>	05021
ANTON	Antonio Moreno Ta	Antonio Moreno	Owner	Mataderos 2312	México D.F.	<NULL>	05023
AROUT	Around the Horn	Thomas Hardy	Sales Representati	120 Hanover Sq.	London	<NULL>	WA1 1DP
BERGS	Berglunds snabbkö	Christina Berglund	Order Administrato	Berguvsvägen 8	Luleå	<NULL>	S-958 22
BLAUS	Blauer See Delikate	Hanna Moos	Sales Representati	Forsterstr. 57	Mannheim	<NULL>	68306
BLONP	Blondesddsl père et	Frédérique Citeaux	Marketing Manager	24, place Kléber	Strasbourg	<NULL>	67000
BOLID	Bólido Comidas pre	Martín Sommer	Owner	C/ Araquil, 67	Madrid	<NULL>	28023
BONAP	Bon app'	Laurence Lebihan	Owner	12, rue des Bouche	Marseille	<NULL>	13008
BOTTM	Bottom-Dollar Mark	Elizabeth Lincoln	Accounting Manage	23 Tsawassen Blvd	Tsawassen	BC	T2F 8M4
BSBEV	B's Beverages	Victoria Ashworth	Sales Representati	Fauntleroy Circus	London	<NULL>	EC2 5NT
CACTU	Cactus Comidas pa	Patricio Simpson	Sales Agent	Cerrito 333	Buenos Aires	<NULL>	1010
CENTC	Centro comercial M	Francisco Chang	Marketing Manager	Sierras de Granada	México D.F.	<NULL>	05022
CHOPS	Chop-suey Chinese	Yang Wang	Owner	Hauptstr. 29	Bern	<NULL>	3012
COMMI	Comércio Mineiro	Pedro Afonso	Sales Associate	Av. dos Lusíadas, 2	Sao Paulo	SP	05432-043
CONSH	Consolidated Holdir	Elizabeth Brown	Sales Representati	Berkeley Gardens 1	London	<NULL>	WX1 6LT
DRACD	Drachenblut Delikat	Sven Ottlieb	Order Administrato	Walserweg 21	Aachen	<NULL>	52066
DUMON	Du monde entier	Janine Labrune	Owner	67, rue des Cinqua	Nantes	<NULL>	44000
EASTC	Eastern Connectior	Ann Devon	Sales Agent	35 King George	London	<NULL>	WX3 6FW
ERNSH	Ernst Handel	Roland Mendel	Sales Manager	Kirchgasse 6	Graz	<NULL>	8010
FAMIA	Familia Arquibaldo	Aria Cruz	Marketing Assistan	Rua Orós, 92	Sao Paulo	SP	05442-030
FISSA	FISSA Fabrica Inter	Diego Roel	Accounting Manage	C/ Moralzarzal, 86	Madrid	<NULL>	28034
FOLIG	Folies gourmandes	Martine Rancé	Assistant Sales Age	184, chaussée de T	Lille	<NULL>	59000
FOLKO	Folk och fä HB	Maria Larsson	Owner	Åkergatan 24	Bräcke	<NULL>	S-844 67
FRANK	Frankenversand	Peter Franken	Marketing Manager	Berliner Platz 43	München	<NULL>	80805
FRANR	France restauratior	Carine Schmitt	Marketing Manager	54, rue Royale	Nantes	<NULL>	44000
FRANS	Franchi S.p.A.	Paolo Accorti	Sales Representati	Via Monte Bianco 3	Torino	<NULL>	10100
FURIB	Furia Bacalhau e Fr	Lino Rodriguez	Sales Manager	Jardim das rosas n.	Lisboa	<NULL>	1675
GALED	Galería del gastrón	Eduardo Saavedra	Marketing Manager	Rambla de Cataluñ	Barcelona	<NULL>	08022
GODOS	Godos Cocina Típic	José Pedro Freyre	Sales Manager	C/ Romero, 33	Sevilla	<NULL>	41101

Figure 7.5 Viewing the *Customers* table in SQL Enterprise Manager.

6. At this point, the Enterprise Manager will open a new window that will show you the data in the *Customers* table. This screen will look similar to the one in Figure 7.5.
7. Notice that this view of your data is updateable. For example, you can change the name Maria Anders in the *ContactName* field for **CustomerID ALFKI**. To do this, simply edit the cell containing the name Maria Anders to change it to the new value. You can save the new value by simply moving the cursor to another row. Do this by clicking the row below the one you are editing or by using the down arrow key.
8. Other panes available in the Query Designer let you change the data displayed. To see the pane showing the current SQL query, right-click anywhere inside the data. On the menu, select Show Panes|SQL. The Enterprise Manager then changes the window to include a view of the SQL query, as seen in Figure 7.6. You can display or hide this pane by using the Show/Hide SQL Pane button on the toolbar.
9. You can edit the query shown in the SQL pane to be any valid **SELECT** statement. Change the query to read **SELECT CompanyName, ContactName FROM Customers**. To run this new query, right-click inside the query pane and choose Run. Notice that the output changes to match your query.

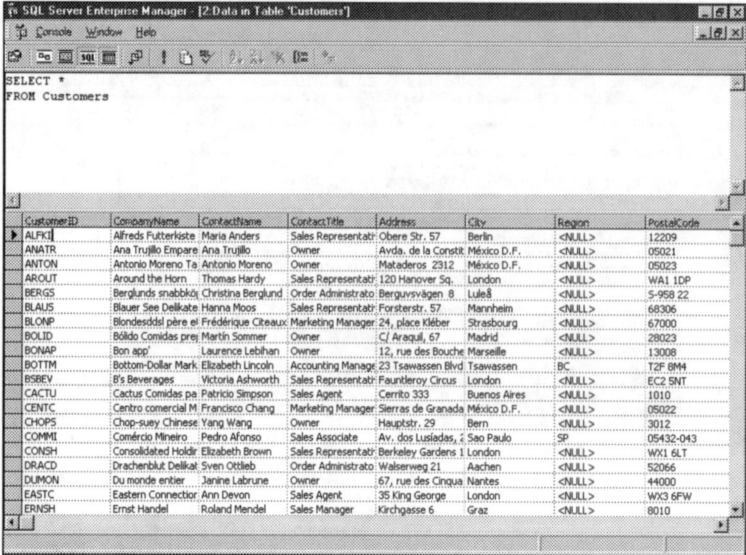

Figure 7.6 Viewing the SQL pane in the Query Design Tool.

10. Display the Diagram pane by right-clicking in the Data pane or the SQL pane and choosing Diagram from the Show Panes submenu. You can also do this by using the buttons on the toolbar. Your screen should now look like the one shown in Figure 7.7. Notice that the two columns named in your query are checked in the Diagram pane, indicating they are included in your query. Check the box next to ContactTitle and notice that it also is

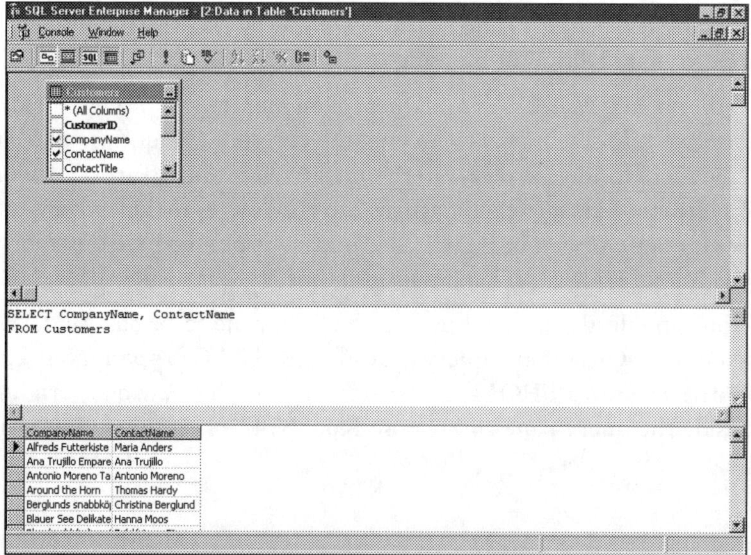

Figure 7.7 Viewing the Diagram, SQL, and Data panes in the Query Design Tool.

checked. At the same time, the query in the SQL pane is changed to reflect the change to your query. In addition, the data is grayed out to indicate that you have changed your query definition and cannot update data until you run your new query. Run this new query by right-clicking an unused space inside the Diagram pane and choosing Run from the menu.

11. You can add more tables to the query to perform joins. Right-click an unused space inside the Diagram pane and choose Add Table. SQL Enterprise Manager will display a list of the tables and views in the *Northwind* database. To add the *Orders* table to your query, select *Orders* from the table list, and then click the Add button. Next, click the Close button to exit the Add Table dialog box. Your screen will now look like the one in Figure 7.8. Notice that SQL Enterprise Manager has automatically joined the tables based on the foreign keys that are declared in the database. You may also notice that the *Orders* table contains a column named *IDENTITYCOL*, although no column has this name in the table definition. The **IDENTITYCOL** keyword is a valid alias for any column name with the *identity* column, and the *Orders* table has an *identity* column.

12. It is easy to add more tables to create complex joins. Figure 7.9 shows a complex four-table join that was quickly generated using the Query Tool. Using such a tool greatly increases both the speed and the accuracy of developing such queries.

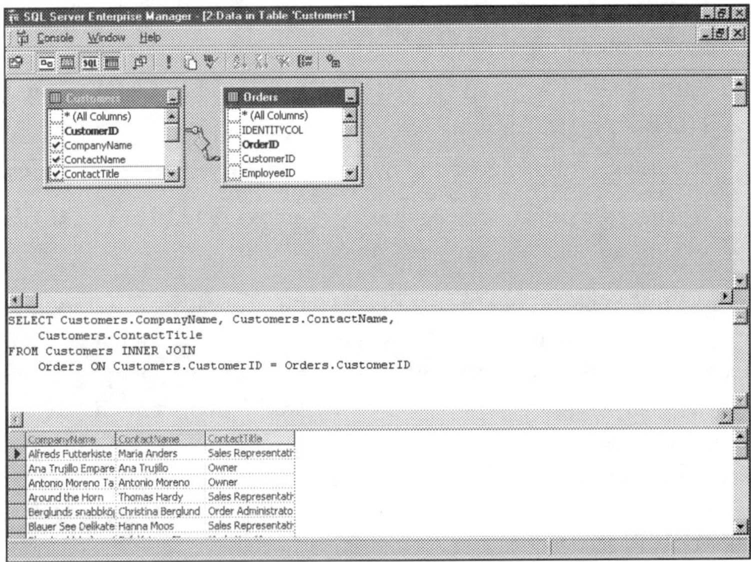

Figure 7.8 Adding a second table in the Query Design Tool.

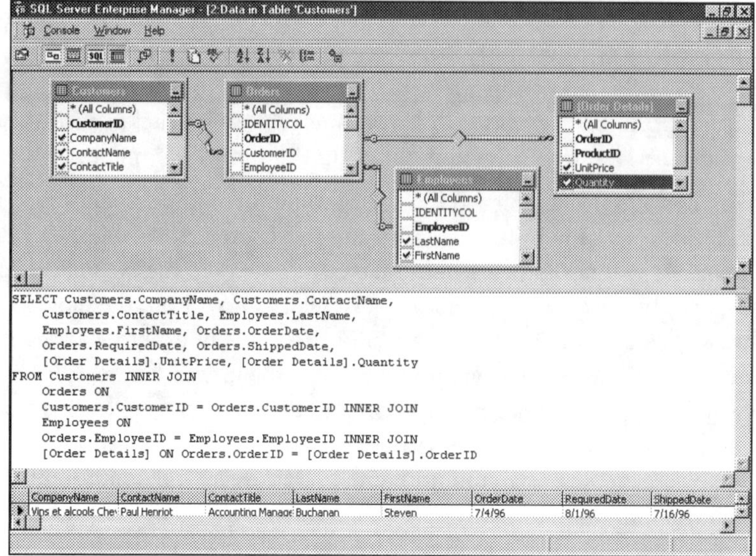

Figure 7.9 A complex query generated with the Query Design Tool.

13. Experiment further with the Query Design Tool to familiarize yourself with its capabilities. See if you can accomplish the following tasks:
    a. Parse a query to verify its syntax.
    b. Use the Grid Pane to add criteria to the **WHERE** clause. Can you add two criteria joined by **OR**?
    c. Change the query type to generate a **CREATE TABLE** statement.
    d. Use the Query Tool with your new table. Change the query type to add rows to your new table by generating **INSERT** statements.
    e. Change the query type again to generate **UPDATE** or **DELETE** statements against your new table.

Greg came to Susan the next morning. "Thanks for all your help yesterday—I learned a lot. One thing, though. I usually use a modem to dial in from home and work late. When I tried to use the Graphical Query Analyzer it was really slow. Is there anything I can do to make it faster?" Susan smiled. "There sure is," she said. "You can use a command-line utility so that you don't have to use all the graphical overhead over the phone line."

Project 7.2

Using *osql* to execute queries.

This short exercise gives you practice running queries using *osql*. You can also execute these examples with *isql* if you wish.

1. Open a command prompt. One way to do this is to click on the Start button and choose Run. Type "command" and press Enter to launch the new command prompt window.
2. At the command prompt, run **osql -?** to see all of the options available with this program.
3. Execute **osql -S MyServer -E -Q "SELECT CompanyName, ContactName FROM Northwind..Customers"** and view the results. Run this against a SQL Server that will grant you a trusted connection, and substitute the name of your SQL Server where the example says **MyServer**.
4. To view the results one screen at a time, pipe the output to the more command by executing **osql -S MyServer -E -Q "SELECT CompanyName, ContactName FROM Northwind..Customers"|more**.
5. Next, we will use the **-o** option to redirect the query output to a file for later viewing. We will also use the **-d** option to specify the database name so that we do not need to qualify the table name. The command that implements these changes is **osql -S MyServer -E -Q "SELECT CompanyName, ContactName FROM Customers" -d Northwind -o SqlOutput.txt**.
6. Use Notepad to view the file SqlOutput.txt you just created by typing the command **notepad SqlOutput.txt**. Exit from Notepad when you are done inspecting the file.
7. Run the command **osql -S MyServer -E -Q "SELECT * FROM Customers" -d Northwind -o SqlOutput2.txt**. Run the command **notepad SqlOutput2.txt** to inspect the new output file. Notice that the output file is hard to read because the output is wrapped at 80 characters, which is the *osql* default. Exit from Notepad when you are done inspecting the file.
8. Use the **-w** option to change the width of the output lines. Also, use the **-h** option to cause the column headers to be repeated for every 50 lines of output. Implement these changes by running the command **osql -S MyServer -E -Q "SELECT * FROM Customers" -d Northwind -o SqlOutput3.txt -w 1000 -h 10**. Open the new output file with the command **notepad SqlOutput3.txt** and notice that it is much easier to read, because an entire row now fits on one line. If you notice characters on your screen that are difficult to display, they are due to the use of international characters in the data. Notice also that the column headers repeat every 10 lines, as specified. Close Notepad when you are finished viewing the file.

7

9. Experiment further with *osql* to familiarize yourself with its functionality. In particular, try to perform these tasks:

    a. Log on to SQL Server using a SQL login ID instead of a trusted connection.

    b. Use *osql* to display a list of available SQL Servers.

    c. Tell *osql* to run a query from an input file (you will first need to create such a file using a text editor, such as Notepad or the SQL Server Query Analyzer).

    d. Have *osql* display performance statistics after it prints out the query output.

    e. Use *osql* to create a comma-delimited file containing the contents of the *Customers* table.

CHAPTER 8

TRANSACT-SQL SCRIPTING AND COMMAND BATCHES

After Reading This Chapter And Completing The Exercises, You Will Be Able To:

- Define Transact-SQL batches and explain their significance
- Understand the relationship between Transact-SQL batches and scripts
- Declare and use local variables to store and retrieve information within a batch
- Include appropriate line and block comments in your scripts
- Use Transact-SQL control-of-flow keywords to manipulate the order of command execution within a batch
- Employ cursors to perform row-by-row processing of a result set
- Use built-in functions, such as **@@ERROR** and **@@ROWCOUNT** to retrieve important information from SQL Server
- Detect and recover from error conditions

Up to this point in the book, you have learned several useful Transact-SQL statements. You are now able to create tables and indexes in SQL Server tables. You can insert, modify, and delete data in the tables you create, and you can retrieve information from the tables using a variety of query techniques. In this chapter, you will learn techniques for linking pieces of Transact-SQL together to build complex and useful batches and scripts.

Putting The Pieces Together

Although you have learned how to do many things using single Transact-SQL statements, you'll find that it is often necessary to have multiple statements work together in a meaningful way. For example, consider the following *functional requirements*. In a nightly maintenance program, you must first find out the current date and the day of the week. If it is a Sunday, you must create a report summarizing weekly sales. If it is the last Sunday of the month, you need to archive old production data so the database doesn't grow too large. On days other than Sundays, you should only run a summary report of that day's sales.

This kind of job cannot be run using individual isolated Transact-SQL statements. It requires that information retrieved by one statement (such as the day of the week) be available for use by a later statement. It also requires that certain statements (such as the monthly archiving) should not execute every time the job runs.

A good example of this is a jigsaw puzzle. The goal of solving a jigsaw puzzle is clear: You need to put all those little pieces together so that they look like the picture on the box. Transact-SQL batches are similar to a jigsaw puzzle, because you need all of the pieces to fit together correctly in order to accomplish the task. The pieces needed to complete the puzzle are the individual Transact-SQL statements you have learned so far, and the picture you are trying to build is specified by the functional requirements.

Batches And Scripts

A *batch* is simply a group of Transact-SQL statements that are executed together. Whenever a client program sends Transact-SQL statements to SQL Server, those statements are sent in batches. SQL Server compiles a batch as a single unit, producing a single *execution plan*. This execution plan tells SQL Server how to execute that particular batch of Transact-SQL statements. In the SQL Server Query Analyzer (as well as other Microsoft-supplied SQL Server utilities), the reserved keyword **GO** is used to separate batches. Listing 8.1 shows three batches of Transact-SQL commands.

Listing 8.1 Transact-SQL command batches separated by **GO**.

```
PRINT 'This is the first command batch.'
GO
WAITFOR DELAY '00:00:05'
GO
PRINT 'The previous command batch contained a five-second delay.'
GO
```

```
Results:
This is the first command batch.
The previous command batch contained a five-second delay.
```

The **PRINT** command used in Listing 8.1 is a way to output a line of text. It is frequently used in Transact-SQL scripts to output diagnostic information or to monitor progress of the script.

Notice that the second batch in Listing 8.1 pauses the execution for five seconds using the **WAITFOR** statement (which is covered later in this chapter). If you execute Listing 8.1 on your computer, you will notice a five-second delay between the output of the two **PRINT** statements. Now try this experiment: Remove the **GO** keywords and run the same code again.

When you run this code without the **GO** statements, a five-second delay occurs before you see *any* output from *either* print statement. The output of the two **PRINT** statements appears simultaneously. The difference in behavior is due the presence (or absence) of the **GO** statements. With the **GO** statements in place, the first **PRINT** statement is considered by SQL Server to be its own batch. This means that the entire batch will execute (and return its output to your screen) before SQL Server even compiles the **WAITFOR** statement. However, without the **GO** statements, the **PRINT-WAITFOR-PRINT** command sequence would be a single batch. Because the amount of output generated by this batch is small, SQL Server buffers the output and sends it back to the client program all at once, after the batch has completed. This is why the output from the two **PRINT** statements appears at the same time, even though the first **PRINT** statement executes five seconds before the other one.

The **GO** reserved keyword is *not* a Transact-SQL command. Rather, it is used as a batch delimiter by some client programs, including *osql*, *isql*, and the SQL Server Query Analyzer. **GO** is a command that tells these programs to take the preceding Transact-SQL statements and submit them as a command batch for execution. In these programs, you can change the batch delimiter from **GO** to something else. For example, in the SQL Server Query Analyzer, click on Query|Current Connection Options. On the General tab you can change the batch delimiter by typing the new delimiter into the field labeled TSQL Batch Separator.

Because a batch is a single compilation unit, a syntax error in any part of the batch prevents compilation of the entire batch. This means that a compilation error results in none of the batch's statements executing at all.

Runtime errors within batches have a less predictable effect. Runtime errors occur when the batch was successfully compiled but cannot be successfully executed. All runtime errors cause the current statement to fail. Runtime errors leave previous (successful) statements unaffected, unless the previous statements were part of a transaction that is rolled back due to the runtime error. Most (but not all) runtime errors cause the batch to terminate so that none of the statements following the runtime error is executed. However, some runtime errors, such as constraint and permission violations, terminate only the current statement, allowing the remainder of the batch to execute. Because of these nuances, it is important to understand how to use error-handling techniques in Transact-SQL.

The batch is a fundamental concept in SQL Server programming. SQL Server always executes one batch of commands at a time. Another important concept is the idea of a *script*, which is simply a group of one or more batches grouped together, usually in the same source file. Whereas the term *batch* has a very well-defined technical definition in SQL Server, the use of the term *script* is more of a convention. You could say that Listing 8.1 is a Transact-SQL script containing three Transact-SQL batches. Database administrators performing administration or maintenance tasks often use lengthy scripts of complicated Transact-SQL batches. A file of commands in another language, such as Windows NT's command language or a batch control language such as VBScript, is also sometimes called a SQL script if it contains embedded Transact-SQL statements. The common denominator between these different meanings is that the term *Transact-SQL script* always refers to a source file run by a client program that will result in one or more batches being executed by a SQL Server. Even when a script consisting of several Transact-SQL batches is run as a single unit by a client program, the parts of the script using SQL Server are still run one batch at a time. The way to write good Transact-SQL scripts is to write good Transact-SQL batches.

SQL Server Enterprise Manager can generate some scripts for you. To use this built-in scripting tool, right-click on a database in the SQL Server Enterprise Manager, choose All Tasks from the pop-up menu, and then choose Generate SQL Scripts. Alternatively, select a database and then, using the menu bar, select Tools|Database Scripting. These scripts are useful for documenting the content of your databases. They also provide a good way to be prepared in case you need to re-create database objects.

Local Variables

When speaking on the telephone, you may often take notes on a piece of scratch paper to help you remember important information. You might write down names, telephone numbers, or other information so that you can use it later. A similar situation occurs in Transact-SQL scripting, because you often store data for use later in the batch. One of the ways you can accomplish this in SQL Server is by using *local variables*. A local variable is like a small piece of scratch paper where we can write down one piece of information for later use.

Declaring Local Variables

Before you can use a local variable, you must declare it. The syntax for declaring a local variable is simple:

```
DECLARE @variable_name data_type [, @variable_name data_type ...]
```


You must supply a name for the variable as well as a data type. The name always begins with the @ character. The data type, as described in Chapter 3, determines what kinds of values can be stored in the variable as well as what operations can be performed on it. For example, the following snippet declares an integer variable:

```
DECLARE @MaxItems INT
```

Using Local Variables

When a local variable is first declared, it has a **NULL** value assigned to it. To assign non-**NULL** values to a local variable, you can use **SET** or **SELECT** statements. You can use a single **SET** statement to assign a value to only one variable, whereas you can use **SELECT** to assign multiple variables in a single statement. Local variables can store literal (hard-coded) values, values retrieved from tables, or values returned by Transact-SQL functions. All of these methods are illustrated in Listing 8.2.

Listing 8.2 Assigning values to local variables.

```
/* assigning variables using literal values: */
SET    @MaxItems = 100
SELECT @LastName = 'Thompson'

/* assigning variables using functions: */
SET    @Now = GETDATE()

/* assigning variables by querying tables: */
SELECT @LastName = LastName
FROM   Employees
WHERE  EmployeeID = 7
```

Once local variables have been assigned values, you can use them in Transact-SQL expressions. Many ways exist to use local variables in Transact-SQL. For example, variable names can be used in place of either column names or constants in most queries.

Scope Of Local Variable Names

The *scope* of variable names in SQL Server is the batch (or stored procedure) in which it is declared. After you declare a variable, you can refer to it, as long as you have not left the batch that created it. In the Listing 8.3, the first **SELECT** will succeed, but the second one (which is in a different batch) will fail.

Listing 8.3 Demonstrating variable scope.

```
DECLARE @x INT
SET     @x = 5
SELECT  @x AS [Legal Reference]
GO
SELECT  @x AS [Illegal Reference]

Results:
Legal Reference
---------------
5

Server: Msg 137, Level 15, State 2, Line 1
Must declare the variable '@x'.
```

Dynamic Batch Execution

You can use the **EXECUTE** statement and the **sp_executesql** stored procedure to execute Transact-SQL contained in a string or a string variable. For example, you may need to build a query based dynamically on values you look up in a table. When either **EXECUTE** or **sp_executesql** statements are used in this way, the Transact-SQL executed will be sent to SQL Server *as an individual batch* and compiled into its own execution plan.

Listing 8.4 shows three batches separated by the **GO** keyword. The first batch uses **EXECUTE** to run dynamically a SQL batch stored in a string. The second batch uses **sp_executesql** to dynamically execute a Transact-SQL batch contained in a string variable. Both of these batches will succeed. The third batch illustrates a common error beginning Transact-SQL programmers make when using dynamic batch execution. After printing a message stating that it will fail, this third batch then attempts to use **sp_executesql** to dynamically execute a literal string. The reason the execution of the string fails is that the string contains a reference to the local variable **@table_name**. Because the string will be compiled as an individual batch, this variable is no longer in scope when SQL Server tries to compile the string.

Listing 8.4 Dynamic string execution.

```
EXECUTE ('PRINT "This batch will succeed!"')
GO

DECLARE @sql_command NVARCHAR(100)
SET     @sql_command = N'PRINT "This batch will also succeed!"'
EXECUTE sp_executesql @sql_command
GO

PRINT  'This batch will FAIL!'
DECLARE @table_name NVARCHAR(256)
SET     @table_name = 'Orders'
EXECUTE ('sp_help @table_name')

Results:
This batch will succeed!
This batch will also succeed!
This batch will FAIL!
Server: Msg 137, Level 15, State 2, Line 1
Must declare the variable '@table_name'.
```

Notice that the error message from the third batch says that the variable **@table_name** has not been declared. This is because the entire batch sent to **sp_executesql** is the string **'sp_help @table_name'** and the variable **@table_name** is not declared anywhere in that batch.

For information on using **EXECUTE** to run stored procedures, refer to the discussion of stored procedures in Chapter 12.

Transact-SQL Comments

No Transact-SQL design book would be complete without encouraging good comments. Although comments are not required in Transact-SQL scripts, comments assist a future reader of the script in understanding the purpose and structure of your code. SQL Server supports two types of comments: *block comments* and *line comments*. Block comments begin with /* and end with */. Everything in between these two markers is treated as a comment and is not compiled by the SQL Server compiler. This type of comment is called a block comment because blocks of text several lines long can be included in a single comment. Many companies have a standard block comment format that should be used at the top of a script file. Listing 8.5 shows a block comment that might appear at the top of a script file.

Listing 8.5 Beginning a script with a block comment.

```
/*
 *         Name: Sample Script
 *     Filename: \\SqlSource\Scripts\SampleScript.sql
 *      Purpose: Demonstrate block comments
 *       Author: Leonard, Chris
 *         Date: July 02, 1999
 *
 *     Modified: Woody, Buck
 *      Purpose: Added code to create a log file of our activity.
 */
```

Notice that the begin-comment marker (/*) is on the first line and that no end-comment marker (*/) displays until the last line. This means that all other text in between these symbols is a comment. The asterisks on the other lines serve only as visual helpers so that the reader can quickly see where the block comment begins and ends. This is one of several common styles of block comments. Block comments can also be confined to a single line, such as the one in the following snippet:

```
/* Initialize variables: */
   SET @min = 1, @max = 100
```

The other type of comment is a line comment; it begins with two hyphens (--). These hyphens mark the beginning of the comment, which is automatically terminated at the end of the current line. The following line of code ends with a line comment:

```
SELECT @MaxItems = 100    -- cannot have more than 100 items
```

Many companies have internal standards regarding the use of comments. If yours does not, here are some guidelines to help you decide on appropriate commenting patterns:

- Put a block comment at the beginning of every Transact-SQL source file you create. Create a standard format for this introductory comment that you can use repeatedly. As a minimum, include your name, the date, the script or procedure name, and its purpose. You could also document the script's input and output. For complicated scripts, you could give an outline of the logic used in the script. Later modifications to the source file could be documented in this opening block comment. You can see a modification documented in Listing 8.5.

- A line comment should refer to the code that precedes it on the same line.
- You can end a comment with a colon if it refers to code that follows the comment. This helps the reader know to look ahead in the text for the pertinent code. This is sometimes called an *introductory comment.*
- Use introductory comments to summarize the purpose of a long section of code.
- Don't use comments to explain things that can be read in your code. You should assume that your reader knows how to read Transact-SQL just as well as they read English. In general, you should comment on the purpose of the code, explaining your *process,* but not your *syntax*. Listing 8.6 illustrates this idea.

Listing 8.6 Comment on your process, not your syntax.

```
Useless comment:
/* Divide @nHits by @nAtBats: */
SELECT @BAvg = @nHits / @nAtBats

Better comment:
/* Calculate batting average: */
SELECT @BAvg = @nHits / @nAtBats
```

No enforced standards exist regarding the use of comments, but these guidelines will help you begin to build good commenting habits. Be sure to check whether your company already has documentation guidelines that specify how you should use comments.

8

Control-Of-Flow Language

Life is full of contexts and rules that we use to determine a course of action. Consider the following sets of instructions:

First set of instructions: Use the interstate to get to the stadium. Take the state highway instead of the interstate.

Second set of instructions: *If you leave before 4:00 P.M., you will miss all of the rush-hour traffic and should* use the interstate to get to the stadium. *Otherwise*, take the state highway instead of the interstate *in order to avoid the rush-hour traffic.*

Both sets of instructions include the appropriate *actions* to help you get to the stadium. However, only the second set of instructions gives you the *context* and *rules* that govern the use of the two actions. The time of day is a context that affects the actions we should take in order to get to the stadium quickly. Without the information in the second set of instructions, you may spend all day just trying to understand the instructions—and then you wouldn't get to the stadium at all.

In a similar fashion, Transact-SQL's *control-of-flow language* lets you control the context and rules that govern the use of specific Transact-SQL actions. Without control-of-flow statements, all statements in a batch would be executed in sequential order each time the batch ran. Control-of-flow language allows you to specify when and under what circumstances specific sections of code are to be executed. You can use *conditional statements*, such as **IF** or **WHILE**, to execute the Transact-SQL statements that are appropriate for the current job context. This feature lets you repeat some sections of code while skipping other sections. With well-thought-out use of control-of-flow language, you can create Transact-SQL batches that intelligently change their behavior from one batch run to the next based on the context of that specific run of the job.

Statements: The Basic Unit For Control-Of-Flow

The simplest concept in flow control is the *statement*. A Transact-SQL statement is any complete Transact-SQL command. We have already discussed many statements, such as the **CREATE TABLE** and **SELECT** statements.

Statement Blocks: Using BEGIN ... END

It is often convenient to group individual statements together so that they can be treated as a single unit for the purposes of flow control. To facilitate this grouping, Transact-SQL includes the **BEGIN** and **END** keywords. These keywords are used like bookends to group all the statements into a single *statement block*. Listing 8.7 shows a short statement block.

Listing 8.7 Using **BEGIN** and **END** to form a statement block.

```
BEGIN
PRINT 'This PRINT statement is in the same statement block ...'
PRINT '... as this one.'
END
```

For control-of-flow purposes, a statement block may be used wherever a statement is expected. Put another way, you can think of a single Transact-SQL statement as being a *simple statement block* with only one statement. When only one statement is in a statement block, the **BEGIN** and **END** keywords are not required. The term *complex statement block* is sometimes used to refer specifically to a statement block that contains more than one statement. A complex statement block must start with **BEGIN** and terminate with **END**.

The *SQL Server Books Online* states that a variable name will go out of scope when a statement block ends. This is not completely accurate. As stated earlier, only batches and stored procedures define the scope of a variable name.

IF ... ELSE

One of the most common control-of-flow constructs is the **IF ... ELSE** statement. This statement allows you to perform a test that will decide which of two possible statement blocks will be executed. The syntax for this statement is shown, along with an example, in Listing 8.8.

Listing 8.8 The **IF** statement.

```
Syntax:
IF Boolean-test
    statement-block-when-true
[ELSE
    statement-block-when-false]

Example:
IF @Today >= '1-1-2000'
    PRINT 'Congratulations! You made it through Y2K!'
```


The *Boolean-test* is a Transact-SQL expression that evaluates to either true or false. If the Boolean test is true, then statement-block-when-true is executed. If the Boolean test is false and the optional **ELSE** clause is specified, then statement-block-when-false is executed.

Listing 8.8 showed a very simple **IF** statement. If the date stored in **@Today** is on or after January 1, 2000, then a congratulatory message is printed; otherwise, it is not. However, the **IF** statement can become much more complex than this. Listing 8.9 shows how a more complex **IF** statement.

Listing 8.9 A slightly more complex **IF** statement.

```
IF @Today >= '1-1-2000'
BEGIN
    PRINT 'Congratulations! You made it through Y2K!'
    /* Find out how much money is left in our account: */
    EXECUTE usp_CheckAccountBalances @MoneyLeft OUTPUT
    IF @MoneyLeft > 0
        PRINT 'Your money is still here.'
    ELSE
        PRINT 'Better call the bank.'
END
ELSE IF @Today >= '12-1-1999'
    PRINT 'It is December 1999. Are you ready for Y2K?'
ELSE /* it is before 12-1-1999 */
    PRINT 'Keep fixing those Y2K bugs while you have time.'
```

The **EXECUTE** statement is covered later in this section.

In this **IF** statement, if the date is on or after January 1, 2000, the code responds by executing a complex (multiple-statement) statement block. This complex statement block consists of a **PRINT** statement, an **EXECUTE** statement, and another **IF** statement. Notice that this second **IF** statement is embedded within the first one. SQL Server allows the nesting of **IF** statements and does not limit how many levels deep this nesting can be. Finally, this example also includes an **ELSE** clause that executes yet another **IF** statement. This technique is commonly referred to as an **ELSE-IF** construct, and it allows you to link together multiple **IF** statements.

WHILE/BREAK/CONTINUE

Another common and useful statement for flow control is the **WHILE** statement. This statement allows code to be executed repeatedly, as long as a certain condition is met. Listing 8.10 shows **WHILE** statement syntax with an example.

Listing 8.10 The **WHILE** statement.

```
Syntax:
WHILE Boolean-test
    statement-block

Example:
DECLARE @i INT
SET @i = 1

WHILE @i <= 3
BEGIN
    PRINT 'This is message number ' + CONVERT(NVARCHAR, @i)
    SET @i = @i + 1
END

Results:
This is message number 1
This is message number 2
This is message number 3
```

The **CONVERT** function, which is covered in Chapter 9, is used here to convert the integer value **@i** to a data type appropriate for printing.

The **WHILE** statement examines a Boolean condition just like the **IF** statement. If the Boolean condition is true, the statement block inside the

WHILE loop is executed. After the statement block is executed, SQL Server evaluates the Boolean condition again, and executes the statement block repeatedly, as long as the Boolean condition remains true. Therefore, it is important to make sure the Boolean condition will eventually change from true to false, or the statement block may be executed indefinitely—a condition known as an *infinite loop*. Listing 8.11 shows an example of an infinite loop, inadvertently created by omitting the statement **SET @i = @i + 1** from the code. You don't have to execute this code, but if you're one of those people who have to touch the stove to see if it's really hot, then to stop the execution you'll need to sever your connection to the SQL Server.

Listing 8.11 An infinite loop.

```
DECLARE @i INT
SET @i = 1

WHILE @i <= 3
BEGIN
    PRINT 'This is message number ' + CONVERT(NVARCHAR, @i)
END

Results:
This is message number 1
This is message number 1
This is message number 1
...
/* message repeats forever, until connection is terminated */
```

The **BREAK** keyword can appear anywhere inside the statement block being executed by a **WHILE** statement. When **BREAK** is encountered, execution jumps to the first statement after the **WHILE** statement. This immediately halts the current execution of the statement block and terminates the **WHILE** statement itself. For example, although the Boolean test in the Listing 8.12 would allow the loop to execute until **@i** is greater than 100, it will execute just three times because of the **BREAK** statement.

Listing 8.12 Using **BREAK** to exit a **WHILE** loop.

```
DECLARE @i INT
SET @i = 1

WHILE @i <= 100
BEGIN
    PRINT 'This is message number ' + CONVERT(NVARCHAR, @i)
    SET @i = @i + 1
    IF @i > 3
        BREAK
END
```

```
Results:
This is message number 1
This is message number 2
This is message number 3
```

Like **BREAK**, the **CONTINUE** keyword can also appear inside a statement block being executed by a **WHILE** loop. When the **CONTINUE** statement is encountered, the remaining statements in the statement block are skipped. This has the effect of moving to the top of the **WHILE** loop, where the Boolean condition is reevaluated to decide whether the statement block should be executed again. Listing 8.13 shows a way to print out a message only when **@i** is odd.

Listing 8.13 Using **CONTINUE** in a **WHILE** loop.

```
DECLARE @i INT
SET @i = 0

WHILE @i < 10
BEGIN
    SET @i = @i + 1
    IF @i % 2 = 0   -- this condition is true when @i is even
        CONTINUE
    PRINT 'This is message number ' + CONVERT(NVARCHAR, @i)
END
```

```
Results:
This is message number 1
This is message number 3
This is message number 5
This is message number 7
This is message number 9
```

The % symbol used in this Listing 8.13 is the *modulus* operator. The expression *x % y* returns the remainder left when dividing x by y. If x % 2 returns 0, this means that x is evenly divisible by 2, and hence even. You can find a table of Transact-SQL operators in Chapter 9.

GOTO

The **GOTO** command causes execution to jump, immediately and unconditionally, to a position specified by a *label*. The label is just a marker placed in the Transact-SQL code. It must be a valid Transact-SQL identifier. When it is defined, a colon is placed at the end of the label name so that SQL Server knows you are defining a label. You do not include the colon when naming the label in the **GOTO** statement. Listing 8.14 shows the **GOTO** syntax with an example showing how a **WHILE** loop could be emulated using **GOTO**.

Listing 8.14 The **GOTO** statement.

```
Syntax:
GOTO label

Example:
DECLARE @i INT
SET @i = 1

/* The label is defined on the next line: */
print_message:
PRINT 'This is message number ' + CONVERT(NVARCHAR, @i)
SET @i = @i + 1
IF @i <= 3
    GOTO print_message

Results:
This is message number 1
This is message number 2
This is message number 3
```


RETURN

You can use the **RETURN** statement to halt execution of the current statement block, stored procedure, or batch. This statement is covered in depth in Chapter 12, where you will learn how to use **RETURN** to pass status information from a stored procedure back to the Transact-SQL code that invoked the procedure. For this chapter, you should know that the **RETURN** statement causes the current batch of commands to be terminated. In Listing 8.15, the first **PRINT** statement produces output, but the second one does not, because the batch is terminated by a **RETURN** statement. The third **PRINT** statement also produces output, because it is located in the next batch, and **RETURN** terminates only the current batch.

Listing 8.15 Terminating a batch with **RETURN**.

```
PRINT 'Message one will be printed.'
RETURN
PRINT 'Message two will NOT be printed.'
GO

print 'Message three will be printed also.'
```

```
Results:
Message one will be printed.
Message three will be printed also.
```

WAITFOR

This statement causes the current SQL Server batch to suspend execution. **WAITFOR** can wait until a specific amount of time passes (such as one minute), or it can wait for a particular time of day (such as 1:30 P.M.) Listing 8.16 shows the **WAITFOR** syntax and examples of both types of **WAITFOR** statements.

Listing 8.16 The **WAITFOR** statement.

```
Syntax:
WAITFOR { DELAY 'hh:mm:ss'|TIME 'hh:mm:ss' }

WAITFOR DELAY example:
PRINT 'About to delay 10 seconds...'
GO
WAITFOR DELAY '00:00:10'
PRINT 'The 10 seconds have elapsed!'

WAITFOR TIME example:
/* Pause execution until 8:00 PM: */
DECLARE @ResumeTime char(8)
SELECT  @ResumeTime = '20:00:00'
SELECT  @ResumeTime
PRINT   'Pausing execution until ' + CAST(@ResumeTime AS VARCHAR)

WAITFOR TIME @ResumeTime
SELECT  GETDATE()        /* will display 8:00 PM */
```

As the examples in Listing 8.16 illustrate, the delay or time of day should be specified as a literal string or a string variable in a 24-hour *hh:mm:ss* format. A **DATETIME** variable can also be used, in which case the date is ignored and only the hours, minutes, and seconds are used to reckon the delay or time of day. The maximum time **WAITFOR** can suspend a batch is 24 hours.

Cursors

In the previous section you read about the **WHILE** statement, which can be used to execute a statement block repeatedly. One common use of the **WHILE** statement is when a query result needs to be processed one row at a time. In this scenario, each iteration of a **WHILE** loop processes one row of a result set until all of the rows have been processed. The mechanism used to process a query result one row at a time is called a *cursor*. Listing 8.17 shows a simple cursor example. Instead of retrieving every employee's name in a single result set, the cursor in Listing 8.17 retrieves each employee's name in a separate, single-row result set.

Listing 8.17 Displaying row-by-row data using a cursor.

```
DECLARE curName CURSOR FOR
SELECT LastName, FirstName
FROM Employees
ORDER BY LastName, FirstName

OPEN curName

FETCH NEXT FROM curName
WHILE @@FETCH_STATUS != -1
BEGIN
      FETCH NEXT FROM curName
END

DEALLOCATE curName

Results:
LastName             FirstName
--------             ---------
Buchanan             Steven

LastName             FirstName
--------             ---------
Callahan             Laura

LastName             FirstName
--------             ---------
Suyama               Michael

LastName             FirstName
--------             ---------
```

8

In the listing, we begin by using **DECLARE CURSOR** to associate a cursor name (**curName**) with a **SELECT** statement. Next we issue the command **OPEN curName**. This causes the **SELECT** statement associated with the cursor **curName** to be executed. However, no results are returned to the client application at this time. Rather, the first result set is returned when the **FETCH NEXT** statement is executed. **FETCH NEXT** is executed repeatedly using a **WHILE** loop until the function **@@FETCH_STATUS** returns -1. When **@@FETCH_STATUS** is -1, SQL Server is telling us that we have tried to retrieve data beyond the result set associated with the cursor.

This is similar to an *end-of-file* condition in other programming languages. In fact, you can tell that we tried to **FETCH** past the end of the cursor's result set by noting that the last result set in the listing's output is empty.

A cursor, then, is used to store the results of a query on the SQL Server. Rows from this *cached result set* can be retrieved one row at a time by using **FETCH** statement. (You may be wondering why you would ever want to do this, and not just display all the results at one time.) Sometimes when designing an *Online Transaction Processing (OLTP)* application, you may want to display only the first part of a large result set, rather than waiting for all of the results to be returned. Using a cursor, a program could fetch only the rows it wanted to display.

However, cursors provide an additional capability that makes them even more useful. Cursors can be used to *retrieve* data instead of *displaying* data. This capability allows us to process a query's result set one row at a time. To show the value of this, we will move beyond the simple cursor example in Listing 8.17. Throughout the remainder of this discussion, we will refer to Listing 8.18, in which a cursor is used to report information about columns.

The Life Cycle Of A Cursor

The following are the four major steps in using a Transact-SQL cursor:

- Step 1: Defining the cursor using the **DECLARE CURSOR** statement
- Step 2: Preparing the cursor's result set with the **OPEN** statement
- Step 3: Retrieving data from the cursor's result set using the **FETCH** statement
- Step 4: Freeing cursor resources with **CLOSE** and **DEALLOCATE**

In Listing 8.18, each of these four steps is preceded by a label in the listing so that you can find each section of code easily.

This section covers Transact-SQL cursors, whose cache result sits on the SQL Server for later retrieval by a client. This type of cursor is most useful when you are writing Transact-SQL code that naturally executes on the SQL Server, such as triggers and stored procedures. Two other types of cursors are supported by SQL Server: *application programming interface (API) server cursors* and *client cursors*. At times, one of these cursor types may be more useful than Transact-SQL cursors. However, because they require the use of a database interface layer such as OLE DB, ODBC, ADO, or DB-Lib, they are outside the scope of this book. For more information on API server cursors and client cursors, consult the *SQL Server Books Online*. A good place to start is the topic Cursors in the section "Accessing And Changing Data."

Listing 8.18 Row-by-row processing with a cursor.

```
DECLARE @TABLE_SCHEMA NVARCHAR(256),
        @TABLE_NAME SYSNAME,
        @COLUMN_NAME SYSNAME,
        @IS_NULLABLE VARCHAR(3),
        @DATA_TYPE NVARCHAR(256),
        @MESSAGE VARCHAR(70)

SET     @TABLE_SCHEMA = N'dbo'
SET     @TABLE_NAME = 'Products'

STEP1_DEFINE:
DECLARE curColumns CURSOR READ_ONLY FOR
SELECT  COLUMN_NAME, IS_NULLABLE, DATA_TYPE
FROM    INFORMATION_SCHEMA.COLUMNS
WHERE   TABLE_SCHEMA = @TABLE_SCHEMA
AND     TABLE_NAME   = @TABLE_NAME
ORDER   BY ORDINAL_POSITION

STEP2_PREPARE:
OPEN curColumns

STEP3A_FETCH:
FETCH NEXT FROM curColumns
INTO @COLUMN_NAME, @IS_NULLABLE, @DATA_TYPE

/* @@FETCH_STATUS = -1 means we've fetched past the last record: */
WHILE @@FETCH_STATUS != -1
BEGIN
   SET @MESSAGE = 'Column ' + @COLUMN_NAME + ' is of data type '
      + @DATA_TYPE
   IF @IS_NULLABLE = 'YES'
      SET @MESSAGE = @MESSAGE + ' and is nullable.'
   ELSE
      SET @MESSAGE = @MESSAGE + ' and is NOT nullable.'

   PRINT @MESSAGE
   STEP3B_FETCH:
   FETCH NEXT FROM curColumns
   INTO @COLUMN_NAME, @IS_NULLABLE, @DATA_TYPE
END

STEP4_FREE_RESOURCES:
CLOSE curColumns
DEALLOCATE curColumns
```

8

```
Results:
Column ProductID is of data type int and is NOT nullable.
Column ProductName is of data type nvarchar and is NOT nullable.
Column SupplierID is of data type int and is nullable.
...
Column ReorderLevel is of data type smallint and is nullable.
Column Discontinued is of data type bit and is NOT nullable.
```

Listing 8.18 begins by declaring local variables. Several of these variables will be used to hold data values returned by the cursor. Note that each local variable has the same data type as the corresponding column that will be read by the cursor. Next, the variables **@SCHEMA_NAME** and **@TABLE_NAME** are initialized. If this code were embodied in a stored procedure, these values might be passed in as parameters. Because we haven't studied stored procedures yet, this script simulates the presence of parameters by using these two variables and initializing them using **SET**. After these variables have been initialized, we are ready to define the cursor.

The **INFORMATION_SCHEMA** views use the term **SCHEMA_NAME** instead of **user**. This is partly due to the fact that these views are created by the ANSI-92 SQL standard. Because this standard is geared toward many database vendors, the terms do not always match those used by SQL Server 7.

Step 1: Defining The Cursor

The **DECLARE CURSOR** statement is used to define the cursor. In Listing 8.18, this statement can be seen just after the label **STEP1_DEFINE**. At this point, no data has been fetched from the view **INFORMATION_SCHEMA. COLUMNS**. Only a cursor definition has been created. As we will see later, several different types of Transact-SQL cursors can be created. By default, this cursor will be *forward-only*, meaning that we can only fetch the rows in sequential order from first to last. Because cursors default to being updatable (which incurs unnecessary overhead on the SQL Server), the **READ_ONLY** option is explicitly specified.

More complete coverage of **DECLARE CURSOR** can be found later in this chapter.

Step 2: Preparing The Cursor's Result Set

The **OPEN** statement (after the **STEP2_PREPARE** label) executes the **SELECT** statement associated with the cursor. However, when the query is executed, the result set is not returned to the client, but is stored, or *cached*, on the

SQL Server. The results are only returned to the client when the client program specifically requests them. One advantage of Transact-SQL cursors is that if a query generates many more result set rows than the client will actually retrieve, network traffic is reduced by storing the (unused) result sets on the server.

Step 3: Retrieving Data From The Cursor

Next, we need to examine the **FETCH** statements that are used to retrieve data from the server where it has been cached by the **OPEN** statement. Two **FETCH** statements exist, found after the labels **STEP3A_FETCH** and **STEP3B_FETCH**. Each **FETCH** returns one row of data. Using a **WHILE** loop, we repeatedly **FETCH** rows until **@@FETCH_STATUS** indicates that no more rows can be retrieved. Notice that each variable retrieved by the cursor's **SELECT** statement has a matching variable in the **FETCH** statement's **INTO** clause. Each of these variables, which have the same data type as the corresponding column in the query, receives the value from an individual row and column every time another row is fetched. Because this is a forward-only cursor, the only type of **FETCH** statement allowed is **FETCH NEXT**. This statement always retrieves the next available row in the result set that has been cached on the server.

You can think of a cursor as a type of pointer: When a cursor is declared, the pointer points to nothing. When the cursor is opened, the cursor points to the beginning of the first row of the result set. Each time **FETCH NEXT** is executed, the row being pointed to is fetched, and the cursor is moved so that it points to the beginning of the *next* row. After the last row is fetched, the cursor points to the end of the result set, and subsequent calls to **FETCH NEXT** will result in **@@FETCH_STATUS** having a value of -1.

Once a single row from a result set has been fetched into the appropriate local variables, those variables can be manipulated just like any other variables in Transact-SQL. The values retrieved by each **FETCH** statement remain in the local variables until they are replaced by the next **FETCH** (or by another SQL statement).

As you have seen, the value of **@@FETCH_STATUS** is 0 after a row is successfully fetched. When we try to **FETCH** another row after the last row has already been retrieved, **@@FETCH_STATUS** will have a value of -1. **@@FETCH_STATUS** can also have a value of -2, but for this example you should concentrate on understanding the meaning of **@@FETCH_STATUS** when it is 0 or -1. You will learn more about this function later in this chapter, and also in Chapter 9.

Step 4: Freeing Cursor Resources

Examine the label **STEP4_FREE_RESOURCES** in Listing 8.18 and the two statements that follow it. These statements free up resources (such as memory) that have been allocated to the cursor. The **CLOSE** statement reverses an **OPEN** statement: It causes the cached result set on the server to be released. After **CLOSE** has executed, the cursor is still defined and can be opened again. If it is reopened, a new result set will be built and stored on the server, just like the first time the cursor was opened.

The **DEALLOCATE** statement reverses the **DECLARE CURSOR** statement: It causes all cursor resources to be released, just as though it were never created. After **DEALLOCATE** has executed, the cursor is undefined. If you want to use a similar cursor you must begin by declaring it again. Table 8.1 summarizes the function of each important cursor-related command used in Listing 8.18.

If you are not going to reopen a cursor, it is not necessary to issue a **CLOSE** command. You can skip to the **DEALLOCATE** statement.

Types Of Cursors

SQL Server 7 supports many different kinds of Transact-SQL cursors. The interaction of the various types of cursors is a topic deserving careful study. You can define a cursor's *scope*, how a cursor may be *navigated*, and the *type of result set* a cursor creates. You can also specify whether the cursor can be used to make changes to the data it retrieves. We begin our exploration of these choices with Listing 8.19, which is a partial syntax diagram for the **DECLARE CURSOR** statement.

Table 8.1 Summary of functions for cursor-related statements used in Listing 8.18.

Cursor-Related Keyword	Function
DECLARE	Creates local variables to hold values fetched by the cursor.
DECLARE CURSOR	Creates the definition of the cursor, but does not execute the associated query.
OPEN	Runs the query associated with the cursor, and caches the result set on the server.
FETCH NEXT	Retrieves the next row from the cached result set on the server and puts individual column values into local variables.
CLOSE	Undoes the **OPEN** command by releasing the cached result set on the server.
DEALLOCATE	Undoes the **DECLARE** command by releasing the system resources allocated to the cursor when it is declared.

Listing 8.19 DECLARE CURSOR syntax.

```
DECLARE cursor_name CURSOR
[LOCAL|GLOBAL]
[FORWARD_ONLY|SCROLL]
[STATIC|KEYSET|DYNAMIC|FAST_FORWARD]
[READ_ONLY|SCROLL_LOCKS|OPTIMISTIC]
FOR select_statement
[FOR UPDATE [ OF column_name1 [, column_name2 ...]]]
```

Cursor declaration compliant with the SQL-92 standard is also supported by SQL Server 7. For more details, consult the "DECLARE CURSOR (T-SQL)" topic in the *SQL Server Books Online*.

As you can see many different kinds of cursors are available for use. Let's examine each of the choices represented in this syntax chart.

LOCAL|GLOBAL

These options are used to specify the scope of the cursor. SQL Server 7 supports *global cursors*, which go out of scope when a connection is terminated, as well as *local cursors*, which go out of scope when the current batch finishes. If you do not specify either **GLOBAL** or **LOCAL** in the **DECLARE CURSOR** statement, the default is controlled by the current value of the database setting **default to local cursor**. This value can be set using the system stored procedure **sp_dboption**.

If you do not **CLOSE** or **DEALLOCATE** a cursor, SQL Server will automatically **DEALLOCATE** it when it goes out of scope.

FORWARD_ONLY|SCROLL

In Listing 8.18, we declared our cursor to be **FORWARD_ONLY**. This means that the only way to navigate the result set was from front to back, one row at a time, using **FETCH NEXT** to retrieve the rows. If **SCROLL** is specified instead, you can use other **FETCH** methods to navigate the result set in a non-sequential manner. The **FETCH** syntax in Listing 8.20 shows all of the cursor navigation options available for use with **SCROLL** cursors.

Listing 8.20 FETCH syntax.

```
FETCH
[NEXT|PRIOR|FIRST|LAST|ABSOLUTE row|RELATIVE rows]
[FROM] cursor_name
[INTO @variable1 [, @variable2, ...]]
```

FETCH PRIOR moves, or *scrolls*, the cursor to the previous record in the result set. Similarly, **FETCH FIRST** and **FETCH LAST**, respectively, retrieve the first and last records in the result set. **FETCH ABSOLUTE n** scrolls the cursor to record number n and **FETCH RELATIVE n** scrolls n rows from the current cursor position, going forward if n is positive and backward if n is negative. For example, **FETCH ABSOLUTE 5** retrieves the fifth record in the result set. **FETCH RELATIVE 5** retrieves the row five rows *beyond* the current cursor position; and **FETCH RELATIVE -5** performs a fetch five rows *before* the current cursor position.

The *SQL Server Books Online* state that **FORWARD_ONLY** is the default option, unless **STATIC**, **KEYSET**, or **DYNAMIC** is specified, in which case the default is **SCROLL**. However, the same documentation also tells us that **FAST_FORWARD** and **FORWARD_ONLY** are mutually exclusive. What this means is that **FORWARD_ONLY** is only the default if you do not specify *any* of **STATIC**, **KEYSET**, **DYNAMIC**, or **FAST_ONLY**.

STATIC|KEYSET|DYNAMIC|FAST_FORWARD

These options represent the type of result set SQL Server stores for a cursor. **STATIC** result sets are implemented by putting an entire copy of the result set into the *tempdb* database. No changes to the original data will be reflected in the cursor, because it is a copy of the original data.

KEYSET cursors are implemented by storing only key values for the rows in the cursor result set. This *keyset*, like a **STATIC** cursor result set, is stored in the *tempdb* database. SQL Server uses these key values to looks up non-key values every time data is fetched. This means that the values fetched from a **KEYSET** cursor reflect any every change to non-key values that occurred before the **FETCH.** However, if a row is deleted before it is fetched, SQL Server will not be able to find the row when the **FETCH** is attempted. This will cause **@@FETCH_STATUS** to return a value of -2. The same thing will happen if key values are changed by another connection in one of the data rows before that row is fetched.

DYNAMIC cursors reflect every change to the underlying data that occurs before a row is fetched. Even newly inserted rows will be reflected in a **DYNAMIC** cursor. **DYNAMIC** cursors do not support the **FETCH ABSOLUTE** statement, even if **SCROLL** is specified. Finally, **FAST_FORWARD** cursors act like **FORWARD_ONLY, READ_ONLY** cursors. This type of cursor is useful for reading through a result set as fast as possible.

READ_ONLY|SCROLL_LOCKS|OPTIMISTIC

These three options control whether a cursor can be used to change data. A **READ_ONLY** cursor is used only to read data, and changes to the data cannot be made through the cursor. The default is for cursors to allow updates unless **READ_ONLY** (or **FAST_FORWARD**) is specified.

SCROLL_LOCKS and **OPTIMISTIC** cursors can both be used to modify data. However, they have different locking strategies. **SCROLL_LOCKS** cursors lock the rows they are eligible to update. For the duration of the cursor, no other connection can modify these rows. This is a *pessimistic* locking strategy. **OPTIMISTIC** cursors, on the other hand, do not lock rows they are eligible to modify until the modification is attempted. This *optimistic* locking strategy uses timestamps or checksums to check whether another user has modified the row since it was read. If another user is found to have modified the row since it was fetched, the cursor's update is disallowed. The mechanism for updating data through cursors, **WHERE CURRENT OF**, is discussed in the next section.

FOR UPDATE [OF column_name1 [, column_name2 ...]]

As we noted, a cursor is updatable unless **READ_ONLY** or **FAST_FORWARD** is specified. An updatable cursor, by default, can be used to modify any column it has retrieved. The **FOR UPDATE** clause can be used to limit the columns that can be updated. The next section tells you how to use cursors to modify data.

Modifying Data With WHERE CURRENT OF

Cursors can be used in conjunction with **DELETE** and **UPDATE** statements to modify data retrieved by the cursor. This is done by using a special **WHERE** clause called **WHERE CURRENT OF**. The syntax for this clause, along with an example of its use, is shown in Listing 8.21.

Listing 8.21 Using **WHERE CURRENT OF** to modify data via a cursor.

```
Syntax:
WHERE CURRENT OF cursor_name

Example:
CREATE TABLE GeometricPlaces
(PlaceCode varchar(3),
 PlaceName varchar(30)
)
GO

/* The following row contains a typo we will correct: */
INSERT INTO GeometricPlaces
VALUES ('AC', 'Artic Circle')

/* The following row will be left as-is: */
INSERT INTO GeometricPlaces
```

```
VALUES ('MSG', 'Madison Square Garden')

/* The following row will (of course) disappear: */
INSERT INTO GeometricPlaces
VALUES ('BT', 'Bermuda Triangle')

DECLARE @PlaceCode VARCHAR(3),
        @PlaceName VARCHAR(30)

DECLARE curGP CURSOR FORWARD_ONLY FOR
SELECT  PlaceCode, PlaceName
FROOM    GeometricPlaces
FOR     UPDATE OF PlaceName

OPEN curGP
FETCH NEXT FROM curGP INTO @PlaceCode, @PlaceName

SELECT PlaceCode AS Code, PlaceName AS [Name Before Cursor]
FROM   GeometricPlaces

WHILE @@FETCH_STATUS != -1
BEGIN
   IF @PlaceCode = 'AC'
      UPDATE GeometricPlaces
      SET PlaceName = 'Arctic Circle'
      WHERE CURRENT OF curGP
 0  ELSE IF @PlaceCode = 'BT'
      DELETE FROM GeometricPlaces
      WHERE CURRENT OF curGP

   FETCH NEXT FROM curGP INTO @PlaceCode, @PlaceName
END

SELECT PlaceCode AS Code, PlaceName AS [Name After Cursor]
FROM   GeometricPlaces

DEALLOCATE curGP
DROP TABLE GeometricPlaces
```

Results:

```
Code Name Before Cursor
---- ------------------
AC   Artic Circle
MSG  Madison Square Garden
BT   Bermuda Triangle
```

```
Code Name After Cursor
---- -----------------
AC   Arctic Circle
MSG  Madison Square Garden
```

In Listing 8.21, a table is declared and populated with rows describing the Arctic Circle, Madison Square Garden, and the Bermuda Triangle. These rows are then retrieved by using a cursor that is declared with a **FOR UPDATE OF PlaceName** clause. When the Arctic Circle record is fetched by the cursor, a **UPDATE ... WHERE CURRENT OF** statement is used to correct a misspelling in the *PlaceName* column. When the Bermuda Triangle record is encountered, it is deleted using **DELETE ... WHERE CURRENT OF**. Two **SELECT** statements in the listing allow us to compare the table's contents before and after the cursor runs, verifying that the intended changes were made successfully.

Grandma's Secret: Making Better Batches

The execution of Transact-SQL statements has something in common with baking chocolate chip cookies: In both cases the work is done one batch at a time. In our family, the best cookies were always made by Grandma. In fact, sometimes they were *so* good that we all would wonder how she did it. "She must not use the same ingredients we do," we would think. "She must be using a *secret ingredient*."

At this point, you may be just beginning to create your first batches of Transact-SQL statements. If so, you need to become acquainted with a few more ingredients commonly used by some of the best Transact-SQL cooks. Several of these missing ingredients are described in other chapters of this book, but we will discuss them briefly here as well. For example, while studying stored procedures in Chapter 12, you learn techniques for responding to *error conditions*. You can query the built-in function **@@ERROR** to find out whether the previous statement completed successfully. You can also examine **@@ROWCOUNT** to find out whether the most recent statement affected the correct number of rows. If one of these methods reveals that an error has occurred, your code can respond by raising an error condition and issuing a **RETURN** statement. These methods, although discussed in Chapter 12 in the context of stored procedures, can be similarly used in batches and scripts.

Transactions and *locking* are also very useful tools for building safe batches and scripts. These concepts are both covered in detail in Chapter 11. Transactions allow you to define a group of statements that will must either all succeed or all fail as a group. If an error is detected at any time during a transaction, the entire transaction can be undone, or *rolled back*. Locks allow you to reserve data so that no other process can change it for the duration of your transaction.

Listing 8.22 illustrates how each of these concepts might apply in a batch environment. The parts of the listing that are highlighted are the places where we are mixing in our new ingredients. Because these topics are covered in more detail in later sections of the book, they are thoroughly commented inside Listing 8.22 to aid your understanding. If this batch looks a little intimidating to you, read the comments carefully. They form the recipe that explains what we are doing with all these new ingredients. You will find that this is actually a fairly simple batch that copies rows from one table to another and performs a simple check to make sure it copied all of the rows successfully.

Listing 8.22 Using error-handling techniques within a batch.

```
DECLARE @SalesCount int

/* Use a transaction so we can undo our work if there are errors: */
BEGIN TRANSACTION
/* Record the number of rows in the table, and hold a shared lock */
/* for the duration of the transaction so that the number won't   */
/* change during our processing:                                  */
   SELECT @SalesCount = COUNT(*)
   FROM   SalesMaster WITH (SERIALIZABLE, TABLOCK)

/* Do the actual copying of rows, deleting the old ones first:    */
   DELETE   FROM SalesCopy
   INSERT   INTO SalesCopy
   SELECT * FROM SalesMaster

/* Finally, use the @@ROWCOUNT and @@ERROR functions to make sure */
/* that the statement completed successfully. Use @@ROWCOUNT to   */
/* make sure that we inserted the same number of rows that we     */
/* counted earlier, and use @@ERROR to make sure SQL Server did   */
/* not return any non-zero error code"                           */
IF (@@ROWCOUNT <> @SalesCount) OR (@@ERROR <> 0)
   BEGIN
      ROLLBACK TRANSACTION
      RAISERROR ("Copy of SalesMaster failed", 16, 1)
      RETURN
   END
   ELSE
      COMMIT TRANSACTION
```

After declaring a local variable, Listing 8.22 starts a transaction so that we can undo our data changes later if necessary. Next, the **COUNT(*)** aggregate function (discussed in Chapter 9) is used to determine how many rows are in the *SalesMaster* table. The syntax **WITH (SERIALIZABLE, TABLOCK)** instructs SQL Server that we need to hold a shared lock on the *SalesMaster* table for the duration of our transaction. Next we use **DELETE** to empty the existing *SalesCopy* table, and then we repopulate it right away using a **INSERT ... SELECT** statement. After that, control-of-flow language works in conjunction with error-handling methods as we examine both **@@ERROR** and **@@ROWCOUNT** to look for unexpected results. The copy was successful if **@@ERROR** is zero and **@@ROWCOUNT** returns the same number that we stored in **@SalesCount** earlier in the batch. If the copy was successful, we **COMMIT** the transaction. Otherwise, we issue a **ROLLBACK TRANSACTION** to cancel the transaction, return error information to the client via **RAISERROR**, and halt the batch with **RETURN**.

The good news is that Transact-SQL has no *secret* ingredients. As Figure 8.1 shows, you can view the source code for any of Microsoft's own system stored procedures by double-clicking on it in the SQL Server Enterprise Manager. This is a great way to learn Transact-SQL programming techniques.

Chapter Summary

In this chapter you learned that SQL Server executes Transact-SQL statements in *batches*, and that the term *script* refers to any source file executed by a client that results in at least one batch being run on the SQL Server. The following points summarize the other key points of this chapter.

➤ *Local variables* have names beginning with the at sign (@) and are used to store and manipulate a single piece of information within a Transact-SQL batch.

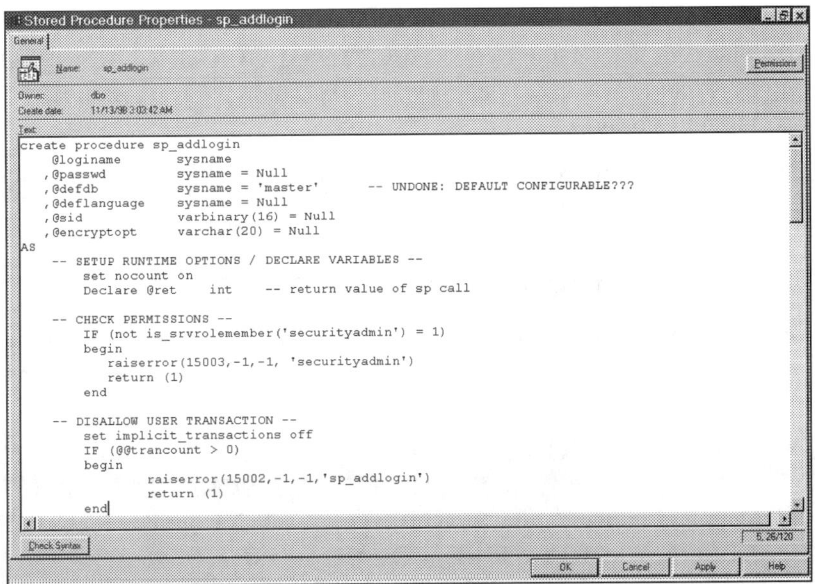
Stored Procedure Properties - sp_addlogin
create procedure sp_addlogin
@loginame sysname
,@passwd sysname = Null
,@defdb sysname = 'master' -- UNDONE: DEFAULT CONFIGURABLE???
,@deflanguage sysname = Null
,@sid varbinary(16) = Null
,@encryptopt varchar(20) = Null
AS
-- SETUP RUNTIME OPTIONS / DECLARE VARIABLES --
set nocount on
Declare @ret int -- return value of sp call
-- CHECK PERMISSIONS --
IF (not is_srvrolemember('securityadmin') = 1)
begin
raiserror(15003,-1,-1, 'securityadmin')
return (1)
end
-- DISALLOW USER TRANSACTION --
set implicit_transactions off
IF (@@trancount > 0)
begin
raiserror(15002,-1,-1,'sp_addlogin')
return (1)
end
Check Syntax
OK
Cancel
Apply
Help

Figure 8.1 Enhance your understanding by studying Microsoft's code.

- Names of local variables are available only for the duration of the batch or procedure that declared them. When the batch or procedure ends, local variable names are said to *go out of scope*.
- The **EXECUTE** statement and the **sp_executesql** stored procedure can be used to dynamically execute the Transact-SQL batch stored in a string. The commands executed in either of these two ways comprise an entire batch and have their own scope for variable names.
- Transact-SQL supports line and block comments. Block comments begin with /* and terminate with */. Line comments begin with two hyphens (--) and automatically terminate at the end of the current line. SQL Server ignores comments when compiling execution plans for a Transact-SQL batch.
- Using **BEGIN** and **END** allows you to create a *statement block* containing multiple statements. A statement block can be used in Transact-SQL code wherever a single statement is expected.
- *Control-of-flow language* keywords, such as **IF**, **WHILE**, **GOTO**, **WAITFOR** and **RETURN**, allow you to choose which statement blocks should be executed and the order of their execution. You can repeatedly execute some statement blocks while skipping others, and you can cause execution to jump from any part of a batch to any other part.
- *Cursors* can be used to facilitate processing one row of a result set at a time. Transact-SQL supports several types of cursors. The type of a cursor determines its *scope*, how it can be *navigated*, and the *type of result set* associated with it.
- The steps involved in using a cursor are **DECLARE CURSOR**, **OPEN**, **FETCH** (this step may be executed repeatedly), **CLOSE**, and **DEALLOCATE**.
- When a cursor's result set is populated by **OPEN**, the cursor itself points to the beginning of the first row.
- The function **@@FETCH_STATUS** can be used to learn whether the most recent **FETCH** statement was executed successfully.
- A **GLOBAL** cursor stays in scope (available for use) until its connection terminates. A **LOCAL** cursor goes out of scope when the current batch terminates.
- A **FORWARD_ONLY** cursor can only be navigated from beginning to end using the statement **FETCH NEXT**. A **SCROLL** cursor can be navigated in many more ways, using the **FETCH** options **FIRST**, **LAST**, **ABSOLUTE**, **RELATIVE**, **PRIOR**, and **NEXT**.
- **STATIC**, **KEYSET**, **DYNAMIC**, and **FAST_FORWARD** cursors are implemented using different types of result sets on the cursor. They also

differ in their ability to reflect changes made to the underlying table data since the cursor was originally opened.

- **READ_ONLY**, **SCROLL_LOCKS**, and **OPTIMISTIC** are keywords that control whether a cursor can be used to modify data and what locking strategies it uses.
- The **UPDATE** and **DELETE** statements both support the **WHERE CURRENT OF** clause, which allows data changes to be made to the base data at the cursor's current position.

Review Questions

1. Which of the following is true regarding the **GO** statement? (Choose all correct answers.)
   a. **GO** is a Transact-SQL command that tells SQL Server to create Transact-SQL batches in the most efficient manner possible.
   b. **GO** is a command that tells SQL Server to create Transact-SQL batches in the manner specified by the Transact-SQL code.
   c. **GO** is a command that tells certain SQL Server client programs to submit a batch for execution.
   d. **GO** is not a Transact-SQL command.

2. If the second statement in a batch of three Transact-SQL statements contains a syntax error, what will happen when you try to execute the batch?
   a. None of the statements will execute.
   b. The first statement will execute, but the batch will abort when the second statement is attempted.
   c. The first and third statements will execute, but the second statement will return an error indicating that a syntax error is present.
   d. After detecting the syntax error, SQL Server will compile this batch as though it contained only the first and third statements.

3. A Transact-SQL batch compiles successfully, but creates a runtime error when it is executed. Which of the following do we know to be true?
   a. The entire batch will be rolled back.
   b. None of the statements before the runtime error will be rolled back.
   c. None of the statements after the runtime error will be executed.
   d. The batch will terminate when the runtime error is encountered.
   e. The exact behavior of a runtime error depends on the specific error encountered, so you must use error-handling to ensure that your code responds appropriately.

4. Each of the following Transact-SQL statements is supposed to assign values to one or more local variables. Which statements will not accomplish this? (Choose all correct answers.)
   a. **SELECT @@ERROR**
   b. **SELECT @ERROR = @@ERROR**
   c. **SET @LastName = 'Smith', @FirstName = 'Bobby'**
   d. **SET @LastName = @param_LastName**
5. Which of the following are valid ways to assign values to Transact-SQL variables? (Choose all correct answers.)
   a. **SELECT @DeptCode = Department**
   FROM Employees
   WHERE EmployeeNumber = 23115
   b. **SET @nRows = @@ROWCOUNT**
   c. **EXECUTE ('ECHO %ERRORLEVEL% > @ERROR')**
   d. **SELECT @Certification = 'MCDBA'**
6. A local variable can only be referenced from within the batch or procedure that created it.
   a. True
   b. False
7. What two standard methods does SQL Server provide that allow you to dynamically execute a Transact-SQL batch stored in a string variable named **@cmd**? (Choose all correct answers.)
   a. **sp_executesql @cmd**
   b. **sp_runthis @cmd**
   c. **EXECUTE @cmd**
   d. **EXECUTE (@cmd)**
8. What are the two types of comments supported by Transact-SQL? (Choose all correct answers.)
   a. Block comments that begin and end with two hyphens (--).
   b. Block comments that begin with /* and end with */.
   c. Line comments that begin with two hyphens (--) and must appear on their own line of code.
   d. Line comments that begin with two hyphens (--) and run to the end of the current line.
   e. Line comments that begin and end with two slashes (//).

9. Comments provide a convenient way to document Transact-SQL code.
    a. True
    b. False

10. What is a complex statement block?
    a. A group of Transact-SQL statements that SQL Server must recompile every time they are run.
    b. A group of Transact-SQL statements, beginning with **BEGIN** and ending with **END**, that can be used in place of a single Transact-SQL statement.
    c. A rule embedded in Transact-SQL code that can block the execution of other code.
    d. Any single Transact-SQL statement.

11. Which of the following are not control-of-flow keywords in Transact-SQL?
    a. **WHILE**
    b. **GOTO**
    c. **CASE**
    d. **IF**

12. Which Transact-SQL control-of-flow statement is used to execute a statement block repeatedly?
    a. **DO WHILE**
    b. **FOR**
    c. **WHILE**
    d. **REPEAT**

13. Which of the following claims about the **GOTO** statement are true?
    a. **GOTO** can cause execution to jump to any other point in a script.
    b. **GOTO** can be used to jump to special error-handling code.
    c. **GOTO 5** will cause execution to jump to line 5 of the batch.
    d. **GOTO 5** will cause execution to terminate after line 5 is reached.

14. What tool does Transact-SQL provide that specifically allows you to program row-by-row handling of result sets?
    a. The SQL Server Query Analyzer
    b. The **WHILE** statement
    c. Cursors
    d. Statement blocks

15. Which of the following can you do with cursors?
    a. Display the results of a single query as separate, one-row result sets.
    b. **FETCH** only the first 50 rows for display so that the client does not have to wait for an entire large data set to be returned.
    c. Update the data that was used to populate the cursor's result set.
    d. Retrieve each value from a result set into Transact-SQL variables for row-by-row processing.
    e. All of the above.

16. What does the **OPEN** statement do?
    a. Retrieves data from the SQL Server to the client for future processing by **FETCH** statements.
    b. Causes the first row of the query to be retrieved from the tables so it is ready for the first **FETCH** statement.
    c. Associates a cursor name with a query definition.
    d. Executes the query associated with the cursor being opened and stores the result set on the server.

17. Which statements could you use with a **SCROLL** cursor to retrieve the row currently pointed to by a cursor and move the cursor position ahead one row? (Choose all correct answers.)
    a. **FETCH NEXT**
    b. **FETCH ABSOLUTE 1**
    c. **FETCH RELATIVE 1**
    d. **FETCH FORWARD**

18. Which statements could you use with a **SCROLL** cursor to retrieve the row before the one currently pointed to by a cursor and move the cursor position backward to point to the row being fetched? (Choose all correct answers.)
    a. **FETCH PREVIOUS**
    b. **FETCH ABSOLUTE -1**
    c. **FETCH RELATIVE -1**
    d. **FETCH PRIOR**

19. Which statements could you use with a **SCROLL** cursor to fetch the row 4 before the current row, thus making that row the cursor's current row?
    a. **FETCH -4**
    b. **FETCH ABSOLUTE -4**
    c. **FETCH RELATIVE -4**
    d. **FETCH (-4)**

20. What does it mean when **@@FETCH_STATUS** returns the value 0?
    a. The **FETCH** was successful.
    b. No rows were available to **FETCH**.
    c. No **FETCH** has been attempted yet.
    d. The cursor has been closed.

21. If you are not going to use a cursor after closing it, you can issue the **DEALLOCATE** command without issuing the **CLOSE** command first.
    a. True
    b. False

22. All cursors are automatically closed and deallocated when they go out of scope.
    a. True
    b. False

23. What type of cursor behaves like a **READ_ONLY, FORWARD_ONLY** cursor?
    a. **STATIC**
    b. **KEYSET**
    c. **DYNAMIC**
    d. **FAST_FORWARD**

24. What type of cursor will reflect all changes made to the underlying data since the time the cursor was opened?
    a. **STATIC**
    b. **KEYSET**
    c. **DYNAMIC**
    d. **FAST_FORWARD**

25. What is the **DECLARE CURSOR** clause that allows the cursor to be used to update the data it retrieves?
    a. **UPDATABLE**
    b. **FOR UPDATE OF**
    c. **WHERE CURRENT OF**
    d. **READ_WRITE**

Hands-On Projects

Susan had been working with the developers on the project, assisting with Transact-SQL statements and syntax. One afternoon the lead developer contacted her through an email.

```
From:          chandlers@email.gbw.com
To:            susans@email.gbw.com
Subject:       Stored Procs.
Date:          Fri, 2 Jul 1999 10:09:59 -0400 (EDT)
Susan -
Bob's not doing well with his flu. I think he's going to be
out about three days with this, so could I get you to help
us with coding some stored procedures for me? He was working
on some code that would do some automatic maintenance
on the database. This is sort of your area anyway. Let me
know if you need any help. I've attached the specs so you
can see what we need done.
Thanks -
Chris
```

Susan thought, "Well, this really *is* my area, and I need to learn how to create the scripts and code to do this for my other databases. Guess I'll dive in."

Project 8.1

Executing **DBCC CHECKTABLE** against all **dbo** tables.

DBCC CHECKTABLE is a Transact-SQL command that invokes the *Database Consistency Checker (DBCC)* to check the internal integrity of a table. In this project, you will use a cursor to retrieve the owner and name of every table in the *Northwind* database. You will then use this information to build an appropriate **DBCC CHECKTABLE** command. This command will be dynamically executed using the **EXEC** command. You will skip any table that is not owned by **dbo**. The following steps walk you through this project:

1. To test that your code works correctly, at least one table must not owned by **dbo**. This requires that you create a SQL Server login and user whose account we will use to create a table. In the SQL Server Query Analyzer, connect to your SQL Server as **sa** and execute the commands in Listing 8.23. This code will create a login and user named **Chapter8User**.

Listing 8.23 Creating a *Northwind* database user called **Chapter8User**.

```
USE Northwind
GO

/* Create the SQL Server login and user: */
EXEC sp_addlogin Chapter8User, Chapter8User, Northwind
EXEC sp_adduser  Chapter8User, Chapter8User, 'public'

Results:
New login created.
Granted database access to 'Chapter8User'.
```

2. Next, you will create a table owned by **Chapter8User**. The code in Listing 8.24 sets a database option allowing you to use the **SELECT INTO** statement. You then use the **SELECT INTO** statement to create a table owned by **Chapter8User**. Notice from the output that the new table has 830 rows in it (which is the same number of rows as the original *Orders* table).

Listing 8.24 Creating a table owned by **Chapter8User**.

```
EXEC sp_dboption Northwind, 'select into', true
GO

SELECT *
INTO   Chapter8User.CopyOfOrders
FROM   dbo.Orders

Results:
Checkpointing database that was changed.
DBCC execution completed. If DBCC printed error messages,
contact your system administrator.

(830 row(s) affected)
```


3. Enter and execute the code shown in Listing 8.25. To help you read the code, this listing uses the same cursor-related labels that were used in Listing 8.18, such as **STEP1_DEFINE**. The code to generate and dynamically executes the **DBCC CHECKTABLE** commands is highlighted so you can find it easily.

Listing 8.25 Executing **DBCC** commands from within a cursor loop.

```
DECLARE @TABLE_SCHEMA NVARCHAR(256),
        @TABLE_NAME   sysname,
        @SQL_COMMAND  NVARCHAR(500)

STEP1_DEFINE:
DECLARE curTables CURSOR FAST_FORWARD FOR
SELECT TABLE_SCHEMA, TABLE_NAME
FROM   INFORMATION_SCHEMA.TABLES
WHERE  TABLE_TYPE = 'BASE TABLE'
ORDER  BY TABLE_SCHEMA, TABLE_NAME

STEP2_OPEN:
OPEN curTables

STEP3A_FETCH:
```

```
FETCH NEXT FROM curTables
INTO @TABLE_SCHEMA, @TABLE_NAME

WHILE @@FETCH_STATUS != -1
BEGIN
   IF @TABLE_SCHEMA = 'dbo'
      BEGIN
         SET @SQL_COMMAND = 'DBCC CHECKTABLE ("' + @TABLE_SCHEMA
                          + '.' + @TABLE_NAME + '")'
                          + ' WITH NO_INFOMSGS'
         PRINT ''
         PRINT 'About to execute command: '
         PRINT @SQL_COMMAND
         PRINT ''
         EXEC (@SQL_COMMAND)
      END
   ELSE
      BEGIN
         PRINT ''
         PRINT 'Skipping table ' + @TABLE_NAME
             + ' owned by ' + @TABLE_SCHEMA
         PRINT ''
      END

   STEP3B_FETCH:
   FETCH NEXT FROM curTables
   INTO @TABLE_SCHEMA, @TABLE_NAME
END

STEP4_FREE_RESOURCES:
DEALLOCATE curTables
PRINT ''
PRINT 'All DBCC commands are complete! '
PRINT 'Please review them for error messages!'
PRINT ''
```

Notice all the different features in this script that represent things you learned in this chapter. For example, every italicized word in the following analysis of this script is a concept covered in this chapter. A *cursor* is declared and associated with a query against a system-defined view. Next the cursor is *opened*, and as long as ***@@FETCH_STATUS*** is not -1, more rows are read and processed using a ***WHILE*** *loop*. (Because this is a ***FAST_FORWARD*** cursor, **@@FETCH_STATUS** will never return -2.) Each fetched row is examined by an ***IF*** *statement* to make sure the table owner is **dbo**. If the owner is **dbo**, then a **DBCC CHECKTABLE** command is built and stored in the *local variable* **@SQL_COMMAND**. Finally, this command is *dynamically executed* using the ***EXEC** statement*. If the user is not **dbo**, then a message is printed explaining that we are skipping this table. The output you receive should look similar to the partial output in Listing 8.26.

Listing 8.26 Partial output from the script in Listing 8.25.

```
Skipping table CopyOfOrders owned by Chapter8User


About to execute command:
DBCC CHECKTABLE ("dbo.Categories") WITH NO_INFOMSGS

DBCC execution completed. If DBCC printed error messages,
contact your system administrator.

About to execute command:
DBCC CHECKTABLE ("dbo.CustomerCustomerDemo") WITH NO_INFOMSGS

DBCC execution completed. If DBCC printed error messages,
contact your system administrator.

...

About to execute command:
DBCC CHECKTABLE ("dbo.Territories") WITH NO_INFOMSGS

DBCC execution completed. If DBCC printed error messages,
contact your system administrator.

All DBCC commands are complete!
Please review them for error messages!
```

It is easy to see how cursors and control-of-flow language can be used together to build very powerful Transact-SQL batches. Study Listing 8.26 until you understand it well. Experiment with it and try to make changes. For example, see if you can change the code so that **EXEC sp_help @TABLE_NAME** is run for each **dbo**-owned table instead of **DBCC CHECKTABLE**.

When you are through with this project, you may want to run the code in Listing 8.27 to drop the table, user, and login created in this project.

Listing 8.27 Clean-up code for Project 8.1.

```
DROP TABLE Chapter8User.CopyOfOrders
EXEC sp_dropuser Chapter8User
EXEC sp_droplogin Chapter8User
```

```
Results:
User has been dropped from current database.
Login dropped.
```

"Great work," Chris exclaimed. "I think I'll have you help out with a few more stored procedures, if you're up to it." Susan was pleased that the lead developer thought she did a good job with her first stab at stored procedures. "I especially liked the comments you put in. That will really help if we ever have to add or change the code later. By the way," Chris went on, " have you created all the scripts for the creating the database yet?" Susan was surprised. "I thought if we had a good backup we wouldn't need database scripts." "Yes, well sometimes you still do. Actually it's a deliverable on this project." Susan had seen a menu option to do this; she had just never tried it. "I'll make a script now," she told him.

Project 8.2

Generating a script with SQL Server Enterprise Manager.

During this chapter, it was mentioned that the SQL Server Enterprise Manager can create scripts to re-create database objects and permissions. In this project, you will create a simple script using the Enterprise Manager so that you can start to become familiar with this tool:

1. Open the SQL Server Enterprise Manager, expand your server group and server, and open the Databases folder. Select the *Northwind* database, and then choose Tools|Database Scripting on the menu. Alternatively, right-click on the *Northwind* database and choose All Tasks|Generate SQL Scripts from the pop-up menu. Either way, you should end up at a dialog box like the one in Figure 8.2.

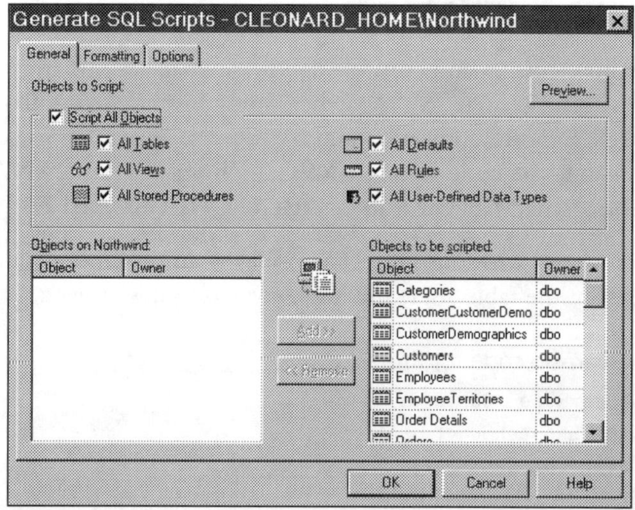

Figure 8.2 Generating SQL Scripts with SQL Server Enterprise Manager.

2. Explore this dialog box to become familiar with its layout and contents. Note the three tabs: General, Formatting, and Options. Click on each of them and observe the different choices that each one offers. Notice that the default configuration of this dialog box will script every object in the database (General tab), scripting both **DROP** and **CREATE** statements (Formatting tab), but without including any security information, table indexes, triggers, or constraints (Options tab).
3. On the General tab, clear the checkbox labeled Script All Objects. Notice that on the bottom portion of the dialog box, all objects move automatically from the Objects To Be Scripted grid to the Objects On *Northwind* grid.
4. Next, select the *Order Details* table and click the Add button to move this table back to the Objects To Be Scripted grid. Your screen should now look similar to the one in Figure 8.3.
5. At this point, click the Preview button on the General tab. A dialog box displays, like the one in Figure 8.4, containing a preview of the requested script. You can permanently save a script by choosing the OK button (from any of the three tabs) instead of the Preview button, or by choosing Save As from inside the Object Scripting Preview window. Notice that you may have to scroll down or to the right in order to see the entire script. For now, examine the script and then choose Close.
6. Click on the Formatting tab and select the checkbox labeled Include Descriptive Headers In The Script Files to include a comment with a date and time in the script file.

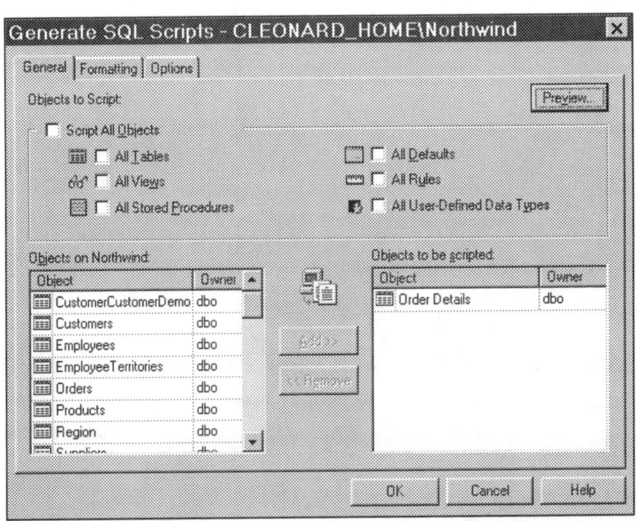

Figure 8.3 Preparing to script the *Order Details* table.

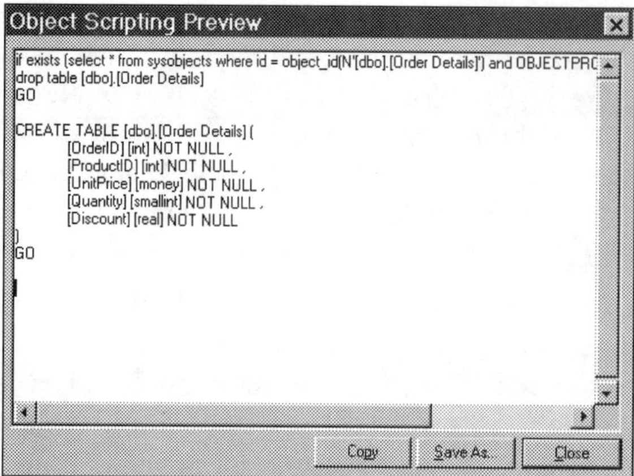

Figure 8.4 Viewing a preview of the *Order Details* script.

7. Click on the Options tab and select the checkboxes labeled Script Object-Level Permissions, Script Indexes, and Script **PRIMARY** Keys, **FOREIGN** Keys, Defaults And Check Constraints.
8. Go back to the General tab and click the Preview button again. Notice how each of the options that you selected caused additional scripting to be performed. At this point, your Object Scripting Preview window should look something like the one in Figure 8.5.

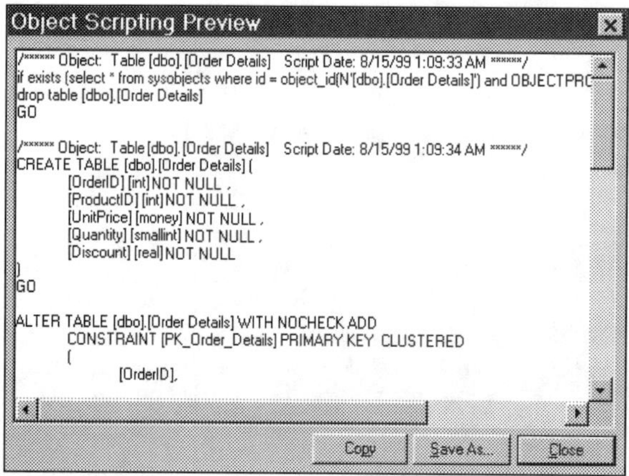

Figure 8.5 Viewing a script preview with more scripting options enabled.

Notice the comments that have been added to the script, as you requested. Also, after the **CREATE TABLE** statement, you should see an **ALTER TABLE** statement that creates the primary key, a **CREATE INDEX** statement, and a **GRANT** statement that gives the *public* role permissions to this table. Experiment with the other options in the Generate SQL Scripts dialog box to understand what all the options do. For example, you can generate a script for all database objects and read it to understand what has been scripted.

Susan finished her scripting of the database and was surprised by how easy it was to create. She saved the files in a folder, and gave the folder a title that indicated the date. "That way," she thought to herself, "I'll be able to version the scripts as we go. If the developers ask for any changes, I'll know what's changed by comparing the scripts."

Chapter Nine

9

Summarizing And Transforming Data

After Reading This Chapter And Completing The Exercises, You Will Be Able To:

- Transform data values by applying scalar functions
- Summarize data by using aggregate functions to group data from different rows
- Perform calculations by using Transact-SQL operators
- Restrict the amount of data returned by a query by using the **TOP** keyword
- Present multiple data groupings simultaneously by using the **ROLLUP** and **CUBE** functions

We have learned to extract data from SQL 7 databases with standard **SELECT** queries. While these queries provide a very powerful way to locate and retrieve data, SQL Server 7 provides many functions to query information not explicitly stored as data. In this chapter we will learn how to obtain aggregate and derived data.

Going Beyond Rows And Columns

You have learned many valuable query techniques thus far in the book. You learned how to restrict which rows or columns are included in a result set, and how to query multiple tables simultaneously in a meaningful way by writing *joins*. However, these data-retrieval methods enable you to retrieve only data that is explicitly stored in the database. These queries are called *row-and-column queries* because they enable you to retrieve data only if it is physically stored in a certain row and column of a certain table. However, not all useful data is explicitly stored in the database.

You may want to retrieve data that is not stored in the database, but that can be derived from information in the database. For example, if the database stores sales amounts for each individual order, you may want the total sales for an entire region. Certainly, you can derive this information from the stored data. You could resort to a labor-intensive strategy of writing a client program to do this. You would first retrieve the stored data into the client program and then use that client program to calculate the desired data.

The problem with this approach is that the programming requires a substantial effort, even for relatively simple data queries. A better way exists to approach such problems. To facilitate queries that retrieve derived data, Microsoft has included several useful functions in the Transact-SQL (T-SQL) language. This chapter looks at those functions and at other methods for restricting and modifying the data returned by a query.

Manipulating Data With Scalar Functions

Microsoft includes many functions in T-SQL that enable you to manipulate data values. Functions that take single-valued arguments and return a single-valued result are called *scalar functions*. Single-valued arguments are the key to identifying scalar functions—if a function can act on more than one value at a time, it is an *aggregate function*. Aggregate functions are discussed later in this chapter.

Because scalar functions return a single value, they can frequently be used in place of constant or column expressions. For example, a query can use a scalar function instead of a column name in the **SELECT** list. Scalar functions can be broken into several categories, which are summarized in Table 9.1. This chapter discusses each of these scalar function categories, particularly the types of functions that are most useful in T-SQL coding.

Configuration Functions

Configuration functions return information about the current configuration of your SQL Server. Not all of these functions are used frequently in database

Table 9.1 Types of scalar functions.

Scalar Function Category	Purpose
Configuration functions	Return information about the current SQL Server configuration
Cursor functions	Return information useful for cursor processing
Date and time functions	Return the current system date and allow manipulations of **DATETIME** values
Mathematical functions	Perform mathematical calculations and return numeric values
Metadata functions	Provide information about the database and the objects within it
Security functions	Return information about logins, users, and roles
String functions	Allow a query to manipulate character strings
System functions	General utility functions provided for use on a system-wide basis
System statistical functions	Return statistical and performance information about the database server
Text and image functions	Provide a way to work with information stored as **TEXT** or **IMAGE** values
Rowset functions	Used in place of table names in queries

applications, but some are very useful, and you should be aware of each of the configuration functions that are available. Configuration functions, like some other scalar functions, are all in the format **@@FUNCTION_NAME**, which is the format for global variables in SQL Server 6.5. In SQL Server 7, global variables are implemented as scalar functions, but they still carry the @@ prefix for backward compatibility. The following sections describe each of the configuration functions.

@@CONNECTIONS

This function returns the number of connection attempts that the SQL Server has processed since the last time it was restarted. This can be very useful information if you are diagnosing a problem that you suspect is related to failed connections. The value of the **@@CONNECTIONS** function increments by one even for failed connection attempts—such as incorrect logins.

@@DATEFIRST

SQL Server can be directed to consider any day of the week to be the first day of the week for business purposes. The function **@@DATEFIRST** can be used to find out what the first day of the week is for a particular SQL Server. The function returns **1** for Monday, **2** for Tuesday, and so on. The default for

U.S. English SQL Servers is **7**, or Sunday. Changing this option with the **SET DATEFIRST** command affects the values returned by certain other functions, such as when **DATEPART** is asked to return the current day of the week.

@@DBTS

This function returns the most recently used timestamp for the database. A *timestamp* is a column (with the data type **TIMESTAMP**) that is automatically updated by SQL Server. The value of a timestamp is automatically assigned whenever a row containing a timestamp column is inserted or updated. Each timestamp value is guaranteed to be larger than the previous one used in the database, so a timestamp fills two possible roles:

- It can be used to obtain a value that is guaranteed to be unique within a database forever.
- If a table has a *timestamp* column, then you can tell which rows in the table were most recently inserted or updated by sorting on that column.

If you have not used timestamps before, Listing 9.1 demonstrates how they work.

Listing 9.1 Using *timestamp* columns.

```
IF EXISTS (SELECT * FROM sysobjects
WHERE NAME = 'DBTS_DEMO' AND TYPE = 'U')
     DROP TABLE DBTS_DEMO
GO

CREATE TABLE DBTS_DEMO
     (RowID INT IDENTITY(1,1),
      TS TIMESTAMP)

SELECT @@DBTS AS "Timestamp Before Insert"

INSERT  INTO DBTS_DEMO
DEFAULT VALUES

SELECT * FROM DBTS_DEMO

SELECT @@DBTS AS "Timestamp After Insert"

DROP TABLE DBTS_DEMO

Results:
Timestamp Before Insert
-----------------------
—0x0000000000000191
```

```
RowID       TS
-----       ------------------
1           0x0000000000000192

Timestamp After Insert
----------------------
0x0000000000000192
```

Prior to SQL Server 7, the value of **@@DBTS** changed every time any data in the database was modified—whether the data modification actually affected a *timestamp* column or not. This was due to the way in which these timestamps were linked to a special table called *syslogs*. In previous versions of SQL Server, *syslogs* was used to record and manage any changes to data in the database. When a timestamp value was generated, it actually pointed to the location in *syslogs* where that change was logged. Because logical page numbers in *syslogs* always increased, the timestamp values generated in this way were guaranteed to be unique.

However, in SQL Server 7, the *syslogs* table is no longer used. Rather, the database log is stored in a separate operating system file. This means that the system log can no longer be queried by T-SQL in the way that it could before. Therefore, no reason exists to associate timestamp values with system log locations. Because of this, in SQL Server 7, the value of **@@DBTS** changes only when a row containing a *timestamp* column is changed or inserted.

9

@@LANGID, @@LANGUAGE

These functions return the language setting in use by SQL Server. **@@LANGUAGE** returns a textual description for the language (such as **us_english**), and **@@LANGID** returns the internal code used to represent the language (which is **0** for **us_english**). The current language can be changed by using the **SET LANGUAGE** command. This does not translate all SQL Server messages into the selected language, but it does affect the way dates and system messages are handled, since dates are handled differently by each language.

@@LOCK_TIMEOUT

If a connection needs to use a resource that is currently in use by another connection, the first connection waits up to **@@LOCK_TIMEOUT** milliseconds for the resource to become available. The value of **@@LOCK_TIMEOUT** can be changed with the **SET LOCK_TIMEOUT** command. The **@@LOCK_TIMEOUT** function is new to SQL Server 7. Locking and related topics are covered in Chapter 11.

@@MAX_CONNECTIONS

This function tells you how many concurrent user connections can be accommodated by the SQL Server. This setting can be changed by running the system stored procedure **sp_configure** and then executing the **RECOMPILE** command.

@@MAX_PRECISION

This function tells you the number of significant digits used by this SQL Server when working with **DECIMAL** or **NUMERIC** data types. This value can only be changed by restarting SQL Server using the **/p** parameter.

@@OPTIONS

This function reports the value of several options that each user can configure with the **SET** command. The **@@OPTIONS** function returns a bitmap telling you which options are set. For example, a user can issue the **SET NOCOUNT ON** command to turn off the messages regarding how many rows a query affected. The value for this option, found in the system table *spt_values* in the *master* database, is 512. To interrogate whether the **NOCOUNT** option is currently set, you can issue the following query:

```
IF (@@OPTIONS & 512) = 512
     PRINT 'NOCOUNT' option is set!
ELSE
     PRINT 'NOCOUNT option is not set!'
```

@@NESTLEVEL

When one stored procedure calls another, the stored procedure calls are said to be *nested*. The **@@NESTLEVEL** function can be used to determine the nesting level of the current stored procedure. If no stored procedure has been invoked, the value of **@@NESTLEVEL** is 0. When a stored procedure is called, the value of this function changes to 1. It then increments by one each time a nested stored procedure call is made, and decrements by one each time a nested stored procedure call returns.

@@REMSERVER

If a stored procedure is invoked via a remote stored procedure call, this function returns the name of the remote server from which the procedure was called. This is useful if a stored procedure will be invoked from several other servers, and the procedure records the calling server's name in a *log* table.

@@SPID

SPID stands for *Server Process ID* and is a unique session identifier for every concurrent user connection on a SQL Server. The SPID is also reported in the system table *sysprocesses* and by the system stored procedure **sp_who**. This value is very useful for database administrators. This function can be used to diagnose or even stop a problematic process.

When developing SQL Server applications, the **@@SPID** function can be useful in retrieving information about the current connection. By using this value, your program can look up its own row in the system catalog table *master..sysprocesses*, which contains information about all current SQL Server connections. Use any of the following three queries to retrieve infor-mation from this table for the current connection:

```
/* first query, returns basic connection information: */
EXEC master..sp_who  @@SPID

/* second query, returns more connection information: */
EXEC master..sp_who2 @@SPID

/* third query, returns extensive connection information: */
SELECT *
FROM   master..sysprocesses
WHERE  spid = @@SPID
```


@@SERVERNAME

The name of your SQL Server is recorded in the *master* database in a table called *sysservers*. The function **@@SERVERNAME** returns this name for you. Selecting **@@SERVERNAME** is equivalent to running the following query:

```
SELECT NAME
FROM   master..sysservers
WHERE  SRVID = 0
```

@@SERVICENAME

This function returns the name of the Windows NT Service that is running your SQL Server. This name is useful because it can be used to start and stop the SQL Server programmatically by using the Windows NT commands **net start** and **net stop**. The default name for this service is MSSQLServer. The **@@SERVICENAME** function is new in SQL Server 7.

@@TEXTSIZE

This function tells you the maximum number of bytes that a **SELECT** statement will return for columns that have the data type **TEXT**, **NTEXT**, or **IMAGE**. The value of **@@TEXTSIZE** can be changed with the **SET TEXTSIZE** command.

@@VERSION

Selecting this function gives you very specific information regarding the current version of your SQL Server installation. This information is very useful when verifying that all of your SQL Servers are running the correct version and service pack. It is also required information when working with Microsoft's Technical Support. For example, if you are running the originally released version of SQL Server 7, the version information returned is as follows:

```
SELECT @@VERSION
-------------------------------------------------

Microsoft SQL Server  7.00 - 7.00.623 (Intel X86)
     Nov 27 1998 22:20:07
     Copyright (c) 1988-1998 Microsoft Corporation
     Desktop Edition on Windows NT 4 (Build 1381: Service Pack 4)
```

Cursor Functions

Cursors are a means by which the result set of a query can be processed one row at a time. The use of cursors is covered in Chapter 8. Here, we briefly review the use of the three cursor functions provided by T-SQL.

@@CURSOR_ROWS

This function returns the number of rows that qualify for inclusion in the last cursor that was opened by the current connection. You must be careful when using this function if you have more than one cursor open at a time, because the value for **@@CURSOR_ROWS** refers only to the *last* cursor opened. Also, if you open any cursors asynchronously, the value of **@@CURSOR_ROWS** is reported differently. Table 9.2 lists the possible values of **@@CURSOR_ROWS**.

Table 9.2 Interpreting **@@CURSOR_ROWS** values.

Value	Meaning
-1	This value is returned for dynamic cursors, which are able to retrieve rows that qualify for the cursor, even if those rows did not qualify at the time the cursor was declared and opened. Because this is true, the total number of rows qualifying for the cursor can never be stated with finality.
-X	A negative number is returned for cursors that are being populated asynchronously but have not yet been fully populated. Currently, X rows have been populated in the cursor, but more rows are still being retrieved. After the cursor is fully populated, a positive number is returned.
X	A positive number indicates that a cursor has been fully populated and contains X qualifying rows.
0	A value of 0 for **@@CURSOR_ROWS** means either that no cursors are currently open or that the last cursor opened had 0 qualifying rows.

CURSOR_STATUS (cursor_type, cursor_name)

In SQL Server 7, a stored procedure may return a cursor as an **OUTPUT** variable. The function **CURSOR_STATUS** may be invoked after the stored procedure returns, to determine whether the **CURSOR** variable contains a valid open cursor. This function takes two parameters:

- ***cursor_type*** Either **global**, **local**, or **variable**.
- ***cursor_name*** Names the cursor or the **OUTPUT CURSOR** variable that you want to know about.

Possible values for **CURSOR_STATUS** appear in Table 9.3.

@@FETCH_STATUS

This function returns the status of the last **FETCH** statement executed by this connection against a currently open cursor. You must take care if either more than one cursor is open within the connection or a stored procedure has been called that may have also processed cursors. The safest practice is to interrogate **@@FETCH_STATUS** immediately after the **FETCH** statement. Possible values are explained in Table 9.4.

9

Table 9.3 Interpreting **CURSOR_STATUS** values.

Value	Meaning
-3	The value for the **cursor_variable** parameter is invalid.
-2	No allocated cursor is assigned to the given **cursor_variable**.
-1	The cursor assigned to the given **cursor_variable** is closed.
0	The **cursor_variable** is assigned to an open, nondynamic cursor, but that cursor's resultset is empty.
1	The **cursor_variable** is assigned to an open cursor, and either the cursor is dynamic or at least one row is in the cursor's result set.

Table 9.4 Interpreting **@@FETCH_STATUS** values.

Value	Meaning
-2	The row to be fetched is no longer available for inclusion in the cursor's resultset. This can happen if, for a dynamic cursor, the row to be fetched existed when the cursor was opened but has since been deleted.
-1	The fetch requested a row beyond the end of the cursor's result set. This is analogous to an end-of-file condition in other programming languages.
0	The fetch successfully retrieved data from the appropriate row in the cursor's result set.

Date And Time Functions

Date and time functions are important to any application that is concerned with time-sensitive data. The practice of storing date and time information as **(N)CHAR** or **(N)VARCHAR** variables produces wasted space and lost precision when storing date and time values. If you want to manipulate date and time information stored as character strings, you must either **CAST** or **CONVERT** them back to **DATETIME** values. You could also write code to replace the built-in **DATETIME** functions. It is a much better practice to use the standard **DATETIME** data type along with its associated functions for date and time values. As always, however, an exception exists: You should use **DATETIME** to store dates only since January 1, 1753. You must use character data to represent dates earlier than this.

Specifying datepart Arguments

Many of the date and time functions require a **datepart** argument, which refers to a standard set of names and abbreviations used by SQL Server to refer to different parts of a date—months, years, seconds, and so on. When a **datepart** argument is required, you can specify either a full **datepart** name or one of its acceptable abbreviations. Table 9.5 lists the possible values that you can use as **datepart** arguments.

GETDATE ( )

The most commonly used date and time function is **GETDATE**, which returns the current date and time, as determined by the system clock of the computer on which SQL Server is running. SQL Server can format the system time in several ways, by using the **CONVERT** function (see **CONVERT**, later in this

Table 9.5 Datepart arguments.

datepart	Acceptable Abbreviations
year	yyyy or yy
quarter	qq or q
month	mm or m
week	wk or ww
dayofyear	dy or y
weekday	dw
day	dd or d
hour	hh
minute	mi or n
second	ss or s
millisecond	ms

chapter, in the section "System Functions"). **GETDATE** requires no arguments, but remember to include the parentheses so that SQL Server understands that you are invoking a function and not naming a column.

DATEADD (datepart, number, date)

The **DATEADD** function enables you to change a **DATETIME** value by adding (or subtracting) a certain amount of time to it. You specify the amount of time by naming an acceptable **datepart** argument, which is the unit of time to be added or subtracted, and then indicating how many of these units you want to add to the given date. To subtract from the date, use a negative number. For example, to return the time exactly one hour ago, you would write the following query:

```
SELECT DATEADD(hour, -1, GETDATE( ))
```

DATEDIFF (datepart, start_date, end_date)

The **DATEDIFF** function defines how many **datepart** boundaries must be crossed to get from **start_date** to **end_date**. For example, the following T-SQL batch returns the number of day boundaries (midnights) crossed since January 1, 1900:


```
DECLARE @Date1 DATETIME, @Date2 DATETIME
SELECT  @Date1 = '1/1/1900'
SELECT  @Date2 = GETDATE( )

SELECT  @Date2 AS 'Now',
        DATEDIFF(day, @Date1, @Date2) AS 'Days Since 1900'

Results:
Now                        Days Since 1900
-----------------------    ---------------
1999-05-14 21:36:25.457    36292
```

DATEPART (datepart, date)

This function can be used to create custom date formats. It returns the numeric value of any part of a date. For the same reason, this function can be helpful if you need to perform custom calculations on **DATETIME** data that isn't easily accomplished using the built-in date and time functions. If **datepart** is **weekday** (or **dw**), then the number returned by this function is affected by the current setting of **@@DATEFIRST**.

DATENAME (datepart, date)

This function behaves just like **DATEPART** unless the **datepart** argument is **weekday** or **month**. In those cases, it returns a character string representing the appropriate month or weekday name according to the current **@@LANGUAGE** setting, as shown in Listing 9.2. This makes the **DATENAME** function particularly useful for making custom date formats for reports.

Listing 9.2 Using **DATENAME** and **@@LANGUAGE**.

```
SET    LANGUAGE 'us_english'
SELECT DATENAME( weekday , GETDATE( ))
SET    LANGUAGE 'deutsch'
SELECT DATENAME( weekday , GETDATE( ))

Results:
Changed language setting to us_english.

---------------
Friday

Changed language setting to Deutsch.

---------------
Freitag
```

Shortcut Date And Time Functions

Three other date and time functions are available in SQL Server 7, but these are just shortcuts to specific uses of a function already presented. The **DAY**, **MONTH**, and **YEAR** functions are all replacements for special cases of the **DATEPART** function. Table 9.6 lists sample uses of these three functions, along with the equivalent use of **DATEPART**.

Mathematical Functions

SQL Server 7 has numerous mathematical functions available for use in T-SQL code. These can be very useful in the right circumstances. However, remember that SQL Server is primarily optimized for the storage and retrieval of data in accordance with the relational model, not as a library of mathematical functions. Although the mathematical library in SQL Server is useful and well tuned, it does not offer the same level of functionality that can be found in more specialized math libraries. However, some applications will function correctly based on their ability to calculate efficiently a high volume of data through complex mathematical

Table 9.6 Shortcut date and time functions.

Shortcut Function	DATEPART Equivalent
SELECT DAY(GETDATE( ))	SELECT DATEPART(DD, GETDATE( ))
SELECT MONTH(GETDATE( ))	SELECT DATEPART(MM, GETDATE( ))
SELECT YEAR(GETDATE( ))	SELECT DATEPART(YY, GETDATE( ))

procedures. If you are designing such an application, you should consider other strategies, where appropriate. For example, suppose that you have a highly specialized C++ math library that fits the needs of your application exactly. In this case, it might be more efficient to retrieve the base data from SQL Server and then to perform the mathematical calculations within the client program by using the specialized math library. In many cases, the mathematical functions provided by SQL Server will fit your needs. The available mathematical functions are summarized in Table 9.7.

Table 9.7 Mathematical functions.

Bounding Functions	Use
CEILING (number)	Returns the smallest integer (cast to the same data type as **number**) that is greater than or equal to the given **number**.
FLOOR (number)	Returns the largest integer (cast to the same data type as **number**) that is less than or equal to the given **number**.
Trigonometric Functions	**Use**
COS (float)	Returns the cosine of an angle, measured in radians.
COT (float)	Returns the cotangent of an angle, measured in radians.
SIN (float)	Returns the sine of an angle, measured in radians.
TAN (float)	Returns the tangent of an angle, measured in radians.
Inverse Trigonometric Functions	**Use**
ACOS (float)	Returns the angle (in radians) whose cosine is the given **float**.
ASIN (float)	Returns the angle (in radians) whose sine is the given **float**.
ATAN (float)	Returns the angle (in radians) whose tangent is the given **float**.
ATN2 (float1, float2)	Returns the angle (in radians) defined by the x-axis and the Cartesian point **(float1, float2)**.
Angle Conversion Functions	**Use**
DEGREES (number)	Converts an angle from radians to degrees.
RADIANS (number)	Converts an angle from degrees to radians.
Powers Functions	**Use**
POWER (number, n)	Returns the value of **number** raised to the power **n**.
EXP (n)	Returns the value of **e** raised to the power **n** (**e** is the base of natural logarithms and is approximately 2.71828).

(continued)

9

Table 9.7 Mathematical functions *(continued)*.

Powers Functions	Use
SQUARE (float)	Returns **float** * **float**. Equivalent to **POWER (float, 2)**.
SQRT (float)	Returns the square root of **float**. Equivalent to **POWER (float, 0.5)**.
LOG (float)	Returns the natural logarithm of the given **float**. That is, **POWER (e, LOG(float)) = float**.
LOG10 (float)	Returns the base-10 logarithm of the given **float**. That is, **POWER (10, LOG10(float)) = float**.
Other Mathematical Functions	**Use**
ABS (number)	Returns the absolute value of **number** (that is, **number** stripped of any sign).
PI ( )	Returns an approximation of pi, which is about 3.14159.
RAND (int)	Returns random numbers between 0 and 1. The optional **int** is a seed value that can be used to control the random series that is initiated. This seed value should usually be supplied only the first time **RAND** is called.
SIGN (number)	Returns the sign of the given **number**. **SIGN** returns -1 if **number** is less than 0, 1 if **number** is greater than 0, and 0 if **number** equals 0.
ROUND (number, places, type)	Rounds or truncates the given **number**, which is rounded if **type** is 0 or is omitted. Otherwise, the given **number** is truncated. The degree of the rounding or truncation is given by **places**. Starting at the decimal point, **ROUND** moves **places** positions and then rounds or truncates from that position to the left. When **places** is positive, the movement is to the right from the decimal point. When **places** is negative, the movement is to the left from the decimal point.

Metadata Functions

SQL Server's Enterprise Manager must be aware of the names of tables, columns, and procedures stored within the database. This tool and others must also know the names of database objects that are not a part of the standard SQL Server setup, but rather are objects that you created. The way this knowledge is passed to these tools lies in the concept of *metadata*. Metadata is a term that means *data about data*. In the context of relational databases, metadata refers to the definitions of the database objects, such as the names of all available tables, the columns in each table, the parameters accepted by a stored procedure, and so forth. Microsoft SQL Server stores metadata in tables just as it stores any other data. The metadata describing the databases on the server is stored in the *system catalog* tables in the *master* database. The metadata describing the objects in an individual database is stored inside that particular database in a special set of system tables called the *database catalog* tables. Information about the tables in the system and database catalogs can be found in Chapter 5.

The information in these catalogs may be queried just as information stored in any other table is queried. For example, the following query returns the names of all the tables in the current database (type **'U'** in **sysobjects** is the way SQL Server identifies a *User* table):

```
SELECT name
FROM   sysobjects
WHERE  type = 'U'
ORDER  BY name

Results:
name
--------------------
Categories
CustomerCustomerDemo
...
Suppliers
Territories
```


Queries that interrogate the data catalog directly can become much more difficult than the preceding simple example. Although queries such as this are frequently performed by experienced database administrators (DBAs), expecting a developer to remember the location of each piece of information in the database catalog usually is unreasonable. Additionally, the database catalog may change from one release of SQL Server to another, requiring any catalog queries in use by an application to be rewritten. For this reason, SQL Server 7 includes numerous metadata functions, listed in Table 9.8, which can assist you in obtaining metadata from the data catalog without needing to know exactly how this information is stored. Because these procedures and functions are part of the supported SQL Server interface, they are more likely to be supported in future versions of the product, even if the underlying catalog structures change.

Notes On Using Metadata Functions

Metadata functions can often be used in combination with each other. For example, you may want to know the name of the current database. Because **DB_NAME** requires the database ID as a parameter, you can use the **DB_ID** function to supply this value, as in the following query:

```
SELECT DB_NAME(DB_ID())
-----------------------
Northwind
```

Table 9.8 The metadata functions.

Column Functions	Use
COL_LENGTH(table_name, column)	Returns the declared length of a column.
COL_NAME(table_id, column_id)	Returns the name of the specified column.
COLUMNPROPERTY (object_id, col_id, property)	Returns the state of a particular property for a column or stored procedure parameter.
Database Functions	**Use**
DB_ID([db_name])	Returns the database ID for the specified database, or for the current database if none is specified.
DB_NAME(db_id)	Returns the name of the specified database.
DATABASEPROPERTY (db_name, property)	Returns the state of a particular property for the specified database.
File Functions	**Use**
FILE_ID(file_name)	Returns the file ID for the specified file name.
FILE_NAME(file_id)	Returns the file name for the specified file ID.
FILEPROPERTY(file_name, property)	Returns the state of a particular property for the specified file.
Filegroup Functions	**Use**
FILEGROUP_ID (filegroup_name)	Returns the filegroup ID for the specified file group.
FILEGROUP_NAME (filegroup_id)	Returns the filegroup name for the specified file group.
FILEGROUPPROPERTY (filegroup_name, property)	Returns the state of a particular property for the specified file group.
Full-text Search Functions	**Use**
FULLTEXTCATALOG PROPERTY(catalog_name, property)	Returns the state of a particular property for the specified full-text catalog.
FULLTEXTSERVICE PROPERTY(property)	Returns the state of a particular property for the full-text Microsoft Search Service.
Index Functions	**Use**
INDEX_COL(table_name, index_id, key_id)	Returns the name of the column occupying a particular position **(key_id)** in the index specified.
INDEXPROPERTY(table_id, index_name, property)	Returns the state of a particular property for the specified index.
Object Functions	**Use**
OBJECT_ID(object_name)	Returns the object ID for the given object name.
OBJECT_NAME(object_id)	Returns the object name for the given object ID.
OBJECTPROPERTY (object_id, property)	Returns the state of a particular property for the object specified.
Other Metadata Functions	**Use**
@@PROCID	Returns the object ID of the stored procedure that is currently running.
TYPEPROPERTY(type_name, property)	Returns the state of a particular property for the data type specified.

The usefulness of metadata functions is more readily apparent by examining the more involved example in Listing 9.3. This listing uses the **OBJECT_NAME**, **COLUMNPROPERTY**, and **OBJECTPROPERTY** metadata functions to report on all the columns in objects that are nonsystem tables and to determine whether or not each column accepts **NULL** values.

Listing 9.3 Using metadata functions.

```
SELECT 'The column [' + OBJECT_NAME(id) + '].[' + name + ']'
     + CASE COLUMNPROPERTY(id, name, 'AllowsNull')
            WHEN 1 THEN ' allows'
            ELSE ' does NOT allow'
       END
     + ' NULLS.'
FROM   syscolumns
WHERE  OBJECTPROPERTY(id, 'IsSystemTable') = 0
AND    OBJECTPROPERTY(id, 'IsTable') = 1
ORDER  BY OBJECT_NAME(id), colid

Results:
The column [Categories].[CategoryID] does NOT allow NULLS.
The column [Categories].[CategoryName] does NOT allow NULLS.
The column [Categories].[Description] allows NULLS.
The column [Categories].[Picture] allows NULLS.
The column [CustomerCustomerDemo].[CustomerID] does NOT allow NULLS.
...
The column [Suppliers].[HomePage] allows NULLS.
The column [Territories].[TerritoryID] does NOT allow NULLS.
The column [Territories].[TerritoryDescription] does NOT allow NULLS.
The column [Territories].[RegionID] does NOT allow NULLS.
```

It is often desirable to disable certain indexes or constraints before performing a large batch of **INSERT** statements against a table. Prior to SQL Server 7, the only way to do this was to drop the constraints by using the command **ALTER TABLE**, perform the inserts, and then use **ALTER TABLE** to add the constraints again. This method required having a reliable way to extract scripts for the constraints to be dropped and added.

SQL Server 7 provides some relief from this scenario by allowing constraints to be disabled and enabled *on the fly*, without actually dropping and adding them. The example in Listing 9.4 shows how you might use metadata functions to detect the existence of certain constraints. You could then disable the constraints, perform a group of inserts, and re-enable the constraints.

Listing 9.4 Detecting, disabling, and reenabling constraints.

```
DECLARE @HowManyConstraints INT

SELECT @HowManyConstraints =
        OBJECTPROPERTY(OBJECT_ID('Orders'), 'TableHasForeignKey')
      + OBJECTPROPERTY(OBJECT_ID('Orders'), 'TableHasCheckCnst')
SELECT @HowManyConstraints AS "Foreign Key and Check Constraints"

IF @HowManyConstraints > 0
      ALTER TABLE Orders NOCHECK CONSTRAINT ALL

/* PERFORM INSERTS HERE */

IF @HowManyConstraints > 0
      ALTER TABLE Orders CHECK CONSTRAINT ALL

Results:
Foreign Key and Check Constraints
---------------------------------
1
```

Security Functions

In SQL Server 7, permissions can be granted to SQL Server users, SQL Server roles, Windows NT user accounts, and even Windows NT groups. Security functions enable you to discover a user's name or *security identifier (SID)*. These functions can also be used to determine whether a particular SQL Server user is a member of a given group or role. The security functions are summarized in Table 9.9.

Table 9.9 Security functions.

Group Or Role Functions	Use
IS_MEMBER (group_or_role_name)	Returns 1 if the current user is a member of the specified role or group, and 0 if not. A **NULL** value returned indicates an invalid value was passed for **group_or_role_name**.
IS_SRVROLEMEMBER (role_name, [login_name])	Returns 1 if the **login_name** provided is a member of the specified **role_name**, and 0 if not. This **role_name** is one of the standard server roles (**sysadmin**, **dbcreator**, **diskadmin**, **processadmin**, **serveradmin**, **setupadmin**, and **securityadmin**). If **login_name** is omitted, the current session's login is used. A **NULL** value returned indicates an invalid value was passed for **role_name** or **login_name**.

(continued)

Table 9.9 Security functions *(continued)*.

System ID Functions	Use
SUSER_SID([login_name])	Returns the *sysxlogins.sid* value for the given **login_name**, which corresponds to the column *sysxlogins.name*. If **login_name** is omitted, the current session's login name is used.
SUSER_SNAME ([server_user_sid])	Returns the *sysxlogins.name* value for the given **server_user_sid**, which corresponds to the column *sysxlogins.sid*. If the **server_user_sid** is omitted, the current session's system identifier is used.
System User ID Functions	**Use**
SUSER_ID([login_name])	Returns the *syslogins.suid* value for the given **login_name**, which corresponds to the column *syslogins.name*. If **login_name** is omitted, the current session's login is used.
SUSER_NAME ([server_user_id])	Returns the *syslogins.name* value for the given **server_user_id**, which corresponds to the column *syslogins.suid*. If **server_user_id** is omitted, the current session's server user ID is used.
Database User Functions	**Use**
USER_ID([user_name])	Returns the *sysusers.uid* value for the given **user_name**, which corresponds to the column *sysusers.name*. If the **user_name** is omitted, the current username is assumed.
USER	Returns the **sysusers.name** value for the current session. This function is a *niladic function*, meaning that its argument list is nonexistent. Even coding **USER( )** causes an error, because an empty argument list is not the same thing as a nonexistent argument list. Simply code the keyword **USER** by itself. Other niladic functions in T-SQL are discussed later in the chapter, in the section "System Functions." **USER** is equivalent to using the System Function **USER_NAME( )** with an empty argument list.

Security Differences Between SQL Server Versions 6.5 And 7

In SQL Server 6.5 and prior versions, the column *syslogins.suid* in the *master* database was used to give each SQL Server account a unique **server user id**. Beginning in SQL Server 7, the **suid** has been replaced by the column *master.dbo.sysxlogins.sid*, which represents a unique **system identifier**. Although the two concepts may seem similar, the use of **syslogins** will always have an extra associated cost in version 7, because **syslogins** is now implemented as a *view* rather than as a *table*, and the column *syslogins.suid* is now a *calculated value* based on the data in *sysxlogins.sid*.

Notes On Using Security Functions

Security functions are used by Microsoft's own system stored procedures to control their functionality. It is possible to grant the *execute* privilege to the **public** group for a stored procedure and to change the functionality inside the procedure based on the results of various security stored procedures. For example, Listing 9.5 shows a snippet of Microsoft's own code from the procedure **sp_addlogin**, showing how the **IS_SRVROLEMEMBER** function is invoked to determine whether the current user can add a new SQL Server login.

Listing 9.5 Controlling functionality with security functions.

```
EXEC SP_HELPTEXT sp_addlogin

Results:
Text
--------------------------------
create procedure sp_addlogin ...
...
— CHECK PERMISSIONS —
      IF (not is_srvrolemember('securityadmin') = 1)
      begin
          raiserror(15003,-1,-1, 'securityadmin')
          return (1)
      end
...
```

Okay, maybe a single best way doesn't exist to become a real T-SQL expert. Some people may prefer to learn at their own pace, using self-study materials (such as this book), while others may choose to enroll in appropriate classes to get started in their learning. Another option is to pay very close attention to the coding habits of someone who is already a Certified TSG (T-SQL Guru). If no such mentor can be found in your company, you need to look only as far as your own SQL Server. SQL Server stores the code for stored procedures in a table called syscomments, and the code for the various system stored procedures are stored just like the code that you create. That's why we were able to use the stored procedure sp_helptext to look at the technique Microsoft's own engineers used to control access to sp_addlogin. This is the same mechanism used by the SQL Server Enterprise Manager to show you the code behind a stored procedure. If you truly want to learn from the best, use this trick to peek inside Microsoft's own code.

String Functions

SQL Server 7 has several different data types for storing string data. These data types include **CHAR** and **VARCHAR**, along with their Unicode counterparts **NCHAR** and **NVARCHAR**. These string data types are very flexible, because they can store any valid character strings. However, this flexibility means that the values stored as string data is very hard to predict. Because of this, you need a set of general functions to help you parse and transform string data. Suppose that you need to extract the second word from a string value. Perhaps your application requires you to transform name data from **last_name, first_name** format to **first_name last_name**. The process for accomplishing these tasks involves the use of the *string functions* provided by SQL Server 7. String functions are very commonly used in T-SQL and are powerful tools for examining and transforming string data. Descriptions of the string functions follow.

ASCII (string) And UNICODE (nstring)

These functions return the ASCII or Unicode value for the character string passed into the function. If the **string** or **nstring** passed is longer than one character in length, only the first character is evaluated. The value passed in to these functions is converted to the appropriate type of string (Unicode or ASCII) whenever possible. Because characters 0 to 255 are the same for ASCII and Unicode, you should use the **UNICODE** function whenever you need maximum flexibility. For example, the following queries all return the value 68. The difference is that the first and third examples require an implicit data conversion, whereas the second and fourth do not:

```
SELECT ASCII    ('D')
SELECT UNICODE  ('D')
SELECT ASCII   (N'D')
SELECT UNICODE (N'D')
```

CHAR (int) And NCHAR (int)

These functions are like **ASCII** and **UNICODE** run backward: They take an ASCII or Unicode value and return the appropriate character. A system stored procedure called **sp_helpsort** lists the characteristics of your server's current character set and sort order and then displays all ASCII characters sorted by that sort order. Listing 9.6 shows how to use the **CHAR** function to generate a similar list of ASCII characters sorted according to the current sort order. The only information **sp_helpsort** gives you that this query does not is that certain characters may be considered equivalent for sorting purposes, such as 'D' and 'd'. This depends on the sort order in effect on your server. Be aware that the order of the characters listed is different from the order of their ASCII values. This reordering is due to the sort order that is in effect.

Listing 9.6 Listing ASCII characters by the server's sort order.

```
/* for reference, run sp_helpsort first: */
PRINT 'Running sp_helpsort...'
EXEC sp_helpsort

PRINT 'Generating table of ASCII characters...'
SET NOCOUNT ON
DECLARE @i INT

CREATE TABLE #AsciiTable ([Ascii Code] INT, [Ascii Character] CHAR)

/* SPACE is the lowest-ranking character in sp_helpsort output: */
SET @i = ASCII (' ')

WHILE @i <= 255
BEGIN
      INSERT INTO #AsciiTable
      VALUES (@i, CHAR(@i))
      SET @i = @i + 1
END

PRINT 'Selecting characters from table of ASCII characters...'
SELECT *
FROM #AsciiTable
ORDER BY [Ascii Character]

DROP TABLE #AsciiTable

Results:
Running sp_helpsort...
...
Characters, in Order
-----------------------------------------------------------------
   ! " # $ % & ' ( ) * + , - . / : ; < = > ? @ [ \ ] ^ _ ` { | }
 ~   ¡ ¢ £ ¤ ¥ ¦ § ¨ © ª « ¬ _ ® ¯ ° ± ² ³ ´ µ ¶ · ¸ ¹ º » ¼ ½ ¾
 ¿ x ÷ 0 1 2 3 4 5 6 7 8 9 A=a À=à Á=á Â=â Ã=ã Ä=ä Å=å Æ=æ B=b C
 =c Ç=ç D=d E=e È=è É=é Ê=ê Ë=ë F=f G=g H=h I=i Ì=ì Í=í Î=î Ï=ï J
 =j K=k L=l M=m N=n Ñ=ñ O=o Ò=ò Ó=ó Ô=ô Õ=õ Ö=ö Ø=ø P=p Q=q R=r S
 =s ß T=t U=u Ù=ù Ú=ú Û=û Ü=ü V=v W=w X=x Y=y Ý=ý ÿ Z=z Ð=ð Þ=þ
...
Generating table of ASCII characters...
Selecting characters from table of ASCII characters...
Ascii Code  Ascii Character
----------  ---------------
```

```
32
33          !
34          "
35          #
36          $
37          %
38          &
39          '
40          (
41          )
...
122         z
208         Đ
240         ð
222         Þ
254         þ
```


CHARINDEX (string_to_find, string_to_search [, start_position]) And PATINDEX (pattern_to_find, string_to_search)

The **CHARINDEX** and **PATINDEX** functions enable you to search for a string within another string. **CHARINDEX** returns the first starting position of the **string_to_find** within the **string_to_search**. If the **string_to_find** is not contained within the **string_to_search**, **CHARINDEX** returns 0.

CHARINDEX also enables you to specify an optional **start_position**, in which case it returns the first matching starting position that is greater than the specified **start_position**. Notice the following example:

```
SELECT CHARINDEX
('er', 'MS SQL Server 7.0')     /* returns 9  */
SELECT CHARINDEX
('aa', 'MS SQL Server 7.0')     /* returns 0  */
SELECT CHARINDEX
('er', 'MS SQL Server 7.0', 10) /* returns 12 */
```

PATINDEX behaves a lot like **CHARINDEX**. The main differences are that **PATINDEX** matches patterns and does not accept a **start_position**. Also, **PATINDEX** works on **TEXT** and **NTEXT** data, as well as string data.

```
SELECT PATINDEX ('er',    'MS SQL Server 7.0')     /* returns 0  */
SELECT PATINDEX ('%er%',  'MS SQL Server 7.0')     /* returns 9  */
SELECT PATINDEX ('%aa%',  'MS SQL Server 7.0')     /* returns 0  */
SELECT PATINDEX ('MS %',  'MS SQL Server 7.0')     /* returns 1  */
SELECT PATINDEX ('%7.0',  'MS SQL Server 7.0')     /* returns 15 */
SELECT PATINDEX ('%S_L%', 'MS SQL Server 7.0')     /* returns 4  */
```

Note that **PATINDEX ('%pattern%', @string1)** always returns the same value as **CHARINDEX ('pattern', @string1)**. However, the functions can't always be interchanged easily. If you want to do a simple string match, either function works well, although **CHARINDEX** may be easier to read. If you need to specify a **start_position**, **CHARINDEX** is your only choice. If you are looking for either combinations of strings in a certain order or a pattern at the beginning or end of a string only, **PATINDEX** may be easier to use.

The following example shows how to use **CHARINDEX** to break up a string into individual words. It also uses the **RIGHT** and **SUBSTRING** functions, which are introduced later in this chapter.

```
SET NOCOUNT ON

DECLARE @position INT, @sentence VARCHAR(80)
SET @position = -1
SET @sentence = 'The quick brown fox jumped over the lazy dog, SIR!'

CREATE TABLE Sentence
     (Position INT IDENTITY (1,1),
      Word     VARCHAR(255))

WHILE @position != 0
BEGIN
     SET @position = CHARINDEX(' ', @sentence)
     IF @position != 0
          BEGIN
               INSERT INTO Sentence (Word)
               VALUES (SUBSTRING(@sentence, 1, @position - 1))
               SET @sentence =
               RIGHT(@sentence, len(@sentence) - @position)
          END
END

/* retrieve last word: */
INSERT INTO Sentence (Word)
VALUES (@sentence)

SELECT *
FROM Sentence
ORDER BY Position

DROP TABLE Sentence
```

```
Results:
Position    Word
--------    ----
1           The
2           quick
3           brown
4           fox
5           jumped
6           over
7           the
8           lazy
9           dog,
10          SIR!
```

DIFFERENCE (string1, string2) And SOUNDEX (string)

The **SOUNDEX** function assigns a *sound index* to a string, based on the first letter of the string and the consonants in the remainder of the string. By itself, **SOUNDEX** usually isn't very useful unless you have a lot of expertise understanding these sound indexes. However, the **DIFFERENCE** function calculates the sound index for both strings that it receives and summarizes how alike or different they are. This can be useful in applications that need to find a row based on an approximate spelling of a value. An example of such an application is a telephone operator's console. A caller may be trying to reach someone, without knowing the exact spelling of a name. **DIFFERENCE** returns values from 0 to 4, with 0 indicating that the strings are identical with respect to their first letter and subsequent consonants, and 4 indicating that the strings are very different.

These functions have their limitations. Notice that in the following example, both the second and third queries return 0, meaning that the words are thought to sound alike, because the sound index is constructed based on the first letter and subsequent consonants only—so both *gauge* and *gag* are reduced to *gg* for the purpose of comparison.

```
SELECT DIFFERENCE ('democrat', 'republican') /* returns 4 */
SELECT DIFFERENCE ('great', 'grate')         /* returns 0 */
SELECT DIFFERENCE ('gauge', 'gag')           /* also returns 0 */
```

LEN (string)

The **LEN** function returns the number of characters in the specified string, whether the string is given in Unicode or ASCII format. Note the difference between this behavior and the behavior of the system function **DATALENGTH**, which returns the number of bytes needed to represent the string:

```
SELECT LEN('abcd')            /* returns 4... */
```

```
SELECT LEN(N'abcd')          /* returns 4... */
SELECT DATALENGTH('abcd')    /* returns 4... */
SELECT DATALENGTH(N'abcd')   /* returns 8!   */
```

LOWER (string) And UPPER (string)

These functions are used to convert strings to all uppercase or lowercase letters, respectively. In many applications, for the sake of personalizing the data, you may allow users to enter text however they please, yet store the data in various forms of capitalization.

A common example of this is the storage of last names. You may want users to enter their name with the capitalization they are used to, such as *Van Der Hoeff*. This name may be stored in all uppercase letters in your database for sorting and retrieval purposes. In this case, a query similar to the following snippet would help you to match the user's input to the information stored in your database:

```
SELECT AccountID
FROM   UserList
WHERE  UPPER(@last_name_input) = LastName
```

LTRIM (string) And RTRIM (string)

LTRIM removes (trims) leading spaces from strings, and **RTRIM** removes trailing spaces. To trim all outer spaces from a string, you can use both functions, as in the following example:

```
SELECT @MyString = LTRIM(RTRIM(@MyString))
```

QUOTENAME (string, delimiter)

QUOTENAME has a limited application, but it can be used in certain situations in which optimal flexibility is required when naming database objects. For example, you could use **QUOTENAME** in applications that generate scripts or that allow a user to specify the definition of database objects through a graphical user interface (GUI). **QUOTENAME** accepts any string and returns another string that can serve as a delimited identifier. The delimiter used is specified by delimiter and must be a square brace, a single quote, or a double quote. Note in the following examples that the delimiter is *included in the query output*, which is different from the normal treatment of strings by SQL Server.

This first example shows how the same string can be delimited in different ways:

```
SELECT QUOTENAME("Fred's Aunt [Helen]", '[') AS [First String]
SELECT QUOTENAME("Fred's Aunt [Helen]", "'") AS [Second String]
SELECT QUOTENAME("Fred's Aunt [Helen]", '"') AS [Third String]
```

```
Results:
First String
------------
[Fred's Aunt [Helen]]]

Second String
-------------
'Fred''s Aunt [Helen]'

Third String
------------
"Fred's Aunt [Helen]"
```

In the next example, a script is generated that could then be executed to check the size of every table in the current database:

```
SELECT 'EXEC sp_spaceused ' + QUOTENAME(name, '[')
FROM    sysobjects
WHERE   type = 'U'
ORDER   BY name

Results:
EXEC sp_spaceused [Categories]
EXEC sp_spaceused [CustomerCustomerDemo]
EXEC sp_spaceused [CustomerDemographics]
...
EXEC sp_spaceused [Territories]
```


REPLACE (string, marker_string, insertion_string) And STUFF (string, start_position, deletion_count, insertion_string)

The **REPLACE** function can help to accomplish such tasks as generating form letters. **REPLACE** searches the given string for the **marker_string** and replaces the **marker_string** with the **insertion_string**. Here's an example of how it works:

```
SELECT REPLACE ('Dear [empname],
                congratulations on your new raise!',
                '[empname]',
                FirstName + ' ' + LastName) AS Salutation
FROM  Employees

Results:
```

```
Salutation
------------------------------------------------------
Dear Nancy Davolio, congratulations on your new raise!
Dear Andrew Fuller, congratulations on your new raise!
...
Dear Anne Dodsworth, congratulations on your new raise!
```

STUFF performs a task similar to **REPLACE**. Instead of specifying a **marker_string** to indicate where to insert text, you specify a **start_position**. Whereas **REPLACE** automatically deletes the **marker_string** from the result, **STUFF** enables you to specify the **deletion_count** characters that should be deleted, starting at the **start_position**. This means that you don't necessarily have to store a **marker_string**, and this could save you storage space in a large application. Here is a similar example for **STUFF** that inserts text without deleting any text first:

```
SELECT STUFF ('Dear , congratulations again!',
             6, 0,
             FirstName + ' ' + LastName
            ) AS [Salutation 2]
FROM Employees

Results:
Salutation 2
--------------------------------------------
Dear Nancy Davolio, congratulations again!
Dear Andrew Fuller, congratulations again!
Dear Janet Leverling, congratulations again!
Dear Margaret Peacock, congratulations again!
Dear Steven Buchanan, congratulations again!
Dear Michael Suyama, congratulations again!
Dear Robert King, congratulations again!
Dear Laura Callahan, congratulations again!
Dear Anne Dodsworth, congratulations again!
```

REPLICATE (string_to_repeat, repitition_count) And SPACE (repititions_count)

These functions simply return a string repeated **repetition_count** times. This can be useful when formatting output for reports. Consider the following example, which uses **REPLICATE** to produce *dot leaders* in a report:

```
SELECT FirstName + ' ' + LastName + ' '
     + REPLICATE('.', 40 - LEN(firstname + lastname)) + ' '
```

```
    + Title AS [Employee .............................. Title]
FROM Employees
ORDER BY LastName, FirstName

Results:
Employee .............................. Title
------------------------------------------------------------
Steven Buchanan ....................... Sales Manager
Laura Callahan ........................ Inside Sales Coordinator
...
Michael Suyama ........................ Sales Representative
```

SPACE is a special case of **REPLICATE**, in which the **string_to_repeat** is always a single blank space. It could therefore be used to emulate tabs in the previous report instead of dot leaders:

```
SELECT FirstName + ' ' + LastName
    + SPACE (40 - LEN(firstname + lastname))
    + Title AS [Employee                              Title]
FROM Employees
ORDER BY LastName, FirstName

Results:
Employee                                      Title
------------------------------------------------------------
Steven Buchanan                               Sales Manager
Laura Callahan                                Inside Sales Coordinator
...
Michael Suyama                                Sales Representative
```

9

REVERSE (string_to_reverse)

This functions simply returns the **string_to_reverse** backward:

```
SELECT REVERSE ("!FFOTFIL ,1 ,2 ,3") AS Launch

Results:
Launch
-----------------
3, 2, 1, LIFTOFF!
```

STR (float_value, string_length, decimal_places)

Sometimes, you may want to include formatted numbers in your query output. The system functions **CAST** and **CONVERT** can be useful for this task. **CAST** and **CONVERT** do not give you a way to specify the precision with which a

float_value is converted to a string. That is the purpose of the **STR** function. For example, to print the value of pi to five decimal places, you could use the following query:

```
SELECT STR(PI( ), 7, 5) as PI

Results:
PI
--------
3.14159
```

SUBSTRING (string, start, length), LEFT (string, length), And RIGHT (string, length)

Use these functions to return part of a string. The **SUBSTRING** function returns **length** characters from the given **string**, beginning at position **start**.

LEFT and **RIGHT** return the first and last parts of a string, respectively. These functions are special cases of **SUBSTRING**. **LEFT (string, length)** is equivalent to **SUBSTRING (string, 1, length)**, and **RIGHT (string, length)** is equivalent to the expression **SUBSTRING (string, LEN (string) - length + 1, length)**.

```
SELECT SUBSTRING (N'ABCDEFG', 3, 2) /* returns 'CD'  */
SELECT LEFT      (N'ABCDEFG', 3)    /* returns 'ABC' */
SELECT RIGHT     (N'ABCDEFG', 3)    /* returns 'EFG' */
```

System Functions

T-SQL includes a group of general utility functions called *system functions*. The *Books Online* states that this category designates functions that give you access to system tables, without having to query them directly. This description is a bit misleading. Many of the other function groups, especially configuration, metadata, security, and system statistical functions also give you access to values stored in system tables. Moreover, many of the system functions, such as **CASE**, **CAST**, and **ISNULL** do not. The best way to think of the system functions is as a group of generally useful functions that don't fit into one of the other function groups.

APP_NAME ( )

The **APP_NAME** function returns the name of the client program that has established the current SQL Server session. Be sure to note the required parentheses. This name must be set by the client program. The **APP_NAME** values returned for various SQL Server utilities are shown in Table 9.10.

Table 9.10 APP_NAME values.

APP_NAME ( ) Value	SQL Server Utility
ISQL-32	isql.exe
OSQL-32	osql.exe
MS SQLEM	SQL Server Enterprise Manager
DTS Wizard	Import and Export Data (dtswiz.exe)
SQL Server Profiler: TraceCtrl	Profiler-session (sqltrace.exe)
SQL Server Profiler: Trace	Profiler-trace (sqltrace.exe)
MS SQL Query Analyzer	Query Analyzer (isqlw.exe)

CASE: Simple CASE Function

```
CASE evaluated_expression
WHEN choice1 THEN value1
WHEN choice2 THEN value2
...
ELSE value_else
END
```


CASE: Searched CASE Function

```
CASE
WHEN boolean_expression1 THEN value1
WHEN boolean_expression2 THEN value2
...
ELSE value_else
END
```

CASE functions provide a very flexible way to transform data values. A simple **CASE** function compares an **evaluated_expression** to a list of possible choices. Each choice is given in the **WHEN** part of a separate **WHEN-THEN** clause. A simple **CASE** function returns the **THEN** value corresponding to the first **WHEN** clause whose choice matches the evaluated expression. In Listing 9.7, a simple **CASE** function is used to transform the column *TitleOfCourtesy* into inferred gender information.

Listing 9.7 Using simple **CASE** functions.

```
SELECT TitleOfCourtesy + ' ' + FirstName + ' ' + LastName AS Name,
       CASE TitleOfCourtesy
            WHEN 'Ms.' THEN 'Female'
            WHEN 'Mrs.' THEN 'Female'
            WHEN 'Mr.'  THEN 'Male'
            ELSE 'Not Inferred'
       END  AS InferredGender
FROM   Employees
```

```
Results:
Name                       InferredGender
---------------------      -------------
Ms. Nancy Davolio          Female
Dr. Andrew Fuller          Not Inferred
Ms. Janet Leverling        Female
Mrs. Margaret Peacock      Female
Mr. Steven Buchanan        Male
Mr. Michael Suyama         Male
Mr. Robert King            Male
Ms. Laura Callahan         Female
Ms. Anne Dodsworth         Female
```

Notice the use of an **ELSE** clause, which specifies what value to return when none of the **WHERE** clauses matches the value of the *TitleOfCourtesy* column. Omitting the **ELSE** clause is the same thing as specifying **ELSE NULL**.

A searched **CASE** function differs in two ways from a simple **CASE** function:

- No **evaluated_expression** follows the **CASE** keyword.
- **WHEN** clauses always list Boolean (True-False) predicates. A searched **CASE** function returns the first **THEN** value associated with a **WHEN** clause that evaluates to **TRUE**.

Listing 9.8 gives T-SQL code that interrogates the *BirthDate* column and classifies employees with respect to the Baby Boom (which the U.S. Census Bureau specifies as having lasted from 1946 until 1964).

This example uses the **CONVERT** function, which is explained in the next section.

Listing 9.8 Using searched **CASE** functions.

```
SELECT TitleOfCourtesy + ' ' + FirstName + ' ' + LastName AS Name,
       CONVERT(VARCHAR, BirthDate, 107) AS [Birth Date],
       CASE
            WHEN BirthDate <  '1-1-1946' THEN 'Born BEFORE Baby Boom'
            WHEN BirthDate <  '1-1-1965' THEN 'Born During Baby Boom'
            WHEN BirthDate >= '1-1-1965' THEN 'Born AFTER Baby Boom'
            ELSE 'Date Of Birth Unknown'
       END  AS BabyBoomStatus
FROM   Employees
select * from Employees
```

```
Results:
Name                    Birth Date     BabyBoomStatus
---------------------   ------------   ---------------------
Ms. Nancy Davolio       Dec 08, 1948   Born During Baby Boom
Dr. Andrew Fuller       Feb 19, 1952   Born During Baby Boom
Ms. Janet Leverling     Aug 30, 1963   Born During Baby Boom
Mrs. Margaret Peacock   Sep 19, 1937   Born BEFORE Baby Boom
Mr. Steven Buchanan     Mar 04, 1955   Born During Baby Boom
Mr. Michael Suyama      Jul 02, 1963   Born During Baby Boom
Mr. Robert King         May 29, 1960   Born During Baby Boom
Ms. Laura Callahan      Jan 09, 1958   Born During Baby Boom
Ms. Anne Dodsworth      Jan 27, 1966   Born AFTER Baby Boom
```

CAST (expression AS data_type) And CONVERT (data_type, expression [, style])

CAST and **CONVERT** are T-SQL's general-purpose data-conversion functions. If you have used T-SQL for SQL Server 6.5, you already know about the **CONVERT** function. The **CAST** function is new for SQL Server 7. Both are straightforward in their basic use, as demonstrated here:

9

```
SELECT 'May is month ' + CAST(5 AS VARCHAR) + '.' AS CAST_5
SELECT 'May is month ' + CONVERT(VARCHAR, 5) + '.' AS CONVERT_5

Results:
CAST_5
--------------
May is month 5.

CONVERT_5
--------------
May is month 5.
```

The optional **style** parameter for **CONVERT** enables you to specify a predefined style constant when converting date, number, or currency values to string values. A total of 17 predefined styles exist for dates, three predefined styles exist for **floats** and **reals**, and three more exist for **currency** values. These styles are well documented in the *Books Online*, under the topic **CAST** and **CONVERT** (T-SQL). The examples in Listings 9.9, 9.10, and 9.11 will help you understand the types of style choices that are available.

Listing 9.9 Using **CAST** and **CONVERT** with date values.

```
DECLARE @Y2K DATETIME
SELECT  @Y2K = '1/1/2000'
SELECT  CAST(@Y2K AS VARCHAR)  [CAST DATE],
        CONVERT(VARCHAR, @Y2K) [CONVERT DATE]
```

```
SELECT  CONVERT(VARCHAR, @Y2K, 109) [FULL 12-HR DATE],
        CONVERT(VARCHAR, @Y2K, 101) [USA DATE]

Results:
CAST DATE                       CONVERT DATE
-------------------             -------------------
Jan  1 2000 12:00AM             Jan  1 2000 12:00AM
```

Listing 9.10 Using **CAST** and **CONVERT** with money values.

```
FULL 12-HR DATE                 USA DATE
--------------------------      ----------
Jan  1 2000 12:00:00:000AM      01/01/2000

DECLARE @1M MONEY
SELECT  @1M = $1000000
SELECT  CAST (@1M AS VARCHAR)  [CAST MONEY],
        CONVERT (VARCHAR, @1M) [CONVERT MONEY]
SELECT  CONVERT (VARCHAR, @1M, 1) [MONEY WITH COMMAS],
        CONVERT (VARCHAR, @1M, 2) [FRACTIONAL MONEY]

Results:
CAST MONEY                      CONVERT MONEY
----------                      -------------
1000000.00                      1000000.00

MONEY WITH COMMAS               FRACTIONAL MONEY
-----------------               ----------------
1,000,000.00                    1000000.0000
```

Listing 9.11 Using **CAST** and **CONVERT** with **float** and **real** values.

```
SELECT  CAST (PI() AS VARCHAR)  [CAST PI()],
        CONVERT (VARCHAR, PI()) [CONVERT PI()]
SELECT  CONVERT (VARCHAR, PI(), 1) [PI() SHORT SCIENTIFIC],
        CONVERT (VARCHAR, PI(), 2) [PI() LONG SCIENTIFIC]

Results:
CAST PI()                       CONVERT PI()
---------                       ------------
3.14159                         3.14159

PI() SHORT SCIENTIFIC           PI() LONG SCIENTIFIC
---------------------           ----------------------
3.1415927e+000                  3.141592653589793e+000
```

COALESCE (expression1, expression2, ..., expression_last)

COALESCE simply returns the first non-**NULL** expression in its argument list. Thus, it is equivalent to a searched **CASE** function of the following form:

```
CASE
WHEN expression1 IS NOT NULL THEN expression1
WHEN expression1 IS NOT NULL THEN expression1
...
WHEN expression_last IS NOT NULL THEN expression_last
END
```

Notice that this construct has no **ELSE** clause. If all the values passed to **COALESCE** are **NULL**, an error message is returned.

Niladic Functions

A *niladic function* is one that has no argument list. Even coding the parentheses that go around an argument list produces an error, because an *empty* argument list is not the same as a *nonexistent* argument list. Niladic functions are frequently used to define **DEFAULT** constraints.

9

You have already seen one niladic function in this chapter, **USER**, when reviewing security functions. That discussion noted that the niladic function **USER** was equivalent to the non-niladic function **USER_NAME( )**. Each of the other niladic functions is also a shortcut for a non-niladic function, as shown in Table 9.11.

DATALENGTH (expression)

This returns the number of bytes used to store the given expression. Note that for **NTEXT** data, **DATALENGTH (expression) = 2 * LEN (expression)**. Refer to the example for **LEN** in the earlier section, "String Functions."

Table 9.11 Niladic functions.

Niladic Function	Non-Niladic Function Equivalent
CURRENT_TIMESTAMP	GETDATE( )
CURRENT_USER	USER_NAME( )
SESSION_USER	USER_NAME( )
SYSTEM_USER	SUSER_NAME( ) or SUSER_SNAME( )
USER	USER_NAME( )

@@ERROR

This function returns the error code for the last operation requested. A successful operation always returns **@@ERROR = 0**. This enables you to trap for errors in T-SQL, as shown in this code snippet:

```
SELECT * FROM TABLE1
IF @@ERROR != 0
     /* handle error condition here */

INSERT INTO TABLE2 VALUES ('X', 123)
IF @@ERROR != 0
     /* handle error condition here */
```

Be sure to invoke **@@ERROR** immediately after the statement in question, because even seemingly innocuous statements, such as **SET @MyName = 'Chris'**, will change values.

FORMATMESSAGE (msg_number, param1, param2, ..., param_last)

This function enables you to create an error message without actually invoking the **RAISERROR** statement to create the error condition. This enables you to format the error message further to meet your own needs. The **msg_number** should be at least **50000** and must be at least **13000**:

```
SELECT FORMATMESSAGE (15035, 'BAD_DEVICE_NAME')

Results:
'BAD_DEVICE_NAME' is not a database device.
```

GETANSINULL (['database_name'])

The **ANSI NULL** behavior determines whether a column in a newly created table allows **NULL** values by default, if its nullability is not explicitly declared. This function returns 1 if the columns created during this session in the given database will allow **NULL** values by default. It returns 0 otherwise.

HOST_ID ( ) And HOST_NAME ( )

The numeric **HOST_ID** and the machine name returned by **HOST_NAME** can be useful if you are either trying to group connections by host computer or trying to determine where a specific connection originated. This can be done when a particular connection or group of connections is causing or having trouble on the SQL Server, or an application could collect this information to include in an activity log.

@@IDENTITY, IDENT_INCR (table_name), And IDENT_SEED (table_name)

These three functions return information about *Identity* columns. The **IDENT_INCR** and **IDENT_SEED** functions return the **seed** and **increment** values for a given table. The **seed** value for an *Identity* column is the identity value for the first row inserted into that table. The **increment** value for an *Identity* column is the amount by which the *Identity* columns increase for each subsequent insert. (For more information on table creation, see Chapter 5.)

The **@@IDENTITY** function returns the value of the last *Identity* column populated by the current connection. This is often very important information to have in an application. Because *Identity* columns are frequently used as surrogate or artificial keys, a table with an *Identity* column frequently does not have a *natural* key. If this is the case, you may insert a row for which the *Identity* column is the only unique identifier. If you don't know what identity value was used for your row, no guarantee exists that you can correctly retrieve it to work with it later. The following code saves the identity value in a variable for later use:


```
DECLARE @ShipperID int

INSERT  INTO Shippers (CompanyName, Phone)
VALUES ('Coriolis Express', '(999) 999-1234')

SELECT  @ShipperID = @@IDENTITY
```

Several reasons exist to be careful when retrieving identity values by using **@@IDENTITY**. First, if your insert completes but is then rolled back, the **@@IDENTITY** value is still updated as though the transaction had been committed. Second, if you insert multiple rows using **INSERT INTO/SELECT**, **@@IDENTITY** tells you only the identity value of the last row inserted. The final consideration is the trickiest. Suppose an insert trigger is on the table into which you inserted a row. If that trigger inserts a row into another table that has an *Identity* column in it, the **@@IDENTITY** function returns the identity value for this second table. In any of these situations, you must be careful to interpret the value of **@@IDENTITY** correctly.

IDENTITY (data_type, [seed, increment]) AS column_name

This **IDENTITY** function has a very specialized purpose: It is used to create *Identity* columns in tables created with the **SELECT/INTO** statement. For example, the following query makes a copy of the *Customers* table and adds an *Identity* column to it:

```
SELECT IDENTITY (INT) AS CustomerIdentity, *
INTO   Customers_COPY
FROM   Customers
```

ISDATE (expression) And ISNUMERIC (expression)

These functions return whether a given **expression** can be successfully converted into a date or numeric value, respectively. These functions are useful for data-input validation.

ISNULL (expression, replacement)

ISNULL evaluates the given **expression** and replaces it with **replacement** if **expression** contains a **NULL** value. It is roughly equivalent to the following **CASE** statement:

```
CASE
WHEN expression IS NULL THEN replacement
ELSE expression
END
```

NULLIF (expression1, expression2)

NULLIF returns **NULL** if **expression1** equals **expression2**. It is roughly equivalent to the following **CASE** statement:

```
CASE
WHEN expression1 = expression2 THEN NULL
ELSE expression1
END
```

NEWID ( )

The **NEWID** function returns a new value of the data type **UNIQUEIDENTIFIER**. Each **UNIQUEIDENTIFIER** value is guaranteed to be unique across every SQL Server database in the world. **NEWID** is frequently used as a **DEFAULT** constraint for a table containing **UNIQUEIDENTIFIER** data.

PARSENAME (object_name, object_name_component)

For SQL Server 7, a fully qualified object name is in the form *server.database.owner .object*. For example, the fully qualified name SQL7.Northwind.dbo.Employee refers to the Employee object owned by the user **dbo** in the *Northwind* database on the SQL 7 server. **PARSENAME** enables you to take a fully qualified name in string form and extract any component of the fully qualified object name from it. The argument **object_name_component** should be 1 to request the object name, 2 to request the owner name, 3 to request the database name, and 4 to request the server name. **PARSENAME** returns **NULL** for any **object_name_component** that is not *explicitly* specified in the **object_name**. For example:

```
SELECT PARSENAME('Northwind..Employees', 1)  /* returns 'Employees' */
SELECT PARSENAME('Northwind..Employees', 2)  /* returns NULL        */
```

PERMISSIONS ([object_id] [, column_name])

This function can be used to interrogate the current user's permissions. If **object_id** is omitted, information about statement permissions is returned. If **object_id** is specified but **column_name** is not, then object permissions are returned. If **object_id** and **column_name** are both specified, column-level permissions are returned. The returned value is a bitmap, where each bit is turned on or off to represent the presence or absence of that permission. For example, if column-level permissions are requested and bit 0x2 is turned on in the result, this means that the current user has update permissions for that column, as the following example illustrates:

```
IF PERMISSIONS (OBJECT_ID('Employees'), 'LastName') & 0x2 = 0x2
   PRINT 'Current user can update Employees.LastName.'
ELSE
   PRINT 'Current user cannot update Employees.LastName.'
```

For a complete list of the bit values returned for each permission, see the **PERMISSIONS** function in the *Books Online*.

@@ROWCOUNT

This function returns the number of rows affected by the last statement. It is useful for verifying that a statement affected the number of rows expected. For example, if an **UPDATE** statement specifies a table's entire primary key in its **WHERE** clause, **@@ROWCOUNT** can be used to verify that exactly one row was updated.

Be sure to invoke **@@ROWCOUNT** immediately after the statement in question, because even seemingly innocuous statements, such as **SET @MyName = 'Chris'**, change their value.

STATS_DATE (table_id, index_id)

This function displays the last time statistics were updated for the given index. SQL Server 7 now automatically maintains statistics and may update them at any time unless you have set it not to for a specific case. If many updates occur in a table but the statistics are not updated, index selection and other optimizer functions may be impaired. For more information on creating and maintaining statistics, see Chapter 6.

@@TRANCOUNT

This function returns how many open transactions currently exist for your connection. Because transactions can be nested, this value may be greater than 1. The following code rolls back all open transactions for the current connection:

```
WHILE @@TRANCOUNT > 0
   ROLLBACK TRANSACTION
```

USER_NAME ([user_id])

If the **user_id** argument is not specified, the **USER_NAME** function returns the name of the current database user. If **user_id** is specified, the function is equivalent to the following query:

```
SELECT name FROM sysusers WHERE uid = user_id
```

System Statistical Functions

The final category of T-SQL scalar functions is system statistical functions. These functions, all of which have a @@ prefix (like the SQL 6.5 global variables), are usually used to diagnose performance problems on SQL Server. As such, typical Online Transaction Processing (OLTP) or Decision Support Service (DSS) programs do not make frequent use of these functions. Most of the information returned by these functions is also found in the output of the **sp_monitor** system stored procedure. For reference, the information returned by these functions is summarized in Table 9.12.

Table 9.12 System statistical functions.

System Statistical Function	Information Returned
@@CPU_BUSY	The amount of CPU time, in milliseconds, used by SQL Server since it last started
@@IDLE	The number of milliseconds that SQL Server has been idle since it last started
@@IO_BUSY	The number of milliseconds that SQL Server has spent performing I/O operations since it last started
@@PACK_RECEIVED	The number of network packets received by SQL Server since it last started
@@PACK_SENT	The number of network packets sent by SQL Server since it last started

(continued)

Table 9.12 System statistical functions *(continued)*.

System Statistical Function	Information Returned
@@PACKET_ERRORS	The number of errors SQL Server has encountered while processing network packets since it last started
@@TIMETICKS	The number of milliseconds per operating system tick on this computer
@@TOTAL_ERRORS	The number of disk I/O errors SQL Server has encountered since it was last started
@@TOTAL_READ	The number of physical disk reads performed by SQL Server since it was last started
@@TOTAL_WRITE	The number of disk writes issued by SQL Server since it was last started

Text And Image Functions

Although string and binary data provide a great deal of functionality, those data types sometimes are not large enough for the job at hand. A **CHAR** value can hold a maximum of 8,000 characters. Although 8,000 characters may be enough for many situations, sometimes even longer strings must be stored. For example, you may want to use the **CHAR** data type to store the entire text from a 30-minute speech. If you were clever (and had lots of free time), you could create a linked list of **CHAR** values in your database and then link them back together upon retrieval. However, SQL Server 7 provides an easier way to accomplish this, using the **TEXT** data type. **TEXT** columns can hold 2GB of ASCII character data. In addition to **TEXT**, SQL Server also provides **NTEXT** for Unicode data, and **IMAGE** to hold large amounts of binary data (such as word-processing documents or bitmaps).

These three data types, **TEXT**, **NTEXT**, and **IMAGE**, have special statements associated with them: **READTEXT**, **WRITETEXT**, and **UPDATETEXT**. To use these special statements, you must first understand the functions **TEXTPTR** and **TEXTVALID**. This section explains what these functions do and shows a basic example that uses these functions.

The **PATINDEX** function also operates on **TEXT** and **NTEXT** data. For a discussion of **PATINDEX**, see the "String Functions" section earlier in this chapter.

TEXTPTR (column_name)

TEXTPTR returns a pointer to a column that has one of the **TEXT** or **IMAGE** data types. The pointer always points to the beginning of its column. The value of the pointer should be stored in a local variable of type **BINARY(16)**. The text and image statements **READTEXT**, **WRITETEXT**, and **UPDATETEXT**

can then use this pointer to select, insert, and update specific portions of the data stored in that column.

Because the value of the pointer is stored in a local variable, text and image processing is typically done one row at a time.

TEXTVALID ('table_name.column_name', @text_pointer)

TEXTVALID enables you to check whether a text pointer variable holds a valid reference to a particular *Text* or *Image* column. This function returns 1 if the text pointer reference is valid, and returns 0 otherwise.

Example Of Text And Image Functions

Listing 9.12 uses **TEXTPTR** to obtain a text pointer. Then, after verifying that the text pointer is valid by using **TEXTVALID**, it retrieves data from an **NTEXT** column 200 characters at a time. Note in the output how each chunk of retrieved **NTEXT** picks up right where the previously retrieved chunk left off.

Typically, you process more than 200 characters at a time when working with text and image statements. However, this example fetches 200 characters at a time, to be portable. Many client applications restrict the amount of text and image data that can be retrieved at one time. In fact, even the SQL Server Query Optimizer, by default, allows only 256 characters to be returned for any given column. If you select Query|Current Connection Options and then select the Advanced tab, you can modify this setting in the field labeled Maximum Characters Per Column. For example, you could set this field to 1024 and then modify the following example to retrieve 1,024 characters at a time. If you do this, the entire **NTEXT** column (which has 448 characters when it is initially installed) will be retrieved in one **READTEXT** operation.

Listing 9.12 Using text functions with **READTEXT**.

```
declare @ptr varbinary(16), @len int, @pos int, @size int

/* Establish text pointer and length of ntext column. */
/* Must divide length by 2 because Notes is NTEXT:    */
SELECT @ptr = TEXTPTR(Notes), @len = datalength(Notes) / 2
FROM Employees
WHERE EmployeeID = 2
```

```
IF TEXTVALID('Employees.Notes', @ptr) = 1
BEGIN
    SELECT 'Valid text pointer returned!' [Message]

    SELECT @len [Length Of Field To Read]
    /* loop to read the NTEXT column 1 chunk at a time: */
    SELECT @pos = 0, @size = 200

    WHILE @pos < @len
    BEGIN        SELECT @pos [Read Start], @size [Read Size]
        READTEXT Employees.Notes @ptr @pos @size
        SET @pos = @pos + @size
        IF @pos + @size > @len
            SET @size = @len - @pos
    END
END
ELSE
    SELECT
    'Invalid text pointer returned.' [Message]

Results:
Message
----------------------------
Valid text pointer returned!

Length Of Field To Read
-----------------------
448

Read Start  Read Size
----------  ---------
0           200

Notes
----------------------------------------------
Andrew received his BTS commercial in 1974 and
a Ph.D. in international marketing from the
University of Dallas in 1981. He is fluent in
French and Italian and reads German. He joined
the company as

Read Start  Read Size
----------  ---------
200         200
```

9

```
Notes
------------------------------------------------
a sales representative, was promoted to sales
manager in January 1992 and to vice president of
sales in March 1993. Andrew is a member of the
Sales Management Roundtable, the Seattle Chamber
of Comm

Read Start  Read Size
----------  ---------
400         48

Notes
------------------------------------------------
erce, and the Pacific Rim Importers Association.
```

For a more complete discussion of text and image manipulation, refer to the topics **READTEXT**, **WRITETEXT**, and **UPDATETEXT** in the *SQL Server Books Online*.

Summarizing Data With Aggregate Functions

Recall that *scalar* functions are functions that operate on single values and return a single value. *Aggregate* functions are another type of function available in T-SQL. Aggregate functions return a single value, just as scalar functions do. However, aggregate functions work on a *set of values* as input, and they summarize that set of values to produce the result they return. Aggregate functions are very useful in reporting and data summarization. This discussion uses aggregate functions in **SELECT** lists to illustrate most points. Aggregate functions are allowed only in **SELECT** lists, **HAVING** clauses, and **COMPUTE [BY]** clauses. Table 9.13 lists all the available aggregate functions.

Table 9.13 The aggregate functions.

Aggregate Function	Meaning
AVG ([ALL|DISTINCT] expression)	Returns the mean of the values associate with **expression**. Uses unique values only if **DISTINCT** is specified.
COUNT ([ALL|DISTINCT] expression]|*)	Counts the number of values associated with **expression**. Counts unique expressions only if **DISTINCT** is specified. If **COUNT(*)** is specified, **COUNT** returns the number of rows in the group.

(continued)

Table 9.13 The aggregate functions *(continued)*.

Aggregate Function	Meaning
GROUPING (column_name)	Used to distinguish **NULL** values from summary information in **CUBE** and **ROLLUP** output.
MAX (expression)	Returns the largest value associated with **expression**.
MIN (expression)	Returns the smallest value associated with **expression**.
SUM ([ALL|DISTINCT] expression)	Returns the sum of the values associated with **expression**. Sums unique values only if **DISTINCT** is specified.
STDEV (expression)	Returns the standard deviation for the values associated with **expression**, treating those values as a sample.
STDEVP (expression)	Returns the standard deviation for the values associated with **expression**, treating those values as an entire population.
VAR (expression)	Returns the variance for the values associated with **expression**, treating those values as a sample.
VARP (expression)	Returns the variance for the values associated with **expression**, treating those values as an entire population.

9

Scalar Aggregation

In a query that uses *scalar aggregation*, only aggregate functions are specified in the **SELECT** list, and aggregation occurs for the entire set of rows that the query would return if it were not aggregating. In other words, the entire result set is treated a single group, and each aggregate function operates on all the values in a given column.

This first example uses scalar aggregation to count the number of rows in the *Employees* table:

```
SELECT COUNT(*) AS [Number of Employees]
FROM Employees

Results:
Number of Employees
-------------------
9
```

More than one aggregate function can be used in the same **SELECT** list. The next query illustrates this by simultaneously retrieving the number of orders and the total sales amount of all orders. The sales amount for each row is obtained by multiplying the *UnitPrice* times the *Quantity*. Then, **SUM** is used to total these values. Finally, the **STR** function is used to control the format of the total sales amounts.

```
SELECT COUNT(DISTINCT OrderID) AS [Orders],
       STR(SUM(UnitPrice * Quantity), 15, 2)
       AS [Total Sales]
FROM  [Order Details]


Results:
Orders      Total Sales
------      -----------
830         1354458.59
```

Vector Aggregation And GROUP BY

In a scalar aggregation query, each aggregate function returns one value for the entire query. Such queries adequately perform simple summarization of data, but *vector aggregation* is needed to compute results that are more sophisticated. With vector aggregation, you create subgroups of data by including a **GROUP BY** clause in the **SELECT** statement. This **GROUP BY** clause names columns or other expressions that will define subsets of the data. For example, you might want to group your sales data by region, or list the highest-paid employee in each department. The next example modifies the previous query, to group the sales amounts by *OrderID*:

```
SELECT OrderID,
STR(SUM(UnitPrice * Quantity), 15, 2) AS [Total Sales]
FROM   [Order Details]
GROUP  BY OrderID
ORDER  BY OrderID

Results:
OrderID     Total Sales
-------     -----------
10248       440.00
10249       1863.40
10250       1813.00
...
11077       1374.60
```

By grouping the data by the *OrderID* column, we are able to calculate the **SUM** of *Total Sales* for each order individually. Without the **GROUP BY** clause, we could only calculate the total **SUM** for all orders.

For vector aggregation, the **GROUP BY** clause is required. In most situations, the expressions that appear in the **GROUP BY** clause also appear in the **SELECT** list, although technically this is not required. However, when you are using aggregate functions, if you specify anything other than an aggregate function in the **SELECT** list, that expression is required to appear in an **ORDER BY** as well. So, in the preceding query, it would be acceptible (although not necessarily sensible) to omit *OrderID* from the **SELECT** list while leaving it in the **GROUP BY** clause. However, it would be an error to delete it from the **GROUP BY** clause without also deleting it from the **SELECT** list.

You can specify more than one column or expression in the **GROUP BY** clause. The following example groups *Orders* by both *EmployeeID* and *CustomerID*, to count the number of *Orders* that each *EmployeeID* has placed for each *CustomerID*:

```
SELECT EmployeeID, CustomerID, COUNT(*) AS Orders
FROM Orders
GROUP BY EmployeeID, CustomerID
ORDER BY EmployeeID, CustomerID, Orders

Results:
EmployeeID  CustomerID  Orders
----------  ----------  ------
1           ALFKI       2
1           ANTON       1
1           AROUT       3
...
9           WELLI       1
```

Using The HAVING Keyword To Limit Query Output

When we executed the previous example, 464 rows were in the result set. Most of these rows were for small numbers of orders. If we wanted to find which combinations of *Employees* and *Customers* are creating the most orders for *Northwind*, we would not be interested in those rows with only a few orders. To find these profitable *Employee-Customer* combinations, we could sort our output by the **COUNT(*)** column. However, in this case, SQL Server would still return all the results, including the ones we are not interested in seeing. If this produces a 700-page printed report and we are interested in only 10 of the rows, we have provided an unacceptable solution.

T-SQL provides a better way of handling this. The **HAVING** clause does for aggregate functions what the **WHERE** clause does for other expressions—it restricts the results included in the result set. Suppose that we want to find only

Employee-Customer combinations that have generated five or more sales. The **HAVING** clause enables us to do this easily, as shown in the following example:

```
SELECT EmployeeID, CustomerID, COUNT(*) AS Orders
FROM   Orders
GROUP  BY EmployeeID, CustomerID
HAVING COUNT(*) >= 5
ORDER  BY Orders DESC, EmployeeID, CustomerID

Results:
EmployeeID  CustomerID  Orders
----------  ----------  ------
1           SAVEA       6
2           QUICK       6
3           BERGS       6
8           FOLKO       6
1           ERNSH       5
1           FRANK       5
1           RATTC       5
3           HUNGO       5
3           QUICK       5
4           ERNSH       5
4           HILAA       5
4           QUICK       5
```

In this case, only 12 rows are returned, so the reader can much more easily identify those employees who have fostered such successful relationships with individual customers.

A similar approach enables us to use **HAVING** to determine our largest sales:

```
SELECT OrderID,
       STR(SUM(UnitPrice * Quantity), 15, 2) AS [Total Sales]
FROM   [Order Details]
GROUP  BY OrderID
HAVING SUM(UnitPrice * Quantity) > 12000
ORDER  BY SUM(UnitPrice * Quantity) DESC

Results:
OrderID     Total Sales
-------     -----------
10865       17250.00
11030       6321.90
10981       15810.00
10372       12281.20
```

Now, instead of having to pore through hundreds of orders looking for the largest ones, we have reduced our report to include only the four largest orders.

In practice, **HAVING** is only used in vector aggregation queries—that is, queries that have a **GROUP BY** clause. Technically, however, the **HAVING** clause can be used in any query. In the absence of a **GROUP BY** clause, **HAVING** is just a fancy restatement of a **WHERE** clause, because without a **GROUP BY** clause, each row in the table being queried is treated as its own group by the **HAVING** clause. This causes the idea of aggregate functions to become trivial. For example, without a **GROUP BY** clause, the clause **HAVING SUM(MyColumn) > 5** has the same effect as the clause **WHERE MyColumn > 5**. Because **WHERE** clauses are so common (and hence easy to read), the query **SELECT MyColumn FROM MyTable HAVING MyColumn > 5** is just going to confuse people, which is one of the main reasons *not* to use **HAVING** without a **GROUP BY** right next to it.

Other Data Summarization Methods

Now that you have learned how to use scalar and aggregate functions, along with the **GROUP BY** and **HAVING** clauses, you should be able to create fairly complex queries to manipulate and summarize your data. The last section of this chapter looks at a few additional summarization methods that can be used independently of scalar and aggregate functions. It looks briefly at T-SQL operators, and discusses a way to calculate aggregate functions at different grouping levels simultaneously. This section begins by looking at how to return only the **TOP** rows returned by a query.

Viewing Only The **TOP** Query Results

TOP is similar to **HAVING** insofar as it lets you restrict the amount of information returned from a query. **TOP** simply specifies how many rows you want SQL Server to return for a query. Specifying **TOP N** tells SQL Server to return only the first N rows of the query output. Similarly, specifying **TOP N PERCENT** tells SQL Server to return only the first N percent of the query output. Previously, you saw a query that used **HAVING** to return information about only those orders whose purchases totaled more than $10,000. The following example uses **TOP** instead of **HAVING**, and returns the largest one percent of the sales orders:

```
SELECT TOP 1 PERCENT
       OrderID,
       STR(SUM(UnitPrice * Quantity), 15, 2) AS [Total Sales]
```

```
FROM   [Order Details]
GROUP  BY OrderID
ORDER  BY SUM(UnitPrice * Quantity) DESC

Results:
OrderID     Total Sales
-------     -----------
10865       17250.00
11030       16321.90
10981       15810.00
10372       12281.20
10424       11493.20
10817       11490.70
10889       11380.00
10417       11283.20
10897       10835.24
```

Although this example uses the **TOP** keyword as an alternative to a **HAVING** clause in a vector aggregation query, **TOP** can actually be used in any query. Typically, using **TOP** makes sense only if the query also has an **ORDER BY** clause. For example, the following query returns information about the first five orders that were shipped on or after July 11, 1996:

```
SELECT TOP 5 OrderID, CustomerID, ShippedDate
FROM   Orders
WHERE  ShippedDate >= '7-11-1996'
ORDER  BY ShippedDate

Results:
OrderID     CustomerID    ShippedDate
-------     ----------    -----------
10252       SUPRD         1996-07-11 00:00:00.000
10250       HANAR         1996-07-12 00:00:00.000
10251       VICTE         1996-07-15 00:00:00.000
10255       RICSU         1996-07-15 00:00:00.000
10248       VINET         1996-07-16 00:00:00.000
```

It is also possible to use the **SET ROWCOUNT N** command in place of a **TOP N** clause to limit the number of rows returned by a query. The difference is that **TOP N** only takes effect for the single query it is included in, whereas **SET ROWCOUNT** affects all statements (not just **SELECT** statements) for the current connection until it is reset by issuing the statement **SET ROWCOUNT 0**.

Many of the examples in this chapter, and throughout the entire book, use T-SQL operators. To facilitate your familiarity with each of these operators, Table 9.14 lists all of them in a quick-study format.

Table 9.14 Transact-SQL operators.

Arithmetic Operator	Meaning	Example
+	Addition	4 + 3 = 7
-	Subtraction	12 - 8 = 4
*	Multiplication	4 * 8 = 32
/	Integer Division	8 / 3 = 2
%	Modulus (remainder)	10 % 7 = 3
Bitwise Operator	**Meaning**	**Example**
&	**AND**	6 & 5 = 4
|	**OR**	6|5 = 7
^	**EXCLUSIVE OR**	6 ^ 5 = 3
Comparison Operator	**Meaning**	**Example**
=	Equal to	5 = 7 returns **FALSE**
>	Greater than	5 > 7 returns **FALSE**
<	Less than	5 < 7 returns **TRUE**
>=	Greater than or equal to	5 >= 7 returns **FALSE**
<=	Less than or equal to	5 <= 7 returns **TRUE**
<>	Not equal to (equivalent to **!=**)	5 <> 7 returns **TRUE**
!=	Not equal to (equivalent to **<>**)	5 != 7 returns **TRUE**
!<	Not less than (equivalent to **>=**)	5 !< 7 returns **FALSE**
!>	Not greater than (equivalent to **<=**)	5 !> 7 returns **TRUE**
Logical Operator	**Syntax**	**Meaning**
ALL	**expression comparison_operator ALL (subquery)**	Used to compare an **expression** to the results of an entire **subquery**. Returns **TRUE** if, and only if, the comparison is true for all rows in the **subquery** result.
AND	**expr1 AND expr2**	Returns **TRUE** if both **expr1** and **expr2** are true.
ANY	**expression comparison_operator ANY (subquery)**	Used to compare an **expression** to the results of an entire **subquery**. Returns **TRUE** if the comparison is true for any row in the **subquery** result.

(continued)

Table 9.14 Transact-SQL operators *(continued)*.

Logical Operator	Syntax	Meaning
BETWEEN	**expr1 BETWEEN expr2 and expr3**	Returns **TRUE** if **expr2 <= expr1 <= expr2**.
EXISTS	**EXISTS (subquery)**	Returns **TRUE** if **subquery** returns at least one row.
IN	**expr1 IN (expr2, expr3, ..., expr_last)**	Returns **TRUE** if **expr1 = expr2 OR expr1 = expr3 OR ... OR expr1 = expr_last**.
LIKE	**expression LIKE 'pattern'**	Returns **TRUE** if **expression** can be matched to **pattern** using SQL Server wildcard matching.
NOT	**NOT expression**	Returns **TRUE** if **expression** is **FALSE**, and returns **FALSE** if **expression** is **TRUE**.
OR	**expr1 OR expr2**	Returns **TRUE** if either of **expr1** or **expr2** is **TRUE**.
SOME	**expression comparison_operator SOME (subquery)**	**SOME** is equivalent to **ANY**. Refer to the preceding definition of **ANY**.
Unary Operator	**Syntax**	**Meaning**
+	**+number**	**number * 1**
-	**-number**	**number * -1**
~	**~number**	**number** with every bit flipped from 0 to 1 or from 1 to 0

Summarizing Multiple Grouping Levels With **CUBE**

Consider the query in Listing 9.13, which retrieves information to summarize sales amounts by *ShipCountry* and *ProductID*. However, the query only considers orders shipped to Portugal, Spain, or Venezuela. Furthermore, the only *Order Detail* records used are those for Products 1, 2, and 4.

Listing 9.13 Retrieving select sales data.

```
SELECT ShipCountry, ProductID,
       STR(SUM(Quantity * UnitPrice), 15, 2) AS [Total Sales]
FROM   [Order Details] D
INNER  JOIN Orders O ON O.OrderID = D.OrderID
WHERE  ShipCountry IN ('Portugal', 'Spain', 'Venezuela')
AND    ProductID   IN (1, 2, 4)
GROUP  BY ShipCountry, ProductID
ORDER  BY ShipCountry, ProductID
```

```
Results:
ShipCountry     ProductID     Total Sales
-----------     ---------     -----------
Portugal        1               216.00
Portugal        4               598.40
Spain           1               180.00
Spain           2               380.00
Spain           4               422.40
Venezuela       1              1332.00
Venezuela       2              1254.00
```

This is just like the other vector aggregation queries earlier in the chapter. It enables you to characterize sales amounts by *Country* and *Product ID*. Suppose, for example, that you also want to know the total sales amount for Product ID 4 in all three countries combined. Perhaps you need to know the total sales for these products in each country.

Several possibilities exist of performing queries to return this data. You could run up a calculator program and manually add the other figures based on the results of this query. This approach would quickly become frustrating, so you might decide to write additional queries to provide the other answers you need. You would need one query grouping by *ShipCountry* and *ProductID*, another grouping by *ShipCountry* only, and a third grouping by *ProductID* only. You would also have to create a query to provide the grand total of the sales. That makes four queries, with the fourth one just being a scalar aggregate on the **SUM** of the amounts.

SQL Server 7 provides an easier way to handle all of these permutations. **CUBE** queries present the requested information at every possible level of grouping. You can demonstrate this by inserting the words **WITH CUBE** right after the **GROUP BY** clause, as in Listing 9.14. In this example, that means the result is the **SUM** of *Sales Amount* by *ShipCountry*, but the **SUM** by *ProductID* is also produced. Furthermore, **CUBE** groups the **SUM** by both *ShipCountry* and *ProductID* simultaneously (the way our original query did), as well as returning the **SUM** of *Sales Amount* regardless of any grouping (this is the grand total).

Listing 9.14 Using **CUBE** to see all possible grouping combinations.

```
SELECT ShipCountry, ProductID,
       STR(SUM(Quantity * UnitPrice), 15, 2) AS [Total Sales]
FROM   [Order Details] D
INNER  JOIN Orders O ON O.OrderID = D.OrderID
WHERE  ShipCountry IN ('Portugal', 'Spain', 'Venezuela')
AND    ProductID   IN (1, 2, 4)
GROUP  BY ShipCountry, ProductID
```

```
WITH  CUBE
ORDER  BY ShipCountry, ProductID

Results:
ShipCountry        ProductID      Total Sales
-----------        ---------      -----------
NULL               NULL           4382.80
NULL               1              1728.00
NULL               2              1634.00
NULL               4              1020.80
Portugal           NULL            814.40
Portugal           1               216.00
Portugal           4               598.40
Spain              NULL            982.40
Spain              1               180.00
Spain              2               380.00
Spain              4               422.40
Venezuela          NULL           2586.00
Venezuela          1              1332.00
Venezuela          2              1254.00
```

Interpreting CUBE Results

The first thing to notice about these results is that all the data from our original query is still there. For example, we can still see that sales of ProductID 4, totaling $422.40, was shipped to Spain. In addition to the previous results, we see additional rows. Each of these additional rows has at least one **NULL** value listed, although we know no **NULL** values were in the original data.

Look at the three rows output for Venezuela. Notice that the *Total Sales* values for *ProductID* 1 ($1,332) and *ProductID 2* ($1,254) add up to the *Total Sales* amount for the **NULL Product ID** ($2,586). The **NULL** values indicate grouping. In this query, any column that has a **NULL** in it is a grouping column for that row. So, for Venezuela, the total *Total Sales* for all products shipped is $2,586. Similarly, the total for *ProductID 2* shipped to all three countries is $1,634, which is found where *ShipCountry* is **NULL** (grouped) and *ProductID = 2*. The total for all products shipped in Spain is $982.40, which is found where *ShipCountry* = **'Spain'** and *ProductID* is **NULL** (grouped). Finally, the grand total of all the sales, *Total Sales* is $4,382.80. This grand total is found in the top row of the output, where both *ShipCountry* and *ProductID* have **NULL** values, indicating that both columns are being used as grouping columns.

ROLLUP—A Hierarchical Subset Of CUBE

Now look at the query in Listing 9.15. This query is identical to the **CUBE** query we just studied, except that the clause **WITH CUBE** has been replaced by **WITH ROLLUP**.

Listing 9.15 Using **ROLLUP** to see hierarchical grouping combinations.

```
SELECT ShipCountry, ProductID,
       STR(SUM(Quantity * UnitPrice), 15, 2) AS [Total Sales]
FROM   [Order Details] D
INNER  JOIN Orders O ON O.OrderID = D.OrderID
WHERE  ShipCountry IN ('Portugal', 'Spain', 'Venezuela')
AND    ProductID   IN (1, 2, 4)
GROUP  BY ShipCountry, ProductID
WITH   ROLLUP
ORDER  BY ShipCountry, ProductID

Results:
ShipCountry      ProductID      Total Sales
-----------      ---------      -----------
NULL             NULL           4382.80
Portugal         NULL            814.40
Portugal         1               216.00
Portugal         4               598.40
Spain            NULL            982.40
Spain            1               180.00
Spain            2               380.00
Spain            4               422.40
Venezuela        NULL           2586.00
Venezuela        1              1332.00
Venezuela        2              1254.00
```


You probably noticed right away that these results look similar to the results we got with **CUBE**. In fact, if you study the results carefully, you'll notice that every row that was returned by this **ROLLUP** query was also included in the **CUBE** output. The converse is not true: Not every row from the **CUBE** output is included in the **ROLLUP** output. **ROLLUP** returns a subset of the rows generated by **CUBE**. Let's look at how this subset is determined.

Recall that **CUBE** generates every possible level of grouping represented by the expressions in the **GROUP BY** clause. However, **ROLLUP** generates only those groupings that make sense hierarchically. So, out of the entire set of possible **GROUP BY** combinations, **ROLLUP** uses only those combinations in which no column is used for grouping unless every column following it in the **GROUP BY** clause is also used for that grouping. A query containing **GROUP BY A, B, C, WITH ROLLUP** generates groupings on **(A, B, C)**, on **(B, C)**, and on **(C)**. It does not produce any of the other groupings that **CUBE** will produce, such as **(A, C)**, **(A, B)**, or **(A)** alone, because no column can be used in a **ROLLUP** grouping unless every column following it in the **GROUP BY** clause is also used. This is how **ROLLUP** returns its information in an orderly, drill-down manner.

Is NULL Really NULL? Using The GROUPING Function

Consider the output of the **CUBE** query in Listing 9.16. You may notice that the first two rows in the result set both have **NULL** for *ShipCountry* and *ShipRegion*. It appears that *two* grand totals are in the result.

The problem is that **NULL** is a legitimate data value for this query. In our previous **CUBE** and **ROLLUP** queries, no **NULL** values were in the underlying data, so no ambiguity occurred when a **NULL** was seen in the query result—it always indicated grouping on that column. However, Venezuela is the only country in this query for which *ShipRegion* data is recorded. Spain and Portugal both list **NULL** for that column, because *ShipRegion* is not a relevant column for those countries. This explains the jumble of **NULL** values in the query output.

Listing 9.16 NULL values in CUBE output.

```
SELECT ShipCountry,
       ShipRegion,
       COUNT(*) AS [Count]
FROM   Orders
WHERE  ShipCountry IN ('Spain', 'Portugal', 'Venezuela')
GROUP  BY ShipCountry, ShipRegion
WITH   CUBE
ORDER  BY ShipCountry, ShipRegion

Results:
ShipCountry      ShipRegion        Count
-----------      ----------        -----
NULL             NULL              82
NULL             NULL              36
NULL             DF                2
NULL             Lara              14
NULL             Nueva Esparta     12
NULL             Táchira           18
Portugal         NULL              13
Portugal         NULL              13
Spain            NULL              23
Spain            NULL              23
Venezuela        NULL              46
Venezuela        DF                2
Venezuela        Lara              14
Venezuela        Nueva Esparta     12
Venezuela        Táchira           18
```

Another aggregate function can help us solve this problem. The **GROUPING** function takes as its only argument the name of an expression listed in a **GROUP**

BY clause. It returns 1 if that expression (usually a column name) is currently being used as a grouping expression, and it returns 0 otherwise.

The query in Listing 9.17 shows how the **GROUPING** function can help us make sense of the previous query. In the output, wherever column G1 is 1, *ShipCountry* is a grouping column. Wherever column G2 is 1, *ShipRegion* is a grouping column. Using these results, it is easier to see, for example, that the true grand total of *Count* is 82, whereas the total of *Count* for **NULL** *ShipRegion* values is 36.

Listing 9.17 Using the **GROUPING** function to detect bonafide **NULL** values.

```
SELECT ShipCountry, GROUPING(ShipCountry) AS G1,
       ShipRegion,  GROUPING(ShipRegion)  AS G2,
       COUNT(*) AS [Count]
FROM   Orders
WHERE  ShipCountry IN ('Spain', 'Portugal', 'Venezuela')
GROUP  BY ShipCountry, ShipRegion
WITH   CUBE
ORDER  BY ShipCountry, ShipRegion

Results:
ShipCountry   G1   ShipRegion      G2   Count
-----------   --   ----------      --   -----
NULL          1    NULL            1    82
NULL          1    NULL            0    36
NULL          1    DF              0    2
NULL          1    Lara            0    14
NULL          1    Nueva Esparta   0    12
NULL          1    Táchira         0    18
Portugal      0    NULL            0    13
Portugal      0    NULL            1    13
Spain         0    NULL            0    23
Spain         0    NULL            1    23
Venezuela     0    NULL            1    46
Venezuela     0    DF              0    2
Venezuela     0    Lara            0    14
Venezuela     0    Nueva Esparta   0    12
Venezuela     0    Táchira         0    18
```

Although this is an improvement, the output still isn't in a very reader-friendly format. We can improve the situation somewhat by combining the **GROUPING** function output with the **CASE** function studied earlier. By using **CASE**, we can print the label **'(TOTAL)'** for any grouping columns and leave the rest of the data unchanged. This technique, which is implemented in Listing 9.18, noticeably improves the readability of the result set. Now, you can easily see that Portugal had 13 orders for which the *Shipping Region* was **NULL**, and Spain had 23 such orders. Venezuela had 46 orders, none of which had a **NULL** *Shipping Region*. The grand total of orders is easily identified as 82, and the value for *Shipping Country* clearly was never **NULL**.

Listing 9.18 Combining **GROUPING** with **CASE** to label grouping columns.

```
SELECT CASE GROUPING(ShipCountry)
            WHEN 1 THEN '(TOTAL)'
            ELSE ShipCountry
       END  AS  [Shipping Country],
       CASE GROUPING(ShipRegion)
            WHEN 1 THEN '(TOTAL)'
            ELSE ShipRegion
       END  AS  [Shipping Region],
       COUNT(*) AS [Count]
FROM   Orders
WHERE  ShipCountry IN ('Spain', 'Portugal', 'Venezuela')
GROUP  BY ShipCountry, ShipRegion
WITH   CUBE
ORDER  BY GROUPING(ShipCountry), ShipCountry,
          GROUPING(ShipRegion),  ShipRegion

Results:
Shipping Country   Shipping Region   Count
----------------   ---------------   -----
Portugal           NULL              13
Portugal           (TOTAL)           13
Spain              NULL              23
Spain              (TOTAL)           23
Venezuela          DF                2
Venezuela          Lara              14
Venezuela          Nueva Esparta     12
Venezuela          Táchira           18
Venezuela          (TOTAL)           46
(TOTAL)            NULL              36
(TOTAL)            DF                2
(TOTAL)            Lara              14
(TOTAL)            Nueva Esparta     12
(TOTAL)            Táchira           18
(TOTAL)            (TOTAL)           82
```

Chapter Summary

In this chapter, you learned T-SQL techniques that take you beyond simple row-and-column queries. Using the methods in this chapter, you can write queries that accurately *derive* data that is not actually *stored* in the database. The key concepts that you learned in this chapter are the following:

- *Scalar functions* are Transact-SQL functions that act on single values and allow you to transform data from one value to another. Scalar functions can be grouped into several categories. Brief descriptions of these categories follow.
- *Configuration functions* return information about SQL Server configuration. **@@SERVERNAME**, **@@DBTS**, and **@@SPID** are examples of configuration functions.
- The *cursor functions* **@@CURSOR_ROWS**, **@@FETCH_STATUS**, and **CURSOR_STATUS** assist you in processing cursors. Cursors enable you to manipulate query results one row at a time. Cursors are covered in greater detail in Chapter 8.
- *Date and time functions,* such as **GETDATE**, **DATEADD**, and **DATEPART**, enable you to retrieve the system time and manipulate **DATETIME** values.
- T-SQL provides a library of *mathematical functions,* such as **PI**, **SIN**, and **POWER**, to assist you in performing calculations.
- *Metadata functions* give you information about the database objects themselves rather than information about the data they contain. Examples of metadata functions include **COLUMNPROPERTY**, **DB_ID**, and **OBJECT_NAME**.
- *Security functions,* such as **IS_MEMBER**, **SUSER_SNAME**, and **USER_ID**, help you interrogate the identity and privileges of SQL Server login accounts and database users.
- Manipulation of the alphanumeric data is accomplished by using the *string functions*. Some of the more useful string functions include **LEN**, **SUBSTRING**, **PATINDEX**, **LTRIM/RTRIM**, and **UPPER/LOWER**.
- The *system functions* have a variety of unique and useful roles. Examples from this diverse group of functions include **HOST_NAME**, **ISNULL**, **CASE**, **CAST/CONVERT**, **@@ROWCOUNT**, and **@@ERROR**.
- *System statistical functions* can be used to help perform basic performance diagnoses, and include functions such as **@@CPU_BUSY**, **@@PACKET_ERRORS**, and **@@TOTAL_WRITE**.
- The *text and image functions* **TEXTVALID** and **TEXTPTR** enable you to establish valid pointers into **TEXT**, **NTEXT**, and **IMAGE** columns, so that you can manipulate them by using functions such as **READTEXT**.
- *Aggregate functions* are used to manipulate groups of values rather than the single values manipulated by scalar functions. Examples of aggregate functions include **SUM**, **COUNT**, and **MAX**.
- *Scalar aggregation* is the term used to describe the use of an aggregate function to summarize a column for an entire result set. When scalar aggregation is used, no **GROUP BY** clause exists. Because of this, a scalar aggregation query has only one row of output.

- The **GROUP BY** clause is used by a *vector aggregation* query to break a result set into subgroups before calculating aggregation functions. Because aggregation is reported for each subgroup defined by the **GROUP BY** clause, a vector aggregation query can have more than one row of output.
- The **HAVING** clause restricts the rows output by an aggregation query. Its effect on groups is similar to the effect of a **WHERE** clause on individual rows in a nonaggregation query.
- The **CUBE** and **ROLLUP** keywords allow the simultaneous presentation of multiple grouping levels in an aggregation query. **CUBE** calculates all aggregation levels that can possibly be generated by the expressions in the **GROUP BY** clause. **ROLLUP** calculates these aggregations in a hierarchical way. Out of all the possible groupings that **CUBE** uses, **ROLLUP** uses only those in which no column is used for grouping unless every column following it in the **GROUP BY** clause is also used for that grouping.
- The **TOP N** and **TOP N PERCENT** clauses give you an easy way to restrict the number of rows returned by a query.

Review Questions

1. Which of the following will result in a query returning only the first five rows of *Employees*? (Choose all correct answers.)
   a. Running **SET ROWCOUNT 5** before running **SELECT * FROM Employees**
   b. Running **SET ROWCOUNT = 5** before running **SELECT * FROM Employees**
   c. Running **SELECT FIRST 5 * FROM Employees**
   d. Running **SELECT TOP 5 * FROM Employees**

2. What information is returned by the query **SELECT @@CONNECTIONS**?
   a. The total number of connections over the history of this SQL Server.
   b. The total number of connections currently in use by the current SQL Server login ID.
   c. The total number of attempted connections since SQL Server was last started.
   d. The maximum number of concurrent user connections SQL Server is configured to allow.

3. Which of the following queries will return the current date and time? (Choose all correct answers.)
   a. **SELECT @@DBTS**
   b. **SELECT DATEADD (day, 0, GETDATE( ))**

   c. **SELECT CURRENT_TIMESTAMP**
   d. **SELECT @@NOW**

4. Which of the following will return the SQL Server Process ID for the current connection?
   a. **SELECT @@CONNECTION**
   b. **SELECT @@SPID**
   c. **SELECT SUSER_SID( )**
   d. **SELECT SUSER_SPID( )**

5. You want to find out whether the characters **'SPOT'** are contained anywhere inside a variable name **@GoodDog**. Which of the following function calls will help you to determine this?
   a. **SELECT CHARINDEX ('SPOT', @GoodDog, 1)**
   b. **SELECT PATINDEX ('SPOT', @GoodDog)**
   c. **SELECT DIFFERENCE ('SPOT', @GoodDog)**
   d. **SELECT SUBSTRING (@GoodDog, 'SPOT', 1)**

6. Which of the following returns the value of your username inside the current database? (Choose all correct answers.)
   a. **SELECT SUSER_SNAME( )**
   b. **SELECT USER_NAME( )**
   c. **SELECT USER**
   d. **SELECT SUSER_NAME( )**

7. You want to know how to write a query that will tell you whether a certain column accepts **NULL** values. However, you can't remember what T-SQL functions might help you to do this. Because you can't remember this information, which category of functions from *Books Online* is the best place to start looking?
   a. Configuration functions
   b. Metadata functions
   c. String functions
   d. System functions

8. Which of the following functions is the first function to use if you want to put error handling into your T-SQL code?
   a. **FORMATMESSAGE**
   b. **RAISERROR**
   c. **@@ROWCOUNT**
   d. **@@ERROR**

9. You have written a query that uses scalar aggregation and includes the function call **SUM (SalesAmount)**. Which of the following statements is true about your query?
   a. The results from your query will contain only one row.
   b. The results from your query may contain any number of rows.
   c. Your query will cause an error because **SUM** cannot be used with scalar aggregation.
   d. Your query will return **SUM** information for the *SalesAmount* column for several different grouping levels.

10. What is the purpose of the **GROUPING** keyword in T-SQL?
    a. To enable you to specify the columns by which the summarized data will be grouped.
    b. To tell SQL Server that a query should use vector aggregation.
    c. To declare, at table-creation time, which columns are eligible for grouping in aggregation queries.
    d. To report on a row-by-row basis in the query output whether a specific column was used as a grouping expression.

11. Which of the following keywords helps you restrict the number of groups included in the output of an aggregation query?
    a. **HAVING**
    b. **ROLLUP**
    c. **GROUPING**
    d. **CUBE**

12. Which clause is always present in a vector aggregation query but not in a scalar aggregation query?
    a. **SELECT**
    b. **FROM**
    c. **WHERE**
    d. **GROUP BY**
    e. **HAVING**

13. You write a query that returns the number of orders by *CustomerID* and *SalespersonID* with the **ROLLUP** option. The first row in the output tells you the number of orders sold by salesperson **'John Smith'** to all customers. Which of the following is a true statement about this row of output?
    a. **GROUPING(CustomerID) = 1 and GROUPING(SalespersonID) = 1**

b. **GROUPING(CustomerID) = 1 and GROUPING(SalespersonID) = 0**
c. **GROUPING(CustomerID) = 0 and GROUPING(SalespersonID) = 1**
d. **GROUPING(CustomerID) = 0 and GROUPING(SalespersonID) = 0**

14. It is possible to use scalar aggregation and vector aggregation in the same query.
    a. True
    b. False

15. Only a SQL Server administrator can use the system functions.
    a. True
    b. False

16. What is returned by the function **NEWID ( )**?
    a. The object ID SQL Server will use the next time that a database object is created.
    b. A new **UNIQUEIDENTIFIER** data value.
    c. Timestamp information for the last transaction logged in the database.
    d. The login ID SQL Server will use the next time that a new SQL Server login is created.

17. Which of the following is *not* a valid data type?
    a. **TEXT**
    b. **NTEXT**
    c. **IMAGE**
    d. **NIMAGE**

18. The language setting used by SQL Server is stored internally within a database and cannot be changed after the database is created.
    a. True
    b. False

19. The value of the **@@DBTS** function will not necessarily change after every **INSERT**, **UPDATE**, or **DELETE** statement executed within the database.
    a. True
    b. False

20. SQL Server lets you write nested procedure calls, but due to the dynamic nature of the nesting, it cannot tell you at runtime whether a procedure call is nested.
    a. True
    b. False

HANDS-ON PROJECTS

Susan has reached the hardest part of the project she has encountered so far. She knows that she is weakest in her ability to summarize data from the database. She decides the best way to tackle the task is to create some rather complex form letters that have been requested by the design team.

Project 9.1

In this project, you will develop a form letter that will be sent to Northwind's employees. This requires creating two tables. The first table, *Template*, stores the sentences in a generic style, along with the order in which the sentences will appear when the letter is printed. To create this table, type and execute the following **CREATE TABLE** statement in the SQL Server Query Analyzer:

```
CREATE TABLE Template
    (SentenceNum INT,
     Sentence    VARCHAR(300)
    )
```

Now, create the second table by running the next **CREATE TABLE** statement. This table, named *Letters*, will hold the sentences in their personalized form, along with the *EmployeeID* the sentence has been personalized for and the order of the sentence in that employee's letter.

```
CREATE TABLE Letters
    (SentenceNum INT,
     EmployeeID INT,
     Sentence VARCHAR(300)
    )
```

Next, you need to populate the *Template* table. To do this, type and execute the following **DECLARE**, **SELECT**, and **INSERT** statements using the Query Analyzer. Notice that many of these sentences have *text markers* that will be replaced by personalized information for each employee.

```
DECLARE @BlankLine CHAR(1)
SELECT  @BlankLine= ' '
```

```
INSERT INTO Template (SentenceNum, Sentence)
VALUES (1, 'Dear [Greeting Name],')

INSERT INTO Template (SentenceNum, Sentence)
VALUES (2, @BlankLine)

INSERT INTO Template (SentenceNum, Sentence)
VALUES (3, 'We at Northwind are proud to have you working '
        +  'with us as [Job Title]. ')
INSERT INTO Template (SentenceNum, Sentence)
VALUES (4, 'Your enthusiasm in the office has not gone '
        +  'unnoticed by [Boss]. ')

INSERT INTO Template (SentenceNum, Sentence)
VALUES
    (5, 'Your efforts have helped us here at Northwind to be '
    +  'extremely profitable over the past year. ')

INSERT INTO Template (SentenceNum, Sentence)
VALUES
    (6, 'In recognition of a job well done, we will be giving '
    +  'you a DOUBLE BONUS at your next review, which is '
    +  'scheduled to be on or about [Review Date]! ')

INSERT INTO Template (SentenceNum, Sentence)
VALUES
     (7, 'Keep up the good work, and start planning what you will '
     +  'do with the extra cash!')

INSERT INTO Template (SentenceNum, Sentence)
VALUES (8, @BlankLine)

INSERT INTO Template (SentenceNum, Sentence)
VALUES (9, 'Sincerely,')

INSERT INTO Template (SentenceNum, Sentence)
VALUES (10, 'The Northwind Management Team')

INSERT INTO Template (SentenceNum, Sentence)
VALUES (11, @BlankLine)
```

At this point, if you were to execute **SELECT * FROM Template**, you would see the following 11 rows. By running this query, you can get an idea of what the final letters will look like.

```
SELECT * FROM Template

Results (text is wrapped for display purposes):
SentenceNum  Sentence
-----------  -----------------------------------------
1            Dear [Greeting Name],
2
3            We at Northwind are proud to have you
             working with us as [Job Title].
4            Your enthusiasm in the office has not
             gone unnoticed by [Boss].
5            Your efforts have helped us here at
             Northwind to be extremely profitable
             over the past year.
6            In recognition of a job well done, we
             will be giving you a DOUBLE BONUS at
             your next review, which is
             scheduled to be on or about [Review Date]!
7            Keep up the good work, and start planning
             what you will do with the extra cash.
8
9            Sincerely,
10           The Northwind Management Team
11
```

The remainder of this exercise consists of storing personalized versions of these sentences for each employee in the *Letters* table. Let's look at how each text marker could be personalized by using T-SQL.

The sentences that need to be personalized are sentences one, three, four, and six. Sentence number one contains the text marker **[Greeting Name]**. To personalize this sentence for each employee and insert the personalized sentence into *Letters*, run the following query:

```
INSERT   INTO Letters
         (SentenceNum, EmployeeID, Sentence)
SELECT   SentenceNum, EmployeeID,
REPLACE  (Sentence, '[Greeting Name]',
         TitleOfCourtesy + ' '
              + FirstName + ' ' + LastName)
FROM     Template, Employees
WHERE    SentenceNum = 1
```

Notice how the **REPLACE** function is used to replace the text marker with the employee's title of courtesy and name.

You may have noticed that this query does *not* join the two tables that it is querying. Although this would usually represent a bad mistake, in this case, it is acceptable because the query selects only one row from *Template* **(SentenceNum = 1)**, so the cross-join results in one row being inserted into *Letters* for each *Employee*, which is the desired result.

Type and execute the following **INSERT** statements to personalize the other text markers:

```
INSERT   INTO Letters
        (SentenceNum, EmployeeID, Sentence)
SELECT   SentenceNum, EmployeeID,
REPLACE (Sentence, '[Job Title]',
         CASE
            WHEN UPPER(SUBSTRING (Title, 1, 1))
                 IN ('A', 'E','I', 'O', 'U')
            THEN 'an ' + Title
            ELSE 'a '  + Title
         END)
FROM     Template, Employees
WHERE    SentenceNum = 3

INSERT   INTO Letters
          (SentenceNum, EmployeeID, Sentence)
SELECT   SentenceNum, Emp.EmployeeID,
REPLACE (Sentence, '[Boss]',
         CASE
            WHEN Emp.ReportsTo IS NULL
            THEN 'the Board of Directors'
            ELSE 'your supervisor, '
                + Boss.TitleOfCourtesy + ' '
                + Boss.FirstName + ' '
                + Boss.LastName
         END)
FROM     Template,
        (Employees Emp LEFT JOIN Employees Boss
         ON Emp.ReportsTo = Boss.EmployeeID)
WHERE    SentenceNum = 4

INSERT   INTO Letters
           (SentenceNum, EmployeeID, Sentence)
SELECT   SentenceNum, EmployeeID,
REPLACE    (Sentence, '[Review Date]',
```

```
         DATENAME(Month, HireDate) + ' ' +
         DATENAME(Day, HireDate))
FROM     Template, Employees
WHERE    SentenceNum = 6
```

Make sure that you understand the sections of these queries that are highlighted. The first of these sections shows that a **CASE** statement is being used to determine whether the job title begins with a vowel. If it does, it is preceded by *a.* If it does not, it is preceded by *an.*

The second highlighted section shows that to get the title and name for the employee's boss, we must join the *Employees* table to itself. One copy of the table *(Emp)* is used for looking up employee information, and the other *(Boss)* is used to look up supervisor information. A **LEFT JOIN** is used so that rows are returned even for employees who do not have supervisors. We detect this situation with yet another **CASE** function, which plugs in a reference to the *Board of Directors* for any employee who does not have a supervisor.

The third and final highlighted section shows how we calculate the month and date of the employee's review by using **DATENAME** to retrieve the month and date of their hire date.

Finally, we can insert all the other sentences into *Letters* simultaneously, because they do not require any customization. To do so, run this query:

```
/* insert rows that do not require any replacement: */
INSERT   INTO Letters
            (SentenceNum, EmployeeID, Sentence)
SELECT   SentenceNum, EmployeeID, Sentence
FROM     Template, Employees
WHERE    SentenceNum IN
            (2, 5, 7, 8, 9, 10, 11)
```

Now, we are ready to print the letters. We have created a template for the letters and stored it in the *Templates* table. Next, we stored one copy of each template sentence for each employee in the *Letters* table, personalized if necessary. Now, we simply retrieve the letters by using the following query:

```
/* print the letters: */
SELECT Sentence AS [Letters]
FROM   Letters
ORDER  BY EmployeeID, SentenceNum

Results (text is wrapped for display purposes):
Letters
-----------------------
```

```
Dear Ms. Nancy Davolio,

We at Northwind are proud to have you working with
us as a Sales Representative. Your enthusiasm in the
office has not gone unnoticed by your supervisor, Dr.
Andrew Fuller. Your efforts have helped us here at
Northwind to be extremely profitable over the past year.
In recognition of a job well done, we will be giving
you a DOUBLE BONUS at your next review, which is
scheduled to be on or about May 1. Keep up the good
work, and start planning what you will do with the
extra cash.

Sincerely,
The Northwind Management Team

...
Dear Ms. Anne Dodsworth,

We at Northwind are proud to have you working with
us as a Sales Representative. Your enthusiasm in
the office has not gone unnoticed by your supervisor,
Mr. Steven Buchanan. Your efforts have helped us here
at Northwind to be extremely profitable over
the past year. In recognition of a job well done,
we will be giving you a DOUBLE BONUS at your next
review, which is scheduled to be on or about November
15. Keep up the good work, and start planning what you
will do with the extra cash.

Sincerely,
The Northwind Management Team
```

So far, the form letter project has worked out well. Now, Susan needs to create a report that determines the top suppliers, ranks them, and displays the ones who are eligible for special incentives.

Project 9.2

Your company has begun a promotion with its suppliers whereby the suppliers will be ranked by your company's total sales of its products. The suppliers who place in the top 25 percent of this ranking will receive special incentives and other offers.

The following code determines which suppliers are to receive the special incentives, and also displays your total sales of their products. Type and execute this query in Query Analyzer and verify your results against this output.

```
SELECT  TOP 25 PERCENT
        CompanyName Supplier,
        STR(SUM(D.Quantity * D.UnitPrice), 15, 2)
        AS Sales
FROM  (([Order Details] D
INNER JOIN Products   P
       ON (D.ProductID = P.ProductID))
INNER JOIN Suppliers  S
        ON (P.SupplierID = S.SupplierID))
GROUP BY CompanyName
ORDER BY Sales DESC

Results:
Supplier                            Sales
--------------------------------    ---------
Aux joyeux ecclésiastiques          163135.00
Plutzer Lebensmittelgroßmärkte AG   155946.55
Gai pâturage                        126582.00
Pavlova, Ltd.                       115386.05
G'day, Mate                          69636.60
Forêts d'érables                     66266.70
Pasta Buttini s.r.l.                 52929.00
Formaggi Fortini s.r.l.              51082.50
```

Notice that the *Order Details* table must be joined to both the *Products* table and the *Suppliers* table to retrieve this information, because although the *Order Details* table has the information needed to derive sales amounts, it does not have supplier information. It only has the *ProductID* for that order line, which must be used to look up the *SupplierID* in the *Products* table. However, you still aren't quite done. Because the requirements state that you are to list the suppliers by name, you must use the *SupplierID* from the *Products* table to look up the *Company Name* in the *Suppliers* table. Finally, the **TOP 25 PERCENT** phrase, combined with the **ORDER BY** clause that puts the largest sales amounts at the top, is the key to retrieving only the most successful 25 percent of our suppliers.

CHAPTER TEN

VIEWS

After Reading This Chapter And Completing The Exercises, You Will Be Able To:

- ➤ Define view restrictions
- ➤ Create a view
- ➤ Alter a view
- ➤ Drop a view
- ➤ Query data through a view
- ➤ Modify data through a view
- ➤ Describe the system views and their purpose

Views have been around in most Relational Database Management Systems for many years. Microsoft has enhanced the use of views in version 7 with many new features. In this chapter we'll explore what views are and how they are used.

Database Views

A *view* is a database object that stores a query and behaves like a table. A view contains a set of columns and rows. The difference between a table and a view is that the data accessed through a view is stored in one or more tables being referenced by a **SELECT** statement. This is why a view is sometimes referred to as a *virtual table*. The table or tables that are being referenced by a view is known as a *base tables*.

The data returned by a view is produced dynamically every time the view is referenced. A view can also be used to update an underlying base table. You can issue **INSERT**, **UPDATE**, and **DELETE** statements against a view, and the base table being referenced by the view will be updated.

When a view references more than one table, the **INSERT**, **UPDATE**, and **DELETE** statements can affect only one base table.

It is important to mention that a view can also reference other views and tables from the current database or even from a different SQL Server database. A view can also reference data from different RDBMS (such as Oracle, DB2, Access, etc.) if the view is defined using a *distributed* query.

SQL Server 7 has two types of views:

- Information schema views
- User views

Information schema views are system-supplied views used to retrieve information from the system tables.

You can create *user views* with the **CREATE VIEW** command or with the Create View Wizard. A good practice to get into is to always test your **SELECT** statements before creating a view in order to ensure the correct result set is returned. The **SELECT** statement that defines the view can return:

- All columns and rows from base tables.
- A subset of columns and/or rows from base tables.
- The result of a union of two or more base tables.
- The result of a join between two or more base tables.
- Summary information from base tables.
- A subset of columns and/or rows from other views.
- A subset of data resulting from a **UNION**, **JOIN**, or data summarization from views and base tables.

Use Of A View

Using a view can offer several advantages. Individual business situations will determine how and when to use views to help with the solution of a business's needs. Some of the advantages offered by views include the following:

- Focusing data for users
- Providing a security mechanism
- Shielding the complexity of data manipulation from the users
- Organizing the importing and export of data
- Working with partitioned data across multiple tables

Focus The Data For Users And As A Security Mechanism

You can create views to show only the data that a user is interested in or that a user is allowed to see. You can accomplish this with views that select only the specific columns the users need access to. For example, suppose an *Employee* table contains the name, address, work phone, department, and salary of all employees of the company. You wish to allow everyone in the company to view all employees' names and display their work phone number, but you don't want everyone to know the salary that each employee is earning. To solve this problem you can create a view that returns only the information required. Listing 10.1 demonstrates how to create a view that restricts the columns retrieved from a table.

Listing 10.1 Creating a view that restricts the columns retrieved from a table.

```
CREATE VIEW vw_AllEmployees AS
SELECT LastName, FirstName, WorkPhone FROM Employees
```

Now suppose that you want the managers to be able to see the salary for the employees of only their department. Creating a view that restricts the users to specific rows can accomplish this goal. Listing 10.2 demonstrates how to create a view that restricts the rows retrieved from a table.

Listing 10.2 Creating a view that restricts the rows returned from a table.

```
CREATE VIEW vw_EmployeesIS AS
SELECT * FROM Employees WHERE DepartmentID = 100
```

You can also create a view that restricts the columns and rows returned at the same time. Restricting the columns and/or rows serves as a way to focus on important data. A view also serves as a security mechanism because you can limit the access to sensitive data.

You can extend the use of views as a security mechanism by granting permissions to the views instead of granting permissions to the base table or tables. This is true as long as the owner of the table and of the view is the same. This works because the *ownership chain* of the objects has not been broken.

In the case where the table owner and the view owner are not the same, permission must be given to both database objects. SQL Server always checks for permissions when the ownership chain is broken.

Shield The Complexity Of Data Manipulation

Once you have fine-tuned a complex query (**JOIN** query, summary query, or lengthy **SELECT** statement) you can define a view using the query. Using the view, you liberate the users from having to memorize and retype all the query conditions each time. For example, imagine that you frequently query the *Northwind* database to find out which orders are due in three days that have not already been shipped. Instead of having to write a query each time you wish to access this data, you can create the following view:

```
CREATE VIEW vw_DueIn3Days AS
SELECT o.OrderID, c.CompanyName, o.RequiredDate,
od.ProductID, p.ProductName, od.Quantity
FROM Orders o
       INNER JOIN Customers c
ON c.CustomerID = o.CustomerID
       INNER JOIN [Order Details] od
ON od.OrderID = o.OrderID
       INNER JOIN Products p
ON p.ProductID = od.ProductID
WHERE o.ShippedDate IS NULL
AND   o.RequiredDate > DATEADD( dd, 3, GETDATE() )
```

and you can use the view as follows:

```
SELECT * FROM vw_DueIn3Days
```

Creating views for queries that summarize data from base tables is also a common practice. For example, suppose you need to know the top 10 products sold at your firm. You can create the following view:

```
CREATE VIEW vw_Top10Products AS
     SELECT TOP 10 p.ProductName, SUM(od.Quantity)
AS [Total Quantity]
```

```
     FROM [Order Details] od
          INNER JOIN Products p
ON p.ProductID = od.ProductID
     GROUP BY p.ProductName
     ORDER BY [Total Quantity] DESC
```

Using views also allows developers to change the database design without having to retrain the users on the table design. A developer can normalize or denormalize tables and change the **SELECT** statement that defines the view without affecting the users' perception of the database. This is the purpose of the *information schema views* introduced by Microsoft in SQL Server 7. If database developers and administrators always query the information schema views to obtain system information, they will not have to retrain themselves on the contents of the system tables if they change in future releases.

Organize Data Import And Export

Views are often used to export data to other databases or applications. Suppose you have another DBMS that needs to obtain data from one of your databases. You can create a view that is based on a **SELECT** statement that joins two or more tables and restricts the columns and rows returned. Then you can export the data using the BCP utility. In the same way, data can be imported into a view using the BCP utility or the **BULK INSERT** statement.

Working With Partitioned Data Across Multiple Tables

It is often convenient to split a large table into subtables. In this case, using a view to display data makes it possible to retrieve data as a single result set. For example, imagine that you have a table that tracks sales per state, and that the table has millions of rows. You may want to create a table per state and specify a **CHECK** constraint on the *Partition* column (is this case, the *State* column) as follows:

```
CREATE TABLE [Sales Florida] (
StoreID integer NOT NULL
CONSTRAINT PK_SalesFL PRIMARY KEY,
Month integer NOT NULL
CHECK (Month BETWEEN 1 and 12),
Year integer NOT NULL,
Sales money NOT NULL,
State char(2) NOT NULL
CONSTRAINT CK_StateFL
CHECK (State = 'FL')
)
GO
```

You can now define a single view that uses **UNION ALL** to retrieve data from the *State* tables as follows:

```
CREATE VIEW vw_Sales AS
SELECT * FROM [Sales California]
UNION ALL
SELECT * FROM [Sales Florida]
UNION ALL
.. .. ..
GO
```

If a search condition on the partition column is specified when referencing the view, the query optimizer uses the **CHECK** constraint to determine which table to select from.

Creating A View

You can create a view with the **CREATE VIEW** command or by using the Create View Wizard. You can create a view only in the current database, but the tables or views that are being referenced by the **SELECT** statement can reside in other databases that reside in the current server or in other servers.

You can also create views through the Enterprise Manager.

A view name must be unique within a database, and cannot be the same as the name of any other tables in that database. The first character of a view name must be a letter as defined in the Unicode Standard 2 or one of the following symbols: _, @. If the view name has embedded spaces, you must delimit it with brackets, such as, [view name]. A view name cannot be a Transact-SQL reserved word.

If the column names of a view are omitted, the columns in the view will inherit the names of the columns in the **SELECT** statement. Additionally, the columns of a view inherit the same data types as the columns that they reference in the **SELECT** statement.

View Definition

A view definition can be viewed with the **sp_helptext <object_name>** system stored procedure. A view's dependencies (base tables on which the view depends and objects that depend on the view, such as stored procedures, triggers, and other views) can be viewed with the **sp_depends <object_name>** system stored procedure.

The definition of a view (such as the **SELECT** statement) is saved in the *Syscomments* system table. The name of the view is stored in the *Sysobjects* system table, the columns defined on the views are stored in the *Syscolumns* system table, and the view dependencies are stored in the *Sysdepends* system table.

Restrictions On Views

Before defining a view you should keep in mind the following restrictions that apply to a view:

- Rules, defaults, and triggers cannot be associated with a view.
- An index cannot be created on a view.
- A view cannot reference a temporary table.
- A view cannot reference more than 1,024 columns.
- The **CREATE VIEW** statement has to be the only statement in the batch that creates the view.
- SQL Server 7 allows 32 levels of nested views.
- The **SELECT** statement that defines the view cannot have an **ORDER BY**, **COMPUTE**, or **COMPUTE BY** clause.
- The **SELECT** statement that defines the view cannot have the **INTO** keyword.

Also keep in mind that the name of a column in the view has to be specified if:

- It is derived from an arithmetic expression, a built-in function, or a constant.
- It has the same name as the name of another column of the joined table(s).
- You want to give a more descriptive name to the column.

Create View Command

The **CREATE VIEW** command is used to define a view. The syntax is as follows:

```
CREATE VIEW <view_name> [(<col1> [,...<coln>])]
[WITH ENCRYPTION]
AS
<select_statement>
[WITH CHECK OPTION]
```

A name for a column in a view can be defined specifying **<col1>,...<coln>**. If you have four columns in your view and you need to specify a name for one of the columns, you must specify the name for the other columns as well (see Listing 10.3). You can also define a column name in the **SELECT** statement.

To protect the definition of a sensitive view, use the **WITH ENCRYPTION** clause. This clause encrypts the entries of the *Syscomments* table that contain the definition (**SELECT** statement) of the view. When you use the **WITH ENCRYPTION** clause, users, including the owner of the view, cannot obtain the view definition (see Listing 10.4).

A statement such as **SELECT * FROM** *Orders* is a valid **SELECT** statement that defines a view. Remember that the **SELECT** statement can query one or more base tables and/or views and that it can restrict the columns and rows returned.

Using the **WITH CHECK OPTION** enforces all **INSERT** and **UPDATE** statements executed against a view to fall within the criteria specified in the **SELECT** statement that defines the view. In other words, the **WITH CHECK OPTION** prevents inserting or updating data through the view that will disappear from the scope of the view (see Listing 10.5). Let's examine this clause using an example. Suppose that the **SELECT** statement that defines the **vw_OrderEmpl_5** view is the following:

```
SELECT OrderID, EmployeeID, OrderDate
FROM Orders
WHERE EmployeeID = 5
```

By default, if the view was created without specifying the **WITH CHECK OPTION**, the following **INSERT** statement will work:

```
INSERT INTO vw_OrderEmpl_5 VALUES( 6, getdate() )
```

If the view was created using the **WITH CHECK OPTION** clause, the statement will give an error because the record added does not meet the criteria **EmployeeID = 5**.

Listing 10.3 Two ways of assigning a name to a column in a view.

```
CREATE VIEW vw_NameColumn1
(OrderID, ProductName, UnitPrice, Quantity, Price)
AS
SELECT
od.OrderID, p.ProductName, od.UnitPrice, od.Quantity,
       (od.UnitPrice * od.Quantity)
FROM [Order Details] od
INNER JOIN Products p
      ON od.ProductID = p.ProductID
WHERE od.Discount = 0
GO

CREATE VIEW vw_NameColumn2
AS
```

```
SELECT
od.OrderID, p.ProductName, od.UnitPrice, od.Quantity,
       (od.UnitPrice * od.Quantity) AS Price
FROM [Order Details] od
INNER JOIN Products p
ON od.ProductID = p.ProductID
WHERE od.Discount = 0
GO
```

In both cases you must give a name to the column derived from the arithmetic expression (**od.UnitPrice * od.Quantity**). In the first **CREATE VIEW** statement, all column names have to be specified. In the second **CREATE VIEW** statement, the column name is assigned in the **SELECT** statement.

Listing 10.4 Encrypting the definition of a view.

```
CREATE VIEW vw_ProductCategory WITH ENCRYPTION
AS
SELECT p.ProductName, c.CategoryName
FROM Products p INNER JOIN Categories c ON p.CategoryID = c.CategoryID
GO

sp_helptext vw_ProductCategory
GO

The object comments have been encrypted.
```


Listing 10.5 Using the **WITH CHECK OPTION** clause to ensure that the data inserted or updated adheres to the criteria set in the **SELECT** statement.

```
CREATE VIEW vw_Employees_1994
AS
SELECT EmployeeID, LastName, FirstName, HireDate
FROM Employees
WHERE HireDate BETWEEN '1994-01-01' AND '1994-12-31'
WITH CHECK OPTION
GO

INSERT INTO vw_Employees_1994
VALUES ( 'Rivas Sanchez', 'Josefina', '1999-03-20' )
GO

Server: Msg 550, Level 16, State 1, Line 1
The attempted insert or update failed because the target view either
specifies WITH CHECK OPTION or spans a view that specifies WITH CHECK
OPTION and one or more rows resulting from the operation did not qualify
under the CHECK OPTION constraint. The statement has been terminated.
```

The **INSERT** statement failed because the *HireDate* does not comply with the query's criteria.

Create View Wizard

You can also create a view using the Create View Wizard. This wizard consists of seven screens that take you step by step through the process of creating a view. You advance from screen to screen by clicking on the Next button. To go back to the prior screen, click on the Back button. The screens are as follows:

- The first screen, Welcome To The Create View Wizard, explains what can be done with the Create View Wizard.
- In the second screen, Select Database, you select the database where the view will be created. The wizard does not allow you to select any system databases (*master*, *model*, *msdb*, *tempdb*).
- In the third screen, Select Tables, you select the table or tables that will participate in the view. Click on the checkbox to include a table in a view (see Figure 10.1).
- In the fourth screen, Select Columns, you select the column or columns for the view to display (see Figure 10.2).
- In the fifth screen, Define Restriction, you can restrict the information the view will display. The information is restricted by defining a **WHERE** clause. If you selected two or more tables, you have to specify a **WHERE** clause in order to avoid a Cartesian product (see Figure 10.3). A Cartesian product is formed when the number of rows in a table is multiplied by the number of rows in another table.

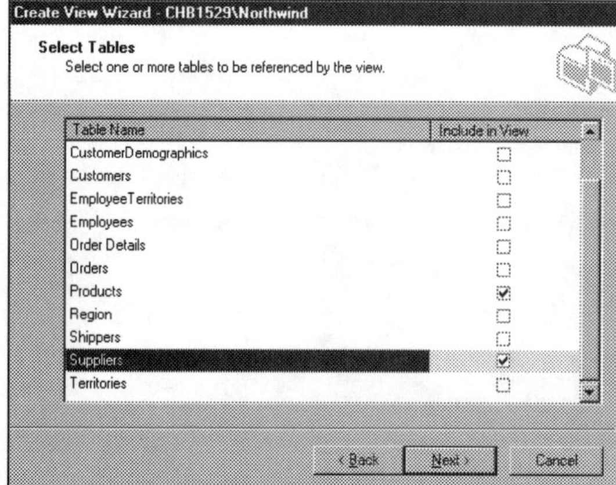

Figure 10.1 The Select Tables screen from the Create View Wizard.

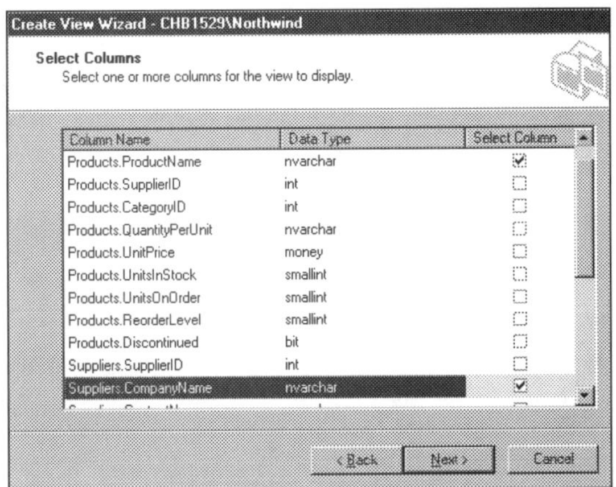

Figure 10.2 The Select Columns screen from the Create View Wizard.

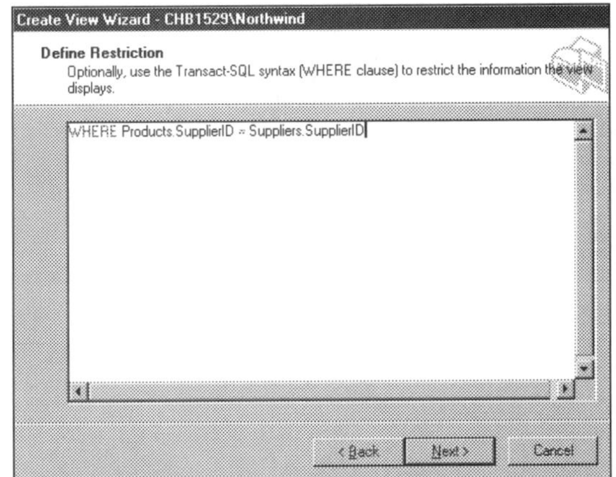

Figure 10.3 The Define Restriction screen from the Create View Wizard.

- In the sixth screen, Name The View, you can specify a name for the view if you do not like the name automatically generated by the wizard (see Figure 10.4).
- The seventh and final screen, Completing The Create View Wizard, displays the **CREATE VIEW** statement created by the wizard. You can edit the statement to reorganize the order the columns will be displayed; add columns (belonging to the base table(s) or derived from an arithmetic expression, system function, or constant); or apply a different name to the columns (see Figure 10.5). Click on the Finish button to create the view.

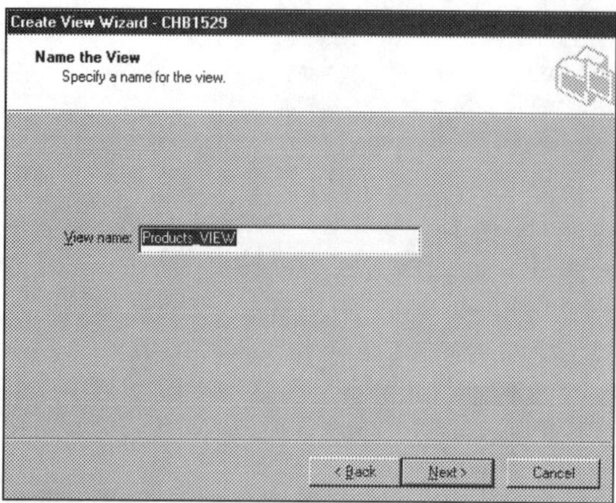

Figure 10.4 The Name The View screen from the Create View Wizard.

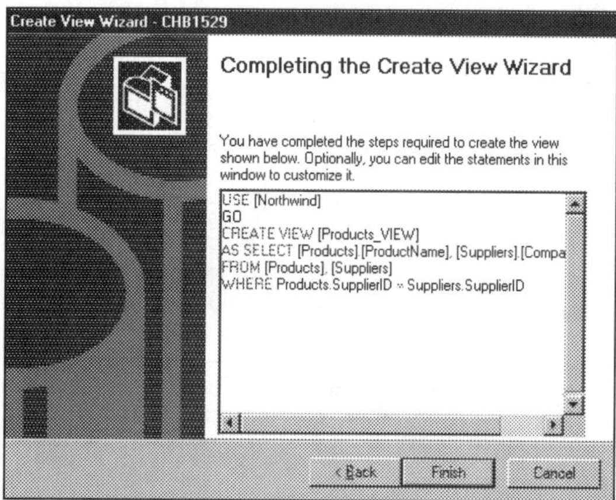

Figure 10.5 Completing The Create View Wizard screen from the Create View Wizard.

ALTERING A VIEW

SQL Server 7 has improved view functionality by adding the ability to change a view dynamically without having to drop and re-create the view. Altering a view does not affect the stored procedures and triggers that depend on it.

The exception to this rule is when the **SELECT** statement that defines the view is changed in such a way that the dependent stored procedures and/or triggers are no longer valid. For example, you could create a view to retrieve the total sales per store of the state of California. If the view is modified to retrieve all stores that have sold more than $100,000, the stored procedures or triggers dependent on the view will also have to change. Altering a view does not affect the permissions associated with the view.

A view is modified with the **ALTER VIEW** command, which allows you to alter:

- The definition of the view (the **SELECT** statement)
- The column names
- The encryption of the view, such as encrypting or not, the view's definition
- The **WITH CHECK OPTION** property of the view, such as enforcing or not enforcing the criteria specified in the queries definition for all inserts and updates executed against the view

The syntax for the **ALTER VIEW** command is as follows:

```
ALTER VIEW <view_name> [(<col1> [,...<coln>])]
[WITH ENCRYPTION]
AS
<select_statement>
[WITH CHECK OPTION]
```

For an explanation of the clauses of the **ALTER VIEW** statement, refer to the **CREATE VIEW** statement.

In order to retain the functionality of the **WITH ENCRYPTION** or **WITH CHECK OPTION** clauses specified in the **CREATE VIEW** statement, you must specify the clauses in the **ALTER VIEW** statement.

Listing 10.6 shows how to alter a view. The first part of the example shows the statement used to create the view. The second part shows how a new column can be added to the view's definition. Because the view was altered and not dropped and re-created, the permission granted to the *public* role is not lost.

Listing 10.6 Altering a view.

```
CREATE VIEW vw_Customers
AS
SELECT CustomerID, CompanyName, Phone
FROM Customers
GO
GRANT SELECT ON vw_Customers TO public
GO

ALTER VIEW vw_Customers
AS
SELECT CustomerID, CompanyName, Phone, Fax
FROM Customers
GO
```

Dropping A View

When a view is dropped, its definition and permissions are removed from the database; however, the tables and data referenced by the view are not affected. You can drop one or more views with the **DROP VIEW** command. Listing 10.7 shows how a view can be dropped.

```
DROP VIEW <view_name1> [,...<view_nameN>]
```

A view will not get removed automatically if the tables that the view references are dropped. You must drop the view explicitly with the **DROP VIEW** command.

Listing 10.7 Dropping a view.

```
IF EXISTS (SELECT TABLE_NAME FROM INFORMATION_SCHEMA.VIEWS
          WHERE TABLE_NAME = 'vw_Customers')
     DROP VIEW vw_Customers
GO
```

Querying Data Through A View

Views are used to query data. The heart of a view is the **SELECT** statement that defines it. The **SELECT** statement can join two or more tables, return the union of two or more tables, or return data from only one table. The **SELECT** statement can access data from *heterogeneous* (other than SQL 7) data sources; additionally, the **SELECT** statement can restrict the number of columns or rows displayed. The query tree of the view is stored in the procedure cache section of memory when it is executed for the first time. The execution plan of a view is recompiled every time the view is accessed.

If a **SELECT *** statement is used to define a view and new columns are added to the base tables, the new columns will *not* appear in the views. For the new columns to appear, you must alter the view or drop and re-create the view.

Modifying Data Through A View

The data retrieved by a view is saved in the base tables that the view references. Therefore, an **INSERT**, **UPDATE** or **DELETE** statement issued against a view is actually modifying the data in the base table. An **INSERT**, **UPDATE**, or **DELETE** statement can only be issued against an *updateable view*.

A view is considered updateable only if the **SELECT** statement that defines the view meets the following restrictions:

- It cannot contain **TOP**, **GROUP BY**, **UNION**, or **DISTINCT** clauses.
- It cannot contain an aggregate function, such as **SUM()**, **COUNT()**, **AVG()**, **MAX()**, **MIN()**, **GROUPING()**, **STDEV()**, **STDEVP()**, **VAR()**, **VARP()**.

Aggregate functions and **TOP**, **GROUP BY**, **UNION**, and **DISTINCT** clauses can be used in the **FROM** clause in a subquery as long as the values are not modified.

- It cannot contain columns that are a result of a calculation or of a function (for example, **GETDATE()**).
- It references at least one table in the **FROM** clause.

For example, the following view is nonupdateable:

```
CREATE VIEW vw_NoFromClause AS
SELECT GETDATE() AS Date
,      SUSER_NAME() AS UserLogged
,      @@RowCount AS [Rows Affected]
GO
```

Furthermore, an **INSERT** or **UPDATE** statement can be executed against an updateable view if:

- It modifies data in only one of the base tables. This is true even if the view displays data from two or more base tables (see Listing 10.8).
- It adheres to the criteria specified in the **SELECT** statement (in the case that the view was created with the **WITH CHECK OPTION** clause).
- All the columns of the base table that do not allow **NULL** values and do not have a **DEFAULT** definition assigned to them have a value specified in the **INSERT** statement.
- The data being modified in the base table complies with all constraints and rules defined on the table. For example, you cannot change a value of a *Salary* column to $500,000 if it has a **CHECK** constraint that does not allow values larger than $100,000.

READTEST And WRITEXT Statements

READTEXT and **WRITEXT** statements cannot be used to modify **TEXT**, **NTEXT**, or **IMAGE** columns in a view.

Listing 10.8 demonstrates a correct and an incorrect **UPDATE** statement issued against the **vw_Orders199607** updateable view that was created using the following statement.

Listing 10.8 A correct and an incorrect **UPDATE** statement on a view.

```
CREATE VIEW vw_Orders199607 AS
SELECT o.OrderID, o.CustomerID, o.OrderDate, od.ProductID,
       od.UnitPrice, od.Quantity, od.Discount
FROM Orders o INNER JOIN [Order Details] od
        ON o.OrderID = od.OrderID
WHERE o.OrderDate BETWEEN '1996-07-01' AND '1996-07-31'
GO
```

The following update statement is valid because it only updates columns from one base table:

```
UPDATE vw_Orders199607 SET OrderDate = '1995-01-01'
GO
```

However, this update statement is invalid because it tries to update columns from two different base tables:

```
UPDATE vw_Orders199607
SET OrderDate = '1995-01-01', Discount = 0.015
GO
```

You can issue a **DELETE** statement against an updateable view if:

- One base table is being referenced in the **FROM** clause of the **SELECT** statement that defines the view.
- All constraints defined on the database are met. For example, you cannot delete rows in a parent table that has a **PRIMARY KEY** constraint defined if child tables have underlying **FOREIGN KEY** constraints that reference those rows.

System Views

Each SQL Server 7 database has a set of *information schema views;* these are system views that can be used to obtain *metadata* (data about data) for all data objects stored in the current database.

The information schema views are independent from the system tables. This means that if the structure of the system tables changes in future releases of SQL Server, these views will be modified to return the same metadata. For this reason you should only reference information schema views in any code you write. A list of all information schema views and a brief explanation of their purpose is provided in Table 10.1.

Table 10.1 Information schema views.

View Name	Brief Description
CHECK_CONSTRAINTS	Returns one row for each **CHECK** constraint owned by the current user
COLUMN_DOMAIN_USAGE	Returns one row for each column that has a user-defined data type and is owned by the current user
COLUMN_PRIVILEGES	Returns one row for each column for which a privilege has been granted to the current user, or for which a privilege has been granted by the current user
COLUMNS	Returns one row for each column that the current user can access
CONSTRAINT_COLUMN_USAGE	Returns one row for those columns that have a constraint defined and are owned by the current user
CONSTRAINT_TABLE_USAGE	Returns one row for those tables that have a constraint defined and are owned by the current user
DOMAIN_CONSTRAINTS	Returns one row for each user-defined data type that has a rule bound to it and that is accessible to the current user
DOMAINS	Returns one row for each user-defined data type that is accessible to the current user
KEY_COLUMN_USAGE	Returns one row for each column that is part of a **PRIMARY KEY**, **FOREIGN KEY**, or **UNIQUE** constraint and that is owned by the current user
REFERENTIAL_CONSTRAINTS	Returns one row for each **FOREIGN KEY** constraint owned by the current user
SCHEMATA	Returns one row for each database that the current user is authorized to access
TABLE_CONSTRAINTS	Returns one row for each table constraint owned by the current user
TABLE_PRIVILEGES	Returns one row for each table for which a privilege has been granted to the current user, or for which a privilege has been granted by the current user
TABLES	Returns one row for each table or view for which permission has been granted to the current user

(continued)

Table 10.1 Information schema views *(continued)*.

View Name	Brief Description
VIEW_COLUMN_USAGE	Returns one row for each column used in a view definition and owned by the current user
VIEW_TABLE_USAGE	Returns one row for each table used in a view definition and owned by the current user
VIEWS	Returns one row for each view that is accessible by the current user

The owner of the information schema views is **INFORMATION_SCHEMA**. Each time you reference an information schema view, you have to specify the owner for example, **INFORMATION_SCHEMA.<information_schema view_name>** (see Listing 10.9).

The **INFORMATION_SCHEMA** user is not displayed in Enterprise Manager, but if you query the *sysusers* system table you will see an entry for the **INFORMATION_SCHEMA** user.

Listing 10.9 shows how to use an information schema view to return all the views owned by **'dbo'** in the current database.

Listing 10.9 Using an information schema view to return all the views owned by **'dbo'** in the current database.

```
SELECT * FROM INFORMATION_SCHEMA.TABLES
WHERE TABLE_TYPE = 'VIEW' AND TABLE_SCHEMA = 'dbo'
ORDER BY TABLE_NAME
```

The result returned from the preceding query is:

```
TABLE_CATALOG  TABLE_SCHEMA  TABLE_NAME                     TABLE_TYPE
-------------  ------------  -----------------------------  ----------
Northwind      dbo           Alphabetical list of products  VIEW
Northwind      dbo           Category Sales for 1997        VIEW
Northwind      dbo           Current Product List           VIEW
.. ..
Northwind      dbo           Customer and Suppliers by City VIEW
Northwind      dbo           sysconstraints                 VIEW
Northwind      dbo           syssegments                    VIEW

(19 row(s) affected)
```

Use Schema Views And System Procedures Provided By SQL Server 7

To ensure that your applications will work correctly in future versions of SQL Server, only use the information schema views and system stored procedures provided by SQL Server 7 to obtain metadata.

To obtain information about views, you can use the following information schema views:

- **INFORMATION_SCHEMA.TABLES**
- **INFORMATION_SCHEMA.VIEWS**
- **INFORMATION_SCHEMA.VIEW_COLUMN_USAGE**
- **INFORMATION_SCHEMA.VIEW_TABLE_USAGE**

Nested Views And Performance

In order to find performance problems quickly, it is not recommended to nest complex views, such as views that join several tables, use the **UNION** operator, or have many expressions on the **WHERE** clause. Nested views tend to hide the complexity of the underlying queries.

For example, it would be extremely difficult to determine what is causing poor performance when we query the following view:

```
CREATE VIEW vw_EmployeeDiscontinued AS
SELECT e.LastName + ', ' + e.FirstName AS [Employee Name],
       o.OrderID, o.OrderDate
FROM Orders o
         INNER JOIN Employees e ON o.EmployeeID = e.EmployeeID
         INNER JOIN vw_ProductsPerOrder vw ON o.OrderID = vw.OrderID
WHERE vw.Discontinued = 1
GO
```

The **vw_EmployeeDiscontinued** view hides the complexity of the **SELECT** statement that defines the **vw_ProductsPerOrder** view. The **vw_ProductsPerOrder** view performs a join of four tables:

```
CREATE VIEW vw_ProductsPerOrder AS
SELECT od.OrderID, p.ProductName,
od.UnitPrice, od.Quantity,
      od.Discount, c.CategoryName,
```

```
s.CompanyName, s.Country,
       p.Discontinued
FROM [Order Details] od
         INNER JOIN Products p
ON od.ProductID = p.ProductID
         INNER JOIN Categories c
ON p.CategoryID = c.CategoryID
         INNER JOIN Suppliers s
ON p.SupplierID = s.SupplierID
GO
```

CHAPTER SUMMARY

In this chapter we have discussed the following items:

- A view stores a query definition. The data accessed through the view is stored in the tables being referenced in the **SELECT** statement.
- Use an **INSERT**, **UPDATE**, or **DELETE** statement to update the underlying base table referenced by the view.
- A view can only be created in the current database.
- A view references tables and views from the current database. A view can also reference data from other databases if it is defined using a distributed query.
- A view can restrict the columns and rows displayed from the base tables or from the views it references.
- Use a view as a security mechanism, to focus the data displayed to the users, to shield the complexity of the queries, to organize import and export of data, and to work with partitioned data across multiple tables.
- Use the **sp_helptext** system stored procedure to display the view's definition.
- Use the **sp_depends** system stored procedure to display the view's dependencies.
- A view can be created with the **CREATE VIEW** statement (only statement allowed in a batch script) or with the Create View Wizard.
- The **SELECT** statement that defines a view cannot have an **ORDER BY**, **COMPUTE**, or **COMPUTE BY** clause and cannot have the **INTO** keyword.
- A view cannot have an index, rule, default, or trigger associated with it.
- You must specify a column name in a view if it is derived from an arithmetic expression.
- A view can be altered with the **ALTER VIEW** statement.

- The **ALTER VIEW** statement does not affect the permissions associated with the view.
- Use the **WITH ENCRYPTION** clause when creating and altering a view, and to encrypt a view's definition.
- Use the **WITH CHECK OPTION** clause when creating and altering a view to enforce that all **INSERT** and **UPDATE** statements executed against the view adhere to the criteria of the **SELECT** statement that defines the view.
- Use the **DROP VIEW** command to drop a view.
- **INSERT**, **UPDATE**, and **DELETE** statements can only be executed against an updateable view.
- Use the information schema views to obtain metadata for all data objects belonging to the current database.
- Nested views can make finding performance problems harder because they can hide the complexity of the underlying queries.
- Data modified through a view can only affect one base table.
- An updateable view cannot contain an aggregate function or the **TOP**, **GROUP BY**, **UNION**, or **DISTINCT** clauses.

Review Questions

1. Which of the following are true about a view?
    a. A view is a database object that stores data.
    b. A view is a database object that stores a query.
    c. A view is a database object that stores data and a query.
    d. None of the above.
2. A view can only reference tables and views in the current database.
    a. True
    b. False
3. A view can:
    a. Restrict the rows displayed
    b. Restrict the columns displayed
    c. Be the result of joining tables
    d. Return summary data
    e. All of the above.

4. A view can be used to shield the complexity of **SELECT** statements.
   a. True
   b. False
5. Which system table(s) store information about views? (Choose all correct answers.)
   a. *Sysdepends*
   b. *Syscomments*
   c. *Sysreferences*
   d. None of the above.
6. Which of the following are true of a view? (Choose all correct answers.)
   a. It cannot have an index.
   b. It cannot reference more than 250 columns.
   c. It cannot have a trigger.
   d. All of the above.
7. A view definition can have an **ORDER BY** and a **COMPUTE** clause.
   a. True
   b. False
8. You can create a view:
   a. With the **CREATE VIEW** statement
   b. With the Create View Wizard
   c. Through the GUI of Enterprise Manager
   d. All of the above.
9. To encrypt a view definition you must:
   a. Use the **WITH ENCRYPTION** clause when creating a view.
   b. Use the **WITH ENCRYPTION** clause when altering a view.
   c. Both a and b.
   d. None of the above.
10. The data returned by a view is:
    a. Saved in the view.
    b. Produced dynamically when the view is referenced.
    c. Both a and b.
    d. None of the above.
11. A view can be used to serve as a security mechanism because: (Choose all correct answers.)

a. It can limit the rows returned.
b. It can limit the columns displayed.
c. Permissions can be assigned only to the view.
d. A view cannot serve as a security mechanism.

12. To get information about the dependencies of a view, which system stored procedure would you use?
    a. **sp_viewdepends**
    b. **sp_viewobjects**
    c. **sp_depends**
    d. None of the above.

13. Which of the following are true?
    a. A view can reference SQL Server tables and views.
    b. A view can reference data from different DBMSs.
    c. Both a and b.
    d. None of the above.

14. If the **vw_Orders** view was created with the following statement:

```
CREATE VIEW vw_Orders AS
SELECT * FROM Orders WHERE CustomerID = 'VINET'
WITH CHECK OPTION
GO
```

What will the following command do?

```
UPDATE vw_Orders SET CustomerID = 'JERS'
GO
```

    a. Update all **CustomerID**s to **'JERS'**.
    b. Return an error.

15. When altering a view you must reset the view's permissions.
    a. True
    b. False

16. Information schema views are owned by:
    a. The **dbo**
    b. The administrator
    c. The **INFORMATION_SCHEMA** user
    d. The **sa**

Hands-On Projects

These activities assume that you are already connected to the *Northwind* database using the Query Analyzer.

After Susan began working with the developers, she realized that views were a superior way to provide access to the data that the program would display in many cases. She had been trying to set permissions such that only certain data would be displayed to the user. The problem was that she needed to restrict not only the data displayed, but also keep the view from being disassembled and the statement revealed. She looked up the **CREATE VIEW** statement for a way to encrypt the view.

Project 10.1

In this activity, you create a view according to the following specifications.

The view needs to return all orders entered by employee 5 and has to display the *OrderID*, *CustomerID*, *EmployeeID*, *OrderDate*, *ProductID*, and *Quantity* columns from the *Orders* and *Order Details* tables. The view definition should be encrypted, and you have to make sure that all data modifications done through the view meet the view's criteria.

In the Query Analyzer, type the following command and execute it.

```
CREATE VIEW vw_OrderEmployee5
WITH ENCRYPTION AS
SELECT Orders.OrderID, CustomerID, EmployeeID,
       OrderDate, ProductID, Quantity
FROM Orders INNER JOIN [Order Details]
             ON Orders.OrderID = [Order Details].OrderID
WHERE EmployeeID = 5
WITH CHECK OPTION
GO
```

Use the **WITH ENCRYPTION** clause to encrypt the view. To make sure that all data modifications done through the view adhere to the criteria specified in the **SELECT** statement, use the **WITH CHECK OPTION** clause.

Once Susan had created the views in her database, she needed to modify some of them. She originally dropped and re-created the views to modify them, but she then had to re-grant permissions on each one. She began to use the **ALTER**

VIEW statement to change them. She remembered to include the **WITH ENCRYPTION** modifier on the views originally created that had them. She remembered to do this after she forgot the first time and the statement was exposed.

Project 10.2

In this activity, you will modify a view definition according to the following specifications.

Instead of displaying the *EmployeeID*, display the full name of the employee. In the Query Analyzer, type the following command and execute it:

```
ALTER VIEW vw_OrderEmployee5
  (OrderID, CustomerID, [Employee Name],
   OrderDate, ProductID, Quantity)
WITH ENCRYPTION AS
SELECT Orders.OrderID, CustomerID,
       LastName + ', ' + FirstName,
       OrderDate, ProductID, Quantity
FROM Orders
   INNER JOIN [Order Details]
     ON Orders.OrderID = [Order Details].OrderID
   INNER JOIN Employees
     ON Orders.EmployeeID = Employees.EmployeeID
WHERE Orders.EmployeeID = 5
WITH CHECK OPTION
GO
```

Now let's delete this view.

In the Query Analyzer, type the following command and execute it:

```
ROP VIEW vw_OrderEmployee5
GO
```

Susan also had a few views that were redundant and unnecessary to the database. She didn't need to look up the statement to get rid of them; they were rather easy to delete.

10

CHAPTER ELEVEN

TRANSACTIONS AND LOCKING

After Reading This Chapter And Completing The Exercises, You Will Be Able To:

- Understand the locking architecture used in SQL Server 7
- Be able to optimize the default dynamic locking behavior
- Be able to define the properties that make up a transaction
- Know when and how to apply transaction management to an application
- Understand the importance of isolation level and when to use each level
- Be able to decide on the proper locking strategy to use for updateable cursors

Locking occurs within all Relational Database Management systems. One of the most difficult tasks a database designer will face is the tradeoff between providing integrity for the data and allowing many users to access that data. One method that helps guarantee the integrity of the data is the use of transactions. We'll take a look at both of these topics in this chapter.

DEFINING A TRANSACTION

SQL Server 7 has made some significant advances in database locking and transaction management over previous versions of the software. This is a topic that can have a far-reaching impact on the success of your design and implementation. For this reason, the certification exam dedicates a number of questions on both the new database locking features and on transaction management.

Definition

As a SQL developer or designer, you are responsible for creating a system that will protect the integrity of the data in your database. Many mechanisms in SQL Server 7 will help you with this task. The list of tools includes Declarative Referential Integrity (DRI), triggers, and transactions. A *transaction* is a method of packaging **SELECT**, **INSERT**, **UPDATE**, and **DELETE** activity in such a way as to protect data consistency. In other words, a transaction is defined as a single logical unit of work.

As a simple example, issuing the SQL statement that follows results in either all of the rows matching the predicate (the **WHERE** clause) to be updated or none at all.

```
UPDATE   Orders
SET      ShipVia = 3
WHERE    OrderID > 10248
```

If the first 10 rows are updated and then an error occurs while updating the eleventh row, the database would cancel the update operation and undo the first 10 updates.

ACID Properties

According to the ANSI SQL-92 definition, one or more SQL statements are considered a transaction if they meet all four of the ACID properties. Table 11.1 lists these four properties of a transaction. You could say that this is the ACID test for databases.

Each of these properties is extremely important in order to protect the integrity of a high-end database system. Fortunately, the server is designed to enforce these properties automatically. But because the isolation property is especially important when designing and implementing databases using SQL Server 7, it can be optimized for a variety of situations.

Table 11.1 The ACID properties of a transaction.

Property	Description
Atomicity	A transaction is a single unit of work. It either completely succeeds or completely fails.
Consistency	Data must be in a consistent state when a transaction finishes. The database cannot be left in an indeterminate state.
Isolation	Each transaction is isolated from all other transactions. Transactions can have varying degrees of isolation; we will study this further in the following section entitled "Isolation Level."
Durable	A transaction is permanent upon completion.

Isolation Level

One of the ACID properties of a transaction is *isolation*. This property states that a transaction must be isolated from all other transactions on the system. In other words, a transaction should be able to complete without regard to what other users are doing on the system. Strict isolation would have a very negative impact on database concurrency, but would provide the highest degree of data integrity. To provide varying degrees of balance between user concurrency and data integrity, four ANSI SQL-92 standard isolation levels have been implemented in SQL Server 7. The four levels are listed in Table 11.2 in order of increasing

Table 11.2 The four ANSI transaction isolation levels.

Isolation Level	Description
Read Uncommitted	Allows users to read data that has not yet been committed. This is also commonly referred to as *dirty reads*. This level provides the best user concurrency and performance, but at the expense of possible data inconsistency.
Read Committed	This is the default isolation level for SQL Server 7, and is the best balance between user concurrency and data consistency. Users can only read data that has been committed to the database. Shared locks are released immediately after completion of a **SELECT** statement, even when executed within the scope of a longer-running transaction.
Repeatable Read	Reads are guaranteed to produce the same results during the scope of a transaction. The only exception is a situation known as a *phantom row*, where another user inserts a new row between two reads. In other words, shared locks are held for the duration of the transaction.
Serializable	Provides the best possible data consistency, but at the expense of user concurrency and performance. This isolation level was not fully implemented in SQL Server 6.5, but conforms to ANSI standards in version 7. This level provides the same behavior as **Repeatable Read**, but also protects against the phantom row problem.

isolation, or decreasing database concurrency. You will need to learn when to use each of these levels in order to design the optimal database solution.

Each isolation level is described in detail in the next section. A good rule of thumb that should be used when deciding which of the four levels to use in your design is to choose the lowest isolation level that will result in consistently accurate data for the application. You'll want to do this to provide the greatest level of integrity for the data while allowing the widest concurrency for the users.

Read Uncommitted

This isolation level allows uncommitted data to be read by another process and applies only to **SELECT** statements. The database is forced to bypass issuing any form of shared locking (see the section on "Database Locking") and to ignore exclusive locks. The reduced locking eases overhead and can therefore improve performance. However, a danger exists in designing a system with this isolation level. Users can read information that has not been committed to the database. For example, if user #1 is running the following command:

```
UPDATE Customers
SET    Region = "Europe"
WHERE  Country in ("Spain", "Germany")
```

and at the same time user #2 is running the command:

```
SELECT Region,
       "#Customers" = count(*)
FROM   Customers (NOLOCK)
GROUP BY Region
ORDER BY Region
```

The possibility exists, if the **UPDATE** statement failed or is not finished at the time that user #2's report is running, then the report will have invalid information. Thus, this isolation level should not be used in cases where applications are updating data.

In the previous **SELECT** statement, both **GROUP BY** and **ORDER BY** clauses are specified. This probably looks strange for most experienced DBAs because you would think that the database would naturally return data in the order of the **GROUP BY** clause. Such an assumption is true for the previous version of the database, as well as most other products. However, Microsoft SQL Server 7 includes advanced parallel query processing technology to speed up queries like this. Each thread that is used to process the query will process the data in the order of the **GROUP BY** clause. However, the threads may complete in any order, resulting in no guarantee for the sort order of the final results. Therefore, if you want to ensure that data is returned in sorted order, you must specify the order in an **ORDER BY** clause.

However, other situations may arise where this isolation should be considered. For example, with *Decision Support Systems (DSS)* or *Online Analytical Processing (OLAP)* systems, most of the database activity is centered on reporting. In these systems most or all of the update activity is confined to various forms of replication from external data sources, most commonly on a once-a-day schedule. In this case, a very low risk exists for reading processes to encounter data problems related to dirty reads. It does not make sense to burden the database with the extra overhead of maintaining shared locking or to contend with the batch updating processes. In this case it may be better to write reporting queries using the uncommitted read isolation level.

Designers and developers may be tempted to use **Read Uncommitted** to improve performance when reading from static lookup tables. However, SQL Server 7 provides a better way to do this. The **sp_indexoption** stored procedure allows you to specify which locks are *not* used on a table. Using this option, you can specify that row and page lock locks are not used to satisfy queries. This forces the optimizer to use table locks, which still reduces overhead and improves performance, but does not require a session-level setting or optimizer hint to be used. Using this method in place of explicitly using a session-level **SET** option or optimizer hint prevents code changes in the future if the nature of the table changes.

You can set this isolation level in two ways: using the **SET** command, and using optimizer hints. The following statement can be included in stored procedures or SQL batches:

```
SET TRANSACTION ISOLATION LEVEL Read Uncommitted
```

The other method is to include the **NOLOCK** optimizer hint in the **FROM** clause of a **SELECT** statement. For example:

```
SELECT *
FROM   Orders (NOLOCK)
```

Read Committed

This is the default setting for SQL Server 7. When this isolation level is used, a **SELECT** statement cannot read information that is being updated by another process. This level would result in consistently accurate results for the example shown previously in the "**Read Uncommitted**" section. You should use this isolation level for most of your applications, unless special circumstances require you to change it.

With **Read Committed**, the database will create shared locks (see "Database Locking" in a later section) during **SELECT** statements. Any **UPDATE** or **INSERT** statement that is working with the same element of data will block these shared locks. At the same time, the shared locks will block other processes from updating the rows that are being read. The locks are released immediately when the **SELECT** statement is finished, even when it is within an explicit transaction construct. For example, the following statement shows that no object-level locks are in the *Northwinds* database, even though the **SELECT** statement is run within a transaction:

```
SET TRANSACTION ISOLATION LEVEL READ COMITTED
BEGIN  TRANSACTION
select *
from   Shippers
exec   sp_lock @@spid
COMMIT
```

That is because the shared locks are released immediately after the **SELECT** statement finishes. Any other process that is updating the *Shippers* table would be blocked only while the **SELECT** statement is running.

You can set this isolation level using both the **SET** command and using optimizer hints. The **SET** command is:

```
SET  TRANSACTION  ISOLATION  LEVEL  Read  Committed
```

An example of using an optimizer hint to set this level is:

```
SELECT *
FROM   Orders (READCOMMITTED)
```

Repeatable Read

Occasionally it is necessary to make sure that shared locks are held for the duration of a transaction rather than being released immediately. In these cases you should use the **Repeatable Read** isolation level. Consider the situation where two users are looking at the same customer's information on an application screen at the same time. User #1 modifies the customer name and submits the changes to the database. User #2 also modifies the customer's name and submits the changes to the database. Unfortunately, user #2 misspells the name slightly and overwrites the changes made by user #1. You can prevent this situation in many ways, including the use of **Repeatable Read** isolation level.

When **Repeatable Read** is used in this situation, both users would retain *shared* locks on the customer data while it is being reviewed and edited. For each person, this would prevent the other user from making changes to the customer record in the database. The first user who submits the changes to the database would be blocked until the second user releases the shared locks. Unfortunately, once the second user tries to submit changes, a deadlock (a type of repeating lock) would result. (See the "Deadlocking" section later in this chapter.) In this case the **Repeatable Read** setting is not a good way to solve this particular problem.

What happened to my changes? Database users sometimes ask this question. Unfortunately, the answer lies in one of two problems in the way the application was designed. The first problem is the lack of adequate error handling in the application and the second is not protecting against parallel updates. Although **Repeatable Read** is not a good way to protect against parallel updates, you should consider using a row versioning technique, such as adding a timestamp column to see if any changes arose since the data was first read.

Other situations do lend themselves to using this isolation level. One such situation is the need to make multiple passes through the same set of data in order to do an iterative calculation. If this is the case, and it is important to make sure that the information does not change between each pass, the **Repeatable Read** isolation level would be appropriate to use.

This isolation level can be set using both the **SET** command and using optimizer hints. The **SET** command is:

```
SET TRANSACTION ISOLATION LEVEL Repeatable Read
```

An example of using an optimizer hint to set this level is as follows:

```
SELECT *
FROM   Orders (REPEATABLEREAD)
```

Serializable

The **Serializable** isolation level is essentially the same as the **Repeatable Read** except for one important difference. The **Repeatable Read** does not protect against the phantom row problem. While using the **Repeatable Read** isolation level, another user could insert a row into the range that is being read. When the data is read again using a range select query, the new row will appear. For example:

```
SELECT *
FROM   Customers
WHERE  PostalCode BETWEEN '30000' AND '50000'
```

If this situation can produce inconsistent results in the data, you should use the **Serializable** isolation level. Like the **Repeatable Read**, the database uses shared locks and keeps them active for the duration of the transaction. However, the database also uses something referred to as a **RANGE-KEY** lock (see "Database Locking"). If one or more indexes are used in satisfying the **SELECT** statement, the database issues a range lock for the pages, extents, or for the entire table as necessary. All other users are prevented from inserting new rows into the protected range. If a table does not have any indexes, or none were used to satisfy the **SELECT** statement, the database issues a shared table lock to prevent any inserts or updates for the entire table. You should use extra precaution when using **Serializable** reads so that excessive blocking does not occur.

You can set this isolation level using both the **SET** command and using optimizer hints. The **SET** command is as follows:

```
SET TRANSACTION ISOLATION LEVEL Serializable
```

An example of using an optimizer hint to set this level is as follows:

```
SELECT *
FROM    Orders (Serializable)
```

Database Locking

Before we look further into programming transactions, we need to understand how the database handles resource locking. A lock is mechanism that is used by the database to prevent conflicting actions for a single resource. Database locking is a fundamental building block for transaction management. The locking implementation used in SQL Server 7 is very sophisticated and is much different from prior versions and other products. It is essential to understand the advanced locking features of SQL Server 7 in order to achieve a successful database design.

Locking Scope

SQL Server 7 implements six different levels of resource locking. The levels progress from the individual row all the way up to the entire database. Table 11.3 describes the six levels of locking.

Table 11.3 Resource locking levels in SQL 7.

Level	Description
RID	Specifies that an individual row is locked. This is also referred to as RID locking, where RID represents the row identifier.
PAGE	Used to lock an 8K page. A *page* can contain one to n rows.
EXTENT	Locks an extent, which is made up of eight pages.
TABLE	Specifies that the entire table is locked.
KEY-RANGE	Used to lock a range of values in support of the **Serializable** transaction isolation level. If an index is specified for one or more columns in the predicate of a **SELECT** statement, the server places a **KEY-RANGE** lock on the index. If an index does not exist for one or more predicate columns, or if a predicate is not specified in the **SELECT** statement, the server escalates the lock to a table lock. This is only used for **Serializable** transactions.
DB	Allows for the entire database to be locked.

Types Of Locking

The database implements eight different types of locks. It is possible for the database to issue any of these types of locks against any of the resources described previously. The database automatically decides which type of lock is appropriate for the current action. Table 11.4 describes these eight types of locks.

Table 11.4 Available locking modes.

Mode	Description
INTENT SHARED (IS)	Designates the possibility for a shared lock to be placed either at or below the resource where this lock is placed. In other words, if an **IS** lock is placed on a page, the possibility exists that the database may issue a shared lock on the page or row on that page.
INTENT EXCLUSIVE (IX)	Indicates the likelihood that the database will issue an exclusive lock at or below the resource locked using **IX**.
SHARED WITH INTENT EXCLUSIVE (SIX)	Used when a process will be reading all or some of the data lower down in the resource hierarchy and modify only some of the data lower down.
INTENT SCHEMA (SCH)	Two types of **SCH** locks exist. An **Intent Shared Schema (SCH-S)** lock is used to prevent any changes to a database object structure while a dependent process is running. An **Intent Modification Schema (SCH-M)** lock is used to change any database objects.
SHARED (S)	Issues a shared lock on the database resource. This is not compatible with update or exclusive locks.

(continued)

Table 11.4 Available locking modes *(continued)*.

Mode	Description
UPDATE (U)	Used when a resource is being read and may be updated later. This is not compatible with other update or exclusive locks. The lock is often upgraded to an exclusive lock when updates are made. However, because shared locks can be placed on objects that also have update locks, the database must wait until all shared locks clear before upgrading to an exclusive lock.
EXCLUSIVE (X)	Exclusively locks the database resource while the resource is modified. Not compatible with any other type of locking.
BULK UPDATE (BU)	This is used to lock an entire table when bulk copying data into the table. This type of lock is not compatible with other types of locking.

Some types of locks are intent locks; these improve performance in the database and help prevent deadlocking. Intent locks are placed on the resources higher in the hierarchy and can be examined at these higher levels. If an *intent* lock is placed at the table level, the database needs to check only at this level to see if it can lock a table exclusively.

Sometimes when many RID locks are being issued, the database will upgrade the lock to the next higher level—either pages or tables. Using *intent* locking at higher levels in the hierarchy lowers the possibility for deadlocking when trading up. This does not mean that the higher-level locks cannot not be blocked by other processes.

Observing Database Locks

When trying to resolve locking problems or analyze a complex design, it is sometimes beneficial to see what locks the database is currently using. The system stored procedure **sp_lock** is used to see current locks issued by the database. In addition, the SQL Profiler utility can be used to trap table and index scans that occur within the database. Running the SQL batch:

```
BEGIN TRAN
UPDATE [Order Details]
SET    Quantity = 1
EXEC   sp_lock @@spid
ROLLBACK
```

Using the *Northwind* sample database gives the following results:

```
spid   dbid   ObjId       IndId   Type   Resource   Mode   Status
----   ----   -----       -----   ----   --------   ----   ------
10     1      0           0       DB                S      GRANT
10     2      0           0       DB                S      GRANT
10     6      0           0       DB                S      GRANT
10     6      661577395   1       PAG    1:231      IX     GRANT
10     6      661577395   1       PAG    1:177      IX     GRANT
10     6      661577395   1       PAG    1:256      IX     GRANT
10     6      661577395   0       TAB               X      GRANT
10     1      117575457   0       TAB               IS     GRANT
```

The results show that the database escalated to a table-level exclusive lock. It also shows that three exclusive page locks are on the clustered index at the node level. Experiment with different SQL statements and use the **sp_lock** procedure to see what sort of locks are being placed on the database. Remember, if you want to see shared locks, set your connection to use **Repeatable Read** or **Serializable** isolation levels first. Otherwise, the locks will be gone before you can see them. Table 11.5 describes the output from the **sp_lock** stored procedure.

Table 11.5 Output from the **sp_lock** system stored procedure.

Column	Description
Spid	This shows the **System Process ID** of the connection that is holding the lock. Each connection has a unique **SPID** number.
Dbid	The database identifier indicates which database the lock is being held in. The database name can be determined from this value by the command **SELECT db_name(<dbid>)**.
Objid	Each object in a database is given a **unique object ID**. This number shows which object is being locked. The object name can be determined by using the command **SELECT object_name(<objid>)**.
Indid	Indicates which index is being locked. A 0 in this column means that a data *page* is being locked. A value of 1 is used for clustered indexes and usually points to node pages of the index. Values greater than 1 are used for nonclustered indexes.
Type	Indicates the resource being locked. Valid values are **RID** (row lock), **PAG** (8K page lock), **EXT** (extent of eight pages), **TAB** (table), **DB** (database), and **KEY** (key range).
Mode	Type of lock being held. Valid values are **S** (shared), **X** (exclusive), **U** (update), **IS** (intent shared), **IX** (intent exclusive), **SIX** (shared with intent exclusive), **SCH** (schema), and **BU** (bulk copy update).
Status	Shows the current status of the lock. **GRANT** = the lock is granted on the resource; **WAIT** = the lock is being blocked by a conflicting type of lock; **CONV** = the lock is in the progress of converting to a higher-level lock (such as, a page lock is becoming a table lock).

Dynamic Locking

If you have experimented with the locking as suggested previously, you have probably noticed the dynamic locking behavior of SQL Server. *Dynamic locking* describes the ability of the database to automatically use the correct granularity of locking. The database will automatically balance user concurrency with performance.

The closer to row-level locking, the better the concurrency. The closer to table-level locking, the better the performance.

As a query uses more and more locks, the database will automatically see that a higher-level lock is more efficient. When a threshold of lower-level locks is met, the query engine will escalate the higher-level intent lock to a regular resource lock and subsequently release the lower-level locks. For example, updating 761 rows in the *Northwind, dbo.* [*Order Details*] table will result in row- and page-level locking. However, updating 762 rows results in a table-level lock.

No complex tuning parameters are available in order to get dynamic locking to work efficiently, but you can override the default behavior in a few ways.

Overriding Default Locking Behavior

Changing the default locking behavior is not recommended because the database engine is tuned for optimal dynamic locking performance. However, special circumstances may come up from time to time that require you to override the default behavior. The designers of SQL Server 7 have provided a robust set of tools you can use to alter the default locking behavior, including the use of server-wide configuration values, optimizer hints, session-level settings, and table options.

Server Configuration Settings

By default, the server is set up to dynamically allocate locking resources.

When the server starts, 2 percent of the available memory is allocated to a locking resource pool, but no more than 40 percent of the currently available memory will be used for this purpose.

SQL Server 7 will dynamically increase the number of locks allocated in the pool as the number of used locks increases. In some cases it may be desirable to statically allocate the locking resource pool using the **sp_configure** command. When using this command remember that each lock uses 96 bytes of memory.

For example, to change the default configuration to statically allocate 500,000 locks, run the following command:

```
EXEC sp_configure "locks", 500000
```

Connection Settings

Two settings are configurable only at the session level. These cannot be set for the entire server or database, but instead are managed for each individual connection.

```
SET LOCK_TIMEOUT
```

By default, when a connection is waiting for another process to finish before it can be granted its locks, the database will wait forever. This is referred to as *blocking* in the database. In most cases, waiting forever is the desired behavior. However, you may encounter cases when you do not want the query to wait more than a certain length of time before an error is returned to the application. To achieve this behavior, use the **SET LOCK_TIMEOUT** command. Once the setting is made, it remains until either the connection is terminated or the setting is changed again. Issue the following command if you want to designate that the database detect and cancel a query once it has waited for 10 seconds for a lock:


```
SET LOCK_TIMEOUT 10000
```

Notice that the value for **SET LOCK_TIMEOUT** is specified in milliseconds.

When the connection times out waiting for a resource lock, the database cancels the current command and returns the following error back to the application:

```
Server: Msg 1222, Level 16, State 50, Line 1
Lock request time out period exceeded.
```

Another setting that impacts locking at for the individual connection is the **SET TRANSACTION ISOLATION LEVEL**.

Table Settings

Changing individual table options is another tool you can use to modify default locking algorithms. By default, the database will issue **RID**, **PAG**, **EXT**, or **TAB** level locks for a given table. However, you can specify whether or not the database should grant **PAG** and/or **RID** locks.

Consider the case when you have a lookup table of state codes. Because the table is not likely to change very often, it does not make sense for the database to keep issuing page locks whenever a lookup is performed. You can specify that page and row locks not be granted on the table, which effectively forces the database to use more efficient table locks. The following commands instruct the database to not use row and page locks on the *Territories* table in the *Northwind* database:

```
EXEC sp_indexoption "Territories", "allowpagelocks", false
EXEC sp_indexoption "Territories", "allowrowlocks", false
```

Notice that this is really an index option setting rather than a table option. That is because the setting is made by changing the *Lockflags* column in the *Sysindexes system* table. Table 11.5 lists the possible values for the *Lockflags* column. In the preceding example, only the table name is specified, which instructs the **sp_indexoption** command to update all the rows in the *Sysindexes* table. You can also specify individual indexes. The following command tells the database not to use page locks on the clustered index. If a table does not have an index, the command still updates the *sysindexes* row for that table and the expected locking behavior is still achieved.

```
EXEC sp_indexoption "Territories.PK_Territories", "allowpagelocks", true
```

Optimizer Hints

The final—and perhaps most powerful and flexible—way to change the default locking behavior is through the use of *optimizer hints*. Optimizer hints can be used with **SELECT**, **INSERT**, **UPDATE**, and **DELETE** statements to indicate the type of locking or isolation level to use for each individual table. For example, the following script specifies that no locking be used for the *Customers* table even though the necessary exclusive locks will still be granted for the *Orders* table during the **UPDATE**:

```
UPDATE Orders
SET    ShipName = C.CompanyName
FROM   Orders O
JOIN   Customers C (NOLOCK)
  ON   O.CustomerID = C.CustomerID
```

Another example is the statement:

```
SELECT *
FROM   Orders WITH (ROWLOCK)
```

This statement specifies that the database use row locking even though every row in the table will be retrieved. Without the optimizer hint, the database would escalate to a table lock for more efficient processing. However, forcing the use of row locks may be necessary due to address concurrency issues.

The following optimizer hints can be used in order to change locking behavior:

```
HOLDLOCK
PAGLOCK
READCOMMITTED
REPEATABLEREAD
ROWLOCK
Serializable
TABLOCK
TABLOCKX
```

DEADLOCKING

Suppose your boss says she will give you a raise if you pass the MCDBA certification tests. You reply that you will pass the MCDBA certification if your boss gives you a raise, because you will need the raise in order to pay for the tests. In database terms, this is a deadlock.

A *deadlock* occurs when one process has a resource that the another process wants, but the other process has a resource that the first process wants, and neither is giving up its resource until it gets the other's resource. SQL Server 7 employs a periodic scanning process that looks for circular lock references. When a circular reference is found, the database determines which process is the least expensive transaction to undo. If you are the victim (and if your application developer programmed error reporting correctly), your query will be terminated and rolled back. You will also receive the message:


```
Server: Msg 1205, Level 13, State 1, Line 1
Your transaction (process ID #12) was deadlocked with another process
and has been chosen as the deadlock victim. Rerun your transaction.
```

If this condition occurs while you are running a long script containing multiple **GO** statements, only the current batch will be terminated. The osql utility will continue executing the remaining batches. For this reason, use caution when running long scripts in a database that may be susceptible to deadlocking.

You can use particular strategies to reduce deadlocking. However, it is not usually completely possible to prevent deadlocks. It is very important that you code applications to handle deadlocks properly. At a minimum, the application should present the user with the error and ask if the task should be retried.

Listing 11.1 shows two batches of code that can be used to generate a deadlock in the database. The **DELAY** step is placed in the code so that enough time exists for you to switch to the second Query Analyzer window and run the second batch of code. This guarantees that both windows of code will run at the same time. Although this example shows a very obvious example of how deadlocks can occur, their cause is often much more subtle. Two processes updating the same page or row by using a different index can also cause a deadlock to occur under the right circumstances.

Listing 11.1 Creating a database deadlock.

```
/* CONNECTION #1 */
USE Northwind

BEGIN TRAN
UPDATE Products
SET    Discontinued = 0

WAITFOR DELAY '0:0:5'

UPDATE Suppliers
SET    HomePage = 'http://www.coriolis.com'
ROLLBACK

/* CONNECTION #2 */
USE Northwind

BEGIN TRAN
UPDATE Suppliers
SET    HomePage = 'http://www.coriolis.com'

WAITFOR DELAY '0:0:5'

UPDATE Products
SET    Discontinued = 0
ROLLBACK
```

Observing Deadlock Behavior

Unless you depend on your users to monitor your database (not a good idea), you will probably want to be proactive in looking for deadlocks using the *Windows NT PerfMon* utility. The **Number of Deadlocks /Sec** counter in the **SQL Server:Locks** object will show you how much deadlocking activity is occurring in the database. You should monitor each of the instances (**Page**, **Extend**, **RID**, **Key**, **Table**) in order to see all deadlocks.

Another way to look for deadlock activity is to use the new *SQL Profiler utility*. This is a graphical interface that can be configured to show you every occurrence of locking. It can also show you the application and user names of the processes that are involved in the deadlocks.

Just knowing that excessive deadlocking is occurring in the database is not enough. You will also need to know where the contention is in the database that is causing the deadlocking to occur. For this information you will need to enable the 3605 and 1204 traceflags, which will write the diagnostic information to the SQL error logs. Figure 11.1 shows how these traceflags should be set up for your database. To add these settings, right-click on the server instance icon from Enterprise Manager and choose Properties. In the General tab choose Startup Parameters. You need to stop and restart the server in order for the new settings to become effective.

Once your server has been restarted and these settings take effect, the server will write detailed diagnostic information to the SQL error log when a deadlock occurs. The following is an example of this output produced for the previous example. From the output it is fairly easy to see what is causing the deadlock behavior:

```
*** Deadlock Detected ***
 ==> Process 8 chosen as deadlock victim
 == Deadlock Detected at: 1999-04-18 22:33:02.47
 == Session participant information:
 SPID: 8 ECID: 0 Statement Type: UPDATE Line #: 1
 Input Buf: BEGIN TRAN UPDATE Products
 SPID: 9 ECID: 0 Statement Type: UPDATE Line #: 1
 Input Buf: BEGIN TRAN UPDATESuppliers
 == Deadlock Lock participant information:
 == Lock: KEY: 6:453576654:1 (010001000000)
 Database: Northwind
 Table: Products
 Index: PK_Products
  - Held by: SPID 8 ECID 0 Mode "X"
  - Requested by: SPID 9 ECID 0 Mode "U"
 == Lock: KEY: 6:325576198:1 (130013000000)
 Database: Northwind
 Table: Suppliers
 Index: PK_Suppliers
  - Held by: SPID 9 ECID 0 Mode "X"
  - Requested by: SPID 8 ECID 0 Mode "U"
```

Avoiding Deadlocks

As the database takes on more of a load, deadlocks cannot be avoided entirely. But certain techniques greatly reduce the chances of their occurrence.

The first rule is to make sure that all queries are accessing the same data elements in the same order. Correcting the deadlock scenario depicted in Listing 11.1 is easily accomplished by making sure that both queries access the tables in the same order.

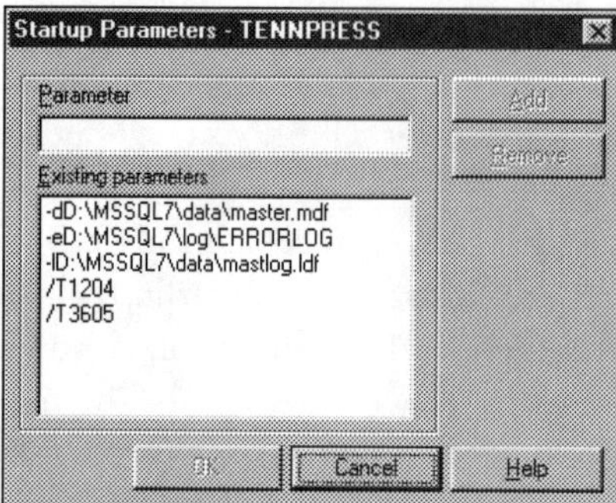

Figure 11.1 Adding traceflags 3605 and 1204 to the database settings.

It is also important to try to make sure that updating and reading processes are using the same indexes to access data. If these processes use different indexes, it is possible that a deadlock problem could occur between two indexes.

This type of analysis and correction is difficult to perform if the code is not all contained within stored procedures. It can be hard to track down SQL code stored away deep down in unknown application modules. This alone is a very good reason to require the use of stored procedures for all database access.

Another way to prevent deadlocking is to ensure that any code running within the context of a transaction completes as quickly as possible. One way to accomplish this is to *prime* the data into cache. For example, suppose you were running the following code:

```
UPDATE Suppliers
SET    HomePage = 'http://www.coriolis.com'
```

This code would invoke a full table scan and would eventually escalate to an exclusive table lock. Unless this information is accessed frequently, it will not be in data cache and the query will take a relatively long time to complete. The time required for the **UPDATE** to finish could be drastically reduced by first running a **SELECT** statement to *pre-fetch* the data into cache. The overall operation may take slightly longer, but the amount of time that an *exclusive* lock is held on the table is greatly reduced. The reduced time for the exclusive lock helps prevent both blocking and deadlocking. In the following modified sample, notice that only a single column is fetched (to reduce I/O in **tempdb**) and that the **SELECT** statement uses a **NOLOCK** optimizer hint:

```
SELECT SupplierID
INTO   #tmp
FROM   Suppliers (NOLOCK)

UPDATE Suppliers
SET    HomePage = 'http://www.coriolis.com'
```

Programming Transactions

To accurately take advantage of transactions, you'll need to understand the various ways that SQL Server handles transactions. We'll examine these modes, and describe the ways that programs can be coded to use transactions.

Implicit, Explicit, And Autocommit Transactions

By default, when SQL Server 7 is installed, it operates in a mode described by Microsoft as *autocommit*. That means that each individual SQL instruction is treated as a transaction and the database automatically issues a **COMMIT** after the instruction successfully completes. This is a very convenient feature for the designer and developer because they do not have to concern themselves with remembering to manually send **COMMIT** instructions after each instruction.

Autocommit is not the ANSI SQL-92 standard behavior.

The ANSI standard specifies that the database operates in an *implicit* transaction mode. In this mode, each SQL statement following a **COMMIT** or **ROLLBACK** instruction automatically marks the start of a transaction, but the database does not automatically **COMMIT**. The implicit transaction mode is rarely used.

Setting the implicit transaction mode can be accomplished by using the **SET** command, which is a connection-level setting:

```
SET IMPLICIT_TRANSACTIONS ON     -- Uses implicit transactions mode
SET IMPLICIT_TRANSACTIONS OFF    -- Uses autocommit transactions mode
```

This mode will also be set when the following command is submitted to the database:

```
SET ANSI DEFAULTS ON
```

If you want to use the implicit transaction mode for all users, you can set the **user options** configuration parameters. For implicit transaction mode, you must set bit 2. Do so by using the following command:

```
EXEC sp_configure "user options", <value>
```

The **BEGIN TRANSACTION** and **COMMIT or ROLLBACK** instructions define explicit transactions. You can use these commands to manage a transaction whether the database is in implicit transaction mode or autocommit mode. Using these explicit statements is the recommended way to manage transactions in the database.

You should demarcate only those SQL statements that absolutely need to be protected by a transaction. If the integrity of the information does not depend on a series of statements to be combined in a transaction, they should be run as individual commands. This is so that the blocking and deadlocking in the database is kept to a minimum. Following this rule also maximizes user concurrency and throughput in the database.

Naming Transactions

In addition to the standard transaction delimiters, SQL Server allows you to name your units of work. Although naming a transaction is not necessary, it is a very good practice to consider. The following example names the unit of work:

```
BEGIN TRAN EXAMTEST
UPDATE Orders
SET    ShipName = "Test Order"
ROLLBACK TRAN EXAMTEST
```

This can be useful if you want to monitor transaction activity in the database. You can do this in two ways.

First, you can use the SQL Profiler utility, which can be configured either to display details for each transaction event or to see counts for each transaction name. This can be a very good diagnostic tool.

Second, you can find out the oldest open transaction in the database by using the following:

```
DBCC OPENTRAN( Northwind )
```

This is important if you suspect a long-running transaction may cause the database logs to fill up. If an open transaction is named, it is easy to determine to what process the transaction belongs. Otherwise it can be rather difficult to find the offending process.

A word of caution, however, regarding the use of transaction names. A **COMMIT** statement that has a misspelled transaction name will still work correctly. But a **ROLLBACK** with a misspelled transaction name will return an error without rolling back the transaction. Because most testing is *positive-pass testing*—that is, testing only to see if the code works under normal circumstances—a typo in a **ROLLBACK** transaction name statement may not be immediately evident. It is very important to test the **ROLLBACK** condition, because a misspelling can cause transactions to remain unexpectedly open. This condition can lead to the log filling up and can cause severe blocking if additional commands are subsequently executed with the same connection.

Nesting

In the practical application of managing transactions in a large database system, it is common for them to become nested several levels deep. Sometimes knowing where you are within a nested set of transactions can become difficult. It is important for you understand how the **COMMIT** and **ROLLBACK** statements impact nested transactions and how you can properly code your stored procedures to handle them.

First, let's take a look at some of the ways that transactions become nested in a database design. Some applications may issue a **BEGIN TRANSACTION** or **SET IMPLICIT TRANSACTIONS ON** when a connection to the database is opened. This is especially true of third-party application packages that support multiple database vendors and 4GL development systems. Many stored procedures also employ the use of explicit transactions to protect data integrity. Stored procedures can sometimes execute other stored procedures that may also employ the use of explicit transactions. In these ways any given stored procedure may become deeply nested within a series of transactions. So what will happen if an error occurs and a **ROLLBACK** is issued?

In order to answer that question, run the following SQL statements in the *Northwind* practice database:


```
BEGIN TRANSACTION OuterTran
INSERT CustomerDemographics
VALUES ("BigCust", "These are my large accounts.")

   BEGIN TRANSACTION InnerTran
   INSERT Region
   VALUES (777, "Big Customer Region")

   select @@trancount
   /* Oops, there must be an error */
   ROLLBACK TRAN InnerTran
   select @@trancount
ROLLBACK
select @@trancount
```

Did you catch the error 6401 in the middle of the results? This is caused by the fact that the first **ROLLBACK** contains the name of the inner transaction, but the database keeps track only of the name of the outer transaction name.

The **@@TRANCOUNT** global variable shows you how many levels deep you are nested, and returns 0 if no open transaction exists.

The **ROLLBACK** statement by itself implicitly refers to the outer transaction, because it rolled back both the inner and outer transactions. Remember that a **ROLLBACK** goes all the way back to the outermost transaction.

A **COMMIT** statement ignores any transaction name associated with it and operates on the innermost transaction name. If you have transactions nested 10 levels deep, you need 10 **COMMIT** statements in order to close all the transactions. This is true whether or not the **COMMIT** statements refer to transaction names, even if the **COMMIT** statements reference the name of the outermost transaction name. However, you will need only a single **ROLLBACK** statement to undo the whole bunch.

If a procedure executes another procedure, it is possible that the inner procedure also uses transactions. If an error occurs in the inner procedure and the transaction is rolled back, the **COMMIT** or **ROLLBACK** in the outer procedure will cause yet another error to be raised because no active transaction exists any longer. For this reason, it is best to code **COMMIT** and **ROLLACK** statements, along with the **@@TRANCOUNT** global variable. For example:

```
IF @@TRANCOUNT > 0 COMMIT
```

Savepoints Within A Transaction

Occasionally it may be necessary to save your work within a transaction and provide the opportunity to undo only a portion of a transaction without losing your ability to **ROLLBACK** the entire transaction. SQL Server 7 provides just this functionality for you. You can create what is referred to as a *savepoint* and can **ROLLBACK** to that point if it becomes necessary. The following example illustrates this feature:

```
BEGIN TRAN OUTERTRAN
INSERT Shippers
VALUES ("The Lords Shipping", "1-800-I-ACCEPT")

SAVE TRAN SAVE_SHIPPER

INSERT Territories
VALUES ("Certified", "Certified DBA's", 1000)

if @@error . = 0
      ROLLBACK TRAN SAVE_SHIPPER

COMMIT
```

Note that it is not necessary to **COMMIT** the savepoint; it is more like a bookmark that you can use to go back to if necessary.

Transaction Behavior Within Triggers

When we first introduced the topic of database transactions, we made the point that all SQL statements are treated as an implicit transaction, even if you do not explicitly specify a **BEGIN TRAN** instruction. But what if a single SQL statement was an **INSERT** or **UPDATE** to a table that has a trigger? Because the statement is a single instruction in its outermost form and it is defined as a transaction, it must fit into ACID properties of a transaction. Namely, it must be treated a single logical unit of work where everything or nothing at all completes. This holds true whether or not a trigger exists on a table.

For this reason, a trigger always runs within the context of a transaction. If the trigger executes a **ROLLBACK**, the initiating **INSERT** or **UPDATE** command will also be rolled back. If the trigger completes successfully, the entire transaction completes successfully, because any constraints (such as, **FOREIGN KEY** or **CHECK** constraint) are validated before the trigger is fired.

The subject of triggers is covered in more detail in Chapter 3.

Distributed Transactions

SQL Server 7 is a database engine that is very capable of hosting mission-critical enterprise software applications. It is very likely that you will see, or perhaps even design, complex applications involving multiple database servers hosting the same application. One possible scenario is a design where information must be written to more than one server at the same time in order to ensure the integrity of the overall system. For example, if a banking deposit is written to one server, it must also be written to another server. Let's examine how can you protect against failures on either one of the servers.

11

The solution lies in two-phase commit technology and the concept of *distributed transactions*. SQL Server 7 includes a transaction monitor process known as the *Distributed Transaction Coordinator*, or *DTC*. This program manages the two-phase commit protocol between two resources and communicates the status of the transaction back to the initiating process. A distributed transaction extends the concepts of transaction management from a single server to multiple servers. The concepts and rules remain the same.

Before starting a distributed transaction, you must first be sure that the DTC service is installed and running on the database server. It needs to be active only on the server that is initiating the two-phase commit.

Once the DTC service is active, defining a distributed transaction involves two steps. First, the **BEGIN TRANSACTION** is changed to **BEGIN**

DISTRIBUTED TRANSACTION. The latter statement is the hook that automatically invokes the DTC service without any complicated programming on your part. Second, the update on the remote server must be made in the form of a remote stored procedure call. It is recommended that all update activities on remote servers be contained within stored procedures. The following is a sample of a code segment that invokes a distributed transaction:

```
BEGIN DISTRIBUTED TRANSACTION
EXECUTE TENNPRESS.Northwind.dbo.sp_sqlexec
      'INSERT Shippers VALUES ("The Lords Shipping", "1-800-I-ACCEPT")'
IF @@error . = 0
      ROLLBACK
ELSE
      COMMIT
```

It is not possible to execute directly an **INSERT** or **UPDATE** statement on a remote server. However, SQL Server 7 includes a system stored procedure that can be used to execute dynamic SQL statements on a remote server. In the preceding example, the **sp_sqlexec** procedure is used to execute the **INSERT** statement. Ideally, the table insert should be written in a stored procedure. Even so, using the **sp_sqlexec** system stored procedure can be very convenient at times. It can even be reliably used within a distributed transaction, as shown.

Cursors And Optimistic Locking

An extensive and flexible server-side cursor architecture is supported in SQL Server 7. Although the topic of server-side cursors in handled in significantly more detail in another chapter, it is worthy of mention here because it is very important to understand how cursors implement locking and transaction control. The wrong use of concurrency control within a cursor can have far-reaching effects in the database. Not only can you end up with data errors, but you could also end up with a database design that promotes extensive blocking and deadlocking.

So what is the correct way to implement concurrency control within server-side cursors? You should be familiar with the scrolling mechanism of cursors and the difference between read-only and updateable cursors, and we will review these differences and examine the under-the-covers locking behavior for each.

A *read-only cursor* uses shared locks on the database resources only for the duration of each individual fetch when the transaction isolation level is left at the default

Read Committed. If the isolation level is set to **Read Uncommitted**, no locks are used. The main focus here is for cursors that are created for update. A lot of processing can occur in the cursor fetch loop between the time the fetch is made into variables and the time the update is made in the database. Ample opportunity exists for a fetched row to be updated by another process. Allowing the cursor update to proceed in this case would create the "where is my data?" problem described earlier in this chapter.

Because you have to contend with many different scenarios, SQL Server 7 provides for two general categories of cursor locking behavior in update cursors: *optimistic* and *pessimistic*. *Optimistic locking* goes on the premise that the likelihood of underlying data to change between the time of the fetch and the update is low. *Pessimistic locking* presumes that the data will almost certainly change before you update it.

Although you can implement optimistic locking in two ways, T-SQL cursors support only one of those methods. Both methods are different forms of row versioning—the ability to tell whether a row has changed since it was read. ADO and ODBC clients support a value detection versioning mode. In this mode, the client re-reads the data and determines if any data changes have occurred. The other mode, which is supported in T-SQL cursors, relies on a *timestamp* column to be in the source table. SQL Server automatically updates *timestamp* columns when a row is updated, and can easily compare this value with a value that is internally stored when a fetch is made.

Either way, when the Transaction Isolation Level is **read commited**, a cursor that is declared with optimistic locking issues shared locks only for the duration of the fetch. This is the same behavior seen with read-only cursors. But if the server detects that the data has changed before the update you will see the following error:

```
Server: Msg 16934, Level 10, State 1, Line 1093055397
Optimistic concurrency check failed. The row was modified outside of
this cursor.
```

Pessimistic locking behavior is created when the cursor is opened with **SCROLL**. In this mode, an update lock is placed on the row until the next fetch is made, which prevents updates by other processes. But if the cursor is run from within a transaction, the update lock is held until a **COMMIT** or **ROLLBACK** is issued. This mode of cursor concurrency should only be used if necessary, because extensive database blocking can potentially occur.

Chapter Summary

We have discussed the following items in this chapter:

- Database transactions, along with declarative referential integrity and triggers, are the features that provide you with the ability to design a database to protect the integrity of your data.
- According to the ANSI SQL-92 standards, a transaction is comprised of one or more data modification statements that possess all four ACID properties: Atomicity, Consistency, Isolation, and Durability.
- Four levels of transaction isolation levels exist, each of which impacts data consistency inversely with database concurrency: **Read Uncommitted**, **Read Committed**, **Repeatable Read**, and **Serializable**.
- **Read Committed** is the default transaction isolation level for SQL Server 7.
- The **Read Uncommitted** isolation level specifies that shared locks will not be issued and exclusive locks will not be honored. **Read Uncommitted** is the best performance option and also the best concurrency option, but it is the worst option for data consistency.
- The **Read Committed** isolation level specifies that shared locks will be issued and exclusive locks will be honored for the duration of only the **SELECT** statement.
- The **Repeatable Read** isolation level specifies that shared locks will be issued and exclusive locks will be honored for the duration of the transaction.
- The **Serializable** isolation level specifies that shared locks will be issued, exclusive locks will be honored, and inserts within the key range will be prohibited for the duration of the transaction. This is the best option for data consistency, but is the worst option for performance and concurrency.
- The lowest isolation level possible that will still protect the integrity of the data should be used.
- The isolation level can be set using either the **SET TRANSACTION ISOLATION LEVEL** command or through the use of optimizer hints.
- A database lock is a semaphore used to secure a database resource and protect data integrity.
- Six database resources can be locked: **RID** (or **Row**), **Page**, **Extent**, **Table**, **Key-Range**, and **Database (DB)**.
- Eight modes of locking the database resources exist: **(IS)** intent shared, **(IX)** intent exclusive, **(SIX)** shared with intent exclusive, **(SCM)** shared or modified schema, **(S)** shared, **(U)** update, **(X)** exclusive, and **(BU)** bulk update.

- For each lock on a database resource, a related *intent* lock is issued for each resource up the hierarchy.
- Database locks can be observed by using the **sp_lock** system stored procedure or by using the Management|Current Activity|Locks/Object selection in the Enterprise Manager.
- SQL Server 7 implements dynamic locking, which is the ability of the server to automatically select the appropriate level of resource to lock and to escalate the level of resource locked as becomes appropriate for performance.
- Lock escalation behavior cannot be tuned in SQL Server 7.
- It is recommended to leave the **sp_configure "locks"** setting to the default value of 0, which allows the server to dynamically configure the memory heaps allocated to locking structures.
- The **SET LOCK_TIMEOUT** session-level setting can be used to force a query to timeout if it is blocked for a specified period of time.
- The **sp_indexoption** system stored procedure can be used to prevent the server from creating either or both **RID** locks or page locks on a given table or index.
- You can use eight optimizer hints to change default locking behavior: **HOLDLOCK**, **PAGLOCK**, **READCOMMITTED**, **REPEATABLEREAD**, **ROWLOCK**, **Serializable**, **TABLOCK**, **TABLOCKX**.
- A deadlock occurs when two processes are blocking each other in a circular-locking pattern.
- All applications should check for and handle the 1205 deadlock error message.
- You can detect deadlocking using the Windows NT Perfmon utility, SQL Profiler, or by checking the SQL error log.
- You can observe detailed deadlocks in the SQL error log by setting both the 3605 and 1204 traceflags on.
- Deadlock avoidance techniques include keeping transactions as short as possible, accessing the data in the same order, and priming the data into cache.
- Transactions are delimited using the **BEGIN TRAN**, **COMMIT TRAN**, and **ROLLBACK TRAN** statements.
- The ANSI SQL-92 standard specifies that the database should run in implicit transaction mode.
- SQL Server 7 defaults to autocommit transaction processing mode.
- The autocommit transaction processing mode can be turned off by using the **SET IMPLICIT_TRANSATIONS ON** command.

- For convenience, transactions can be given optional names for easy monitoring.
- You can nest transactions.
- All procedures should issue the command **if @@trancount > 0 rollback** when an error is detected.
- You can specify transaction savepoints using the **SAVE TRAN <savepoint name>** command.
- Triggers always run within the context of a transaction.
- A **ROLLBACK** statement cancels all changes to the outermost transaction.
- A **COMMIT** statement commits the work for only the innermost transaction.
- A distributed transaction uses the two-phase commit protocol to enforce transactional consistency across two or more database servers.
- The Distributed Transaction Coordinator (DTC) is a Windows NT service that installs with SQL Server 7 and is used to manage and monitor the two-phase commit distributed transaction protocol between two or more SQL servers.
- The DTC service is required only to be running on servers that are initiating a distributed transaction.
- Two types of locking behavior are supported for updateable T-SQL cursors: optimistic locking and pessimistic locking. Optimistic locking is the best choice for user concurrency and is implemented using timestamp columns and row-versioning. Pessimistic locking is the best choice for data integrity and is implemented using scroll locks (or hold locks) for the duration of the transaction.
- A database error is generated if a row is updated between the **FETCH** and **UPDATE** commands when optimistic locking is specified.

REVIEW QUESTIONS

1. **Read Uncommitted** is the best isolation level to use as a general rule of thumb.
   a. True
   b. False

2. The default isolation level for SQL Sever 7 is: (Choose all correct answers.)
   a. Row-level locking
   b. Dirty reads
   c. **Read Committed**
   d. Autocommit

3. The best way to select the optimal isolation level for your design is to:
   a. Use the lowest level that still provides data integrity.
   b. Use the highest level that still provides data integrity.
   c. Use the level that will provide the best performance.
   d. Use the level that will provide the best consistency.

4. SQL Server defaults to using which of the following types of locks? (Choose all correct answers.)
   a. **RID**
   b. **Page**
   c. **Uncommitted**
   d. **Table**

5. An intent shared lock is used to:
   a. Indicate possible additional update locks lower in the resource hierarchy.
   b. Indicate possible additional shared locks higher in the resource hierarchy.
   c. Force the use of a shared lock.
   d. Indicate possible additional shared locks lower in the resource hierarchy.

6. The database will escalate a **RID** lock to a table lock dynamically.
   a. True
   b. False

7. Techniques used to prevent deadlocking include: (Choose all correct answers.)
   a. Keep transactions as short as possible.
   b. Pre-fetch data into cache.
   c. Access data in the same order.
   d. Use the lowest isolation level possible while still protecting data integrity.
   e. All of the above.

8. Which of the following commands increment the **@@TRANCOUNT** variable by 1? (Choose all correct answers.)
   a. **SAVE TRANSACTION**
   b. **BEGIN DISTRIBUTED TRANSACTION**
   c. **COMMIT TRANSACTION**
   d. **ROLLBACK TRANSACTION**

9. A traceflag does not need to be set in order to detect deadlocks in the database.
   a. True
   b. False

10. The autocommit transaction mode:
    a. Automatically issues a savepoint after every SQL command.
    b. Automatically issues a **COMMIT** after every SQL command.
    c. Explicitly begins a transaction after every SQL command.
    d. Automatically issues a **ROLLBACK** after every error.

11. A database application should always: (Choose all correct answers.)
    a. Issue a **COMMIT** before exiting a stored procedure.
    b. Issue a **if @@trancount > 0 rollback** after a fatal error.
    c. Check for and appropriately handle a 1205 deadlock error message.
    d. **SET IMPLICIT_TRANSACTIONS ON**.

12. **A WAITFOR DELAY** statement can be used in a transaction to prevent deadlocks.
    a. True
    b. False

Hands-On Projects

The lead programmer, Chris, had called Susan. "Hey," he said, "I'm seeing a lot of locking errors returning from my code. Can you come take a look at this?"

Susan grabbed her notebook and a pen and headed for Chris's cubicle. She watched as Chris's code encountered error after error regarding locked data. And this was even before any significant load was put on the database. She went back to her workstation and observed the locks from the database perspective.

Project 11.1

In this example we will work with a couple different update statements that will allow you to observe the dynamic locking behavior of SQL Server 7:

1. Open a new window in Query Analyzer.
2. Change database to *Northwind*.
3. Type and execute the code in Listing 11.2.
4. Notice that an exclusive lock is on a single row, but *IX* locks are on the next higher page and again at the table level.
5. Type and execute the code in Listing 11.3.
6. This query updates 500 rows in the *Order Details* table. Notice how SQL Server is still uses page locking.
7. Type and execute the code in Listing 11.4.

8. This query updates 765 rows in the *Order Details* table. SQL Server now upgrades the locks to an exclusive table lock for the data and uses *IX* locks for the index pages.

Listing 11.2 Row locks example #1.

```
BEGIN TRANSACTION
UPDATE  [Order Details]
SET     Discount = 0
WHERE   OrderID  = 10248
AND     ProductID= 11
exec sp_lock @@spid
ROLLBACK
```

Listing 11.3 Row locks example #2.

```
BEGIN TRANSACTION
UPDATE  [Order Details]
SET     Discount = 0
WHERE   OrderID  between 10248 and 10534
exec sp_lock @@spid
ROLLBACK
```

Listing 11.4 **Table** and page locks.

```
BEGIN TRANSACTION
UPDATE  [Order Details]
SET     Discount = 0
WHERE   OrderID  between 10248 and 10535
exec sp_lock @@spid
ROLLBACK
```

11

Project 11.2

In this example, we will take a look at how to use SQL Profiler and Performance Monitor to detect database deadlocking:

1. Select Start|Programs|Administrative Tools|Performance Monitor.
2. Click on the + sign to add new counters to the graph.
3. Select the Object: SQL Server: Locks from the drop-down menu.
4. Select **Number Of Deadlocks/Sec** in the Counters window and highlight all the instances. Refer to Figure 11.2.
5. Click on Add and Done to add the counters to the Performance Monitor window.
6. Open a new window in Query Analyzer. Type in the code shown in Listing 11.5.
7. Open another new window in Query Analyzer. Type in the code shown in Listing 11.6.

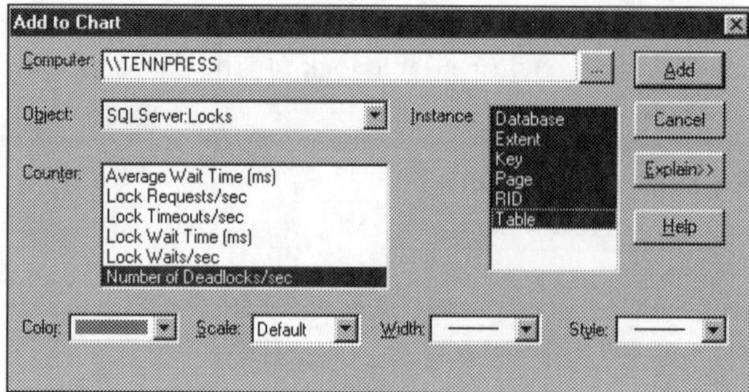

Figure 11.2 Adding deadlock counters to Performance Monitor.

8. Execute the code in the first window, switch to the second window, and execute the code there also.
9. Observe that Performance Monitor has reported a table deadlock.
10. Select Start|Programs|Microsoft SQL Server 7|Profiler.
11. Click on the Create Trace Wizard icon.
12. Click on Next and select Identify The Cause Of A Deadlock in the Problem drop-down menu.
13. Click on Next, Next, and Finish to create the trace profile.
14. Again, execute the code in the Query Analyzer from Listing 11.5.
15. Quickly, execute the code in the Query Analyzer from Listing 11.6.
16. Observe the deadlocking in the Profiler and the SQL statements that contributed to the deadlock condition.

Listing 11.5 Deadlock-producing code #1.

```
begin transaction
update  [Orders]
set     Freight = 0
waitfor delay '0:0:1'
update  [Order Details]
set     Discount = 0
rollback
```

Listing 11.6 Deadlock-producing code #2.

```
begin transaction
update  [Order Details]
set     Discount = 0
waitfor delay '0:0:1'
update  [Orders]
set     Freight = 0
rollback
```

See Figure 11.2 for an example of using Performance Monitor to check for deadlocks.

Susan also wondered if the data being locked was causing other problems. Sure enough, some of the data the user sent from the client screen wasn't making it into the database. Using the SQL Server Profiler tool to create a trace on the calls to the database, she saw that the data had been sent to the database, but had been rejected by one of her constraints. When she examined the tables, she found that some of the data did make it through to the database, and now she had bigger problems. The data that had gotten through didn't violate any referential integrity on the database, but it wasn't particularly useful without all of the data. She decided to group the data into transactions. "This way," she thought, " if it all doesn't go, none of it will." Chris had his team modify their code to take advantage of the transactions and to handle the errors generated by the rejections. The transactions also prevented most of the locking errors she saw in the database.

CHAPTER TWELVE

STORED PROCEDURES

After Reading This Chapter And Completing The Exercises, You Will Be Able To:

- Define the benefits of using stored procedures
- Define a stored procedure and its types
- Define input and output parameters
- Create a stored procedure
- Alter a stored procedure
- Drop a stored procedure
- Execute a stored procedure
- Use the **RAISERROR** statement
- Define the system views and their purpose

Stored procedures are SQL statements that are stored on the server to be enacted by programs or triggers later. Advantages for using stored procedures include ease of security, speed of operations, and business rules enforcement. We'll learn about these advantages and more in this chapter, as well as how to create stored procedures and modify them.

Stored Procedures

A *stored procedure* is a database object that contains one or more Transact-SQL statements. Stored procedures are used to process data on the server. If you have a programming background, you can relate SQL Server 7 stored procedures to procedures in programming languages, such as Visual Basic. SQL Server stored procedures:

- Perform operations in the database
- Can call other stored procedures
- Can accept input parameters
- Can return multiple values
- Can return a status that indicates success or failure of execution. In case of failure, it also returns a reason for the failure.

Use the **RETURN [<integer_expression>]** statement to return a status of the execution of a stored procedure.

Why Use A Stored Procedure?

Some of the advantages to using stored procedures are:

- Stored procedures can be used as a security mechanism. If the data stored in the database is accessed and modified through stored procedures, you can grant execute permissions on the stored procedures without granting permissions to the underlying tables and views.
- Stored procedures can be used to simplify business applications. Business logic, rules, and policies can be designed, programmed, and tested once in stored procedures and shared by different applications. This not only ensures consistency in how the data is accessed and altered but also makes it possible to make only one change if the business logic, rules, or policies change.
- Stored procedures increase performance. A stored procedure is compiled the first time it is executed, and its execution plan will remain in the cache. Stored procedures reduce network traffic because only the call of the stored procedure and the final result are sent over the network, rather than multiple SQL statements and the results of those SQL statements.

Prior versions of SQL Server stored a partially compiled execution plan of the Transact-SQL statements when the stored procedure was created. This behavior has changed in SQL Server 7. Many performance benefits that applied only to stored procedures in prior versions have been extended to processing of Transact-SQL statements. The most important of these benefits is that each time a statement is executed, SQL Server compares the statement with statements for which it already has created execution plans. If SQL Server finds a match, it will reuse the execution plan.

- Stored procedures shift *application* logic from the client to the server, which allows the use of the more powerful resources located on the server.
- Stored procedures can automatically execute processes (such as a notification that the server was restarted, etc.) when SQL Server is started.

Stored procedures are automatically executed only after all databases have been recovered. Use the **sp_procoption** system stored procedure to set stored procedures to execute automatically at startup.

Types Of Stored Procedures

Five types of stored procedures exist in SQL Server 7:

- System stored procedures
- Extended stored procedures
- Local (user) stored procedures
- Remote stored procedures
- Temporary stored procedures

System Stored Procedures

System stored procedures are identified by the **sp_** prefix. They are stored in the *master* database, but can be executed from any database without specifying the database qualifier name. System stored procedures are used to:

- Retrieve data from system tables.
- Update system tables.
- Perform administrative tasks.

If a stored procedure prefixed with **sp_** is executed, SQL Server will try to find the stored procedure in the following order:

- The *master* database
- The specified database if a database qualifier was provided
- The current database

It is not recommended to prefix user stored procedures with **sp_**. If a user stored procedure has the same name as a system stored procedure, it will *never* be executed.

For example, to create a stored procedure named **sp_who** in the *Northwind* database use the following statement:

```
CREATE PROCEDURE sp_who AS
SELECT * FROM Orders
RETURN
GO
```

Even if you try to run the stored procedure specifying the database qualifier as follows:

```
EXECUTE Northwind..sp_who
GO
```

the **sp_who** system stored procedure stored in the *master* database will be executed.

Extended Stored Procedures

Extended stored procedures are identified by the **xp_** prefix. They are stored in the *master* database. To execute an extended stored procedure from any other database you must qualify the database name, such as **master..<extended_stored_procedure>**.

As their name suggests, extended stored procedures are used to extend SQL Server capabilities. Although SQL Server contains many extended stored procedures, you can create your own external routine with a programming language like C++ and save it as a dynamic link library (DLL) so that SQL Server can load and execute it. Examples of this type of stored procedure include operating system calls that load a particular tape library, or other hardware extensions.

Extended stored procedures can only be added to the *master* database.

Local (User) Stored Procedures

Local stored procedures are stored procedures created in user databases. Generally, they are used to implement business logic, rules, and policies. They are created with the **CREATE PROCEDURE** statement explained later in this chapter.

Remote Stored Procedures

Remote stored procedures are stored procedures that exist in remote SQL Servers and are called in the current server. You can execute a system, extended, or local stored procedure from a remote SQL Server.

To call a stored procedure that exists in another SQL Server, the server must be a linked server or defined as a remote server.

Temporary Stored Procedures

Temporary stored procedures are created in the *tempdb* database. A temporary stored procedure can be:

- **Local** A local temporary stored procedure is indicated by the # (pound) sign preceding the procedure name, that is, **#<stored_procedure_name>**. A local stored procedure is only visible to the session that created it and is automatically deleted when the session is closed.
- **Global** A global temporary stored procedure is indicated by the ## sign preceding the procedure name, that is, **##<stored_procedure_name>**. A global stored procedure is visible to all sessions; it is automatically deleted when the session that created it is closed and any currently executing versions of the stored procedure being executed by other sessions complete.

You should use temporary stored procedures only when connecting to prior versions of SQL Server because those versions cannot reuse Transact-SQL statements execution plans found in cache. If you are connecting to a SQL Server 7 database, use the **sp_executesql** system stored procedure instead of creating temporary stored procedures.

Deferred Name Resolution And Compilation Of Stored Procedures

A stored procedure goes through different stages, which will be explained next. These stages are parsing, resolution, optimization, and compilation.

Parsing

The first thing that occurs when a stored procedure is created is that the Transact-SQL statements that define the procedure are checked for syntactical accuracy. This process is known as *parsing*. If SQL Server 7 finds a syntax error in any of the statements, an error is returned and the stored procedure is not created. If no syntax error is found, the text definition of the stored procedure is stored in the *syscomments* system table and an entry is created in the *sysobjects* system table.

A major difference between prior versions of SQL Server and version 7 is that a stored procedure can be created even if the objects it references do not exist. This is called *deferred name resolution.*

In prior versions of SQL Server, when a stored procedure was created, a normalized plan was saved in the *sysprocedures* system table. With deferred name resolution, a normalized plan is not created. In SQL Server 7 the *sysprocedures* table no longer exists.

Resolution

The first thing that occurs when a stored procedure is executed for the first time or when a stored procedure is recompiled is a process called *resolution*. During this process SQL Server 7 performs several activities:

- It reads the definition of the stored procedure found in the *syscomments* system table.
- It checks that the objects referenced by the Transact-SQL statements that define the procedure exist.
- It checks the compatibility of data types between table columns and variables.

If an error is encountered, the stored procedure will not be executed and an error message will be returned. Stored procedures are recompiled when:

- The statistics of an index or table that it references changes.
- A new index is created on a table that it references.
- A table that it references is altered.
- The stored procedure is executed with the **WITH RECOMPILE** option (see "Executing A Stored Procedure" later in this chapter).
- The stored procedure was created with the **WITH RECOMPILE** clause (see "Creating A Stored Procedure" later in this chapter).
- The **sp_recompile** system stored procedure is run against any table that the procedure references.

Optimization

If no errors were found during the resolution stage, the SQL Server query optimizer analyzes the Transact-SQL statements that define the stored procedure and creates a plan defining the fastest way to access the data and execute the procedure. This process is known as *optimization of a stored procedure*. In order to create the best execution plan, the optimizer analyzes:

- The amount of data in the referenced tables
- The existing indexes of the tables and their distribution statistics

- The distribution statistics of nonindexed columns
- The **WHERE** clause(s) of the Transact-SQL statements
- If any **UNION**, **GROUP BY**, or **ORDER BY** clauses are used

Compilation

In the last process, *compilation*, SQL Server places the compiled and optimized execution plan in procedure cache. This compiled and optimized execution plan that is placed in memory will be used when the stored procedure is executed.

The execution plan of a stored procedure will stay in procedure cache unless the space in memory is needed for another object or unless SQL Server is stopped. If the optimized and compiled plan stays in memory, all other executions of the stored procedure will run faster because they do not have to go through the resolution, optimization, and compilation processes.

Creating A Stored Procedure

You can create a stored procedure with the **CREATE PROCEDURE** statement and with the Create Stored Procedure Wizard. Before you create a stored procedure you should test all the statements that will define it to make sure they return the expected results. Stored procedures can only be created in the current database, except for temporary stored procedures, which are created in the *tempdb* database.

12

The following Transact-SQL statements cannot be included in a stored procedure definition:

- **CREATE DEFAULT**
- **CREATE PROCEDURE**
- **CREATE RULE**
- **CREATE TRIGGER**
- **CREATE VIEW**
- **SET SHOWPLAN_TEXT**
- **SET SHOWPLAN_ALL**

When creating a stored procedure keep in mind:

- SQL Server 7 allows the creation of stored procedures that reference tables and views that are not defined.

Though a stored procedure that references nonexistent tables and views can be created, it cannot be executed if those objects do not exist.

- The maximum size of a stored procedure is 128MB.
- The **CREATE PROCEDURE** statement must be the only statement in the batch that defines the stored procedure.
- Stored procedures can execute other stored procedures and can reference tables and views.
- The first character of a stored procedure name has to be a letter as defined in the Unicode Standard 2 or one of the following symbols: _, @. If the stored procedure name has embedded spaces, you must delimit it with brackets, such as [**stored procedure name**]. The stored procedure name can have 128 characters.

The first character of a temporary stored procedure name is the # (pound) sign (a single # denotes a local temporary stored procedure, and two ## denote a global temporary stored procedure).

- A local temporary table created in a stored procedure is only visible within the stored procedure. When the procedure finishes executing, the local temporary table will be dropped.
- By default, database owners (members of the *db_owner* role), system administrators (members of the *sysadmin* role), and DDL administrators (members of the *db_ddladmin* role) are the only roles authorized to create stored procedures.

To avoid broken ownership chains (where the owner of a stored procedure and owner of the table or view that is referenced differs), create all database objects as the database owner.

- It is a good practice to have the stored procedure return a success or failure status. In case of a failure, the stored procedure should also return the reason for failure.
- Do not prefix user-defined stored procedures with **sp_**; this prefix is used by system stored procedures.
- It is a good practice to keep stored procedures simple. Have each stored procedure accomplish a single task. Create more small stored procedures rather than fewer larger ones.
- A **SET** option specified in a stored procedure stays current only while the stored procedure is running.
- Change the status of the settings of **SET QUOTED_IDENTIFIER** and **SET ANSI_NULLS** to the desired values at the time the stored procedure is created. These settings are used when the stored procedure is executed, no matter what the settings are in the client calling the procedure. All other **SET**

Table 12.1 System stored procedures used to view stored procedure information.

View Name	Brief Description
sp_depends	Returns a list of database objects (tables, views, other stored procedures) dependent on a stored procedure
sp_help	Returns a list of parameters of a stored procedure
sp_helptext	Returns the stored procedure definition
sp_stored_procedures	Returns a list of stored procedures in the current database

options are not saved and should be specified in the stored procedure. Table 12.1 shows system stored procedures used to view information about stored procedures.

Grouping Stored Procedures

You can group stored procedures logically. To group stored procedures together, name them the same, but specify a different identification number using the following syntax:

```
<procedure_name>[;<number>]
```

For example, you might create two stored procedures that are used to delete an order from a database. These two stored procedures might depend on each other, meaning that the first one executes the other. You would name these stored procedures in the following manner:

```
usp_DeleteOrders;1
usp_DeleteOrders;2
```

Grouping stored procedures allows them to be dropped at the same time with one drop statement (see "Dropping A Stored Procedure" later in this chapter). Once stored procedures are grouped, you cannot drop an individual stored procedure without dropping all stored procedures within the group.

CREATE PROCEDURE Statement

The **CREATE PROCEDURE** statement is used to define a stored procedure. The syntax is as follows:

```
CREATE PROC[EDURE] <stored_procedure_name>[;<number>]
[ @<parameter1> <data_type> [VARYING] [=<default_value>] [OUTPUT]
  [...[, @<parameterN> <data_type> [VARYING]
    [=<default_value>] [OUTPUT] ] ]
  ]
[WITH { [RECOMPILE] [,] [ENCRYPTION] ]
[FOR REPLICATION]
```

```
AS
<Transact-SQL statement1>
[... <Transact-SQL statementN>]
```

For information about **@<parameters>** see "Stored Procedure Parameters" later in this chapter.

The **RECOMPILE** clause is used to instruct SQL Server to recompile the stored procedure every time it is executed. This clause prevents the execution plan of the procedure to be cached. Listing 12.1 shows how to use the **RECOMPILE** clause.

If a stored procedure receives parameters by which it performs a range search, it is a good practice to use the **RECOMPILE** clause to have a current execution plan. For example, if you have created a stored procedure with the following statement:

```
CREATE PROCEDURE usp_OrdersByDate
     @StartDate    datetime = '1900-01-01',
     @EndDate      datetime = '2999-01-01'
AS
SELECT * FROM Orders
WHERE OrderDate BETWEEN @StartDate AND @EndDate
RETURN
GO
```

And the first time it is executed with the following statement:

```
EXECUTE usp_OrdersByDate '1996-07-01', '1996-07-15'
GO
```

the query optimizer might create an execution plan using an index. The second time it is executed with a wider range: '1990-01-01', '1999-12-31'. SQL Server already finds the plan in cache that uses an index and will use it, even though for this date range it might be better to perform a table scan. Listing 12.1 shows how to use the **RECOMPILE** clause.

Listing 12.1 Using the **RECOMPILE** clause.

```
CREATE PROCEDURE usp_CustomersByName
     @Name    nvarchar(40) = '%'
WITH RECOMPILE
AS
SELECT * FROM Customers
WHERE CompanyName LIKE @Name
ORDER BY CompanyName
RETURN
GO
```

To protect the definition of a sensitive stored procedure, use the **ENCRYPTION** clause. This clause encrypts the entries of the *syscomments* table that contain the definition (Transact-SQL statements) of the stored procedure. By using the **WITH ENCRYPTION** clause, users (including the owner of the view) cannot view the stored procedure definition (see Listing 12.2).

The **FOR REPLICATION** clause is used for stored procedures executed only by replication. Stored procedures created with this clause cannot be executed on a subscribing server (see Listing 12.3 for how to store group stored procedures).

The **FOR REPLICATION** and **RECOMPILE** clauses are mutually exclusive.

Listing 12.2 Encrypting the definition of a stored procedure.

```
CREATE PROCEDURE usp_OrderDetails
     @OrderID      integer = NULL
WITH ENCRYPTION
AS
IF @OrderID = NULL
   RETURN -1
SELECT * FROM [Order Details] WHERE OrderID = @OrderID
RETURN
GO

sp_helptext usp_OrderDetails
GO

The object comments have been encrypted.
```

Listing 12.3 Grouping stored procedures.

```
CREATE PROCEDURE usp_DeleteOrder;1
          @OrderID    integer = NULL
AS
IF @OrderID = NULL
     RETURN -1
DELETE [Order Details] WHERE OrderID = @OrderID
RETURN
GO
CREATE PROCEDURE usp_DeleteOrder;2
          @OrderID    integer = NULL
AS
IF @OrderID = NULL
     RETURN -1
DELETE Orders WHERE OrderID = @OrderID
RETURN
GO
```

12

Create Stored Procedure Wizard

You can also create a stored procedure using the Create Stored Procedure Wizard. The wizard consists of four main screens and two subscreens that take you step by step through the process. You advance from screen to screen by clicking on the Next button and move to a prior screen by clicking the Back button. Use the Create Stored Procedure Wizard to quickly create procedures that insert, update, or delete rows to a single table. The wizard screens are as follows:

- The first screen, Welcome To The Create Stored Procedure Wizard, explains what can be done with the create stored procedure wizard.
- In the second screen, Select Database, you select the database in which you want the stored procedure to be created. The wizard does not allow you to select any system databases (*master, model, msdb, tempdb*).
- In the third screen, Select Stored Procedures, you select the table(s) and action(s) (insert, update, row) for which you want to generate a stored procedure (see Figure 12.1). For example, if you select one table and click on the Insert and Delete checkboxes, two stored procedures will be generated, one for inserting a row and another for deleting a row.
- The fourth screen, Completing The Create Stored Procedure Wizard, displays the name of the stored procedures that will be generated and a brief description of what they do (see Figure 12.2). To generate the stored procedures, click on the Finish button. To change the name of the stored procedure that will be generated or to view or edit the script that will be generated, click on the Edit button.

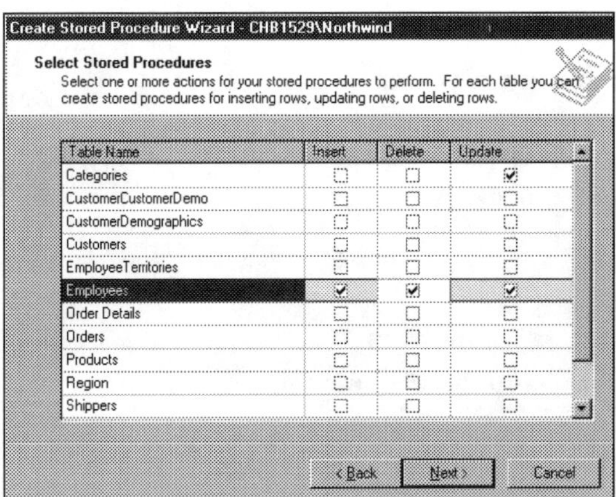

Figure 12.1 The Select Stored Procedures screen from the Create Stored Procedure Wizard.

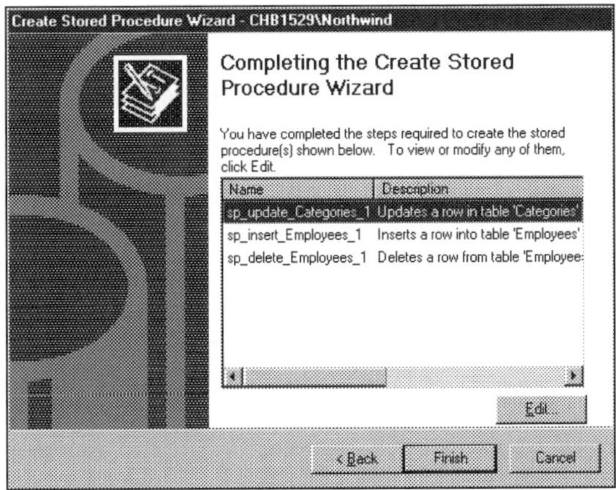

Figure 12.2 The Completing The Create Stored Procedure Wizard screen.

- In the fifth screen, Edit Stored Procedure Properties, you can change the name of the stored procedure and, depending on the action of the stored procedure, select the columns that will be selected, updated, or be defined as part of the **WHERE** clause (see Figure 12.3). To edit the Transact-SQL statements that define the stored procedure, click on the Edit SQL button.
- In the sixth screen, Edit Stored Procedure SQL, you can modify the definition of the stored procedure (see Figure 12.4).

Nesting Stored Procedures

A stored procedure is said to be *nested* when it is executed from within another stored procedure. Stored procedures can be nested up to 32 levels. The nesting level increments each time a stored procedure is called and decreases when it

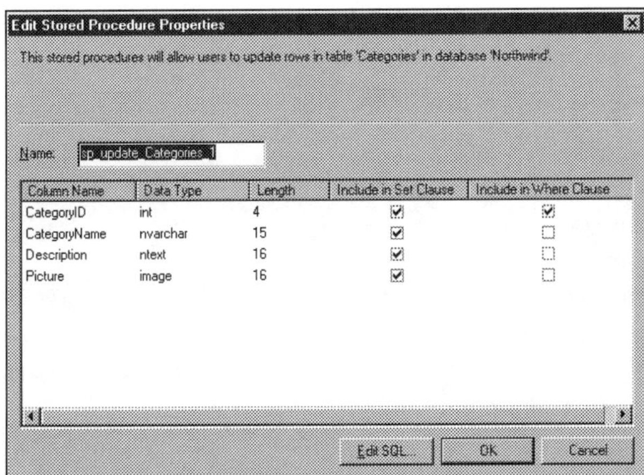

Figure 12.3 The Edit Stored Procedure Properties screen from the Create Stored Procedure Wizard.

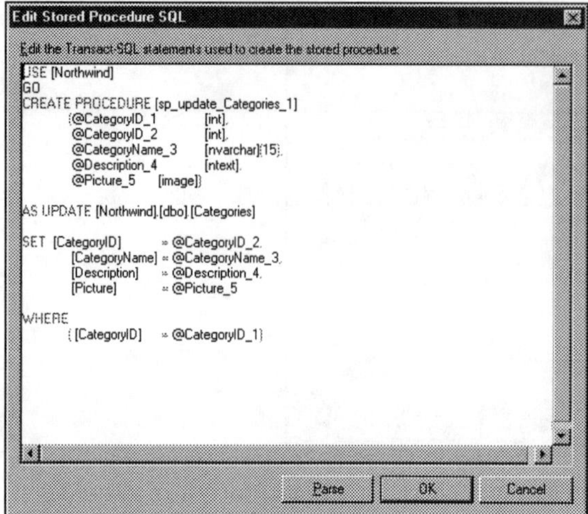

Figure 12.4 The Edit Stored Procedure SQL screen from the Create Stored Procedure Wizard.

finishes execution. Use the system function **@@NESTLEVEL** to determine what the current nesting level is for the stored procedure being executed. Listing 12.4 shows how nested stored procedures can use objects created in prior nested levels and how the nesting level increases and decreases. First let us create four stored procedures, three of which are nested. Next, we will execute the main stored procedures and look at the results.

A stored procedure that calls itself is also a nested stored procedure and increments the current nesting level.

Listing 12.4 Nested stored procedures using objects created in prior nested levels.

```
CREATE PROCEDURE usp_proc4
AS
SELECT 'Stored procedure: usp_proc4; nesting level: ', @@NESTLEVEL
RETURN
GO
CREATE PROCEDURE usp_proc3
AS
SELECT 'Stored procedure: usp_proc3; nesting level: ', @@NESTLEVEL
SELECT * FROM #test
RETURN
GO
CREATE PROCEDURE usp_proc2
AS
SELECT 'Stored procedure: usp_proc2; nesting level: ', @@NESTLEVEL
INSERT INTO #test VALUES (99)
EXEC usp_proc3
```

```
RETURN
GO
CREATE PROCEDURE usp_proc1
AS
SELECT 'Stored procedure: usp_proc1; nesting level: ', @@NESTLEVEL
CREATE TABLE #test (col1 int)
EXEC usp_proc2
EXEC usp_proc4
RETURN
GO

EXECUTE usp_proc1
GO

Results:
----------- --
Store procedure: usp_proc1; nesting level:  1
----------- --
Store procedure: usp_proc2; nesting level:  2
----------- --
Store procedure: usp_proc3; nesting level:  3

col1
--
99
----------- --
Store procedure: usp_proc4; nesting level:  2
```

As you can see, stored procedure **usp_proc3** can use the table created in stored procedure **usp_proc1**. Notice how the nesting level increases each time a procedure is called and how it decreases when a procedure finishes executing.

Stored Procedures' Parameters

Parameters are used to pass information between a stored procedure and the process that executed the stored procedure. Information about stored procedures' parameters is stored in the **syscolumns** system stored procedure. The two types of parameters are:

- Input parameters
- Output parameters

The maximum number of parameters (input and output) allowed in a stored procedure is 1,024.

Input Parameters

Input parameters are used to pass information into a stored procedure. The scope of an input parameter is the stored procedure where it is defined. Input parameters are defined when a stored procedure is created. Listing 12.5 demonstrates how input parameters can be defined. The syntax for defining input parameters is:

```
@<input_parameter>   <data_type> [= <default_value>]
```

You can allow a user to not specify a value for the input parameter when executing a stored procedure. In this case, a default value should be assigned to the input parameter.

Listing 12.5 Defining input parameters for a stored procedure.

```
CREATE PROCEDURE usp_CustomerOrdersByDate
     @dt_StartDate     datetime = '1900-01-01'
,     @dt_EndDate       datetime = '2999-12-31'
AS
SELECT * FROM Orders
WHERE OrderDate >= @dt_StartDate
AND   OrderDate <= @dt_EndDate
ORDER BY OrderDate, CustomerID
RETURN
GO
```

A good practice to use when writing stored procedures is to check the input parameters at the beginning of the procedure for missing and invalid values. Listing 12.6 shows how you can do this.

Listing 12.6 Checking for missing and invalid input parameters.

```
CREATE PROCEDURE usp_EmployeesByCountry
     @nvc_Country    nvarchar(15) = NULL
AS
IF @nvc_Country IS NULL OR LEFT( @nvc_Country, 1 ) = '%'
BEGIN
     PRINT 'ERROR: A Country must be specified'
     RETURN -1
END
SELECT * FROM Employees
WHERE Country LIKE UPPER( @nvc_Country )
ORDER BY LastName, FirstName
RETURN
GO
```

Output Parameters

Output parameters are used to pass data or a cursor variable to the process that executed the stored procedure. An input value can be assigned an output parameter. The stored procedure can then change the value of the output parameter and return it (by creating a variable storing the value) to a program. To define an output parameter you must specify the **OUTPUT** keyword when creating the stored procedure as follows:

```
@<output_parameter>   <data_type> OUTPUT
```

To define an output parameter of **CURSOR** data type you must specify the **CURSOR VARYING OUTPUT** keywords when creating the stored procedure as follows. Listing 12.7 demonstrates how to return and use a cursor value.

```
@<output_parameter>   <data_type> CURSOR VARYING OUTPUT
```

The process that is calling the stored procedure must specify the **OUTPUT** keyword when executing the procedure in order to be able to use the value returned. If the **OUTPUT** keyword is not specified, no error will be returned, and the value returned by the stored procedure is lost. For example, create a stored procedure that assigns the product name to an output parameter for a given product ID using the following statement:

```
CREATE PROCEDURE usp_ProductName
     @i_ProductID     int = NULL
,     @outpar           nvarchar(40) OUTPUT
AS
IF @i_ProductID = NULL
BEGIN
     PRINT 'ERROR: A Product ID must be specified'
     RETURN -1
END
SELECT @outpar = ProductName FROM Products
WHERE ProductID = @i_ProductID
RETURN
GO
```

Next, call the stored procedure two times, the first time specifying the **OUTPUT** keyword, and the next time without specifying it.

```
SET NOCOUNT ON
DECLARE @case1_with_OUTPUT    nvarchar(40),
        @case2_without_OUTPUT nvarchar(40)
EXEC usp_ProductName 5,
```

12

```
        @case1_with_OUTPUT OUTPUT
SELECT 'OUTPUT keyword is specified: ',
        @case1_with_OUTPUT
EXEC usp_ProductName 5, @case2_without_OUTPUT
SELECT 'OUTPUT keyword is NOT specified: ',
        @case2_without_OUTPUT
GO
Results:
-------- --------
OUTPUT keyword is specified:  Chef Anton's Gumbo Mix
-------- --------
OUTPUT keyword is NOT specified:  NULL
```

As you can see from this example, the first time the stored procedure is called, the value assigned by the stored procedure is retained. The second time the procedure is called this value is lost because the **OUTPUT** keyword was not specified when executing the stored procedure.

Listing 12.7 Returning a cursor value as an output parameter.

```
Create procedure statement:
CREATE PROCEDURE usp_Cursor
     @cc          CURSOR VARYING OUTPUT
AS
SET @cc = CURSOR FOR
  SELECT EmployeeID, LastName + ', ' + FirstName
   AS [Employee Name]
  FROM Employees ORDER BY [Employee Name]
OPEN @cc
RETURN
GO
Calling script:
DECLARE @cur CURSOR
DECLARE @id  int,
        @Name nvarchar(30)
exec usp_Cursor @cur OUTPUT
FETCH @cur into @id, @Name
WHILE @@fetch_status = 0
BEGIN
     SELECT @Name, @id
     FETCH @cur into @id, @Name
END
CLOSE @cur
GO
Result:
-------- --
Buchanan, Steven               5
```

```
-------- --
Callahan, Laura               8
-------- --
Davolio, Nancy                1
-------- --
Dodsworth, Anne               9
-------- --
Fuller, Andrew                2
-------- --
King, Robert                  7
-------- --
Leverling, Janet              3
-------- --
Peacock, Margaret             4
-------- --
Suyama, Michael               6
```

Returning Data From Stored Procedures

SQL Server 7 stored procedures can return data to the calling program in different ways:

- As data through an output parameter
- As a cursor variable through an output parameter (see the topic "Output Parameters" in this chapter)
- As a return code—Stored procedures always return an integer value. If no explicit value is returned, the return code is 0. Return codes are generally used to indicate the success or failure of a stored procedure (by convention, a return code of 0 indicates that no error was encountered) or to indicate that the processing was not performed.

Use the **RETURN [<integer_expression>]** statement to return an explicit value. If **<integer_expression>** is not specified, the return code will be 0.

- As a result set from each **SELECT** statement defined in the stored procedure

Result sets for each **SELECT** statement in nested stored procedures will also be returned.

- As a global cursor

12

The following two examples show how data can be returned from stored procedures. Listing 12.8 demonstrates a stored procedure that returns data in three different ways. It returns a list of all customer orders done after a certain date (through a result set of a **SELECT** statement), the total amount of orders (using an output parameter), and a return code of success or failure (using the **RETURN** statement).

Listing 12.8 Returning data from a stored procedure.

```
CREATE PROCEDURE usp_OrdersByDate
     @DateOfOrder      datetime = NULL,
     @TotalOrders      integer OUTPUT
AS
IF @DateOfOrder IS NULL
BEGIN
     PRINT 'A Date Of Order must be specified'
     RETURN -1
END
SELECT c.CompanyName, o.OrderID,
       CONVERT( nvarchar, o.RequiredDate, 1)
              AS Required,
       ISNULL( CONVERT( nvarchar, o.ShippedDate, 1),
               'NOT SHIPPED')
              AS Shipped,
       [Customer Is] = CASE
             WHEN o.RequiredDate >= o.ShippedDate
             AND o.RequiredDate >= GETDATE()
             THEN 'HAPPY'
             ELSE 'ANGRY !!!'
       END
FROM Orders o
INNER JOIN Customers c
ON o.CustomerID = c.CustomerID
WHERE o.OrderDate >= @DateOfOrder
ORDER BY c.CompanyName
SELECT @TotalOrders = @@rowcount
RETURN 0
GO
```

The results of executing the following script is:

```
DECLARE @out         int,
        @return_code int
EXEC @return_code = usp_OrdersByDate '1998-05-06',
        @out OUTPUT
IF @return_code <> 0
     PRINT 'ERROR'
ELSE
```

```
    SELECT 'Total Orders: ', @out
GO
CompanyName                  OrderID  Required  Shipped      Customer
                                                             Is
-------                      ---      ---       ----         ----
Bon app'                     11076    06/03/98  NOT SHIPPED  ANGRY !!!
Rattlesnake Canyon Grocery   11077    06/03/98  NOT SHIPPED  ANGRY !!!
Richter Supermarkt           11075    06/03/98  NOT SHIPPED  ANGRY !!!
Simons bistro                11074    06/03/98  NOT SHIPPED  ANGRY !!!
----- ---
Total Orders:  4
```

Listing 12.9 shows a stored procedure that returns a global cursor. Notice that the cursor is *not* assigned to an output parameter.

Listing 12.9 Returing a global cursor from a stored procedure.

```
CREATE PROCEDURE usp_GlobalCursor
AS
DECLARE Cursor_Product CURSOR FOR
SELECT p.ProductName, s.CompanyName AS Supplier,
       c.CategoryName AS Category,
       'Discontinued' = CASE
       WHEN p.Discontinued = 1 THEN 'YES'
       ELSE ' '
       END
FROM Products p
        INNER JOIN Suppliers s
        ON p.SupplierID = s.SupplierID
        INNER JOIN Categories c
        ON p.CategoryID = c.CategoryID
ORDER BY p.ProductName
OPEN Cursor_Product
GO
```

12

Altering A Stored Procedure

SQL Server 7 has the ability to dynamically change a stored procedure without having to drop (delete) and re-create the procedure. When you drop and re-create a stored procedure, all permission assignments are lost. When you alter a stored procedure, all permission assignments are retained.

A stored procedure is modified with the **ALTER PROCEDURE** command; using this command you can alter:

- The definition of the stored procedure (the Transact-SQL statements)
- The encryption of the stored procedure (encrypt or not the procedure definition)

➤ The recompilation behavior of the stored procedure (recompile or not the procedure each time it is executed)

The syntax for the **ALTER PROCEDURE** command is as follows:

```
ALTER PROC[EDURE] <stored_procedure_name>[;<number>]
[ @<parameter1> <data_type> [VARYING] [=<default_value>] [OUTPUT]
  [...[, @<parameterN> <data_type> [VARYING] [=<default_value>] [OUTPUT] ]
]
]
[WITH { [RECOMPILE] [,] [ENCRYPTION] ]
[FOR REPLICATION]
AS
<Transact-SQL statement1>
[... <Transact-SQL statementN>]
```

For an explanation of the clauses of the **ALTER PROCEDURE** statement, refer to the **CREATE PROCEDURE** statement.

In order to retain the functionality of the **WITH RECOMPILE** and/or **WITH ENCRYPTION** clauses specified in the **CREATE PROCEDURE** statement, you must also specify the clauses in the **ALTER PROCEUDRE** statement.

Listing 12.10 shows how to alter a stored procedure. The first part of the example shows the statement used to create the procedure. The second part shows how new Transact-SQL statements can be added. In order to keep the stored procedure definition encrypted, the **ENCRYPTION** clause is also specified when altering the procedure. Because the stored procedure was altered and not dropped and re-created, the permission granted to the *public* role is not lost.

Listing 12.10 Altering a stored procedure.

```
CREATE PROC usp_OneOrder
     @OrderID    int
WITH ENCRYPTION AS
SELECT o.OrderID, o.CustomerID, o.EmployeeID,
       od.ProductID, od.UnitPrice,
       od.Quantity, od.Discount
FROM Orders o JOIN [Order Details] od
ON o.OrderID = od.OrderID
WHERE o.OrderID = @OrderID
GO
GRANT EXECUTE ON usp_OneOrder TO public
GO

ALTER PROC usp_OneOrder
     @OrderID    int = NULL
WITH ENCRYPTION AS
```

```
IF @OrderID IS NULL
BEGIN
   PRINT '***ERROR: An Order ID must be specified'
   RETURN -1
END
SELECT o.OrderID, o.CustomerID, o.EmployeeID,
       od.ProductID, od.UnitPrice,
       od.Quantity, od.Discount
FROM Orders o JOIN [Order Details] od
ON o.OrderID = od.OrderID
WHERE o.OrderID = @OrderID
RETURN
GO
```

Dropping A Stored Procedure

When a stored procedure is dropped, the procedure's definition and permissions are removed from the database. Use the **DROP PROCEDURE** command to delete stored procedures or stored procedure groups. The syntax is as follows:

```
DROP PROC[EDURE] <stored_proc_name1> [,...<stored_proced_nameN>]
```

You cannot drop an individual stored procedure within a group. You have to drop the stored procedure group, which will drop all stored procedures of the group.

12

Listing 12.11 shows how a stored procedure (**usp_OrderDetails**—created in Listing 12.2) and a stored procedure group (**usp_DeleteOrder**—created in Listing 12.3 has two stored procedures: **usp_DeleteOrder;1** and **usp_DeleteOrder;2**) can be dropped in one statement.

Listing 12.11 Dropping stored procedures.

```
DROP PROC usp_OrderDetails, usp_DeleteOrder
GO
```

Executing A Stored Procedure

Use the **EXECUTE** statement to execute a stored procedure. The syntax of the **EXECUTE** statement is:

```
EXEC[UTE] [@<return_status>=]
            { <proc_name>[;<number]|@<proc_name_var> }
            [[<@parameter1>=] {<value>|@<variable> [OUTPUT]|[DEFAULT]}
             [...
```

```
                 [,<@parameterN>=] {<value>|@<variable>
[OUTPUT]|[DEFAULT]} ]]
              ]
              [WITH RECOMPILE]
```

It is not necessary to specify the **EXECUTE** keyword if the stored procedure is executed by the first statement of a batch.

If you want to capture the return status of the stored procedure use **@<return_status>** (see Listing 12.12 that appears later in this chapter).

To execute a stored procedure you must specify a procedure name **(<proc_name**>) or a variable that represents a procedure name (**@<proc_name_var>**). To execute a remote procedure (see Listing 12.13 that appears later) specify the fully qualified name of the stored procedure in the following format:

```
<server_name>.<database_name>.<object_owner>.<stored_procedure_name>
```

To execute an individual stored procedure in a group you must specify the procedure identification number (**<number>**) (see Listing 12.14 that appears later). **<value>** is used to pass a constant to a stored procedure.

@<variable> can be a variable that stores a value to be passed to a stored procedure or a variable that will store a return parameter. If **@<variable>** stores a return parameter, you must specify the **OUTPUT** keyword and the parameter must be defined in the stored procedure also with the **OUTPUT** keyword (see "Stored Procedure Parameters" in this chapter).

The **DEFAULT** keyword supplies the default value of a parameter in the stored procedure. A default value must have been specified when the procedure was defined. Parameters can be passed to a stored procedure by reference or by position.

When passing parameters by reference, you can specify the parameters in any order, and you can omit parameters that have a default value or allow **NULL** values. To pass parameters by reference you must specify the parameter name. For example, in a stored procedure created with the following script:

```
CREATE PROC usp_Order
     @CustID     nchar(5),
     @EmplID     int = 6,
     @OrderDate  datetime = NULL
AS
SELECT * FROM Orders
```

```
WHERE (CustomerID LIKE @CustID
       OR EmployeeID = @EmplID)
AND   OrderDate >= @OrderDate
RETURN @@rowcount
GO
```

parameters can be passed by reference as follows:

```
EXEC usp_Order @EmplID = 5, @CustID = 'VINET',
     @OrderDate = '1998-01-01'
GO
```

or:

```
EXEC usp_Order @CustID = 'VINET', @OrderDate = '1998-01-01'
GO
```

Notice that the second parameter **EmplID** is not specified, and the default value of 6 will be used.

When passing parameters by position, the parameters must be passed in the order defined in the stored procedure. You can omit parameters that have a default value or accept a **NULL**, but you cannot specify any other parameter after it. For example, the following first two execute statements are correct, but the third will return an error because the second parameter was omitted and the third was specified.

12

```
EXEC usp_Order 'VINET', 5, '1998-01-01'
EXEC usp_Order 'VINET', 5
EXEC usp_Order 'VINET', '1998-01-01'
GO
```

To force SQL Server to recompile the stored procedure at execution time, specify the **WITH RECOMPILE** keywords. This will cause a new execution plan to be created in the procedure cache.

Always use the **WITH RECOMPILE** keywords if the values passed to the stored procedure differ greatly from the values usually passed. For example, a five-year search will require a different execution plan than a two-day search.

The **sp_recompile <table_name>** system stored procedure causes all procedures that reference the table to be recompiled the next time they are executed.

Listing 12.12 shows how to store the return status of a stored procedure.

Listing 12.12 Storing the return status of a stored procedure.

```
DECLARE @TotalOrders integer
EXEC @TotalOrders = usp_Order @EmplID = 5,
     @CustID = 'VINET', @OrderDate = '1998-01-01'
SELECT 'Total Orders returned:', @TotalOrders
GO
```

Listing 12.13 shows how to execute a remote stored procedure. This example executes the **usp_Remote** stored procedure found in the *RemoteDB* database on the remote server **SQLREMOTE**.

Listing 12.13 Executing a remote stored procedure.

```
EXECUTE SQLREMOTE.RemoteDB..usp_Remote
GO
```

Listing 12.14 shows how to execute an individual stored procedure in a group. The stored procedure that will be executed is the second stored procedure that was created in Listing 12.3. Note that the **EXECUTE** keyword doesn't have to be specified because the execution of the stored procedure is the first statement in the batch.

Listing 12.14 Executing an individual stored procedure in a group.

```
usp_DeleteOrder;2
GO
```

Listing 12.15 shows how to execute an extended stored procedure.

Listing 12.15 Executing an extended stored procedure.

```
EXEC master..xp_cmdshell 'dir'
GO
```

Enforcing Business Rules With Stored Procedures

Using stored procedures to enforce business rules is highly recommended because stored procedures provide an extra insulation layer between an application and the database. Imagine that your database administrator decides to make design changes to the database in order to provide better performance. If your business rules had been programmed in each application, it would be a major operation to make and test the changes in each application. On the other hand, if the business rules had been programmed in stored procedures, the changes would have to be made and tested only in one place. As long as the stored procedures return the same information, the applications do not have to make any changes. Enforcing business rules through stored procedures ensures consistency in how data is accessed and modified.

THE RAISERROR STATEMENT

Error checking and handling is an important part of stored procedures. When writing a stored procedure keep in mind the following recommendations:

- Each stored procedure should return a success or failure status of its execution. Use the **RETURN** statement for this purpose.
- Use the **@@ERROR** function immediately after each statement you want to error check.

The value of **@@ERROR** changes after each statement.

- Use the **RAISERROR** statement to return error messages to the process that executed the stored procedure.

You can also use the **PRINT** statement to return messages to the calling process.

The **RAISERROR** statement not only returns an error message but also sets a system flag to record that an error has occurred (the error number is stored in **@@ERROR** function). The **RAISERROR** statement can return a message string or a user-defined error message (see Listing 12.16).

User-defined error messages are added to SQL Server with the **sp_addmessage** system stored procedure and are stored in the *sysmessages* system table in the *master* database.

The partial syntax for the **RAISERROR** statement is:

```
RAISERROR ( <messageID>|<message_string>, <severity>, <state>)
[WITH LOG|NOWAIT|SETERROR]
```

To return a user-defined error message, specify the message number (**<messageID>**). User-defined error messages should be greater than 50,000. To return an error message string, specify the error text (**<message_string>**). **<severity>** is used to associate an error message with a severity level. SQL

Server has 25 severity levels: Levels 0 through 18 can be used by any user; levels 19 through 25 are used only by system administrators.

Levels 20 through 25 are fatal severity levels. They will terminate the client connection.

<state> represents information on the invocation state of the error. It can be a number between 1 and 127. Negative numbers are equivalent to 1. To log the error in the SQL Server error log and in the NT application log, specify the **WITH LOG** keywords. To send a message to the client immediately, specify the **WITH NOWAIT** keywords. To set the **@@ERROR** function value to the message number (**<messageID>**) or to 50,000, specify the **WITH SETERROR** keywords.

Listing 12.16 shows the **RAISERROR** statement used in a stored procedure to return a user-defined message and a message string. Before creating the stored procedure, a user-defined message will be added to the server using **sp_addmessage**.

Listing 12.16 Using the **RAISERROR** statement in a stored procedure to return a user-defined message and a message string.

```
EXEC sp_addmessage 50101, 9, 'Employee ID does not exist'
GO

CREATE PROC usp_UpdateEmployeeHireDate
     @HireDate      datetime = NULL,
     @EmployeeID     integer  = 0
AS
IF @HireDate IS NULL
BEGIN
     RAISERROR ( 'Hire date cannot be NULL', 9, -1 )
     RETURN
END

IF EXISTS (SELECT * FROM Employees
           WHERE EmployeeID = @EmployeeID)
     UPDATE Employees
     SET HireDate = @HireDate
     WHERE EmployeeID = @EmployeeID
ELSE
     RAISERROR ( 50101, 9, -1 )
RETURN
GO
```

Chapter Summary

In this chapter we have discussed the following items:

- Use of stored procedures as a security mechanism, to simplify business applications, to increase performance, and to enforce business rules.
- System stored procedures are prefixed with **sp_** and are stored in the *master* database (do not prefix user-defined stored procedures with **sp_**). They are used to perform administrative tasks and retrieve and update data from system tables.
- Extended stored procedures are prefixed with **xp_** and are stored in the *master* database. They are used to extend SQL Server capabilities.
- Local stored procedures are used to implement business rules and policies.
- Remote stored procedures are procedures located on remote or linked SQL Servers and are called from the current server.
- Temporary stored procedures are prefixed with a # sign (local temporary stored procedure) or with a ## sign (global temporary stored procedure).
- Use the **sp_executesql** system stored procedure instead of temporary tables if connecting to a SQL Server 7 database.
- When a stored procedure is created, it is checked for syntactical accuracy. This process is known as *parsing*.
- A stored procedure can be created even if the tables and views that it references do not exist. This is called *deferred name resolution*.
- The first time a stored procedure is executed SQL Server 7 checks that the objects referenced exist and the compatibility between columns and variables. This process is known as *resolution*.
- If the resolution process is successful, SQL Server 7 optimizes the execution plan and compiles it in procedure cache.
- To create a stored procedure, use the **CREATE PROCEDURE** statement or the Create Stored Procedure Wizard.
- The **CREATE PROCEDURE** statement has to be the only statement in the batch that defines the procedure.
- **CREATE DEFAULT**, **CREATE PROCEDURE**, **CREATE RULE**, **CREATE TRIGGER**, **CREATE VIEW**, **SET SHOWPLAN_TEXT**, and **SET SHOWPLAN_ALL** statements cannot be part of a stored procedure definition.
- To obtain information about a stored procedure, use the **sp_depends**, **sp_help**, **sp_helptext**, and **sp_stored_procedures** system stored procedures.

12

- Stored procedures definition can be encrypted specifying the **WITH ENCRYPTION** clause when they are created or modified.
- To force a stored procedure to be recompiled every time it is executed, specify the **WITH RECOMPILE** clause when creating or modifying the procedure.
- To force a stored procedure to be recompiled, specify the **WITH RECOMPILE** clause when executing it or run the **sp_recompile** system stored procedure against any table being referenced by the procedure.
- Stored procedures can be nested 32 levels.
- Information can be passed between a stored procedure and the process that called it through input and/or output parameters.
- Define output parameters with the **OUTPUT** keyword. The **OUTPUT** keyword also has to be specified when calling the stored procedure.
- A stored procedure returns data to the calling program as an output parameter, cursor variable, return code, or result set from **SELECT** statements.
- Modify a stored procedure using the **ALTER PROCEDURE** statement.
- Drop a stored procedure using the **DROP PROCEDURE** statement.
- Use the **EXECUTE** statement to execute a stored procedure.
- Use the **RAISERROR** statement to return an error message to the calling program.

Review Questions

1. Which of the following are true about stored procedures? (Choose all correct answers.)
    a. They return only one output parameter.
    b. They are compiled when created.
    c. They can be used as a security mechanism.
    d. They can be used to simplify business applications.
2. Which of the following statements about system stored procedures are true? (Choose all correct answers.)
    a. They are stored in the *model* database.
    b. They are stored in the *master* database.
    c. They are used to update system tables.
    d. They can only be executed within a system database.

3. Which of the following statements about extended stored procedures are true? (Choose all correct answers.)
   a. They are used to extend SQL Server capabilities.
   b. They can be added to any database.
   c. They are identified by the **xp_** prefix.
   d. They are supported for backward compatibility.

4. Which of the following statements about temporary stored procedures are true?
   a. They are supported for backward compatibility.
   b. They can be local or global.
   c. They are dentified by the **temp_** prefix.
   d. They are stored in the current database.

5. Which of the following system tables stores information about stored procedures? (Choose all correct answers.)
   a. *sysprocedures*
   b. *syscomments*
   c. *syscolumns*
   d. *sysindexes*

6. When is a stored procedure compiled? (Choose all correct answers.)
   a. If it is executed with the **WITH RECOMPILE** option
   b. If an index is created on a table that it references
   c. If the **sp_recompile** stored procedure is executed against a table that it references
   d. Never

7. Which of the following Transact-SQL statements cannot be included in a stored procedure? (Choose all correct answers.)
   a. **CREATE INDEX**
   b. **CREATE TRIGGER**
   c. **UPDATE STATISTICS**
   d. **SET SHOWPLAN_TEXT**

8. Which of the following system stored procedures are used to view information about stored procedures? (Choose all correct answers.)
   a. **sp_helptext**
   b. **sp_depends**
   c. **sp_text_stored_procedure**
   d. **sp_stored_procedures_text**

9. The **WITH RECOMPILE** clause of the **CREATE PROCEDURE** statement is used to:
   a. Cause the compilation of the stored procedure when it is created
   b. Cause the compilation of the stored procedure each time it is executed
   c. Recompile the stored procedure if call from a remote server
   d. Not supported

10. Which of the following are true about stored procedure parameters? (Choose all correct answers.)
    a. The maximum number allowed is 255.
    b. The maximum number allowed is 1,024.
    c. A SQL Server cursor can be an input parameter.
    d. A SQL Server cursor can be an output parameter.

11. A stored procedure can be modified by:
    a. Using the **ALTER PROCEDURE** statement
    b. Using the **MODIFY PROCEDURE** statement
    c. Only by dropping and re-creating the procedure

12. Which statement is used to delete a stored procedure?
    a. **DELETE PROCEDURE**
    b. **DROP PROCEDURE**
    c. **sp_dropprocedure**
    d. **sp_deleteprocedure**

13. Which of the following statements can be used to execute the **usp_Test** stored procedure? (Choose all correct answers.)

```
CREATE PROCEDURE usp_Test
@par1      int = 3,
@par2      int = 2,
@par3      smallint OUTPUT
AS
...
```

    a. **EXECUTE usp_Test @var1, @var2, @var3 OUTPUT**
    b. **EXECUTE usp_Test @par1=@var1, @par2=@var2,@par3=@var3 OUTPUT**
    c. **EXECUTE usp_Test @var1, @var3 OUTPUT**
    d. **EXECUTE usp_Test @par3=@var3 OUTPUT, @par2=@var2**

14. Which clause of the **RAISERROR** statement is used to log the error in the Windows NT application log?
    a. **WITH NOWAIT**
    b. **WITH LOG**
    c. **WITH SETERROR**
    d. **WITH NT_LOG**

15. Which of the following statements returns an error to the client immediately? (Choose all correct answers.)
    a. **RAISERROR** ('Error updating table', 9, -1) **WITH NOWAIT**
    b. **RAISERROR** (50001, 9, -1) **WITH NOWAIT**
    c. **RAISERROR** ('Error updating table', 9, -1) **WITH CLIENT**
    d. **RAISERROR** (50001, 9, -1) **WITH CLIENT**

HANDS-ON PROJECTS

These activities assume that you are already connected to the *Northwind* database using the Query Analyzer.

12

Susan had never been formally trained in programming. She was a little apprehensive when she was told that because she had been learning most of the Transact-SQL statements, her company would appreciate her lending a hand at developing some stored procedures to assist in the development process. She had learned that many times the database administrator was tasked to perform this job. Once again she thought, "I guess this will help me pass the exam as well." She began practicing by creating some procedures in the *Northwind* database.

Project 12.1

In this activity, you create a stored procedure according to the following specifications.

The stored procedure needs to return the *OrderID*, *CustomerID*, *OrderDate*, *ProductID*, and the *Quantity* of the product of all orders entered by an employee. The *EmployeeID* will be passed to the procedure. The procedure should also return the total amount of orders (one for each item) entered by the employee. The stored procedure definition should be encrypted.

In the Query Analyzer, type the following command and execute it:

```
CREATE PROCEDURE usp_OrdersByEmployee
     @EmployeeID      int,
     @TotalOrder      int OUTPUT
WITH ENCRYPTION AS
SELECT Orders.OrderID, CustomerID, EmployeeID,
       OrderDate, ProductID, Quantity
FROM Orders INNER JOIN [Order Details]
              ON Orders.OrderID = [Order Details].OrderID
WHERE EmployeeID = @EmployeeID
SET @TotalOrder = @@rowcount
RETURN
GO
```

To encrypt the stored procedure the **WITH ENCRYPTION** clause is used.

Project 12.2

In this activity, you will modify a stored procedure definition according to the following specifications, and then execute it. The stored procedure should return an error message if the *EmployeeID* is not passed to the procedure.

In the Query Analyzer, type the following command and execute it:

```
ALTER PROCEDURE usp_OrdersByEmployee
     @EmployeeID      int = NULL,
     @TotalOrder      int = 0 OUTPUT
WITH ENCRYPTION AS
IF @EmployeeID IS NULL
BEGIN
     RAISERROR ( 'Stored procedure is expecting an EmployeeID.',
                 16, -1 )
     RETURN -1
END
SELECT Orders.OrderID, CustomerID, EmployeeID,
       OrderDate, ProductID, Quantity
FROM Orders INNER JOIN [Order Details]
              ON Orders.OrderID = [Order Details].OrderID
WHERE EmployeeID = @EmployeeID
SET @TotalOrder = @@rowcount
RETURN
GO
```

Execute the **usp_OrdersByEmployee** stored procedure. Pass an *EmployeeID* of 5. Display the total amount of orders. The stored procedure should be recompiled.

In the Query Analyzer, type the following command and execute it:

```
SET NOCOUNT ON
DECLARE @TotOrd int
EXEC usp_OrdersByEmployee 5, @TotOrd OUTPUT WITH RECOMPILE
SELECT 'Total amount of orders: ', @TotOrd
GO
```

CHAPTER THIRTEEN

TRIGGERS

After Reading This Chapter And Completing The Exercises, You Will Be Able To:

- Define a trigger and its types
- Define the benefits of using triggers
- Create a trigger
- Alter a trigger
- Drop a trigger

A *trigger* is a database object that contains one or more Transact-SQL statements and is invoked when data in the table is modified in some way. Triggers are used to extend the power of a SQL database. A trigger evokes the image of a gun firing a bullet. The comparison is quite accurate, because a trigger in a database is attached to a table and *fires* a series of SQL statements to perform database activities against another table. These triggers are used to provide referential integrity or to delete child records from a dependent table. In this chapter you'll learn how to create, modify, delete, and apply these triggers, as well as become aware of their limitations and proper use.

WHAT'S A TRIGGER?

A trigger is a special kind of stored procedure that is defined on a table and is fired automatically when an **INSERT**, **UPDATE**, or **DELETE** statement is executed against the table. A major difference between a trigger and a stored procedure is that a trigger cannot have parameters and cannot be executed directly. Triggers also should not return a result set. Triggers can only be created on permanent tables; they cannot be defined on a view or on a temporary table. The table on which a trigger is defined is called a *trigger table*.

When using triggers in SQL Server 7, you should keep in mind that constraints defined on the table are always checked before the trigger is fired. If a constraint is violated, the trigger is not fired. A trigger is only fired after the **INSERT**, **UPDATE**, or **DELETE** statement that fires it is completed.

Triggers are not fired by BCP operations.

Triggers are mainly used to:

- Enforce complex business rules. You can use triggers to enforce business rules that are more complex than the rules that are defined using **CHECK** constraints and rule definitions. Triggers are used if the business rules depend on the values of columns in other tables.

Remember, **CHECK** constraints cannot reference columns in other tables.

- Perform cascade deletes and/or updates.
- Maintain denormalized data, such as creating ancillary denormalized tables for reporting purposes.

TYPES OF TRIGGERS

Triggers are classified in one of three types, depending on which action causes the trigger to fire:

- **Insert triggers** Fired when an **INSERT** statement is executed against a table.
- **Update triggers** Fired when an **UPDATE** statement is executed against a table.
- **Delete triggers** Fired when a **DELETE** statement is executed against a table.

A delete trigger is not fired if data is deleted from a table using the **TRUNCATE TABLE** statement. This is because the **TRUNCATE TABLE** statement removes all rows from a table without logging the individual row deletes.

New for SQL Server 7 is the feature that allows the definition of multiple triggers of a given type on a table. For example, more than one **DELETE** trigger can be defined for a table. You should be aware that if multiple triggers for an action are defined on a table, they are not fired in any particular order. The following trigger will be fired every time a row is inserted or updated in the *Order Details* table:

```
CREATE TRIGGER OrderDetails_InsertUpdate
ON [Order Details] FOR INSERT, UPDATE AS
UPDATE Products
SET UnitsInStock = UnitsInStock - Quantity
     FROM Products p
     INNER JOIN inserted i
     ON p.ProductID = i.ProductID
IF (SELECT UnitsInStock
     FROM Products p
     JOIN inserted i
     ON p.ProductID = i.ProductID) < 0
ROLLBACK TRANSACTION
RETURN
```


Special Tables: Deleted Table And Inserted Table

Two special temporary tables are used in triggers. It's very important to understand how these tables are used during the trigger process:

- **Deleted table** This table stores a copy of the rows that are deleted during a **DELETE** statement and a copy of the original rows (before image) that were updated during an **UPDATE** statement. The rows stored in the deleted table cannot be found in the trigger table because they have already been removed.
- **Inserted table** This table stores a copy of the rows that are inserted during an **INSERT** statement, and a copy of the rows that were updated (after image) during an **UPDATE** statement. The rows stored in the inserted table are a copy of the rows just added to the trigger table.

Notice that these temporary tables do not have the # (pound) sign as the first character in their names. Think of an **UPDATE** statement as a delete step (that stores the original data or before image data in the deleted table) followed by an insert step (that stores the modified data or after image data in the inserted table).

The deleted and inserted tables have the same structure as the table on which the trigger is defined.

Access to the data stored in the deleted and inserted tables is fast because these tables are always stored in cache. The data stored in the deleted and inserted tables cannot be modified. The deleted and inserted tables cannot reference columns of **TEXT**, **NTEXT**, or **IMAGE** data types.

It makes no sense to reference the inserted table in a delete trigger and the deleted table in an insert trigger because these tables will be empty.

Creating A Trigger

Before you create a trigger you should test all the statements that will define the trigger to ensure that they return the expected results. When creating a trigger, keep the following facts in mind:

- Triggers cannot be created on temporary tables or views.
- Triggers can only be created in the current database.
- Triggers can reference database objects outside the current database.
- Only the table owner, the database owner (members of the *db_owner* role), and the system administrator (members of the *sysadmin* role) are authorized to create, alter, and drop triggers.
- SQL Server 7 allows the creation of triggers that reference tables and views that are not defined. This is a new feature.

Though a trigger that references nonexistent tables and views can be created, it will not execute if those objects do not exist. This is called *deferred name resolution*.

- A trigger name must be unique within the database. The first character of a trigger name must be a letter as defined in the Unicode Standard 2 or one of the following symbols: _, @. If the trigger name has embedded spaces, you must delimit it with brackets, such as [trigger name]. The trigger name can have up to 128 characters.

- User-defined triggers cannot be created on system tables.
- The **TRUNCATE TABLE** statement does not cause the **DELETE** triggers to fire.
- The **WRITETEXT** statement does not cause the **INSERT** and **UPDATE** triggers to fire.
- A trigger is fired only once per statement. This is true even if more than one row is updated.

In order to determine if the statement modified any data, check the value of the **@@rowcount** variable at the beginning of the trigger. Listing 13.1 shows how to use **@@rowcount**.

- Specify **SET NOCOUNT ON** at the beginning of the trigger to prevent any results being returned by a trigger when variable assignment occurs in it.
- SQL Server 7 allows multiple triggers to be created for any given action (**INSERT**, **UPDATE**, or **DELETE** statement).
- Constraints are checked before a trigger is fired. If the constraint is violated, the trigger will not be fired.
- Information about a trigger is stored in the *sysobjects* and *syscomments* system tables.

Listing 13.1 shows how to use the **@@rowcount** variable to check for data modification.

13

Listing 13.1 Using the **@@rowcount** variable to check for data modification.

```
CREATE TRIGGER OrderDetails_update
ON [Order Details] FOR UPDATE
AS
- If no rows where inserted, stop processing
IF @@rowcount = 0
RETURN
IF (SELECT count(*)
    FROM Products p
    JOIN inserted i
    ON p.ProductID = i.ProductID
       AND p.Discontinued = 1) > 0
BEGIN
RAISERROR
    ( 'Discontinued product cannot be updated', 15, 1)
ROLLBACK TRANSACTION
END
RETURN
GO
```

The following Transact-SQL statements cannot be included in a trigger definition:

- All **ALTER** statements (**ALTER DATABASE, ALTER PROCEDURE, ALTER TABLE, ALTER TRIGGER**, and **ALTER VIEW**)
- All **CREATE** statements (**CREATE DATABASE, CREATE DEFAULT, CREATE INDEX, CREATE PROCEDURE, CREATE RULE, CREATE SCHEMA, CREATE TABLE, CREATE TRIGGER**, and **CREATE VIEW**)
- All **DROP** statements (**DROP DATABASE, DROP DEFAULT, DROP INDEX, DROP PROCEDURE, DROP RULE, DROP TABLE, DROP TRIGGER**, and **DROP VIEW**)
- All permission statements (**DENY, GRANT, REVOKE**)
- All restore database and restore log statements (**RESTORE DATABASE, RESTORE LOG**)
- **RECONFIGURE**
- **TRUNCATE TABLE**
- **UPDATE STATISTICS**

Table 13.1 shows system stored procedures used to view information about triggers.

CREATE TRIGGER Statement

To define a trigger, use the **CREATE TRIGGER** statement. It must be the first statement in any batch statement that defines the trigger. The syntax is as follows:

```
CREATE TRIGGER <trigger_name>
ON <trigger_table_name>
[WITH ENCRYPTION]
FOR { [INSERT] [,] [UPDATE] [,] [DELETE] }
[WITH APPEND]
[NOT FOR REPLICATION]
AS
<Transact-SQL statement1>
[... <Transact-SQL statementN>]
```

<trigger_table_name> specifies the table on which the trigger is executed.

Table 13.1 System stored procedures used to view trigger information.

View Name	Brief Description
sp_depends	Returns a list of the columns of tables and views that the trigger depends on
sp_helptext	Returns the triggers definition
sp_helptrigger	Returns a list of triggers and their types for the specified table
sp_help	Returns information about the specified trigger

In previous versions of SQL Server, when you created a trigger with the same name as one that existed in the database, the old trigger was deleted and a new one was created. In SQL Server 7 this behavior has changed. If you try to create a trigger with the same name as an existing trigger, an error will be returned, and the creation will fail. To protect the definition (the SQL statements you used to create the trigger) of a sensitive trigger from being displayed, use the **ENCRYPTION** clause. This clause encrypts the entries of the *syscomments* table that contains the definition of the trigger. By using the **WITH ENCRYPTION** clause, users, including the owner of the table (and thus the trigger), cannot view the trigger definition (see Listing 13.2).

The [**INSERT**] [,] [**UPDATE**] [,] [**DELETE**] keywords are used to specify the type of trigger. At least one of them must be specified. For the trigger to fire for more than one action, specify the desired combination of keywords. Listing 13.3 shows how to define a trigger to be fired when data is inserted or updated in a table. The **WITH APPEND** keyword is used with compatibility level set to 6.5 or 6.0 to specify that an additional trigger of an existing type will be added.

Use the **NOT FOR REPLICATION** clause to disable the trigger from firing when a replication process modifies the data of the table. Listing 13.2 shows how the definition of a trigger can be encrypted. A user who tries to view the definition of the trigger with the **sp_helptext** system stored procedure will receive a message that the trigger has been encrypted.

Listing 13.2 Encrypting the definition of a trigger.

```
CREATE TRIGGER OrderDetails_insert
ON [Order Details]
WITH ENCRYPTION
FOR INSERT
AS
SET NOCOUNT ON
IF @@rowcount = 0
RETURN
IF (SELECT count(*)
    FROM Products p
    JOIN inserted i
    ON p.ProductID = i.ProductID
    AND p.UnitPrice <> i.UnitPrice) > 0
BEGIN
RAISERROR
( 'Unit Price of one or more products is incorrect', 15, 1)
ROLLBACK TRANSACTION
END
RETURN
GO
```

```
sp_helptext OrderDetails_insert
GO

The object comments have been encrypted.
```

Listing 13.3 shows how to create a trigger that will be fired every time data is inserted or updated. In order to achieve this, the trigger was created with the keywords **FOR INSERT, UPDATE**. After running this script, the *Order Details* table will have one update trigger (**OrderDetails_insupd**) and two insert triggers (**OrderDetails_insupd** and **OrderDetails_insert** created in Listing 13.2). To verify that this is true we will run the **sp_helptrigger** system stored procedure on the *Order Details* table.

Listing 13.3 Creating a trigger that will be fired every time data is inserted or updated.

```
CREATE TRIGGER OrderDetails_insupd
ON [Order Details]
FOR INSERT, UPDATE
AS
UPDATE Products
SET UnitsInStock = p.UnitsInStock - i.Quantity
FROM Products p JOIN inserted i ON p.ProductID = i.ProductID
RETURN
GO

sp_helptrigger [Order Details]
GO
trigger_name          trigger_owner   isupdate   isdelete   isinsert
------------------    -------------   --------   --------   --------
OrderDetails_insert   dbo             0          0          1
OrderDetails_insupd   dbo             1          0          1

(2 row(s) affected)
```

Altering A Trigger

SQL Server 7 has the ability to dynamically change a trigger's definition without having to drop and re-create the trigger. A trigger is modified with the **ALTER TRIGGER** command; with this command you can alter the following:

- The definition of the trigger (the T-SQL statements)
- The encryption of the trigger (encrypt or not the trigger definition)
- The execution of the trigger when fired by a replication process
- The type of trigger

The syntax for the **ALTER TRIGGER** statement is as follows:

```
ALTER TRIGGER <trigger_name>
ON <trigger_table_name>
[WITH ENCRYPTION]
FOR { [INSERT] [,] [UPDATE] [,] [DELETE] }
[NOT FOR REPLICATION]
AS
<Transact-SQL statement1>
[... <Transact-SQL statementN>]
```

For an explanation of the clauses of the **ALTER TRIGGER** statement, refer to the **CREATE TRIGGER** statement discussed earlier.

In order to retain the functionality of the **WITH ENCRYPTION** and/or **NOT FOR REPLICATION** clauses specified in the **CREATE TRIGGER** statement, you must also specify these clauses in the **ALTER TRIGGER** statement. If the [**INSERT**] [,] [**UPDATE**] [,] [**DELETE**] clauses specified are different from the ones used in the **CREATE TRIGGER** statement, the **ALTER TRIGGER** statement overrides the create statement. Listing 13.4 shows how to alter the trigger created in Listing 13.3 to be fired only when data is inserted into the table. In order to achieve this, the trigger was altered with the keyword **FOR INSERT** only. Additional logic is added to the trigger to ensure that enough product is in stock to allow the order.

Listing 13.4 Altering a trigger.

```
ALTER TRIGGER OrderDetails_insupd
ON [Order Details]
FOR INSERT
AS
UPDATE Products
SET UnitsInStock = p.UnitsInStock - i.Quantity
     FROM Products p
     JOIN inserted i
     ON p.ProductID = i.ProductID
 IF (SELECT UnitsInStock
     FROM Products p
     JOIN inserted i
     ON p.ProductID = i.ProductID) < 0
BEGIN
RAISERROR ( 'Not enough product in stock', 15, -10)
ROLLBACK TRANSACTION
END
RETURN
GO
```

Dropping A Trigger

Whenever a table is dropped from a database, SQL Server 7 automatically drops all the triggers on the table. To drop one or more triggers explicitly from the current database, use the **DROP TRIGGER** statement. When a trigger is dropped, the trigger table and table's data are not affected. The syntax for the **DROP TRIGGER** statement is as follows:

```
DROP TRIGGER <trigger_name1> [, …<trigger_nameN>]
```

Listing 13.5 shows how to drop two triggers (trigger **OrderDetails_insert** created in Listing 13.2 and trigger **OrderDetails_insupd** altered in Listing 13.4) in a single drop statement.

Listing 13.5 Dropping two triggers in a single drop statement.

```
DROP TRIGGER OrderDetails_insert, OrderDetails_insupd
GO
```

Checking For Changes To A Column

In some instances in an **UPDATE** trigger, you might need to check if a specific column has been modified. To accomplish this you can use the **IF UPDATE (<column>)** or **IF COLUMN_UPDATED()** functions. These functions are not used in **DELETE** triggers.

IF UPDATE (<column_name>)

To check in a trigger if one or more columns were updated, place the following syntax within the trigger's definition:

```
IF UPDATE (<column_name1>)
[ {AND|OR} UPDATE (<column_name2>
[... {AND|OR} UPDATE (<column_nameN>)]
  ]
```

Listing 13.6 shows how to use **IF UPDATE(<column_name>)** to check if a column has been updated. First, the trigger checks if the *Quantity* column has been updated in order to adjust the *UnitsInStock* column of the *Products* table. Second, if either the *UnitPrice* or *Discount* columns have been updated, it checks if the product is discontinued, in which case it returns an error.

Listing 13.6 Using **IF UPDATE(<column_name>)** to check if a column has been updated.

```
CREATE TRIGGER OrderDetails_update
ON [Order Details]
FOR UPDATE AS
```

```
IF @@rowcount = 0
   RETURN
IF UPDATE(Quantity)
   UPDATE Products
   SET UnitsInStock = p.UnitsInStock - i.Quantity + d.Quantity
   FROM Products p
   JOIN inserted i
   ON p.ProductID = i.ProductID
   JOIN deleted d
   ON i.ProductID = d.ProductID
IF UPDATE(UnitPrice) OR UPDATE(Discount)
   --  If Product is discontinued return error
IF (SELECT COUNT(*)
   FROM Products p
   INNER JOIN inserted i
   ON p.ProductID = i.ProductID
   AND p.Discontinued = 1) > 0
   BEGIN
   RAISERROR
   ('Cannot change an Order of a discontinued product',16, -1)
   ROLLBACK TRANSACTION
END
RETURN
GO
```

IF COLUMNS_UPDATED()

You can also use the **COLUMNS_UPDATED()** function in a trigger to check if one or more columns has been updated. The **COLUMNS_UPDATED()** function returns a binary bit pattern that indicates the columns that have been updated. The syntax is as follows:

```
IF (COLUMNS_UPDATED() <bitwise_operator> <columns_updated_bitmask>)
<comparison_operator> <column_bitmask>
```

The bitwise operators can be one of the following: **&** (bitwise AND), **|** (bitwise OR), **^** (bitwise exclusive OR), **~** (bitwise NOT).

The comparison operator can be one of the following: **>** (greater than), **<** (less than), **=** (equals), **<=** (less than or equal to), **>=** (greater than or equal to), **!=** (not equal to), **<>** (not equal to), **!<** (not less than), **!>** (not greater than). **<columns_updated_bitmask>** represents the integer bitmask of the updated columns. **<column_bitmask>** represents the integer bitmask of the columns to check if they were updated or not. To obtain the integer bitmask value use the following formula:

```
<bitmask> = power(2,(<col1>-1)) + power(2,(<col2>-1)) + ... +
power(2,(<colN>-1))
```

Where **<col1>**, **<col2>**, **<colN>** represent the position of the column in the table.

Let's look at an example to clarify how to calculate a bitmask. The *Categories* table of the *Northwind* database has four columns: *CategoryID, CategoryName, Description,* and *Picture*. Using the formula previously described you would calculate the integer bitmask of columns *CategoryID* (first column) and *Description* (third column) as follows:

```
<bitmask> = power(2,(1-1)) + power(2,(3-1))
<bitmask> = 1 + 4 = 21
```

Listing 13.7 shows how Listing 13.6 can be written using **IF COLUMNS_UPDATED()**. The structure of the *Order Details* table is:

```
Column #1: OrderID
Column #2: ProductID
Column #3: UnitPrice
Column #4: Quantity
Column #5: Discount
```

Listing 13.7 Using **IF COLUMNS_UPDATED()**.

```
CREATE TRIGGER OrderDetails_update
ON [Order Details]
FOR UPDATE AS
IF @@rowcount = 0
   RETURN
-       Check if Quantity column was modified
-     <bitmask> = power(2,(4-1)) = 8
IF (COLUMNS_UPDATED() & 8) = 8
   UPDATE Products
   SET UnitsInStock = p.UnitsInStock - i.Quantity + d.Quantity
   FROM Products p
   JOIN inserted i
   ON p.ProductID = i.ProductID
   JOIN deleted d
   ON i.ProductID = d.ProductID
-     Check if UnitPrice column or Discount column was modified
-     <bitmask> = power(2,(3-1)) + power(2,(5-1)) = 20
IF (COLUMNS_UPDATED() & 20) > 0
-      If Product is discontinued return error
IF (SELECT COUNT(*)
    FROM Products p INNER JOIN inserted i
    ON p.ProductID = i.ProductID AND p.Discontinued = 1) > 0
    BEGIN
    RAISERROR
```

```
    ('Cannot change an Order of a discontinued
      product',16, -1)
    ROLLBACK TRANSACTION
END
RETURN
GO
```

Triggers And Transactions

The trigger and the **INSERT**, **UPDATE**, or **DELETE** statement that fires it are always treated as a single transaction. This means that when a **ROLLBACK TRANSACTION** statement is executed in a trigger, all data modifications performed in the transaction are rolled back. For example, if you create the following insert trigger:

```
CREATE TRIGGER ti_OrderDetails
ON [Order Details] FOR INSERT AS
UPDATE Products
SET UnitsInStock = UnitsInStock - Quantity
FROM Products p
INNER JOIN inserted i
ON p.ProductID = i.ProductID
IF (SELECT UnitsInStock
    FROM Products p
    JOIN inserted i
    ON p.ProductID = i.ProductID) < 0
    ROLLBACK TRANSACTION
RETURN
```

And then try to insert the following rows (the second **INSERT** statement causes the *UnitsInStock* value to be lower than 0):

```
BEGIN TRANSACTION
INSERT INTO [Order Details]
(OrderID, ProductID, UnitPrice, Quantity, Discount)
VALUES (10248, 2, 99, 1, 0)
INSERT INTO [Order Details]
(OrderID, ProductID, UnitPrice, Quantity, Discount)
VALUES (10248, 1, 99, 45, 0)
```

The **ROLLBACK TRANSACTION** executed in the trigger rolls back the update to the *Products* table and both inserts to the *Order Details* table.

If an explicit **BEGIN TRANSACTION** statement is not included, the **INSERT**, **UPDATE**, or **DELETE** statement that invokes the trigger is considered the beginning of an implicit transaction.

13

A **ROLLBACK TRANSACTION** statement issued in a trigger that is fired from within a batch causes the entire batch to be canceled. For example, if the following batch is run in a Query Analyzer window, and the **UPDATE** statement fires a trigger that issues a **ROLLBACK TRANSACTION** statement, the **INSERT** statement is not executed because the batch is canceled by the rollback statement:

```
UPDATE Products SET UnitsInStock = UnitsInStock - 38
WHERE ProductID = 1
INSERT INTO Categories (CategoryName)
VALUES ('This is a test')
GO
```

NESTED TRIGGERS

Triggers are said to be *nested* when a trigger performs an **INSERT**, **UPDATE**, or **DELETE** on another table that fires a trigger. Triggers can be nested up to 32 levels. The trigger nesting level increments each time a trigger performs an operation that fires another trigger and decreases each time a fired trigger finishes execution. If the maximum nesting level is exceeded, the trigger returns an error and rolls back the entire transaction.

A trigger that recursively calls itself is also a nested trigger and increments the current nesting level. Recursive triggers are discussed later in this chapter.

Nested triggers is a server-wide configuration option. By default, nested triggers are enabled. You enable or disable the **nested triggers** configuration option with the **sp_configure** system stored procedure.

To disable nested triggers, run the following code:

```
sp_configure 'nested triggers', 0
GO
reconfigure with override
GO
```

To enable nested triggers, run the following code:

```
sp_configure 'nested triggers', 1
GO
reconfigure with override
GO
```

Recursive Triggers

A trigger that performs an action that causes the same trigger to fire again is called a *recursive trigger*. These are controlled on a database level through the database option **recursive triggers**. By default, recursive triggers are disabled; to enable them run the following code:

```
sp_dboption <database_name>, 'recursive triggers', ON
GO
```

For recursive triggers to work, the **nested triggers** server-wide configuration option must be enabled.

TRIGGER_NESTLEVEL() Function

To find out the current nesting level of a trigger use **TRIGGER_NESTLEVEL()**. The syntax is as follows:

```
TRIGGER_NESTLEVEL( [<trigger_id>] )
```

To obtain the object ID of this trigger (**<trigger_id>**) use the **object_id(<object_ name>)** system stored procedure.

Depending on the **<trigger_id>** value specified, **TRIGGER_NESTLEVEL()** returns different procedures:

- If a valid **<trigger_id>** is specified, it returns the nesting level of the specified trigger.
- If **<trigger_id>** is not specified, it returns the current nesting level.
- If an invalid **<trigger_id>** is specified, it returns 0.

13

Listing 13.8 shows how you can use nested triggers. For the purpose of the example, a *Discontinued* column is added to the *Categories* table of the *Northwind* database, an update trigger is added to the *Categories* tables that discontinues all products associated with the discontinued *Category*, and an update trigger is added to the *Products* table that sends an email to **Manager_Maggie** of all discontinued products. For illustrative purposes the values returned by the **TRIGGER_ NESTLEVEL()** function are shown.

Listing 13.8 Using nested triggers.

```
– Add Discontinued column to the Categories table
ALTER TABLE [dbo].[Categories]
ADD Discontinued BIT NOT NULL
CONSTRAINT DF_CategDiscon DEFAULT (0)
GO
–   Create update trigger on Categories table
```

```
CREATE TRIGGER Categories_update
ON Categories
FOR UPDATE AS
IF @@rowcount = 0
    RETURN
SET NOCOUNT ON
SELECT
   'Categories_update: Trigger nesting level:',
    TRIGGER_NESTLEVEL()
IF UPDATE( Discontinued )
-  Discontinue all Products of discontinued Category
UPDATE Products
SET Discontinued = 1
FROM Products p
INNER JOIN inserted i
ON p.CategoryID = i.CategoryID
AND i.Discontinued = 1
RETURN
GO
-  Create update trigger on Products table
CREATE TRIGGER Products_update
ON Products
FOR UPDATE AS
IF @@rowcount = 0
   RETURN
SET NOCOUNT ON
SELECT
   'Products_update: Trigger nesting level:',
   TRIGGER_NESTLEVEL()
SELECT
   'Products_update: Trigger "Categories_update" nesting level:',
    TRIGGER_NESTLEVEL(object_id('Categories_update'))
IF UPDATE( Discontinued )
    BEGIN
    INSERT INTO DiscontProd
    SELECT CAST(p.ProductID AS nvarchar(50))
    FROM Products p
    JOIN inserted i
    ON p.ProductID = i.ProductID
    JOIN deleted d
    ON i.ProductID = d.ProductID
    AND i.Discontinued = 1
    AND d.Discontinued = 0
    IF @@rowcount > 0
       EXEC master..xp_sendmail @recipients
       = 'Manager_Maggie',
       @message = 'Discontinued Products: ',
       @query = 'SELECT * FROM DiscontProd'
```

```
END
RETURN
GO

-- Discontinue a Category
UPDATE Categories SET Discontinued = 1 WHERE CategoryID = 1
GO
Results:
----------------- -----------------------
Categories_update: Trigger nesting level: 1
---------------- -----------------------
Products_update: Trigger nesting level: 2
---------------- ---------------------------------------
Products_update: Trigger "Categories_update" nesting level: 1
```

Enforcing Business Rules And Data Integrity With Triggers

As explained in prior chapters, in SQL Server 7, business rules and data integrity can be enforced through constraints. For example, entity integrity can be enforced through **PRIMARY KEY** and **UNIQUE** constraints, domain integrity through **CHECK** constraints, and referential integrity through **FOREIGN KEY** constraints. However, constraints are not very flexible.

Business rules and data integrity can also be enforced through triggers. Triggers, as is the case with constraints, can be used to enforce entity, domain, and referential integrity.

13

Even though triggers are flexible, whenever possible use constraints to enforce integrity, because they have better performance than triggers.

Triggers can also be used to enforce complex business rules that cannot be enforced through constraints. For example, use triggers when you need to:

- Validate a column against a column in another table (the table can be in the same database or in another database) (see Listing 13.9).

CHECK constraints can only validate a column against a value in another column of the same table, or against a logical expresion.

- Perform cascading deletes or cascading updates (explained later in this chapter).

FOREIGN KEY constraints do not allow cascading deletes or cascading updates.

- Return customized error messages (see Listing 13.10).
- Perform an operation based on the before and after image rows in a table.

Listing 13.9 shows how triggers can be used to enforce business rules. An insert trigger is created on the *Order Details* table of the *Northwind* database that checks if the product ordered is discontinued or not. If the product is discontinued, it rolls back the transaction. This cannot be done with a **CHECK** constraint because it has to check a value from a different table.

Listing 13.9 Using triggers to enforce business rules.

```
CREATE TRIGGER [Order Details - Insert]
ON [Order Details]
FOR INSERT AS
IF @@rowcount = 0
   RETURN
SET NOCOUNT ON
IF EXISTS (SELECT *
   FROM Products p
   INNER JOIN inserted i
   ON p.ProductID = i.Productid
   AND p.Discontinued = 1)
   ROLLBACK
RETURN
GO
```

Listing 13.10 shows how triggers can be used to return customized error messages. For this example let's suppose that the employees can only be from Florida, California, New York, and Texas. First, we create the table. Second, we create a trigger that checks the states entered. Third, we try to insert a record that has a nonallowed state. This can be enforced through a **CHECK** constraint, but it would return a standard error message such as:

```
INSERT statement conflicted with COLUMN CHECK constraint 'CK_State'.
```

Listing 13.10 Using triggers to return customized error messages.

```
-  First let's create the Employees table
CREATE TABLE [dbo].[Employees] (
[EmployeeID] [int] IDENTITY (1, 1) NOT NULL
CONSTRAINT [PK_Employee] PRIMARY KEY CLUSTERED,
[LastName] [nvarchar] (20) NOT NULL ,
[FirstName] [nvarchar] (10) NOT NULL ,
```

```
[Address] [nvarchar] (60) NOT NULL ,
[City] [nvarchar] (15) NOT NULL ,
[State] [nchar] (2) NOT NULL
)
GO
–  Next, let's create the trigger
CREATE TRIGGER Employees_InsUpd
ON Employees
FOR INSERT, UPDATE AS
IF @@rowcount = 0
   RETURN
SET NOCOUNT ON
IF UPDATE( State )
IF EXISTS (SELECT * FROM inserted
   WHERE State NOT IN ('FL', 'CA', 'NY', 'TX'))
   BEGIN
   RAISERROR('States allowed are: FL, CA, NY, TX', 16, -1)
   ROLLBACK TRANSACTION
END
RETURN
GO
– Finally, let's test the trigger
INSERT INTO [Employees]
  (LastName, FirstName, Address, City, State)
  VALUES
  ('Amado-Blanco', 'Carlos', '1306 Ocean', 'Tampa', 'PA')
GO
Results:
Server: Msg 50000, Level 16, State 1, Procedure Employ_InsUpd, Line 12
States allowed are: FL, CA, NY, TX
```

13

Cascading Updates And Cascading Deletes

One of the most common uses of triggers is to perform cascading updates and deletes. **FOREIGN KEY** constraints in SQL Server 7 do not allow cascading updates and deletes. For example, when a delete or update is performed in the parent table and all corresponding records of the child table need to be deleted or updated, you would use triggers (see Listing 13.11).

Listing 13.11 shows how triggers can be used to perform cascading deletes. Let's suppose that the application business rule requires that when an order is deleted from the *Orders* table in the *Northwind* database, all corresponding order details are deleted from the *Order Details* table. Please note that for this example to work, the **FOREIGN KEY** constraint *FK_Order_Details_Orders* between *the Order Details* and *Orders* tables has to be dropped. Otherwise the constraint would be checked first, return an error, and the trigger would not be fired.

Listing 13.11 Using triggers to perform cascading deletes.

```
– Drop FOREIGN KEY constraint for the trigger to be fired
ALTER TABLE [Order Details]
DROP CONSTRAINT FK_Order_Details_Orders
GO
–      Create the trigger
CREATE TRIGGER [Orders DeleteTrigger]
ON [Orders]
FOR DELETE AS
IF @@rowcount = 0
   RETURN
SET NOCOUNT ON
DELETE [Order Details]
FROM [Order Details] od
INNER JOIN deleted d
ON od.OrderID = d.OrderID
RETURN
GO
```

Coding Triggers

The way you code your trigger will vary, depending on the number of rows affected by the statement that fires the trigger. For example, suppose that you decide to add a *TotalProducts* table in the *Northwind* database that will track the total quantity ordered per product. Each time a row is inserted in the *Order Details* table, the *YTDQuantity* must be updated:

```
CREATE TABLE TotalProducts
    (ProductID int, YTDQuantity int)
GO
```

The following trigger only works for **INSERT** statements that add only one row:

```
CREATE TRIGGER OrderDetail_SingleInsert
ON [Order Details]
FOR INSERT AS
IF @@rowcount = 0
   RETURN
UPDATE TotalProducts
SET YTDQuantity = tp.YTDQuantity + i.Quantity
FROM TotalProducts tp
JOIN inserted i
ON tp.ProductID = i.ProductID
RETURN
GO
```

The following trigger works for **INSERT** statements that add one row and for **INSERT** statements that add multiple rows (**INSERT INTO... SELECT**):

```
CREATE TRIGGER OrderDetail_MultiInsert
ON [Order Details]
FOR INSERT AS
IF @@rowcount = 0
   RETURN
UPDATE TotalProducts
SET YTDQuantity
= TotalProducts.YTDQuantity +
  (SELECT SUM(Quantity)
   FROM inserted
   WHERE TotalProducts.ProductID = inserted.ProductID)
   FROM inserted i
   WHERE TotalProducts.ProductID = i.ProductID
RETURN
GO
```

Chapter Summary

We have covered the following items in this chapter:

- Triggers can be created only on a permanent table.
- Triggers can not be created on system tables.
- Triggers can be created only on the current database.
- A trigger is fired when an **INSERT**, **UPDATE**, or **DELETE** statement is executed against the table.
- Triggers cannot be executed directly.
- A trigger cannot have parameters.
- A trigger is treated as part of the transaction of the statement that fired it.
- A trigger should not return a result set. Use the **SET NOCOUNT ON** statement at the beginning of a trigger's definition to avoid returning results when variable assignments occur in the trigger.
- Use triggers to perform cascade deletes and/or updates, maintain denormalized data, and return customized error messages.
- Use triggers to enforce business rules that cannot be enforced through constraints.
- Triggers are not fired if a constraint (**PRIMARY KEY, FOREIGN KEY, CHECK, UNIQUE**) is violated. Constraints are checked before a trigger is fired.

- An insert trigger is fired when an **INSERT** statement is executed against the table.
- An update trigger is fired when an **UPDATE** statement is executed against the table.
- A delete trigger is fired when a **DELETE** statement is executed against the table.
- Multiple triggers of a given action (insert, update, or delete) can be defined on a table. They are not fired in any particular order.
- A trigger can be defined to fire for more than one action.
- Two special temporary tables are used in triggers: a deleted table (stores a copy of rows deleted from a table, or the before image of rows updated) and an inserted table (stores a copy of rows inserted into a table, or the after image of rows updated).
- The deleted and inserted tables have the same structure as the table on which the trigger is defined. They are stored in cache.
- **TRUNCATE TABLE** does not cause the delete triggers to fire.
- Use the **CREATE TRIGGER** statement to create a trigger.
- All **ALTER**, **CREATE**, **DROP**, and restore statements cannot be part of a triggers definition. **DENY**, **GRANT**, **REVOKE**, **RECONFIGURE**, **TRUNCATE TABLE**, and **UPDATE STATISTICS** statements cannot be part of a triggers definition either.
- To obtain information about a trigger use the **sp_depends**, **sp_help**, **sp_helptext**, and **sp_helptrigger** system stored procedures.
- Triggers definition can be encrypted specifying the **WITH ENCRYPTION** clause when they are created or modified.
- Triggers can be disabled from firing during a replication process specifying the **NOT FOR REPLICATION** clause when they are created or modified.
- A trigger is modified using the **ALTER TRIGGER** statement.
- A trigger is dropped using the **DROP TRIGGER** statement.
- To check in a trigger if a specific column was modified, use the **UPDATE()** function or the **COLUMNS_UPDATED()** function.
- Triggers can be nested 32 levels if the nested triggers server-wide configuration option is enabled.
- To find out the current nesting level of a trigger, use the **TRIGGER_NESTLEVEL()** function.
- To enable recursive triggers the database option **recursive triggers** has to be set on, and **trigger nesting** must be enabled.

REVIEW QUESTIONS

1. Which of the following statements is true about triggers?
   a. Triggers can have input parameters.
   b. Triggers can have output parameters.
   c. Triggers can have input and output parameters.
   d. None of the above.

2. Triggers are mainly used for: (choose all correct answers.)
   a. Enforcing business rules.
   b. Substituting constraints whenever possible.
   c. Performing cascading deletes and updates.
   d. Improving performance.

3. An insert trigger is fired:
   a. When an **INSERT** statement is executed and a constraint fails validation
   b. When an **INSERT** statement is executed and all constraints pass validation
   c. Always when an **INSERT** statement is executed
   d. When the trigger is directly invoked

4. For table *Table1* you define, in the following order, two update triggers: **Table1_UpdateTrigg1** and **Table1_UpdateTrigg2**. If the following statement is executed:

```
UPDATE Table1 SET col1 = 1
```

   Which trigger is fired first?

   a. **Trigger Table1_UpdateTrigg1** because it was the first defined.
   b. It depends on which trigger was fired first for the prior update. One time trigger **Table1_UpdateTrigg1** is fired first, and another trigger **Table1_UpdateTrigg2** is fired first.
   c. **Trigger Table1_UpdateTrigg2** because it was the last one defined and it overwrote the first trigger.
   d. It is unknown; they are not fired in any particular order.

5. Which temporary tables can be defined for a trigger that is defined with the following statement? (Choose all correct answers.)

```
CREATE TRIGGER Order_trigger
ON Orders FOR INSERT, UPDATE, DELETE
AS
<statements>
```

   a. The deleted table.
   b. The inserted table.
   c. The updated table.
   d. None, these are not temporary tables.

6. Which of the following statements is true about triggers? (Choose all correct answers.)
   a. User-triggers can be created on system tables.
   b. Triggers can only be created in the current database.
   c. Triggers information is stored in the *sysobjects* and *syscomments* system tables.
   d. Only one trigger can be created for a given action (**INSERT**, **UPDATE**, or **DELETE** statement).

7. Table *Employees* has an insert trigger. If the following statement inserts five rows, how many times is the insert trigger fired?

```
INSERT INTO Employees
SELECT col1, col2 FROM OtherDB..Employees
```

   a. 1
   b. 5
   c. 2
   d. 0

8. Which of the following T-SQL statements cannot be part of a trigger definition?
   a. **ALTER TABLE**
   b. **UPDATE STATISTICS**
   c. **GRANT**
   d. **DROP VIEW**
   e. All of the above

9. Which of the following system tables stores information about triggers?
   a. *sysindexes*
   b. *sysprocedures*

c. *syscolumns*

d. *syscomments*

10. Which of the following system stored procedures can be used to view information about a trigger(s)? (Choose all correct answers.)

    a. **sp_help**

    b. **sp_helptrigger**

    c. **sp_text_trigger**

    d. **sp_helptext**

11. Which of the following statement encrypts a trigger definition?

    a. **CREATE TRIGGER ti_test ON TEST**
    WITH ENCRYPTION FOR INSERT AS
    <statements>

    b. **ALTER TRIGGER ti_test ON TEST**
    WITH ENCRYPTION FOR INSERT AS
    <statements>

    c. Both a and b.

    d. A trigger definition cannot be encrypted.

12. Which statement will successfully delete the *Orders* table trigger **Orders_Delete** from the database?

    a. **DELETE Orders.dbo.Orders_Delete**

    b. **DROP Orders.dbo.Orders_Delete**

    c. **DELETE dbo.Orders_Delete**

    d. **DROP dbo.Orders_Delete**

13. Which functions can be used in an update trigger to check if a column was changed? (Choose all correct answers.)

    a. **IF UPDATE(<column_name>)**

    b. **IF COLUMNS_UPDATED()**

    c. **IF COLUMN_CHANGED(<column_name>)**

    d. None of the above.

14. According to the following code:

```
CREATE TABLE Table1 ( col1 int, col'2 int)
CREATE TABLE Table2 ( col1 int, col2 int)
GO
CREATE TRIGGER trigg_Table1 ON Table1 FOR INSERT AS
DECLARE @col2 int
```

```
INSERT INTO Table2 SELECT * FROM inserted
SELECT @col2 = col2 FROM inserted
IF @col2 > 50 ROLLBACK TRANSACTION
RETURN
GO
```

What will be the result of this batch?

```
BEGIN TRANSACTION
INSERT INTO Table1 VALUES (1, 51)
COMMIT TRANSACTION
GO
```

a. Table *Table1* will have one row inserted.
b. Table *Table2* will have one row inserted.
c. Both a and b.
d. No rows will be inserted.

15. According to the following code:

```
CREATE TABLE Employee (
     LName nvarchar(20),
     Fname nvarchar(20),
     Status bit )
CREATE TABLE Employee_BKP (
     LName nvarchar(20),
     Fname nvarchar(20),
     Status bit )
GO
CREATE TRIGGER trigg_Employee ON Employee FOR INSERT AS
DECLARE @status bit
INSERT INTO Employee_BKP SELECT * FROM inserted
SELECT @status = Status FROM inserted
IF @status = 0 ROLLBACK TRANSACTION
RETURN
GO
```

What will be the result of this batch?

```
INSERT INTO Employee VALUES ('Smith', 'Joe', 0)
INSERT INTO Employee VALUES ('Brown', 'Karen', 1)
GO
```

a. Table *Employee* and *Employee_BKP* will have two rows inserted.
b. Table *Employee* will have two rows inserted and table *Employee_BKP* will have one row inserted.

c. Table *Employee* will have two rows inserted and table *Employee_BKP* will have zero rows inserted.

d. No rows will be inserted into tables *Employee* and *Employee_BKP*.

HANDS-ON PROJECTS

Susan found during her report design phase that certain reports would require an excessive amount of joins and would cause too many locks to be taken on her database. She fought the problems using every tool she had, but couldn't get the performance she needed. She pushed back from her desk and grabbed the phone, punching numbers. "Jose, you got a minute?" she asked. Jose was a database guru she spoke with often. "I'm having a tough time with this database design. I'm trying to get some reports designed in this thing and I'm taking way too many locks. What should I do?" After some discussion, Jose explained to her that she might want to denormalize some of her tables and create ancillary tables to report on. "Okay" she thought, "I'll get the design for those tables, but how do I populate them?" She spoke further with Jose who explained to her the use of triggers to create those tables.

These activities assume that you are already connected to the *Northwind* database using the Query Analyzer.

Project 13.1

In this activity, you create an insert trigger according to the following specifications:

13

Add a summary table to keep track of the dollar amount sold per category during each month. This table has to be updated automatically each time a record is inserted into the *Order Details* table. The **INSERT** statements used to add data to the *Order Details* table inserts only one row.

First let's create the summary table. In the Query Analyzer, type the following command and execute it:

```
CREATE TABLE SalesPerCategory (
CategoryID int,
D_year smallint,
D_Month tinyint,
Sold money,
CONSTRAINT PK_SalesPerCategory
PRIMARY KEY CLUSTERED (CategoryID, D_year, D_Month)
)
GO
```

Second, let's create the insert trigger. In the Query Analyzer, type the following command and execute it:

```
CREATE TRIGGER OrderDetail_Category
ON [Order Details]
FOR INSERT
AS
IF @@rowcount = 0
RETURN
DECLARE @i_year   int
,       @i_month  int
,       @i_catid  int
,       @sold     money

SELECT @i_year  = YEAR( o.OrderDate )
,      @i_month = MONTH( o.OrderDate )
,      @i_catid = p.CategoryID
,      @sold = i.UnitPrice * i.Quantity * (1 - i.Discount)
FROM inserted i
JOIN Orders o ON o.OrderID = i.OrderID
JOIN Products p ON p.ProductID = i.ProductID
UPDATE SalesPerCategory
SET Sold = Sold + @sold
WHERE CategoryID = @i_catid AND D_year = @i_year AND D_Month = @i_month

IF @@rowcount = 0 — Row for CategoryID, Year, Month doesn't exist
INSERT INTO SalesPerCategory (CategoryID, D_year, D_Month, Sold)
VALUES ( @i_catid, @i_year, @i_month, @sold )
RETURN
GO
```

Project 13.2

In this activity, you will modify a trigger definition according to the following specifications:

Encrypt the definition of the **OrderDetail_Category** trigger created previously. In the Query Analyzer, type the following command and execute it:

```
ALTER TRIGGER OrderDetail_Category
ON [Order Details]
WITH ENCRYPTION
FOR INSERT
AS
IF @@rowcount = 0
RETURN
```

```
DECLARE @i_year   int
,       @i_month  int
,       @i_catid  int
,       @sold     money

SELECT @i_year  = YEAR( o.OrderDate )
,      @i_month = MONTH( o.OrderDate )
,      @i_catid = p.CategoryID
,      @sold = i.UnitPrice * i.Quantity * (1 - i.Discount)
FROM inserted i
JOIN Orders o ON o.OrderID = i.OrderID
JOIN Products p ON p.ProductID = i.ProductID
UPDATE SalesPerCategory
SET Sold = Sold + @sold
WHERE CategoryID = @i_catid AND D_year = @i_year AND D_Month = @i_month

IF @@rowcount = 0 — Row for CategoryID, Year, Month doesn't exist
INSERT INTO SalesPerCategory (CategoryID, D_year, D_Month, Sold)
VALUES ( @i_catid, @i_year, @i_month, @sold )
RETURN
GO
```

Now let's drop the **OrderDetail_Category** trigger created earlier.

In the Query Analyzer, type the following command and execute it:

```
DROP TRIGGER OrderDetail_Category
GO
```

After Susan created and modified her triggers, she pointed the reports to the new tables, and the design worked flawlessly. She experienced no locks on her original tables because she wasn't accessing them with the reports at all, and the reports ran quickly because the joins were minimized. Susan was very pleased at the design of the database this far. She knew the next step was going to be the actual creation of the objects she had been designing.

Chapter Fourteen

Creating The Physical Database

After Reading This Chapter And Completing The Exercises, You Will Be Able To:

- Understand the data storage structure of a database
- Define files
- Define filegroups
- Create a database
- Add data and transaction files to a database
- Remove data and transaction files from a database
- Modify the definition of data and transaction files
- Drop a database
- Shrink a database
- Set database options
- Attach and detach a database
- Rename a database
- Change the ownership of a database

A *database* consists of a collection of tables, indexes, stored procedures, triggers, views, and constraints. In this chapter we will discuss the physical components that make up a Microsoft SQL Server database.

Sizing SQL Server Database Components

Microsoft SQL Server 7 databases are stored in Microsoft Windows NT operating system files. Before you design and create a SQL Server 7 database, you should you have an understanding of the database storage structure and how data is stored. This understanding will help you prepare for the exam and will help you plan for the proper size of drives on your server.

To help you plan for your database sizing, we will discuss the numbers involved in its storage. The fundamental unit of storage in SQL Server 7 is a *page*. In SQL Server 7, pages are 8K long, which results in 128 pages per megabyte. Eight contiguous pages form an *extent*, which makes an extent 64K. This means that a database can have 16 extents per megabyte.

Tables and indexes are stored in extents, and SQL Server 7 tables can now share these extents with other database objects. A row of data, however, cannot span multiple pages. This limits the maximum size of a row to 8,096 bytes (8,192 bytes page size minus 96 bytes for the row header).

A couple of major differences between SQL Server 7 and prior versions are the 8K pages (versus 2K), and the extent sharing between database objects. Also, in prior versions, an extent could only be owned by one object.

Database File

All Microsoft SQL Server 7 databases consist of the following operating system files:

- **Data files** A file where database objects such as tables, stored procedures, and indexes are stored. There are two types of data files: the *primary data file* (at least one is necessary) and the *secondary data file* (many can exist).
- **Transaction log files** Files that contain all database activity in a sequential format.

Database files are created when the database is created or altered. Here are some important facts to consider about these files:

- A database file cannot be shared between two or more databases and it can only be used by one database.
- Data and transaction log information is always stored in separate files.
- A database file can be placed on a FAT or a NTFS file system. It cannot be placed on a compressed file system.

Database files can also be created on raw partitions. A raw parition might give slightly better performance, but the limitations of raw partitions outweigh the small performance gain. See *Books Online* for a more in-depth discussion on raw partitions.

- A database file has an operating system file name (os_file_name), which is the name of the physical file on the drive media. It also has a logical_file_name, which is the name used in the Transact-SQL statements to refer to the file. For example, the transaction log file of the *Northwind* database has an operating system name of: *C:\MSSQL7\DATA\northwnd.ldf*, and a logical name of *Northwind_log*.
- A file can be a member of only one filegroup. More on filegroups later in this chapter.
- You can specify the following properties of a file: initial size, maximum size, automatic growth, and growth increment (only if automatic growth is allowed). This only applies to data files.

If a database file is set to grow automatically, you should specify the maximum size the file can grow to. This prevents the disk from getting full.

If a data file is part of a filegroup, it will autogrow only after all other data files of the filegroup are full.

Use the **sp_helpfile** system stored procedure to view the properties of all files associated with the current database. For example, the following statement returns all files associated with the *Northwind* database:


```
use Northwind
go
sp_helpfile
go
```

Primary Data File

A *primary data file* is identified by the .mdf extension. It stores the startup information for the database, as well as database objects. Every database has one, and only one, primary file.

Secondary Data File

A secondary data file is identified by the .ndf extension. The *secondary data file* stores database objects. Secondary data files are used when the primary data file cannot store all the data. They are also used in conjunction with filegroups in large databases to balance the disk load (see "Database Filegroups" later in this chapter). Some databases do not have a secondary data file, while other databases may have one or more secondary data files.

Transaction Log File

A *transaction log file* is identified by the .ldf extension; it stores all the information necessary to recover the database in case of a system failure. Every time SQL Server 7 is started, it performs an automatic recovery, using this file.

SQL Server 7 performs the following actions when recovering a database from the transaction log:

- It rolls forward all committed transactions.
- It rolls back all incomplete transactions.

The recovery process is possible because SQL Server uses a *write-ahead* log. This means that the log is written before data is modified in the database. Whenever an **INSERT**, **DELETE**, or **UPDATE** statement is executed against a database, SQL Server performs the following actions:

- Checks if the data pages that are going to be modified are already in cache. If not, it reads them from disk and loads them into memory.
- First writes the changes to the transaction log file. It makes no modifications to the data files.
- When a checkpoint occurs, writes all pages that have been modified in memory to the data files on disk.

By default a transaction log file is 25 percent of the data files. The minimum size of a transaction log file is 512K.

DATABASE FILEGROUPS

A *filegroup* is a collection of data files that are grouped together for allocation and administration purposes. You would normally use filegroups to balance the disk load of your system by spreading data across multiple disks. For example, imagine that your system has two disk drives. You could create a filegroup for each drive, and create your tables on one filegroup and your indexes on the other filegroup (to learn how to create tables and indexes on specific filegroups refer to Chapters 5 and 6).

In small systems you can get the same performance improvements with a RAID stripe set. If you have a system with several sets of RAIDs, planning and correctly placing your files and filegroups can result in better load balancing of your disks, and thus better performance.

You can create filegroups when you create or alter the database. When designing filegroups keep in mind that:

- A database can have up to 256 filegroups.
- A filegroup can only be used by one database.
- A filegroup can only consist of data files; transaction log files cannot be part of a filegroup.

Two different types of filegroups exist:

- *Primary* filegroup
- *User-defined* filegroup

A filegroup can have three properties that are set with the **ALTER DATABASE** statement:

- **READONLY property** No updates are allowed to objects stored in the filegroup.
- **READWRITE property** Updates are allowed to objects stored in the filegroup.
- **DEFAULT property** A database can only have one filegroup with this property set. When a database is created, the primary filegroup is the default filegroup. All tables and indexes created without specifying a filegroup are placed in the default filegroup (see Chapters 5 and 6).

14

Use the **sp_helpfilegroup** system stored procedure to view the properties of all filegroups associated with the current database. The following statement returns all files associated with the *Northwind* database:

```
use Northwind
go
sp_helpfilegroup
go
```

Primary Filegroup

A *primary* filegroup always contains the primary data file. It also contains any other data file that is not specifically assigned to any other filegroup. An important fact to remember is that the system tables are always allocated in the primary filegroup of the database.

User-Defined Filegroup

A *user-defined* filegroup is a filegroup created with the **FILEGROUP** clause in a **CREATE DATABASE** or **ALTER DATABASE** statement. A database can have up to 255 user-defined filegroups.

Creating A Database

You can create a database using the **CREATE DATABASE** statement or by using the Create Database Wizard. Up to 32,767 databases can exist on a single SQL Server 7 installation.

When a database is created without the **FOR ATTACH** clause, SQL Server 7 uses the *model* system database as a template. Any database objects and database settings in the *model* database will be copied to the new database. If you use special objects or user-defined data types in all your databases, you would place them in the *model* database first. All databases you create after that would contain those items. A newly created database's size will be equal to the size of the *model* database if it is created with no size specified. If you specify a size, it must be at least as large as the *model* database.

To ensure that a database object (user-defined data type, table, view, stored procedure, etc.) is always created in a new database, add the database object to the *model* database.

When creating a database, here are some important facts to keep in mind:

- A database has at least one data file (primary data file) and one transaction log file.
- A database always has a primary filegroup.
- The user who creates the database is the owner of the database.
- All database files will be filled with zeros when created.
- Information about all databases on a SQL Server is stored in the *sysdatabases* system table on the *master* system database.
- The database name must be unique within a server and can be up to 128 characters long. The first character of a database name has to be a letter as defined in the Unicode Standard 2 or one of the following symbols: _, @, #. If the database name has embedded spaces, you must delimit it with brackets, for example [database name].

Always back up the *master* system database after creating a database. The *master* database is required to recover a server properly.

You can use the **sp_helpdb [<db_name>]** system stored procedure to view information about many items regarding a database, including the following:

- All databases on the server (database name, size, owner, ID, creation date, and database options).
- A specific database (database name, size, owner, ID, creation date, database options, and properties of all data and transaction log files).

CREATE DATABASE Statement

Let's take a look at the commands used to create a database. The syntax for the **CREATE DATABASE** statement is as follows:

```
CREATE DATABASE <db_name>
[ON [PRIMARY]
     [<data_file1>[, ... <data_fileN>]]
     [, FILEGROUP <filegroup_name1> <data_fileN+1>[, ... <data_fileN+N>]
        [, ... FILEGROUP ...]
     ]
]
[LOG ON <log_file1>[, ... <log_fileN>]]
[FOR LOAD|FOR ATTACH]
```

The **PRIMARY** clause is used to specify the primary filegroup. The first data file specified in the **CREATE** statement always becomes the primary data file.

To specify other filegroups, use the **FILEGROUP** clause. The **LOG ON** clause is used to specify the transaction log files. If this clause is not specified, a transaction log file is created automatically.

The **FOR LOAD** clause is used for backward compatibility. The **FOR ATTACH** clause is used to attach a database from an existing set of database files. This is a new feature, and this clause is used when attaching a database that has more than 16 database files. For more information about attaching and detaching a database see "Attaching And Detaching A Database" later in this chapter.

If no data files and transaction log files are specified in the **CREATE DATABASE** statement, SQL Server 7 creates a database with one primary data file and one transaction log file. When specifying data files **(<data_file1>**, ... **<data_fileN>**) and transaction log files (**<log_file1>**, ... **<log_fileN>**) you can specify the following properties:

```
( [NAME = <logical_file_name>,]
  FILENAME = <os_file_name>
  [, SIZE = <size>]
  [, MAXSIZE = {<max_size>|UNLIMITED}]
  [, FILEGROWTH = <growth_increment>] )
```

The **NAME = <logical_file_name>** clause is used to specify the logical file name of the database file. This is the name used in Transact-SQL statements.

The **FILENAME = <os_file_name>** clause is used to specify the operating system file name. It contains the full path and file name. For example: C:\mssql7\data\northwnd.mdf. The **SIZE = <size>** clause is used to specify the initial file size of the database file. To specify the size in kilobytes use the *KB* suffix. To specify the size in megabytes use the *MB* suffix (this is the default). The minimum value allowed is 512KB. If the **SIZE** clause is omitted when defining a primary data file, then SQL Server 7 creates a primary file the same size as the one of the model database. If the **SIZE** clause is omitted when defining a secondary data file, then SQL Server 7 creates a 1MB file. If the **SIZE** clause is omitted when defining a transaction log file, it creates a file with a size equal to 25 percent of all the data files.

The **MAXSIZE = {<max_size> | UNLIMITED}** clause is used to specify the maximum size to which the database file can grow. To specify the size in kilobytes use the *KB* suffix. To specify the size in megabytes use the *MB* suffix (this is the default). If this clause is not specified, or **UNLIMITED** is specified, the file will grow until the disk fills up.

The **FILEGROWTH = <growth_increment>** clause is used to specify the amount of space that will be added to the file each time it auto-grows. The **<growth_increment>** can be specified in kilobytes (KB suffix), megabytes (MB suffix; this is the default), or percent (**% suffix**). If this clause is not specified, the file will auto-grow by 10 percent of the current file size. The minimum value by which a file is increased is 64KB. If a value of 0 is specified, no auto-growth will occur.

Listing 14.1 shows how to create a simple database with one data file of 100MB. When more space is needed, the data file will grow by 35MB until it reaches 1GB. Because the transaction log file is not specified, SQL Server creates a log file 25 percent the size of all data files (in this case, 25MB).

Listing 14.1 Creating a simple database.

```
CREATE DATABASE ExPrep
ON
( Name = ExPrep_Data,
  FILENAME = 'c:\mssql7\data\ExPrep_Data.mdf',
  SIZE = 100MB,
  MAXSIZE = 1000MB,
  FILEGROWTH = 35MB)
GO
```

Listing 14.2 shows how to create a database with three data files and two transaction log files. All data files are part of the **PRIMARY** filegroup.

Listing 14.2 Creating a database with three data files and two transaction log files.

```
CREATE DATABASE ExPrep
ON
( Name = ExPrep_Data1, FILENAME = 'c:\mssql7\data\ExPrep_Data1.mdf',
  SIZE = 100MB, MAXSIZE = 1000MB, FILEGROWTH = 35MB),
( Name = ExPrep_Data2, FILENAME = 'c:\mssql7\data\ExPrep_Data2.ndf',
  SIZE = 100MB, MAXSIZE = 500MB, FILEGROWTH = 35MB),
( Name = ExPrep_Data3, FILENAME = 'c:\mssql7\data\ExPrep_Data3.ndf',
  SIZE = 100MB, MAXSIZE = 500MB, FILEGROWTH = 35MB)
LOG ON
( NAME = ExPrep_Log1, FILENAME = 'd:\mssql7\data\ExPrep_Log1.ldf',
  SIZE = 50MB, MAXSIZE = 250MB, FILEGROWTH = 35MB),
( NAME = ExPrep_Log2, FILENAME = 'd:\mssql7\data\ExPrep_Log2.ldf',
  SIZE = 50MB, MAXSIZE = 250MB, FILEGROWTH = 35MB)
GO
```

Listing 14.3 shows how to create a database with several filegroups in order to balance disk load. In this case, three filegroups are created (one on disk C, one disk D, and one on disk E). Next, a table is created on the **PRIMARY** filegroup, but the index is stored on the **Group1** filegroup and the image column on the **Group2** filegroup.

Listing 14.3 Creating a database with several filegroups.

```
CREATE DATABASE ExPrep
ON PRIMARY
( Name = ExPrep_Data1, FILENAME = 'c:\mssql7\data\ExPrep_Data1.mdf',
  SIZE = 100MB, MAXSIZE = 1000MB, FILEGROWTH = 35MB),
FILEGROUP Group1
( Name = ExPrep_Data2, FILENAME = 'd:\mssql7\data\ExPrep_Data2.ndf',
  SIZE = 100MB, MAXSIZE = 500MB, FILEGROWTH = 35MB),
( Name = ExPrep_Data3, FILENAME = 'd:\mssql7\data\ExPrep_Data3.ndf',
  SIZE = 100MB, MAXSIZE = 500MB, FILEGROWTH = 35MB),
FILEGROUP Group2
( Name = ExPrep_Data4, FILENAME = 'e:\mssql7\data\ExPrep_Data4.ndf',
  SIZE = 100MB, MAXSIZE = 500MB, FILEGROWTH = 35MB)
LOG ON
( NAME = ExPrep_Log1, FILENAME = 'e:\mssql7\data\ExPrep_Log1.ldf',
  SIZE = 100MB, MAXSIZE = 250MB, FILEGROWTH = 50MB)
GO

CREATE TABLE Employees (
    Empl_ID     integer identity NOT NULL,
    Empl_LName  nvarchar(30) NOT NULL,
    Empl_FName  nvarchar(15) NOT NULL,
    Empl_Foto   image )
    ON "PRIMARY"
```

```
    TEXTIMAGE_ON "Group2"
GO
CREATE INDEX Empl_Name_IDX ON Employees ( Empl_LName, Empl_FName)
    ON Group1
GO
```

Listing 14.4 shows how to create a database without specifying a data and transaction log file. In this case SQL Server creates one data file the same size as the data file of the *model* database, and one transaction log file the size of 25 percent of the data file.

Listing 14.4 Creating a database without specifying a data and transaction log file.

```
CREATE DATABASE ExPrep
GO
```

Create Database Wizard

You can also create a database using the Create Database Wizard, which consists of seven screens that take you step by step through the process. You advance from screen to screen by clicking on the Next button and you go back to the prior screen by clicking on the Back button. The following describes the Create Database Wizard screens:

- The first screen, Welcome To The Create Database Wizard, explains what can be done with the wizard (name the database, create one or more data files and transaction log files, specify database file growth information).
- On the second screen, Name The Database And Specify Its Location, enter: database name, location of the data file(s), and the location of the transaction log file(s).
- On the third screen, Name The Database Files, enter the data file(s) name and its initial size (see Figure 14.1).
- On the fourth screen, Define The Database File Growth, specify the data file growth options (will auto-growth be allowed, the amount of MB or percent of the growth, and the maximum size of the data files) (see Figure 14.2).
- On the fifth screen, Name The Transaction Log Files enter the transaction log file(s) name and its initial size (see Figure 14.3).
- On the sixth screen, Define The Transaction Log File Growth, specify the transaction log file growth options (will auto-growth be allowed, the amount of MB or percent of the growth, and the maximum size of the data files) (see Figure 14.4).
- The seventh and final screen, Completing The Create Database Wizard, shows the options you have defined for the database. To create the database click on the Finish button.

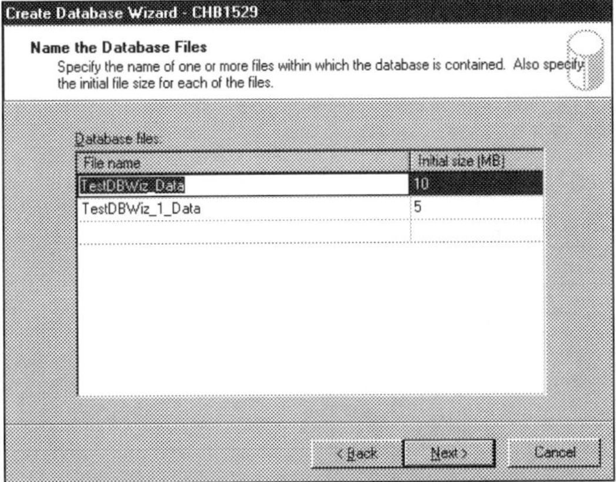

Figure 14.1 Name The Database Files screen from the Create Database Wizard.

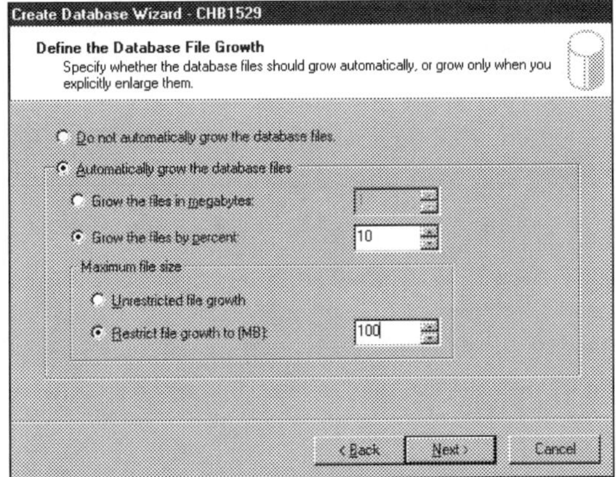

Figure 14.2 Define The Database File Growth screen from the Create Database Wizard.

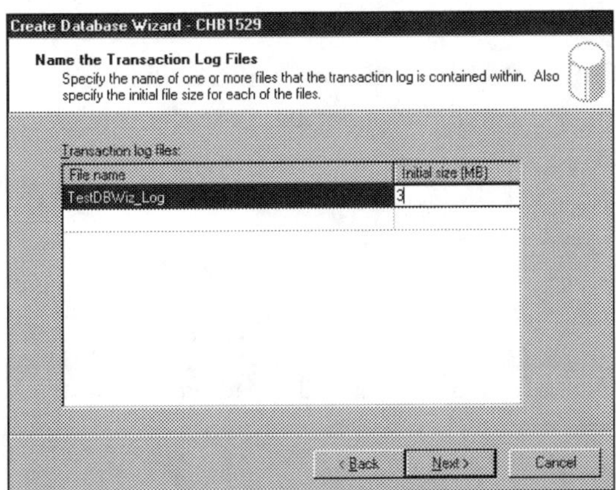

Figure 14.3 Name The Transaction Log Files screen from the Create Database Wizard.

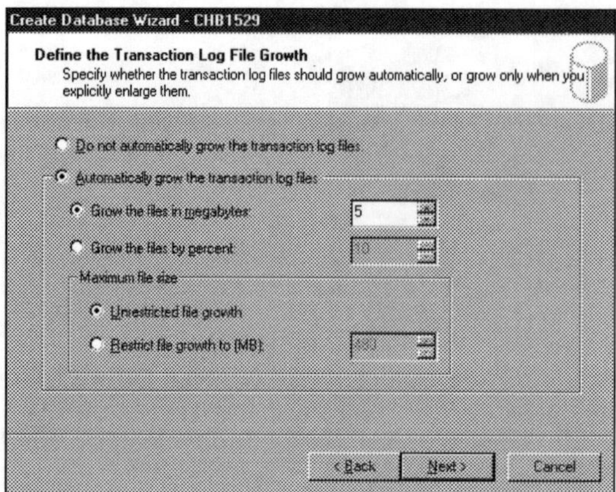

Figure 14.4 Define The Transaction Log File Growth screen from the Create Database Wizard.

Modifying A Database

Once a database has been created, you can modify its structure. The **ALTER DATABASE** statement allows you to perform the following:

- Add data files.
- Add transaction log files.
- Remove a data or transaction log file.
- Modify a data or transaction log file.
- Add a filegroup.
- Remove a filegroup.
- Modify a filegroup property.

Adding Data Files

Using a single **ALTER DATABASE** statement, you can add more than one data file to a database. To add a data file to a database use the following syntax:

```
ALTER DATABASE <db_name> ADD FILE <data_file1>[, ... <data_fileN>]
     [TO FILEGROUP <filegroup_name>]
```

When adding a data file you can specify which filegroup it will belong on (the filegroup must already exist in the database). If the **TO FILEGROUP <filegroup_name>** is not specified, the data file will be added to the **PRIMARY** filegroup. A single command cannot be used to add two data files to two different filegroups. See Listing 14.5.

For an explanation of **<data_file1>[, ... <data_fileN>]** refer to the **CREATE DATABASE** statement.

Listing 14.5 Adding two data files to a database.

```
ALTER DATABASE ExPrep ADD FILE
( Name = ExPrep_Data2, FILENAME = 'c:\mssql7\data\ExPrep_Data2.ndf',
  SIZE = 50MB, MAXSIZE = 200MB),
( Name = ExPrep_Data3, FILENAME = 'c:\mssql7\data\ExPrep_Data3.ndf',
  SIZE = 25MB, MAXSIZE = 100MB, FILEGROWTH = 35MB)
GO
```

Adding Transaction Log Files

With a single **ALTER DATABASE** statement, you can add more than one transaction log data file to a database. See Listing 14.6 for a demonstration of this command. Use the following syntax:

```
ALTER DATABASE <db_name> ADD LOG FILE <log_file1>[, ... <log_fileN>]
```

For an explanation of **<log_file1>[, ... <log_fileN>]** refer to the **CREATE DATABASE** statement.

Listing 14.6 Adding a transaction log file to a database.

```
ALTER DATABASE ExPrep ADD LOG FILE
( NAME = ExPrep_Log2, FILENAME = 'd:\mssql7\data\ExPrep_Log2.ldf',
  SIZE = 50MB, MAXSIZE = UNLIMITED)
GO
```

Removing A Data Or Transaction Log File

A data or transaction log file cannot be removed from the database unless it is empty. A file that is removed from the database is also deleted from disk. To remove a data or transaction log file use the following syntax:

14

```
ALTER DATABASE <db_name> REMOVE FILE {<data_file>|<log_file>}
```

The following command shows how to remove a data file from a database:

```
ALTER DATABASE ExPrep REMOVE FILE ExPrep_Data3
GO
```

Modifying A Data Or Transaction Log File

You can use the **ALTER DATABASE** statement to change the following properties of a data or transaction log file (only one property per statement can be modified):

- **FILENAME** Physical file name. Can be specified only for a file that is part of the *tempdb* system database.
- **SIZE** File size. The new size has to be larger than the current size of the file.

- **FILEGROWTH** File growth.
- **MAXSIZE** File's maximum size.

The syntax to modify a file is as follows:

```
ALTER DATABASE <db_name>
     MODIFY FILE ( NAME = < file_name>,
                                        { FILENAME = <os_file_name>|
                                          SIZE = <size>|
                                          MAXSIZE = {<max_size>|UNLIMITED}|
                                          FILEGROWTH = <growth_increment>  }
)
```

For an explanation of file's properties, refer to the **CREATE DATABASE** statement.

The following shows how to modify a property of a data file. In this case, the **MAXSIZE** property of file is set to grow unlimited:

```
ALTER DATABASE ExPrep MODIFY FILE
( Name = ExPrep_Data2, MAXSIZE = UNLIMITED )
GO
```

Adding A Filegroup

To add a data filegroup to a database, use the following syntax:

```
ALTER DATABASE <db_name> ADD FILEGROUP <filegroup_name>
```

Listing 14.7 shows how to add a filegroup to a database. After the filegroup is created, a data file is added and associated with the filegroup.

Listing 14.7 Adding a filegroup to a database.

```
ALTER DATABASE ExPrep ADD FILEGROUP Group9
GO
ALTER DATABASE ExPrep ADD FILE
( Name = ExPrep_Data4, FILENAME = 'c:\mssql7\data\ExPrep_Data4.ndf',
  SIZE = 100MB, FILEGROWTH = 0) TO FILEGROUP Group9
GO
```

Removing A Filegroup

A filegroup can only be removed from a database when it is empty, that is, when there are no files associated with it. The syntax for removing a filegroup is as follows:

```
ALTER DATABASE <db_name> REMOVE FILEGROUP <filegroup_name>
```

Listing 14.8 shows how to remove a filegroup from a database. First, all files associated with filegroup must be dropped.

Listing 14.8 Removing a filegroup from a database.

```
ALTER DATABASE ExPrep REMOVE FILE ExPrep_Data4
GO
ALTER DATABASE ExPrep REMOVE FILEGROUP Group9
GO
```

Modifying A Filegroup Property (READONLY, READWRITE, DEFAULT)

To modify a property of a filegroup use the following syntax:

```
ALTER DATABASE <db_name> MODIFY FILEGROUP <filegroup_name>
     {READONLY|READWRITE|DEFAULT}
```

You can change only one property at a time. For an explanation of filegroup properties refer to the topic "Database Filegroups" in this chapter.

You cannot modify a filegroup property if it doesn't have at least one data file associated with it.

The following syntax shows how to change the default filegroup for a database.

```
ALTER DATABASE ExPrep MODIFY FILEGROUP Group9 DEFAULT
GO
```


Dropping A Database

Only databases that are not being used can be dropped. To drop one or more databases use the following statement:

```
DROP DATABASE <db_name1>[, ... <db_nameN>]
```

Dropping a database will remove the database from SQL Server and will delete all the data and transaction log files from disk.

Always backup the *master* system database after dropping a database.

Listing 14.9 shows how to drop multiple database with one **DROP DATABASE** statement.

Listing 14.9 Dropping multiple database with one **DROP DATABASE** statement.

```
DROP DATABASE ExPrep, ExPrep_Old
GO
```

Expanding A Database

SQL Server 7 allows three ways of expanding a database:

- Configure each data and transaction log file to grow automatically.

Remember, a data file that is part of a filegroup will not automatically grow unless all the files of the filegroup are full.

- Increase the size of an existing data or transaction log file with the **ALTER DATABASE** statement.
- Add data and transaction log files with the **ALTER DATABASE** statement.

For more on how to set the file growth property of a file, increase the size of a file, and add files to a database, refer to "Creating A Database," "Adding Data Files," "Adding Transaction Log Files," and "Modifying A Filegroup Property" in this chapter.

Shrinking A Database

The process of recovering space not being used by the database is called *shrinking a database*. Space can be recovered from both the data and transaction log files. SQL Server 7 allows three ways to shrink a database:

- Automatically shrink the database.
- Manually shrink the entire database.
- Manually shrink individual files.

An entire database cannot be shrunk to a size smaller than its original size; however, a data or transaction log file can be shrunk to a size smaller than its original size.

Automatically Shrinking A Databse

For a database to shrink automatically, you can set the **autoshrink** database option with the **sp_dboption** system stored procedure (see "Database Options" later in this chapter). SQL Server will automatically shrink the database whenever there is a significant amount of unused space in the database.

DBCC SHRINKDATABASE Statement

To manually shrink a database, use the **DBCC SHRINKDATABASE** statement. The syntax is as follows:

```
DBCC SHRINKDATABASE (  <db_name>
                                              [, <target_%>]
                                              [, {NOTRUNCATE|
TRUNCATEONLY}] )
```

To specify the desired percentage of free space left after shrinking the database, specify **<target_%>**. To shrink to the maximum, do not specify a **<target_%>**.

If the **NOTRUNCATE** clause is specified, the recovered free space is retained in the database. If not specified, it is released to the operating system. The only effect is the relocation of used pages to free up space.

If the **TRUNCATEONLY** clause is specified, the recovered free space is released to the operating system. Specifying this clause frees up the unused space at the end of the files. The **<target_%>** clause is ignored if it is specified. Listing 14.10 shows how to shrink a database. The desired percentage of free space left in the *Northwind* database is 10 percent.

Listing 14.10 Shrinking a database.

```
DBCC SHRINKDATABASE ( Northwind, 10 )
GO
```

DBCC SHRINKFILE Statement

To manually shrink individual files use the **DBCC SHRINKFILE** statement. The syntax is as follows:

14

```
DBCC SHRINKFILE ( <logical_file_name>|<file_id>
                                    { [, <target_size>]
                                      [,
{EMPTYFILE|NOTRUNCATE|TRUNCATEONLY}]
                                     } )
```

You can shrink only the files that are part of the current database.

You can either specify the logical file name of the data or transaction log file, or you can specify the file identification number.

You can obtain the file identification number by using the **FILE_ID()** function.

Use the **<target_size>** clause to specify the desired file size in MB. For example, if 20 is specified, SQL Server 7 will try to shrink the file until its size is 20MB.

Use the **EMPTYFILE** clause to have SQL Server migrate all the data of the specified file to other files of the same filegroup, or disable any future data placement on the file. After shrinking the file with the **EMPTYFILE** clause, the file can be dropped with the **ALTER DATABASE** statement.

If the **NOTRUNCATE** clause is specified, the recovered free space is retained in the file. If not specified, it is released to the operating system. The only effect is the relocation of used pages to free up space.

If the **TRUNCATEONLY** clause is specified, the recovered free space is released to the operating system. Specifying this clause releases the unused spaced that is at the end of the file. The **<target_size>** clause is ignored if it is specified. Listing 14.11 demonstrates how to shrink a file. Since no target size is specified, SQL Server shrinks the transaction log file of the *Northwind* database as much as possible.

Listing 14.11 Shrinking a file.

```
DBCC SHRINKFILE ( Northwind_Log )
GO
```

DATABASE OPTIONS

SQL Server allows you to set a number of options that define the characteristics of the database. It is important to remember that database options are specific to each database. For example, setting the *read only* database option on the *Northwind* database does not affect any other database.

Remember, each newly created database will inherit the database options of the *model* system database.

The **sp_dboption** system stored procedure is used to change database options. The syntax is as follows:

```
sp_dboption [@dbname =] '<db_name>'
                        [, [@optname =] '<option_name>']
                        [, [@optvalue =] '<option_value>']
```

The **sp_dboption** system stored procedure accepts three parameters:

- Database name (**<db_name>**). This specifies the database where the option will be set.

- Database option to set (**<option_name>**). If not specified, SQL Server 7 lists all the database options that are set on the database.
- New setting of the database option (**<option_value>**). The setting can be true (on) or false (off). If it is not specified, SQL Server 7 returns the current setting of the database option specified in **<option_name>**.

For a list of all database options see Table 14.1.

Table 14.1 Database options.

Database Option	Description
ANSI **NULL** default	If set to true, all columns that are not explicitly defined as **NOT NULL** default to allowing **NULL** values. If set to false, they do not allow **NULL** values. The default is true.
ANSI **NULL**s	If set to true, all comparisons to a **NULL** value evaluate to false. If set to false, the comparison of two **NULL** nonunicode values evaluate to true. The default is false.
ANSI warnings	If set to true, error or warning messages are returned when a *divide by zero* condition occurs, and when an aggregate function encounters a **NULL** value. If set to false, no errors or warnings are returned. The default is false.
auto create statistics	If set to true, any statistic that SQL Server needs for optimization is automatically created. If set to false, they are not created. The default is true.
auto update statistics	If set to true, existing statistics are updated when needed. If set to false, they are not updated automatically. The default value is true.
autoclose	If set to true, the database is shut down automatically by SQL Server when no users are connected to the database and no processes are running against the database. If set to false, the database is not shut down. The default is false for all SQL Server editions except for the Desktop Edition.
autoshrink	If set to true, the database is automatically shrunk when unused space is available. If set to false, the database is not shrunk automatically. The default is false for all SQL Server editions except for the Desktop Edition.
concat **NULL** yields **NULL**	If set to true, if there is a **NULL** operand in a concatenation operation the result is a **NULL** value. If set to false, the **NULL** operand is ignored. The default is false.
cursor close on commit	If set to true, opened cursors are closed when the transaction is committed. If set to false, they stay open. The default is false.

(continued)

Table 14.1 Database options *(continued)*.

Database Option	Description
dbo use only	If set to true, only the database owner can use the database (active connections remain active even if they belong to nondatabase owners). If set to false, any user who has permission can access the database. The default is false.
default to local cursor	If set to true, cursor declarations default to **LOCAL** unless otherwise specified. If set to false, they default to **GLOBAL**. The default is true.
merge publish	If set to true, the database can be published for a merge replication. If set to false, it cannot. The default is false.
offline	If set to true, the database is closed and marked as offline. If set to false, the database is online and can be used. The default is false.
published	If set to true, publication is enabled. If set to false, tables of the database are not published. The default is false.
quote identifier	If set to true, identifiers can be delimited by double quotation marks, strings must be delimited by single quotation marks. If set to false, identifiers cannot be delimited by quotation marks, strings can be delimited by double or single quotation marks. The default is false.
read only	If set to true, data in the database can only be read (database cannot be shrunk, no locking will occur). If set to false, data in the database can be read and modified. The default is false.
recursive triggers	If set to true, triggers can fire recursively (the nested triggers server wide configuration option must be enabled too). If set to false, triggers cannot fire recursively. The default is false.
select into/bulkcopy	If set to true, nonlogged operations are allowed (**SELECT INTO** statements and fast bulk copies). If set to false, nonlogged operations are not allowed (bulk copies are logged). The default is false.
single user	If set to true, only one user can access the database. If set to false, all database users that are connected to SQL Server can access it. The default is false.
subscribed	If set to true, the database can be subscribed for publication. If set to false, the database cannot be subscribed for publication. The default is false.
torn page detection	If set to true, SQL Server 7 detects incomplete pages. If set to false, incomplete pages are not detected. The default is false.

(continued)

Table 14.1 Database options *(continued)*.

Database Option	Description
trunc. log on chkpt.	If set to true, every time a checkpoint is issued, the inactive part of the transaction log is truncated. If set to false, the inactive part of the log is not truncated after a checkpoint. The default is false for all SQL Server editions except for the Desktop Edition. (If true, the transaction log cannot be backed up.)The *tempdb* database always has this option set to true.

The only database option that can be set on the *master* database is **trunc. log on chkpt**.

Listing 14.12 shows how to set database options. In this case the **select into/bulk copy** and **trunc. log on chkpt**. options of the *Northwind* database are set to true.

Listing 14.12 Setting database options.

```
sp_dboption "Northwind", "select into/bulkcopy", TRUE
GO
sp_dboption "Northwind", "trunc. log on chkpt.", TRUE
GO
```

Attaching And Detaching A Database

A brand new feature of SQL Server 7 is the ability to attach or detach a database. When a database is detached, SQL Server 7 closes the database and removes it from the server. The physical files (data and transaction log) still remain on disk. These files can then be used to attach the database to any other server running SQL Server 7.

14

This technique is widely used when moving a database from one computer to another, moving a database from one disk to another or recovering from a damaged master database.

Though *Books Online* does not state that you can attach a database that has not been previously detached, it can be done successfully. In numerous master recovery exercises, we have done this without incident.

sp_detach_db

A SQL Server 7 database is detached using the **sp_detach_db** system stored procedure. A database that is being used cannot be detached. The syntax for detaching a database is as follows:

```
sp_detach_db  <db_name> [, {TRUE|FALSE} ]
```

To have all distribution statistics updated before the database is detached, specify **TRUE**.

For example, to update the statistics from all tables of the *Northwind* database and then detach it, run the following statement:

```
sp_detach_db 'Northwind', 'TRUE'
go
```

sp_attach_db

The **sp_attach_db** system stored procedure is used to attach a database that has previously been detached, and that has 16 or less database files (data + transaction log files). The syntax is as follows:

```
sp_attach_db  <db_name>, [@filename1 =] <file_name1>[, ...
<file_name16>]
```

<file_name1>[, ... <file_name16>] represents the physical location of the file. For example, C:\mssql7\data\northwnd.mdf.

To attach a database that has more than 16 database files, use the **CREATE DATABASE** statement with the **FOR ATTACH** clause.

The primary data file must always be specified because it contains the system tables that store information about the other database files. Any file moved from its previous location must also be included.

For example, the *TAttach* database was created with the following statement:

```
CREATE DATABASE TAttach
ON
(name = TAttach_D1, filename = 'c:\mssql7\data\TAttach_D1.mdf'),
(name = TAttach_D2, filename = 'c:\mssql7\data\TAttach_D2.ndf'),
(name = TAttach_D3, filename = 'c:\mssql7\data\TAttach_D3.ndf')
LOG ON
(name = TAttach_L, filename = 'c:\mssql7\data\TAttach_L.ldf')
go
```

In this case another disk can be used to place the log file apart from the data files. In this case, you would detach the database, copy the log file to its new location: D:\TrLogFiles, and attach the database with one of the following statements:

```
Statement #1 (specifying all the files)
sp_attach_db TAttach,
```

```
             'c:\mssql7\data\TAttach_D1.mdf',
             'c:\mssql7\data\TAttach_D2.ndf',
             'c:\mssql7\data\TAttach_D3.ndf',
             'D:\TrLogFiles\TAttach_L.ldf'
go

Statement #2 (specifying the primary file and the file that has been
moved)
sp_attach_db TAttach,
             'c:\mssql7\data\TAttach_D1.mdf',
             'D:\TrLogFiles\TAttach_L.ldf'
go
```

Because information about the other files is contained in the primary data file, you don't need to specify them if they haven't been moved.

Renaming A Database

A SQL Server 7 database can only be renamed if no one is currently using it, and if it has the **single user database** option set to **true** (see "Database Options" earlier in this chapter). Renaming a database does not affect the physical name of the data and transaction log files.

To rename a database use the **sp_renamedb** system stored procedure. The syntax is as follows:

```
sp_renamedb  [@old_name =] <old_db_name>, [@new_name =] <new_db_name]
```


Listing 14.13 shows how to rename a database. Before renaming it, set the database option to single user mode. After the database is renamed, set the option to multiuser mode.

Listing 14.13 Renaming a database.

```
sp_dboption ExPrep, 'single user', TRUE
GO
sp_renamedb ExPrep, [ExamPrep 70-029]
GO
sp_dboption [ExamPrep 70-029], 'single user', FALSE
GO
```

DATABASE OWNER

The *owner* of a database is the login who created it. The database owner is known as the *dbo*. The dbo has all permissions to perform all activities in the database.

Use the **sp_changedbowner** system stored procedure to change the owner of the current database. The syntax is as follows:

```
sp_changedbowner [@loginname =] <login_name>
                               [, [@map =]  {TRUE|FALSE}]
```

<login_name> is the login that will become the new owner of the current database. This login cannot have any permissions to the database (that is, it cannot be a user of the database, and it cannot be an alias to another user of the database).

The **[@map =] {TRUE|FALSE}** clause is used to indicate if the aliases dependent on the old database owner will be dropped or mapped to the new dbo. If **TRUE** is specified, or the parameter is omitted, all aliases will be remapped. If **FALSE** is specified, all aliases will be dropped.

The owner of the *master*, *model*, and *tempdb* system databases cannot be changed.

SYSTEM DATABASES

When SQL Server 7 is installed, it creates four system databases and two sample databases. By default, the data and transaction log files of these databases are located in the \Mssql7\Data directory. Table 14.2 shows these automatically installed databases and their data and log files.

Table 14.2 Databases installed by the SQL Server 7 Setup.

Database	Type	Data File	Transaction Log File
master	System	master.mdf	mastlog.ldf
model	System	model.mdf	modellog.ldf
msdb	System	msdbdata.mdf	msdblog.ldf
tempdb	System	Tempdb.mdf	Templog.ldf
Northwind	Sample	northwnd.mdf	northwnd.ldf
Pubs	Sample	pubs.mdf	pubs_log.ldf

If the server is configured as a replication distributor, SQL Server also creates the *distribution* system database.

master Database

The *master* system database is the *heart* of SQL Server 7. In it SQL Server stores the following *metadata* (data about data):

- System configurations settings
- Login accounts
- Information about all databases
- All system errors
- Information about remote and linked servers

model Database

The *model* system database is used as a *template* whenever a new database is created. It is a good practice to create any company standards for objects, logins, datatypes, and so forth in the *model* database, because they will be duplicated into all future databases.

msdb Database

The *msdb* system database stores all information about jobs, schedules, and SQL Server operators. This information is used by the SQL Server Agent service.

tempdb Database

The *tempdb* system database is used by SQL Server to store temporary tables created by users, stored procedures created by users, and work tables created automatically by SQL Server.

The *tempdb* system database is re-created each time SQL Server is started.

Storage Options And RAID Levels

An important step when designing and implementing a database server is deciding where to store the SQL Server software, and where to store the data and transaction log files of the system and user databases. The goal is to obtain good performance and for the installation to be fault tolerant. If a drive failure occurs, no data can be lost and the system should continue to function.

The most common method to manage disk storage is using hardware-based *Redundant Array of Independent Disks* (*RAID*). This consists of multiple (arrays of) disk drives that are configured to provide high performance, reliability, and capacity. Basically, six levels (0–5) of RAID systems exist, depend on the algorithm used to implement the fault tolerance. The most commonly used levels of RAID implemented with SQL Server are the following:

- **RAID 0 (or level 0)** This level of RAID is known as *disk striping*.
  - Data is striped across all the disks in the array, allowing I/O operations to be performed simultaneously and independently. This is the level with the best performance, but it doesn't give any fault tolerance. If one disk fails, the data becomes inaccessible. This requires a minimum of two disks.
- **RAID 1 (or level 1)** This level of RAID is known as *disk mirroring*.
  - Data of the primary disk is mirrored into a second (mirror) disk. This RAID level improves read performance, bit it may degrade on write operations. If the primary goes bad, it switches automatically to the mirror disk. This requires a minimum of two disks.

RAID 1 performs well on operations that sequentially read and write data. For optimal performance, place your transaction log files on a RAID 1 disk.

For better performance, the primary and mirror disks should be on different disk controllers, or on the same disk controller, but on different channels.

- **RAID 5 (or level 5)** This level of RAID is known as *striping with parity*.
  - Data and parity is striped across the disks in the array. No disk in the arrayis dedicated exclusively to store data or parity information. The redundancy algorithm ensures that the parity information is stored on different disks on each write operation. This requires a minimum of three disks.

RAID 5 performs very well on operations that randomly access the disk. For optimal performance, place your data files on a RAID 5 disk. Most RAID 5 allows the possibility to replace a disk while the system is running. This is known as a *hot swap*.

For better data protection, do not place transaction log files and data files on the same physical disk.

Fast and reliable hard drives and disk configurations are not a substitute for good design. A database with poorly designed tables, indexes, and queries will never perform well, regardless of the speed of the drives.

Chapter Summary

- The fundamental unit of storage in SQL Server 7 is a page. Eight contiguous pages form an extent (64K).
- Tables and indexes are stored in extents. Small tables can share extents.
- SQL Server 7 databases are stored in operating system files. They can be on a FAT or NTFS file system, or on a raw partition.
- A database file has a logical file name and an operating system file name. A database file has the following properties: initial size, maximum size, automatic growth, and growth increment.
- A database has at least one data file and one transaction log file. A database file cannot be shared among databases.
- The **sp_helpfile** system stored procedure returns the properties of all files (data and transaction log) of the current database.
- A database has one and only one primary data file. This file stores the startup information for the database and database objects. It is identified by the .mdf extension.
- Secondary data files store database objects. They are identified by the .ndf extension. Not all databases have secondary data files.
- A database has at least one transaction log file; it stores all information necessary to recover a database. It is identified by the .ldf extension. SQL Server 7 uses a write-ahead log.
- A data file can be a member of only one filegroup.
- Transaction log files cannot be part of a filegroup.
- Filegroups are used to balance the disk load of your system by spreading data across multiple disks.
- The **sp_helpfilegroup** system stored procedure returns the properties of all filegroups of the current database.
- Only one filegroup of the database can be the default filegroup.
- A database always has a primary filegroup that contains the primary file. System tables are always allocated in the primary filegroup.
- To create a database, use the **CREATE DATABASE** statement or the Create Database Wizard.

- SQL Server 7 uses the *model* database as a template when creating a database.
- The **sp_helpdb** system stored procedure is used to view information about all databases on the current server, or to view information about a specific database.
- Use the **ALTER DATABASE** statement to modify a database's definition. This statement allows you to add, remove, and/or modify data files, transaction log files, and filegroups.
- Use the **DROP DATABASE** statement to drop one or more databases.
- To expand a database manually you can increase the size of an existing data or transaction log file, or you can add a new file by using the **ALTER DATABASE** statement.
- To expand a database automatically, configure each database file to grow automatically.
- To shrink a database manually you can shrink the entire database using the **DBCC SHRINKDATABASE** statement, or you can shrink the data and/or transaction log file(s) using **DBCC SHRINKFILE** statement.
- To shrink a database automatically, set the **autoshrink** database option to **TRUE**.
- The **sp_dboption** system stored procedure is used to set or review database options.
- Detach and attach a database when moving a database from one computer to another, when moving a database from one disk to another, and when recovering from a damaged *master* database.
- The **sp_detach_db** system stored procedure is used to detach a database. The database cannot be in use.
- The **sp_attach_db** system stored procedure is used to attach a database that has 16 or less database files. Use the **CREATE DATABASE** statement with the **FOR ATTACH** clause to attach a database with more than 16 database files.
- The **sp_renamedb** system stored procedure is used to rename a database. The database must be in single user mode.
- The **sp_changedbowner** system stored procedure is used to change the owner of a database.
- SQL Server 7 has 4 system databases: *master*, *model*, *msdb*, and *tempdb*. If the server is configured as a replication distributor, SQL Server 7 creates another system database named *distribution*.

Review Questions

1. A page in SQL Server 7 is ___ long.
   a. 2K
   b. 8K
   c. 64K
   d. 1,024 bytes

2. Which of the following are true about database files? (Choose all correct answers.)
   a. Small databases store data and log on the same files in order to save space.
   b. A database file can be placed on FAT and NTFS file systems and on raw partitions.
   c. Data files, generally, are members of one or two filegroups.
   d. When defining a database file you must specify a logical file name to use with Transact-SQL statements.

3. Which of the following database objects does a data file store? (Choose all correct answers.)
   a. Tables
   b. Indexes
   c. Logs
   d. Stored procedures definitions

4. Select the statements that apply to database filegroups:
   a. A database filegroup has three properties: **READONLY**, **READWRITE**, **DEFAULT**.
   b. Transaction log files are never part of a database filegroup.
   c. A database can have up to 256 filegroups.
   d. The primary filegroup always contains the primary data file.
   e. All of the above.

5. Which of the following statements are true about databases and SQL Server 7? (Choose all correct answers.)
   a. A SQL Server 7 installation can have 32,767 databases.
   b. Database information is stored in the *sysdatabases* system table on the *master* database.
   c. All objects defined in the *model* database are created on new databases.
   d. A database always has one primary filegroup and one log filegroup.

6. According to the following statement, what will be the configuration of the database?

```
CREATE DATABASE Test
ON (name = Test_Data,
    filename = 'c:\mssql7\data\Test_Data.mdf',
    size = 100MB,
    maxsize = 200MB,
    filegrowth = 10MB)
GO
```

   a. The database will have one file with the data and log on it. The initial size of the file is 100MB, and it will auto-grow by 10MB each time more space is needed until it is 200MB.
   b. The database will have one data file and one transaction log file with the same properties: the initial size of the file is 100MB, the maximum size is 200MB, and it will auto-grow by 10MB each time it needs more space.
   c. The database will have one data and one transaction log file. The initial size of the data file is 100MB, and it will auto-grow by 10MB each time more space is needed until it reaches 200MB. The initial size of the transaction log size is the same as the log of the *model* database.
   d. The database will have one data and one transaction log file. The initial size of the data file is 100MB, and it will auto-grow by 10MB each time more space is needed until it reaches 200MB. The initial size of the transaction log size is 25MB.

7. Which of the following statements adds a data file the will grow unlimited to the TQ database? (Choose all correct answers.)
   a. `ALTER DATABASE TQ ADD FILE (name = Ugrow, maxsize = UNLIMITED)`
   b. `ALTER DATABASE TQ ADD FILE (name = Ugrow,`
      `filename = 'c:\Ugrow.ndf', maxsize = UNLIMITED)`
   c. `ALTER DATABASE TQ ADD FILE (name = Ugrow,`
      `filename = 'c:\Ugrow.ndf', size = 10MB, maxsize = UNLIMITED)`
   d. All of the above.

8. Which of the following statements adds a transaction log file to the **NewFG** filegroup in the *TQ* database (the file must grow by 10 percent)?
   a. `ALTER DATABASE TQ ADD FILE (name = Ugrow, maxsize = UNLIMITED)`
   b. `ALTER DATABASE TQ ADD FILE (name = Ugrow,`
      `filename = 'c:\Ugrow.ndf', maxsize = UNLIMITED) TO FILEGROUP`
      `NewFG`

c. `ALTER DATABASE TQ .ADD FILE (name = Ugrow,`
```
    filename = 'c:Ugrow.ndf', size = 10MB, maxsize = UNLIMITED)
```
d. Cannot be done.

9. You need to drop the data file Dfile1 from the DA database. The data file is associated with the **FGFiles** filegroup. Select the statement that can drop the file.

    a. `ALTER DATABASE DA DROP FILE Dfile1 FROM FILEGROUP FGFiles`

    b. `ALTER DATABASE DA DELETE FILE Dfile1 FROM FILEGROUP FGFiles`

    c. `ALTER DATABASE DA REMOVE FILE Dfile1 FROM FILEGROUP FGFiles`

    d. `ALTER DATABASE DA REMOVE FILE Dfile1`

10. Which of the following statements correctly modifies a property of the Tlog transaction log file of the *KB* database? (Choose all correct answers.)

    a. To move the file to a new location:
    ```
    ALTER DATABASE KB MODIFY FILE
    (name = Tlog, filename = 'd:\Nloc\Tlog.ldf')
    ```
    b. To modify the maximum size to 500MB:
    ```
    ALTER DATABASE KB MODIFY FILE
    (name = Tlog, maxsize = 500MB)
    ```
    c. To move to a new location and modify the maximum size:
    ```
    ALTER DATABASE KB MODIFY FILE
    (name = Tlog, filename = 'd:\Nloc\Tlog.ldf', maxsize = 500MB)
    ```
    d. To change the filegrowth increment to 100K:
    ```
    ALTER DATABASE KB MODIFY FILE
    (name = Tlog, filegrowth = 100KB)
    ```


11. To recover some free space from a database you can: (Choose all correct answers.)

    a. Back up the database, re-create it with a smaller size, and restore the database.

    b. Configure the database to shrink automatically.

    c. Use the **DBCC SHRINKDATABASE** statement.

    d. Shrink the data and log files one at a time.

12. For which situations would you use the **sp_attach_db** system stored procedure?

    a. To move the database to a new location

    b. To attach a newly created transaction log file

    c. To restore a backed up database

    d. To attach a newly created data file

13. Select the statement(s) that can be used to remove the *DB3* database.
    a. `DROP DATABASE DB3`
    b. `REMOVE DATABASE DB3`
    c. `DELETE DATABASE DB3`
    d. `DBCC DBREPAIR(DB3, DROPDB)`

14. Select the correct statements about database options. (Choose all correct answers.)
    a. The **auto update statistics** database option controls when the distribution statistics of the indexes are updated.
    b. One of the conditions that must be met to perform a fast BCP is that the database option **select into/bulkcopy** must be set to **TRUE**.
    c. Database options can only be set when a database is created.
    d. For a database option to be set in future databases, you must set the option in the *model* database.

15. You have a database that has three disks (C, D, E). One of your future tables will be heavily used. Which of the following configuration is the best?
    a. Create one data file on each disk and the transaction log file on one disk.
    b. Create one data file and one transaction log file on each disk.
    c. Create one data file on disk C associated with the **PRIMARY** filegroup; another data file on disk D associated with a different filegroup; and the transaction log file on the E disk. Place the heavily used table on the D drive (no other tables will be placed on D).
    d. All of the above.

HANDS-ON PROJECTS

Susan hung up the phone. The project lead had just called her to ask her "professional opinion" on the type of server they should purchase. The IT networking staff had selected the computer brand, but various models had various hard drive configurations. Now the IT networking staff wanted to know which model to pick based on these drive sizes, and asked the developers. The developers weren't sure how large the database component was, and called Susan.

She was a little taken aback, because she didn't consider herself a "professional" yet, and because she wasn't exactly sure how to begin to figure out the size of the database. She contacted a friend who had some large servers in her organization and asked her how they picked a size for them. "I'm not really sure," her friend started, "but I wish they would have spent a little more time on it. We ended up with some really proprietary hardware that's going to cost us a fortune to upgrade.

At first everything was fine" her friend went on, "but then the database got huge, and now we're running out of space. The server we bought was fine, but it's a bit old, and now the drive types are hard to find, or something like that." "Thanks" Susan said as she hung up. Now she was nervous. How would she determine the right size? She then hit on an idea. "I could start by figuring out what all the sizes are for the individual pieces of the database, and then try and estimate what we have now. Then I'll try and predict a growth rate and see what I come up with."

That exercise gave Susan a working number. She added some space for growth, and then, based on those numbers, she created a test database.

These activities assume that you are already connected to a computer running SQL Server 7 through Query Analyzer. You'll also need several hundred megabytes available, and a physical or logical drive D: on your practice system.

Project 14.1

In this activity, you will create a database with the following specifications:

The database must have one data file and one transaction file. Both files will be on the C: drive in the \mssql7\data directory. The properties of the data file are: 100MB initial size, 500MB maximum size, 50MB growth increment. The properties of the transaction log file are: 40MB initial size, unlimited maximum size, 20 percent growth increment.

In the Query Analyzer type the following command and execute it:

```
CREATE DATABASE Hands_On_Project
ON PRIMARY
( NAME = Hands_On_Project_Data,
  FILENAME = 'C:\MSSQL7\DATA\Hands_On_Project_Data.mdf',
  SIZE = 100MB,
  MAXSIZE = 500MB,
  FILEGROWTH = 50MB )
LOG ON
( NAME = Hands_On_Project_Log,
  FILENAME = 'C:\MSSQL7\DATA\Hands_On_Project_Log.ldf',
  SIZE = 40MB,
  MAXSIZE = UNLIMITED,
  FILEGROWTH = 20% )
GO
```

After Susan created her database, she moved it around a bit to better suit her needs.

Next we'll limit the maximum size of the transaction log file to 150MB. Add a data file to the **FGROUP1** filegroup. The properties of the data file are: 130MB initial size, 600MB maximum size, 50MB growth increment. The data file should be placed on the D: drive in the \Data directory. All image columns will be stored on the added data file.

In the Query Analyzer, type the following commands and execute them:

```
ALTER DATABASE Hands_On_Project MODIFY FILE
( NAME = Hands_On_Project_Log, MAXSIZE = 150MB )
GO
ALTER DATABASE Hands_On_Project ADD FILEGROUP FGROUP1
GO
ALTER DATABASE Hands_On_Project ADD FILE
( NAME = Hands_On_Project_Data2,
  FILENAME = 'D:\DATA\Hands_On_Project_Data2.Ndf',
  SIZE = 130MB,
  MAXSIZE = 600MB,
  FILEGROWTH = 50MB )
GO
```

Project 14.2

In this activity, you will move a database file to a new location.

In order to balance the disk load on your system, move the transaction log file to the \Log directory on the E: drive. To do this, you must perform the following steps in the specified order:

1. Detach the database.
2. Copy the transaction log file to the new location.
3. Attach the database.

In the Query Analyzer, type the following commands and execute them:

```
sp_detach_db Hands_On_Project
GO

*** Copy the transaction log file (Hands_On_Project_Log.ldf) from
C:\MSSQL7\DATA\ to E:\Log.

sp_attach_db Hands_On_Project,
             'C:\MSSQL7\DATA\Hands_On_Project_Data.mdf',
             'D:\DATA\Hands_On_Project_Data2.Ndf',
             'E:\LOG\Hands_On_Project_Log.ldf'
GO
```

When Susan was finished with her testing, she felt she had a working size to start with. She called the project lead and told him, "I created a report based on some tests, and I just sent that over in an email." There was a slight pause as he checked his email. "Looks like I've got it here... Wow!"

Susan thought for a moment that he might have thought the sizes were a bit off. "This is really good stuff. I wouldn't have known where to start, but this report gives us the ammunition to go after the server we really need. Thanks, Susan!" Susan hung up the phone, thinking, "Maybe I am getting a little better at this."

CHAPTER FIFTEEN

15

REMOTE DATA SOURCES

After Reading This Chapter And Completing The Exercises, You Will Be Able To:

- Understand the difference between old-style remote servers and the newer linked server metaphor
- Set up and configure SQL Server, Oracle, ODBC, and MS Access linked servers
- Design and execute both local and remote queries against linked-server data
- Understand when you can update remotely stored information and how to do it

Corporate computing environments are becoming increasingly complex. Valuable corporate information is stored not only in a variety of high-end database systems but also in Excel spreadsheets, Microsoft Access databases, and other applications. Importing all this information into a common database for reporting and updating can be difficult and can produce data inconsistencies. That is why SQL Server 7 provides a robust set of features that allows database designers to query (and in some cases even update) data that remains stored in external applications.

Remote Data Sources

A remote data source is any database or information that is accessed from SQL Server 7 and is not a native SQL Server 7 database on that server. With this definition, even other SQL Server databases are considered remote if they are not located on the server on which you are working. Microsoft SQL Server has in previous versions allowed connection to these types of sources, but version 7 provides even more functionality.

Remote Server Architecture

In previous versions of SQL Server, Microsoft used a somewhat limited method of accessing remote information. That method relied on the configuration of remote server entries and used the Open Data Services API to connect to the remote server. The remote server needed to be able to receive *db-library* requests and the higher-level *Open Database Services (ODS)* calls in order for this solution to work correctly. Limitations of this architecture included the following:

- Only other SQL Servers and a small number of ODS-compliant gateways could be configured as remote servers.
- Remote queries had to be in the form of stored procedures on the remote server.
- Remote tables could not be included in SQL statements.

Although the use of remote servers in Microsoft SQL Server has largely been superseded though the new linked-server architecture, it is retained for backward compatibility. Even so, a word of caution is called for. SQL Server uses a completely new version of the *Tabular Data Stream (TDS)* to communicate with remote servers. Many older ODS-compliant servers and gateways will not be able to understand the new TDS format. For example, trying to access SQL Server version 4.2 servers and Micro Decisionware (MDI) gateways from SQL 7 gives the following results:

```
Server: Msg 7399, Level 16, State 1, Line 1
OLE DB provider 'SQLOLEDB' reported an error.
[OLE/DB provider returned message: The data source can not be used,
because it DBMS version is less than 6.5.0.]
```

This error message correctly implies that the backward-compatible remote server functionality has been implemented using the new OLE DB linked server communication structure. The only difference between setting up a linked server and a remote server are some status flags in the *master..sysservers* table. These status flags enable the older style user login mapping and turn off the ability to include the provider name in a SQL query.

Linked Servers

The use of remote servers has been superseded by the new *linked server* architecture. Linked servers support all the features of remote servers plus an enhanced set of capabilities.

Configuring A Remote Server

Setting up a remote server is a straightforward task that involves the same system stored procedures used in previous versions. For example, enter and execute the following command to add a remote server named **GEMINI**:

```
Exec sp_addserver GEMINI
```

This adds a row into the *master..sysservers* catalog table. You can also set up and use a server alias as in prior versions. This could be useful if you have stored procedures that reference the **RemoteServer** system, but the real server name is **GEMINI**. In this case, you would set up a remote server entry using the following commands:

```
Exec sp_addserver RemoteServer
Exec sp_setnetname RemoteServer, GEMINI
```

If you need to set your SQL Server 7 server to be able to receive remote procedure calls from an older-style system, you have two choices. You can either set up a remote server as described, or you can set up and configure a *linked* server. Configuring a linked server also allows you to be able to receive remote procedure requests from older systems.

In order to set up your server to receive remote procedure requests from another server using the remote server architecture, you must first set up the far system as a remote server in the local system. Next, you need to set up the remote logins that will be used to authenticate the remote connections. In the following example, we will set up a remote server named **HOSTSERVER**, and map the **ACCTUSR** user account. We will also enable trusted connections between the servers for this user in case the passwords are not the same between the two systems:

```
Exec sp_addserver HOSTSERVER
Exec sp_addremotelogin HOSTSERVER, ACCTUSR, ACCTUSR
Exec sp_remoteoption HOSTSERVER, ACCTUSR, ACCTUSR, trusted, true
```

Remote Server Setup

Remote server setup and configuration is identical to SQL Server 6.5.

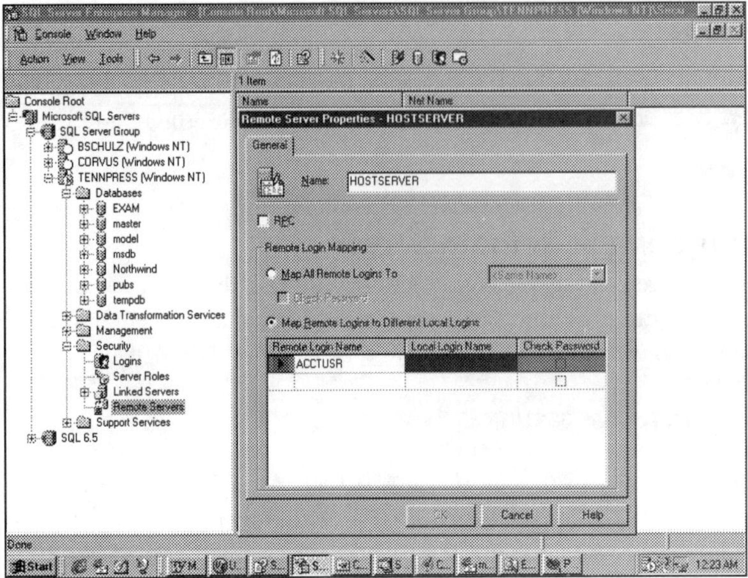

Figure 15.1 Using Enterprise Manager to configure a remote server and logins.

You can also use the Enterprise Manager graphical interface to perform the same setup. Figure 15.1 shows this usage.

Executing Remote Procedures

Using the remote server architecture limits you to being able to execute stored procedures on the remote server. For example, the following command executes the **sp_who2** stored procedure on the remote server named **REMOTESERVER**:

```
Exec REMOTESERVER.master.dbo.sp_who2
```

Because the new linked server architecture supports this same functionality, this subject will be examined more closely in the following section.

Linked Server Architecture

The previous remote server structure worked for many situations. However, it did not allow database applications to work directly with non-ODS data sources. The new structure has solved that problem through the use of OLE DB data providers. The ODS layer now interfaces with the remote data source via the *Object Linking and Embedding For Databases (OLE DB)* provider layer (see Figure 15.2).

The OLE DB structure is similar in concept to *Open Database Connectivity (ODBC)* where a single *Application Programming Interface (API)* can interface

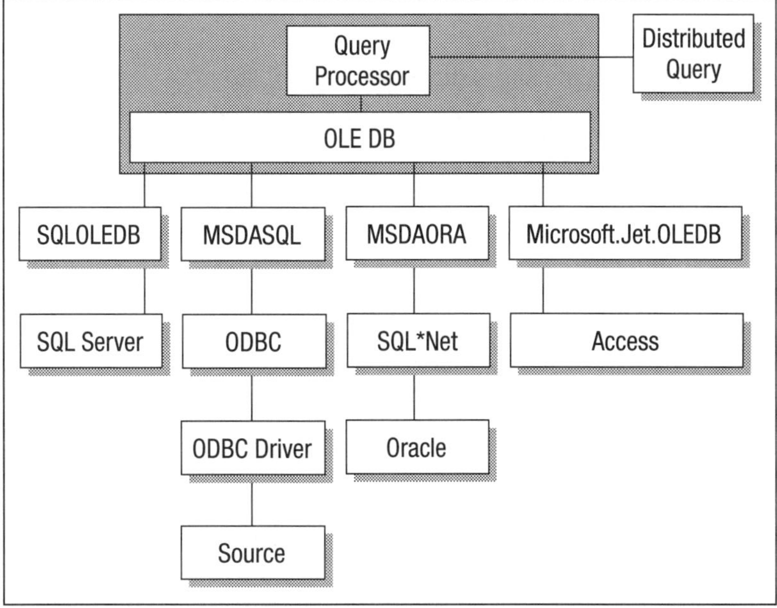

Figure 15.2 Linked server communication architecture.

with multiple data sources. But the older ODBC API does not support the new data types, Unicode data, or new functionality, such as OLAP services. SQL Server 7 includes a number of OLE DB providers, including the following:

- A SQL Server provider for connecting to version 6.5 and 7 databases.
- An ODBC provider that allows connectivity to many data sources through the diverse selection of existing ODBC drivers.
- An Oracle provider allowing SQL*Net connectivity to Oracle 7 and 8 databases.
- A Jet database provider for connecting to MS Access databases.
- A Data Transformation Services (DTS) Packages provider that allows accessing data setup as a DTS package (see Chapter 16).

The setup and configuration for linked servers is covered in a later section in this chapter. In order to follow along in the ensuing examples, enter and run the following commands from a Query Analyzer window on your server. These commands will set up two linked servers, **Server1** and **Server2**, which will be used in later examples. The **Server1** and **Server2** names are called *alias* names because the physical server names are different than the logical server names. Also, because these linked servers point back to your current local server, they are called *loopback* servers. They are the method through which queries are executed through the OLE DB provider and they use a separate connection.

N'SQL Server

Let's examine what the 'N' means in the **N'SQL Server'** literal shown to the right. This form of specifying a string converts the string to its Unicode equivalent data type.

The commands are as follows:

```
exec sp_addlinkedserver N'Server1', N'SQL Server'
exec sp_addlinkedserver N'Server2', N'SQL Server'
exec sp_setnetname Server1, @@servername
exec sp_setnetname Server2, @@servername
```

Seamless SELECT

Another feature of the new linked server architecture is the ability to include tables from a remote data provider directly in a **SELECT** statement. This is a very powerful feature. Suppose you have a database server in two different locations. Each server stores orders for the customers serviced by the respective locations, and you wish to see if any customers have placed orders at both locations (assuming that customer numbers are unique for all locations). The following query could be run from a third server and would give you the results you are looking for:

```
select distinct CustomerID
from  Server1.Northwind.dbo.Orders
union
select distinct CustomerID
from  Server2.Northwind.dbo.Orders
```

As you can see from this example, tables stored in a remote data source that has been configured as a linked server can be accessed directly from a **SELECT** statement. The remote table must be specified in the format:

```
Linked_Server.Catalog.Schema.Object
```

You can also include remote tables in **JOIN** statements. The following example joins data from two remote tables stored on **Server1** with one remote table stored on **Server2**:

```
select *
from  Server1.Northwind.dbo.Orders Orders
join  Server1.Northwind.dbo.[Order Details] Details
 on   Orders.OrderID = Details.OrderID
join  Server2.Northwind.dbo.Customers Customers
 on   Orders.CustomerID = Customers.CustomerID
```

Let's take a more detailed look to examine how this process works. It is important that you understand how the server resolves queries such as this because they can have performance implications for your system. Figure 15.3 shows the execution plan for this query. Notice that the plan shows two remote queries, indicating that the server exported the join for the *Orders* and *Order Details* tables to **Server1** as a single query. A simple **SELECT** statement was issued to **Server2** to return the rows from the *Customers* table. The results of both queries were then combined in a merge join executed on the local server. Overall this is an efficient process. However, the operation would be fetching a lot of unnecessary information from **Server2** if the number of matching rows from the *Customers* table were small relative to its total size. Therefore, whenever you design a distributed query you should consider whether alternative methods would be more efficient.

Some restrictions apply when referencing linked servers in **SELECT** statements. These restrictions apply even when the remote server is another version 7 SQL Server. Such restrictions include the following:

- An **ORDER BY** clause cannot be specified when a **text** or **image** data type is specified in the select list.
- The **IS NULL** and **IS NOT NULL** operators cannot be specified on a column defined as text or image.
- An **INTO** clause is not permitted where the target table is located on a remote server.
- Data Definition Language (DDL) statements cannot be run on linked servers.

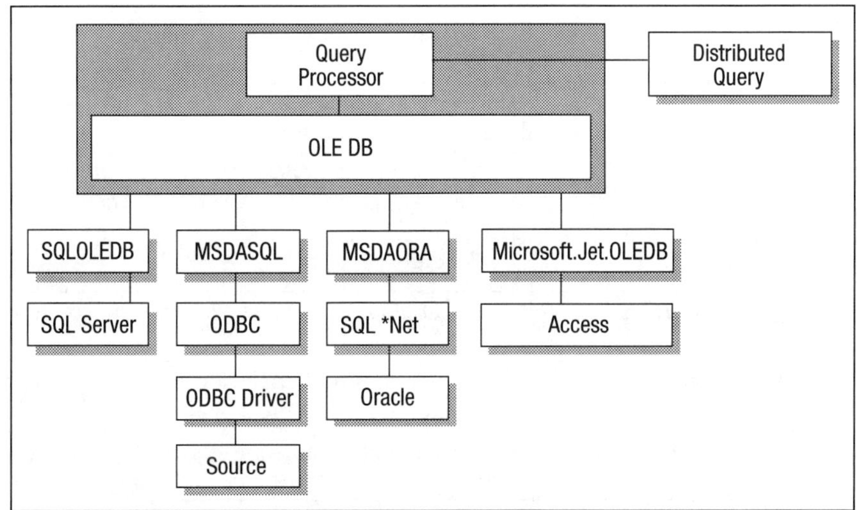

Figure 15.3 Distributed query execution plan.

15

- The **GROUP BY** clause cannot be included in a distributed query.
- Only **STATIC**, **INSENSITIVE**, and **KEYSET** cursors can be used with a remote table.

Metadata

In the previous example, the initiating server is executing a number of extra procedures on each of the remote servers. These queries are used to return information about the table structure, data types, and indexes, all of which are referred to as *metadata*. The specific metadata that is available depends largely on the specific OLE DB provider being used. If you find it necessary to obtain metadata from a linked server, a number of system stored procedures are supported for any OLE DB provider. Table 15.1 lists the procedures that are available.

FREQUENT OPENQUERY

When a table is referenced directly in a **SELECT** statement, the server automatically creates a dynamic **SELECT** statement that is issued on the linked server. For remote data sources that do not have a query engine, the dynamic queries are fulfilled by either the OLE DB provider or by the ODBC driver if the ODBC provider is being used. In any case, much control is lost by allowing the server to build the remote query dynamically. Also, you may need to be able to

Table 15.1 Supported stored procedures for retrieving metadata from a linked server.

Procedure	Description
sp_catalogs	Returns a listing of catalogs on the remote server. A catalog is the second part in a four-part remote object specification and is equivalent to a SQL Server database.
sp_columns_ex	Returns a list of table privileges that have been set up on the linked server for the specified table.
sp_foreignkeys	Lists the columns that are included as part of the foreign keys for the specified server, catalog, schema, and table.
sp_indexes	Displays the indexes that exists for the specified server, catalog, schema, and table.
sp_linkedservers	Returns a listing of linked servers that are configured on the local server.
sp_primarykeys	Lists the columns that are included as part of the primary key for the specified server, catalog, schema, and table.
sp_tables_ex	Displays a listing of table information for the specified linked server, catalog, schema, and table.

create a query that can be passed *through* to the source in order to get the correct data. For these reasons the **OPENQUERY** function is provided.

OPENQUERY accepts the name of a configured linked server and a pass-through query, and then returns a table-like result set to the optimizer engine. In this way you can use the **OPENQUERY** function where a table would normally be specified. The following is an example of using this function as part of a simple **SELECT** statement:

```
select *
from  OPENQUERY(Server2,
       'select * from Northwind..Customers')
```

In this statement, the **Server2** linked server name needs to be defined and configured prior to using the **OPENQUERY** function. It is also possible to use the **OPENQUERY** function as the target of an **UPDATE**, **INSERT**, or **DELETE** statements, such as the following:

```
insert OPENQUERY(Server2, 'select * from Northwind..Region')
select RegionID = 321, RegionDescription = 'My Remote Test Region'

update OPENQUERY(Server2, 'select * from Northwind..Region')
set RegionDescription = 'Test UPDATE Region'
where RegionID = 321

delete OPENQUERY(Server2,
'select * from Northwind..Region where RegionID = 321')
```

However, only those OLE DB providers that meet the conditions discussed later in "Undeniable Updates" will allow update operations. As can be observed by these examples, the syntax for this function is as follows:

```
OPENQUERY(<Linked_Server_Name>, <Query>)
```


Occasional OPENROWSET

Although the **OPENQUERY** function provides for the ability to create ad-hoc queries, it only works for preconfigured linked servers. Sometimes you may need to produce a report or query using data sources that are not configured as a linked server. For example, you may need to join existing data in a database with spreadsheet information for a one-time report. In cases like this it is not practical to configure a linked server to a temporary data source for the purpose of creating a one-time query. For these situations the designers of SQL Server 7 have included the **OPENROWSET** function.

The **OPENROWSET** function is similar to the **OPENQUERY** function; you can use it anywhere where a table reference is normally used. The **OPENROWSET** function allows you to access a data source through an OLE DB provider by dynamically specifying the configuration parameters. Because the server has the increased overhead of resolving the linked server configuration whenever the function is used, you should only use this function for single queries. The following is an example of using the **OPENROWSET** function within a **SELECT** statement to access a Microsoft Access database:

```
select *
FROM OPENROWSET( "Microsoft.Jet.OLEDB.4.0",
'd:\inetpub\aspsamp\advworks\advworks.mdb';"Admin";"",
'select * from Customers')
```

You can also use this function where table names are referenced in **INSERT**, **UPDATE**, and **DELETE** statements if the OLE DB provider meets the necessary criteria. The provider requirements necessary for updating is discussed in more detail in the following section titled "Undeniable Updates." The syntax for the **OPENROWSET** function is as follows:

```
OPENROWSET(
    <'Provider_Name'>,
    <'datasource';'user_id';'password'> OR <'provider_string'>,
    <[catalog.][schema.]object> OR <'query'>
)
```

Leaving Locality

Let's examine where the queries execute when you reference a remote data source using one of the three methods described previously. We have described the underlying database behavior earlier, and we will explore this topic further. In addition to understanding where the queries execute, you need to understand issues related to data type mapping and locking behavior.

For queries and updates that use the **OPENQUERY** or **OPENROWSET** functions, the SQL statements are passed through directly to the provider. This allows for a lot of control over how queries are distributed. For example, try running the query while the Profiler application is running (**SERVER2** is a loopback linked server pointing to the local server):

```
update SERVER2.Northwind.dbo.Customers
set    Region    = 'Northwest'
where  CustomerID = 'ALFKI'
```

You will see that all the rows from the *Customers* table are returned back from the remote server and that the predicate is evaluated locally. You can see this behavior even more clearly by reviewing the execution plan generated by SQL Analyzer. The interesting thing here is that the rows are brought back one at a time using a cursor. Using the **OPENQUERY** function you can design a much more efficient query:

```
update OPENQUERY
    (
      SERVER2,
      "select *
        from  Northwind.dbo.Customers
        where  CustomerID = 'ALFKI'"
    )
set Region = 'Northwest'
```

In the revised query, the **SELECT** statement passed to the **OPENQUERY** function is passed through to the remote server. Only the single row that we wish to update is returned to the local server for updating. This is a much more efficient statement for the server to process. You can use this to your advantage when designing and implementing distributed queries.

When the **OPENQUERY** and **OPENROWSET** functions are not used, SQL Server attempts to determine the capabilities of the provider and weighs that information against the request that is being made. The server attempts to decide which part of the query can be passed through to the remote server. However, as we saw above, the server cannot always determine the most efficient implementation for distributed queries. Optimizing distributed queries is a very complicated subject; you should be sure that any distributed queries you implement are operating as efficiently as you expect them to be.

Data Type Mapping

Although being able to access remote data sources through the use of distributed queries seems simple, a great number of details must be worked out by SQL Server. One of these is data type mapping between the local server and the remote source. Many different sources of information can be used, many of them using different data types. In order to solve this problem, Microsoft has created a data type map.

Each individual OLE DB provider is required to expose the source data types using one of several dozen standard data types used in the conversion map. The definition of the standard data types can be found in *Books Online*.

Undeniable Updates

We have already seen that update statements can contain references to linked server data sources. SQL Server has the responsibility to ensure data congruity with these updates and enforce the rules of transaction integrity. Because transaction management, locking behavior, and scope of the operation can have far-reaching impacts on overall database design, it is important to examine this topic in greater detail.

Update operations are permitted on any OLE DB data source that supports transaction support local to that provider. In other words, the provider must be able to ensure the integrity of a write operation and report the results of the operation back the SQL Server. When a write operation is begun and the connection is made to the remote data source, SQL Server automatically sets the implicit transaction mode on for the secondary connection. This is necessary so that the query engine can be sure that any other operations that are part of the same query complete successfully before committing the updates. If an error occurs, the server issues a **ROLLBACK** command.

Of course, exceptions to the rule are always present. The transaction settings for the local connection prior to the remote update operation can change this default behavior. One other setting that can change this behavior is the *Non-transacted updates* OLE DB provider option, which is described later in the section entitled "Additional Configuration Settings."

Effect Of Autocommit And Explicit Transactions

By default, SQL Server automatically commits implicit transactions after each SQL statement. This is a mode of operation referred to as autocommit. You can change this setting that using the command:

```
Set implicit_transactions [On|Off]
```

See Chapter 11 for more information on this and other transaction processing commands. Setting autocommit off is also referred to as *implicit transaction processing* mode. In this mode, a transaction is started implicitly after each SQL statement; you must end it with a **COMMIT** or **ROLLBACK** command. When the database is either in *implicit* transaction mode, or an *explicit* **BEGIN TRAN** statement is executed, the behavior for updates involving remote data sources changes substantially. The database then uses the two-phase commit approach of transactional integrity.

Two-Phase Commit

If an update is executed against a remote data source while inside a transaction, SQL Server attempts to export the transaction using the *Distributed Transaction*

Coordinator (DTC) service. If the OLE DB provider does not support two-phase commit transactions, an error is produced and the command is aborted. If support for distributed transactions is provided, DTC initiates the remote transaction using the two-phase commit protocol. If this happens, it is not necessary for the query engine to set implicit transaction mode on the remote data source.

The two-phase commit protocol involves a multistep process for ensuring transactional integrity across multiple data sources. First the relevant **SELECT** or **UPDATE** statement is executed on each of the data sources. Next, the *protocol manager* (in this case DTC) asks each data source to prepare to make the changes. At this stage, if the provider must be able to guarantee that the write operation will succeed if a **COMMIT** instruction is executed. If not, it must return an error and the entire distributed transaction will be aborted. Once each of the participating data sources responds back to the coordinator, the **COMMIT** is executed for each location.

One final important note about the handling of distributed transactions is warranted here. The ***XACT_ABORT*** setting effects how transactions respond to runtime errors. If ***XACT_ABORT*** is turned on, a transaction should abort if a runtime error occurs. If it is turned off, only the command that raised the runtime error is aborted, but the transaction remains open. Thus, if ***XACT_ABORT*** is enabled while an update is requested against a remote data source, the server forces the use of two-phase commit regardless of whether autocommit is enabled or not. This is necessary to protect distributed transactional integrity.

Configuring Linked Servers

The typical installation of SQL Server 7 includes a number of pretested OLE DB providers for the most common data sources. Almost certainly additional drivers will be developed and released by third-party vendors. Until then, Microsoft has included a general ODBC provider as a catchall, because many ODBC drivers are already available. Unfortunately, two drawbacks exist to using the ODBC provider. First, the communication architecture includes an extra layer (refer back to Figure 15.2) that adds to the processing overhead and makes for slower response times compared with using a native OLE DB interface. Also, the ODBC provider does not support the new features of SQL Server, including the use of Unicode data types, column widths greater than 255 characters, and OLAP services. The added convenience and power that are delivered through the new distributed query architecture will generally diminish these two negative points.

The following sections describe how to configure linked servers using the included providers.

SQL Server Data Sources

Adding another SQL Server database as a linked server is perhaps the easiest type to set up. You only need to provide the linked server name and the product name. You can set up the linked server using either a system stored procedure or by using the Enterprise Manager graphical interface. You should take the time to understand how to use both methods to set up a linked server for the exam and for actual use.

To set up a linked server using the system stored procedures, execute the **sp_addlinkedserver** stored procedure. The following example demonstrates how to set up a linked server named **ACCTSRV**:

```
Exec sp_addlinkedserver 'ACCTSRV', 'SQL Server'
```

Another common situation is the use of server alias names. An alias allows you to reference a static server name in your code, but the actual physical name of the server can change without impacting your design. In our earlier examples in this chapter, we have been referencing the **Server1** and **Server2** aliases. In order to setup a linked server using an alias, the same stored procedure is used. After the linked server alias is set up, you need to configure it to point to the physical server name using the **sp_setnetname** stored procedure. Thus, in order to setup a linked server alias named **Server1** that points to the physical server **ACCTSRV** you would run the following commands:

```
Exec sp_addlinkedserver 'Server1', 'SQL Server'
Go
Exec sp_setnetname 'Server1', 'ACCTSRV'
```

In this example, the **ACCTSRV** does not need to be set up previously as a linked server. Figure 15.1 shows this setup using the Enterprise Manager interface. Note that you must use the command line **sp_setnetname** to change the network name, because the graphical interface does not support changing the network name.

SQL Server 6.x

You can use the same OLE DB provider for 7, 6.5, and 6 versions of the database. However, for versions prior to 7, the database catalog needs to be upgraded in order to support the distributed query features (running remote stored procedures will work whether or not the catalog has been updated). To find out if the catalog has been updated, execute the command from a Query Analyzer window:

```
Exec sp_server_info
```

Observe the value of the **SYS_SPROC_VERSION** parameter—it should be version 7.00 or higher. If the catalog has not been updated, run the following command at the command prompt:

```
C:\> Isql -S<server> -Usa -P<password> -n -
ic:\MSSQL7\Install\instcat.sql
```

Security Settings

When using a linked server for remote stored procedure calls, the receiving server bears the burden of mapping remote login ID's to local login ID's. In contrast to this operation, the distributed query mechanism *pushes* the login mapping back to the originating server. Figure 15.4 illustrates this behavior.

Suppose that you have **SERVER7** as the originating SQL 7 server and you wish to execute remote stored procedure calls to **SERVER6**, which is a SQL 6.5 server. The user is logging in to **SERVER7** using the **WWWUSR** login. In order to map this login to a user of the same name on **SERVER6**, you would run the following commands in a Query Analyzer window on **SERVER6**:

```
Exec sp_addserver SERVER7
Exec sp_addremotelogin SERVER7, WWWUSR, WWWUSR
```

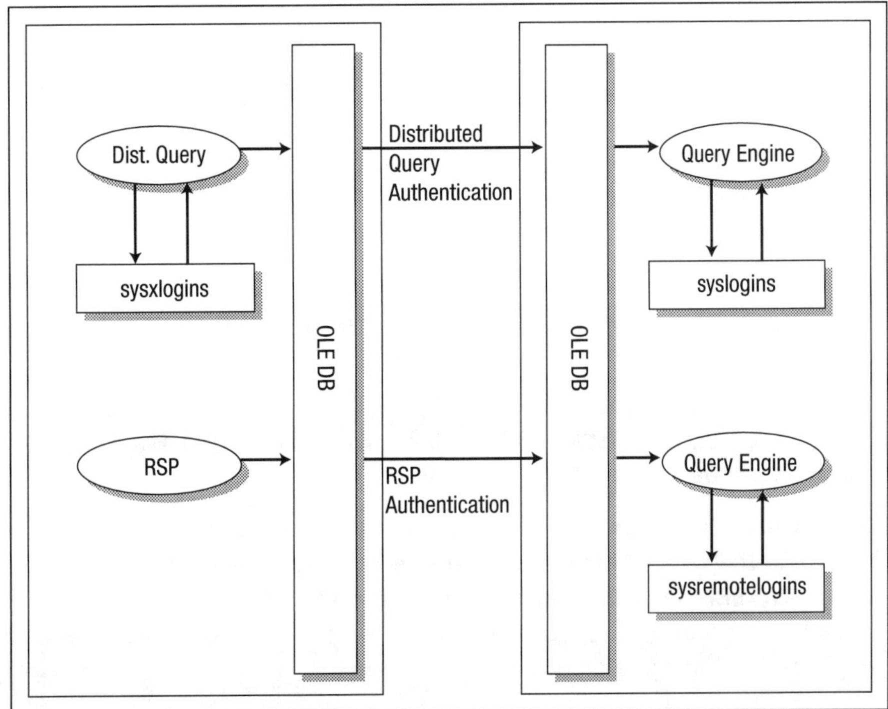

Figure 15.4 Linked server login mapping behavior.

The Difference Between A Distributed Query And An RSP

It is important to remember the difference between a distributed query and a remote procedure call. A *distributed query* refers to the use of a linked server object directly in a **SELECT**, **INSERT**, **UPDATE**, or **DELETE** statement, including the use of **OPENQUERY** and **OPENROWSET** functions. On the other hand, a *remote procedure* call refers to the execution of a stored procedure on the remote server using the **EXEC** syntax.

If the passwords vary between **SERVER7** and **SERVER6**, you will also need to turn on the **trusted** option. To do this run following additional command on **SERVER6**:

```
Exec sp_serveroption SERVER7, WWWUSR, WWWUSR, trusted, true
```

Consider that you are using the same two servers, but you also want to reference **SERVER6** in distributed query commands. You will now need to set up the login mapping on the initiating server **SERVER7**. The following commands will map the **WWWUSR** account to the login of the same name on the remote server:

```
Exec sp_addlinkedsrvlogin SERVER6, false, WWWUSR, WWWUSR
```

This example assumes that the passwords for the account are the same on both servers. If they are not, you must specify the remote password as the fourth parameter (not shown). If users are logging into **SERVER7** using NT security, you must map the NT account to a database login on the remote server. For instance, if the user logs into the server with the NT account **DOMAIN\DonnaSue**, you would map the logins using the command:

```
Exec sp_addlinkedsrvlogin SERVER6, false, DOMAIN\DonnaSue, WWWUSR
```

Figure 15.5 shows this task being performed using the Enterprise Manager interface.

Including Your Local NT SQLServer Account In Your Security Mapping

Depending on how your servers are configured, if your initiating server uses an NT account for the SQL Server service, you may need to also map this account. For example, if your **SERVER7** SQL Server service logs in using the NT account **SQLServer** instead of the **LocalSystem** account, you may need to include the local NT **SQLServer** account in your security mapping.

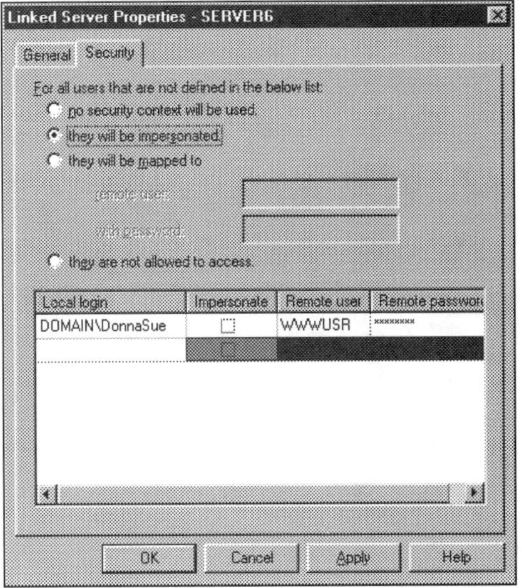

Figure 15.5 Mapping user IDs to the remote database.

MS Access Data Sources

Microsoft also provides an OLE DB provider for Jet database sources, which provides access to MS Access and Excel spreadsheets. This makes it very convenient and easy to join information from both sources without importing SQL Server information into Access or importing the Access data into SQL Server. Let's begin this exercise by setting up a linked server to the **AdvWorks** database that is included with Internet Information Server (see Figure 15.6):

```
exec sp_addlinkedserver
  @server    = 'AdvWorks',
  @srvproduct = 'Access 97',
  @provider   = 'Microsoft.Jet.OLEDB.4.0',
  @datasrc    = 'd:\InetPub\ASPSamp\AdvWorks\AdvWorks.mdb'

exec sp_addlinkedsrvlogin
  @rmtsrvname = 'AdvWorks',
  @useself    = false,
  @locallogin = null,
  @rmtuser    = 'Admin',
  @rmtpassword= NULL
```

The remote login setup previously shown maps all local logins (**@locallogin=null**) to the username **Admin** with no password. This is the technique used when the Access database does not have security enforced. Otherwise, you would use the username and password that has permissions set up in the *system* database.

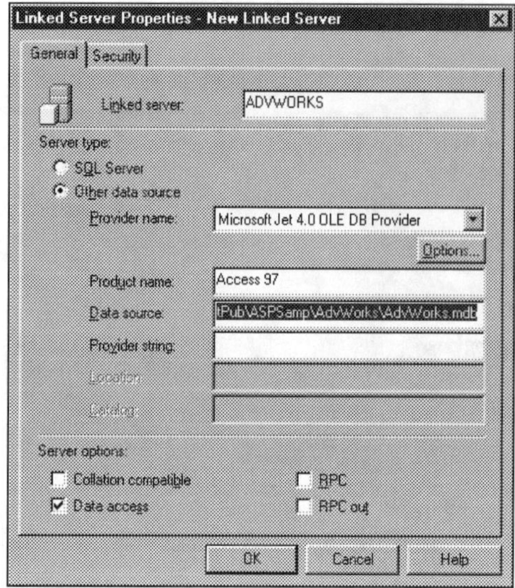

Figure 15.6 Using Enterprise Manager to configure the AdvWorks linked server.

Now we can see if any duplicate product IDs are between the *Northwind* and *AdvWorks* databases by joining the *Products* tables from both sources:

```
Select A.ProductID, A.ProductName, N.ProductID, N.ProductName
from  AdvWorks...Products A
join  Products N
 on  A.ProductID = N.ProductID

ADVWorks  ProductName        Northwind  ProductName
--------  -----------------  ---------  --------------------
1         North Face Sunspot 1          Chai
2         Polar Star         2          Chang
3         Big Sur            3          Aniseed Syrup
4         One Nighter        4          Chef Anton's Cajun S
5         Everglades         5          Chef Anton's Gumbo M
7         Rockies            7          Uncle Bob's Organic
9         Sierras            9          Mishi Kobe Niku
```

Oracle Data Sources

Recognizing that you may have some information in an Oracle database that you may need to integrate, Microsoft has included a robust Oracle provider. Once set up properly, querying and updating Oracle databases is as seamless and easy as working with SQL Server data. You need to follow some prerequisites to get the distributed query interface to function properly.

First, you need to install the SQL*Net client software (from Oracle) on the same computer as the SQL Server installation where the distributed queries will be executed. According to Microsoft documentation, you must have version 7.3.3.4.0 or later. For this example, Net8 was installed. Next you need to add a SQL*Net database alias, also referred to as a *service name* in Oracle documentation. You can do this by using the Net8 Easy Config utility that is included with the enterprise edition of Oracle 8. In this case we will use the alias name **ScottyDB**.

We are now ready to add the linked server in SQL Server. The following command demonstrates how to setup the linked server with the name **OrclDB** and the SQL*Net alias of **ScottyDB**. We will also map all local logins to the **SCOTT/TIGER** demo Oracle username:

```
exec sp_addlinkedserver
  @server = 'OrclDB',
  @srvproduct = 'Oracle',
  @provider = 'MSDAORA',
  @datasrc = 'ScottyDB'

exec sp_addlinkedsrvlogin
  @rmtsrvname = 'OrclDB',
  @useself = false,
  @locallogin = null,
  @rmtuser = 'SCOTT',
  @rmtpassword = 'TIGER'
```

Now let's give someone in the employee table a raise. Mr. Smith was formerly a clerk, but because he reads all the company mail, he has come to understand the business and made significant contributions. Let's make him the CEO:

```
update OrclDB..SCOTT.EMP
set   JOB = 'CEO',
    MRG = NULL,
    SAL = 10000
where  EMPNO = 7369

select EMPNO, ENAME, JOB, SAL from OrclDB..SCOTT.EMP

EMPNO   ENAME    JOB        SAL
-----   ------   --------   --------
7369    SMITH    CEO        10000.00
7499    ALLEN    SALESMAN   1600.00
7521    WARD     SALESMAN   1250.00
7566    JONES    MANAGER    2975.00
7654    MARTIN   SALESMAN   1250.00
```

15

```
7698    BLAKE    MANAGER    2850.00
7782    CLARK    MANAGER    2450.00
7788    SCOTT    ANALYST    3000.00
7839    KING     PRESIDENT  5000.00
7844    TURNER   SALESMAN   1500.00
7876    ADAMS    CLERK      1100.00
7900    JAMES    CLERK      950.00
7902    FORD     ANALYST    3000.00
7934    MILLER   CLERK      1300.00
```

Other Data Sources

Although the SQL Server, Jet, and Oracle OLE DB providers that are included with SQL Server will cover most of the situations where distributed queries are needed, you can also link with any ODBC data source using the general ODBC provider. This provider provides an interface with nearly any ODBC data source. You need to consider some limitations when using this interface, however:

- The ODBC provider does not support any Unicode data types.
- Column widths greater than 255 characters are truncated.
- **Text** and **image** data types are not supported.

Microsoft also includes a couple of special-purpose providers. A provider is also available for interfacing with the Microsoft Indexing Service that is the facility through which Web site searches are made. Another provider interfaces with DTS packages.

Additional Configuration Settings

You can set a few configuration settings for each provider that is used. The settings are stored in the Windows NT Registry and apply to all linked servers that use the given provider. Figure 15.7 shows how these settings are made from Enterprise Manager, which is the only place they can be made. You can't use any system stored procedures to make these changes. How these are set depends on the capabilities of each specific provider. The settings are described in Table 15.2.

Forcing OLE DB To Use The Lowest Level Interface

When configuring a linked server for many ODBC sources, you will need to force OLE DB to use the lowest level interface. You accomplish this by setting the Level Zero Only provider option using Enterprise Manager. Changing the provider settings is described in the "Additional Configuration Settings" section that follows. For example, you must use this setting to use the ODBC Access drivers.

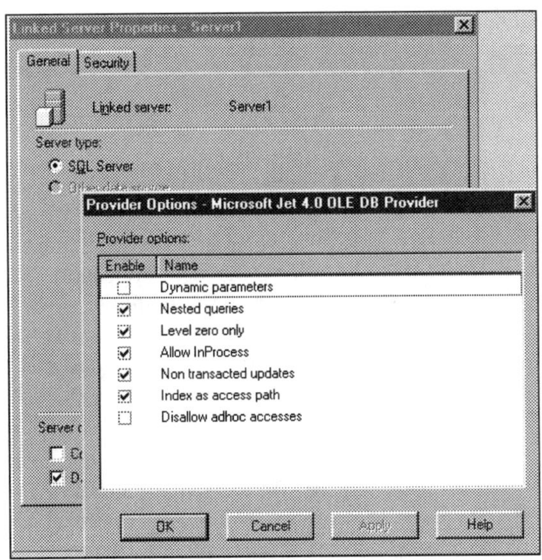

Figure 15.7 Setting OLE DB provider settings in Enterprise Manager.

Table 15.2 OLE DB provider settings.

Option	Description
Dynamic Parameters	Set this option if the provider allows parameterized queries. A *parameterized query* is one that replaces normal parameters with a ? as a marker for each parameter. This allows the source to compile and bind the execution plan for the query and just substitute parameters as needed, similar to the performance benefits for a stored procedure.
Nested Query	If the provider supports nested queries, or subqueries, setting this option can help SQL Server optimize that use a correlated subquery in certain instances. The setting allows SQL Server to pass the full query and subquery through to the data source for execution in one statement. Otherwise, the server issues two separate queries and then evaluates the results locally.
Level Zero Only	Setting this option forces SQL Server to use only the lowest level interface with the provider, even if the provider supports additional interfaces and features.
Allow In Process	By default, this option is enabled when setting up a linked server, which specifies that the distributed query will be executed in the same thread owned by SQL Server that is servicing the local query. Although this default behavior results in slight performance benefits, any error in the provider code can potentially cause SQL Server to crash. For example if the remote request hangs,

(continued)

15

Table 15.2 OLE DB provider settings *(continued)*.

Option	Description
Allow In Process	because only a single thread is used, control would never return to SQL Server to allow it to clean up the connection and memory structures. It is easy to see how this could create a problem for the server. It is recommended that you disable this option where possible, which allows SQL Server to issue a separate child thread to process the remote portion of the query, even though there is a slight increase in overhead associated with the allocation and management of the additional thread. The only other downside is that out-of-process requests cannot update or insert to **text** or **image** data types.
Non Transacted Updates	By default,an OLE DB provider must support local transactions in order to receive updates. If the Non Transacted Updates option is enabled, SQL Server allows update operations, even if the provider does not support local transactions. Even with this option enabled, SQL Server attempts to enable implicit transactions on the provider if possible.
Index As Access Path	If this option is not enabled, SQL Server exposes indexes on the data source only for metadata information and will not attempt to use any available indexes for faster retrieval of information. Enabling this option requests that SQL Server attempt to use any available indexes for more efficient data access. If the source has an optimizer engine, such as another SQL Server, and the engine automatically uses the appropriate indexes, setting this option is of no value.
Disallow Adhoc Access	Setting this option prevents the *ad hoc* use of the **OPENROWSET** function. However, any stored procedure that uses the **OPENROWSET** function and that has already been compiled when the option is enabled can still be executed successfully.

In addition to the previously mentioned settings, you can configure server-specific settings as described in Table 15.3. These apply to each individual, defined, linked server rather than to the OLE DB provider. The options are set using the **sp_serveroption** system stored procedure. For example, to enable **Server1** for inbound Remote Procedure Call (RPC), execute the command:

```
Exec sp_serveroption
  @server = 'Server1',
  @optname = 'rpc',
  @optvalue = 'TRUE'
```

Table 15.3 Server-specific linked server options.

Option	Description
collation compatible	When SQL Server exports a query to a remote server it has no knowledge of the character set or sort order of the remote server. Therefore, SQL Server performs any sorting and comparisons on the initiating server. If you know that the remote server has the same character set and sort order as the local server, turning on this flag can save some overhead and increase performance for distributed queries.
data access	This option enables distributed query access for the linked server. If this option is turned off, the linked server cannot be referenced in **SELECT**, **INSERT**, **UPDATE**, **DELETE**, or **OPENQUERY** statements.
Dist	Flags the linked server as a distributor in a replication scheme.
Dpub	Flags the linked server as a publisher to a remote distributor in a replication scheme.
Pub	Designates the linked server as a replication publisher.
Rpc	Allows remote procedure calls to be received from the linked server.
Rpc out	Allows remote procedure calls to be issued to the linked server.
Sub	Designates the linked server as a replication subscriber.
System	As per MS documentation, this is system use only.

Chapter Summary

In this chapter we have presented and discussed the following items:

- The use of remote server functionality is used only for backward compatibility.
- You can use remote servers only to execute and receive remote stored procedure calls.
- New linked servers include all old remote server functionality in addition to distributed query functionality.
- The linked server architecture uses OLE DB providers to communicate with linked server data sources.
- SQL Server 7 includes several OLE DB providers: SQL Server, Jet, Oracle, ODBC, Indexing Service, and Data Transformation Services (DTS) packages.
- A loopback server is a linked server that points back to the local server and is useful for testing distributed queries.

- OLE DB supports new data types, Unicode data, columns longer than 255 characters, and new features of SQL Server 7. These are not supported with ODBC.
- When a linked server data source is used in a join, the server retrieves all rows from the remote source and evaluates that rows matching the join locally.
- The **OPENQUERY** function is used with predefined linked servers and can occur anywhere a table name can appear within a SQL statement. This function allows SQL commands to be passed through to the OLE DB provider.
- You can complete remote *ad hoc* queries using the **OPENROWSET** function. This function works with nonconfigured linked servers and passes SQL queries through to the remote data source.
- The OLE DB provider must convert data types, sort order, and character sets between the data source and SQL Server.
- A provider must support local transactions in order to perform an update operation on a remote data source.
- If implicit or explicit transactions are used, update operations occur within a distributed transaction using the Distributed Transaction Coordinator (DTC) utility.
- The database catalog must be updated for remote servers prior to version 7 that will participate in distributed queries.
- For distributed queries, security is accomplished by mapping logins on the local server. For remote stored procedure calls, logins are mapped on the remote server.

Review Questions

1. If you want to be able to execute remote stored procedures, you should configure:
   a. A remote server
   b. A linked server
   c. A OLE DB server

2. You should configure a remote server when:
   a. No more linked servers are available.
   b. The remote data source does not support linked servers.
   c. You need to load balance your system.
   d. You need backward compatibility.

3. A linked server table can be included directly in a **SELECT** statement.
   a. True
   b. False

4. Which of the following *cannot* be included in a distributed query? (Choose all correct answers.)
   a. **JOIN**
   b. **CREATE**
   c. **GROUP BY**
   d. All the above.

5. **OPENQUERY** should only be used for occasional *ad hoc* queries.
   a. True
   b. False

6. When a linked server data source is included in a SQL statement, which of the following statements are true?
   a. Some SQL statements are passed through and executed on the provider.
   b. The local SQL Server may evaluation part of the SQL statement locally.
   c. The provider is responsible for exposing data types to one of the defined OLE DB data types.
   d. SQL Server is not aware of the character set and sort order for the remote server and therefore must perform comparisons locally.
   e. All of the above.

7. Which of the following should you do if you want to force the use of a distributed transaction in a remote update operation?
   a. Enable an explicit or implicit transaction.
   b. Set implicit transactions off.
   c. Execute a remote stored procedure on the target server.
   d. Use the **OPENQUERY** function.

8. Which of the following data sources can be configured as a linked server?
   a. Oracle
   b. SQL Server 6.5
   c. DB2
   d. Text file
   e. All of the above.

9. The **sp_serveroption** settings apply to all linked servers using the specified OLE DB provider.

a. True
b. False

10. Which of the following remote server settings impact performance?
    a. RPC Out
    b. Dpub
    c. Collation compatible
    d. Data access
11. To link a SQL Server to another SQL Server, you need:
    a. The ODBC string and login information.
    b. The linked server name, the product name, and the ODBC string.
    c. The ODBC string only.
    d. The linked server name and the product name.
12. Using the ODBC provider for linking servers does not support which features of SQL Server 7?
    a. The use of Unicode data types.
    b. Column widths greater than 255 characters.
    c. OLAP services.
    d. All of the above.
13. By default, SQL Server automatically commits implicit transactions after each SQL statement.
    a. True
    b. False
14. Which queries and updates are passed through directly to the ODBC provider (choose two)?
    a. **OPENQUERY**
    b. **FULLTEXT**
    c. **PASSTHROUGH**
    d. **OPENROWSET**
15. Which stored procedure displays a listing of table information for the specified linked server, catalog, schema, and table?
    a. **sp_catalogs**
    b. **sp_tables_ex**
    c. **sp_columns_ex**
    d. **sp_linkedservers**

Hands-On Projects

Susan got a call from the lead programmer on the project. "We've gotten a request to do some comparisons for data we have in the database and an Excel spreadsheet from Finance. I think I read somewhere that SQL 7 can do that, right?" Susan smiled. "Yup," she said, "just read up on it yesterday. Send me over what you want done."

Project 15.1

In this project, you will create a linked server to an Excel spreadsheet. The spreadsheet will be used to update the product prices in the *Northwind* database. A sample spreadsheet for this exercise is included on the CD and is named Example15-1.xls.

You will first need to prepare the spreadsheet for use as a linked data source. This preparation step is not specific to the use of linked servers and must be done before the worksheet can be used in any ODBC query that references it. Open the sample spreadsheet using Microsoft Excel. The references in this example are from using version 97 with SR-1 applied.

Highlight all the data in the worksheet. One way to do this is to press Ctrl+Home, which takes you to cell A1. Next, press and hold the Shift key and double-click on the right-hand side of the cell border. This highlights all the cells in row 1 that have data. While continuing to depress the Shift key, double-click the bottom border of the selected cells. Now you should have all the cells containing data highlighted.

Next, you need to define a named range. While the data cells remain highlighted, select Insert|Name|Define, and type in the name "Products" (see Figure 15.8). This named range will take the place of the table name.

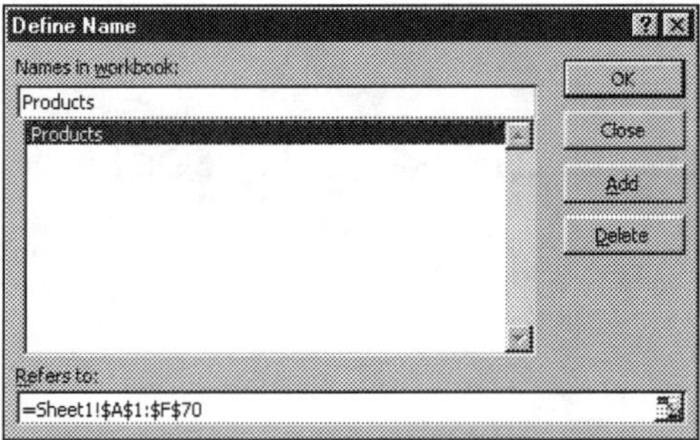

Figure 15.8 Creating a named range in Microsoft Excel.

15

Now, save the worksheet on your local hard drive and close the Excel application. For this example, we have saved the spreadsheet in D:\SQLBOOK\Example15-1.wks.

Because this will be a one time query and Excel spreadsheets are temporary in nature, we will use the **OPENROWSET()** function to access the data source. First we will build the **OPENROWSET()** command and test the data source with a select statement. Open a new window in Query Analyzer and type in the SQL command and execute it:

```
select * from
OPENROWSET(
'MSDASQL',
"DRIVER={Microsoft Excel Driver (*.xls)};
 UID=admin;PWD=;DBQ=D:\sqlbook\Example15-1.xls",
"select * from Products")
```

Project 15.2

Now that we are sure about the **OPENROWSET()** command and the data source, we will use the spreadsheet information to update the prices in the *Product* table. Open a new window in Query Analyzer and select the *Northwind* database. Type in and execute the following SQL command:

```
update Products
  set UnitPrice = E.NextYearPrice
 from Products P
 join OPENROWSET(
    'MSDASQL',
    "DRIVER={Microsoft Excel Driver (*.xls)};
    UID=admin;PWD=;DBQ=D:\sqlbook\Example15-1.xls",
    "select * from Products") E
  on E.ProductID = P.ProductID
 where P.Discontinued = 0
```

You've now successfully linked an Excel spreadsheet with SQL Server 7.

CHAPTER 16

DATA TRANSFERS

After Reading This Chapter And Completing The Exercises, You Will Be Able To:

- Identify the tools used to transfer data into and out of SQL Server
- Decide which is the best transfer tool for the task
- Know how to use Bulk Copy to import and export from the database
- Know how to use **BULK INSERT** to import into the database
- Understand the Data Transformation Service, Import and Export Wizard, and DTS Designer

We have examined SQL Server's ability to obtain data from programs and users or even derive the data from a database. Many times, however, the data resides in text files, Microsoft Access databases, Microsoft Excel spreadsheets, or other data formats. Microsoft SQL Server previously loaded data from sources such as these with a utility called the Bulk Copy Program (bcp). Microsoft SQL 7 has included not only the bcp utility but also a new powerful set of tools to obtain and transfer data from a variety of sources. In this chapter, we'll detail the steps to transfer data into and out of a SQL Server 7 database using these tools.

Importing And Exporting

Chapter 15 explained how to use the distributed query features of SQL Server 7. Linked servers and distributed queries enable you to read and write from other sources of information, including other SQL Servers, Access databases, and Excel spreadsheets. The tools examined in Chapter 15 generally aren't the best fit for importing and exporting data into and out of a database. This chapter focuses on the tools and methods that are better suited for moving information into and out of the SQL Server database.

A variety of situations require you to import information into a database. The list includes migrating from another database system, importing information from an *Online Transaction Processing* (*OLTP*) system into an *Online Analytical Processing (OLAP)* system, importing information from customers or vendors, and importing heavily used information from another source, to speed access to that information.

Many other situations require you to export information from the database. For example, you may need to send information from your database to customers and vendors, or perhaps you may need to export information that will be used by other systems in specialized processing tasks or for use in building static Web pages. Whatever the situation, Microsoft SQL Server provides a very complete and robust set of tools to enable you to get the job done.

Deciding Between Transfer Tools

Deciding which is the best tool to use for a particular situation may seem difficult because so many are available. Although overlap occurs between the capabilities of each of the tools, a brief look at the strong points for each method helps in deciding the best one to use. To review the items in your toolbox that you can use to move information between two sources, Table 16.1 lists the tools and provides a brief description of each.

Table 16.1 Data transfer tools.

Tool	Description
Bulk Copy Program (bcp)	The fastest way to move information into and out of the database. It works only with flat text files and provides very limited support for column mapping and handling various formats. Nonetheless, it is widely used because of its fast load and unload speeds.

(continued)

Table 16.1 Data transfer tools *(continued)*.

Tool	Description
BULK INSERT A	T-SQL statement that works by invoking the OLE DB bulk copy APIs. It provides identical functionality to the bcp utility, but works only for database loads.
Data Transformation Service (DTS)	Provides the best all-around solution for importing and exporting information. It enables you to execute custom data transformations, scripting, and migration of database objects, and works with virtually any data source or destination.
Distributed query	Remote data sources can be included with local data sources in SQL statements. This method is very convenient, but it's slow and not a good method for importing and exporting information.
Remote stored procedure	Executes a stored procedure on a remote server and returns the results. Combined with an **INSERT** statement, the **EXEC** statement can be used to import data from a remote source. A remote stored procedure can also be called repetitively, to write information on the remote system. This method is not the best tool for performance and does not provide much flexibility to cleanse and format information.
Replication	The new replication system is very robust and can be used to move changed data to other systems. Generally, the replication system captures and stages only data changes. It does not provide a means for applying updates to flat-file or other nondatabase subscribers. Furthermore, it does not facilitate importing data into the database.

The bcp and DTS utilities are best suited for, and have been optimized for, importing and exporting information from the database. The bcp utility is the best tool to use when you are importing from or exporting into flat files and need the fastest possible operation. When you need flexibility, or the source or destination is something other than a flat file, you should use the DTS system. The following sections describe the features of these two utilities.

BULK COPY

The Bulk Copy Program (also referred to as the *bcp utility*) is the fastest method for loading information into and unloading information from the database. The new version is reportedly two times faster than the previous version. This performance improvement is the result of using the query processor to optimize the use of database resources. Figure 16.1 illustrates the new bcp architecture. Note that the bcp requests are routed through the database engine's query processor. The query processor makes the most efficient use of the database resources, including coordinating the use of Read Ahead, indexes, and locking strategies.

The bcp utility works only with flat files. A *flat file* is a host file that usually is stored as an ASCII text file, but can also be stored either as a Unicode text file or in a SQL Server native data type format. If it is stored in a SQL Server native format, it can be read only by the bcp utility. The bcp utility is a standalone executable file that is run from a command window—this utility doesn't have a graphical interface. The bcp utility is located in \MSSQL7\BINN\bcp.exe. The syntax for the command follows:

```
usage: bcp {dbtable|query}
           {in|out|queryout|format}
           datafile
/* Load Options */          /* Connection Options */
[-b batchsize]              [-S server name]
[-e errfile]                [-U username]
[-E keep identity values]   [-P password]
[-F firstrow]               [-T trusted connection]
[-L lastrow]
[-h "load hints"]           /* Host File Options */
[-k keep null values]       [-c character type]
[-R regional enable]        [-w wide character type]
                            [-t field terminator]
/* Process Options */       [-r row terminator]
[-m maxerrors]              [-n native type]
[-i inputfile]              [-N keep non-text native]
[-o outfile]                [-6 6x file format]
[-v version]                [-C code page specifier]
[-q quoted identifier]      [-f formatfile]
[-a packetsize]
```

As an example, suppose that you need to unload a file of *ProductIDs* and descriptions for all products that fall into the *Seafood* category in the *Northwind* database. The following bcp command creates the file **Seafood_Products.dat**:

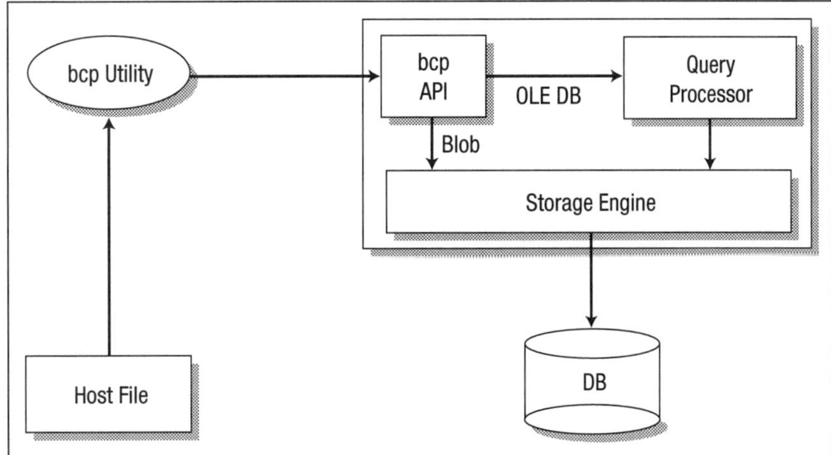

Figure 16.1 bcp architecture.

```
D:\wip\>bcp "select ProductID, ProductName
from Northwind..Products where CategoryID=8"
queryout Seafood_Products.dat -T -c
```

As this example shows, the bcp command can be executed by using a query rather than a table or view name. The next example shows how to unload the entire *Products* table by specifying only the table name:

```
D:\wip\>bcp Northwind..Products out All_Products.dat -T -c
```

The **-T** option specifies a connection to the local server (because an **-S** option was not used) using trusted security. The output file is in standard ASCII character format, due to the **-c** option being used. These options are explained further in the next section to follow. Table 16.2 lists the core command-line parameters that must be specified.

Specifying Connection Information

Running bcp.exe without specifying any connection information defaults to using the local server. If a local server does not exist, the command fails; otherwise, the connection is made and is authenticated using trusted security. To load data to or from a remote server, you must supply the server name. You must also specify either standard SQL Server authentication information or a trusted connection. A *trusted connection* uses the network login to authenticate the user. For example, the following bcp command unloads the *Customers* table from the Acct server, using standard security:

Table 16.2 Core bcp command-line parameters.

Parameter	Description
Dbtable	Specifies the database table that is to be loaded or unloaded. The table is in the format database. owner.table. A global temporary table can be specified by using the format **##temporary_table**.
Query	Instead of specifying a **dbtable** parameter, the results of a query can be used as input to an unload operation. The query can be a join or even a distributed query.
In	Specified if you are importing into the database from the data file.
Out	Used when you are exporting from the database and are providing the **dbtable** parameter rather than a query.
Queryout	Used when you are exporting from the database and are using a query rather than a direct table reference.

```
D:\wip\>bcp Northwind..Customers out customers.dat
-SAcct -Ubean -Pcounter -c
```

Table 16.3 lists the connection parameters and their descriptions.

Working With The Host File

Several command-line options are used to specify the format of the host file or flat file. If the format of the host file is not specified when unloading or loading data to or from the database, you are prompted for formatting information for each column. The files can be ASCII text, Unicode text, standard native format, or a Unicode native format (see Table 16.4 for host file options).

Specifying the **-c** option instructs the utility that the host file is in ASCII text format. When using the **-c** option (or the **-w**, **-n**, and **-N** options, described

Table 16.3 bcp connection parameters.

Parameter	Description
-S	Used to specify the server name. If not specified, the default is the local server.
-U	Specifies the SQL Server standard security login ID with which to authenticate the connection. If not specified, trusted security is assumed.
-P	Gives the password for the user specified with the **-U** option.
-T	Instructs the utility to authenticate the connection using the network login credentials.

later), the default field delimiter is the tab character (**\t**) and the default row delimiter is the *newline* character (**\n**). These defaults can be changed by specifying the **-t** and **-r** options (see Table 16.4 for more information). Using a standard text file is useful if you either need to be able to edit the host file by using a text editor or are exporting data to be used on another system.

If you are unloading data to a standard text file, the server converts character information to the Original Equipment Manufacturer (OEM) code page (default = 437). Conversely, when data is loaded into the database, the server converts character information to the ANSI (ACP) code page (default = 1252). For Windows 95/98/NT systems, these default code page settings are stored in the HKEY_LOCAL_MACHINE/System/CurrentControlSet/Control/Nls/ Codepage Registry tree. Extended character information can be lost as a result of this back-and-forth code-page conversion. To solve this problem, the host file can be stored in Unicode format by specifying the **-w** option (wide format) in place of the **-c** option. Aside from the fact that many editors do not understand Unicode data, the only downside to using the **-w** format is that each character takes up two bytes of storage as opposed to the single byte for **-c** type files.

For both the **-c** and **-w** file format options, the server converts all data types to character data. These conversions add processing overhead to the load and unload process. For the best performance, a bcp option enables you to specify that data are stored using the native binary SQL storage formats. Again, you have two choices for native file formats:

- **Standard** The **-n** option specifies that noncharacter data is stored in the native binary structures and that character data is stored as standard text. This option poses a potential loss of extended character information due to the conversion of strings to OEM and ACP code pages.
- **Unicode** The **-N** option specifies that noncharacter data is stored in the native binary structures and that character data is stored as Unicode information, thus preventing possible loss of data.

As discussed earlier, character data can be stored as Unicode information to prevent the possible loss of extended character information. An alternative to using the two-bytes-per-character Unicode format is to specify the code page that data will be converted to (see the **-C** option in Table 16.4).

Format Files

A format file is used only during import operations. When data is exported from the database, the host file always contains all the columns in the same order as the source table, view, or query. The delimiters and storage formats for export files can be specified by the **-c**, **-w**, **-n**, **-N**, **-r**, and **-t** bcp parameters.

Table 16.4 Host file bcp parameters.

Parameter	Description
-c	All data types are converted to ASCII characters in the host file. These files can usually be viewed or edited using virtually any editor. This format is most useful for sharing information with other systems or prior database versions.
-w	Specifies that all data types are converted to Unicode characters in the host file. This prevents any possible loss of extended characters due to code-page conversions. Unicode characters are stored using two bytes instead of the usual one byte, and thus use twice as much storage space. Host files containing Unicode information cannot be loaded into prior versions of the database.
-t	Provides the field terminator to be used. By default, the field terminator is the tab (**\t**) character with the **-c**, **-w**, **-n**, or **-N** storage types.
-r	Designates the row terminator. By default, the row terminator is the newline (**\n**) character for the **-c**, **-w**, **-n**, or **-N** storage types.
-n	All noncharacter information is stored in SQL Server native binary formats, and all character data is converted to standard ASCII characters. This storage option provides the faster bcp operation, because very little conversion activity is performed. Host files stored in this format cannot be viewed or edited, and can be used only with other SQL Server 7 databases.
-N	Like the **-n** option, all noncharacter information is stored in SQL Server native binary formats. However, all character data is stored as Unicode information. Host files stored in this format cannot be viewed or edited and can be used only with other SQL Server 7 databases.
-6	Used only with either the **-c** or **-n** file types. When loading data into v6.5 databases, this option causes datatypes to be backward-compatible.

(continued)

Table 16.4 Host file bcp parameters *(continued)*.

Parameter	Description
-C	Provides the ability to specify the code page that is stored in the host file. For export operations, this option instructs the server to convert character data types to this code page instead of the default OEM code page (default = 437). For import processes, this option instructs the server which code page for the character data stored is stored in the host file. This can help to prevent the loss of extended character information when converting between two different code pages. Valid values for this option include **ACP**, **OEM**, **RAW**, and a specific code page number. **RAW** specifies that no code-page conversion is to take place, which is the fastest option.
-f	Designates the format file to be used during a Bulk Copy operation. This is in place of specifying one of the **-c**, **-w**, **-n**, or **-N** host file format options.

In situations where the format of the host file cannot be described by using the **-c**, **-w**, **-n**, or **-N** parameters, the bcp provides the ability to create a format file. A *format* file also allows column mapping between the source host file and the target database table. If none of the formatting options are specified on the command line, bcp prompts for all the formatting information. After you respond to all prompts, you have the chance to save the settings as a format file. This method is the easiest way to create a format file. The following is an example of creating a format file using this method:

```
D:\wip>bcp Northwind..EmployeeTerritories in ET.home -T

Enter the file storage type of
field EmployeeID [int]: char
Enter prefix-length of field EmployeeID [1]: 0
Enter length of field EmployeeID [12]: 10
Enter field terminator [none]:|

Enter the file storage type of
field TerritoryID [nvarchar]: char
Enter prefix-length of field TerritoryID [1]: 0
Enter length of field TerritoryID [96]: 40
Enter field terminator [none]:|\n
Do you want to save this format
information in a file? [Y/n] Y
Host filename [bcp.fmt]: ET.fmt

Starting copy...
```

```
49 rows copied.
Network packet size (bytes): 4096
Clock Time (ms.):
total         1 Avg       0 (49000.00 rows per sec.)

D:\wip>type ET.fmt
7.0
2
1    SQLCHAR   0   10  "|"      1  EmployeeID
2    SQLCHAR   0   40  "|\r\n"  2  TerritoryID
```

In this example, four prompts for each field determine the format of the host data file. The first prompt is for the storage type of the field. Valid values include any of the SQL Server data types. Only the **CHAR**, **NCHAR**, or **TEXT** datatypes are readable in the host file. Other formats (such as **INT** and **FLOAT**) indicate that information is stored in propriety binary structures. The second prompt is for the number of prefix characters that are stored prior to the actual data. Prefix characters are used only for storing proprietary formats, and hold the number of bytes that are contained in the ensuing field data. The third prompt is for the actual length of the field, and the final prompt is for the field delimiter. The preceding example uses a field delimiter of a vertical bar, and a row delimiter of a newline character **\n**.

Now that you have created your first format file, take a look at the contents of the file. Figure 16.2 illustrates the various sections of the format file. After you create the file, you can edit it to customize the host file layout or to change the mapping of database table columns to host file columns. A one-to-one mapping isn't required between the two data sources—columns can appear in any order.

The best way to learn how to map columns between the host file and the target database table is to work through an example. Consider the situation depicted

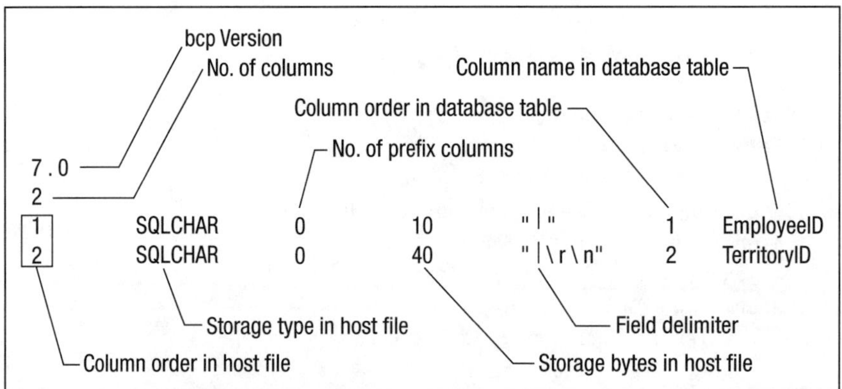

Figure 16.2 Sections of the bcp format file.

in Figure 16.3. The host file contains four columns that map to the target database table, but in a different order. The host file contains an additional column that is not stored in the database. Likewise, the database table contains information that is not stored in the host file.

When you create the format file to handle this situation, remember that the column numbers for the host file are always numbered sequentially (refer to Figure 16.2). In situations where the target database table contains columns that are not represented in the host file, you have two options. You can either create a placeholder in the format file for the target table columns or skip them altogether. If you choose to create a placeholder for the columns, you should set the field length to 0 and the field delimiter to an empty string ("") to indicate that the information is not stored in the host file. You choose to skip the placeholders if you follow the bcp interactive prompting to create and save the initial format file. In the example shown in Figure 16.3, the placeholders have been removed.

The other situation depicted by Figure 16.3 is the existence of information in the host file that is not stored in the database table. For this situation, you must represent the data element by placing a row in the format file. However, the database column number should be set to 0. You also need to specify a fictitious name for the column. In this case, the column is named *Comments*, but any unique name will suffice, because it is not used in the import process.

The following is output in a format file that has been created to satisfy the example presented in Figure 16.3. Pay particular attention to how the column mapping has been implemented for the *CustState* and *CustStartDate* columns, because they appear in different orders.

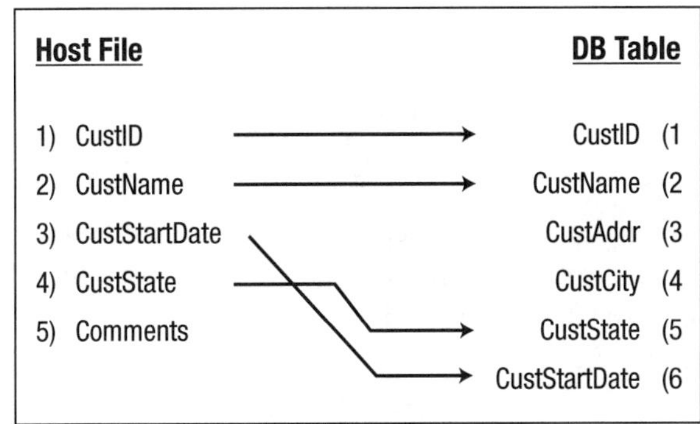

Figure 16.3 Mapping columns between the source and target tables.

16

```
7.0
5
1       SQLCHAR     0     10     ","     1     CustID
2       SQLCHAR     0     25     ","     2     CustName
3       SQLCHAR     0     2      ","     6     CustStartDate
4       SQLCHAR     0     8      ","     5     CustState
5       SQLCHAR     0     20     "\n"    0     Comments
```

For any situation in which more sophisticated data cleansing, decoding, or transformations are necessary, you need to use Data Transformation Services, described later in this chapter.

Bulk Loads

By now, you should understand how to perform basic import and export operations using bcp, including how to specify connection options and work with various host file formats. Now, we will examine the bcp parameters that apply only to database loads. These parameters are an important part of the bcp utility, especially for large import operations. Table 16.5 lists the parameters specific to load operations.

If the batch size (**-b**) is not specified, the entire import operation is treated as a single transaction in the database. During the load, bcp prints a message for every 1,000 rows loaded into the database. A common mistake is to interpret this message to mean that the batch size defaults to 1,000 rows. This is not true, however, because the default is to treat the entire operation as a single batch.

In the bcp examples presented thus far, the import operation has been treated as a single transaction. If you are importing large quantities of information, you'll quickly notice that the transaction log fills up quickly, even halting the import of the data if the log fills completely. The bcp utility provides the **-b** parameter, which can force multiple commits to be issued as data is loaded into the database. This is one of the most common parameters in bcp operations. The higher the batch size is set, the faster the bcp utility operations complete. However, if the batch size is set too high, the transaction log will fill up, or an extensive rollback will occur if an error is encountered. Thus, a reasonable limit should be used for the **-b** parameter.

Optimizer Hints

Because the new bcp utility imports information through the database Query Optimizer, query hints can be used to improve significantly the speed of database loads. Five different optimizer hints can be specified by using the **-h** bcp parameter. If more than one hint is used, they should be separated by a comma.

Table 16.5 bcp load parameters.

Parameter	Description
-b	Specifies the batch size to use. If no batch size is specified, the default is to treat the entire load operation as a single batch and transaction. If the batch size is specified, a **COMMIT** is issued after each batch of rows has been imported.
-e	Used to designate an error file that will contain all rows that could not be imported due to an error. If not specified, no record exists of which rows did not get imported into the database.
-E	Used to enable **SET IDENTITY_INSERT ON** for the target table if the host file contains identity values that you want to import into the target table.
-F	Indicates the first row to be imported. This is useful if a large bcp operation fails and you need to restart at a particular row. The default is **-F1**.
-L	Indicates the last row to be imported. This is useful in concert with the **-F** parameter if only a certain range of rows from the host file needs to be imported. The default is for all rows to be imported into the database.
-h	Allows certain optimizer hints to be used to improve the performance of a bcp operation. Optimizer hints are described in more detail in the next section.
-k	Using the **-k** parameter specifies that the **NULL** value should be retained even if a default is defined for the target column. If the target column does not allow **NULL**s, then the attempt to import the row results in an error and the row is not imported. By default, if the host file contains an empty string for a particular column, the Query Optimizer replaces the **NULL** value with the default value of the column, if defined.
-R	Instructs the query processor to use the locale settings from the bcp client in place of the server or connection locale settings. The locale settings determine the format for date, time, and currency information.

16

If the target table contains a clustered index, and the source host file is sorted in the same order as the index, the load operation can occur significantly faster. Use the hint to let the Query Optimizer know that the host file is in the same sorted order as the clustered index:

```
-h"ORDER(COLUMN1 ASC|DESC, COLUMN2 ASC|DESC, ...)"
```

This option has no effect if either no clustered index exists or the order specified in the hint does not match the index order exactly.

We have already examined the **-b** parameter that is used to specify the batch size for a database load. The same information can be specified by using an optimizer hint. Using one method over the other offers no advantage. Use the following syntax to specify the batch size as part of the **-h** parameter:

```
-h"ROWS_PER_BATCH=10000"
```

If you are not sure of the number of rows to use for the batch size, you may alternatively want to specify a number of bytes as a batch size. The optimizer determines how many rows correspond to the size specified. For example, to specify that a batch size of 2MB be used, use the following hint:

```
-h"KILOBYTES_PER_BATCH=2048"
```

Regardless of whether the batch size is specified, the database grants and holds row-level locks during Bulk Insert operations. For large transfers, that is an enormous amount of locking overhead for the database server. You can remove the overhead associated with locking by using the table lock (**TABLOCK**) hint. If the table lock hint is not used, the database may still use a table lock if the table lock on bulk load table option is set by using the **sp_tableoption** stored procedure. An example of using the table lock hint follows:

```
-h"TABLOCK"
```

The last hint that is available to you pertains to whether the query engine checks for constraint violations when bulk loading data. The default behavior ignores any constraint checking, which is the fastest option. However, you may encounter situations in which you need to make sure that constraints are not violated. In this case, use the following hint:

```
-h"CHECK_CONSTRAINTS"
```

Processing Options

In addition to bcp parameters that are used to specify connections, host file options, and database loads, a handful of other parameters are available, which are administrative in nature. Table 16.6 lists this final set of parameters.

Optimizing Performance

We have already seen how the bcp utility includes the ability to specify optimizer hints and how these hints can improve performance of a data load. In addition to the Query Optimizers, you can do a few other things to achieve a much faster bcp performance. This section looks at how to enable a nonlogged bulk load operation and how to perform parallel loads.

Table 16.6 Miscellaneous bcp parameters.

Parameter	Description
-m	Designates that the bcp should terminate after this number of errors. Each row that can't be copied is considered an error. If **-m** is not specified, the default is 10 errors.
-i	Gives the full path and file name for a response file, which is used to answer the interactive format questions.
-o	Designates the file name of an output file that will contain the redirected output from bcp.
-v	Returns the version and copyright information of the bcp utility.
-q	Turns on the quoted identifier option. This is used when the table or view contains spaces or special characters. If this option is used, the table or view name should be enclosed in quotation marks.
-a	Specifies the network packet size. By default, the default database server packet size is used. Increasing the network packet size sometimes can improve bcp performance.

One of the primary features of an enterprise database system is that it logs every change to the database, enabling the database to guarantee transactional consistency and the ability to recover from a disk failure. During a *Bulk Load* operation, the extra overhead associated with the database logging activity can significantly increase the time it takes to complete the operation. In addition to performance considerations, logging bulk data transfers has the additional possibility of filling the transaction logs rapidly. The query processor decides whether or not the bcp operation is logged based on several factors. If the following conditions are met, then the bcp will not be logged, thus improving performance significantly:

- The target database must have the select into/bulkcopy option enabled.
- The bcp must use a table lock on the target table. This can be set by using either the bcp optimizer hint or the **sp_tableoption** setting.
- The target table cannot be marked for replication.
- The target table must either be empty or lack any indexes.

16

Backing Up The Database Log

After a nonlogged operation is run in a database, the database log cannot be backed up until a full backup or a differential backup is completed.

If all of these conditions are met, the Query Optimizer can complete the bcp operation without logging. If the target table does not have any indexes, you can also structure several bcp client sessions to run in parallel. The load of these operations scales linearly with the number of processors, thus, the number of client bcp sessions should not exceed the number of processors available to the database server. Taking advantage of parallel loading into the target table also requires you to use separate host files for each bcp client.

Other factors that we have examined that impact bcp performance include setting the batch size, using constraint checking, using ordered host files, code page conversion, ignoring column **DEFAULT** definitions, and the use of optimizer hints.

BULK INSERT

The bcp is a very robust utility that provides the fastest way to get data into and out of the database. The bcp functionality is exposed through the bcp.exe executable file, ODBC, OLE DB, and SQL-DMO APIs, and also through the T-SQL **BULK INSERT** statement. The **BULK INSERT** statement provides the same functionality as the bcp.exe utility, except that it works only for loading data into the database.

The following is the syntax of the **BULK INSERT** statement:

```
BULK INSERT [['database_name'.]['owner'].]{'table_name'
FROM data_file}
[WITH (
[ BATCHSIZE [= batch_size]]
[[,] CHECK_CONSTRAINTS]
[[,] CODEPAGE [='ACP'|'OEM'|'RAW'|'code_page']]
[[,] DATAFILETYPE [=
        {'char'|
        'native'|
        'widechar'|
        'widenative'}]]
[[,] FIELDTERMINATOR [= 'field_terminator']]
[[,] FIRSTROW [= first_row]]
[[,] FORMATFILE [= 'format_file_path']]
[[,] KEEPIDENTITY]
[[,] KEEPNULLS]
[[,] KILOBYTES_PER_BATCH [= kilobytes_per_batch]]
[[,] LASTROW [= last_row]]
[[,] MAXERRORS [= max_errors]]
[[,] ORDER ({column [ASC|DESC]} [,...n])]
[[,] ROWS_PER_BATCH [= rows_per_batch]]
[[,] ROWTERMINATOR [= 'row_terminator']]
[[,] TABLOCK]
)]
```

Although the syntax is necessarily different from bcp, the functionality is identical. We won't spend time here explaining the same bcp features, but you are advised to follow along with the examples demonstrated, substituting the **BULK INSERT** statement for the bcp utility. This will give you a good idea of how to accomplish bulk load operations using either utility.

Data Transformation Services

The bulk copy utilities are very powerful tools in the SQL Server 7 repertoire, yet bcp cannot perform sophisticated data transformations or data cleansing, which are important functions for database applications, such as data warehousing. That is why Microsoft has delivered the sophisticated *Data Transformation Services (DTS)* utility to serve these needs. DTS provides a flexible framework for defining and storing all data transformations in a central location, including bcp operations.

DTS is a standalone suite of utilities that includes the ability to define import, export, and custom transformations between any two OLE DB or ODBC data sources. Transformations can consist of multiple steps and are stored as a single package. *Packages* are groups of steps and commands that can be run by using the DTS utility. Packages can be executed from Enterprise Manager, scheduled with SQL Server Agent, or referenced through an external application, such as Visual Basic or Java.

Import And Export Wizard

The Import and Export Wizards are really a single tool that enables you to move data from any OLE DB or ODBC provider to any other OLE DB or ODBC provider. DTS includes two wizards to make it easy to get up and running quickly with very little understanding of the DTS packages. The Import and Export Wizards prompt you through a series of questions and quickly create a DTS package for importing and exporting information into and out of SQL Server. To start the Import Wizard, open Enterprise Manager and click on the wizard icon, expand the DTS tree, and select either the Import or Export Wizard. Selecting one or the other really makes no difference, because both enable you to copy data from one OLE DB provider to another, regardless of whether the source or target is a SQL Server. The Import Wizard can also be started by running the dtswiz.exe utility from the command prompt.

When you first run the Import Wizard, you are prompted to choose the data source (see Figure 16.4). The drop-down box lists all available OLE DB providers and ODBC drivers on the system. For example, on this server, the choices are as follows:

- dBase III, IV, and 5
- Microsoft Access
- Microsoft Data Link
- Microsoft Excel 3, 4, 5, and 8
- Oracle (OLE DB and ODBC)
- SQL Server (OLE DB and ODBC)
- Visual FoxPro
- Paradox 3, 4, and 5
- Text file
- Other ODBC source

The remaining properties that are displayed depend on the specific data source that you choose. Choosing the OLE DB provider for SQL Server prompts for the server name, authentication protocol, and database.

Next, you choose a destination for your data. You can choose from the same OLE DB and ODBC providers as in the first step. A DTS package can be created for copying data from a text file to a Microsoft Access database, between two SQL Servers, or between SQL Server and an Oracle instance. When choosing an OLE DB provider for the source or destination, you may need to set several advanced options, for a successful connection. These options are exposed by and vary per provider. In most cases, you will not need to change these settings unless the provider documentation instructs you to make modifications. Refer to the documentation included with the referred RDBMS for any specific parameters needed to transfer the data.

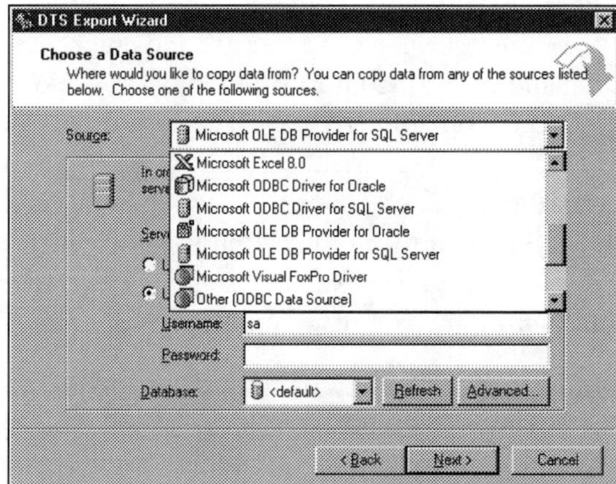

Figure 16.4 Choosing a data source.

If the source is a database or understands a SQL dialect, you are prompted to either copy tables or provide a query to specify the data to copy. In addition, if both the source and destination sources are SQL Servers, you can designate database objects to migrate along with the data. Finally, you choose whether to run the package now or schedule it for later execution. You can also save the package so that you can run the transformation at a later time, or even on a regular basis.

The Import/Export Wizard creates a simple DTS package that can be saved for later use or additional editing. You can save a package to any one of the following:

- **The *msdb* database** Within the SQL Server metadata location.
- **A Microsoft Repository** Can be used along with other metadata to create a data mart or data warehouse.
- **A local file** Has the advantage of being easy to distribute with packaged solutions.

Any DTS package created by one of the wizards can be further edited and modified by using the DTS Designer component in the Enterprise Manager utility. The prompts presented by the wizards are part of the package components and are discussed in greater detail in the next section.

DTS Designer

The heart and soul of the DTS utility is the Designer, a GUI that you use to create or edit a package. Using a drag-and-drop approach, you can add connections, tasks, and workflow objects to a package. Packages created by the wizards have only a few components, but a complex set of transformations can be engineered using the Designer.

To start the package Designer, right-click on the DTS folder of a server tree (see Figure 16.5) and select the New Package option from the pop-up menu. Alternately, you can select either Local Packages or Repository Packages from the Data Transformation Services menu tree and double-click on an existing saved package. After you are in the Designer, you can add as many connections, tasks, and workflow objects as necessary to complete the package.

When you are creating a new package, you may want to review and change the package properties. Click on the Package drop-down menu and choose Properties. The package description is saved with each individual package version and is a good way of distinguishing between versions. You can also set the name and location of the error file that is used to log package errors during execution, as well as various other options. The transaction options on the Advanced tab are of particular interest because you can specify how transactions are used for the transformation and what the isolation level should be.

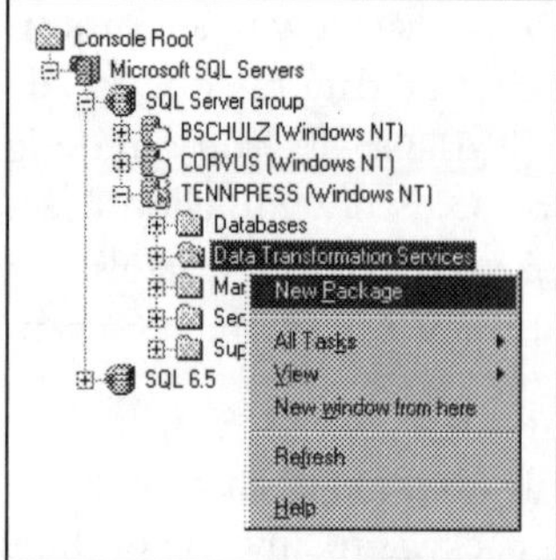

Figure 16.5 Creating a new DTS package.

Connections

The first step when designing a new package is to add one or more connections. A connection object usually should be configured prior to adding any tasks to the package. Many tasks require at least two connections to be added to a package—one for the source and another for the destination. A connection can be configured for any OLE DB provider or ODBC driver. A connection can also be reused, by specifying an existing connection when adding a new connection object. A task that requires both a source and destination requires two separate connections.

Connection objects are predefined for the following data sources or destinations:

- SQL Server
- MS Access
- Excel 8
- dBase 5
- Paradox 5
- Text source/destination
- Oracle
- MS Data Link
- Other (ODBC DSN)

These connection objects are really all the same OLE DB connection object. Choosing the provider or ODBC driver from the drop-down list changes the displayed icon and the available connection properties. When adding a connection, choose either New Connection or Existing Connection. Specifying an existing connection by selecting from the drop-down list results in adding a second connection icon to the Designer desktop.

If the data source is an OLE DB provider, the Connection Properties dialog box has an Advanced Settings button. The advanced settings that you can select after clicking this button are specific to each provider. In most cases, these advanced options don't need to be changed. In certain circumstances, the advanced settings may need to be modified to make a reliable connection to the data source. This will normally be required based on the level of compatibility the data source has made to the ODBC or OLE-DB standard.

Figure 16.6 shows the Connection Properties dialog box for adding a new SQL Server connection. A new connection is established and the connection name is changed from the default to TENNPRESS—*Northwind*. Performing a test such as the one shown will help you to identify the correct connection in a complex transformation that has numerous connections. Figure 16. 6 shows that we have also elected to use Windows NT authentication and have selected the *Northwind* database.

Tasks

The Designer includes eight tasks that you can add to your transformation package, four of which require one or more connections to be established first. Table 16.7 lists the tasks and provides a brief description of each one. So that you can understand these tasks in more depth, the details of how to use each task are provided following Table 16.7.

The *Data Pump* task is the primary method for moving information between two SQL Servers, and requires both a source and destination connection to be configured. If you are looking at the DTS Designer for the Data Pump task, you might have a hard time finding it. Interestingly, it is not located with the other tasks on either the Task drop-down menu or in the Task toolbox. Click on the Transform Data icon on the toolbar or select the Add Transform menu

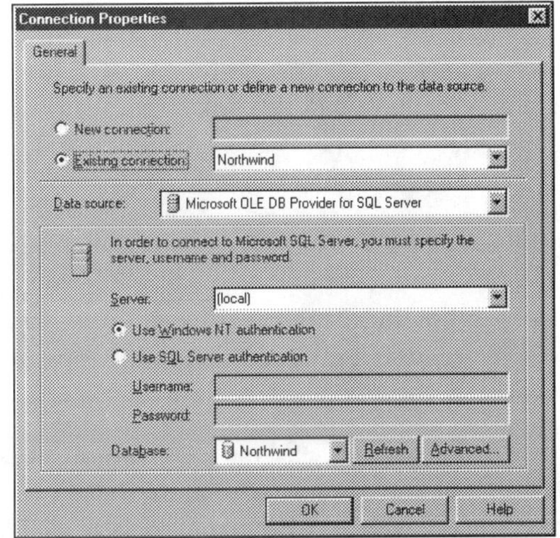

Figure 16.6 SQL Server Connection Properties dialog box.

Table 16.7 DTS tasks.

Task	Description
Data Pump	Probably the most commonly used task, it enables you to specify a source table or query, a destination table, and a transformation.
ActiveX Script	Enables you to create an ActiveX script to customize the transformation process. The script can conditionally execute certain workflow steps of the transformation, create or modify global variables, or perform administrative functions, such as logging transformation results to a SQL table.
Execute Process	Enables you to execute any executable program or batch script command.
Execute SQL	Provides the capability to execute one or more SQL commands on a connection.
Data Driven Query	Very similar to the Data Pump task, but does not support bulk transfers. Enables you to specify how data is moved into the target, by using stored procedures or queries for inserts, updates, or deletes into or out of the target table(s).
Transfer SQL Server Objects	Useful for transferring database objects from one SQL Server to another. This cannot be used to transfer database objects to non-SQL Server destinations.
Send Mail	Allows a mail message to be sent as part of the transformation. This is a convenient way to notify operators of problems with a transformation step or convey the results of a transformation to an email address.
Bulk Insert	Provides a way to bulk insert information into the destination SQL Server.

item in the Workflow drop-down menu to add this task to the worksheet. With this task, you determine a source table (or query) and a target table. This table can be created if it does not already exist.

Figure 16.7 shows the Transformations tab for a Data Pump, which is where all the magic happens. The default column mappings are created for you automatically. You can use this window to map the source columns to any destination columns, choosing either a straightforward column copy or an ActiveX Script transformation.

Suppose that you need to copy the *Categories* table from the *Northwind* database to another destination. In this case, you do not want to have a straightforward copy operation, but instead want to strip all the spaces out of the *Description* column along with the transfer. Instead of the column copy transformation, you can create a simple

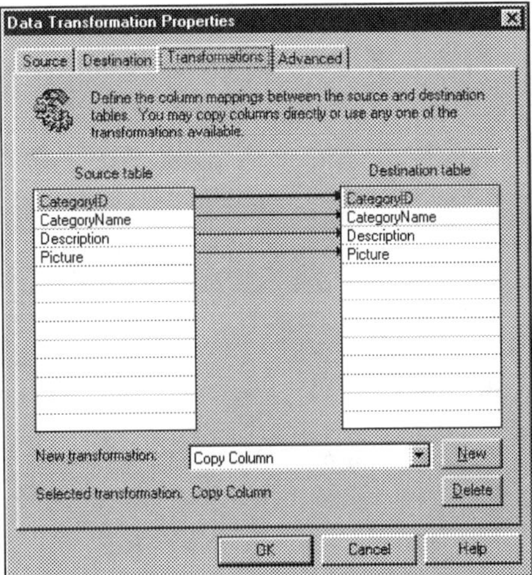

Figure 16.7 Data Pump transformations.

ActiveX Script transformation to perform this operation for you. Figure 16.8 shows a sample ActiveX Perl script that will do the trick. In this example, we could have used the ActiveX script to transform only the *Description* column and used the standard column copy transformation for everything else. But, because we are invoking the ActiveX script anyway, it is just as fast to transform everything all in one place.

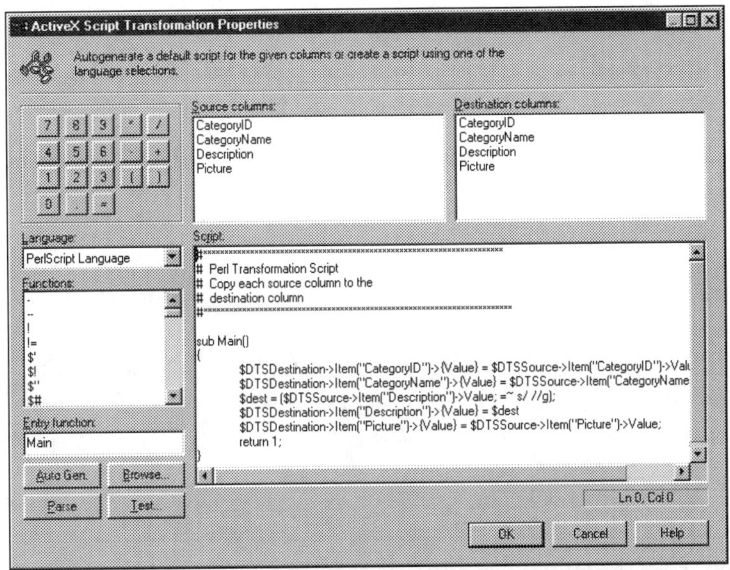

Figure 16.8 Using an ActiveX PerlScript transformation.

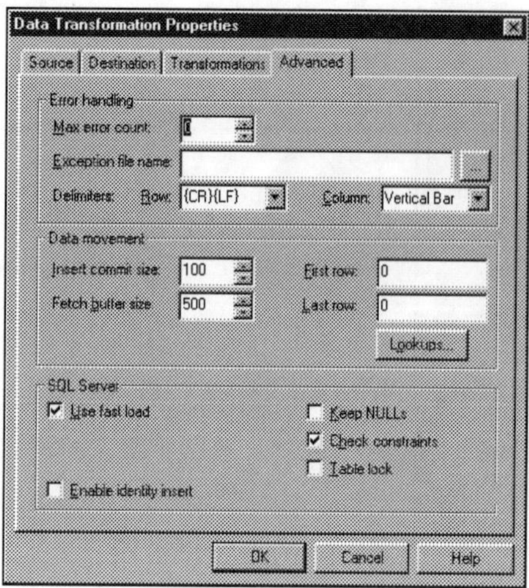

Figure 16.9 Data Pump Advanced settings tab.

The Advanced Settings tab includes some additional options for the overall transformation operation (see Figure 16.9), including error handling settings, data movement settings, and bulk copy settings. Data movement settings are very similar to some of the bulk copy parameters. You can set the insert commit size, which is similar to the batch size in bcp. The number of rows that will be fetched at a time from the source connection can also be set independently. Selecting the Fast Load option allows the use of the OLE DB provider fast load interface. For SQL Server destinations, this will use the Bulk Copy interface, which significantly improves the performance of the transfer.

Another transformation task that is commonly used is the *Data Driven Query*. This is very similar to the Data Pump operation, previously described. The primary difference is the method used to insert or update the target table. By default, the transformation for a Data Driven Query is an ActiveX script. Within the script, after executing the column transformations and mappings, the script returns control by indicating whether the type of operation is an **INSERT**, **UPDATE**, or **DELETE**. For example, if the ActiveX script returns the value then the transformation object will execute the insert query defined in the Queries tab (see Figure 16.10):

```
Main = DTSTransformstat_InsertQuery
```

The query can be an explicit **INSERT** statement, as shown, or it can be a stored procedure that contains the necessary logic for updating the destination. This capability adds a great deal of flexibility to the transformation process, but it comes at the cost of performance. A Data Driven Query is most likely to be used for maintaining a data warehouse.

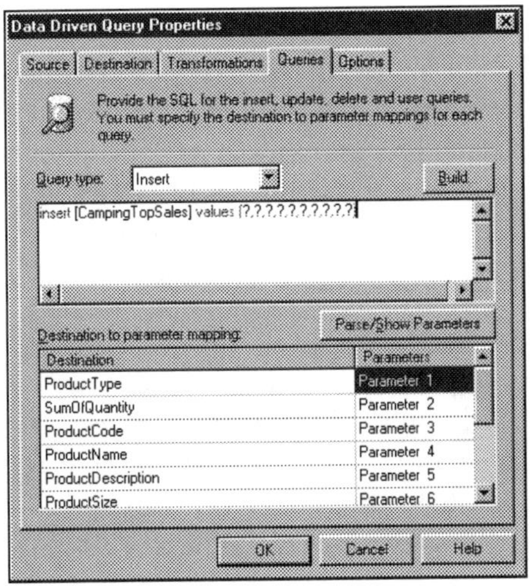

Figure 16.10 Defining a query in the Data Driven Query Properties dialog box.

The next task to consider is the Execute SQL task. Using this function, you can execute any SQL statement on any defined connection. You can use this task to prepare data that will be copied to a destination, log the transformation activity to a database table, or perhaps even create the destination table prior to execution of a Data Pump task. The Execute SQL task object supports the **GO** statement, just like the Query Analyzer, so several SQL statements can be included in a single task. For example, the following two statements drop and re-create a table on the destination connection:

```
if exists
(   select *
    from sysobjects
    where id = object_id( [CampingTopSales] )
)
     drop table [CampingTopSales]
go
CREATE TABLE [CampingTopSales] (
[ProductType] nvarchar (20) NULL,
[SumOfQuantity] float NULL,
[ProductCode] nvarchar (10) NULL,
[ProductName] nvarchar (50) NULL,
[ProductDescription] nvarchar (255) NULL,
[ProductSize] nvarchar (5) NULL,
[ProductImageURL] nvarchar (255) NULL,
[UnitPrice] float NULL,
[OnSale] bit NOT NULL,
[ProductIntroductionDate] smalldatetime NULL )
```

As part of a transformation sequence, suppose that you need to run an external program that will export information out of an application. To do this, you can add the Execute Process to your worksheet and run the program to write information to a text file. The Execute Process task can execute any program or batch file. This would be a good way to run the bcp.exe utility to do a fast unload from a SQL Server data source. Of course, you could also run bcp.exe to run a fast load into a SQL Server, but a separate Bulk Insert transformation task is available that can be used to do that.

The Bulk Insert transformation task provides a graphical interface for specifying a bulk load operation. This task works only with SQL Server destinations. All the bcp.exe options that are available for loads are exposed in the Properties dialog box, including using a format file, setting the batch size, and designating code page conversions. The only thing missing is the ability to designate an error file for storing input data rows that generate an error.

Another very handy transformation task is the Transfer SQL Server Objects function. If the transformation includes the need to move many database objects, it would be very tedious to build the scripts manually. Using the Transfer SQL Server Objects function, you can select the objects that you want to transfer to the destination SQL Server, including logins, users, permissions, and other scripting options. You can even use this task to move the data to the destination. The interface for this object is very similar to the Database/Object Transfer tool that was included with SQL Server 6.5. The database connections are defined within the task, so you don't need to explicitly create source and destination connection objects first. Encapsulated within this task is everything that is necessary to copy a database completely from one server to another.

If the standard DTS components are not enough to meet your needs, you can also create your own DTS tasks by using Visual Basic or Visual C++. A custom transform is registered as a task in the DTS Designer from the Task drop-down menu. An example of a custom task might be a utility that can run bcp out of a SQL Server and bcp back into another SQL Server without first saving the data in a text file. Even if designing a custom task is more than you need, you can use ActiveX scripting to enhance your DTS package and do some complex tasks.

ActiveX Scripting

The DTS suite includes an ActiveX scripting engine that makes it very easy to add sophisticated validation and cleansing to your package. ActiveX scripting also makes it possible to change the parameters of connections and tasks dynamically, create new instances of COM objects, or retry connection attempts. For example, using a VBScript file you can prompt the user for the name of a target server when a package is executed, and then set the connection properties accordingly. A script could conditionally bypass certain transformation workflow steps.

The scripting engine supports VBScript, JScript, and PerlScript languages. The Perl language is not installed with either Windows NT or SQL Server. Installing a third-party Perl interpreter is a prerequisite for using this language. Both the VBScript and JScript scripting engines are installed with Internet Explorer.

ActiveX scripts can be used in several places within a DTS package. You saw earlier in this section how ActiveX scripts can be used to create custom transformations in the Data Pump and Data Driven Query tasks. Scripts can also be used in workflow steps and as a standalone script task. When used in a workflow step, the ActiveX script executes before the step completes. This allows the script to change conditionally the properties for the workflow, bypass it, or run it multiple times.

The **DTSGlobalVariables** collection is always exposed in a DTS ActiveX script, regardless of whether it is used in a task, a workflow step, or as a transformation. This collection provides access to variables that are visible to any object in the DTS package and exist until the package finishes execution. You can also use this collection to retrieve an object reference to the parent DTS package object, which can then be used to reference various package collections. For example:

```
'*** VB Script ***
Function Main()
...
Dim DTSPackage, Connection
DTSPackage = DTSGlobalVariables.Parent
Connection = DTSPackage.connections(1)
...
End Function
```

Referencing a global variable that does not exist results in the creation of the variable. Upon creation, a variable is automatically initialized to a value of 0. Common uses for global variables include using a counter to keep track of how many times a loop occurs, or storing the error code from the last task that executed. Another possible use is to create an instance of a COM object, such as an ADO connection, and store the object reference in a global variable. This way, you could create the object as the first task of a package, and subsequent ActiveX scripts can still reference the same object.

Scripts, when they occur as part of a data column transformation in either a Data Pump or Data Driven Query task, also contain automatic references to the **DTSSource** and **DTSDestination** collections. These collections are the paths for setting and getting the column values for the transformation. The specific column values can be referenced by using either the column name or the ordinal column number. Using the ordinal column number results in a much faster script. This code snippet shows an example of validating data by using an ActiveX Script transformation:

```
'**** VB Script ****
Functin Main()
...
DTSDestination("CustomerID") = DTSSource("ID")
DTSDestination(2) = DTSSource(2)
...
End Function
```

A script that is used as a data transformation should end by returning one of several return codes. Tables 16.8, 16.9, and 16.10 list the valid return codes for ActiveX scripts used within a column transformation, a workflow step, and a task, respectively.

Table 16.8 ActiveX return codes from a column transformation.

Return Code	Description
DTSTransformStat_OK	Transformation succeeded.
DTSTransformStat_SkipRow	Cancel processing of the current row. Basically, this is the same as a success return code, except that no data is written to the destination.
DTSTransformStat_SkipFetch	Do not fetch the next row. Instead, process the current row again. Useful for when you want to process the same row multiple times.
DTSTransformStat_SkipInsert	Continues processing the current row, but does not write information to the destination.
DTSTransformStat_Info	The current row processing is successful, but additional information exists.
DTSTransformStat_OKInfo	Combination return code of **DTSTransformStat_OK** plus **DTSTransformStat_Info**.
DTSTransformStat_SkipRowInfo	Combination return code of **DTSTransformStat_SkipRow** plus **DTSTransformStat_Info**.
DTSTransformStat_Error	An error has occurred with processing the current row.
DTSTransformStat_ErrorSkipRow	An error has occurred in the current row, and the remainder of the row processing should be skipped. No data is to be written to the destination.
DTSTransformStat_AbortPump	Aborts all further processing of rows.
DTSTransformStat_NoMoreRows	The Data Pump operation is finished.

Table 16.9 ActiveX return codes from workflow step.

Return Code	Description
DTSStepScriptResult_DontExecute Task	The workflow step should not be executed.
DTSStepScriptResult_ExecuteTask	The workflow step should be started.
DTSStepScriptResult_RetryLater	Postpone the task until later.

Table 16.10 ActiveX return codes from a script task.

Return Code	Description
DTSTaskExecResult_Failure	The task failed.
DTSTaskExecResult_Success	The task succeeded.

Workflow

The workflow steps are the final element of a DTS package. These are individual objects, just like the connection and task objects. A workflow step connects two tasks together to control the flow of a multistep transformation package. Figure 16.11 demonstrates the use of workflow in a package. The striped lines are the workflow steps. The solid line between the Source and Destination connections is a Data Pump task, which has built-in workflow properties. The workflow objects provide a means of determining when each task starts relative to other tasks.

A few different methods, at least, can be used to create the workflow objects. The first method involves selecting the predecessor and successor tasks and choosing the appropriate start condition from the Workflow drop-down menu. Alternately, you can right-click on the successor task, select Workflow Properties, and then enter the dependencies and start conditions. The latter method also allows you to set workflow options on the Options tab.

Start conditions can include On Completion, On Success, or On Failure. Custom logic can easily be introduced by using an ActiveX script to control conditionally the start logic. Select the Options tab on the workflow properties of a successor task (see Figure 16.12) to add the ActiveX script. This also is where you set the advanced workflow options. Table 16.11 lists the description for each of these options.

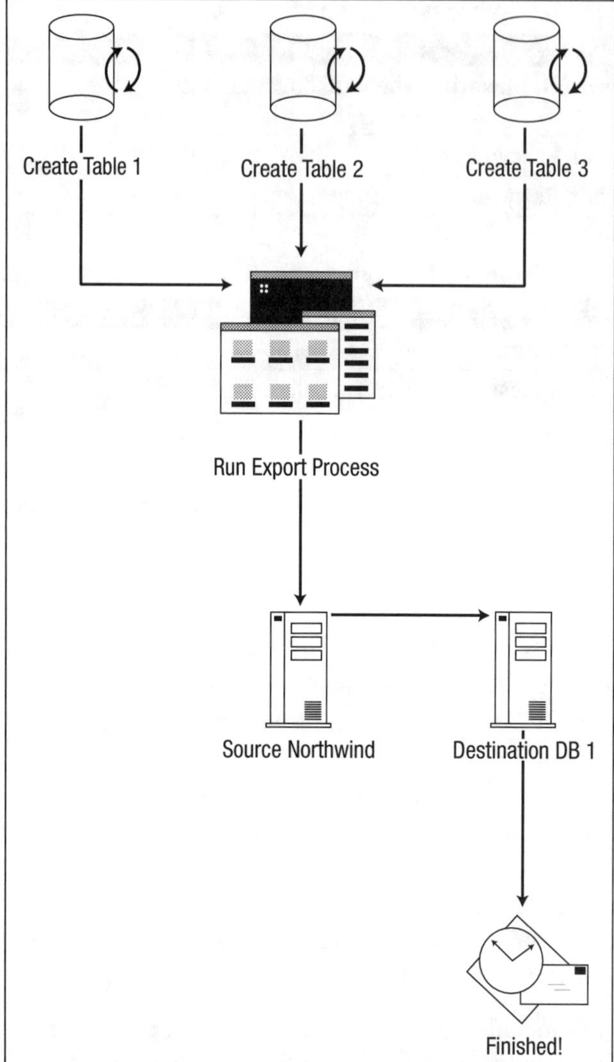

Figure 16.11 A workflow in a DTS package.

Table 16.11 Advanced workflow options.

Option	Description
Join Transaction If Present	A join transaction uses the Distributed Transaction Coordinator (DTC) to use the two-phase commit approach. This may be useful, for example, if you are removing source data rows after you move them to a destination. In this case, you would want to be sure that everything either succeeds or rolls back. Both source and destination OLE DB providers need to support distributed transactions, and DTC needs to be configured and running.

(continued)

Table 16.11 Advanced workflow options *(continued)*.

Option	Description
Commit Transaction On Successful Completion Of This Step.	Specifies that a commit should be issued after this step. You may want to do this even if you are not using distributed transactions if the destination is using implicit transaction mode.
Rollback Transaction On Failure	If the current step fails, a rollback will be issued.
Execute On Main Package Thread	Specifies that the current step should not run on its own thread. Setting this option is useful for debugging, or if the providers don't support multiple connections, and more than one task possibly could attempt to connect to the provider simultaneously.
DSO Rowset Provider	Creates a new data source that can be used with the OLE DB provider for DTS packages. If this option is enabled, the output of this step becomes available to the OLE DB provider and can be configured as a linked server, enabling you to join with scrubbed or transformed information within SQL Server without necessarily needing to move the information into the server.
Close Connection On Completion	Closes the connection on completion of the current step.
Disable This Step	Bypasses the current step. This can also be conditionally controlled by using ActiveX scripts.

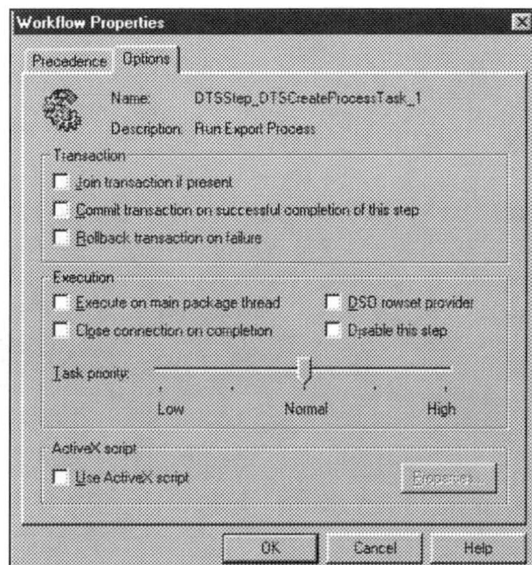

Figure 16.12 Setting advanced options in the workflow step.

16

Transactions In Packages

One additional topic warrants a brief mention here. Because the use of transactions can have far-reaching impact on your systems, it is important to understand how transactions are used within DTS packages. The primary purpose of creating a package is to move information from one place to another, so you must be able to ensure transactional consistency. For example, consider that you have a package that copies changes from two related tables to a destination. You want to be sure that a transfer failure in one of the tables does not introduce broken relationships on the destination connection. At the same time, you don't want to use extensive transactions if doing so isn't necessary to maintain data consistency; otherwise, you lock database resources and could potentially cause the transaction log to fill quickly.

You just saw how distributed transactions can be set up in the workflow step. Transaction use can also be controlled at the package level. From within DTS Designer, choose Package Properties from the drop-down menu and select the Advanced tab. If the Transactions option is enabled, each connection will automatically have implicit transactions enabled. Selecting the Auto Commit Transaction option indicates that the SQL 7 autocommit feature is turned on, which simply means that a commit will automatically be issued after each workflow step. Disabling the Use Transactions option effectively enables the SQL 7 autocommit feature. The isolation level can also be set in this dialog box. Review the chapter on transaction handling and be sure to use the lowest transaction level that still provides data consistency.

CHAPTER SUMMARY

This chapter examined how to import and export information from the database. You also learned:

- Which methods you can use to move, create, and export data from the database.
- How to decide which method is best for what you are trying to do.
- Bulk Copy is the fastest method to get information into and out of the server.
- A Bulk Copy can be completed by using the bcp utility, **BULK INSERT**, or DTS, or from an application using OLE DB and ODBC application programming interfaces.
- Bulk Copy only transfers information between a SQL Server and a text file.
- Data Transformation Services is a flexible framework for defining and storing all data transformations into and out of the database, including bcp operations, and can facilitate transferring data to/from any OLE DB or ODBC data source.

- DTS includes easy-to-use Import and Export Wizards that navigate you through creating a simple transformation package.
- Packages can be stored in the *msdb* database, in the MS Repository, or as a COM object file, and can be executed through the SQL Server Agent.
- DTS Designer includes the Data Pump and Data Driven Query transformation objects, which are the most widely used methods to cleanse and transform data from DTS.
- A DTS package includes connection, task, and workflow objects.
- ActiveX scripting provides a powerful way to customize cleansing and transformations, as well as conditionally alter the task flow.

REVIEW QUESTIONS

1. You are asked to send to another department a one-time text file containing all information from the *Customers* table for the accounts located in the United States. The file will be used to load the information into another database. The best way to complete this task would be to:
   a. Execute an appropriate **SELECT** statement in a Query Analyzer window and save the results as a text file.
   b. Create a DTS package by using the Export Wizard.
   c. Construct a bcp by using the **tableout** option.
   d. Construct a bcp by using the **queryout** option.

2. When using bcp, the **–b*n*** option is used to: (Choose all correct answers.)
   a. Help prevent the transaction log from overflowing.
   b. Issue a commit after every *n* rows.
   c. Give a hint to the optimizer.
   d. This is not a valid bcp command-line option.

3. For Bulk Copy operations, a format file is generally used to: (Choose all correct answers.)
   a. Map table columns to text file columns.
   b. Specify the storage type for text file columns.
   c. Change the row and column delimiters of the text file.
   d. Specify the code page that the data will be converted to.

4. For bcp, which of the following command-line options results in faster operation?
   a. **-CACP**
   b. **-hintTABLOCK**
   c. **-k**
   d. **-x**

5. You can set up a bcp operation by using the DTS Import Wizard.
   a. True
   b. False

6. The DTS package-wide transaction settings are located in:
   a. The Workflow Properties dialog box.
   b. The DTS properties advanced options dialog box.
   c. An ActiveX script.
   d. None exist.

7. The differences between the Data Pump and the Data Driven Query tasks include: (Choose all correct answers.)
   a. The Data Pump includes a Fast Load option, but the Data Driven Query does not.
   b. The Data Pump does not allow a query to be used to supply the source rowset for the transformation, but the Data Driven Query does.
   c. You can use ActiveX scripts to clean information in the Data Driven Query but not in the Data Pump.
   d. Only the Data Driven Query allows you to use stored procedures for inserting into the target table.

8. Using ActiveX scripts can speed the performance of a DTS package.
   a. True
   b. False

9. A Data Pump task is being used to copy data from the *Categories* table. The first two columns in this table are *CategoryID* and *CategoryDescription*. Which of the following statements are valid for retrieving the *CategoryID* source column in an ActiveX script? (Choose all correct answers.)
   a. **cValue = DTSSource(0)**
   b. **cValue = DTSSource(1)**
   c. **cValue = DTSSource().Item(*CategoryID*)**
   d. **cValue = DTSSource(*CategoryID*)**

10. Which of the following statements are true regarding a workflow object in a DTS package? (Choose all correct answers.)
    a. Determines whether a task executes on the main package thread.
    b. Determines the order in which tasks run.
    c. Must be included in a DTS package.
    d. Workflow properties determine package-wide transaction settings.

11. Where can you save a package?
    a. The *msdb* database.
    b. A Microsoft Repository.
    c. A local file.
    d. All of the above.

12. You set the options for a bcp operation not to be logged. The operation fails. What could be a cause?
    a. The target table is marked for replication.
    b. The bcp service is not started.
    c. The **PASSAUTHENT** option has not been set.
    d. None of the above.

13. After a nonlogged operation is run in a database, what must you do to backup the database log?
    a. Modify the *msdb* database to allow log backups.
    b. Change the truncate on checkpoint setting to true for that database.
    c. Perform a full backup or a differential backup.
    d. You can't backup the log after a nonlogged operation.

14. What parameter do you use to specify optimizer hints for the bcp utility?
    a. **-o**
    b. **-f**
    c. **-h**
    d. **-b**

16

15. When using a bcp format file, what should you remember?
    a. The bcp utility cannot read a text file for formats.
    b. The column numbers for the host file are always numbered sequentially.
    c. The bcp format file must be in all caps.
    d. The format file should be located in the same directory as the bcp utility.

HANDS-ON PROJECTS

Brad Shill had been the marketing director for Fitness Unlimited and had been promoted to Acquisitions just one week prior to receiving important news. The CEO wanted talk to him about a takeover of a firm that provided exercise equipment for one of the major U.S. hotel chains. One of the CEO's main concerns was that the data from the company be merged into the new information system that Fitness Unlimited was designing.

The CEO called Susan and asked her to get in touch with the systems people at the new company and "make it happen." Susan determined that the other firm had a fair amount of data in an Oracle database that she would need to add to her own. She contacted the IT manager at the new acquisition and had a copy of some sample data from that company's system put on a tape and sent to her. She had it sent over both in the native database format and as a text file output. Susan first tried to use bcp to transfer data from the sample text file into her database.

Project 16.1

In this project, you will create a script to bcp out all the tables in a database, and then use the bcp utility to move that information back into another database. The data source will be the *Northwind* database on Server1, and the destination will be the *Northwind* database on Server2.

1. Open a new Query Analyzer window and change databases to the *Northwind* database.
2. Type and execute the following query. The results should not be in a grid, but instead should be in plain text:

```
SELECT "bcp Northwind..[" + rtrim(name) + "] out "
       + rtrim(name) + ".dat -c -SServer1 -T"
FROM   sysobjects
Where  type = 'U'
And    uid = 1
```

3. This generates a bcp for each table owned by dbo in the *Northwind* database. Save the results as Scriptbcp.bat in a directory with plenty of free space.
4. Choose Start|Programs|Command Prompt. Change directories to the location where you saved your script is Step 3. Run the script:

```
D:\WIP> Scriptbcp.bat <ENTER>
```

5. Assuming that your target database has already been prepared, we will copy the data back into Server2. Open a new Query Analyzer window and change databases to *Northwind*.
6. Type and execute the following query. The results should not be in a grid, but instead should be in plain text:

```
SELECT  "bcp " + rtrim(name) + ".dat in Northwind..["
        + rtrim(name) + "] -c -SServer2 -T -E"
FROM    sysobjects
where   type = 'U'
and     uid = 1
```

7. Notice in the preceding query that the **–E** option is used, because some of the tables use *Identity* columns, and we want to insert into those columns. Save your results as **Scriptbcpin.bat** in the same directory used for Step 3.
8. From the command prompt, run the script:

```
D:\WIP> Scriptbcpin.bat <ENTER>
```

9. You will see some errors due to using the **–E** option for tables that don't contain *Identity* columns. Don't worry about these messages—they are only warnings. The bcp operation will still succeed.
10. Verify the information in your new database.

The transfer of the text file worked properly, but after another call to the new company's IT staff, Susan found out that some of the data would be from a Microsoft SQL Server 7. "Hey," she thought, "I could use Data Transformation Services!" She spoke with the IT staff and asked whether anyone had used DTS before. "Nope, sorry," came the inevitable answer. "Oh well, I'll have to learn it for the exam anyway." Susan felt that DTS would be a great way to deal with the constant transfer of the data, because some of the DBAs that would be working with the data would be new to SQL Server, and would rather use a GUI to transfer the data. She also felt that having the data in a graphical package that could be modified easily later would help.

16

Project 16.2

Now, we will perform the same task using DTS. We will use the Import Wizard to create a package that uses the Transfer SQL Server Objects task. This package will build the tables, move the data, and copy over all the stored procedures.

1. Open Enterprise Manager and connect to your source server. Choose Tools|Data Transformation Services|Export Data to start the DTS Import and Export Wizard.

2. Click on Next and select Microsoft OLE DB Provider for SQL Server as the source. Type your server name and authentication information. Select the *Northwind* database and click on Next.
3. Enter the same information for the destination. Type the server name of your second server and choose the database that you want to copy to. For this sample, we use the same server with the *tempdb* database. Click on Next to continue.
4. Choose the option labeled Transfer Objects And Data Between SQL Server 7 Databases, and then click on Next.
5. The next screen prompts you to select the objects you want to transfer. The default choices are good for this example. The only items we will modify are the default scripting options. Uncheck the Use Default Options checkbox and click on the associated Options button. All checkboxes should be unchecked except for the following:
   - Transfer Object-Level Permissions
   - Transfer Indexes
   - Transfer Triggers
   - Transfer **PRIMARY** And **FOREIGN** Keys
   - Use Quoted Identifiers When Transferring Objects
6. Click on OK and then click on Next. You now have the option of running the package immediately or scheduling it to run at a later time. Select Run immediately, and save the package on your local SQL Server.
7. The Transferring Data status box is displayed, which gives the status for saving and executing the package.
8. You now have a copy of the *Northwind* database in your *tempdb* database. You can also open the new package and view or modify the settings.

CHAPTER SEVENTEEN

17

IMPLEMENTING FULL-TEXT SEARCH

After Reading This Chapter And Completing The Exercises, You Will Be Able To:

- Understand the difference between a full-text index and a standard index
- Understand the architecture of the full-text search feature
- Install Microsoft Search and configure a new full-text catalog using either SQL commands or the Full-Text Search Wizard
- Create maintenance jobs to keep your full-text catalogs up to date
- Design flexible full-text search queries that use phrases and phrase operators

You have probably seen Web pages where you can enter a phrase and the search function automatically finds all forms of the noun, and then the results are weighted. Previously this type of function was provided by complex programming functions. SQL 7's new full-text search engine gives you tremendous flexibility to implement those types of searches against structured database information.

Full-text searching extends the capabilities of the structured storage engine by allowing you to create special indexes of text and character data. This design also includes new stored procedures and a wizard to make administration easy. Finally, the full-text search adds four powerful query functions to Transact-SQL (T-SQL) that allow you to search on single words, parts of a word, conjugate forms, phrases, and complex combinations of those.

Full-Text Architecture

A *declension* word form is an alternate form of a root word. This translates to variations of tense for verbs, and either singular or plural forms of nouns. For example, alternate forms of the word *computer* includes the words *computers, computing, computed*. This also applies to verbs; for example alternates of *run* include *ran*, *running*, and *runs*.

The traditional ANSI-92 SQL language is designed for standard row and column storage of information. Although you can build indexes on character columns, it is not efficient to search for individual words or phrases within the text. The **LIKE** operator allows you to search for character patterns, but if your search clause is something like **%computer%**, an index on the text column cannot be used. Using the **LIKE** operator, a weighted search, or something like *computer* NEAR *software* is not possible. Rather than character patterns, the full-text engine allows you to search for word patterns, phrase patterns, and declension word forms in either character or text columns. Because these types of searches cannot be efficiently handled in a traditional index structure, a new indexing service has been added—*Microsoft Search*.

The Microsoft Search service is not installed when completing a *typical* or *minimal* installation of SQL Server. To install the full-text search components, you must select the *custom installation* setup and check the *Full-Text* option, which is only available when installing the full edition of SQL Server on an NT Server platform (see Figure 17.1). The full-text components cannot be installed on Windows 95, Windows 98, or NT Workstation installations. If you

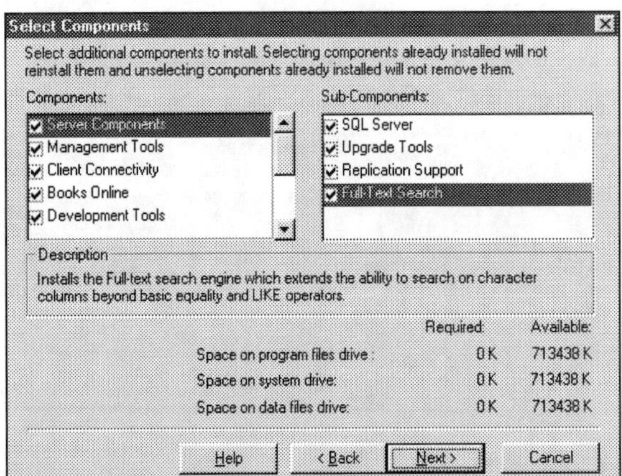

Figure 17.1 Installing full-text search components.

have already installed SQL Server without the full-text components, run the setup from the installation CD again. Select the Full-Text Search component from the Server component menu to add these files to your installation.

Microsoft Search is a service that runs independently from SQL Server, MS Agent, or MS DTC. Think of this service as a specialized index engine for hosting full-text catalogs. It serves two primary purposes:

- **Storage engine** Microsoft Search builds the physical index structures and manages the reads, writes, and caching for the full-text catalogs.
- **Query engine** The service is also a query parser because it determines the most efficient way to implement the requested query.

Figure 17.2 shows the relationship of the service to other database components. During an index refresh or rebuild, the storage engine passes the character-based columns from the source table, along with primary key values and other information, to Microsoft Search. Microsoft Search in turn parses the character strings, builds statistics used in the search process, and stores the index information in special operating system files. The illustration shows another interface between

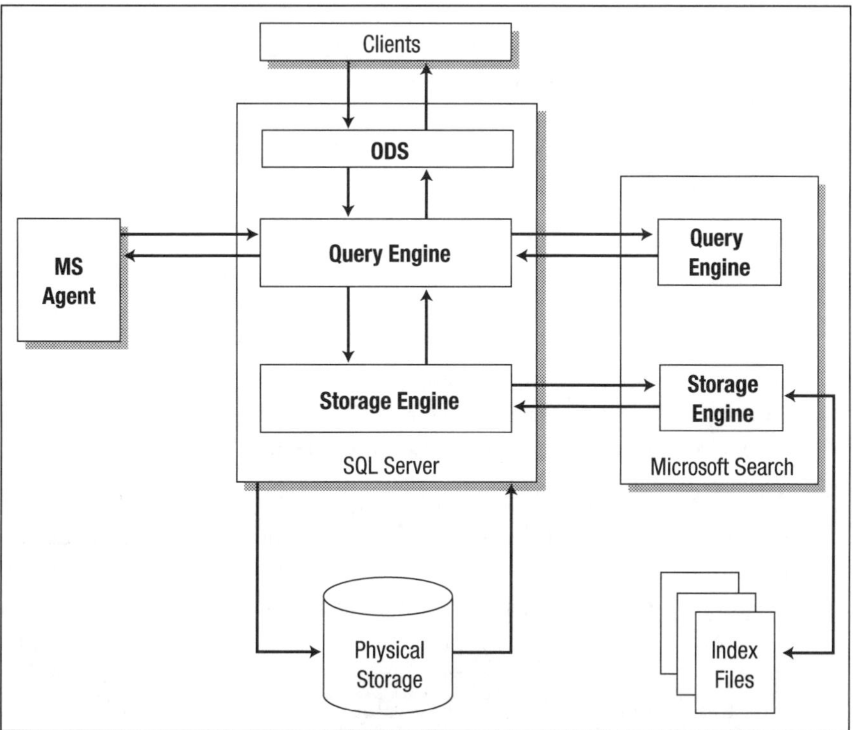

Figure 17.2 Full-text searching architecture.

the database query engine and the search service. When a query is run that references a full-text index, the query engine passes the full-text search request to the search service for processing.

In a query that uses a regular internal index, the query engine traverses a binary tree structure to find the data values contained in the predicate. The leaf-node index pages contain pointers that are used by the query processor to retrieve the data page and row containing the resultant row. The index and pointers are automatically kept updated by the database engine at the same time as the associated data rows. For a review of these concepts refer back to Chapter 6.

A full-text index is not kept updated synchronously with the data rows. The overhead needed for parsing the character strings into words, converting code pages, compiling statistics and the like is far too high. Updating the full-text index synchronously would have a significant negative impact on database performance. Therefore, a full-text index is updated as a scheduled background process during periods of low activity.

Because a full-text index is not always in sync with the latest version of data, the index cannot use pointers to refer back to the physical location of the data rows. That is because the physical pages that data rows are stored on can change as updates to the data are made. For example, updating the key value for a clustered index is one condition that could change the page on which a row is stored. Another situation is page splitting that can occur as new rows are added to a page. In any case, regular pointers would not work because full-text indexes are not updated in real time.

A full-text index references the underlying data source by referencing unique primary key values. Having a unique primary key index is a requirement for defining a full-text index on a table. As the Microsoft Search engine executes a full-text search, the primary key values are passed back into the query engine and are used for resolving the result set of the text search with the rows from the base table. Figure 17.3 illustrates the difference between the use of a full-text index and an internal index in resolving queries.

Although the physical structure of a full-text index is proprietary and unknown, we can derive its logical structure from the functionality it provides. A full-text index includes a reference to a primary key into the source table, words from the original character or text columns, and word positions in the original text. Although a full-text index is probably not stored in strict row and column format, Figure 17.4 is a reasonably good logical representation of what the index looks like. The primary key values are used to join with the data table and produce the results. Index key values, of course, are made up of the decomposed words from the source string and are used for locating the primary key values. A word location exists that facilitates **NEAR** searches. Some usage statistics enable weighted results to be returned.

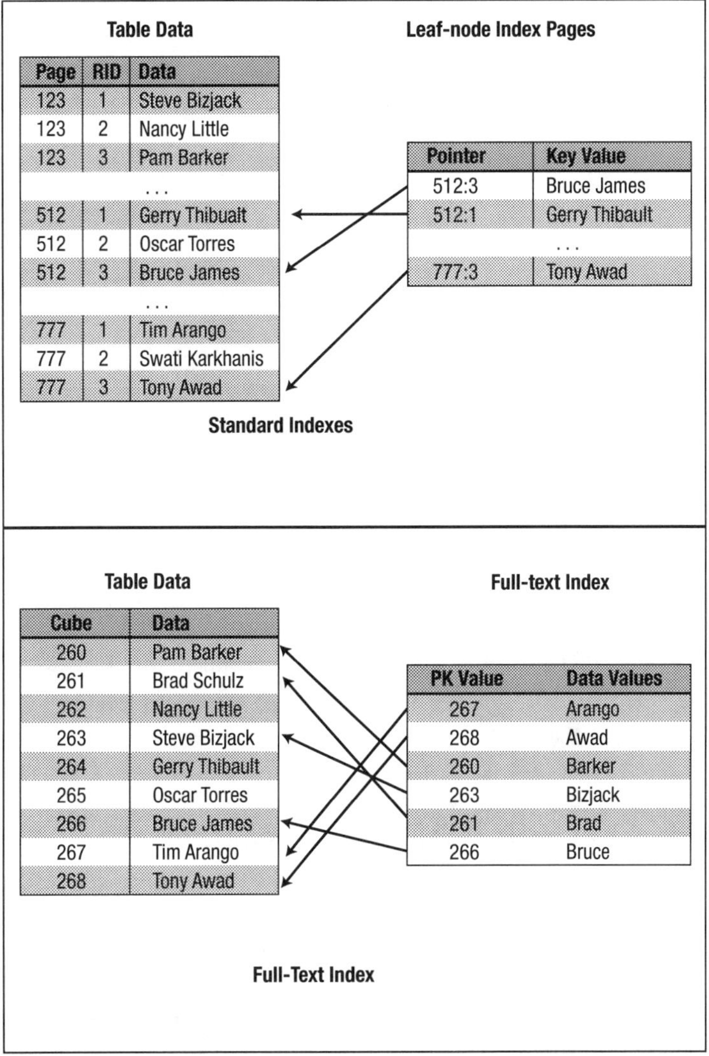

Figure 17.3 Full-text index resolution.

A database can be associated with one or more full-text catalogs, but a catalog can only be related to a single database. Likewise, a catalog can be related to one or more tables, but a table can only be associated to one catalog. Accordingly, within a table, multiple columns can be configured for full-text indexing, although all columns will be contained within the single catalog. Each column that is tagged for full-text indexing results in the creation of an index structure within the catalog. Figure 17.5 illustrates the relationships between databases, catalogs, tables, and columns.

So far, we have examined the components that make up a full-text search. We have looked at Microsoft Search and how it interfaces with data database engine.

ID	DESCRIPTION
38573	SQL LINK 1.0 SYBASE SQL
97414	SQL EMBEDDED SQL TOOLKIT

KEY	WORD	POSITION	STATISTICS
38573	SQL	1	???
38573	LINK	2	???
38573	1.0	3	???
38573	SYBASE	4	???
38573	SQL	5	???
97414	SQL	1	???
97414	EMBEDDED	2	???
97414	SQL	3	???
97414	TOOLKIT	4	???
...			

Figure 17.4 The structure of a full-text index.

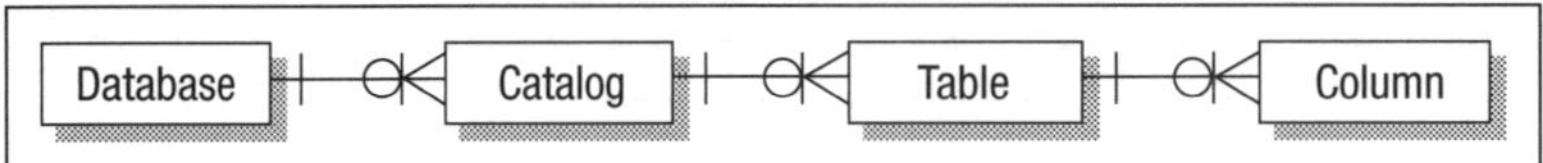

Figure 17.5 Catalog relationships.

We have even looked at the intricacies of how the full-text index operates. Next we will explain how to set up the full-text services, create a catalog, and perform maintenance on those catalogs.

Full-Text Catalog Administration

We have learned that a full-text catalog is not always synchronized with the data rows. A catalog is rebuilt or updated as a scheduled back-ground task. A background task needs some way of knowing which databases, tables, and columns need to be maintained, so in this section we will discuss how to create the *metadata* (data about data) that defines a full-text catalog. We will also learn how to use the setup wizard, set up the background tasks, and fine-tune the Microsoft Search service.

Metadata defining a catalog is stored in many different places. A database is enabled for full-text searching by changing the *status* column in the *sysdatabases* table. Catalogs are defined within a database in the *sysfulltextcatalogs* system table. Once a catalog is defined, tables are tagged as belonging to a full-text catalog by setting the *ftcatid* column in the *sysobjects* system table and the *status* column for the primary key in *sysindexes*. Finally, a column is identified as belonging to a full-text index by setting the *colstat* column in the *syscolumns* system table.

Fortunately, you won't need to learn and manipulate all this metadata manually. A robust set of stored procedures and system functions can be used to simplify setup. Some administrative functions can also be performed from the SQL Server Enterprise Manager. A wizard also makes setting up a catalog a snap.

A number of system stored procedures are provided both for querying the status of database objects relative to full-text indexing and to set up and administrate a full-text catalog. Table 17.1 lists the procedures that can be used.

In addition to these stored procedures, some new systems functions allow you to query the status of the search service or interrogate the properties for database objects in SQL 7. These system functions can be used in T-SQL statements when administrating or researching the system status. Table 17.2 lists the new functions.

Table 17.1 Administration stored procedures.

Procedures Used For Querying Status	
Procedure	**Description**
sp_help_fulltext_catalogs	Retrieves catalog information regarding all catalogs in the current database, or for the catalog specified. If a catalog is specified, it must be defined in the current database.
sp_help_fulltext_columns	Provides a list of columns that are enabled for full-text indexing on the specified table. Alternatively, if a table name is not specified, the procedure will list all tables and columns in the current database and that have been configured for full-text indexing.
sp_help_fulltext_tables	Returns a list of tables set up for full-text searching the specified catalog. If no catalog is given, a list of all tables and the associated catalogs will be given.
Procedures Used For Administering Full-Text Catalogs	
Procedure	**Description**
sp_fulltext_catalog	Used for setting up and maintaining a catalog in a database that has already been enabled for full-text searching. Valid actions include **create**, **drop**, **start_full**, **start_incremental**, **stop**, and **rebuild**.
sp_fulltext_column	Used for adding or dropping a column from a full-text enabled table. Valid actions are **add** or **drop**.
sp_fulltext_database	Enables or disables the current database for full-text searching. If either action is specified, any catalogs, tables, and columns defined for full-text searching in the database are dropped. Valid actions are **enable** or **disable**.
sp_fulltext_service	Establishes service parameters for Microsoft Search. The service priority can be set along with the connection timeout. A third option cleans up catalog files that are no longer in use. Valid actions are **resource_usage**, **clean_up**, and **connect_timeout**.
sp_fulltext_table	Adds or drops a table from a full-text catalog definition. Full-text searching can also be temporarily disabled while maintenance on the index is being performed, or a new column is added or dropped. Valid actions include **add**, **drop**, **enable**, and **disable**.

Table 17.2 System functions.

Function	Description
FullTextServiceProperty()	Returns information about the Microsoft Search service. This can be used to determine if the service has been installed on the system, the current service priority, and the connection timeout.
FullTextCatalogProperty()	Interrogates physical characteristics of a particular catalog. The available properties include the current status of the content, the number of items in the catalog, the size of the index, the size of the log, and so on. This function can also be used to determine the last time the catalog was updated.
DatabaseProperty()	Determines if a database is full-text enabled.
ObjectProperty()	Can be used to determine if a table has an active full-text index, or to determine the primary key used in the full-text catalog.
ColumnProperty()	Can be used to determine if a column is enabled for full-text indexing.

Now let's take a look at how to perform the most common administrative tasks.

Configuring A New Catalog

In most of the examples we have been using the *Northwind* database. However, for these next few examples we will be referring to the *pubs* practice database. This database contains good candidates for full-text indexing. Consider that you are the publisher for all the very best books on SQL 7 and you have set up an Internet searching interface to browse your books. Users would probably want to use full-text searching so they can easily find the books they are looking for. Let's look at how to set up a catalog that can do this.

The first thing we need to do is verify that the full-text search service is properly installed on your system. Run the query to determine if the service is installed on your system:

```
Select FullTextServiceProperty('IsFulltextInstalled')

------
0
```

The query will return a 1 if it is installed, or a 0 if not. As you can see from the preceding example, the full-text service has not been installed on this server. The next step for this server would be to install the full-text indexing components. Assuming the service is installed, we need to enable the database for full-text searching. To do this, open a new Query Analyzer window and run the following T-SQL commands:

```
use pubs
go
sp_fulltext_database @action = 'enable'
go
```

Verify that your database is set up correctly:

```
Select DatabaseProperty('pubs', 'IsFulltextEnabled')
```

If the database is ready, the command will return a 1, or 0 if it is not. Next we need to determine how to set up your catalog. A catalog can contain numerous indexes and can be stored in its own directory structure. You would not want to place several heavily used indexes in the same catalog because that would create a *hot spot* (a location on the drive that is accessed too often for various forms of data) on your disk. It is better to separate heavily used indexes onto separate disks. In this case we will create a catalog just for the *titles* table. Run the following code to create the catalog:

```
Exec sp_fulltext_catalog @ftcat = 'titles_catalog',
                         @action = 'create',
                         @path = 'h:\SpecialTitlesCatalogFolder\FTData'
```

Next, we need to add the *titles* table and *title* column to the newly created catalog, and then activate the catalog. See Listing 17.1.

Listing 17.1 Adding the tables and columns.

```
/*** add the table ***/
Exec sp_fulltext_table @tabname = 'titles',
                       @action = 'create',
                       @ftcat = 'titles_catalog',
                       @keyname = 'UPKCL_titleidind'
go

/*** add the titles column ***/
exec sp_fulltext_column @tabname = 'titles',
                        @colname = 'title',
                        @action = 'add'
go

/*** activate the table ***/
exec sp_fulltext_table @tabname = 'titles',
                       @action = 'activate'
```

We now have a full-text catalog. Let's try a simple query against the new catalog to see how it works. If a user is looking for a good book on the effect of fear on life, they could run this query:

```
Select * from titles where CONTAINS(title, "fear NEAR life")
```

Notice that no data is returned. This might appear strange, because we have successfully completed the setup of the **titles_catalog**. Recall that in the architecture section we determined that a full-text index is not updated synchronously with the data rows. We need to start manually the asynchronous task to repopulate the catalog. Run the following commands to start the process and wait until it is finished.

```
Exec sp_fulltext_catalog @ftcat = 'titles_catalog',
                         @action = 'start_full'
go
while
  (
    select FullTextCatalogProperty
('titles_catalog', 'PopulateStatus')
  ) != 0
    WAITFOR DELAY "00:00:05"
Print "The catalog rebuild is finished!"
```

The catalog should now be fully rebuilt and ready to go. If we run the initial query again we should see a positive result.

Using The Full-Text Catalog Wizard

Instead of using T-SQL commands to set up a new catalog, you can also run the *Full-Text Wizard* to quickly create a new catalog. From the Enterprise Manager console, select the server on which you want to set up a catalog, and then select Tools | Wizards. Within the database tree select the Full-Text Indexing Wizard option.

In the current production release of SQL Server 7, with no service packs installed, the index you use for setting up a table for full-text indexing must be a single-column index. In order words, you cannot use a composite index consisting of more than one column, although it may be unique. Microsoft documentation contains some references to this. Even so, Microsoft has listed this condition as a bug and will allow composite key unique indexes to be used in full-text searching in a later build. In the mean time, if you want to create a full-text index on a table that does not have any single columns that can be used as a unique key, consider altering the table and adding an identity column along with a unique index.

Once inside the wizard, you are asked to select a database on which you want to enable full-text indexing. Next, you select an existing user table defined in the database. Because full-text indexing requires a unique index to exist for the table, you also need to select the unique index that will be used for cross-referencing from the index back to the table. All these choices are presented in an easy-to-use drop-list.

The wizard subsequently displays all columns in the table that have a data type of **CHAR**, **NCHAR**, **TEXT**, or **NTEXT**. Columns defined only as one of these data types can be selected for inclusion in a full-text catalog. Figure 17.6 illustrates the selection of table columns for indexing. If the catalog already existed when run-ning the query and the table you chose was already configured, any columns that already existed in the full-text catalog are also shown.

If you have not set up any catalogs for this database previously, you will need to choose a name for your catalog. If you have already set up one or more catalogs, you can choose one of the existing catalogs or create a new one. Keep in mind the previous discussion regarding the distribution of tables across multiple catalogs. It is not wise to place two highly used tables in the same catalog, or even in two different catalogs on the same disk. That would create unnecessary disk contention.

The final task in using the wizard to help you configure a new index or to modify an existing index, is to create scheduled jobs for building and maintaining the catalogs. The jobs are scheduled at the catalog level and operate on all tables that are placed in that catalog. Remember that individual columns that are placed into a catalog are referred to as *indexes*. A job can be established to fully repopulate a catalog or to incrementally update the catalog. Refer to the following section on catalog maintenance.

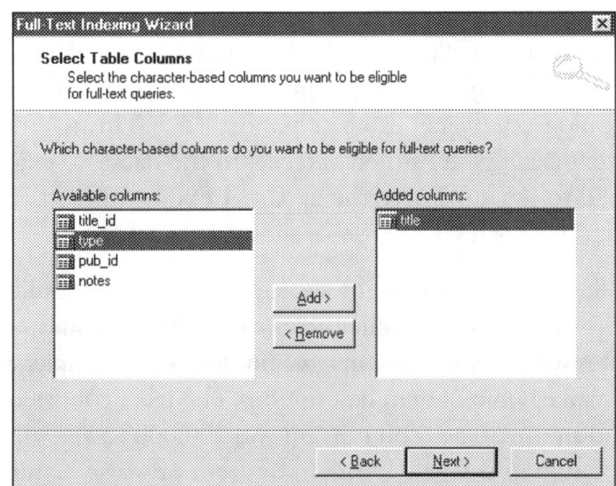

Figure 17.6 Selecting columns to include in the full-text catalog.

17

You are not required to set up refresh jobs at this point. Setting them up or changing them at a later date is reasonable. If you do choose to forgo setting up jobs within the wizard, the catalog will not contain any information when you are finished. Any attempt to run a query will result in this message:

```
Server: Msg 7623, Level 17, State 1, Line 1
Full-text query failed because full-text
catalog 'titles_catalog' is not yet
ready for queries.
```

The best thing to do if you get this message is to manually start a rebuild of the catalog. You can specify full or incremental using the **sp_fulltext_catalog** stored procedure. If you start an incremental rebuild and a table does not have a *timestamp* column, then a full refresh will be used. Run the following command from a Query Analyzer window to begin an incremental update:

```
Exec sp_fulltext_catalog @ftcat = 'titles_catalog',
     @action = 'start_incremental'
```

Even though the incremental mode was specified, a full refresh is implemented, because the table does not have a *timestamp* column.

Maintaining The Catalog

Once you have created a full-text catalog, you will need to keep it updated and perform administrative activities. At some point you will likely want to index more tables and columns. You may also want to turn off full-text search capability on a particular table for a period of time. In this section we will examine how to perform these activities.

Refreshing Catalog Indexes

We have already discussed the need for full-text catalogs to be updated asynchronously from the base table. This is because the overhead associated with building a catalog would slow overall database performance. This is also one of the reasons the full-text catalogs are stored external to the database engine. In any case, you will need to schedule periodic updates of your full-text catalogs. You can use two types of updates: a *full refresh*, and *incremental updates*.

A full repopulating of a catalog is time and resource intensive and should be done only during times of low usage. Even while the catalog is being rebuilt, searches can still be issued, but results may be incomplete and slow. For example, we have created a catalog on a small table of item descriptions. The table consisted of only an *identity* column and the *description* column and was 100,000 rows—a little under 4MB of information in database terms. In our test, we started a full refresh job, and ten minutes later our computer was still working on building the catalog.

Queries against the catalog worked, but were slow. The results contain more rows each time the query is executed while the catalog is rebuilding.

Alternatively, you could also create an incremental update job to maintain a full-text catalog. There is one requirement exists for doing this: The source table must contain a *timestamp* column. As the catalog is updated, only those rows with a timestamp greater than the last time the catalog was rebuilt will be updated. In addition to updating the catalog, if a new column was added or if the catalog has never been built, the incremental update will perform a full refresh. This is another good reason for placing tables in their own catalogs. You would not want to trigger a full refresh of a catalog that hosts a several-million-row table when you decide you want to index a new column.

Creating a job for either type of update is very simple. Either a full refresh or an incremental update can be started with a single T-SQL command. The following command triggers a full refresh:

```
Exec sp_fulltext_catalog @ftcat = '<insert catalog name>',
                         @action = 'start_full'
```

In similar fashion, an incremental refresh is started using this command:

```
Exec sp_fulltext_catalog @ftcat = '<insert catalog name>',
                         @action = 'start_incremental'
```

When you create a job using SQL Agent, you only need to create a single step with one of these commands configured as a T-SQL script. In determining the schedule for the job(s), you need to consider the time that the job will run and how long it will take. Even though database activity might be very low at 7:00 A.M. when the update is begun, if the job runs three hours and user activity picks up heavily at 8:00 A.M., you should reconsider your schedule. The updates should be run when activity on the server is low. You will also want to consider how current the catalog indexes need to be kept. For example, if you run an incremental update once per day, users should understand that changes made today would not be seen in the search results until tomorrow. To solve this problem, you could schedule the incremental update to run more than once per day, for example, noon and midnight. One job should be set up for each catalog placed in service.

Your SQL Agent jobs for updates will complete very quickly, possibly within seconds. This is because these jobs only serve to initiate the background task that updates the full-text catalogs. Using the SQL Agent task history will not give a good indication of how long updates are taking. Using the Windows NT Performance Monitor is perhaps the only reliable method to determine how long refresh jobs are actually taking. The Microsoft Search Indexer Catalogs object within the Performance Monitor contains a build in progress counter. If you

Table 17.3 Catalog populate status values.

Status	Description
0	The catalog is idle. This indicates that a rebuild job is not currently running. A status of 0 does not indicate that the catalog is actually built, however.
1	A population is in progress.
2	Update process has been paused.
3	Indexing has been throttled.
4	Service is recovering.
5	Service is shut down.
6	Incremental update in progress.
7	A full or refresh build is in progress.

monitor the catalog during your update job, you can figure out how long it is taking. Aside from using Performance Monitor, you can run a T-SQL script to determine the current state of the catalog. Table 17.3 lists the possible status values that can be returned. Running the following command provides the current status of the catalog:

```
select FullTextCatalogProperty('titles_catalog', 'PopulateStatus')
```

At some point, you will probably want to be able to determine when a catalog was last updated. The following command will give you that information:

```
select FullTextCatalogProperty
       (
         'titles_catalog',
         'PopulateCompletionAge'
       )
```

However, this command returns the number of seconds that have elapsed between the time the catalog was last rebuilt and midnight on the date 1/1/1900. If you want to return the rebuild date in a more readable format, try the following:

```
declare @secs int
select @secs = FullTextCatalogProperty
              (
                'titles_catalog',
                'PopulateCompletionAge'
              )
select dateadd(ss, @secs, '1/1/90') as LastRebuildDate

LastRebuildDate
```

```
-------------
1999-06-20 14:29:16.000
```

Adding A Column To An Existing Index

The time will probably come when you will want to add additional columns to full-text indexes. Consider the *titles* table that we worked with earlier in this chapter when we created our first full-text index. At that time, we choose to index only the *title* column. However, another column would be favorable to be able to search on: The *notes* column contains comments and additional information regarding the publication.

The first step in adding this column is deactivating full-text search on the *titles* table. A new column cannot be added to an active catalog. To disable full-text searching run:

```
exec sp_fulltext_table 'titles', 'deactivate'
```

Next, add the new column and reactivate the index:

```
exec sp_fulltext_column 'titles', 'notes', 'add'
exec sp_fulltext_table 'titles', 'activate'
```

Once this command is run, users can begin searching against the index. Queries referencing the *notes* column will succeed, but will not return any results. This seems to conflict with the results we saw when the catalog was first created. In that case, querying against the catalog returned the following error:

```
Server: Msg 7623, Level 17, State 1, Line 1
Full-text query failed because full-text catalog 'titles_catalog'
is not yet ready for queries.
```

You will not receive that error when the newly indexed *notes* column is referenced. That is because the catalog was previously populated and contains information, even though no index data is specifically related to this column. To repopulate the catalog with the new data, run the following script:

17

```
exec sp_fulltext_catalog 'titles_catalog', 'start_incremental'
```

Because the *titles* table does not contain a *timestamp* column, the entire **titles_catalog** will be repopulated.

Dropping A Catalog

If you decide that users are not using your new full-text catalog, you can easily remove it. Removing a full-text catalog is as easy as building it and requires only a few commands. First, drop the tables that are enabled in the catalog you want to drop. Dropping the table automatically deactivates the index and removes the associated columns. To drop the *titles* table from our catalog, run the following:

```
exec sp_fulltext_table 'titles', 'drop'
```

This is the only table associated with the *titles_catalog* catalog. We are ready to drop the catalog. To drop the catalog, run:

```
exec sp_fulltext_catalog 'titles_catalog', 'drop'
```

This command will work even if the Microsoft Search service is not active at the time. However, if this happens, the catalog metadata will be out of sync with the actual search service files and you will need a facility to clean up the orphaned files. The following command will remove any catalog files that do not have corresponding entries in *sysfulltextcatalogs*:

```
Exec sp_fulltext_service @action = 'clean_up'
```

Catalog Backup And Restore

Because the full-text indexes reside external to the database, they are not backed up during a regular database backup or restore. None of the database backup mechanisms—full database, differential, log, or file group—will back up the full-text index files. This is important to know when planning a full-text search system or a disaster recovery plan.

In order to back up the full-text catalog files, you first need to stop the Microsoft Search service. Stopping the service closes the operating system files and enables them to be read by backup software. Each catalog can be stored in different file folders, so it is necessary to catalog the directory paths when planning a backup strategy. To determine the path for each catalog, query the *sysfulltextcatalogs* table in each database in which a catalog exists. The *path* column contains the parent folder name for the catalog files. If the path has a **NULL** value in this table, the default path is used. A default path is established when the search service is installed. Its location can be retrieved from the registry by issuing the command:

```
exec master..xp_regread 'HKEY_LOCAL_MACHINE',
                        'SOFTWARE\Microsoft\MSSQLServer\MSSQLServer',
                        'FulltextDefaultPath'
```

Alternately, you can right-click on the Full-Text Services icon in the Support Services tree within Enterprise Manager. The default path is displayed on the General tab.

In any case, once you know where the catalog information is stored, you are ready to perform a backup. This type of backup is commonly referred to as a *file-system backup* because it is based on backing up the physical operating system files rather than the logical information as in a database backup. You can choose between the native backup utility that is installed with Windows NT and third-party backup software.

If a restore of this backup becomes necessary, it must be restored to the same file path. You cannot use this method to back up a large full-text catalog and restore it to another location. If the catalog needs to be moved, you will need to drop the catalog and rebuild it in the other location. This can be a lengthy process if the base table is large. This point should be a consideration when planning the location for full-text catalogs.

QUERYING

Most sections of this book use either the *Northwind* or *pubs* practice databases for the examples so you can follow along. However, those practice databases don't contain much data. For this section, we are using part of a table from a real-world application in the examples. The information necessary to create this practice table is included on the CD-ROM, and the first hands-on practice at the end of this chapter provides instructions for creating this table on your system.

So now you have studied the architecture of full-text searching, have built your first catalog, and know how to administer it, and are ready to learn how to use the full-text indexes in queries and unleash full-text searching in your applications. SQL Server 7 provides four new system functions that deal specifically with full-text searching. In the sections that follow we will take a look at each of the functions individually. Many elements of each function are common to the others and will be covered in the **CONTAINS** section.

Full-text search capabilities have two primary forms. The first method uses the **CONTAINS** predicate function for resolving searches. This form, although flexible, is more precise and surgical than other methods. For example, using **CONTAINS** to search for the phrase *tower computers* with *gray cabinets* would return all rows that contain this exact phrase. Alternatively, you could use the **FREETEXT** predicate function for completing this search. Using **FREETEXT** breaks up the phrase into individual words, including inflectional forms of the words, and compiles a weighted response.

CONTAINS

The **CONTAINS** function is used as part of the **WHERE** clause in a **SELECT** statement to specify a full-text search condition to the query engine. The syntax for this function is somewhat complex:

```
CONTAINS( <column>|*, <search condition> )

Where

<search condition> is one of the following:

1.   <simple term>           e.g. 'computer'
2.   <multiple simple term>  e.g. 'computer OR software'
3.   <phrase>                e.g. ' "computer software" '
4.   <proximity>             e.g. 'computer NEAR software'
5.   <prefix>                e.g. ' "computer*" '
6.   <inflectional>          e.g. 'FORMSOF(INFLECTIONAL, computer)'
7.   <weighted>              e.g. 'ISABOUT( computer weight(.8) )'
```

Let's take a few of these methods of specifying the search condition. Consider a situation where you simply want to find all the products that contain the word *computer*. You could execute this query:

```
SELECT *
FROM   INVENTORY_HEADER
WHERE  CONTAINS( *, 'computer' )

id          Description
------      ------------------------
8494        COMPUTER SPEAKER PAIR
8513        COMPUTER SPK PR W/
8514        COMPUTER SPK SYS SUBWOOF
10940       GREAT COMPUTER ADVENTURE
10953       COMPUTER CARNIVAL
15963       CGS 250  250 VA COMPUTER
15964       CGS 350  350 VA COMPUTER
...
```

Notice that the search condition is given in lowercase, but the query found items that contain the keyword in uppercase. The full-text search is not case sensitive. In this example, an * is given in place of a column name. If more than one column from the *INVENTORY_HEADER* table is enabled for full-text indexing, the search will search in each of the columns.

This was a fairly straightforward search. But suppose you want to look for any form of the word *computer*, including *computers*, *compute*, or *computing*. For this, let's try using the *inflectional* word search:

```
SELECT *
FROM   INVENTORY_HEADER
WHERE  CONTAINS
         ( *,
           'FORMSOF( INFLECTIONAL, computers )'
         )

id          Description
------      ---------------------
7993        HOW COMPUTERS WORK
98419       THE WAY COMPUTERS AND

(2 row(s) affected)
```

In this case, the keyword was changed from *computer* to *computers* to illustrate a point. Notice that only two items were returned, and that all the items containing the word *computer* disappeared from the results. For nouns, the inflectional search is designed to find the singular and plural of the word, and for verbs to find different forms of the tense and case. However, this time it appears that did not happen. This is because the Microsoft Search service does not include the word *computer* in its internal dictionary. In order to get the desired results you need to format the query as follows:

```
SELECT *
FROM   INVENTORY_HEADER
WHERE  CONTAINS( *, 'comput*' )

id          Description
------      ------------------------
7993        HOW COMPUTERS WORK
8494        COMPUTER SPEAKER PAIR
30174       COMPUTEREASY DRAW WIN 3.5
46385       COMPUTONE ATVANTAGE 4
48103       8MB PWR COMPUTING POWER
...

(91 row(s) affected)
```


Let's try something a little more sophisticated. Suppose you wish to find all the fax modems in your tables. A normal binary search for any word returns 982 rows. However, you can use this search incrementally:

```
SELECT *
FROM   INVENTORY_HEADER
WHERE  CONTAINS( *, 'fax NEAR modem')
```

Replacing the **NEAR** keyword with **AND** returns the same results in this case. Another way to accomplish this is to weight the search words. Consider the following:

```
select *
from   INVENTORY_HEADER
where  CONTAINS( *, 'ISABOUT (fax weight (.9), modem weight(.1) )')

id          Description
-----       -------------------------
59751       MODEM T1 850 MM 15DB
57735       336 SPANISH EXT MODEM
57558       RJ45 TO DB25 MODEM CABLE
44039       CC MAIL FAX SVR MAINT RWL
43655       FAX SVR FOR NOTES LIC/
...
(982 row(s) affected)
```

Notice that the first three results contain the word *modem* but do not contain the word *fax*. You might think that the rows containing both *fax* and *modem* would appear near the top of the returns, because they are weighted more heavily. However, in this situation the results are not sorted in any particular order. To sort the results by their weighting you will use the **CONTAINSTABLE** function described below.

Let's try our search one more time. This time we will simply search for the phrase *fax modem*. Here are the results:

```
SELECT *
FROM   INVENTORY_HEADER
WHERE  CONTAINS( *, ' "fax modem" ')

id          Description
-----       ------------------------
41511       14.4 INT. FAX/MODEM BULK
79495       PCMCIA FAX MODEM 24/96
53479       PAGEMARQ INT FAX MODEM
41510       14.4 INT. FAX/MODEM BULK
41353       28.8 FAX MODEM EXT
41368       28.8 EXTERNAL FAX MODEM
41367       28.8 INTERNAL FAX MODEM

(110 row(s) affected)
```

You have seen most forms of searching with the **CONTAINS** function. In addition to these examples, you can also combine these methods together. For example, you can sandwich a **NEAR** between two **FORMSOF()** statements. Like-wise, within a **ISABOUT()**, you can use phrases or expressions in place of the simple single words that are being weighted.

FREETEXT

Another form of full-text searching is a little less rigid on the syntax. Using the **FULLTEXT** function, you can simply give *fuzzy* (less precise) phrases that you want to search on. The **FULLTEXT** algorithm breaks the phrases down into individual words, including their inflectional forms, and executes the equivalent of a binary **OR** search. We saw above that using **CONTAINS** to search for the phrase *fax modem* returns 110 rows. If we perform the same phrase search using **FREETEXT**, we see 982 rows returned.

Try running this query:

```
SELECT *
FROM   INVENTORY_HEADER
where  FREETEXT( *, ' "I want a mobile phone and airplane!" ')

id          Description
-----       ----------------------
43432       CC:MAIL MOBILE MAINT
43076       CC:MAIL MOBILE TO NOTES
...
42343       PHONE NOTES MAIN/INST
...

(186 row(s) affected)
```

The **FREETEXT** function does not recognize any of the special search operators that can be used with **CONTAINS**. Operators include, **AND**, **OR**, **NEAR**, *, **&**, |, and ~. It also ignores noise words and punctuation. Although the function is not an English phrase parser, you can enter full sentences and get the desired search results. However, the matching algorithm for **FREETEXT** is much more liberal than that used with **CONTAINS**. If you are using **FREETEXT** and are getting frustrated with meaningless results, you should be using **CONTAINS**.

17

CONTAINSTABLE

Instead of being used in the predicate section of a **SELECT** statement, the **CONTAINSTABLE** function is used in place of a table. It has nearly identical syntax as the **CONTAINS** predicate function, but returns a rowset containing the key value and rank of the results. The only difference in the syntax of the function is that the table name must be supplied as the first parameter. All other parameters and options are the same. Consider the following query:

```
SELECT *
FROM   CONTAINSTABLE
        (
          INVENTORY_HEADER, *,
          'ISABOUT (fax weight (.9), modem weight(.1) )'
        )

KEY          RANK
-----        ----
59751        13
57735        13
57558        13
44039        137

(982 row(s) affected)
```

This is the information that normally is returned by the search service to the query engine to resolve a full-text search. In an earlier section we discussed the difference between a full-text index and a regular internal database index. The *key* column contains the primary key values of the base table and can be used to join with the base table. In the following query, the query will be turned into a more usable format:

```
SELECT ih.id, ih.Description, ft.RANK
FROM   CONTAINSTABLE
        (
          INVENTORY_HEADER, *,
          'ISABOUT (fax weight (.9), modem weight(.1) )'
        ) ft
JOIN   INVENTORY_HEADER ih
  ON   ft.[KEY] = ih.id
ORDER BY RANK desc

id       Description                 RANK
-----    -------------------------   ----
57592    FAX MODEM INT W/FAX WORKS   317
57594    FAX MODEM EXT W/FAX WORKS   317
37635    FAX 625 THERM FAX           301
41511    14.4 INT. FAX/MODEM BULK    152
79495    PCMCIA FAX MODEM 24/96      152
53479    PAGEMARQ INT FAX MODEM      152
...
(982 row(s) affected)
```

Executing full-text queries in this fashion adds a powerful means of ranking and sorting results. You can also add a predicate to limit the rows coming back based on rank. In other words, you could add the predicate to limit the number of rows returned:

```
WHERE RANK > 100
```

Doing this may not improve the performance of the query, because all the rows from Microsoft Search still need to be returned so that the query optimizer can apply the predicate condition.

FREETEXTTABLE

Like the **CONTAINSTABLE** statement, the **FREETEXTTABLE** statement is used in place of a table in the query statement and returns the key and rank from the search results. The syntax and usage is exactly like the **FREETEXT** predicate function, with the exception that the first parameter must be the table name. Listing 17.2 is an example.

Listing 17.2 Using the **FREETEXT** statement

```
select  id, Description, RANK
from    FREETEXTTABLE
        (
           INVENTORY_HEADER, *,
           ' "I want a good SQL book" '
        ) ft
join    INVENTORY_HEADER ih
  on    ft.[KEY] = ih.id
order by RANK desc

id       Description               RANK
-----    -----------------------   ----
38573    SQL LINK 1.0 SYBASE SQL   122
97414    SQL EMBEDDED SQL TOOLKIT  122
94272    4MB POWER BOOK 230 UPGRD  85
94037    6MB APPLE PWR BOOK 100    85
74567    FERN GULLY COLORING BOOK  85
...
```


Chapter Summary

In this chapter you learned about the exciting new full-text indexing capabilities of SQL 7. You also learned the following:

- The difference between the character-oriented **LIKE** search and the word-oriented full-text search.

- A full-text index is stored external to the database.
- A full-text index is not backed up as part of a database backup.
- Full-text indexes are not updated realtime with data updates; they are updated via scheduled batch jobs.
- A full-text index requires the existence of a single-column primary key.
- How to create a full-text catalog using both catalog stored procedures and the Full-Text Wizard.
- How to add additional columns to an existing full-text catalog.
- How to schedule jobs to incrementally or fully repopulate a full-text catalog.
- How to design queries that use full-text searching features, including **CONTAINS**, **FREETEXT**, **CONTAINSTABLE**, and **FREETEXTTABLE**.

Review Questions

1. You are responsible for administrating a large database system. Part of the system includes databases named *Customer*, *Product*, and *Ordering*. A user is running the following query:

   ```
   select * from CUSTOMER..CUSTOMER_MASTER cm left join
   ORDERING..[Order Details] od on cm.customerID = od.customerID join
   PRODUCT..PARTS p on p.productID  = od.productID where contains
   (p.Description, 'fax AND modem')
   ```

   The user has called the help desk to report that a particular part number is not showing up in the results. Which of the following is the most likely reason the item is not showing up?

   a. The Microsoft Search service is not running.

   b. A full-text catalog can only be associated with a single database.

   c. An incremental update needs to be run on the catalog containing the *Description* column.

   d. A full refresh needs to be run on the catalog containing the *Order Details* table.

2. Your company is located in Miami, Florida, and because an active hurricane season is forecast, your company is making business recovery plans. You are asked to make recovery plans for the database servers. You already have data-base backup tapes sent to the recovery site on a daily basis, and have weekly backups of the file system sent there also. Which of the following tasks would you add to your recovery plan in order to restore a full-text index?

a. Restore the full-text catalog directories and subsequently run a full refresh of the full-text catalogs.

b. Bypass restoring the full-text catalog directories and run a full refresh of the full-text catalogs.

c. Restore the database and subsequently run an incremental update on the full-text catalogs.

d. None of the above.

3. You are setting up a full-text catalog to give Web users the ability to run flexible searches against your product catalog. As part of this activity you run the following script:

```
exec sp_fulltext_table @tabname = 'products', @action = 'create',
@ftcat = 'product_catalog', @keyname = 'PK_productid'
go
exec sp_fulltext_column @tabname = 'products', @action = 'add',
@colname = 'description'
go
exec sp_fulltext_catalog @ftcat = 'products', @action = 'start_full'
go
```

What is the most likely reason that a query against the newly created catalog fails?

a. The full-text catalog is not enabled.

b. The table is not activated.

c. Microsoft Search is not running.

d. The preceding create script contains a syntax error.

4. You are a developer and have been given the task of providing the ability to provide character pattern searching. You want to be able to search on two very large tables in your database. The first table, *Titles*, contains over 10 million published titles that your company sells. The second table, *Reviews*, contains over 50 million reviews for these titles. Which of the following is the best way to design the system?

a. Create two separate full-text catalogs. One catalog is placed on the C:\ drive, and the other catalog is placed on the D:\ drive.

b. Create two separate full-text catalogs. One catalog is placed in the C:\CATALOGS\CATALOG1 directory, and the other catalog is placed in the C:\CATALOGS\CATALOG2 directory.

c. A full-text catalog is not needed. Create a regular database index on both the *Titles* and *Reviews* tables.

d. None of the above is a good design.

5. Your company provides data processing services for law enforcement offices around the country. One service that your company provides is the ability to perform a text search on a national database of crime events. The users need to be able to find crime events as soon as they occur and are logged into the database so that they can correlate possible suspects as they are spotted on the streets. Search activity is heavy between 8:00 A.M. and 9:00 P.M. EST, but greatly tapers off after that. The best way to design this system is:
   a. Create a full-text catalog and set up two update jobs per day. One will be at noon and the other at midnight. Explain to users that crimes logged into the system between these times will not be available until the next update.
   b. Create a full-text catalog and set up one update job that will run between 9:00 P.M. and 8:00 A.M. EST.
   c. Create a full-text catalog and schedule incremental updates once each hour, because an update can be run at the same time that users are searching the system. Explain to users that there could be a one-hour latency time after a crime is entered into the system.
   d. Create a full-text catalog and set up a full-refresh job every morning at 7:00 A.M. before the heavy search activity begins.

6. A very large database in your department contains a list of all publications that can be purchased through **www.WhatsThatRiver.com**. The server name is *BIGBOOKS* and contains a database named *DATABASEBOOKS*. You discover that you cannot connect to the server using named pipes, but are able to connect using TCP/IP. The president of the company is out of town trying to pick up additional contracts for selling more titles, but wants each subject stored in a different database. Your favorite user, who has never used SQL Server before, calls and want you to teach him how to design a query for selecting SQL Server books with good reviews. Millions of titles exist, but the number of titles with good reviews is very small. The table containing that information has two relevant columns. The first one, *titles*, contains descriptions for all of the books. The second, *comments*, contains a summary of the book reviews. Which of the following queries is the best design for the user?
   a. `select * from CONTAINSTABLE('sqlbooks', *, 'SQL ~ good')`
   b. `select * from FREETEXTTABLE('sqlbooks', *, 'I want to find all good SQL books')`
   c. `select * from sqlbooks where CONTAINS( *, 'SQL AND good')`
   d.
   ```
   select * from sqlbooks where CONTAINS( titles, 'SQL*')
   union all
   select * from sqlbooks where CONTAINS( comments,
   'FORMSOF(INFLECTIONAL, good)' )
   ```

7. You are designing a query for a good friend, who wants to know which homes have either or both a pool and hot tub. However, he is most interested in having a pool. Which of the following will return such a list prioritized to favor pools?

   a. ```
      select * from homes h join containstable(homes, features,
      'ISABOUT(pool weight(0.9), hot tub* weight (0.5))' ft
          on ft.[KEY] = h.[KEY]
          order by RANK desc
      ```

   b. ```
      select * from homes h join freetexttable(homes, features, 'homes
      with both pool and hot tub') ft
          on ft.[KEY] = h.[KEY]
          order by RANK desc
      ```

   c. ```
      select * from homes where contains(features, 'ISABOUT(pool
      weight(0.9), hot tub* weight (0.5))'
          order by RANK desc
      ```

   d. All the above.

8. The differences between **CONTAINS()** and **FREETEXT()** include: (Choose all correct answers.)

   a. You cannot perform a weighted search using **CONTAINS()**.
   b. You cannot search for a sentence using **CONTAINS()**.
   c. **FREETEXT()** breaks the phrase into individual words.
   d. **NEAR** is not a search operator in **FREETEXT()**.

9. Which function returns a rowset containing the key value and rank of the results?

   a. **CONTAINSTABLE**
   b. **CONTAINS**
   c. **HAVING**
   d. **ROWSET()**

10. The **FREETEXT** function does not recognize any of the special search operators that can be used with **CONTAINS**.

    a. True
    b. False
      ```

11. The full-text search:

```
SELECT *
FROM INVENTORY_HEADER
WHERE CONTAINS ( *,'FORMSOF( INFLECTIONAL, computer )')
```

could return which of the following?

   a. computers, computer, COMPUTERS
   b. COMPUTERS, COMPUTER, COMPUTERS
   c. computers, computer
   d. All of the above.

12. To remove the full-text catalog from the titles table, which command should you execute?
   a. **exec sp_fulltext_table titles, drop**
   b. **DROP TEXTINDEX** 'titles'
   c. **exec sp_fulltext_table'titles', 'drop'**
   d. **DROP TEXTINDEX ON** titles

13. What should you do first when you wish to add a column to an existing full-text index?
   a. Run the command **exec sp_fulltext_table 'tablename', 'add_column'**
   b. Deactivate the full-text search on the table.
   c. Remove all Primary Key references to the table.
   d. Change the session-level **'COLUMN_REF'** to **'TRUE'** for the table.

14. Why would using the SQL Agent task history not give a good indication of how long updates are taking to maintain a full-text catalog?
   a. The Agent cannot be used to maintain a full-text catalog.
   b. Agent jobs serve only to initiate the background task that updates the full-text catalogs.
   c. The Agent will not report the process until the refresh process is complete.
   d. The system clock may not be an accurate gauge for this activity.

15. When using the wizard to create a full-text index, which columns are displayed for inclusion?
   a. **CHAR, NCHAR, TEXT, NTEXT**
   b. **CHAR, NCHAR, TEXT, MEMO**
   c. **CHAR, NCHAR, NTEXT**
   d. **TEXT, NTEXT**

HANDS-ON PROJECTS

Susan wanted to provide some "oomph" in her database and had been researching the full-text function. She knew that the programmers would not want an additional load placed on their requirements by asking them to create a full-text search function, but she knew from her reading that she could create one within the database. First, she set her server to use the Full-Text Service.

Project 17.1

In this project, you will create a new table in the *Northwind* database. Sample data is included on the CD-ROM accompanying this book. You will then create a full-text catalog that can be used to follow the examples in the "Querying" section of this chapter. The data file that is included on the CD-ROM is a little under 3MB. However, the table in the database will take up a little more than 4MB. Be sure your file group for the *Northwind* database is set to allow autogrowth. Also, the full-text catalog will consume approximately 130MB of disk space once it is fully built. Be sure you have a drive with plenty of free space before attempting this project.

1. This first step involves creating the table in the *Northwind* database. Place the CD-ROM that came with this book in your CD-ROM drive. For this project we will use D: as the drive letter for your CD-ROM drive. If your drive letter is different, substitute the actual drive letter wherever D: appears in the instructions.
2. Open a new Query Analyzer window and log in to your database server.
3. Choose File | Open from the drop-down menus and open the file D:\Projects\Chapter17\Project1\INVENTORY_HEADER.sql.
4. You should now have a script on your screen. Running this script will create the *INVENTORY_HEADER* table in your *Northwind* database. Go ahead and execute the script now.
5. Now we need to load the table with data. To do this, open a Command Prompt window.
6. Type: "CD /D D:\Projects\Chapter17\Project1" and press Enter.

   Type in and run the following BCP command, substituting your server name for the -S parameter:

```
BCP Northwind..INVENTORY_HEADER in INVENTORY_HEADER.dat
-STENNPRESS -T -f inventory_header.fmt -b 10000
```

   This should result in over 100,000 rows being added to the *INVENTORY_HEADER* table.

17

7. Verify the number of rows in the table. Open a new Query Analyzer window and run the command: **Exec sp_spaceused INVENTORY_HEADER**. If are fewer than 100,000 rows result, please check the output from Steps 1 through 6 and repeat as necessary.
8. Now create the full-text catalog. Open a new Query Analyzer window.
9. Make sure the full-text components are installed. From a Query Analyzer window, type in and run the command:

```
Select FullTextServiceProperty('IsFullTextInstalled')
```

   If this does not return 1 you do not have the full-text services installed. Please install the full-text search components.

Next, Susan tested her new functionality. She knew if this worked properly, she would have quite the feather in her database cap.

Project 17.2

1. Make sure the Microsoft Search service is running. Open the SQL Server Service Manager and select Microsoft Search. If it is not shown to be running, start the service by clicking the Start/Continue button.
2. From a Query Analyzer window, type in and execute the following script:

```
Use Northwind
go

/*** enable the database for full-text searching ***/
exec sp_fulltext_database @action = 'enable'
go

/*** create a new catalog ***/
exec sp_fulltext_catalog @ftcat = 'Northwind', @action = 'create',
@path = 'C:\MSSql7\FTDATA'
go

/*** create the table index ***/
exec sp_fulltext_table @tabname = 'INVENTORY_HEADER',
@action = 'create', @ftcat = 'Northwind', @keyname = 'I1'
go

/*** add the column to the index ***/
exec sp_fulltext_column @tabname = 'INVENTORY_HEADER',
@colname = 'Description', @action = 'add'
go
```

```
/*** activate the table ***/
exec sp_fulltext_table @tabname = 'INVENTORY_HEADER',
@action = 'activate'

/*** start a full refresh ***/
exec sp_fulltext_catalog @ftcat = Northwind,
@action = 'start_full'
go
```

3. You now have a full-text catalog configured for the practice table. Depending on the speed of your server, the rebuild of the catalog might take some time.

CHAPTER EIGHTEEN

18

MAINTAINING A DATABASE

After Reading This Chapter And Completing The Exercises, You Will Be Able To:

- Gain a better understanding of the storage architecture
- Understand the issues behind database consistency checking
- Plan appropriate consistency checking for your database
- Identify the existence of database fragmentation and be able to plan corrective action
- Recognize the symptoms of out-of-date index statistics and be able to take corrective action

Although this text will help you prepare for the SQL developer exam, you need to understand some of the key considerations of database administration that can impact your design and performance. A well-maintained database is like the speakers in a high-fidelity sound system. Even with the best amplifier and sound source in the world, the sound quality won't be very good if the speakers aren't performing well. The same holds true with database design. All too often, developers understand the basics of design and implementation, but if they do not have a good understanding of maintenance and problem solving, the system is not going to reach its potential. The topics covered in these next two chapters make up one of the five major topics in the certification exam.

Database Consistency

Webster's dictionary defines *consistency* as a "condition of adhering together, as the parts of a body; firmness; coherence." By now you understand that a database system is a sophisticated, highly structured system for storing and retrieving information. It is very important that all the elements of user data, system catalog information, and storage structures be made completely consistent with one another. When errors creep into storage structures, or catalog information gets out of sync with user data, performance can severely degrade. You could even experience loss of data. It is important to study the recommended maintenance activities for a database.

Traditional database systems require a great deal of performance tuning and maintenance. SQL Server 7 has made significant progress by providing automated tuning parameters and self maintenance. Some database maintenance still needs to be performed manually, and you need to understand these required maintenance activities. In addition, you may want to disable the automated maintenance options so you can exercise more control over the database environment.

A particular collection of Transact-SQL commands is used for checking database consist-ency; it is referred to as the *Database Consistency Checking* (*DBCC*) commands. Each command is prefaced by the **DBCC** keyword and should be run on regular intervals to verify database structural integrity. Before we delve into the details for these commands, we will examine a brief primer of the related database storage architecture. Gaining a deeper understanding in this area will help you make better maintenance plans and allow you to be able to define the concepts behind the maintenance.

Storage Primer

Earlier chapters in this book covered the higher-level structures for the database, including databases, filegroups, files, tables, indexes, and pages. Now we will explore these concepts a bit further, examining how pages are used and allocated within the files and are associated with database objects. Remember that a page contains 8,096 bytes (8K) of storage, and that eight contiguous pages are organized into a unit referred to as an *extent*. A page is the basic building block for storage in the database, and an extent is the primary unit, or container, with which space is managed in the database.

Table 18.1 lists the seven types of pages found in a SQL 7 database. A page can be allocated to a single database object. Multiple tables cannot share the same data page, and an extent usually belongs to a single object. However, because an extent is 64K of storage, the database may decide to share the extent between several smaller objects to conserve space.

Table 18.1 The SQL 7 page types.

Page Type	Description
Data	Contains rows for a table, including all columns except for **TEXT**, **NTEXT**, and **IMAGE** datatypes. These column types are stored in separate page structures.
Index	Contains data for indexes.
Text/Image	Contains data for **TEXT**, **NTEXT**, and **IMAGE** datatypes.
Global Allocation Map (GAM)	Contains an extent allocation bitmap for up to 64,000 extents in the current datafile.
Shared Global Allocation Map (SGAM)	Contains an extent allocation bitmap for up to 64,000 extents in the current datafile. The bitmap indicates which extents are allocated for shared use and whether any space exists in the extent.
Page Free Space (PFS)	Contains a bitmap of how much space is available on each page.
Index Allocation Map (IAM)	For each table or index, the IAM pages contain a bitmap of extents that are allocated to that object.

The first pages in each file are made up of the file header, GAM, SGAM, and PFS pages. An additional PFS page is located throughout the database file every 1,000 extents. Additional GAM and SGAM pages are also located every 64,000 extents in the file. Figure 18.1 shows this relationship between these page structures. The GAM and SGAM pages are bitmaps showing which of the next 64,000 extents (500Mb) are allocated. Each bit has a 0 value if the associated extent is allocated, or a 1 if it is free. This structure allows the database to find free space quickly. In

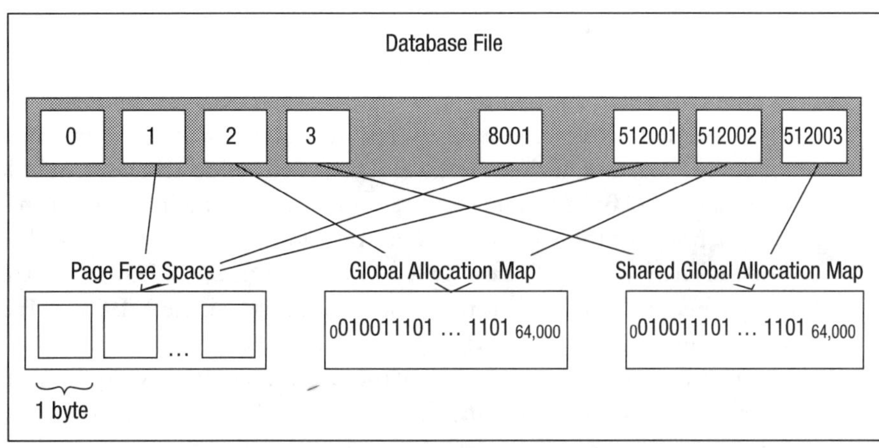

Figure 18.1 Relationship between allocation page structures.

18

the case of SGAM pages, the bitmap indicates if an extent is being shared between database objects and has some space available. When the database finds an available extent, it then needs to find a page with sufficient empty space. A PFS page contains one byte per page indicating how much space is available on each of 8,000 pages.

In addition to these allocation-tracking structures, a need also exists to identify to which extents a particular object belongs. That is the role of the *Index Allocation Map (IAM)*. This map is an associative entity between the database object and the Global Allocation Map. It is a bitmap structure that determines which of up to 64,000 extents are allocated to a particular table. At least one IAM page exists for each 64,000 extents that are allocated to a table. In addition, at least one IAM page must be present for each database file that contains allocated extents for a table. As the name suggests, the IAM page also stores allocation information for index objects.

The *sysindexes* table contains a pointer to the offset of the first IAM page for the table or index. Each IAM page contains a pointer to the next IAM page for the table or index. This is the only chain construct within the allocation mechanism of the database, which is very good news because page chaining is the one area that is most susceptible to corruption when multiple processes are trying to update the allocation maps at the same time. With this new design, little opportunity for corruption exists. In fact, some have even said that they think consistency checking is a thing of the past and is no longer needed. Contrary to that opinion, we are going along with Microsoft's recommendations to check your database for possible problems on a regular basis.

DBCC Commands

I'm sure that the storage architecture is now clear as mud to you. In any case, you should understand enough to appreciate that the storage constructs are very complex and that it is important to ensure that everything is properly allocated and linked together. If the extents are incorrectly allocated, you could lose data. A number of **DBCC** commands are used to check the integrity of this information. Many of these commands do the same things; they differ only in the scope of their analysis. For example, running a **DBCC CHECKTABLE** on every table in the database is the same as running a single **DBCC CHECKDB**. Sometimes working on individual tables may be desirable if you wish to have better control over the scheduling. Most of these commands require shared table locks to run and they result in a large amount of I/O on the processor.

Table 18.2 lists the **DBCC** commands that relate to consistency checking. Many additional **DBCC** commands are used to perform other types of maintenance or return database status information. We will look at many of these commands throughout the remainder of this chapter. For now, we will concentrate on the commands that check the database for consistency in the storage structures.

Table 18.2 DBCC commands for checking storage consistency.

DBCC Command	Description
DBCC CHECKALLOC	Checks allocation and use of all pages and extents in the specified database.
DBCC CHECKCATALOG	Checks the system catalog tables for consistency.
DBCC CHECKDB	Checks the entire database for consistency, including allocation pages and data storage pages.
DBCC CHECKFILEGROUP	Same as **CHECKDB** except checks only the objects in the specified filegroup. Because the entire database is not being checked, allocation structure consistency is not included in the analysis. Also, you will need to run **CHECKALLOC** and **CHECKCATALOG** if you opt for this command.
DBCC CHECKTABLE	Again, same as **CHECKDB** except checks only the specified table. Because the entire database is not being checked, allocation structure consistency is not included in the analysis. Also, you will need to run **CHECKALLOC** and **CHECKCATALOG** if you opt for this command.
DBCC TEXTALL	Executes **TEXTALLOC** for every table in the database that contains a **TEXT**, **NTEXT**, or **IMAGE** column. The functionality provided by this command is now included in **CHECKDB**.
DBCC TEXTALLOC	Checks the specified table for consistency in the text, ntext, or image data storage. The functionality provided by this command is now included in the **CHECKTABLE** statement. Thus, it is recommended that this command be replaced by **CHECKTABLE**.

DBCC CHECKALLOC

In the previous storage primer we described the complex mapping of extents and pages, and how they relate to tables and indexes. Although the storage mechanism seems very complex, it is quite simple compared to previous versions of the data-base. It is unlikely that this information will become corrupted. It is nevertheless a wise decision to check the accuracy of the allocation structures. That is the pur-pose of the **DBCC CHECKALLOC** command. The format of the command is as follows:

18

```
DBCC CHECKALLOC
   ( 'database_name'
     [, NOINDEX|
     { REPAIR_ALLOW_DATA_LOSS|REPAIR_FAST|REPAIR_REBUILD}]
   )
[WITH {ALL_ERRORMSGS|NO_INFOMSGS}]
```

This consistency check looks for problems in the PFS, GAM, SGAM, and IAM pages for the entire database. It is not necessary to run this command if you are running the **DBCC CHECKDB** command, because it is a subset of the checking done with the more comprehensive command. Giving the **NOINDEX** option instructs the database to bypass checking the allocation of index pages. Sometimes the checking of index structures is bypassed to save time. Bypassing these checks is not recommended, because this check is very efficient and it is important to catch any errors that may exist in the indexes. Notice that you cannot bypass index checking if you instruct the engine to fix database errors.

Normally, you should run **DBCC** commands without data fix options so you can see what errors are present in the database. After you review and analyze the reported errors, you can make an appropriate decision to rerun the **DBCC** command with error correction enabled. Unless you are very familiar with particluar errors and understand their impact on your database, you should consult with your technical support resource before correcting error conditions.

The **CHECKALLOC** command issues schema locks in the database while it is running. Only the **CREATE**, **DROP**, or **ALTER** statements will be blocked while you are checking allocation structures. Normal **SELECT**, **INSERT**, **UPDATE**, and **DELETE** activity can continue unhindered. On large databases you will probably want to run your **DBCC** commands with the **NO INFOMSGS** option to suppress noncritical information. That will make your analysis of the results much easier. Correcting errors is beyond the scope of this book, and you should consult your technical support resources if you find errors in your database.

DBCC CHECKCATALOG

Metadata about the database, such as what tables and indexes exist, as well as the columns and datatypes included in tables, is stored in the system catalogs. This information is very important to keep accurate. The **DBCC CHECKCATALOG** command checks the consistency of these catalog tables. Every table must have a row in *sysobjects* and have at least one row in *sysindexes* and *syscolumns*. Checking the catalog will ensure that rules such as this exist for every object in the database. Any problems with the relationships between the catalog tables will be reported.

In addition to checking catalog table relationships, the **DBCC CHECKCATALOG** command also verifies that the information within these tables is reasonable. We discussed earlier that the *sysindexes* table contains a pointer to the first IAM page and the first datapage for each table. The catalog-checking algorithm verifies that the values for these pointers are within the logical page number range for the database.

The format for this command is as follows:

```
DBCC CHECKCATALOG ( 'database_name' )
[WITH NO_INFOMSGS]
```

You should run this command periodically along with any other **DBCC** commands that you regularly schedule.

DBCC CHECKDB

The only two consistency checks that you need to run on a regular basis are **DBCC CHECKCATALOG** and **DBCC CHECKDB**. The **CHECKDB** command is a superset of **CHECKALLOC** and the other commands. The only checking that is not performed by this powerful analysis tool is verification of the catalog tables, which is why you still need to include **CHECKCATALOG** in your maintenance plan.

The format for this command is:

```
DBCC CHECKDB
   ( 'database_name' [, NOINDEX|
     { REPAIR_ALLOW_DATA_LOSS|REPAIR_FAST|REPAIR_REBUILD }]
   )
[WITH {ALL_ERRORMSGS|NO_INFOMSGS}]
```

When this command is run, it checks the allocation structures and subsequently checks the integrity of the data pages for every table in the database. It places shared table locks on each table as it is checking table structures. Because of this, **INSERT**, **UPDATE**, and **DELETE** activity will be blocked while an individual table is being scrutinized. For small tables the blocking will be inconsequential, but for large tables blocking could be extensive and lengthy if the check is done during hours of user activity. For this reason you may want to consider using other consistency checking commands for large databases or databases approaching 24×7 availability. In this manner you will be able to determine more accurately which tables are scanned at which time and effectively minimize impact to users or system availability.

Using **CHECKTABLE** or **CHECKFILEGROUP** over **CHECKDB** also has the added advantage of completing the consistency checking in parallel. Two or more tables or filegroups can be scheduled to run concurrently, thereby decreasing the time it takes to complete the consistency checking.

A good rule of thumb to use for running consistency checks is to check the database every time you do a complete database backup. Run the **DBCC** before the database is backed up so that you are certain you are not backing up errors.

In prior versions of the database it was important to do this because the allocation structures were not centrally stored and were composed of large page chains. The backups simply moved along the page chains and wrote the information to tape. If any errors were in the links, the backup would be unusable. SQL Server 7 has a much different architecture that does not lend to the occurrence of the same problems. It is still important to check database consistency and the best time to do that is prior to the backup.

DBCC CHECKFILEGROUP And DBCC CHECKTABLE

When you use **DBCC CHECKDB** each table in the database is checked serially for consistency. Checking two or more tables simultaneously may help improve performance. When checking the entire database you have little control over the order in which tables are checked. For this reason you cannot readily predict when a table will be locked and scanned. In some cases, you may have large tables in a database that you only want to check every month or so due to their size. In these cases you should consider using **CHECKFILEGROUP** or **CHECKTABLE** in place of **CHECKDB**.

One filegroup in the database will be listed as the *primary filegroup* when it is created. A primary filegroup is the default storage location for tables and indexes. For large or complex database designs you will probably designate multiple filegroups in the database. Each filegroup can store data for one or many different tables and indexes. In some cases you may even place individual tables or indexes on their very own filegroup. For more information about filegroups and how you should use them, refer to Chapter 14. If you are using filegroups to manage your tables and need a finer granularity of control in your maintenance plan, then using the **CHECKFILEGROUP** option of **DBCC** may be a good option for your database.

The **DBCC CHECKFILEGROUP** statement executes a consistency check on each table stored in that filegroup. You can schedule two or more **DBCC CHECKFILEGROUP** statements to run concurrently on different filegroups. If you schedule too many checks to run concurrently you may lose the parallel read efficiency built in to the database engine and slow down performance. Running a **CHECKFILEGROUP** on each filegroup in the database, along with a **CHECKALLOC**, is equivalent to running a single **CHECKDB**.

In the case where your database is not separated into multiple filegroups, or if you need to be able to control your maintenance plan at the table level, you will need to use the **DBCC CHECKTABLE** command. This command is identical to the **CHECKFILEGROUP** version, except that it operates only on the single table specified. With **CHECKTABLE** you may also find performance gains by running two or more table checks concurrently, but the same caution previously mentioned applies—running too many may cause you to lose the advantages of parallel reads.

If a table is located in a filegroup that has more than one file, the database can issue one parallel read thread for each file. Parallel reads are only used for scan operations, such as **DBCC** commands or queries where table scans are implemented. For example, if a table is located on filegroup **PRIMARY** that contains three files, the database can use three simultaneous read threads, one for each file, to complete the I/O intensive operation more quickly.

Even if you use **CHECKDB**, you may still find a use for the **CHECKTABLE** or **CHECKFILEGROUP** commands. Consider that you regularly schedule **CHECKDB** for your database system. If your results show corruption on a particular table and your support contact instructs you to use **DBCC** to correct the problem (as opposed to restoring from a backup), you could use **CHECKTABLE** with one of the fix options enabled. Using this approach will eliminate unnecessary scanning of valid information and will quickly correct the problem in many circumstances.

Because both **CHECKTABLE** and **CHECKFILEGROUP** are performing the same checks as **CHECKDB**, they will also issue shared table locks when scanning a table. Locking a table is necessary in order to have a condition of quiescence for accurate error checking and reporting. If it is simply not possible to check certain tables in your database for consistency because of their size and your requirements for system availability, another option is available. You can periodically back up and load your database to another computer and run the consistency checks there. Using this method has several advantages. You will avoid interruption for your users, verify the usability of your backups, and still be able to check the consistency of your storage structures.

DBCC TEXTALL And DBCC TEXTALLOC

For tables containing **TEXT**, **NTEXT**, and **IMAGE** data, special consistency checks are required. Data rows in these tables are stored in data pages, but the data pages do not store the actual column values for these datatypes. Instead, the rows contain pointers to separate page chains that contain the column data, allowing very large blocks of information to be stored. If the row pointers become corrupt, the **TEXT**, **NTEXT**, or **IMAGE** information related to that row will be lost.

The **DBCC TEXTALLOC** checks these pointers for the specified table and reports any corruption or cross-linkages that exist. In place of running that command for each table in the database, **DBCC TEXTALL** executes **TEXTALLOC** for each table in the database that contains a **TEXT**, **NTEXT**, or **IMAGE** column. A new feature that is implemented in SQL Server 7 is the inclusion of pointer checking with the **CHECKDB**, **CHECKFILEGROUP**, and **CHECKTABLE** commands. Because of this, the **TEXTALL** and **TEXTALLOC** checks are not longer needed and are included only for backward compatibility.

Efficiency—Contiguous Storage

Imagine that you are a filing clerk with a large law firm, and you regularly re-sort large case files—the type of files that take up multiple file cabinet drawers. You already know and realize the benefits of indexing your case files. But as you reclassify papers and add new reports to your system, your folders become disordered and cluttered. The indexing system makes filing new motions and briefs fast and easy. As files become more cluttered, it takes longer to retrieve important information. That is because the files are no longer physically ordered correctly, nor is related information stored contiguously. At this point it is necessary to clean out the old folders and reorganize the papers.

This is a very close analogy to a computerized database system. During the normal course of user activity, the database does not waste much time keeping data neat and tidy. The RDBMS engine's primary goal is to execute the transactions as quickly as possible. After a considerable amount of **INSERT**, **UPDATE**, and **DELETE** activity, the data becomes very fragmented, especially for tables with clustered indexes. Clustered indexes cause the data rows to be physically stored in sorted order, and they become fragmented because of *page splitting*.

Consider the table of employees illustrated in Figure 18.2. The table has a clustered index with an order of *EmpDate* and is stored currently on two data

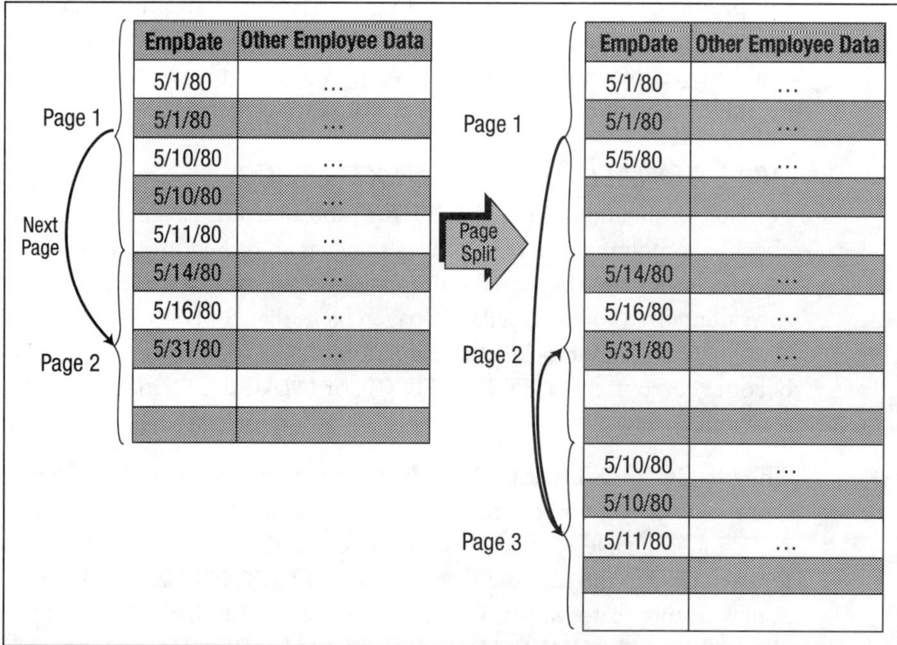

Figure 18.2 Page splitting.

pages. Because each row is 1,500 bytes, only five rows can fit on a page. Page one already has five rows stored on it, and page two has three rows. When a new row is inserted into the table, the clustered index order places the row between rows two and three, but no physical place is available to put the new data. This condition causes a page split to occur. The storage engine will allocate page three in the current extent and change page one's next page pointer to page three. Likewise, page three's next page pointer will be changed to page two. The logical order of the pages after the page split is one-three-two. Regardless of the fill factor (it is used only for index reorganizations), the storage engine will move existing rows three through five to the new page, and the new row will be added as row three on page one.

Try to imagine what the physical order of pages looks like after a very busy day of activity on a table. In order to read the data in the table in the order of the clustered index, the storage engine will be very inefficient, jumping from page to page over the filegroup. In effect, a severely fragmented table can convert very fast sequential I/O into very slow random I/O. That is why it is very important to check regularly for fragmented tables and reorganize them.

Overlooking table fragmentation is a common mistake that often leads to severe performance degradation. Although detecting and correcting fragmentation is the job of the database administrator in most shops, the developer and designer should be aware of the symptoms and should include table reorganization in the maintenance plan.

Although the earlier examples explained page splitting on data pages, the same condition also occurs with index pages. As inserts and updates are made to a table, the index pages can become very fragmented. Even node pages (nonleaf pages) can become severely fragmented, resulting in significant degradation of performance. Because database fragmentation is often overlooked and misunderstood, a good number of the certification exam questions on database maintenance relate to this topic.

DBCC SHOWCONTIG

18

The **DBCC SHOWCONTIG** command allows you to check for table and index fragmentation. The need to do this on a regular basis cannot be emphasized enough. Following is the syntax for this command:

```
DBCC SHOWCONTIG ( table_id [, index_id] )
```

The table ID represents the object ID for the table object. This can be determined by running:

```
SELECT object_id( "Employees" ) as "table_id"
```

The index ID is the ID for the index you want to check. This ID comes from the *sysindexes* table. If the index ID is not given, or if it is 0, the command returns information on the table data pages. The following query returns the list of index names and ID's for the *Products* table:

```
SELECT  indid, convert(char(20), name) as name
from    sysindexes
where   id = object_id( "Products" )
and     indid > 0

indid  name
-----  ------------------
1      PK_Products
2      CategoriesProducts
3      CategoryID
4      ProductName
5      SupplierID
6      SuppliersProducts

(6 row(s) affected)
```

As mentioned earlier, fragmentation can occur on both data pages and index pages. It is a good practice to check fragmentation on both data and index structures. If a table has a clustered index, it is normally acceptable to check the clustered index. The only exception to this practice is observed if a lot of updates to nonclustered index keys exist, which would not cause page splitting for the clustered index, but would result in fragmentation for the nonclustered index. Listing 18.1 shows a query to generate **DBCC SHOWCONTIG** commands for each index on the *Products* table. The highlighted portion of the listing also shows the results for the clustered index.

Listing 18.1 DBCC SHOWCONTIG.

```
select 'DBCC SHOWCONTIG( '
       + convert(char(10), object_id( "Products" ))
       + ', '
       + convert(char(10), indid)
       + ')'
from    sysindexes
where   id = object_id( "Products" )
and     indid > 0

---------------------------------------

DBCC SHOWCONTIG( 453576654 , 1         )
DBCC SHOWCONTIG( 453576654 , 2         )
```

```
DBCC SHOWCONTIG( 453576654 , 3          )
DBCC SHOWCONTIG( 453576654 , 4          )
DBCC SHOWCONTIG( 453576654 , 5          )
DBCC SHOWCONTIG( 453576654 , 6          )

(6 row(s) affected)

DBCC SHOWCONTIG scanning 'Products' table...
Table: 'Products' (453576654); index ID: 1, database ID: 6
TABLE level scan performed.
- Pages Scanned................................: 1
- Extents Scanned..............................: 1
- Extent Switches..............................: 0
- Avg. Pages per Extent........................: 1.0
- Scan Density [Best Count:Actual Count].......: 100.00% [1:1]
- Logical Scan Fragmentation ..................: 0.00%
- Extent Scan Fragmentation ...................: 0.00%
- Avg. Bytes Free per Page.....................: 1.0
- Avg. Page Density (full).....................: 99.99%
DBCC execution completed. If DBCC printed error messages,
contact your system administrator.
```

This is a very small table, so not much useful information is available from the **SHOWCONTIG** output. Listing 18.2 shows the final **DBCC** output from Project 18.1 using the test data and scripts provided on the CD-ROM. A lot of information can be gleamed from this report, the most significant of which is the *Scan Density* (highlighted in the listing). Let's examine the output piece by piece to determine what it means.

Listing 18.2 SHOWCONTIG output.

```
DBCC SHOWCONTIG scanning 'ShowContigSample' table...
Table: 'ShowContigSample' (1813581499); index ID: 1, database ID: 6
TABLE level scan performed.
- Pages Scanned................................: 5065
- Extents Scanned..............................: 637
- Extent Switches..............................: 1564
- Avg. Pages per Extent........................: 8.0
- Scan Density [Best Count:Actual Count].......: 40.51% [634:1565]
- Logical Scan Fragmentation ..................: 21.34%
- Extent Scan Fragmentation ...................: 0.16%
- Avg. Bytes Free per Page.....................: 2408.3
- Avg. Page Density (full).....................: 70.25%
DBCC execution completed. If DBCC printed error messages,
contact your system administrator.
```

18

The first piece of information is the number of pages that were scanned (in this case 5,065). This is the number of pages allocated to the storage of the table. If the output were for an index, this would be the number of pages allocated to the storage of the index, including both leaf and nonleaf pages. The next number indicates how many extents were scanned. Dividing the *Pages Scanned* by eight pages per extent equals 634 extents (rounding up). But the **SHOWCONTIG** output shows that we scanned 637 extents. This simply indicates that four extents are allocated to the table with only some of the pages on those extents allocated to the table.

Extent Switches is a count of how many times the storage engine switched between extents while traversing the data or index pages. If this number is greater than the number of extents allocated to the table, the pages are not contiguous. The ratio between the number of *Extents Scanned* and *Extent Switches* provides the Scan Density, or fragmentation. The actual fragmentation can actually be greater than this ratio, because only extent switches are measured. Additional fragmentation can occur on the pages within extents, although this type of fragmentation is not as bad as extent switching fragmentation, because the database performs I/O operations in extent-sized blocks.

The Scan Density shows these extent values that make up the ratio: the *Best Count* and the *Actual Count*. For this example, if the table were 100 percent contiguous, the database would need to make 634 reads (one per extent) to scan the entire table. Because it is very fragmented, it needs to make 1,565 reads to get the job done, an increase of 931 reads, or 242 percent. Even though this table is only 32MB in size, the severe fragmentation shown can make a large performance difference if it is heavily used.

Avg. Pages per Extent indicates how many pages per extent are allocated to the table on the average. If this number is less than eight and the table is very large, this could indicate that a large number of pages allocated to the table resides in extents shared with other tables or indexes. This should not be the case, however, because the database engine is not supposed to share extents for large tables. The other possible explanation is that the page splitting for a clustered index has resulted in the allocation of a large number of extents that are only partially used. A low Scan Density number would also indicate this condition.

Logical Scan Fragmentation and *Extent Scan Fragmentation* numbers are valid only when reporting on indexes. These numbers simply add to the picture of what the index pages and extents look like. Scan Density is still the primary number to look at for fragmentation.

The final two numbers indicate how full each page is. *Avg. Bytes Free per Page* is an average measurement of free bytes per page for every page allocated to the table or index. *Avg. Page Density* is simply the same information expressed as a percentage of the page size (1—Avg. Bytes Free per Page * 100/8,096 bytes per page), in this case 70 percent full. It is important to exercise caution when considering this number. For example, in Listing 18.2 each data row is 3,004 bytes, so only two rows will fit on a page (6,008 bytes used). If each page had two rows on it, 2,088 bytes would be free on each page, even though the pages are really 100 percent full. The average bytes free (2,408) less the nominal bytes free per page (2,088) leaves an excess of 320 bytes of free space on each page. Dividing that number by the maximum bytes that can be used, we observe that these numbers really indicate that the pages are 94 percent full for our specific situation.

The page density is also an important number to analyze when tuning your database. The higher the page density, the better performance read operations will have because fewer extents will be fetched for the same amount of data retrieved. On the other hand, inserts and updates often cause page splitting, as discussed earlier. Page splitting can slow down transaction throughput, because the number of I/O operations is increased substantially. Increasing the amount of free space per page can have a significant positive impact on performance for **INSERT** and **UPDATE** statements. A balance between reading and writing processes must be maintained to arrive at the optimal page density. This topic is discussed more fully in Chapter 6 in the section discussing **FILLFACTOR**.

DBCC Reindex

When you determine that either your table is too fragmented or your page density is too high or low, you need to undertake a reorganization of your data for the affected tables. In practical terms this means you will need to rebuild the indexes on your tables. If you are concerned about excessive fragmentation on data pages for a table that does not have a clustered index, you may need to unload the data, truncate the table, and reload the information. Because most large tables in SQL Server 7 will have clustered indexes for performance reasons, we will consider only the situation where rebuilding indexes will solve the fragmentation or page density problem.

On tables that have both clustered indexes and nonclustered indexes, most often you will be checking only for fragmentation of the clustered index, unless knowledge of the application usage profile directs you to do otherwise. Chapter 6 revealed the fact that nonclustered indexes actually point to clustered index keys rather than physical pointers to data pages. Therefore, rebuilding a clustered index forces the database to automatically rebuild all nonclustered indexes for a given table so the key pointers can be synchronized to the new values.

Two approaches exist to rebuilding a clustered index. The first approach requires the index to be dropped and subsequently recreated. Although effective, this approach results in any nonclustered indexes being rebuilt twice—once when the clustered index is dropped, and again when the clustered index is re-created. The better approach is to use the **DBCC REINDEX** command. With this command, the nonclustered index will be rebuilt only one time, on completion of the clustered index reorganization. You will not have to drop and re-create primary key or unique constraints that exist on a table.

The syntax for the command is:

```
DBCC DBREINDEX
   ( 'database.owner.table_name' [, index_name [, fillfactor ] ] )
[WITH NO_INFOMSGS]
```

If this command is executed without an index name, all indexes on the table are rebuilt. Additionally, a fill factor can be specified to override the default fill factor for the indexes. If no fill factor is supplied, and no fill factor was specified during index creation, the default server-wide fill factor is used. For more information regarding the use of this command, refer to Chapter 6, where it is discussed in more detail.

Identity Columns

Consider a situation where you have a table of names and you need to create a unique value that can be used as a primary key. Because names are not usually good candidates for primary keys, you must use a different approach. One way to solve this problem is to create a table where one of the columns is given the **IDENTITY** property. This property indicates that the database will automatically generate sequential values for the column. If the column datatype is **INT**, by default the values will start at one and increment sequentially. Using the **IDENTITY** property is very convenient in these situations.

The database keeps an internal counter of the last number used for the table. If an insert to the table is made and aborted, the internal counter is incremented, but the corresponding data row will not exist in the table. Such an occurrence is not usually a problem, because the next row that is inserted successfully will simply skip a number and is still unique. The problem is when this internal counter becomes out of sync with the actual data in the table. Consider that the maximum value for an *IDENTITY* column in a table is 30, but the internal last used counter is set to 25. The next insert to the table would attempt to use the value 26, which is already in the table, violating the primary key (most *IDENTITY* columns are used as primary keys). Problems like this often occur if you are loading and unloading data from tables that contain *IDENTITY* columns or replicate such tables to other servers.

The **DBCC CHECKIDENT** command provides both a reporting facility for detecting this problem and a corrective facility to re-seed the internal counter if necessary. The syntax for this command is as follows:

```
DBCC CHECKIDENT
   ( 'table_name' [, { NORESEED|{RESEED [, new_reseed_value]} }] )
```

To get a list of tables in your database that have *IDENTITY* columns, run this command:

```
select  distinct object_name(id)  as "Tables with
  IDENTITY values"
from    syscolumns
where   status & 0x80 = 0x80
```

To report the value of the internal last used counter for the *Employees* table run the following command:

```
dbcc checkident( 'Shippers' )

Checking identity information: current identity value '15',
current column value '15'.
DBCC execution completed. If DBCC printed error messages,
contact your system administrator.
```

If you find that the current identity value does not match the current column value, you will need to re-seed the internal last used counter. You can re-seed a table's counter even if no inconsistency exists between the counter and the table data. For example, to re-seed the counter for the *Shippers* back to the original value of nine, execute the command:

```
dbcc checkident( 'Shippers', reseed, 9 )

Checking identity information: current identity value '15',
current column value '9'.
DBCC execution completed. If DBCC printed error messages,
contact your system administrator.
```

18

As you can see, we had previously inserted some rows in our *Shippers* table and we have succeeded in getting the **IDENTITY** counter out of sync with the data in the table.

Distribution Statistics

Another major area of database maintenance that is often overlooked is the area of *index distribution statistics*. Although this topic was covered in Chapter 6, we will go a little deeper into this topic here in this chapter. Just like politicians, a database lives and dies by statistics—and of course, in both cases, the statistics are compiled by polls.

Suppose you are a query engine and a user asks you to run this query:

```
SELECT  *
FROM    Births
WHERE   BirthDate between "Jan 1, 2000 00:00:00"
                      and "Jan 1, 2000 23:59:59"
AND     State = 'FL'
```

And two of the indexes on the *Births* table look like this:

```
CREATE INDEX BirthDate on Births (BirthDate, State)
CREATE INDEX State on Births (State, Birthdate)
```

You would probably want to know if fewer births occurred in Florida or on January 1, 2000. If you knew that information, you would use the index on which the first column returned the fewest records for the given criteria. That is good logic, but if you were informed that only ten births were recorded in the table, the logic doesn't work. With this new information you would not use the index at all, but would simply read all ten rows in a single extent I/O operation. These are the types of decisions that must be made by the query engine.

Statistics Primer

The query engine relies on the availability of up-to-date distribution statistics for each index in the database, including clustered indexes. To see just what information is contained in these statistics, use the following **DBCC** command that allows you to see the information stored on the statistics page. The following command shows statistics for the *OrderID* index on the *Order Details* table:

```
DBCC SHOW_STATISTICS ([Order Details], OrderID)

Statistics for INDEX 'OrderID'.
Updated              Rows      Rows Sampled   Steps
-----------          ----      ------------   -----
Jul 13 1999  7:24PM  2155      2155           270

        Density                  Average key length
        ------------             ------------------
        1.1922787E-3             7.9999347
```

```
(1 row(s) affected)

All density          Columns
------------         ------------------
1.2048193E-3         OrderID
4.6403712E-4         OrderID, ProductID

(2 row(s) affected)

Steps
-----
10248
10251
...
11077
11077

(270 row(s) affected)

DBCC execution completed. If DBCC printed error messages, contact
your system administrator.
```

If you are following along and have run the previous **DBCC** command on your system in the *Northwind* database, you may not have seen these results. Not to worry, it will be your goal as you read through the rest of this section to figure out why and correct the problem.

Looking at the statistics information that was reported, notice that three separate sections exist. First, general information regarding the index is listed. Next it also shows density information on the index keys, and finally a sampling of the values in the table. This last sampling section is often referred to as the *histogram*, or described as the *shape* of the index. This is because this section paints a picture of how the key values are distributed within the table. Let's examine what all this information means and how it is derived.

Starting at the top, the statistics include the date that the statistics were last updated. This date is modified whether the statistics where updated manually or automatically by the database (discussed shortly). This is very useful to refer to if you are researching a poorly executing query and suspect that the statistics may be out of date. Also reported are the number of rows in the table and the number of rows sampled when building the statistics. New to SQL Server 7 is the performance-enhancing ability to sample a certain number or percentage of the rows in a table from which the index statistics can be derived. The alternative is to sample all the rows in the table, which can generate a significant amount of I/O requests, because every row in the table would need to be scanned. It has been determined that sampling can provide nearly the same statistics at a much lower cost than reading the entire table.

The next pieces of information reported are the number of steps, the index density, and average key length. *Steps* refer to the histogram at the bottom of the printout. This is simply the number of values from the table that are stored in the statistics page. The *index density* is an overall average ratio that is used to determine how many unique index key values are in the table (more on this later). Finally, the *average key length* describes how long the index key values are, in this case 8 bytes (two integer columns at 4 bytes each).

Next we come to the result set that lists the *All Density* and *Columns* for each combination of columns contained in the key. In this case, two columns are in the key. If one column were in the key, only one row would be shown. The density value is the inverse of the number of distinct values for the key combination. The *Order Details* table has 830 distinct *OrderID* values. The density value shown for this column is calculated by taking 1/830 = 1.2048193E-3. The combination of *OrderID* + *ProductID* has 2,155 unique values, giving a ratio of 1/2155 = 4.6403712E-4. Whenever the query engine resolves an exact value predicate (using = operator) it uses the density values to compute the estimated query cost. To illustrate, consider this query:

```
SELECT  *
FROM    [Order Details]
WHERE   OrderID = 10248
```

The optimizer will estimate the cost of using the index to evaluate the query compared with the cost of using other indexes or no indexes. To do that it uses the density values to estimate how many rows will be returned using a given index. Because *OrderID* is contained in the predicate, the optimizer will compute the estimated rows by multiplying the total number of rows in the table (2,155) by the density value (1.2048193E-3) to arrive at 2.6. This number can be converted into I/O operations by determining the number of rows on a page (from *syscolumns*) and calculating the number of extents that would need to be read. This method is very straightforward, but if the query is something like this:

```
SELECT  *
FROM    [Order Details]
WHERE   OrderID BETWEEN 10248 AND 10252
```

The optimizer knows that an average of 2.6 rows would be returned for each *OrderID*, but it does not know how many *OrderIDs* lie between 10,248 and 10,252. At this point the optimizer turns to the histogram. The optimizer can determine the number of steps that would be traversed in the table by comparing the values. This query needs two steps. Because 2,155 rows are in the table and 270 steps listed, an average of 7.98 (2,155/270) rows would be returned per steps traversed or approximately 16 rows in our example. This is a very good estimate—the actual number of rows returned in this query is 14.

Without distribution statistics, the optimizer would be guessing at which plan is the most efficient query plan to use. It is vital to have accurate statistics maintained for each index. Similar logic is used when trying to determine the best way to resolve a join between two tables. If accurate statistics are not available, then the optimizer is likely to make bad decisions, and as a result you will end up with a slow database.

Creating Statistics On Columns

Creating statistics on nonindexed columns is a new concept in SQL Server 7. Previously, distribution statistics have made sense only for indexes. But with a much smarter cost-based optimizer and with two additional join methods, providing histogram and density information on nonindexed columns can sometimes add value. The more indexes you have on a table, the slower insert and update operations will be, and slower transactions can lead to blocking and deadlocking more in a database. Indexes also take up valuable disk storage space and memory cache. Having exactly the necessary indexes is the best choice, and adding statistics on nonindexed columns to those can help a great deal in query optimization.

Let's look at a couple situations where the optimizer can make good use of having statistics available on nonindexed columns. Suppose that you have the following table and index:

```
CREATE TABLE TerritorySalesSummary
(
   Territory     char(10),
   CustomerID    int,
   Month         char(6),      - yyyymm
   SalesAmt      money
)
CREATE INDEX TerritoryMonth on TerritorySalesSummary(Territory, Month)
```

18

Also consider the following query:

```
SELECT  *
FROM    TerritorySalesSummary
WHERE   Territory  = 'Southwest'
AND     Month      BETWEEN '199901' AND '199912'
```

Although the index *TerritoryMonth* has density values for the combination of *Territory* and *Month*, a histogram exists only on the column *Territory*. Suppose the density values indicate that over 40 percent of the rows in the table would be returned by just the predicate; the optimizer may choose to use a table scan rather than use the index:

```
Territory = 'Southwest'
```

Nevertheless, the query is supposedly more selective, because it also contains a second predicate. The *Month* column has no histogram, so the optimizer does not have any indication of how many rows may qualify for the **BETWEEN** clause. This is where creating statistics on the *Month* column could help by providing histogram information by which the optimizer could estimate the number of qualifying rows. This estimated number of rows, combined with the composite density values for *Territory* and *Month* from the index, would give the optimizer the information it needs to decide on the least costly access path.

Perhaps an even more beneficial use for column statistics would be to help the optimizer choose between join methods, or to select the table with the smallest number of qualifying rows for the outer table in a join. For example, consider the following two tables and their respective indexes:

```
CREATE TABLE Book
(
  ISBN           int,
  Title          varchar(50),
  PublishDate    datetime
)
CREATE INDEX ISBN on Book(ISBN)
go

CREATE TABLE AuthorBook
(
  ISBN           int,
  AuthorID       int,
)
CREATE INDEX AuthorBook on AuthorBook(ISBN, AuthorID)
go

CREATE TABLE Author
(
  AuthorID       int,
  FirstName      varchar(25),
  LastName       varchar(25),
  Famous         char(1)
)
```

```
CREATE INDEX AuthorID on Author(AuthorID)
go
```

Given these tables, consider this query:

```
SELECT   *
  FROM   Book as B
  JOIN   AuthorBook as AB
    ON   AB.ISBN = B.ISBN
  JOIN   Author as A
    ON   A.AuthorID = AB.AuthorID
 WHERE   B.PublishDate BETWEEN 'Jan 1, 1950' AND 'Jan 1, 1951'
   AND   A.Famous = 'Y'
```

You are looking for all the books published in 1950 from one or more famous authors. Given that the *Book* table has 100,000 rows and that the *Author* table has 300,000 rows, it might be difficult to determine which table would be the best outer table in the join. It is difficult to be sure, because you don't know how many books were published in 1950 or how many famous authors exist. Availability of this information would be very beneficial for selecting the most efficient join order. That is where creating column statistics becomes important. Having a histogram available for the *PublishDate* would provide an estimate of the number of rows that qualify for that predicate. Likewise, having the density value for the *Famous* attribute would provide the same information for the other predicate. The following statements could be used to create this statistical distribution information for the hypothetical example given:

```
CREATE STATISTICS Famous on AuthorTitle(Famous)
go
CREATE STATISTICS PublishDate on Book(PublishDate)
go
```

Updating Statistics

If a table is populated fully when an index is created, the statistics are created automatically. However, a common mistake is to create the table with the indexes, and subsequently load the data into the table. In this case, the statistics page would be blank and the optimizer will be left guessing. In this case, you will want to create the statistics manually. To do this for the *Order Details* table, run this command:

18

```
UPDATE STATISTICS [Order Details]
```

With this version of the command, the database will determine the best way to compile the statistics. We already mentioned that either a full scan of the table can be made, or alternatively, a sampling of the information in the table can be used. The following command illustrates the full syntax for this command:

```
UPDATE STATISTICS table [index|(statistics_name[,...n]) ]
[ WITH [[FULLSCAN]|SAMPLE number {PERCENT|ROWS}]]
       [[,] [ALL|COLUMNS|INDEX]
       [[,] NORECOMPUTE]]
```

The **SAMPLE** option can be used to give an actual number of rows that you want the database to sample, or you can state a percentage. If at least a minimal number of rows is not given, the server will adjust automatically the number of scanned rows to a number that will produce reasonably accurate statistics. Higher numbers will produce more accurate statistics and histogram data and possibly better query plans. The query processor makes the basic assumption when reading statistics information that every unique value that will be stored in the table has been seen. In most cases, allowing the database engine to determine the optimal number of rows will result in a good balance between accurate statistics and fast processing time. Updating statistics produces a shared table lock. It is not normally a good idea to update statistics during periods of high activity.

As we have seen, it is also possible to create index statistics on columns that are not indexed. By default, running **UPDATE STATISTICS** on a table with no options will update the statistics on all indexes and all columns that have statistics defined on them. Optionally, special circumstances may exist where you only want to update statistics only on certain indexes or columns, which can be done by individually naming the index or column, or by using the **COLUMNS** or **INDEX** options. The **NORECOMPUTE** clause prevents the statistics from being automatically updated in the future by the database engine if **auto update statistics** is turned on.

Auto-Update Statistics

In previous versions of the database it was necessary to rely solely on manually created and updated maintenance plans to keep statistics up to date. Whereas manually created plans allow a wide degree of flexibility and control, SQL Server 7 brings another option. As part of working toward the goal of a self-maintaining database engine, Microsoft has provided the ability for the server to update statistics automatically. This setting can be determined for each individual database. If set, every minute during periods of low activity the server will scan for and update out-of-date statistics.

To show how the server knows when statistics become out of date, open a new query window in the *Northwind* database and run this statement:

```
SELECT rowmodctr
FROM   sysindexes
```

```
WHERE  object_name(id) = 'Orders'
AND    indid = 1

rowmodctr
---------
0
```

Next, type in and run these two queries:

```
UPDATE Orders
SET    ShippedDate = getdate()

SELECT rowmodctr
FROM   sysindexes
WHERE  object_name(id) = 'Orders'
AND    indid = 1

(830 row(s) affected)

rowmodctr
---------
830

(1 row(s) affected)
```

Each time a row is inserted, updated, or deleted, the *rowmodctr* column in the *sysindexes* table is incremented. If a high enough percentage of rows have been modified, the database will automatically update the statistics. The only problem with allowing this to occur automatically is that the database does not know your environment. In the middle of peak time, the server could automatically start updating statistics on one or more tables. This scenario would be bad because users who are updating data would be blocked until the process is finished. The statistics algorithm can use sampling to speed up the process greatly, reducing the blocking time. Even with the sampling process, updating statistics on a table with several million rows in the middle of the day could be a bad choice.

Two different strategies are available that you can use to manage such a situation. First, you can set the **NORECOMPUTE** attribute for individual indexes or column statistics, or you can set the attribute at the table level. The automatic update processes bypasses and indexes or tables with this attribute turned on. If you do this, be sure to remember to schedule a job to update these statistics. Setting **NORECOMPUTE** can be accomplished in different ways. The most common way is to use the **sp_autostats** catalog stored procedure. The following T-SQL statement sets the option for the *Orders* table:


```
EXEC sp_autostats Orders, 'OFF'
```

The other method you can use is to disable automatic statistics updating in the database. You would need to create a maintenance plan for your database that includes updating statistics. The advantage of manually maintaining statistics for large or highly utilized databases is being able to determine exactly which statistics get updated at what time.

Telltale Performance Problem Signs

Updating statistics on a regular basis is very important for the highest performing database possible. Many designers fail to plan for regular database maintenance such as this and realize the consequences too late. Let's detail the symptoms for poorly maintained index statistics. A query or procedure that has historically performed well and suddenly begins to show deteriorating performance is one sign that the statistics are not updated. Users might complain of slow performance. You might later discover that a large amount of data has been added to the table. Situations like these are a sure sign of out-of-date statistics.

Suppose you have a report that has been working fine, but all of the sudden users are reporting that it has started running slow the first few times it runs each day. After those first few times, however, the performance is restored. Two situations could actually be causing this problem. First, the automatic statistics update could be turned off, and after the first few executions the data is cached, resulting in fast execution of the report. Another possibility is that a batch update of the underlying table data is taking place in the morning, causing the statistics to become dated and the report to run slowly. During the morning the server automatically updates the statistics, after which query performance returns to normal.

Database Maintenance Planning Wizard

Microsoft has greatly expanded the use of wizards in SQL Server 7. One wizard that is very useful in these situations can set up database maintenance plans automatically. You can use this very robust wizard to help you easily set up your database maintenance activities. The Database Maintenance Plan Wizard steps through the options of updating statistics, backups, log maintenance, and shrinking databases. It even helps you schedule database consistency checks. This wizard-planning tool is very useful for smaller or medium size databases.

To run the wizard, click the wizards icon from Enterprise Manager toolbar. Then select Maintenance|Database Maintenance Plan Wizard. The wizard guides you through selecting the database(s) that you want to develop a maintenance plan for. Once you have selected the database, you decide if you want the planning wizard to set up tasks for reorganizing data and index pages (**DBCC REINDEX**), updating statistics (not necessary if you schedule reorganizations), and remove unused space from the database files. Next you choose whether to run database integrity checks (such as **DBCC CHECKDB**). Other options include backups for both the database and log files, deciding how much maintenance history information to keep, and where.You would probably not want to use this wizard for larger databases, because you do not have the granularity of control for types of **DBCCs** to run, only reorganizing certain tables, and so forth.

CHAPTER SUMMARY

In this chapter you learned about the various elements of database maintenance and how important they are to your design. Here are the main points we have covered:

- The storage structures in SQL Server 7 are much better than previous versions and as a result are less susceptible to corruption.
- **DBCC CHECKDB** and **DBCC CHECKCATALOG** perform all the necessary consistency checking in the database.
- **DBCC CHECKTABLE** and **DBCC CHECKFILEGROUP** are alternatives to using **DBCC CHECKDB**. However, if you opt for either of these, you will also need to run **DBCC CHECKALLOC**.
- Consistency checking should be completed prior to a full database backup.
- Database fragmentation is a result of normal operations, but can severely degrade performance by effectively converting sequential I/O to random I/O.
- **DBCC SHOWCONTIG** reports data and index fragmentation. Check this frequently.
- **DBCC REINDEX** reorganizes index and table pages into contiguous streams of data.
- **DBCC CHECKIDENT** verifies and corrects problems with *IDENTITY* column counters.
- Indexes have distribution statistics to help the optimizer select the best data access path.
- Distribution statistics can also be created for nonindexed columns. Like index statistics, these help the optimizer make better decisions for query plans.
- The **UPDATE STATISTICS** command either executes a full table scan or uses a sampling algorithm to update index and column statistics.
- By default, databases automatically update statistics and create column statistics as needed.

Review Questions

1. Which two consistency checking commands together perform all the checking that is necessary in the database?
   a. **DBCC CHECKCATALOG** and **DBCC CHECKDB**
   b. **DBCC CHECKDB** and **DBCC CHECKALLOC**
   c. **DBCC CHECKCONTIG** and **DBCC CHECKDB**
   d. **DBCC CHECKSYS** and **DBCC CHECKALLOC**

2. If you run **DBCC CHECKTABLE** on every table in the database, which two other **DBCC** checks should you also run?
   a. **DBCC CHECKDB** and **DBCC CHECKALLOC**
   b. **DBCC CHECKCATALOG** and **DBCC CHECKALLOC**
   c. **DBCC CHECKFILEGROUP** and **DBCC CHECKCATALOG**
   d. **DBCC CHECKALLOC** and **DBCC CHECKIDENT**

3. Look at the following **DBCC SHOWCONTIG** output, then check all the statements that are true:

```
DBCC SHOWCONTIG scanning 'ShowContigSample' table...
Table: 'ShowContigSample' (1861581670); index ID: 1, database ID: 6
TABLE level scan performed.
  Pages Scanned................................: 4000
- Extents Scanned..............................: 504
- Extent Switches..............................: 504
- Avg. Pages per Extent........................: 7.9
- Scan Density [Best Count:Actual Count].......: 99.01% [500:505]
- Logical Scan Fragmentation ..................: 0.07%
- Extent Scan Fragmentation ...................: 0.40%
- Avg. Bytes Free per Page.....................: 2068.8
- Avg. Page Density (full).....................: 74.44%
DBCC execution completed. If DBCC printed error messages, contact
your system administrator.
```

   a. The *ShowContigSample* table is 40 percent fragmented.
   b. The pages in the *ShowContigSample* table can hold 26 percent more rows.
   c. The index statistics are out of date and should be updated.
   d. The *ShowContigSample* table is contiguous.

4. Given that each row in *ShowContigSample* is 3,004 bytes long, and seeing the following **DBCC SHOWCONTIG** output, on average, how many rows are stored on each data page?

```
DBCC SHOWCONTIG scanning 'ShowContigSample' table...
Table: 'ShowContigSample' (1861581670); index ID: 1, database ID: 6
TABLE level scan performed.
- Pages Scanned................................: 4000
- Extents Scanned..............................: 504
- Extent Switches..............................: 504
- Avg. Pages per Extent........................: 7.9
- Scan Density [Best Count:Actual Count].......: 99.01% [500:505]
- Logical Scan Fragmentation ..................: 0.07%
- Extent Scan Fragmentation ...................: 0.40%
- Avg. Bytes Free per Page.....................: 4096
- Avg. Page Density (full).....................: 50%
DBCC execution completed. If DBCC printed error messages, contact
your system administrator.
```

a. One row per page.

b. Two rows per page.

c. Three rows per page.

d. Four rows per page.

5. Looking at the following **DBCC SHOWCONTIG** output, how fragmented is the table?

```
DBCC SHOWCONTIG scanning 'ShowContigSample' table...
Table: 'ShowContigSample' (1813581499); index ID: 1, database ID: 6
TABLE level scan performed.
- Pages Scanned................................: 5065
- Extents Scanned..............................: 637
- Extent Switches..............................: 1564
- Avg. Pages per Extent........................: 8.0
- Scan Density [Best Count:Actual Count].......: 40.51% [634:1565]
- Logical Scan Fragmentation ..................: 21.34%
- Extent Scan Fragmentation ...................: 0.16%
- Avg. Bytes Free per Page.....................: 2408.3
- Avg. Page Density (full).....................: 70.25%
DBCC execution completed. If DBCC printed error messages, contact
your system administrator.
```

a. 21.34 percent

b. 0.16 percent

c. 40.51 percent

d. 70.25 percent

6. Assuming that the *ShowContigSample* table is severely fragmented, which of the following remedies should be taken to correct the problem?
   a. Enable auto-update statistics for the database.
   b. Run **DBCC DBREINDEX**.
   c. Enable the auto-update fragmentation option for the database.
   d. Run **DBCC SHOWCONTIG** with the **FIX** option.

7. A user notifies you that a query that was has been running fine in the past is now running very slowly. Which of the following commands should you run to find out the problem? (Choose all correct answers.)
   a. **DBCC CHECKDB** and **DBCC CHECKCATALOG**
   b. **DBCC SHOWCONTIG**
   c. **DBCC SHOW_STATISTICS**
   d. **DBCC CHECKIDENT**

8. After inserting several thousand rows into a table, why should statistics be updated?
   a. Page splitting may cause the database to become fragmented.
   b. The indexes may need to be rebuilt to reflect the new keys.
   c. The histogram for the indexes will no longer be accurate.
   d. The table will now be more densely populated.

9. What are some reasons you might turn off auto-updating of statistics for a database?
   a. To control when statistics will be updated better, so that user activity is not impacted.
   b. If a table grows during the day and is truncated at night.
   c. Because you need to disable statistics updating for certain tables.
   d. All of the above.

10. Which of the following conditions can mask the problems created by out-of-date statistics?
    a. Data caching
    b. Fragmented pages
    c. High transaction rates
    d. All the above.

11. You should use the database maintenance wizard for all databases and not try to run maintenance by hand on any tables.
    a. True
    b. False

12. Which of the following options can you use to give an actual number of rows that you want the database to sample?
    a. **ROW**
    b. **SAMPLE**
    c. **PERCENT**
    d. **ALL**

13. By default, what will running **UPDATE STATISTICS** on a table with no options do?
    a. Nothing.
    b. Update statistics only on tables that have statistics defined on them.
    c. Update statistics only on indexes that have statistics defined on them.
    d. Update the statistics on all indexes and all columns that have statistics defined on them.

14. When should you create statistics?
    a. Before loading data into the tables
    b. After loading data into the tables
    c. After creating the table
    d. After creating the table and then the indexes

15. SQL Server 7 has the capability to update statistics automatically. This is always desirable because the database engine has been designed to know when to do this.
    a. True
    b. False

HANDS-ON PROJECTS

Susan had designed the database with proper joins, optimized indexes, and normalized and denormalized table structures as required. She nervously delivered the database to the testing staff that had been working with her on the project. The testers loaded the database with several megabytes of data and created test scripts that inserted randomly, updated, and deleted data from the database, using the application and software designed for that purpose. At the next project review, the testers made their report. "Well," the testing representative said, "the program runs fine at first, but as you can see here," he pointed to a chart showing a graph with a severely declining red line, "at about 10,000 transactions performance tanks." The programmers and Susan scribbled some notes. The day after the meeting, the lead of the testing staff approached Susan and said, "The developers tell me that they don't have anything in the code that would explain the dropoff in performance at that point. Guess the ball's in your court." Susan went back to her cubicle and opened the Query Analyzer on the database. "I guess the first place to start is to check the fragmentation," she thought.

Project 18.1

In this project, you will create a test table to examine the effects of fragmentation on performance. Note that your results from the following queries may differ slightly from the results displayed here.

1. Open a new Query Analyzer window and select *tempdb* as the active database. We are using *tempdb* so that the table we are going to create will be removed automatically when the database is recycled. Alternatively, you can use any database you would like; just remember to remove that table at the end.

2. Create the *ShowContigSample* table using the following **CREATE** statement:

```
create table ShowContigSample
(
    id          int,
    bigdata     char(3000),
    primary key clustered (id)
)
```

3. Next we need to populate the table with lots of data. The following script can be used to create 8,000 rows in the table (this will be 32MB of data):

```
set nocount on
declare @numrows int
select  @numrows = 1
while   (@numrows < 8000)    – this is 500 extents, or 4000 pages,
begin                        – or 31.25Mb of data
    insert ShowContigSample values (@numrows, 'bigdata')
    select @numrows = @numrows + 1
end
```

4. Next, let's take a look at the table fragmentation after adding so many rows. Run the following command and see if the table is fragmented. The results in this test are highlighted below the script:

```
/*** initial showcontig as baseline ***/
declare @id int
select  @id = object_id( "ShowContigSample" )
dbcc showcontig( @id )
```

```
DBCC SHOWCONTIG scanning 'ShowContigSample' table...
Table: 'ShowContigSample' (1813581499); index ID: 1, database ID: 6
TABLE level scan performed.
- Pages Scanned................................: 4000
- Extents Scanned..............................: 503
- Extent Switches..............................: 502
- Avg. Pages per Extent........................: 8.0
- Scan Density [Best Count:Actual Count].......: 99.40% [500:503]
- Logical Scan Fragmentation ..................: 0.13%
- Extent Scan Fragmentation ...................: 0.20%
- Avg. Bytes Free per Page.....................: 2068.8
- Avg. Page Density (full).....................: 74.44%
DBCC execution completed. If DBCC printed error messages, contact
your system administrator.
```

5. The table is not fragmented because we were adding a number of rows where the key was incrementing sequentially in the same order as the clustered index. Next we want to devise a performance test that we can run now and again later on when the table is fragmented to compare results. The following script will force a number of table scans on our newly created table. The total time is accumulated and averaged to give us an average number of milliseconds for each iteration. Using this approach will normalize effects, such as caching and fluctuations in CPU resources. Type in and run this script in your database. The test results we obtained are highlighted below the script.

```
/*** initial performance test as baseline ***/
set nocount on
declare @start datetime,
        @Iterations int,
        @count int,
        @elapsedtime int
select  @Iterations = 1, @start = getdate()
while   (@Iterations < 1000)
begin
    select  @count = count(*)
    from    ShowContigSample
    with    (index=0)

    select  @Iterations = @Iterations + 1
end
select  @elapsedtime = datediff(ms, @start, getdate())
select  @elapsedtime / 1000.0000 as TotalScanTime
```

```
TotalScanTime
------------
40.870000000
```

18

Project 18.2

In this project, you will look at the effects of fragmentation on performance. Note that your results from the following queries may differ slightly than the results displayed here.

1. We need to generate a lot of update activity on the table in order to produce fragmentation. The following script accomplishes that by randomly selecting 2,000 keys from the table and changing their values. Type in and run this script:

```
/*** lots of update statements to modify the key ***/
set nocount on
declare @OldId int,
        @Iterations int,
        @NewId int
select  @Iterations = 1
while   (@Iterations < 2000)
begin
    select  @OldId = ceiling( rand() * 8000)
    select  @NewId = ceiling( rand() * 8000) + 10000

    if not exists( select * from ShowContigSample where id = @NewId )
        update  ShowContigSample
        set id = @NewId
        where   id = @OldId

    select  @Iterations = @Iterations + 1
end
```

2. Next, let's look at the **SHOWCONTIG** output again to verify that we have indeed fragmented the table. Type in and run the following script. Again the test results are shown highlighted:

```
/*** new showcontig ***/
declare @id int
select  @id = object_id( "ShowContigSample" )
dbcc showcontig( @id )
```

```
DBCC SHOWCONTIG scanning 'ShowContigSample' table...
Table: 'ShowContigSample' (1813581499); index ID: 1, database ID: 6
TABLE level scan performed.
- Pages Scanned................................: 5065
- Extents Scanned..............................: 637
- Extent Switches..............................: 1564
- Avg. Pages per Extent........................: 8.0
- Scan Density [Best Count:Actual Count].......: 40.51% [634:1565]
```

```
- Logical Scan Fragmentation ..................: 21.34%
- Extent Scan Fragmentation ...................: 0.16%
- Avg. Bytes Free per Page.....................: 2408.3
- Avg. Page Density (full).....................: 70.25%
DBCC execution completed. If DBCC printed error messages, contact
your system administrator.
```

3. Now we want to run our performance test again. Rerun the performance test listed previously and see what your results are. Here are the results:

```
TotalScanTime
-------------
56.643000000
```

4. Remember to drop your table.:

```
drop table ShowContigSample
```

5. Even though the data from this table was 100 percent in cache on the computer for this author, the performance degraded by 40 percent as a result of fragmentation. Now you can see that your database performance will suffer significantly if you do not properly maintain it. It is interesting that the performance degraded by the same percentage that the table is fragmented. Although this is not always the case, it probably reflects the randomness of the updates that were made to the table to make it fragmented. As a side observation, if you run the update script several more times, the average page density will approach 50 percent (plus or minus some due to the row size). That is because the storage engine moves 50 percent of the rows to a new page during a page split.

Susan ran all her tests and found that the database was indeed highly fragmented. She set up a full maintenance plan using the database maintenance wizard and had the testers run their tests again, with various stop points in the testing for the maintenance. From those results she found that the best place for the maintenance was at about 18,000 transactions. The developers estimated that they would see that many transactions per day, so she estimated that general maintenance would need to be run every three nights, and on some tables and indexes nightly.

CHAPTER NINETEEN

19

DIAGNOSING PROBLEMS AND IMPROVING QUERY PERFORMANCE

After Reading This Chapter And Completing The Exercises, You Will Be Able To:

- Understand how to read and use text and graphical query plans to analyze queries
- Gain an understanding of the Index Tuning Wizard and how to use it to prevent performance problems
- Learn the common uses for SQL Profiler and how it can help you pinpoint database problems
- Be able to use Performance Monitor to benchmark and track database performance trends
- Discover the biggest problem when manually migrating existing applications from other database packages

We have learned about the basic server architecture, tables, stored procedures, views, triggers, transaction management, and many other aspects of designing and implementing solutions using SQL Server 7. We complete our study of SQL Server design and implementation with a look at potential problems and performance improvements.

Query Plans

A *query optimizer* engine within a database product is the part of the program that is responsible for determining the fastest, most accurate route to the data. The query optimizer for SQL Server 7 is a *cost-based optimizer*. This means that as the optimizer evaluates different indexes, join orders, and join algorithms, it assigns a *costing* value to each option, where the cost is expressed as an approximate amount of time it will take to complete the query. In some cases, the optimizer determines that it will be more efficient to do a table *scan* (look at each record in the table one at a time) as opposed to using an index to locate the data. Other situations will result in the optimizer choosing a series of indexes in an index *intersection* to resolve the query. In each case, the optimizer evaluates each access path and chooses the path that has the lowest overall cost.

You might be interested in the optimizer's decision-making process. SQL Server provides a very sophisticated interface into the query optimizer that returns information about how your query is going to be executed. It also returns costing information at each step of the way so you can see the information the optimizer used to make its decision. Learning to use this information is very important, as it is one of the more powerful ways to identify and solve query problems.

Simple Text Query Plans

You can use a couple of different methods to display query plan information. Let's start with the simplest first. Before running your query, set the **SHOWPLAN_TEXT** connection property on. You do this by running the command:

```
SET SHOWPLAN_TEXT ON
go
```

from your current session window in the Query Analyzer tool. If this setting is turned on, your query will not be executed when you instruct the system to run it. Instead, information regarding the estimated query plan will be returned to you in a text format. You can observe this behavior by opening a new Query Analyzer window in the *Northwind* database and executing the following commands:

```
SET SHOWPLAN_TEXT ON
go
SELECT  c.CustomerID, c.CompanyName, o.OrderID,
        o.ShippedDate, o.ShipVia, o.ShipName
FROM    Orders o
join    Customers c
```

```
  on     o.CustomerID = c.CustomerID
where    o.OrderID = 10248
go
SET SHOWPLAN_TEXT Off
```

When you run this query with **SHOWPLAN_TEXT** turned on, you will see a hierarchical query plan returned. The output is very wide, so we will try to wrap it while still keeping it as readable as possible below:

```
StmtText
-------------------------
|-Nested Loops(Inner Join)
 |-Clustered Index Seek(OBJECT:([Northwind].[dbo].[Orders].[PK_Orders]
    AS [o]), SEEK:([o].[OrderID]=10248) ORDERED)
 |-Clustered Index Seek(OBJECT:([Northwind].[dbo].[Customers]
    [PK_Customers] AS [c]), SEEK:([c].[CustomerID]=[o].[CustomerID])
    ORDERED)
```

Although a lot of the details, such as costing values, are not shown, enough information is available to determine what the optimizer is doing with your query. In this case, we see that the optimizer has chosen the *nested loops* join method, and that the *Orders* table has been placed as the outer table (since it is the first table listed). A nested loop join loops through each qualifying row in the outer table, and for each row in the outer loop, it loops through the inner table to find all matching rows. This type of join is usually used when the number of qualifying rows in the outer table is small, and the inner table is indexed on the join criteria. A clustered index is used to resolve both the outer and inner tables.

The italic statements in the **SHOWPLAN** output, such as *Clustered Index Seek*, are referred to as *physical* operators because they indicate a physical index seek by the database. Also, *logical* operators are shown for other types of queries; for example, *Compute Scalar*, which indicates that the optimizer is evaluating a statement to compute a scalar value. Let's look at another example that shows other operators:

```
StmtText
---------------------------------------------
SELECT  c.CustomerID, c.CompanyName, count(*)
FROM    Orders o
join    Customers c
  on    o.CustomerID = c.CustomerID
where   o.OrderID = 10248
group by c.CustomerID, c.CompanyName

(1 row(s) affected)
```

19

```
StmtText
-------------------------------------------
|--Stream Aggregate(GROUP BY:([c].[CompanyName],
   [c].[CustomerID]) DEFINE:([Expr1002]=Count(*)))
   |--Nested Loops(Inner Join,
      WHERE:([c].[CustomerID]=[o].[CustomerID]))
      |--Sort(ORDER BY:([c].[CompanyName] ASC, [c].[CustomerID] ASC))
      |  |--Table Scan(OBJECT:([Northwind].[dbo].[Customers] AS [c]))
      |--Table Spool
         |--Table Scan(OBJECT:([Northwind].[dbo].[Orders] AS [o]),
            WHERE:([o].[OrderID]=10248))
```

This time, the optimizer shows a very different query plan. A query plan like this might be produced if the index statistics became out of date. Notice that table scans are being done on both input tables. The output of the first table scan is being sorted so it can be used as the outer table in a nested loop join. A temporary table (*Table Spool*) is created to store the output from the inner table in the join. The optimizer does this to make the join more efficient when no index is available for its use.

Comprehensive Text Query Plans

The **SHOWPLAN_TEXT** output is simple and suffices for most situations. This format was intended for looking at simple queries, and for use from tools such as osql.exe. Other formats exist for viewing the optimizer activity. Another method is to set the **SHOWPLAN_ALL** option. This is simply an expanded format of the same type of information returned by **SHOWPLAN_TEXT**. In fact, the same hierarchical query plan information is also contained in the **SHOWPLAN_ALL** output. The difference is that costing information is also reported. Try running the same query we looked at earlier using this format. Because the output is over 750 bytes wide, we won't show the results here. Fortunately, an easier way is available to view this information.

Graphical Query Plans

Query Analyzer includes a graphical interpreter that displays the **SHOWPLAN_ALL** information in an easy-to-read graphical format. As the **SHOWPLAN** output is returned, Query Analyzer interprets the physical (for example, **SEEK**) and logical (for example, nested loops) operators into icons. The icons are organized into an information flow diagram showing the steps the optimizer will use to resolve the query. Related costing information is associated with each icon and is displayed when the pointer is hovered. In your Query Analyzer window, highlight the query and press Ctrl+L (or select Query|Display Estimated Execution Plan from the pull-down menu). Figure 19.1 shows the results.

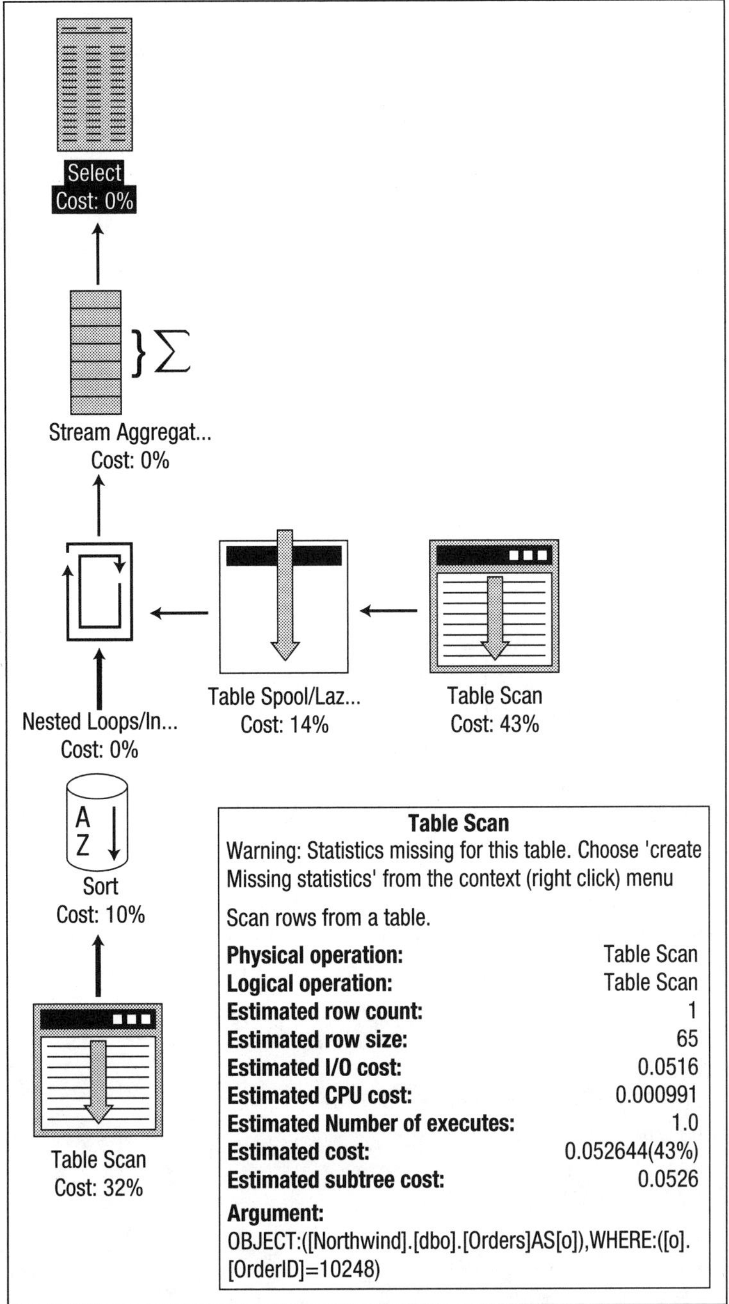

Figure 19.1 Example of graphical **SHOWPLAN** output.

You should pay particular attention to a couple of items in Figure 19.1. First, notice the pop-up window. These windows appear whenever you hold the mouse pointer over any of the icons or lines. Costing and detailed information about the underlying step is displayed. In addition, this pop-up window provides a warning message regarding missing statistics. Such a message is displayed whenever the optimizer could benefit from creating statistics. Missing statistics can be created automatically by right-clicking the icon and selecting Create Missing Statistics. Opening the Create Statistics window also gives you the opportunity to see what statistics the optimizer is asking for.

Next, notice the two Table Scan icons, as seen in the diagram, that have arrows leading to the Nested Loops icon. The uppermost Table Scan icon has arrows that are a little bolder than the icon on the bottom of the diagram. Bolder arrows indicate that the table represented by the icon is the outer table in the join. The other table is the inner, or *probe*, table. This is an important observation, because the table that will return the fewest number of rows should be the outer table. If you see that this is not the case, the optimizer is not selecting the best query plan for your situation.

Finally, each icon in the illustration has a "Cost: %" below it. Each step in the query plan includes an estimate of the amount of time that it will take to complete the step. The displayed percentage indicates how much of the total cost of the query the individual step represents. By looking at this graphical query plan output and paying attention to the "Cost: %," it is very easy to spot which steps are the most costly. When performance is not what you want it to be, you can focus your attention on optimizing these steps.

Let's examine another graphical query plan. We are trying to grow the Northwind seafood business and want to determine the top ten customers for these products. The following query has been designed to return this information:

```
select  top 10
        C.CompanyName,
        sum(Quantity) as NumberOrdered
from    Customers C
join    Orders O
on      C.CustomerID = O.CustomerID
join    [Order Details] D
on      D.OrderID = O.OrderID
join    Products P
on      P.ProductID = D.ProductID
where   P.CategoryID = 8
group by C.CompanyName
order by NumberOrdered desc
```

Figure 19.2 shows the graphical query plan that this query produces. What types of joins are being used to satisfy this query? Are clustered indexes being used?

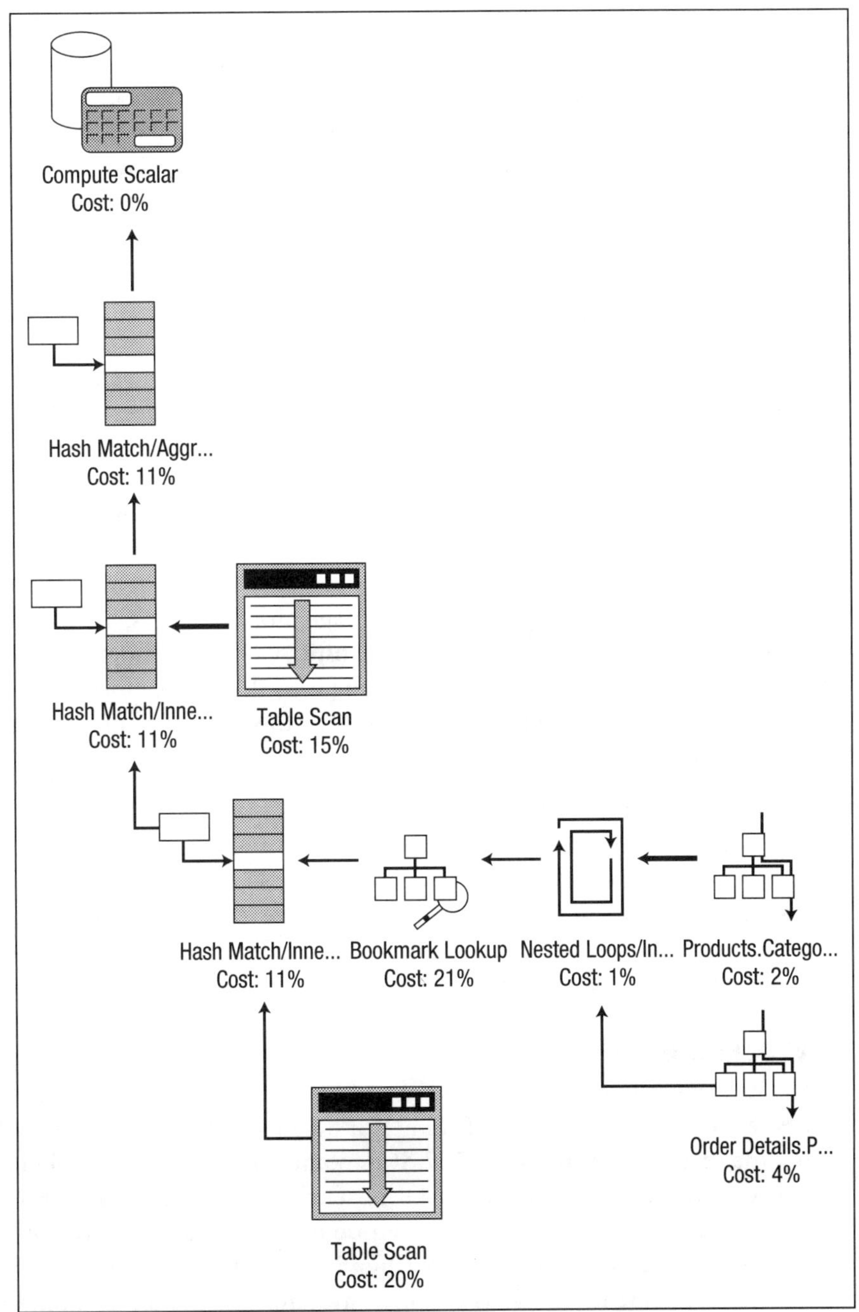

Figure 19.2 Graphical **SHOWPLAN** output.

These questions can be easily discerned by looking at the icons representing each of the steps. A nested loop join is being used to resolve the *Products* and *Order Details* table join. The resultant rows are then combined with the table scan input of the *Orders* table in a hash match join. Finally, these rows are combined in another hash join with the *Customers* table. Table 19.1 shows the most frequently used symbols in the graphical **SHOWPLAN**. Be sure to familiarize yourself with the index access symbols. These symbols can be further researched in *Books Online*.

Index Tuning Wizard

One of the more challenging tasks for a DBA to perform is to analyze the workload of a database in relation to the schema and available indexes. During the initial design, a database designer typically avoids placing indexes on tables where they are not essential. This is usually done to avoid the extra overhead associated with updating extra indexes during **INSERT**, **UPDATE**, and **DELETE** operations. Too many indexes result in slow performance for updates, whereas too few indexes result in table scans and poor performance for data retrieval operations. As the size of a database grows and the usage profile changes, it may become necessary to add additional indexes or statistics to keep the applications running at their optimum performance. Due to the high degree of effort and time it takes to complete such an analysis, often even the most diligent DBAs do not make such a practice a routine occurrence.

SQL Server 7 has added a valuable time-saving wizard to help you determine if it would be wise to create or drop indexes or statistics as a result of current workloads. By using this utility in conjunction with NT's PerfMon and SQL Server's Profiler, it becomes much more feasible to analyze databases regularly and workloads for possible performance gains. The Index Tuning Wizard is an easy-to-use application wizard that steps you through conducting a thorough index analysis.

Workload Files

Creating a workload file is an important fundamental step in achieving the desired results with the Index Tuning Wizard. A workload file is a SQL Profiler log file that contains up to 32,767 SQL commands. A SQL statement may be a stored procedure call or a direct DML statement (**SELECT**, **INSERT**, **UPDATE**, **DELETE**). The basic premise behind the analyzer is that a query plan is generated several times for each individual SQL statement in the batch. For each statement, the wizard works through the possible combinations of indexes and statistics that could exist on the table and that are referenced by the query plan. The execution cost for each combination is reviewed and analyzed to determine the best possible method of access. After each SQL statement is reviewed in this fashion, the optimal index and statistics configuration for the workload is compared with the indexes that already exist to produce a change recommendation.

Table 19.1 Most commonly used graphical **SHOWPLAN** icons.

Data Access Methods Symbol	Description
	*Index scan* (clustered or nonclustered)
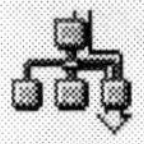	*Index seek* (clustered or nonclustered)
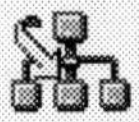	*Index spool*—A temporary table is created to hold the contents of a table scan or index scan for the purpose of creating an alternate index on the data. Most often this indicates that an appropriate index does not exist.
	*Table scan*—No indexes are used.
	*Table spool*—The results of a table scan are stored in a temporary table.
Join Methods Symbol	**Description**
	*Nested loops*—The inner table is scanned for each row in the outer table.
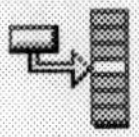	*Hash match*—The optimizer assigns the smaller result set to be designated as the build input; the larger result set is termed the probe input.
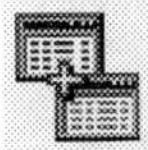	*Merge join*—Both inputs must be sorted. Each input is scanned and related to the other input. Nonmatching rows are discarded.
Miscellaneous Symbols	**Description**
	Indicates that the optimizer has inserted a parallel query operator. The presence of this operator only indicates that it is possible that the query will be executed in parallel to speed execution. Even though the operator is present in a query plan, the query engine may still determine during execution that it is more efficient to execute the query steps in serial.
	The compute scalar symbol indicates that the optimizer is combining one or more inputs to result in a scalar output.

It is vital to be sure that the workload file is representative of the database usage. If key queries are missing from the workload file, the Index Tuning Wizard will not be able to determine whether any changes to existing indexes may be warranted. Unless you are sure that every query that can be run in the database is included in the workload file, you should check the Keep All Existing Indexes option on the first panel of the wizard. That way the wizard will not generate **DROP** statements for indexes and statistics that were not used in the workload analysis.

To create a workload file, start the SQL Profiler application and create a new trace. After naming your new trace, select the Capture To File: option and provide a file name. The default event objects—Sessions And TSQL—will work fine, although most users usually remove the Sessions events to reduce the clutter and size of the trace file. The default data columns will work sufficiently, but only the text column is really needed. You might also want to filter for certain commands. For example, suppose you only want to review the queries submitted by a certain user or for a certain application. By filtering by this type of criteria, you can run the Index Tuning Wizard on only this subset of queries. Once you have created a sufficient amount of information, you are ready to run the wizard.

Running The Index Tuning Wizard

To start the wizard, select the Tools|Wizards drop-down menu, then select Management|Index Tuning Wizard. Once you are running the wizard, you are asked to select the server and database you wish to analyze. There are two additional options on the first panel that affect the analysis that is going to take place. First, you have the option of instructing the wizard to keep existing indexes. This is usually a good idea unless you are sure that all possible queries are included in the workload file. The second factor to consider is whether to choose the Perform Thorough Analysis option. Selecting the option to perform a thorough analysis forces the wizard to inspect every possible combination of creating indexes and statistics for each query, which takes a very long time. Even if you do not perform an exhaustive index analysis, the wizard will find nearly every situation where index or statistic creation is necessary.

On the next panel you are prompted to choose whether you have already created a workload file or whether you still need to create one. If you select the I Will Create The Workload File On My Own option, the wizard will start SQL Profiler and exit. Select I Have A Saved Workload File to continue with the wizard execution. Click Next and enter the location of your workload information. Here you may also set some advanced options (see Figure 19.3), such as specifying the maximum storage size for all recommended indexes or the maximum number of columns to recommend for an index.

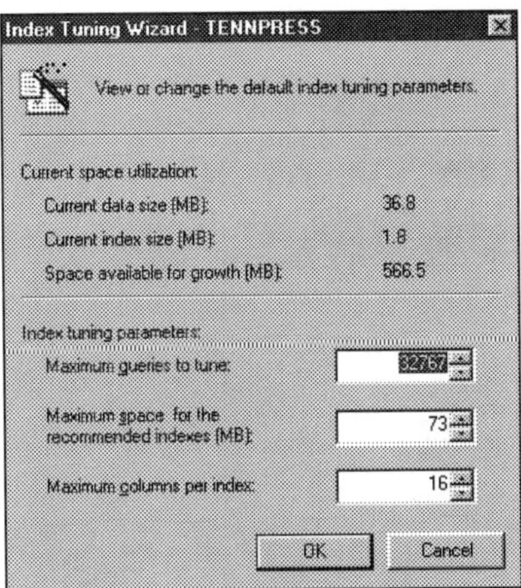

Figure 19.3 Index Tuning Wizard advanced processing options.

Selecting the next panel brings up a list of tables in the database. This screen gives you even more flexibility in specifying where you want the optimizer to spend its energy. If you suspect that certain tables may benefit from new indexes, or other tables are heavily used but you don't want to analyze them, select the tables to include in the index analysis. You are now ready to begin processing the workload file. Clicking Next starts the analysis phase, which might take a very long time. Depending on how many queries and tables are in your database, be prepared to allow the wizard to run for an extended period.

The Index Tuning Wizard can execute several dozen queries for each SQL statement in the workload file during its analysis. Therefore, you should use discretion as to when you run the wizard. For example, it would not be wise to run the wizard on a heavily loaded system during peak processing times.

When the processing completes you will be presented with a table of recommended indexes. Indexes that already exist will be checked. Those that SQL Server recommends to be created as clustered indexes are also checked. You can view a lot of very useful information by clicking the Analysis button. Available reports include index usage for the current and recommended configuration, a table analysis, query cost, and several other reports. Figure 19.4 shows a sample report.

So far we still haven't made any changes to the database structure. The next panel 19
provides the opportunity to apply the recommended changes. Available options include implementing the recommendations immediately (not recommended on busy production systems), scheduling the changes for a certain time using SQL Agent, or saving the DDL in a script file that can be reviewed and executed at a later time.

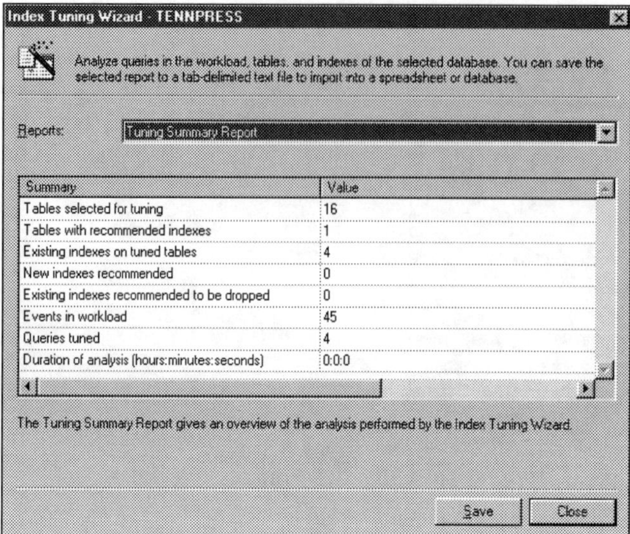

Figure 19.4 Tuning summary report.

Running the tuning wizard on a regular basis will go a long way in providing you with piece of mind that your index design is still optimal. A good interval to run the wizard is once per month, whenever a significant milestone in database growth is reached, or when the application usage profile has changed significantly. For example, when a new application is implemented, it is a good idea to use the wizard to validate the design.

SQL Profiler

SHOWPLAN and the Index Tuning Wizard are valuable tools for SQL 7, but nothing can take the place of SQL Profiler for helping you pinpoint a problem. SQL Profiler is a client application with hooks directly into the query engine; it allows you to capture pertinent information about how applications are interacting with the server. You can determine when users connect, disconnect, execute a query, and many other actions. In this chapter we will not try to provide a complete guide on using the tool, but instead we'll focus on how you can use the tool to help you identify and solve the most common query problems.

Tracing An Application

It is often difficult to determine whether a performance or usage problem is related to the database or an application issue. The interaction between an application and the database is complex, and it is often difficult to trace the source of problems. The user of the application sees only the output and cannot be a source of problem solving, and application developers often point to the database as an issue. Using SQL Profiler is a very valuable way to pinpoint these sorts of problems. As an example, the developers of a WWW application told us that the use of connection pooling was employed, and that the WWW servers would not cycle through connections very often. However, using SQL Profiler we discovered a very high connect/disconnect rate from the WWW servers and helped to uncover a fundamental application problem that the developers were not aware of. Using SQL Profiler as a preventive measure before applications go live can eliminate a lot of problems and headaches later.

The basic events that you will want to capture when examining an application using SQL Profiler include one or more of the items in the TSQL group, such as SQL:BatchCompleted or SQL:BatchStarting. The Starting events record the command or batch before execution commences, while the Completed events record the same information after execution is completed. You will probably want to capture the data before execution starts, because if something takes a very long time, you will still know what commands were sent to the database. You can also capture Connect and Disconnect events, Lock:Deadlock, Prepare SQL, and other such events to help you see what is going on.

Unless you have exclusive use of the database server when tracing an application, you will see data coming from all users, for all applications, in all databases. Using the filter properties of the trace allows you to specify certain criteria to include or exclude from your analysis. For example, you may want to see what user AustinBradleySchulz is doing in the database. To do this, select SQL User Name from the Trace Event Criteria window and enter AustinBradleySchulz in the Include text box (see Figure 19.5). Subsequently, only database activity from this user will show up in the Trace window.

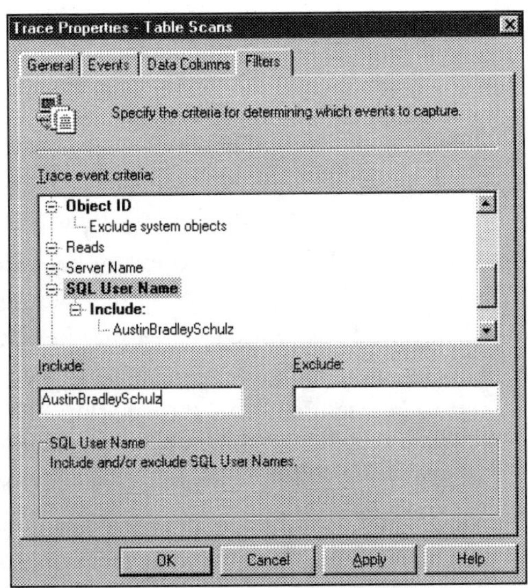

Figure 19.5 Adding filter criteria.

Next we will look at some more specific uses of SQL Profiler in solving common problems.

Table Scans

Let's suppose that an application that you are supporting is not performing correctly and that you suspect the problem is a result of a table scan. You can use SQL Profiler to help you determine for which tables a full scan is being used. The best way to do this is to set up a new trace for just this purpose. Include only the Scan:Started event in the Events pane to trap table scan events. The only other even you may want to consider adding is the SQL:StmtStarting event that traps the execution of DML or stored procedures, although on a busy server the trace output can become very cluttered and confusing.

You can save yourself a lot of time by including the server name, database ID, and object ID in your data columns. If all three of these are included, SQL Profiler automatically looks up the name corresponding to the object name or database name and substitutes those values for the object IDs in the trace output. For example, by doing this you will not need to figure that the object ID of 213575799 corresponds to the *Northwind.Customers* table.

After selecting the events to include, at a minimum you should include the following data columns in your scan:

- Event class
- Server name
- Database ID
- Object ID
- Event subclass

As an alternative, it may be useful to add the server name, database ID, and object ID to form a group (see Figure 19.6). Doing this will give you a summary of the tables that are being used in scans and how often they are being accessed in a table scan. One thing that you will immediately notice when doing this is that the system tables are scanned hundreds of times. Every time the database does any work, it usually starts out scanning the system tables to gather information about what it is about to do. Capturing all this information can clutter and confuse your results, but it is possible to use the filtering features of SQL Profiler and eliminate the unnecessary information. In the Filter tab, select the Object ID in the Trace Event Criteria window. Then check the Exclude System Objects checkbox to filter out any table scans on the system tables.

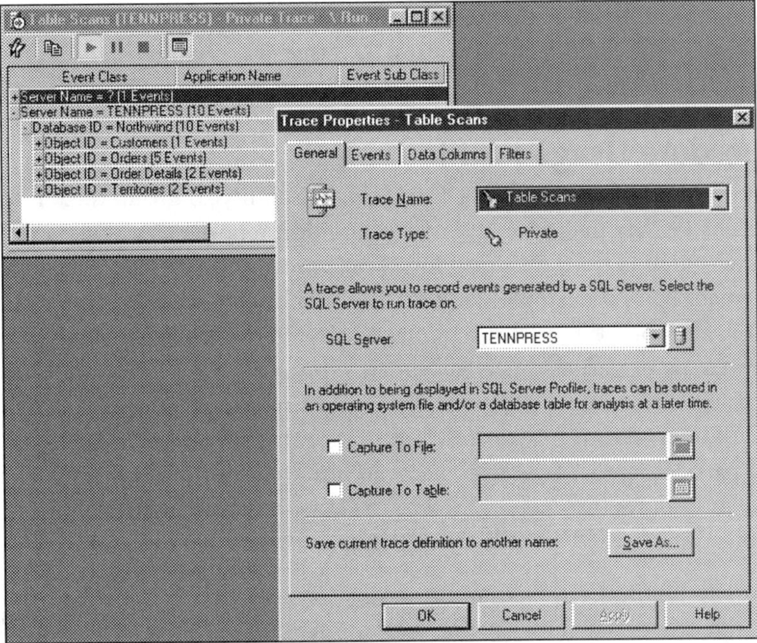

Figure 19.6 SQL Profiler table scans.

Finding Deadlocks

Consider that users are calling you with reports of deadlock errors in an application. If the server is a production server, it is likely that you will not have set the DBCC trace options that will log deadlocking information to the SQL error log, because this option produces excess overhead activity in a live environment. You will need another way to find out what tables are being deadlocked. You can determine this by setting up a SQL Profiler trace and including the Lock:Deadlock and/or Lock:DeadlockChain events. The trace will not let you see deadlock events that have already occurred prior to your starting the trace. However, you will be able to identify those tables that are a party to subsequent deadlock events.

In using SQL Profiler to locate deadlocks, you will only be able to determine the tables that are a part of the deadlock condition on the first pass. You will then need to perform further analysis on connections, users, or applications to determine the root cause of the deadlocking. As in tracing for table scans, tracking for deadlocks is much more effective if the deadlock events are the only ones included in your trace definition. Figure 19.7 shows sample trace results from a deadlock. The Lock:DeadlockChain event shows the sequence leading up to the deadlock. In this case connection 137 acquired a table lock on the *Customers* table. Connection 138 then acquired a table lock on the

Orders table. Finally, both connections tried to get a lock on the other's table, resulting in a deadlock. Connection 138 that was trying to get a table lock on the *Customers* became the victim, as shown by the Lock:Deadlock event.

Procedure Usage Profile

Another useful feature of SQL Profiler is the ability to group trace information together. Rather than have the trace definition report every single event that occurs (much like a transaction log), you can set it up to report only summary information. One example where that can be useful is to determine the profile of how an application uses stored procedures. We were able to use this technique to find a major performance flaw in an application. By looking at which stored procedures were being executed and how many times they were being called over an interval of time, we were able to see that something was not quite right. One particular procedure was executed hundreds of times more frequently than other procedures that were related to the same business function. Further research uncovered very inefficient logic in the application.

To set up a summary trace, add only the SP:Starting event to your definition. Add the event class, server name, database ID, and object ID to the Groups tree under the Select Data window (see Figure 19.8). If you are only interested in profiling a particular user or application, be sure to set the filtering criteria. Figure 19.9 shows the summary output from this type of trace.

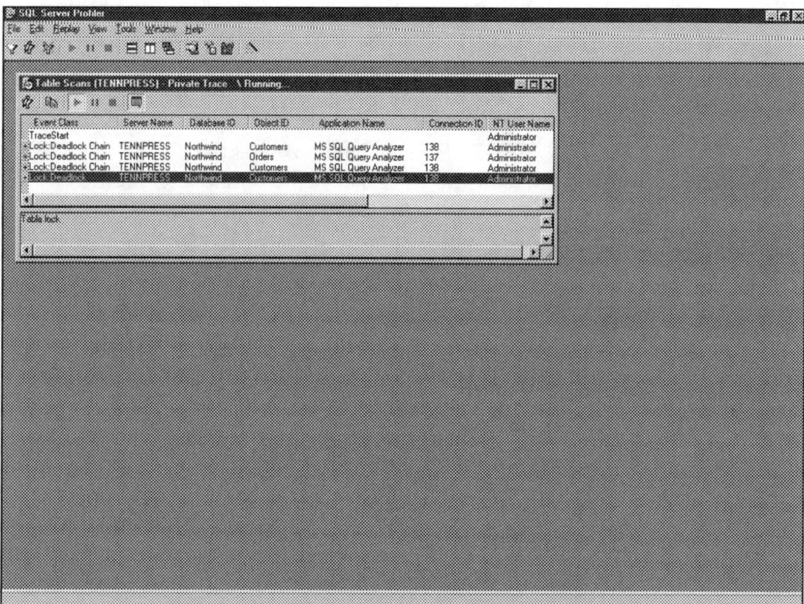

Figure 19.7 Deadlock trace results.

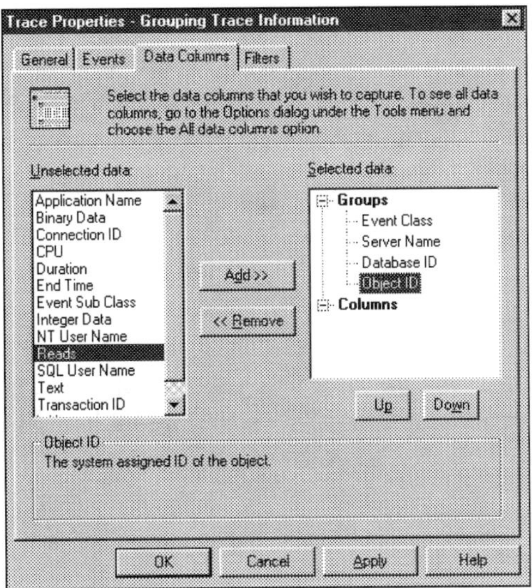

Figure 19.8 Creating a summary trace output.

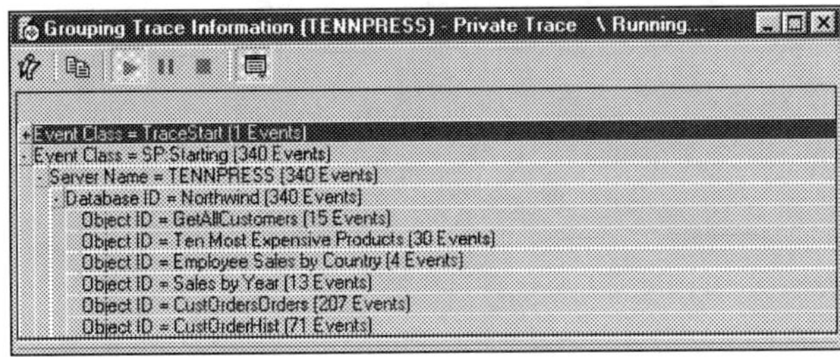

Figure 19.9 Summary trace output.

When creating a summary trace definition, you cannot remove the event class and add it back into the Groups tree. You need to select the event class item and then click Up until it moves up into the Groups section.

Performance Monitor

You are now on your way toward knowing that your queries are as tuned as they possibly can be. Let's examine another tool that shows the areas you can tune to gain more performance out of your system or to help you identify the source of a problem. Windows NT includes a very useful tool called *Performance Monitor*, that gives you insight into the inner workings of your server. Using Performance Monitor, or PerfMon, you can monitor counters, such as the number of page splits per second, work tables created per second,

19

cache hit ration, database and log size, number of user connections, current blocks, current deadlocks, and much more. These items are just a small portion of the many SQL Server counters that you can track. Other NT and hardware-related counters are also important to server performance.

PerfMon is available only on Windows NT computers. To start the program, select the Performance Monitor icon from the Microsoft SQL Server 7 program group. A default set of counters is already provided for you. You can remove these counters by highlighting them and pressing the Delete key. Add new counters by clicking the plus sign in the toolbar at the top of the window. You can also log the output to a file for later viewing, or adjust the counter sampling interval by setting various options. Check the online help for making these changes.

The major counter objects, or containers, that are specific to SQL Server include the following:

- SQLServer:Access Methods
- SQLServer:Backup Device
- SQLServer:Buffer Manager
- SQLServer:Cache Manager
- SQLServer:Databases
- SQLServer:General Statistics
- SQLServer:Latches
- SQLServer:Locks
- SQLServer:Memory Manager
- SQLServer:Replication Agents
- SQLServer:Replication Dist.
- SQLServer:Replication Logreader
- SQLServer:Replication Merger
- SQLServer:Replication Snapshot
- SQLServer:SQL Statistics
- SQLServer:User Settable

Although we cannot cover each of these in detail, we will look at the more commonly used counter objects that relate more to design and implementation as opposed to administration.

Access Methods

The *SQLServer:Access Methods* object contains several counters that are very interesting. However, in this section we focus only on the *Full Scans/sec*, *Page Splits/sec*, and *Worktables Created/sec* counters. Although some overlap exists between some of the information you can mine from both PerfMon and SQL Profiler, PerfMon is more suited to long-term statistics gathering and is a good tool to use to monitor database usage trends. For example, you can glean table scan information from both PerfMon and SQL Profiler. Using PerfMon, you can determine the rate of table scans per second that are being used by the optimizer.

The appearance of table scans is not necessarily a bad thing, because it may take less I/O requests to scan an entire table than it would take to use an index. However, if table scan rates sharply increase or decrease, this could be a cause for concern. Table scans can also be a symptom of poorly written queries or index statistics that are outdated. This makes it difficult to distinguish between healthy and problem table scans, especially for newly designed systems. Once a system has been achieving good performance in production, it is a good idea to get a baseline of key metrics such as *Table Scans/sec* over a designated period of time (for example one week) to use for comparison later on.

In Chapter 18, we talked at length about data and index fragmentation. One primary cause for fragmentation is the occurrence of page splitting, which happens when a page becomes full and the storage engine needs to move half of the data onto a newly allocated page. If you monitor the rate of page split activity in your database, you can get a feel for how fast fragmentation is occurring, and subsequently how often a reorganization of data might be needed. That is the purpose for the Page Splits/sec counter. It measures how many times each second the storage engine is splitting pages. Excessive page splitting can also cause **UPDATE** and **INSERT** statements to perform poorly, more than likely indicating that index pages are too full. So if you are caught researching why **SELECT** statements are performing well, but **INSERT** and **UPDATE** statements are performing poorly, this is one area to look for.

The third counter we want to examine is the number of worktables created per second. A *worktable* is a hidden temporary table that is created by the database engine to resolve certain joins, **ORDER BY**, **GROUP BY**, or **UNION** statements. If a query contains an **ORDER BY** statement and no index is present to satisfy the sorting requirements, the optimizer may choose to create a worktable to reduce the I/O requests needed to sort the results. Although it is sometimes difficult to avoid the creation of queries that create worktables, an excessive use of worktables indicates either poorly written queries or the absence of adequate indexes. In other words, some worktables are acceptable, but too many indicate a likelihood of performance problems. Keep track of how many worktables are being created in your database by including the Worktables Created/sec counter in your PerfMon traces.

Databases

The next counter object we will look at is the *SQLServer:Databases* object. This object contains counters that are specific to individual databases. Information such as the amount of free space in the database and log files is available, along with the number of active transactions, number of transactions occurring per second, and the performance of any active bulk copy operations that are running. These counters are best used to compare with a baseline report of the same information.

Sometimes it is handy to know how many transactions are currently active in a database. Consider that you are researching a situation where excessive blocking occurs in the database. One reason for the blocking could be that applications are explicitly defining transactions and holding locks open for an excessive amount of time. We have observed this situation by a third-party gateway product used to interface with another database. By monitoring the *Active Transactions* counter for the database, we were able to determine that there were transactions staying open for a long period of time. It turned out that the gateway product was running the command **SET IMPLICIT_TRANSACTIONS ON**, which unexpectedly started a transaction each time a stored procedure was executed. Since the stored procedure was doing a lot of work and it took a while to complete, extensive blocking was produced in the database.

A related, but different, counter is the *Transactions/sec* counter. This counter records how many transactions are occurring per second. Because each SQL statement runs as an implicit transaction, this counter tells you how many SQL statements are being executed in addition to how many transactions are being defined in those statements. In relation to the other performance counters, this counter can give you an indication of whether the application profile is more like an OLTP or DSS type of application. A low number of transactions per second combined with a high server utilization indicates that the application is acting more like a DSS system. The opposite is also true; a high number of transactions indicates that the application is more like an OLTP system. By tracking the Transactions/sec over time, you can determine if increased server load is a result of increased drive by the application or results from some other reason.

When planning for a server migration or tracking performance problems with downloads from a mainframe, it can be useful to know the throughput of bulk copy operations. The *Bulk Copy Rows/sec* and *Bulk Copy Throughput/sec* counters indicate the measured performance for a specified database. Suppose that you need to review the cause for long-running data transfers from another server. Assuming that the process includes a bulk copy step and that you have a historical baseline of performance numbers, you can use PerfMon and these two counters to quickly alert you as to whether this step is a contributor to the problem or not. If it is, the root cause could be related to page splitting, or perhaps even a result of a new constraint or trigger being applied to the underlying tables.

General Statistics

We discussed in an earlier section on SQL Profiler an example of a problem whose signature was a high number of user connect/disconnect cycles. Although that problem was discovered using SQL Profiler, PerfMon could have also been used. The *SQLServer:General Statistics* object contains counters to track the number of logins per second, logouts per second, and current user connections. These counters, especially the current number of connections, make good candidates on which to set up alerts. Establishing an alert on the current number of connections can provide advanced warning before the number of licensed user connections is exceeded.

Locks

The *SQLServer:Locks* object contains most of the important counters for discovering problems with blocking or deadlocking. A common misunderstanding is that blocking in a database is bad. Blocking in a database simply indicates that the database is doing its job properly by protecting the integrity of the information stored in it. The counters in this object provide a great deal of useful diagnostic information to determine the difference between a good and bad block. Table 19.2 lists the counters found in this object and a description of each one. Each counter can be monitored for each lock type: *Database, Extent, Key, Page, RID, Table.*

Table 19.2 Performance Monitor Locks counters.

Counter	Description
Average Wait Time (ms)	For each lock request that is waiting to be satisfied, this is the average amount of time that the requester must wait. If blocking is high but this number is low, the locks are healthy and are being serviced normally. However, if this number is high and blocking is occurring, that could indicate explicit transactions that are being held open or performance problems.
Lock Requests/sec	This counter provides the number of lock requests per second that are made to the storage engine. It gives a good indication of the level of locking activity on the server.
Lock Timeouts/sec	A query that is waiting on resources can eventually time out. The setting can be changed using the **sp_configure** stored procedure. This counter indicates how often that is happening. A high number here means that problems are occurring in the database that need to be corrected.
Lock Wait Time (ms)	This is the total lock wait time (in ms).

(continued)

19

Table 19.2 Performance Monitor Locks counters *(continued)*.

Counter	Description
Lock Waits/sec	This is the number of lock requests per second that are placed into a wait state. In other words, this is the number of blocks per second that are occurring.
Number of Deadlocks/sec	Hopefully it will not make sense to record the per-second rate of deadlocks in your database design. But if it does, this counter tells you how many deadlocks you are getting each second.

SQL Statistics

In one software package that used SQL Server, we noted that the query plans for the SQL Statements were not being cached; each time a query was issued the optimizer had to compile the query and generate a new query plan. The poor performance was due to the added compilation time for each SQL command. To find this type of problem you can use the *SQL Compilations/sec* counter. In addition to this counter, several others can help you figure out what is going on in your database server. Table 19.3 lists the counters in the *SQLServer:SQL Statistics* object.

Table 19.3 Performance Monitor SQL Statistics object counters.

Counter	Description
Batch Requests/sec	Provides the number of batch requests that are executed per second. Each batch request can in turn contain multiple SQL statements. This gives an indication of how many instructions are being issued to the database by the application, and should be somewhat related to the Transactions/sec counter.
Failed Auto-Parms/sec	Parameterization describes the ability for SQL Server to reuse query plans and avoid recompilations. This number indicates how many times SQL Server unsuccessfully attempted to reuse a query plan.
Safe Auto-Parms/sec	Most of the time when the server caches a query plan, it can be used to satisfy subsequent queries that are similar. However, sometimes there are conditions that exist that prevent the server from reusing an existing cached plan, which is described as an unsafe parameterization attempt.
SQL Compilations/sec	This is the number of times per second the optimizer must compile a query. This number should be small, because a large number of compilations adds excessive overhead and decreases performance.

(continued)

Table 19.3 Performance Monitor SQL Statistics object counters *(continued)*.

Counter	Description
SQL Re-compilations/sec	A query plan for a stored procedure is normally cached and reused. However, if it was created or executed with the **WITH RECOMPILE** option, it will be recompiled each time it runs, adding to the execution time.
Unsafe Auto-Parms/sec	Most of the time when the server caches a query plan, it can be used to satisfy subsequent queries that are similar. However, sometimes conditions exist that prevent the server from reusing an existing cached plan, which is described as an unsafe parameterization attempt.

User Settable Statistics

In addition to the counters just listed, the server allows you to design your own counters. Counters are implemented using stored procedures that are named **sp_user_counter1** through **sp_user_counter10** in the *master* database. By customizing these counters you can log custom counter information using PerfMon. An example of this might be to see how many Web users are in the system:

```
Use master
go
create procedure sp_user_counter1
as
select count(*) from master..sysprocedures
where suser_name(suid) like 'WWW%'
return
```

Chapter Summary

In this chapter you learned about some of the problem-solving tools and methods that are included with SQL Server 7. You also learned:

- A query plan is a description of the optimizer data access plan and gives you insight into the implementation of a specific query.
- You can determine which indexes are being used by studying the query plan.
- The query plan shows you what kind of join is being used, which table is the outer table, and which table is the inner table.
- The **SHOWPLAN_TEXT** connection property returns a simple but effective query plan.
- When a query plan option is enabled, a query plan is returned, but the query does not execute.

- A merge join is used when one of the inputs is small relative to the other input and the inner table is sorted or indexed.
- A query plan that shows a table scan when an suitable index exists is probably due to the distribution statistics being outdated.
- The **SHOWPLAN_ALL** connection property returns the same information as the **SHOWPLAN_TEXT** property along with additional costing information.
- Query Analyzer has the capability to interpret the **SHOWPLAN_ALL** output and produce a graphical query plan output.
- The Index Tuning Wizard helps you determine if any changes to the indexes in your database are necessary.
- A workload file is created by capturing SQL Profiler output and saving it to a file.
- The Index Tuning Wizard can review up to 32,767 queries in a workload file at a time.
- SQL Profiler captures database activity in realtime and can return either detailed or summary information.
- By using the SQL:BatchStarting, SQL:BatchCompleted, SQL:StmtStarting, or SQL:StmtCompleting events and including the Text column in the output, you can capture SQL commands being executed on the database server.
- SQL Profiler can tell on which tables table scans are occurring.
- SQL Profiler can help you identify on which tables deadlocks are occurring.
- Performance Monitor provides a variety of counters for SQL server, the NT operating system, and the server hardware.

Review Questions

1. Which of the following tools is the best way to discover how the optimizer is implementing a query?
   a. **SET SHOWPLAN_TEXT ON**
   b. SQL Profiler
   c. Performance Monitor
   d. ISQLW
2. Which of the following is *not* provided as part of **SHOWPLAN** output?
   a. Method of join being used.
   b. Which index is being used, if any.

c. Which tables come first in a deadlock

d. Whether a temporary worktable is created

3. Which of the following definitions is the *best* to describe what a Table Spool operator in a **SHOWPLAN** output is?

   a. No suitable index is available and a scan of the table is being made.

   b. A hidden temporary worktable is being created to hold intermediate result information.

   c. Data from the table is being cached in memory.

   d. The query results are being printed to the standard output device.

4. Which of the following results in a graphical **SHOWPLAN** output?

   a. **SET SHOWPLAN_TEXT ON**

   b. **SET SHOWPLAN_ALL ON**

   c. **SET SHOWPLAN_GRAPHICAL ON**

   d. None of the above.

5. Which of the following icons indicates that a nested join is being used?

   a.

   b.

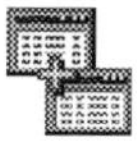

   c.

   d.

6. Which of the following icons indicates the presence of a table scan in a query plan?

   a.

   b.

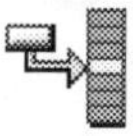

   c.

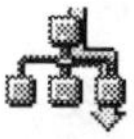

   d.

19

7. The maximum number of commands in a workload file that the Index Tuning Wizard can process is:
   a. User specified in Advanced Options.
   b. Based on the size of the indexes recommended.
   c. 32,767
   d. Unlimited

8. Which of the following events would be used to detect a deadlock using SQL Profiler?
   a. Scan:Started
   b. SQL:StmtStarting
   c. Object ID
   d. None of the above.

9. Which is the *best* tool to use for seeing trends in database performance?
   a. Performance Monitor
   b. SQL Profiler
   c. Index Tuning Wizard
   d. Enterprise Manager

10. What is the most common problem when migrating existing applications to SQL Server 7?
    a. Using Query Analyzer in place of the Upgrade Wizard.
    b. Setting the ANSI **NULLS** setting in the database.
    c. Compiling tables and stored procedures while the **ANSI_NULLS**, **ANSI_PADDING**, and **ANSI_WARNINGS** connection properties are enabled.
    d. None of the above.

11. Which of the following **SHOWPLAN** options displays query costing information?
    a. **SET SHOWPLAN_ALL ON**
    b. **SET SHOWPLAN_TEXT ON**
    c. **SET SHOWPLAN_GRAPHICAL ON**
    d. None of the above.

12. Consider that you are studying the query plan for a query. Given the following query plan output,

```
|--Nested Loops(Inner Join)
|--Clustered Index
Seek(OBJECT:([Northwind].[dbo].[Orders].[PK_Orders]
AS [o]), SEEK:([o].[OrderID]=10248) ORDERED)
```

```
|--Clustered Index
Seek(OBJECT:([Northwind].[dbo].[Customers].
[PK_Customers] AS [c]),
SEEK:([c].[CustomerID]=[o].[CustomerID])
ORDERED)
```

which of the following statements is true?

a. The *Orders* table is being used as the outer table in the join.
b. A **SORT BY** clause is in the query.
c. Both a and b.
d. Neither a nor b.

13. As a general rule of thumb, when running the Index Tuning Wizard you should always drop existing indexes that are not being used to save space and improve performance.

a. True.
b. False.

14. By including the SQL:StmtStarting event in a SQL Profiler definition, which of the following problems will you be able to detect?

a. The application is executing the wrong stored procedure.
b. The application is being deadlocked with another application.
c. Both a and b.
d. None of the above.

15. Which of the following Performance Monitor counters can help you determine how often you might need to rebuild your indexes?

a. Full Scans/sec
b. Page Splits/sec
c. Transactions/sec
d. Lock Timeouts/sec

Hands-On Projects

Susan was near the end of the project. She spent most of her days working on improving the performance of the database (What was it the Microsoft trainer had told her? Oh yes, "Make the pig, then grease the pig") and detecting problems. A tense moment occurred when one of the main stored procedures suddenly stopped returning data from an Oracle database that had been imported. Originally Susan had designed the query with data she generated in a SQL Server table. She then had imported the data from an Oracle database and now it was returning blank rows. Susan opened Query Analyzer and set to work.

Project 19.1

As SQL Server 7 has been out for quite a while now and has proven itself stable and effective. More and more companies are converting existing applications from other database systems to SQL Server. A very robust upgrade wizard is available for converting version 6.5 database to version 7. (Very few issues have arisen when using the wizard to upgrade existing applications.) However, many people are either converting from other database packages, or are converting only small sections of their database applications at a time. As a result, the databases are being scripted out and built manually. In these situations, I have heard about one particular problem repeatedly when doing this: the use of the ANSI default settings.

The symptoms of the problem includes seeing existing queries with **LIKE** clauses that evaluate **NULL** conditions, and other cases not working as anticipated. In addition, it is common to see databases increase dramatically in the amount of space that they consume. In most cases, all these problems are caused by some simple settings that seem very elusive to SQL Server 7 newcomer.

By default, when a new database is created, the following database options are disabled:

- ANSI **NULL** default
- ANSI **NULL**s
- ANSI warnings

Therefore, it would seem that fairly standard stored procedures should work correctly. However, when a table is created or a stored procedure is created, they acquire and keep certain connections settings that are present at the time the **CREATE** or **ALTER** statement is executed. In order to understand an example of this, let's take a look at the ANSI **NULL**s setting. Run the following sample of code from a Query Analyzer window:

```
set ANSI_NULLS OFF
GO
select Region
from Customers
where Region = NULL
go

Region
------
NULL
...
NULL

(60 row(s) affected)
```

Now run this sample of code:

```
set ANSI_NULLS ON
GO
select Region
from Customers
where Region = NULL
go

Region
------

(0 row(s) affected)
```

The only difference is that the **ANSI_NULLS** option is turned on. When the setting is turned on the "=" comparison operator ignores any **NULL** values. You must use the **IS NULL** coding style to get the same results when **ANSI_NULLS** is turned on. The ANSI-compliant way to code this would be:

```
set ANSI_NULLS ON
GO
select Region
from Customers
where Region IS NULL
go

Region
------
NULL
...
NULL

(60 row(s) affected)
```

Next, open a new Query Analyzer window—don't reuse an existing connection or this will not work. Type in and execute the following query to create a new stored procedure (do not change the ANSI settings):

```
Use Northwind
Go
Create procedure MyTest
As
Select Region
From Customers
Where Region = null
Return 0
go
```

```
Exec MyTest

Region
------

(0 row(s) affected)
```

We are assuming that the ANSI **NULL**s are turned on. Let's turn off the setting and run the procedure again to see what happens:

```
SET ANSI_NULLS OFF
Go
Exec MyTest

Region
------

(0 row(s) affected)
```

Same result. This is very confusing and not the same results we had earlier when we were not using a stored procedure. You might think that the system is behaving differently with stored procedures and dynamic SQL statements, but it is not. The problem is that **ANSI_NULLS** setting is *persistent* and stays with the stored procedure after it is compiled. By default, Query Analyzer sets the **ANSI_DEFAULTS** to be on when you open a new connection. Because the procedure was created with the setting turned on, it continues to operate as if the setting were turned on, even if you explicitly turn the setting off.

To correct this problem, be sure to turn off the default ANSI connection setting options in Query Analyzer. To do this, open File|Configure|New Connections and uncheck the box labeled Use ANSI Nulls, Padding, And Warnings. Even after doing this, your current connection will still have the **ANSI_DEFAULT** settings enabled. You will need to open a new connection. Once you are sure that the ANSI settings are disabled, **DROP** and re-create all your database objects to correct the problems.

Project 19.2

In this example we will examine the impact of the sticky **ANSI_PADDING** setting when creating tables.

Type in and run the following script to create a sample table in the *Northwind* database:

```
USE Northwind
Go
SET ANSI_PADDING ON   -- default for Query Analyzer
```

```
Go
CREATE TABLE PaddingTest
(
  Description     VARCHAR(200)
)
go
```

Now we want to add a little data. Note that in the following statement spaces are appended on the data purposely to illustrate a point. Type in and run the follow-ing statements:

```
INSERT PaddingTest VALUES("This is a test value       ")
Select "|" + Description + "|" from PaddingTest

--------------------------------------
|This is a test value           |

(1 row(s) affected)
```

Notice the location of the vertical bar. It indicates that spaces exist at the end of the data value even though the value was stored in a **VARCHAR** column. Now let's re-create the table with **ANSI_PADDING** off and retest the same query. Type in and run the following:

```
SET ANSI_PADDING OFF
Go
drop table PaddingTest
go
CREATE TABLE PaddingTest
(
  Description     VARCHAR(200)
)
go

INSERT PaddingTest VALUES("This is a test value       ")
Select "|" + Description + "|" from PaddingTest

--------------------------------
|This is a test value|

(1 row(s) affected)
```

Now that the table was created with **ANSI_PADDING** off, and that the extra spaces at the end of the data value are truncated. For new applications you probably want to preserve any spaces that occur at the end of data. However, for existing version 6.5 applications you set **ANSI_PADDING** off when creating tables to ensure compatible behavior.

19

Susan ran all her final tests. She bundled up all of her papers, reports, and graphs, and headed off for the conference room. She waited there with a little apprehension as the members of management arrived and took their places. The room dimmed, and the lead developer cleared his throat. "Uh, let's get started," he began. "We're here to take a look at the final run of the system before we go live next week. We've been doing a lot of testing and resolved all the bugs we've run into so far." He continued on for a while on the problems they'd run into and the processes they'd used to solve them. "Susan has been a great help—and even embarrassed a few senior developers who shall remain nameless." One of the developers across the table reddened a bit and Susan smiled. She'd shown the developers a couple of SQL Profiler traces that revealed a rather fundamental flaw that the developers originally claimed couldn't be there.

The meeting went on for a few hours, and at the end Susan's manager stepped up to her. "I want you to know that you did a great job on this project Susan". "I really enjoyed it, and I learned a lot." Susan smiled back at him. She knew she had one more hurdle…

The next day, Susan took her place at the Microsoft testing center. The test began, and Susan took a long breath. An hour later, she waited anxiously at the "Preparing your Score. Please stand by…" screen. There it was. The green bar was longer. She'd passed the test! She was very excited as she showed her manager the score sheet. "Great work again, Susan. I'll run this upstairs and get your paperwork started. You're going to want a little more cash to stay around here after this, I'll bet," he grinned. Susan actually was very pleased with herself. She remembered back at the beginning of the project how frightened she was when she was given the assignment. Now she knew that she had the confidence to work as a database designer, and she had the credentials and experience to prove it.

APPENDIX A

DESIGN ON SQL SERVER 7 EXAM OBJECTIVES

Developing A Logical Data Model	Chapter
Group data into entities by applying normalization rules.	3
Identify primary keys.	3
Choose the foreign key that will enforce a relationship between entities and that will ensure referential integrity.	3
Identify the business rules that relate to data integrity.	3, 4
Incorporate business rules and constraints into the data model.	3, 4
In a given situation, decide whether denormalization is appropriate.	3, 4

Deriving The Physical Design	Chapter
Assess the potential impact of the logical design on performance, maintainability, extensibility, scalability, availability, and security.	4

Creating Data Services	Chapter
Access data by using the dynamic SQL model.	7
Access data by using the stored procedure model.	12
Manipulate data by using Transact-SQL cursors.	11
Choose the appropriate type of cursor.	11
Define the appropriate level of sensitivity to change.	11
Choose the appropriate navigation.	11
Choose the scope of the cursor, specifically global or local.	11
Create and manage explicit, implicit, and distributed transactions to ensure data consistency and recoverability.	11
Define the transaction isolation level.	11
Design transactions of appropriate length.	11
Avoid or handle deadlocks.	11
Use optimistic locking appropriately.	11
Implement error handling by using **@@trancount**.	11
Write **INSERT**, **DELETE**, **UPDATE**, and **SELECT** statements that retrieve and modify data.	7
Write Transact-SQL statements that use joins or subqueries to combine data from multiple tables.	7
Create scripts by using Transact-SQL. Programming elements include control-of-flow techniques, local and global variables, functions, and error-handling techniques.	8

Design, create, use, and alter views.	10
Modify data through a view.	10
Query data through a view.	10
Create and execute stored procedures to enforce business rules, modify data in multiple tables, perform calculations, and use input and output parameters.	12
Implement error handling by using return codes and the **RAISERROR** statement.	12
Choose appropriate recompile options.	12
Create triggers that implement rules, enforce data integrity, and perform cascading updates and cascading deletes.	13
Implement transactional error handling.	11
Create result sets that provide summary data. Query types include **TOP N PERCENT** and **GROUP BY**, specifically **HAVING**, **CUBE**, and **ROLLUP**.	9
Configure session-level settings.	12
Access data from static or dynamic sources by using remote stored procedures, linked servers, and **OPENROWSET**.	15
Evaluate where processing occurs when using **OPENQUERY**.	11

Creating A Physical Database	Chapter
Create and manage files, filegroups, and transaction logs that define a database.	14
Create tables that enforce data integrity and referential integrity.	5
Choose the appropriate data types.	5
Create user-defined data types.	5
Define columns as **NULL** or **NOT NULL**.	5
Define columns to generate values by using the **IDENTITY** property, the **UNIQUEIDENTIFIER** data type, and the **NEWID** function.	5
Implement constraints.	5
Create and maintain indexes.	6
Choose an indexing strategy that will optimize performance.	6
Given a situation, choose the appropriate type of index to create.	6
Choose the column or columns to index.	6
Choose the appropriate index characteristics, specifically **FILLFACTOR**, **DROP_EXISTING**, and **PAD_INDEX**.	6
Populate the database with data from an external data source. Methods include the bulk copy program and Data Transformation Services (DTS).	16
Implement full-text search.	17

Maintaining A Database	Chapter
Evaluate and optimize the performance of an execution plan by using DBCC **SHOWCONTIG**, **SHOWPLAN_TEXT**, **SHOWPLAN_ALL**, and **UPDATE STATISTICS**.	18, 19
Evaluate and optimize the performance of query execution plans.	19
Diagnose and resolve locking problems.	11, 19

Identify SQL Server Events And Performance Problems By Using SQL Server Profiler	Chapter
Identify SQL Server Events And Performance Problems By Using SQL Server Profiler	19

Appendix B

MCSE Requirements

MCSE Requirements*

Core

All 3 of these are required	
Exam 70-067	Implementing and Supporting Microsoft Windows NT Server 4.0
Exam 70-068	Implementing and Supporting Microsoft Windows NT Server 4.0 in the Enterprise
Exam 70-058	Networking Essentials
Choose 1 from this group	
Exam 70-064	Implementing and Supporting Microsoft Windows 95
Exam 70-073	Implementing and Supporting Microsoft Windows NT Workstation 4.0
Exam 70-098	Implementing and Supporting Microsoft Windows 98

Elective

Choose 2 from this group	
Exam 70-088	Implementing and Supporting Microsoft Proxy Server 2.0
Exam 70-079	Implementing and Supporting Microsoft Internet Explorer 4.0 by Using the Internet Explorer Administration Kit
Exam 70-087	Implementing and Supporting Microsoft Internet Information Server 4.0
Exam 70-081	Implementing and Supporting Microsoft Exchange Server 5.5
Exam 70-059	Internetworking with Microsoft TCP/IP on Microsoft Windows NT 4.0
Exam 70-028	Administering Microsoft SQL Server 7.0
➤ Exam 70-029	**Designing and Implementing Databases on Microsoft SQL Server 7.0**
Exam 70-056	Implementing and Supporting Web Sites Using Microsoft Site Server 3.0
Exam 70-086	Implementing and Supporting Microsoft Systems Management Server 2.0
Exam 70-085	Implementing and Supporting Microsoft SNA Server 4.0

* This is not a complete listing—you can still be tested on some earlier versions of these products. However, we have included mainly the most recent versions so that you may test on these versions and thus be certified longer. We have not included any tests that are scheduled to be retired.

MCSE+Internet Requirements*

Core

All 6 of these are required	
Exam 70-067	Implementing and Supporting Microsoft Windows NT Server 4.0
Exam 70-068	Implementing and Supporting Microsoft Windows NT Server 4.0 in the Enterprise
Exam 70-058	Networking Essentials
Exam 70-059	Internetworking with Microsoft TCP/IP on Microsoft Windows NT 4.0
Exam 70-087	Implementing and Supporting Microsoft Internet Information Server 4.0
Exam 70-079	Implementing and Supporting Microsoft Internet Explorer 4.0 by Using the Internet Explorer Administration Kit
Choose 1 from this group	
Exam 70-064	Implementing and Supporting Microsoft Windows 95
Exam 70-073	Implementing and Supporting Microsoft Windows NT Workstation 4.0
Exam 70-098	Implementing and Supporting Microsoft Windows 98

Elective

Choose 2 from this group	
Exam 70-088	Implementing and Supporting Microsoft Proxy Server 2.0
Exam 70-081	Implementing and Supporting Microsoft Exchange Server 5.5
Exam 70-028	Administering Microsoft SQL Server 7.0
Exam 70-029	**Designing and Implementing Databases on Microsoft SQL Server 7.0**
Exam 70-056	Implementing and Supporting Web Sites Using Microsoft Site Server 3.0
Exam 70-085	Implementing and Supporting Microsoft SNA Server 4.0

* This is not a complete listing—you can still be tested on some earlier versions of these products. However, we have included mainly the most recent versions so that you may test on these versions and thus be certified longer. We have not included any tests that are scheduled to be retired.

Glossary

@@ERROR
A function that returns the error code from the last Transact-SQL statement to be executed.

@@FETCH_STATUS
A function that returns status information for the last **FETCH** command to be executed.

ACID
An acronym describing the four properties of a transaction: Atomicity, Consistency, Isolation, and Durability.

ADO
A data access interface used to transfer data to and from any OLE DB-compliant data source.

Aggregate functions
Aggregate functions can act on an entire grouping of data in order to return a single-valued result.

Alert
A notification based on an event that occurs in the database.

ANSI
American National Standards Institute.

ANSI-92
The American National Standards Institute standard dealing with SQL relational databases.

API
See Application Programming Interface.

Application Programming Interface (API)
A set of functions, routines, or methods of SQL access made available for use in other programs. Many APIs are available for enabling programs to access SQL Server.

ASCII
American Standard Code for Information Interchange. A way of representing a character of data as a set of codes ranging from 0 through 255. The ASCII system represents each character of data with one byte, and is large enough to store character information for most individual languages. The ASCII system is not large enough to encode the character sets of all languages simultaneously. The Unicode standard is large enough to do so.

Atomic
A data value is atomic when only one data value can exist for any attribute in any row in a table.

Atomicity
The quality of being at the smallest practical unit of data. Also, one of the ACID properties of a transaction. Indicates that a transaction must act as a single unit of work.

Attach/Detach
The ability to inactivate and reactivate a series of data files to a database server.

Attribute
Corresponds to a column or data element in a row, with each row in a table having one or more attributes.

Autocommit
The default transaction processing mode for SQL Server 7. While in this mode the database automatically issues a **COMMIT** after each SQL statement.

Base table
A table that is being referenced by a view.

Batch
A group of (one or more) Transact-SQL statements that are sent to SQL Server as a unit, compiled by SQL Server into one execution plan, and executed together.

bcp
The native fast load and unload utility is referred to as *bulk copy*. This is the fastest method for importing and exporting from the database.

BEGIN
The Transact-SQL keyword that marks the beginning of a complex statement block.

Block comments
A comment beginning with slash-star (/*) and ending with star-slash (*/).

BREAK
The Transact-SQL keyword that allows execution to jump to the first statement after the current **WHILE** statement. **BREAK** causes the current **WHILE** statement to terminate.

Bulk update
A fast load of information into the database, usually using the bcp utility included with SQL Server.

Cartesian product
The result of joining two tables together with no join condition restricting which rows from each table can be paired together. Also called a cross join, a Cartesian product between a table with x rows and another table with y rows contains x * y rows.

Catalog
The system catalog is a collection of system tables in the *master* database that describes key features of the SQL Server and of all the other databases. The database catalog is a set of system tables in every database that provides important information about that particular database. Other database systems do not use the terms *database* and *owner* when describing separate groupings of database objects. Instead, they use the terms *catalog* and *schema*. When specifying a four-part database name in one of these database products, substitute the schema for the database name and the catalog for the owner name.

CHECK constraints
Defines data values that a column can accept. Enforces domain integrity.

CLOSE
The Transact-SQL statement that releases the result set associated with a cursor. **CLOSE** reverses the action of **OPEN.**

Clustered index
An index that determines the order the data is saved in the table. The leaf pages of a clustered index are the data pages. A table can have only one clustered index.

Column alias
A name used in a query to rename a column or other selected expression for the duration of the query.

Column-level constraint
A property that applies to only one column. It is defined at the same time the column is declared.

COM
See Component Object Model**.**

Comments
Transact-SQL statements that are ignored during compilation and execution. Comments provide a convenient place to document your code.

Compilation
Process that compiles the execution plan for a stored procedure and stores it in procedure cache.

Component Object Model
The framework that Microsoft and other vendors developed designing applications. COM is the underlying architecture that forms software services.

Composite index
An index defined on two or more columns.

Conjugate
An alternate form of a root word. For nouns this consists of both plural and singular forms of the word. For verbs, this includes different tenses of the verb. Synonyms for this word used in this text include inflection and declension.

Consistency
One of the ACID properties of a transaction. Indicates that a transaction must leave data in a consistent state, whether it finishes successfully or fails. Describes the condition of coherency within the database regarding the storage allocation structures, data pages, index pages, and other information.

Constraint
Tools that enforce integrity of data. These tools include **PRIMARY KEY** constraints, **FOREIGN KEY** constraints, **UNIQUE** constraints, **CHECK** constraints, **DEFAULT** definitions, and Nullability.

CONTINUE
The Transact-SQL keyword that allows execution to jump to the Boolean test at the "top" of the current **WHILE** statement. **CONTINUE** causes the current **WHILE** statement to iterate.

Control-of-flow language
The Transact-SQL keywords that allow you to control the flow of execution within a block of code. Control-of-flow keywords include **BEGIN**, **BREAK**, **ELSE**, **END**, **GOTO**, **IF**, **RETURN**, **WAITFOR**, and **WHILE**.

Correlated subquery
A subquery or nested query that depends on its outer query and thus must be run once for each row in the outer query.

Cost-based optimizer
The query optimizer determines the cost, or estimated amount of time to execute a query for each access plan. The query engine then chooses the access plan with the least cost.

Covered index
An index that has all the columns needed to solve a query.

CROSS JOIN
The ANSI-compliant implementation of a Cartesian product.

Cursor
A mechanism in Transact-SQL that allows query results to be stored, or cached, on the SQL Server until they are fetched one row at a time. A cursor is used for special result set processing that allows you to examine and process one row of output at a time.

DAO
An application programming interface available for use in Visual Basic and Visual C++. DAO presents an API layer over the top of ODBC, and is considered a legacy API.

Data
Information (or parts of information) stored in a file.

Data Control Language
SQL syntax that allows rules for data integrity and data security to be defined. The subset of SQL statements, such as **GRANT** or **REVOKE**, that control access to database objects.

Data Definition Language
SQL syntax that defines tables and other supporting elements. The subset of SQL statements, such as **CREATE TABLE** or **DROP PROCEDURE**, are used to control the structure of database objects.

Data file
The operating system file in which data is stored. A database file where database objects (tables, stored procedures, triggers, indexes, view definitions, constraint definitions) are stored. Can be primary or secondary.

Data Manipulation Language
The subset of SQL statements, such as **SELECT** or **INSERT**, used to control the data held in database tables. This is the SQL syntax that specifies methods by which data can be retrieved for viewing or updating.

Data page
Page containing all data except for **TEXT**, **NTEXT**, and **IMAGE** data.

Data source
In SQL syntax, the object that contains the data being queried. A data source can be a table, view, or derived table.

Data transformation
The ability to cause the same information to be represented in different ways. Some examples of data transformations include converting between upper and lower case, converting between metric and English units of measure, combining multiple fields to calculate or derive data, and using Transact-SQL operators to alter data.

Data Transformation Service
A tool that allows data to be moved to and from Microsoft SQL Server 7 using wizards, programs, and scheduling. SQL Server includes a suite of COM objects and utilities referred to as Data Transformation Services. This set of utilities provides the ability to import, export, clean, and transform information to and from the database.

Database
Collection of tables, indexes, stored procedures, triggers, views, and constraints. A database consists of data files and transaction log files.

Database consistency checking
Several options are available with this command that performs maintenance and reports on a database.

Database file
A data or transaction log file that is part of a database. Every database has two or more system files that contain data and log file information.

Database ID
A unique number assigned to each database.

Datum
A single piece of data.

DBCC
See Database Consistency Checking.

DBID
See Database ID.

DB-Library
An application programming interface that natively uses SQL Server's Tabular Data Stream. DB-Library is for use with the C programming language, and is considered a legacy API. DB-Library for Visual Basic provides a wrapper around DB-Library for use in Microsoft Visual Basic.

DCL
See Data Control Language.

DDL
See Data Definition Language.

Deadlock
Two or more processes that are blocking each other in a circular locking pattern.

DEALLOCATE
The Transact-SQL statement that releases all internal resources associated with a cursor, and disassociates it from any query definition. **DEALLOCATE** reverses the action of **DECLARE CURSOR**.

Decision Support System
A system that consists mostly of reading and reporting, as opposed to an online processing system that is at least an equal mix of reads, updates, and inserts.

DECLARE CURSOR
The Transact-SQL statement that associates a cursor name with a query definition.

Declarative Referential Integrity
The ability of the database to support primary key and foreign key constraints.

Declension
An alternate form of a root word. For nouns, this consists of both plural and singular forms of the word. For verbs, this includes different tenses of the verb. Synonyms for this word used in this text include conjugate and inflection.

Default
A value placed in a column when that value is not defined explicitly by the user.

DEFAULT constraint
Defines a value that will be assigned to a column if no value for the column is specified during an insert.

Deferred name resolution
See Resolution.

DELETE
A SQL statement used to remove rows from tables.

DELETE ... FROM
A **DELETE** statement that locates rows to remove from a table by using a **FROM** clause to compare rows between multiple tables.

Delete trigger
Trigger that is fired when a **DELETE** statement is executed against a table.

Deleted table
Special temporary table that stores a copy of the rows deleted by the **DELETE** statement, or a copy of the original (before image) rows modified by the **UPDATE** statement. Has the same structure as the table on which the trigger is defined. The deleted table is stored in cache.

Density
Indicates the selectivity of an index. This number is stored in the distribution statistics page(s) of an index and represents the inverse of the number of unique index key values.

Derived data
Data that is not explicitly stored the database, but is implied by other data stored there. Derived data can be calculated from stored data.

Derived table
A data source for a query based on an embedded query.

Difference operator
Produces a result relation containing all records appearing in the first table but not in the second.

Dirty read
A synonym for Read Uncommitted transaction isolation level.

DISTINCT
A keyword used in the select list indicating that all duplicate values should be eliminated.

Distributed query
A query that accesses data from heterogeneous data sources.

Distributed transaction
One or more SQL instructions that keep the ACID properties of a transaction across two or more different servers.

Distribution statistics
Statistics kept about the distribution values in a column and about the selectivity of the values. Statistics are updated automatically by SQL Server or by using the **UPDATE STATISTICS** command.

Divide operator
Builds a resulting relation of all matches between a two-attribute and a one-attribute relation (or primary key).

DML
See Data Manipulation Language.

Domain
A pool of all possible data values for a specific column or attribute in a table.

DRI
See Declarative Referential Integrity.

Drop
Delete from a database.

DSS
See Decision Support System.

DTS

See Data Transformation Service.

Durable
One of the ACID properties of a transaction. Indicates that the actions of a transaction must be permanent and cannot be undone once committed.

DYNAMIC
A type of cursor that reflects all changes to underlying data for the entire duration of the cursor's life, from **OPEN** to **CLOSE**.

Dynamic execution
The ability to build and execute Transact-SQL statements in an ad hoc manner. The **EXECUTE** statement and the **sp_executesql** stored procedure can both execute Transact-SQL batches that are stored in string literals or string variables.

ELSE
This Transact-SQL clause optionally specifies that action to take if an IF statement's Boolean test is false.

Embedded query
A query that is contained in another query. Also called *subquery*, *nested query*, or *inner query*.

END
The Transact-SQL keyword that marks the termination of a complex statement block.

Entity integrity
No attribute that is either the whole primary key or a part of the primary key is allowed to accept null values.

Entity Relationship Diagrams
A graphical representation of either a logical or physical view of a database.

ERD
See Entity Relationship Diagrams.

EXECUTE
A Transact-SQL keyword that can call stored procedures and dynamically execute strings containing Transact-SQL batches.

Explicit transaction
The specification of a transaction using the **BEGIN TRAN** and either the **COMMIT TRAN** or **ROLLBACK TRAN** delimiters.

Extent
A chain of eight pages, or 64K. Consists of eight contiguous 8K pages (8 × 8K = 64K). Sixteen extents are contained in a megabyte.

FAST_FORWARD
A type of cursor that behaves like a **READ_ONLY, FORWARD_ONLY** cursor and is highly optimized for reading the cursor's result set from front to back without changing any of the underlying

data. The only type of **FETCH** that can be done with a **FAST_FORWARD** cursor is **FETCH NEXT**.

FETCH
The Transact-SQL statement that retrieves a single row from a cursor's result set. Several options are available for use with the **FETCH** statement. **FORWARD_ONLY** cursors can only issue **FETCH NEXT**, whereas **SCROLL** cursors can use the options **PRIOR**, **FIRST**, **LAST**, **ABSOLUTE**, and **RELATIVE** in addition to **NEXT**.

Filegroup
One or more files grouped as a unit of allocation and administration. Collection of data files that are grouped together for allocation and administration purposes. Transaction log files cannot be part of a filegroup. An organization of database files into named groups that can improve placement of data on disk or allow for multiple backup strategies.

Fill factor
An option that controls how full the leaf pages of an index will be after it has been created. Reduces the amount of page splits.

FOR UPDATE OF
This clause is used by the **UPDATE** and **INSERT** commands to modify data associated with a cursor.

Foreign key
An attribute or combination of attributes whose value is required to match that of the primary key of another table.

FOREIGN KEY constraint
A column or set of columns that reference a **PRIMARY KEY** or **UNIQUE** constraint of another table. Enforces referential integrity and identifies relationships between tables.

FORWARD_ONLY
A type of cursor, updateable by default, that can only scroll through the data in a front-to-back manner.

FROM clause
A SQL clause used to specify data sources for a query.

FULL OUTER JOIN
An ANSI-compliant join that will return rows from either table, even if they do not satisfy the join condition.

Full-text search
A flexible word and phrase matching search that uses special indexes. The indexes are stored external to the database, and are maintained by the Microsoft Search service.

Global allocation map page
Records whose extents have been allocated.

GLOBAL cursor
A cursor that is available from anywhere within the connection that created it.

GO
The batch separator for the SQL Server Query Analyzer, *isql*, and several other SQL Server client programs. Technically, it is not a Transact-SQL keyword, because it is used by the client program to know when to group batches.

GOTO
This Transact-SQL control-of-flow command causes code execution to jump unconditionally to a position marked by a label.

GROUP BY
The clause that tells a vector aggregation query how to group the data before applying aggregate functions.

GROUPING
A special aggregate function that tells you how to interpret **NULL** in the output of a

vector aggregation query. If **GROUPING** returns 1 for a column, that column is being used as a grouping column for that row. If **GROUPING** returns 0 for the column, the **NULL** that is displayed represents actual **NULL** values in the database.

HAVING
The clause that is used to restrict what grouping levels will be present in the result set of a vector aggregation query.

Heap table
A table that does not have a clustered index.

Histogram
A sampling of values from an index key stored in the distribution statistics page(s) that provides a picture of the value distribution.

IAM
Index Allocation Map.

***Identity* column**
A column that auto-increments its value every time a record is inserted into the table. Only one *identity* column per table is allowed.

Identity value
A numeric value that SQL Server can automatically assign sequentially to every new row of data in a table.

IF
The Transact-SQL keyword used to choose between two different statement blocks that could be executed.

Implicit transaction
A transaction begun automatically by the database without the use of **BEGIN TRAN**.

Index
Database object that makes it possible to find data in a table quickly.

Index allocation map page
Page containing information about extents used by a table or index.

Index intersection
Condition occurring when more than one index of a table is used to solve a query.

Index page
Page containing index entries.

INDID
Index ID. A unique number assigned to each index for a table. A 0 specifies the table itself, 1 specifies the clustered index, and 255 specifies a text or image structure.

Inflection
An alternate form of a root word. For nouns, this consists of both plural and singular forms of the word. For verbs, this includes different tenses of the verb. Synonyms for this word used in this text include conjugate and declension.

Information schema view
A system supplied view that returns metadata for a data object stored in the current database.

INNER JOIN
An ANSI-compliant join that will only return rows from either table if they satisfy the join condition.

Inner query
A query that is contained in another query. Also called *subquery*, *nested query*, or *embedded query*.

Input parameter
Parameter used to pass information to a stored procedure.

INSERT
A SQL statement used to add rows to tables.

Insert trigger
Trigger that is fired when an **INSERT** statement is executed against a table.

INSERT ... EXEC[UTE]
An **INSERT** statement that gets the rows to be inserted from an **EXEC** or **EXECUTE** statement.

INSERT ... SELECT
An **INSERT** statement that gets the rows to be inserted from a **SELECT** statement.

Inserted table
Special temporary table that stores a copy of the rows inserted by the **INSERT** statement, or a copy of the updated (after image) rows modified by the **UPDATE** statement. Has the same structure as the table on which the trigger is defined. The inserted table is stored in cache.

***Intent* lock**
A type of database locking that indicates that the database may issue a *Shared*, *Update*, or *Exclusive* lock at or below the resource in the database architecture hierarchy.

Intersect operator
Produces a set of all records appearing in two tables.

Isolation
One of the ACID properties of a transaction. Indicates that a transaction must be able to execute in isolation from all other transactions.

Isql
A command-line query processor that uses DB-Library to communicate with SQL Server.

Job
A sequence of events combined to take place on a SQL Server, controlled by the SQL Server Agent.

Join
The general term used to refer to a query that has more than one data source.

Join operator
Builds a resulting relation from two specified relations where the resulting relation contains all possible concatenated pairs of tuples from the two original relations.

Key-Range
A database resource that is used in serializable transactions to prevent inserts from occurring within a range of key values.

KEYSET
A type of cursor whose result set is implemented by storing a set of key values in *tempdb* so that the rest of the row can be looked up when the **FETCH** occurs. **KEYSET** cursors are able to reflect some, but not all, changes to underlying data since the cursor was opened.

Label
A named position in the Transact-SQL code. A label is any valid identifier. When the label position is declared, the label appears on its own line followed by a colon (:). The **GOTO** statement can cause execution to jump directly to any label in the same batch.

LEFT OUTER JOIN
An ANSI-compliant join that will return all rows from the first table defined in the query, even if they do not satisfy the join condition.

LIKE
A SQL keyword used to make wildcard comparisons of text strings. The SQL wildcard for a single character is the underscore (_), and the SQL wildcard for multiple characters is the percent symbol (%).

Line comments
A Transact-SQL comment that begins with a double-hyphen (--) and ends automatically at the end of the current line.

Linked server
A remote data source configured to allow either remote stored procedure requests, or

that can be used to participate in heterogeneous queries. Configuring a linked server supercedes the configuration of a remote server.

LOCAL cursor
A cursor that is only visible from within the batch that created it.

Local variable
A named location in memory that can hold one piece of data of a particular data type. Local variable names begin with the at sign (@), and are visible only within the batch or stored procedure that created them.

Lock
A database semaphore used to secure a database resource and protect data integrity. The ability to prevent one user from accessing the data at the same time as another user.

Log file
A database file containing the transaction log; every database has at least one log file.

MAP
See Global allocation map page.

Metadata
Data about the data. Information about the structure and definition of the various database objects stored in the database. Information that describes database objects and their origins, including column definitions, parameter lists, and indexes defined for a table.

Microsoft Management Console
Microsoft's newest management framework that provides a graphical representation of the SQL Server environment.

Microsoft search
A service that is installed optionally with SQL Server. The service maintains the physical storage for full-text indexes and also parses and implements full-text queries passed by the database engine.

MMC
See Microsoft Management Console.

Multicolumn index
See Composite index.

Nested query
A **SELECT** query that returns a value and is nested inside another **SELECT**, **INSERT**, **UPDATE**, or **DELETE** statement, or inside another query.

Nesting
An inner transaction defined within an outer transaction. This can occur an unlimited number of levels deep.

Nonclustered index
An index in which the logical order of the index does not match the order in which the data is stored. A table can have 249 nonclustered indexes.

Nonunique index
An index that allows duplicate key values.

NULL
A special representation of the lack of data. A **NULL** value is, technically speaking, not a value at all, but is used to represent anyplace in a database where information is missing or not yet known. This value is not the same as nothing or zero.

Object Linking and Embedding
OLE services are used in creating things like compound documents, custom controls, inter-application scripting, data transfer, and other software interactions.

Object Linking and Embedding for Database
An Application Programming Interface (API) that allows COM applications to place and retrieve data from various data sources. This replaces DB-Library as the new native application programming interface for SQL Server 7. An application programming interface that natively uses SQL Server's Tabular Data Stream. OLE DB is for use with the Visual C++

compiler. ADO provides a wrapper around OLE DB for use in Microsoft Visual Basic, Visual C++, and Visual J++.

OBJID
Object ID. A unique number assigned to each object in the database.

ODBC
See Open database connectivity.

OLAP
See Online Analytical Processing.

OLE
See Object Linking and Embedding.

OLE DB
See Object Linking and Embedding for Database.

OLTP
See Online Transaction Processing.

Online Analytical Processing.
A system that services reporting needs and has a very high percentage of read activity. A synonym for a DSS system. Data is stored in a nonnormalized form that provides summarized data for analysis by a Decision Support System (DSS).

Online Transaction Processing
A system that can be described as having mostly very small transactions with a high percentages of writing and little to no *ad hoc* reporting.

OPEN
The Transact-SQL statement that executes the query associated with a cursor and stores (or caches) the result on the SQL server.

Open data services
An application programming interface used to write extended stored procedures. The native connectivity data services used by SQL Server. In version 7, the Open Data Services layer supports connections via DB-Library, ODBC, and OLE DB clients.

Open database connectivity
A natively supported method for communicating with SQL Server. ODBC is used typically in Microsoft Visual C++. ADO and RDO provide wrappers around ODBC, and can be used from Microsoft Visual Basic and Microsoft Visual C++.

Optimistic locking
A type of cursor that is updateable, but does not hold locks before updating data. Rather than holding locks, an **OPTIMISTIC** cursor notes the timestamp or checksum of a row and use this information later when trying to determine if a row has been modified by another user since it was first read. A mode of cursor locking used when the likelihood of an update occurring between a read and update is very low.

Optimization
Process that creates the best execution plan for a stored procedure.

ORDER BY
A SQL clause used to sort a result set.

Osql
A command line utility used to execute Transact-SQL statements and scripts. A command-line query processor that uses ODBC to communicate with SQL Server.

Outer join
The general term for any join that will return rows that do not satisfy the join condition. For more details, see **FULL OUTER JOIN**, **RIGHT OUTER JOIN**, and **LEFT OUTER JOIN**.

Output parameter
Parameter used to return information from a stored procedure.

Package
A group of Data Transformation Services steps, commands, and transforms.

PAD_INDEX
A clause of the **CREATE INDEX** statement that instructs SQL Server to apply the fill factor percentage to the nonleaf index pages.

Page
A 8K database construct. Fundamental unit of storage in SQL Server 7. A page is 8K. Each megabyte has 128 pages.

Page free space page
Page containing information about available free space.

Page split
Process of moving approximately half the rows of an index page to a new page to free space for new entries.

Parsing
Process that checks the syntax of Transact-SQL statements that define a stored procedure. The process occurs when the stored procedure is created.

Predicate
Describes the **WHERE** portion of a query.

Permissions
Permissions represent the ability to perform certain operations in a database. Permissions can be added to or removed from a role or a group by using the **GRANT** and **DENY** statements.

Pessimistic locking
A mode of cursor locking used when the likelihood of an update occurring between a read and update is very high.

Primary data file
A database file containing table, index, and system data; every database must have a primary data file. A data file where the startup information for the database is stored. It also stores database objects.

Primary filegroup
A filegroup that contains the primary data file.

Primary key
A unique identifier for a table made up of one or more columns. Values in the primary key will not be duplicated within the table. It is also a column or minimal set of columns that uniquely identify a row in a table. Enforces entity integrity. The column(s) cannot allow **NULL** values.

Procedure
A set of code stored in a database.

Product operator
Produces a Cartesian product of all possible combinations of pairs of tuples.

Project operator
Extracts a named subset of columns from a table.

Projection
A term describing the filtering of columns represented in a result set.

Query plan
A reentrant, read-only data structure that can be used by any number of users to return data from the database engine.

RAID
See Redundant Array of Independent Disks.

RAS
See Remote Access Service.

RDO
An application programming interface that provides a wrapper around ODBC and can be used from Microsoft Visual Basic and Visual C++.

Read Committed
One of the four-transaction isolation levels. It is also the default for SQL Server 7. The database uses shared locks and honors exclusive locks only for the duration of the **SELECT** statement.

Read Uncommitted
One of the four-transaction isolation levels. Also referred to as *dirty reads*. Forces the

database to forgo the use of shared locks and to not honor exclusive locks. The best option for performance and user concurrency, but the worst option for data integrity.

READ_ONLY
A type of cursor that cannot be used to modify the data on which the cursor's result set is built. By default, cursors are updateable unless **READ_ONLY** (or **FAST_FORWARD**) are specified.

Recursive trigger
A trigger that performs an action that causes the same trigger to fire again.

Redundant Array of Independent Disks
An array of disk drives that is configured to provide high performance, reliability, and capacity.

Referential integrity
If a record in one table references a record in a second table, then the second record must exist.

Relation
A 2D representation of data; this corresponds to a table.

Relational algebra
The set of operators that manipulates one or more relations and produces a new resulting relation.

Relational data model
A theoretical model based on algebra and set theory used to define the principles upon which relational database systems were constructed.

Relational database
A method of storing data that commonly uses the Structured Query Language, or SQL, invented by an IBM researcher in the 1970s. A collection of relations or tables where the data will vary over time.

Remote Access Service
A telephonic method of network communication found in the Windows NT operating system.

Remote server
A remote server that can support remote stored procedure calls. In SQL Server 7, this functionality is superceded by the new linked server.

Repeatable Read
One of the four-transaction isolation levels. Shared locks will be issued and exclusive locks will be honored for the duration of the transaction.

Replication
The movement of data changes from a source to a target table.

Resolution
Process that checks that the objects referenced by a stored procedure exist. Process occurs the first time a stored procedure is executed or when a procedure is recompiled. Allows stored procedures to be created, even if objects that it references do not exist.

RETURN
A Transact-SQL keyword that causes a batch or stored procedure to halt execution unconditionally. When used from inside a stored procedure, a status code may be returned to the code that invoked the stored procedure.

RID
See Row identifier.

RIGHT OUTER JOIN
An ANSI-compliant join that will return rows from the second table, even if they do not satisfy the join condition.

Role
A collection of statement, object, or database permissions. By adding a user to a role, you effectively grant all of the role's privileges to that user.

Row global unique identifier column
An identifier column that is unique across the entire database.

Row identifier
Consists of the file number, page number, and the row location of the data row in the data page.

Row locator
A pointer from the leaf page of a nonclustered index to a data page. Can be a clustered key or a row identifier.

Row-level locking
The ability to prevent one user from accessing the data at the same time as another user, performed one logical record at a time.

Rule
Rules perform some of the same functions as **CHECK** constraints. They are included in SQL 7 for backward compatibility. You should use **CHECK** constraints wherever possible.

Savepoint
A "bookmark" that can be defined within a transaction that allows for rolling back to the savepoint without rolling back the entire transaction.

Scalar aggregation
A query that uses only aggregate functions in its **SELECT** clause and that does not use a **GROUP BY** clause to group the data aggregations.

Scalar functions
Scalar functions act on individual data values (as opposed to lists or arrays) and return single-valued results.

Schema
Some other database systems do not use the terms *database* and *owner* when describing separate groupings of database objects. Instead, they use the terms *catalog* and *schema*. When specifying a four-part database name in one of these database products, substitute the schema for the database name and the catalog for the owner name.

Scope
The code where an object's name is known and the object can be used. Most, but not all, types of objects in SQL Server go out of scope when the batch or stored procedure that created them terminates.

Script
A general term that can have many different meanings, all of which revolve around the idea of combining multiple batches of work into one source file that can be run automatically. Sometimes the term *script* refers to any group of one or more Transact-SQL batches. Alternatively, it can refer to a Perl or operating system script that sends batches of work to SQL Server or a specific type of script that the SQL Server Enterprise Manager can produce for re-creating database objects.

SCROLL
A type of cursor that can use all of the available cursor-navigation options supported by **FETCH**.

SCROLL_LOCKS
A type of cursor that is updateable and holds locks before updating data. A **SCROLL_LOCKS** cursor will lock the data it is loading for update before any update is being attempted. This is also called a *pessimistic locking strategy*.

Secondary data file
A database file containing table, index, and system data; optional, though a database may have many secondary data files.

SELECT
The SQL statement used to retrieve data from tables and other data sources. The **SELECT** statement can also be embedded inside **INSERT**, **DELETE**, and **UPDATE** statements.

Select List
The list of columns or other expressions that will be retrieved by a **SELECT** statement.

SELECT ... INTO
A **SELECT** statement that creates a new table.

Select operator (not SQL select)
Extracts records from a table based on specified criteria; subset of records is returned.

Selection
A term describing the filtering of rows represented in a result set.

Serializable
One of the four transaction isolation levels. *Shared* locks will be issued, *exclusive* locks will be honored, and inserts within the key range will be prohibited for the duration of the transaction. This is the best option for data consistency, but is the worst option for performance and concurrency.

Service
In Windows NT, services are a special class of applications. Services do not require any interactive logon session with the Windows NT computer, but can run automatically as background processes. They can be caused to start whenever Windows NT starts, and they can be given a specific Windows NT user account to use so that they will have an authentication context on other computers.

SGAM
See Shared global allocation map page.

Shared global allocation map page
These pages record which extents are mixed extents and which have at least one unused and available page.

Shrinking a database
Process of recovering free space from the database.

Single column index
An index defined on one column.

sp_executesql
A built-in stored procedure that can dynamically execute Transact-SQL stored in string literals or string variables.

SPID (Server Process ID)
A number assigned by the SQL Server to each SQL Server connection. A SPID is guaranteed to be unique only for the duration of a connection. As soon as the connection is closed, the SPID may be reused by another connection.

SQL-92
The 1992 specification of the American National Standards Institute providing an international standard for Structured Query Language (SQL).

SQL-DMO
An application programming interface that is used to create programs that can manage SQL Server.

SQL Scheduler
The engine that controls dates, times and recurrence patterns for activities to happen within SQL Server 7.

SQL Server Agent
Performs the functions previously served by the SQL Server Executive.

SQL Server Engine
The software responsible for the storage and management of relational data.

SQL Server Enterprise Manager
The graphical utility used to configure and manage all of your SQL Server and SQL Server objects, whether local or not.

SQL Server Profiler
A tool that monitors any events produced by SQL Server, and can filter events based on user-specified criteria.

SQL Server Query Analyzer
A query tool based on the Windows graphical user interface. Among other

things, the SQL Server Query Analyzer can show execution plans and perform index analysis in addition to executing queries.

Statement
Any single, complete Transact-SQL command.

Statement block
This is a group of one or more Transact-SQL statements that can be grouped together for the purpose of flow control. A complex statement block contains more than one statement, starts with **BEGIN**, and terminates with **END**.

STATIC
A type of cursor that creates a complete copy of the data returned by its result set in the *tempdb* database.

Statistics
See Distribution statistics.

Stored data
This is data that is stored physically in the database. Stored data can be retrieved from a single row-and-column location in a particular table.

Stored procedure
Database object that contains one or more Transact-SQL statements.

Subquery
This is a query that is contained in another query. Also called *embedded query*, *nested query*, or *inner query*.

Symmetric multiprocessing
The ability of a computer to use more than one processor at a time for the same activity.

Table
A 2D data structure in which the columns are also known as *attributes* and the rows are known as *instances*. A logical grouping of data that is at its highest level of atomicity.

Table alias
A name used in a query to rename a table or other data source for the duration of the query.

Table-level constraint
A property that applies to one or more columns and is defined independently from the columns definitions.

Tabular Data Stream
This is SQL Server's native data transfer protocol. The implementation of TDS is independent of any particular operating system or network protocol. The client and database servers communicate using a tabular data stream protocol. This protocol defines how requests are sent to the server, and how results, messages, and errors are sent back to the client.

TDS
See Tabular Data Stream.

Text/image page
Page containing **TEXT**, **NTEXT**, and **IMAGE** data.

Timestamp
A special type of system-defined column that is used to support row-versioning. Helps identify whether a row has been modified since the last read. A **BINARY(16)** value that uniquely identifies each transaction in a database. **TIMESTAMP** values can be used by a program for versioning and concurrency control of individual rows.

TOP N, TOP N PERCENT
These are query clauses that restrict the number of rows acted upon by a query.

Transact-SQL
Microsoft's extension, or broadening, of the set of commands available in the Structured Query Language (SQL).

Transaction
A logic unit of work consisting of one or more SQL statements that meet all four of

the ACID transaction properties. Data changes grouped together as a unit, for instance, adding both the client's name and address to several tables at once.

Transaction log
Data written in a sequential fashion prior to being written to the database. All user data that is created, edited, or deleted is done via the transaction log. Reads are done against the database.

Trigger
Actions tied to a table that contain code that "fires" when an event happens in that table. Database object that contains one or more Transact-SQL statements and is invoked when data in the table is modified. Sometimes it is referred to as a special kind of a stored procedure.

Trigger table
A table on which a trigger is defined.

TRUNCATE TABLE
A SQL statement used to quickly deallocate all of a table's pages. This resets a table effectively to a newly created state. **TRUNCATE TABLE** can remove rows quicker than **DELETE**, because it only has to log page deallocations, rather than row deletions. **TRUNCATE TABLE** always removes every row from the table.

T-SQL
See Transact-SQL.

Tuning
Performing various steps including design and maintenance to enable a particular server to run at optimum efficiency.

Tuple
Corresponds to a record or row where each row is a data instance in a table.

Unicode
A special storage format for character information that uses two bytes rather than the usual one byte per character. The extra byte allows the code page information to be stored along with the string value, thereby preventing problems in converting extended characters between different code pages. A way of representing a character of data that uses two bytes of information to represent each character. Because of this, the Unicode standard can represent over 65,000 characters at once, which is enough to simultaneously encode languages from all over the world.

UNION
A SQL statement used to combine the result sets from two queries. By default, **UNION** removes duplicate rows from the final result set.

UNION ALL
A SQL statement used to combine the result sets from two queries that includes all duplicate rows in the final result set.

Union operator
Produces a superset of all records appearing in either or both of two specified tables.

UNIQUE constraint
A column or minimal set of columns that ensure(s) uniqueness of the data in that column or set of columns. Enforces entity integrity on nonprimary keys. The column(s) can allow **NULL** values.

Unique index
An index that does not allow duplicate key values.

UNIQUEIDENTIFIER
A data type that can be generated in such a way as to ensure its worldwide uniqueness.

UPDATE
A SQL statement used to modify existing data in tables.

Update trigger
Trigger that is fired when an **UPDATE** statement is executed against a table.

UPDATE ... FROM
An **UPDATE** statement that uses a **FROM** clause to reference other data sources. This allows the **UPDATE** statement to retrieve values from other data sources or to compare values from multiple data sources when determining how to modify the data.

Updateable view
A view that can be used to modify the data of a base table.

User view
View created by the user with the **CREATE VIEW** statement or through the Create View Wizard.

User-defined data type
A user-defined setup of data stored as a type.

User-defined filegroup
A filegroup created with **FILEGROUP** clause in the **CREATE DATABASE** or **ALTER DATABASE** statement.

Vector aggregation
A query that uses aggregate functions and other expressions in its **SELECT** clause and that also uses a **GROUP BY** clause to group the data aggregations.

View
Database object that stores a query. The data accessed through a view is stored in the base table(s) the view references. A view sometimes is known as a *virtual table*.

WAITFOR
This is a Transact-SQL statement that can pause execution of its connection for up to 24 hours.

WHERE clause
A SQL clause used by **SELECT**, **UPDATE**, and **DELETE** statements, as well as embedded queries in statements such as **INSERT ... SELECT**, that restricts which rows will be retrieved by the current operation.

WHERE CURRENT OF
The clause used by **INSERT** and **DELETE** to modify data retrieved by a cursor.

WHILE
The Transact-SQL statement that allows a statement block to be executed repeatedly.

WITH CUBE, WITH ROLLUP
These two clauses cause SQL Server to summarize multiple grouping levels simultaneously. **CUBE** creates all possible grouping levels based on the **GROUP BY** clause, while **ROLLUP** is a hierarchical subset of **CUBE**.

Wizard
Graphically driven software assistants that guide database administrators and designers through a task. A small stand-alone application that guides the user through the steps needed to complete a task. A wizard usually uses an interview technique to gather the important information and then perform the task, thus shielding the user from the underlying details.

Workload
A sample of work performed on a database by users. A set of **SQL INSERT**, **UPDATE**, and **DELETE** statements and remote procedure calls saved as a SQL script or as a SQL Server Profiler output file or table. A file of SQL statements created by capturing the output of SQL Profiler to a file. This file is used as an input to the Index Tuning Wizard to determine if any changes to existing indexes are recommended.

INDEX

B

D

E

G

H

I

J

K

L

M

Q

S

T

U

V

W

Y

CERTIFIED CRAMMER SOCIETY

A breed apart, a cut above the rest—a true professional. Highly skilled and superbly trained, certified IT professionals are unquestionably the world's most elite computer experts. In an effort to appropriately recognize this privileged crowd, The Coriolis Group is proud to introduce the Certified Crammer Society. If you are a certified IT professional, it is our pleasure to invite you to become a Certified Crammer Society member.

Membership is free to all certified professionals and benefits include a membership kit that contains your official membership card and official Certified Crammer Society blue denim ball cap emblazoned with the Certified Crammer Society crest—proudly displaying the Crammer motto "Phi Slamma Cramma"—and featuring a genuine leather bill. The kit also includes your password to the Certified Crammers-Only Web site containing monthly discreet messages designed to provide you with advance notification about certification testing information, special book excerpts, and inside industry news not found anywhere else; monthly Crammers-Only discounts on selected Coriolis titles; *Ask the Series Editor* Q and A column; cool contests with great prizes; and more.

GUIDELINES FOR MEMBERSHIP

Registration is free to professionals certified in Microsoft, A+, or Oracle DBA. Coming soon: Sun Java, Novell, and Cisco. Send or email your contact information and proof of your certification (test scores, membership card, or official letter) to:

Certified Crammer Society Membership Chairperson
THE CORIOLIS GROUP, LLC
14455 North Hayden Road, Suite 220, Scottsdale, Arizona 85260-6949
Fax: 480.483.0193 • Email: ccs@coriolis.com

APPLICATION

Name: ....

Address: ....

....

Society Alias: ....

Choose a secret code name to correspond with us and other Crammer Society members. Please use no more than eight characters.

Email: ....

What's On The CD-ROM

The *MCSE Database Design on SQL Server 7 Exam Prep's* companion CD-ROM contains elements specifically selected to enhance the usefulness of this book, including:

- Answers to chapter summary questions.
- Two complete practice exams!
- 160 practice exam questions!
- **BCPDirect** A fantastic utility that provides a graphical interface to the bcp utility and allows you to cut your data transfer times in half. This 30-day trial version of the software provides direct BCP transfers between two SQL 7 servers without the intermediate step of creating a host data file, thereby cutting your transfer times in half. Registered versions allow two-way transfers between other RDBMS's, such as Oracle 8 and SQL Server 7 or SQL Server 6.5, as well as several advanced features.
- **ProcedurePro** May save your database programmers or DBA hundreds of hours. With ProcedurePro, users can generate commonly required stored procedures easily for tables on Microsoft® SQL Server™ versions 6.5 and 7. For example, a database containing 100 tables may require several hundred stored procedures to accommodate simple **SELECT**, **INSERT, UPDATE**, and **DELETE** requests. Using ProcedurePro to write this standard set of procedures may decrease the development time for your projects. With ProcedurePro, your programmers and DBA could spend more time on implementing complex business requirements and less time on tedious and basic stored procedures.

System Requirements

Software

- Microsoft Windows 95, Microsoft Windows 98, Microsoft Windows NT 4 Workstation with Service Pack 4 installed, or Microsoft Windows NT 4 Server with Service Pack 4 installed.
- Microsoft Internet Explorer 4.01 or later with Service Pack 1 installed.
- SQL Server 7 Standard Edition is needed to complete all the projects included in this book. However, SQL Server 7 Desktop Edition can also be used to complete many, but not all, of the examples.

Hardware

- PC with Intel Pentium 166MHz or higher.
- 32MB RAM.
- Approximately 200MB of disk space is needed for a Standard Edition installation along with additional data included in Projects.
- Networking support or Microsoft Loopback Adapter (included with Microsoft Windows NT 4 operating systems only) must be installed to complete all the projects.